MW01011720

INVITATION TO
BIBLICAL
THEOLOGY

Exploring the Shape, Storyline,
and Themes of Scripture

INVITATION TO THEOLOGICAL STUDIES SERIES

INVITATION TO THEOLOGICAL STUDIES SERIES

INVITATION TO
BIBLICAL
THEOLOGY

Exploring the Shape, Storyline,
and Themes of Scripture

JEREMY M. KIMBLE

CHED SPELLMAN

 KREGEL
ACADEMIC

Printed in the United States of America

20 21 22 23 24 / 5 4 3 2 1

For our teachers and our students

CONTENTS

INTRODUCTION

A Word about the Purpose of This Book

In writing this volume, we took seriously the task of providing an *invitation* to the discipline and practice of biblical theology. Accordingly, this book is neither a full-scale or exhaustive account of these areas of inquiry, nor only a surface-level introduction to basic elements. Rather, we seek to introduce some of the central aspects of biblical theology as a discipline, explain some of the strategic tools that are used in the practice of biblical theology, and provide a series of studies that highlight the payoff to this approach for understanding the Scriptures. In these discussions, we do take certain positions and make several specific proposals, but the overall aim of the endeavor is to orient you to this type of study and way of thinking about the Bible's message as a whole.

In chapter one, we explore a working definition of biblical theology, provide a brief history of the discipline, and survey contemporary approaches to the discipline. In light of this orienting discussion, in chapter two we propose an approach to biblical theology that centers on the canon, the covenants, and the Christ. We also explore the biblical-theological tools that support this type of framework. In chapter three, we discuss some of the issues involved in seeing that the whole Bible is about Christ. In chapter four, we examine some of the theological commitments we make about Scripture that enable us to approach the study of biblical theology in the way that we have.

In chapters five through ten, we outline of the grand storyline of the Bible from beginning to end. In these chapters, we consider both the basic structure of each major grouping of the canon and also some of the canonical considerations that might impact the way we understand the shape of the narrative storyline that appears in these groupings. Accordingly, the focus of these chapters is the narration and interpretation of redemptive history that the biblical authors provide in their narratives. This focal point is not an explicit or implicit argument that the narrative portions of the biblical canon are more significant than the non-narrative portions (e.g., the psalms, proverbs, or epistles) for the study of biblical theology. Rather than being a feature of this volume's space constraints (though this is a factor!), part of the purpose of this section is to demonstrate the unique role that the many narratives of the biblical collection play in articulating and shaping the big picture of the Bible. Here, we explore "The Grand Storyline of the Bible" as a biblical-theological tool alongside other tools we can employ in the study of biblical theology.

In the next major section (chapters eleven through twenty), we pursue the biblical-theological tool of "tracing a central theme across the canon." In these chapters, we discuss some of the significant biblical-theological topics that are prompted by a reading of the biblical storyline. Whereas "The Bible's Grand Storyline" is tightly focused on biblical narratives, each theme developed in "The Bible's Significant Themes" includes an overview of any relevant texts from the other biblical genres. For example, in examining the storyline of the New Testament, we do not outline the theological themes found in Paul's letters; however, in the development of each central theme, a discussion of Paul's letters is included. This observation will help you see the design of the chapters of this book and also the interconnected nature of biblical theology as a discipline.

The book ends, in chapters twenty-one and twenty-two, with brief reflections on how the study of biblical theology can serve both the church and the academy. In the major parts of this book, then, we endeavor to provide an invitation to the different ways you might approach the biblical-theological task. Our hope is that this volume will be a resource for pastors and students who are seeking to engage in the study of biblical theology and its application in the ministry of the churches.

As an aid to those using this book in a classroom setting, each chapter concludes with a set of discussion questions and a brief list of resources for further study. These reflective questions highlight some of the key issues examined within a given chapter and can also serve as prompts for small group or larger class discussion times. The final chapter also includes a series of case studies and exercises that might be used as small reflective assignments or as parameters for larger research papers. Moreover, the major sections of this volume are designed to complement the usual shape of an academic course. The book unfolds in a way that might structure a class on biblical theology (moving from method to practice to application). In this model, each new section would mark a new phase of the class. Each section could also function as a resource for a particular component of a course. The method chapters (1–4, 11, and 21–22), for example, might be utilized in the first part of a class in order to discuss the discipline and practice of biblical theology. The sections examining the grand storyline and central themes of the Bible could then be utilized as further phases of a course or as resources for students as they develop culminating research projects.

In terms of the production of the book, Ched wrote chapters one through three, five through eleven, and twenty-two. Jeremy wrote chapters four and twelve through twenty-one. Any first-person pronouns in these chapters refer to these authors.

A Word from Jeremy

It has been a joy to work on this book, as it has functioned as a continual invitation to increasingly know, love, and delight in God by means of his Word. There is no greater book than the Bible, and no greater object of meditation than the living God. What a pleasure it is to study, write, teach, and preach about our great God. My prayer is that this work will prove to be of help to readers and that it would be glorifying to the Lord. I give him thanks that he has used his Word and the work of the Holy Spirit to open my blind eyes to "the light of the knowledge of the glory of God in the face of Christ" (2 Cor. 4:6).

I am grateful to our friends at Kregel. To Herb Bateman, thanks so much for listening to the initial ideas for this volume. To Dennis and Paul Hillman, thank you for your encouragement and answering of questions throughout the process. To Shawn Vander Lugt and Robert Hand, I want to express appreciation for your careful eye attending to the details of the manuscript.

To Cedarville University, the administration as well as the School of Biblical and Theological Studies, I am indebted. It is a joy to work in a university setting so dedicated to the Word of God and the testimony of Jesus Christ. I am grateful for an institution that supports faculty engaging in scholarship for the sake of the church. A particular note of thanks to JR Gilhooly, who read and attentively commented on my chapters from this volume. Mom and Dad, you are also constant in your encouragement and prayers; thank you so much for all you do.

And finally, to my amazing family. Hannah and Jonathan, you bring me more delight than you can possibly know. Watching you grow in stature and, more importantly, godliness is a testament to the goodness and grace of God. Always seek to know God by means of his Word, infinite treasures await you! To my wife Rachel, you are one of the greatest kindnesses God has ever bestowed upon me. Thank you for reading through this manuscript several times with a keen eye. More importantly, thank you for your constant desire to follow Jesus wherever he leads. I am constantly instructed as you pursue him day by day. I continue to pray that our marriage is a picture of the Christ-church relationship that we will enjoy in full someday. Until that time, may we endeavor to be a Psalm 1 people, delightfully and constantly meditating on his Word.

A Word from Ched

I'm thankful for the faithful love and support of my wife Leigh Anne; my daughters Hope, Kate, and Claire; and my son Luke. Each of you motivate and inspire me. No book is more important than y'all. I'm also thankful for my mom, who has encouraged me through the whole writing process (and who first taught me to love the Scriptures). I'm grateful for friends and colleagues who have read portions of this manuscript, provided valuable feedback, prayed for me, and encouraged me along the way: Zach Bowden (TX is forever), Billy Marsh (for band of brothers), JR Gilhooly (for cheery optimism), Josh Kira (for Apex Legends carries), Jonathan Watson (for 1. e4), Madison Grace (for milk in a glass), and Matthew Millsap (for ludonarrative dissonance). Joel Wasserstein and Kevin Symonette also took breaks from trolling one another to read and comment on several chapters. I also warmly acknowledge the value of the questions, comments, and discussions with students in my Biblical Theology courses at Cedarville University who have thought carefully about "BT moves" with me over the last several years.

A special word of thanks to Jason Lee. At many points during the composition of these chapters, I recognized the abiding effect of his teaching, scholarship, and approach to the Scriptures. If you have ever sat under his teaching, you will hear echoes of his influence at several points in the chapters that I have written. In the academic community there is often a tendency for scholars to guard their material or hold back some "proprietary insights" in the classroom for later personal publications. This is not Jason's approach to the task of theological education. In many ways, my contribution in this book is a result of his contribution to me through his teaching, guidance, and dialogue in graduate, doctoral, professional, and collegial interactions. It was in his Hermeneutics course years ago that I was first introduced to the idea that the best theology is to be done for the churches and that what God is doing in the world is directly connected to what God is doing in his Word. What I offer in this volume, then, comes with a deep appreciation for what I myself have received.

SECTION I

STUDYING THE BIBLE'S THEOLOGY

CHAPTER I

DEFINING BIBLICAL THEOLOGY

The Need for Biblical Theology

ONE OF THE GOALS OF THIS BOOK IS to increase the number of people who are interested in doing biblical theology. We want you to be biblical theologians, but we also want you to be well-equipped and well-informed biblical theologians. We need a generation of students, teachers, pastors, church leaders, missionaries, and church members who care deeply about biblical theology.

Whether or not you share this vision and passion for biblical theology might very well depend on how you define biblical theology. Just what do we mean when we refer to *biblical theology*? How is this type of study any different than simply reading the Bible? How is this practice different than preaching or systematic theology? What are the prevailing questions that arise in this particular discipline? Answering these preliminary questions helps orient our study, demonstrate its value for pastoral ministry, and justify its place within the academic study of the Bible.

"Do You Understand What You Are Reading?"

In Acts 8:26–40, the Spirit leads Philip to encounter an Ethiopian official departing from Jerusalem. This official was riding home in a chariot while "reading the prophet Isaiah" (8:28). The Spirit tells Philip to go over and join the chariot. At this point, Philip hears the official reading from the book of Isaiah and asks him, "Do you understand what you are reading?" (8:30). The official responds, "How can I, unless someone guides me?" and invites Philip to sit with him (8:31). As Luke recounts, "Now the passage of the Scripture that he was reading was this: 'Like a sheep he was led to the slaughter and like a lamb before its shearer is silent, so he opens not his mouth. In his humiliation justice was denied him. Who can describe his generation? For his life is taken from the earth'" (8:32–33).

After reading Isaiah 53:7–8, the official questions Philip regarding the identity of the suffering servant described in this passage, saying, "About whom, I ask you, does the prophet say this, about himself or about someone else?" (8:34). Philip responds to the official and "beginning with this Scripture [i.e., Isaiah 53] he told him the good news about Jesus" (8:35). In what follows, Philip baptizes the official along the roadside before being carried away by the Spirit to the city of Azotus where he continues preaching the gospel (8:36–40). This rather minor historical episode serves an important role in Luke's narrative in the book of Acts and its account of the Spirit spreading the gospel across geographic and ethnic boundaries. However, this brief but fascinating story also encapsulates several of the themes and distinctive goals of biblical theology.

The official recognizes he needs help interpreting the Scriptures. As Acts 8 emphasizes, this includes not only the details of the passage under investigation (Isaiah 53) but also its broader literary context. The preaching of the gospel is connected to the close reading of the Scriptures. The two questions presented in Acts 8:30–31—"Do you understand what you are reading?" and "How can I, unless someone guides me?"—also highlight what is at stake in biblical theology and deserve enduring consideration.

Several other questions are raised by the details of this scene. What is the message of the Scriptures when considered as a whole? In light of the Bible's overarching message, how do individual passages relate to that broader textual horizon? While Acts 8 provides only a summary of Philip's conversation with the official, Luke does give us a glimpse into Philip's interpretive methodology. According to Acts 8:35, Philip preached the gospel by starting with his interpretation of Isaiah 53. This interpretive approach not only considers the words of the prophet, but also connects these words to the gospel. How are the Prophets related to the Gospels? Do the words of Isaiah really lead to the good news about Jesus? If so, *how* do they do this? What is Philip on about here? These are the types of questions biblical theology seeks to consider.

Defining Biblical Theology

A Working Definition

We begin with a working definition of *biblical theology*, which we define as *the study of the whole Bible on its own terms*. Having a "working definition" of biblical theology is helpful because scholars still debate the precise meaning of the term. A working definition is intentionally brief, easy to understand, and focused on the essential aspects of the term in question. While a working definition may be tentative (or not fully formed), it is also flexible and broad enough to initially *work with*. These features make a working definition useful for orienting someone to a particular discussion or discipline. However, this also means that a working definition must be *unpacked* to provide further definitional clarity. In order to unpack our working definition of biblical theology as the study of the whole Bible on its own terms, we can first think about its relationship to biblical exegesis and systematic theology, and then observe its prevailing concern for the relationship between the Old Testament and the New Testament.

A Tale of Two Senses

The study of biblical theology works within the electrifying dynamic generated by the two poles of biblical and theological studies. These two main components of biblical theology are of course embedded in the expression *biblical theology*, making it both a descriptive yet easily misunderstood term.

On the one hand, the term biblical theology can denote *a theology that is biblical*.[1] In this broad sense, biblical theology describes whether one's reflections about God and all things in relation to God *accord with the Scriptures*. Much as Paul instructs Titus to "teach what accords with sound doctrine" (Titus 2:1), the term here indicates whether a theology is "sound" and agrees with what we find in Scripture. This type of theological correspondence is an important and crucial goal for those who are in ministry.

On the other hand, a more specific or narrow understanding of the phrase biblical theology is *the theology presented in the Scriptures*. In this sense, biblical theology represents "the Bible's theology," or the "theology that we find in the Bible." In other words, when doing biblical theology, the goal is to first *present* the theological reflection that *occurs within* the Scriptures before *producing* theological reflection that *accords with* the Scriptures.

These two senses of biblical theology generate a level of ambiguity that some have said haunts the field.[2] Although failure to recognize this distinction can cause confusion and misunderstanding, the distinction itself can prove helpful as we pursue our study of the

---

1. An often-cited discussion of these two senses of "biblical theology" is Gerhard Ebeling, "The Meaning of 'Biblical Theology'," *Journal of Theological Studies* 6.2 (1955): 210–25. Noting that biblical theology is "in any event no simple idea," Ebeling observes the term means either "the theology contained in the Bible . . . the theology of the Bible itself" or "theology in accordance with the Bible, scriptural theology." However, Ebeling laments that "Both possible meanings are pregnant with a mass of problems." As Ebeling observes, these two senses represent two distinct disciplines: "In the latter sense, 'biblical theology' is a normative concept, in the former sense it is an historical concept. In the one 'biblical theology' means a theology of the right kind, in the other a theology of a particular stamp. Among theologians it is the dogmatic theologian who is concerned with one, the historical theologian who is concerned with the other" (210). Thus, Ebeling highlights the importance of reckoning with the issue of definition.
2. For example, Christine Helmer notes that "the famous definition of biblical theology that Gerhard Ebeling formulated in 1955 identified the fundamental ambiguity haunting the field" ("Introduction: Multivalence in Biblical Theology," in *The Multivalence of Biblical Texts and Theological Meanings*, ed. Christine Helmer, Society of Biblical Literature Symposium Series 37 [Atlanta: Society of Biblical Literature , 2006], 1). For Helmer, "Ebeling's contrast has convincingly set the conceptual parameters for biblical theology. The contrast between historical

Scriptures. This distinction between the broad and narrow senses of biblical theology provides conceptual categories that separate different types of analysis. As Brevard Childs notes, "from one perspective the entire modern history of the discipline of Biblical Theology can be interpreted as the effort to distinguish between these two definitions and to explore the important implications of the distinction."[3]

In broad terms, the process of understanding the Bible includes several areas of emphasis. An important preliminary step involves both *distinguishing* and *relating* biblical theology to the tasks of biblical exegesis and systematic theology. Both biblical theology and systematic theology involve exegetical analysis and also some level of abstraction. Consequently, it is probably inaccurate to say that one of these disciplines is closer to the biblical text than the other.[4] However, we can nevertheless note the distinctive aims of each discipline. Their purpose, goals, and object of study explain why their presentations often seem more or less directly connected to the biblical material. As we will discuss at various points, this does not automatically entail that a given discipline pursues a task wholly disconnected from the biblical text. Rather, it could mean that the purpose of a particular study or presentation of research is more or less suited to an arrangement other than a strict exposition of the biblical writings.

In our focus on biblical theology as *the study of the whole Bible on its own terms*, we will be mindful of the way exegesis, systematic theology, and other disciplines relate to our area of study.

- A working definition of exegesis is *the study of an author's textual intention.*
- A working definition of systematic theology is *the study of God and all things in relation to God according to his Word.*

---

and theological methods, between the object as described historically and the object of theological construction, exposes the braided trajectories of biblical theology's two foundational disciplines" (2).

3. Brevard S. Childs, *Biblical Theology of the Old and New Testaments: Theological Reflection on the Christian Bible* (Minneapolis: Fortress, 1992), 3.

4. For a helpful dialogue on this particular issue, see D. A. Carson, "Systematic Theology and Biblical Theology," in *New Dictionary of Biblical Theology*, ed. T. D. Alexander and Brian S. Rosner (Downers Grove: InterVarsity, 2000), 89–104; and Kevin J. Vanhoozer, "Is the Theology of the New Testament One or Many? Between (the Rock of) Systematic Theology and (the Hard Place of) Historical Occasionalism," in *Reconsidering the Relationship between Biblical and Systematic Theology in the New Testament: Essays by Theologians and New Testament Scholars*, ed. Benjamin E. Reynolds, Brian Lugioyo, and Kevin J. Vanhoozer, Wissenschaftliche Untersuchungen zum Neuen Testament 2.369 (Tübingen: Mohr Siebeck, 2014), 17–38. Still helpful as well is the exchange between Carl Trueman ("Editorial: A Revolutionary Balancing Act," *Themelios* 27.3 [2002]: 1–4) and Graeme Goldsworthy ("Ontology and Biblical Theology. A Response to Carl Trueman's Editorial: *A Revolutionary Balancing Act*," *Themelios* 28.1 [2002]: 37–45). Cf. also the vision for interdisciplinary dialogue in C. Kavin Rowe, "For Future Generations: Worshipping Jesus and the Integration of the Theological Disciplines," *Pro Ecclesia* 17.2 (2008): 186–209.

In some ways, biblical theology shares a family resemblance to exegesis and the close reading of individual biblical texts. Exegesis is the study of an author's textual intention. Recognizing that the mental state of an author is inaccessible to a reader, exegesis focuses upon what the author has in fact expressed in a particular act of written communication. The difference between doing exegesis and biblical theology is often one of scope. Whereas exegetical studies typically focus on individual passages and ask how specific words create meaning by forming sentences, paragraphs, and sections, biblical theology asks how those larger sections of text relate to one another and create book-level meaning. As such, biblical theology examines how the textual intention of one biblical author intersects and interacts with the writings of other biblical authors. When one biblical author draws directly upon another biblical text, we can clearly see just how close the exegetical and biblical-theological tasks are often related within the canon.

In other ways, biblical theology shares a family resemblance to systematic theology. As the study of God and all things in relation to God according to his Word, systematic theology resonates with the broad sense of biblical theology as a "theology that is biblical" and *accords* with the Scriptures.[5] The theological task involves at least three types of activities. First, systematic theology aims to summarize and synthesize what the Bible says about a particular topic in an understandable way.[6] Second, systematic theology seeks to demonstrate the basic coherence and logical connections between the many statements and teachings found in the biblical literature.[7] Third, systematic theology strives to draw out the theological implications of the statements made by the biblical authors in their texts. Whereas part of systematic theology's goal is to summarize, synthesize, and draw out the

---

5. For an articulation of this way of phrasing the definition of systematic theology, see John Webster, "What Makes Theology Theological?" *Journal of Analytic Theology* 3 (2015): 17–28. Webster argues that "the object of Christian theology is twofold: God the Holy Trinity and all other things relative to God" (17). Note also the discussion and distinctions Webster advances in his chapter "Principles of Systematic Theology," in *The Domain of the Word: Scripture and Theological Reason* (London: Bloomsbury, 2012), 133–49. For a further contemporary example of this phrasing, see Craig A. Carter, *Interpreting Scripture with the Great Tradition: Recovering the Genius of Premodern Exegesis* (Grand Rapids: Baker, 2018), 63–64.

6. Along these lines, Vanhoozer notes that systematic theology involves "faith seeking understanding—of God, the world and ourselves—through an ordered presentation of the doctrines implicit in the biblical testimony to the history of creation and redemption." See "Systematic Theology," in *New Dictionary of Theology: Historical and Systematic*, ed. Martin Davie, et al. (Downers Grove: InterVarsity, 2016), 885. Vanhoozer notes further that this theological reflection is "expressed via contemporary idiom and addressed to relevant cultural intellectual issues" (885).

7. Cf. Michael Horton, *The Christian Faith: A Systematic Theology for Pilgrims on the Way* (Grand Rapids: Zondervan, 2011), 29: "To assume that the Bible itself gives us a system of doctrine and practice is simply to acknowledge its organic unity as a single canon: the interdependence and coherence of its various teachings." On the relationship between the disciplines, Horton also notes that "if biblical theology is a topographical map, systematic theology is more like a street map, pointing out the logical connection between various doctrines spread throughout Scripture. Without biblical theology, systematic theology easily surrenders the dynamism of revelation to timeless truths; without systematic theology, biblical theology surrenders the Bible's internal coherence—the relation of the parts to the whole" (29).

theological implications of what the Bible says, biblical theology is mostly focused on how the Bible says what it says and how the biblical authors have composed their books.[8]

Each of these disciplines are critically important and should be constantly related to one another in the context of ministry. They are necessary for the life and practice of the church. To be sure, exegesis, biblical theology, and systematic theology are each required in order to achieve "the whole counsel of God" (Acts 20:27). Consequently, it is counterproductive to set these tasks against each another in some sort of disciplinary combat. Rather, they complement one another, even if the process they move in is not strictly linear. Recognizing its organic connection to both biblical exegesis and systematic theology, the focus of the discipline of biblical theology is to articulate and defend the value and significance of the study of the whole Bible on its own terms as a discernable and discrete task.

A Tale of Two Testaments

This way of understanding biblical theology strikes at the heart of another definitional question: How do the Testaments relate to one another? By defining biblical theology as the study of the *whole* Bible on its own terms, we are required to grapple with this and other related questions. How do the textual connections between the books in these collections impact our area of study? How does the ordering of the canonical collections, alongside the shape and meaning of the individual biblical books, contribute to how we address this relationship? If we define biblical theology the way that we have, these are the questions that we should anticipate.

As we understand the discipline, the aim of biblical theology is to behold the big picture of the biblical writings and convey the inner workings of that big picture. How does the big picture of Genesis, for instance, relate to the big picture of the New Testament? Or, how does the book of Romans fit into the meaning of the rest of Paul's Letters? Biblical theology tells a story from *beginning* to *end*. The story of the Bible begins with the Genesis creation account and ends with the outline of the "last things" in Revelation. These are the bookends of the grand storyline of the Bible. In the beginning, God created the heavens and the earth, and in the end he makes a new heaven and a new earth. This cosmic scope is the staggering perspective that we encounter as we make our way through the biblical narratives. So, when we engage the Scriptures at any level, we must keep in mind the grand storyline that we examine and reflect upon in biblical theology.

---

8. Cf. Karl Barth's understanding of the task of systematic theology (dogmatics) as "the self-examination of the Christian Church in respect of the content of its distinctive talk about God." See *Church Dogmatics, Volume I: The Doctrine of the Word of God, Part One,* trans. G. W. Bromiley (Edinburgh: T&T Clark, 1975), 11. In relation to the other disciplines, Barth later notes that "exegetical theology investigates biblical teaching as the basis of our talk about God" and "dogmatics as such does not ask what the apostles and prophets said but what we must say on the basis of the apostles and the prophets" (16).

These preliminary reflections help us unpack our working definition of biblical theology as *the study of the whole Bible on its own terms.* The discipline of biblical theology can be understood first in relation to biblical exegesis and systematic theology (A Tale of Two Senses), and second by its relentless pursuit of the question about the relationship between the Old Testament and the New Testament (A Tale of Two Testaments). This working definition and these two distinctive areas of emphasis give shape to this discipline and characterize much of the work that flies under the banner of biblical theology.

The History of Biblical Theology as a Discipline

Another useful way to get a handle on what biblical theology is all about is to consider what others in the past have understood this task to entail. This seemingly simple procedure, though, is fraught with difficulty because the history of biblical theology is engrossed in the question of the definition of the discipline. Indeed, while maintaining the coherence of the parameters of our working definitions outlined above, we also recognize that there are a host of challenging and diverse issues involved in the discipline of biblical theology. Nevertheless, a brief survey of how theologians throughout history have engaged these questions can help orient our contemporary pursuit of biblical theology.

Biblical Theology before the Modern Period

According to some, the discipline of biblical theology began with the advent of the modern era of biblical studies. This conclusion, of course, anticipates the question of definition and whether biblical theology should take a predominantly historical or theological approach. Before we address the rise of biblical theology as an independent discipline, we will briefly consider a few historical figures who pursued some of the enduring concerns of the discipline prior to modernity. To our point, it is important to see that leaders and theologians of every age "struggled to find models for dealing theologically with both testaments of Scripture as a revelation of Jesus Christ."[9] As soon as the canon developed, there was a need to describe the unified and consistent theology of the two-testament Christian Bible. Most of the influential leaders in the history of the church were biblical theologians of some sort, or pursued aspects of the biblical-theological task.

Irenaeus on the Order and Connection of the Scriptures

One early example of a premodern biblical theologian is Irenaeus of Lyons, who in the late second century wrote works that defended the Christian faith against false teachings

---

9. Childs, *Biblical Theology*, 30.

as well as articulated the nature of the gospel message for the churches.[10] His major work, *Against Heresies*, partakes in both of these tasks. In this writing, Irenaeus refutes the teaching of Gnosticism, defends the coherence of the Christian faith, and proclaims the gospel message. Throughout *Against Heresies*, Irenaeus employs a "rule of faith" that allows the totality of the biblical witness to God's person and work to inform his defense of the faith and proclamation of the gospel. In order to refute the "story of Gnosticism," Irenaeus articulates the story of redemption that is shaped by the biblical storyline and the revealed character of God's inner being.[11]

One particular teaching Irenaeus sought to counter was the idea that the God of the Old Testament was full of wrath and evil because he created the material world, which was considered corrupt and tainted. Conversely, the Father of Jesus Christ portrayed in the New Testament represented an entirely different divine being, full of love and untainted by having created the material world.[12] Irenaeus argues that this "system" was one which "neither the prophets announced, nor the Lord taught, nor the apostles delivered, but of which they boast that beyond all others they have a perfect knowledge" (*Haer.* 1.8.1). Here Irenaeus emphasizes the priority of special revelation over any "secret" knowledge, the flow of redemptive history, and also the shape of a two-testament witness to Christ.[13] Irenaeus notes that these theological conclusions were built upon a faulty hermeneutical method.

---

10. See John Behr's translation and introduction to *On the Apostolic Preaching* (Crestwood: St Vladimir's Seminary Press, 1997) and Behr, *Irenaeus of Lyons: Identifying Christianity* (Oxford: Oxford University Press, 2013).

11. Childs begins his survey of early Christian examples of biblical theology with Irenaeus, noting in particular the way he "sought to present a comprehensive summary of the Christian faith in terms of the testimony of Scripture as the written form of the church's rule-of-faith" (*Biblical Theology*, 30). Childs summarizes the import of Irenaeus's emphasis on "recapitulation" for biblical theology: "Because of the unity of God's salvation, it was absolutely essential to the faith that the two testaments of the Christian Bible be seen as a harmonious witness to the one redemptive purpose in history" (31).

12. Irenaeus summarizes and confronts different forms of this false teaching throughout his work. For example, see *Haer.* 1.2–8 and 1.23–29. All quotations from this work come from *Against Heresies* in *Ante-Nicene Fathers of the Christian Church*, trans. Alexander Roberts and James Donaldson, ed. Philip Schaff (Edinburgh: T&T Clark, 1896), 1:315–567.

13. Irenaeus draws on this broad shape of the biblical collection regularly. For instance, he says, "Since, therefore, the entire Scriptures, the prophets, and the Gospels, can be clearly, unambiguously, and harmoniously understood by all, although all do not believe them" (*Haer.* 2.27.2). Irenaeus concludes book two of *Against Heresies* by summarizing, "Now, that the preaching of the apostles, the authoritative teaching of the Lord, the announcements of the prophets, the dictated utterances of the apostles, and the ministrations of the law . . . are all in harmony with our statements" and show that "there is but one God, the Maker of all things" (2.35.4). In the middle of this sentence, Irenaeus includes summary affirmations that these diverse sections of Scripture all "praise one and the same Being, the God and Father of all." When Irenaeus characterizes the Scriptures as a whole ("the entire Scriptures"), he shows remarkable sensitivity to the shape of the biblical canon, the notion of theological unity/diversity, the organic relationship between economic development in redemptive history (the prophets, the Lord, and the apostles) and ontological identification (the God of Israel is the Father of Jesus Christ), and the urgency of carefully specifying the proper object of worship across the entire collection of biblical texts. Note also the connection of Irenaeus's phrasing to Peter's comment in 2 Peter 3:1–2. There Peter combats false teaching by reminding his readers of "the predictions of the holy prophets and the commandment of the Lord and Savior through your apostles" (3:2).

They used scriptural words, but re-located them, re-organized them, and fit them into an alternative textual strategy.[14] "In doing so," Irenaeus insists, "they disregard the order and the connection of the Scriptures, and so far as in them lies, dismember and destroy the truth" (*Haer.* 1.8.1).[15]

To illustrate his point, Irenaeus envisions a "skillful artist" who constructs a beautiful image of a king out of a set of precious jewels. When the false teachers take biblical passages out of context and re-interpret them according to a different storyline and an alternative theological worldview, it is like they are taking those precious jewels and re-arranging the image of the beautiful king into an ugly dog or fox (and that "poorly executed"). In this manner, the false teachers "patch together" their theological formulations and then "endeavor, by violently drawing away from their proper connection, words, expressions, and parables whenever found, to adapt the oracles of God to their baseless fictions" (*Haer.* 1.8.1). Irenaeus's metaphor demonstrates how knowing the subject of Scripture as a whole and how the pieces of the Bible fit together can *rule out* these interpretive and theological disasters. Knowing that the final form of the mosaic's pattern will resemble a beautiful king will assist you if you ever start to discern an ugly fox begin to emerge in a given ordering of the gems.

The "rule of faith" is a strategic summary of the message of the biblical writings that functions as a kind of hermeneutical guide for understanding the Scriptures as a whole.[16] In this summary, it is clearly understood that the God of Abraham, Isaac, and Jacob is the God and father of the Lord Jesus Christ. As a summary of the Scriptures, the rule of faith provides an interpretive lens that highlights the interconnections appearing across the Scriptures and the theological relationship between the Father, the Son, and the Holy Spirit. In one instance, Irenaeus describes the content of this rule of faith as belief in:

> One God, the Father Almighty, Maker of heaven, and earth, and the sea, and all things that are in them; and in one Christ Jesus, the Son of God, who became incarnate for our salvation; and in the Holy Spirit, who proclaimed through the prophets the

---

14. As Irenaeus notes, "They gather their views from other sources than the Scriptures; and, to use a common proverb, they strive to weave ropes of sand, while they endeavor to adapt with an air of probability to their own peculiar assertions the parables of the Lord, the sayings of the prophets, and the words of the apostles, in order that their scheme may not seem altogether without support" (*Haer.* 1.8.1).

15. For Irenaeus, the result of this literary disjunction is theologically disastrous: "By transferring passages, and dressing them anew, and making one thing out of another, they succeed in deluding many through their wicked art in adapting the oracles of the Lord to their opinions" (*Haer.* 1.8.1).

16. The scholarly discussion on Irenaeus's rule of faith is vast. Two major perspectives on the rule of faith are: (1) that it provides a summary of Scripture's overarching narrative as a whole; and (2) that it functions as an interpretive summary Scripture's theological message. On the former, see Paul M. Blowers, "The *Regula Fidei* and the Narrative Character of Early Christian Faith," *Pro Ecclesia* 6 (1997): 199–228. On the latter, see Nathan MacDonald, "Israel and the Old Testament Story in Irenaeus's Presentation of the Rule of Faith," *Journal of Theological Interpretation* 3.2 (2009): 281–98.

dispensations of God, and the advents, and the birth from a virgin, and the passion, and the resurrection from the dead, and the ascension into heaven in the flesh of the beloved Christ Jesus, our Lord and His future manifestation from heaven in the glory of the Father "to gather all things in one," and to raise up anew all flesh of the human race, in order that to Christ Jesus, our Lord, and God, and Savior, and King, according to the will of the invisible Father, "every knee should bow, of things in heaven, and things in earth, and things under the earth, and that every tongue should confess" to Him, and that He should execute just judgment towards all. (*Haer.* 1.10.1)

Irenaeus insists throughout his writings that the two-testament portrait of God and redemption in Christ, found in the proclamation of the prophets and apostles, is textually consistent and theologically coherent. For Irenaeus, redemptive history begins with God's creative work and climaxes in Christ's redemptive work on the cross.[17] Because there is a unity in God's plan of redemption, there is a unity in God's character and being. These features of Irenaeus's work make him a valuable resource for those who understand the task of biblical theology to be the study of the whole Bible on its own terms. Accordingly, Irenaeus and other theologians of the early church can serve as fruitful dialogue partners for those engaged in the discipline of biblical theology.

Aquinas on the Shape of the Canon

Another influential thinker who engaged some of the main concerns of biblical theology is Thomas Aquinas. Born in Italy, Aquinas served as a Dominican friar and taught theology and philosophy in Paris and Rome during the mid-thirteenth century. In much of his writing, Aquinas focuses on systematic formulations, the philosophical examination of theological language, and issues of ethics and epistemology. Running throughout his major works, though, is careful consideration of biblical texts and the nature of textual interpretation.[18]

---

17. Cf. MacDonald, "Israel and the Old Testament Story," 293–94: "With his attention to the shape of the canon, we can justly speak of Irenaeus as the first canonical interpreter. There is a genuine diversity to Scripture in the different parts of the canon [for Irenaeus], but the Rule of Faith points to the Scripture's unity in the story of Jesus Christ." Emphasizing the *hermeneutical* function of the rule of faith for Irenaeus, Christopher Seitz argues that the rule is "the scripturally grounded articulation, based upon a proper perception of the hypothesis of Scripture, that Jesus Christ is one with the God who sent him and who is active in the Scriptures inherited, the Holy Spirit being the means of testifying to his active, if hidden, life in the "Old Testament" and our apprehension of that." See his *The Character of Christian Scripture: The Significance of a Two-Testament Bible* (Grand Rapids: Baker, 2011), 198.

18. In addition to his major works such as *Summa Theologica, Summa contra Gentiles,* and *Scriptum super Sententiarum,* Aquinas also wrote commentaries on several Old Testament books (Psalms, Jeremiah, Lamentations, Isaiah, and Job), the Gospels of Matthew and John, and each of the Pauline Epistles (including Hebrews). He also published collections of selected quotations from the patristic era on each of the four Gospels (*Catena Aurea*). For recent scholarship that highlights this aspect of Aquinas's approach to the Bible, see Christopher T. Baglow, "Rediscovering St. Thomas Aquinas as a Biblical Theologian," *Letter and Spirit* 1 (2005): 137–46; Terence McGuckin, "Saint Thomas Aquinas and Theological Exegesis of Sacred Scripture," *New Blackfriars* 74.870 (1993): 197–213;

For example, in one of his inaugural lectures at the University of Paris known as *Hic est Liber* (*This is the Book*), Aquinas provides a "commendation of Sacred Scripture" (part 1) followed by an analysis of the "division of Sacred Scripture" (part 2).[19] In the first part, Aquinas gives a devotional account of Scripture's authority and ability to teach, delight, and motivate its hearers. In the second part, Aquinas speaks about the Scriptures by describing and discussing the ordering of canonical collections and the possible theological reasons behind their literary shape.

Aquinas begins by characterizing the Old Testament as leading people to life "by commanding" and the New Testament leading humans to life "by helping." "The whole of sacred Scripture," Aquinas continues, "is principally divided into two parts, namely, the Old and New Testaments, which are mentioned in the Gospel of Matthew" (citing here Matt. 13:52 and Song 7:13). Focusing first on the Old Testament, Aquinas articulates three ways the Old Testament conveys its message: the precepts of a king; the proclamations of a herald; and the instructions of a father. These three theological images map onto the "three parts" of the Old Testament. First, the Law is "as it were a precept proposed by the king himself" (citing Isa. 33:22). Second, the Prophets are "like messengers and heralds of God, speaking to the people in the person of God and inducing them to the keeping of the law" (citing Hag. 1:13). Third, the "works of the hagiographers" (i.e., the Writings) who were "inspired by the Holy Spirit" serve a "paternal" function (citing Prov. 6:20) by speaking "not on behalf of the Lord, but on their own behalf."[20]

Next, Aquinas further refines his theology of the Old Testament by exploring themes that explain the structure and sequence of each of its "three parts." He starts with the Law, which he divides into the "private law" and the "public law." The "private law" was given to the individuals mentioned in Genesis (e.g., Noah, Abraham). The "public law" was given to the people through a mediator in two steps: "First, the law comes from the Lord to the mediator, and this is contained in three books, namely, Exodus, Leviticus, and Numbers. Hence, in those books we frequently read: *God said to Moses.* The second step is that by which the law is expounded to the people by the mediator, and this is contained in Deuteronomy, which is clear from its beginning" (citing Deut. 1:1).[21]

---

and the essays in Thomas G. Weinandy, Daniel A. Keating, and John P. Yocum, eds., *Aquinas on Scripture: An Introduction to his Biblical Commentaries* (London: T&T Clark, 2005).

19. See *Thomas Aquinas: Selected Writings*, ed. and trans. Ralph McInerny (London: Penguin Books, 1998), 5–17. The *Hic est Liber* lecture has recently been translated by John R. Gilhooly for The Aquinas Institute (available online at https://aquinas.cc/la/en/~HicEst). All quotations from Hic est Liber come from Gilhooly's translation.

20. Aquinas clarifies at this point in *Hic est Liber* that this is the reason why "the hagiographers are called sacred writers or sacred scribes, from 'agios' (that is, sacred) and 'graphia' (that is, writings)." In the subsequent section, Aquinas also discusses how Jerome includes the Apocrypha in his canon and his doubts about these books. Regarding the Apocrypha, he remarks that "they have their strength not from the authority of the authors, but more from the reception by the Church."

21. Aquinas further characterizes the function of these books: "The three books just mentioned are distinguished according to the three ways in which people should be organized. First, in precepts related to the equity of judgment,

Like the Law, the Prophets are also divided by Aquinas into two parts, "according to the tasks that a herald ought to perform." These two tasks are to "expound the goodness of the king to incline men to obedience" and to "declare the rule of the law." Regarding the historical books included among the Prophets, Aquinas views them as prophets who showed divine goodness to the people: Joshua demonstrates the "result of heredity"; Judges exhibits the "destruction of armies"; Ruth shows the private "exaltation of the people"; and Kings conveys the public display of "royal dignity." The other books in the Prophets declare "divine rules for the observance of the law." The Major Prophets do this on a general scale ("sent to the whole people to call them to observe the whole law") whereas the Minor Prophets do this for particular groups ("sent for different reasons to special peoples"). The prophets employ both "promises of goodness" (seen especially in Isaiah) and "the threat of punishment" (seen especially in Jeremiah) as they warn the people about the "condemnation of sins" (seen especially in Ezekiel).[22]

In his final discussion of the Old Testament, Aquinas discusses "the hagiographic and the apocryphal books."[23] Perhaps because this collection is more eclectic, Aquinas uses several categories to describe these books (e.g., ways of training, levels of virtues). Overall, though, these books are ordered under the rubric of the way fathers train their sons in virtue. For example, the Psalms teach "by the mode of speaking to God in prayer." The book of Job "destroys errors" by using the "way of disputation." The Song of Songs instructs a person who spurns the cares of the world and "delights in only the contemplation of wisdom."

As he moves to the New Testament, Aquinas notes that this collection is "ordered to eternal life, not only by precepts, but through the gifts of grace" and is "divided into three parts." The first part, the Gospels, treats the "origin of grace." The second part, Paul's Letters, treats "the strength of grace." The third part, the "remaining books" of the New Testament, discusses "the carrying out of the aforesaid power." For the Gospels, Aquinas describes the unity and diversity of the Gospels by noting the particular prominence of the person of Christ:

> In Christ two natures are considered, namely, a divine; and the gospel of John is principally concerned with this. Hence, it begins: *in the beginning was the Word, and the Word was with God, and the Word was God* (John 1:1). And, a human; and the other

---

and this is in Exodus; second, in sacraments related to the display of worship, and this is in Leviticus; third, in offices related to public administration, and this is in the book of Numbers."

22. He prefaces these characterizations by noting that "these three are all found in each prophet." Pushing further ("they can also be distinguished in another way"), Aquinas notes next the unique way Isaiah "foretells the mystery of the Incarnation, whence the Church reads him during the time of advent." Jeremiah shows the "mystery of the passion" (and is read at Easter). Ezekiel speaks of the "mystery of the resurrection." Aquinas also counts Daniel among the prophets because of his prophetic predictions ("he did not speak to the people from the person of the Lord, he described the divinity of Christ"). In these ways, "the four prophets correspond to the four evangelists, and also the call to judgment."

23. The apocryphal books that Aquinas mentions in this section include Wisdom, Judith, Maccabees, Tobit, and Sirach. He also mentions Joshua again here due to Jerome's inclusion of the book "in the hagiographies."

Evangelists principally treat of this, which are distinguished according to the triple dignity that belongs to Christ as man. Matthew designates his royal dignity; hence, in the beginning of his Gospel he shows that he descended from kings according to the flesh and was adored by the Magi kings. Mark designates his prophetic dignity; hence, he begins with the preaching of the Gospel. Luke designates his priestly dignity; hence, he begins with the temple and the priesthood, and he concludes his Gospel in the temple, and frequently returns to the temple, as the gloss says on Luke 2:46: *they found him in the temple, sitting in the midst of the teachers.*[24]

Aquinas concludes his lecture by outlining the shape of the rest of the New Testament. The "beginning of the Church" is found in the Acts of the Apostles.[25] The "progress of the Church" is delineated in "the apostolic teaching in the canonical epistles." Finally, the "end of the Church" is seen in the Apocalypse, "with the spouse in the chamber of Jesus Christ sharing in the life of glory, to which Jesus Christ himself conducts us." Aquinas notes, too, that in this book, "the content of the whole of sacred Scripture concludes."

There are a number of relevant observations we can make after this brief reflection on Aquinas's *Hic est Liber*. Aquinas here develops the theological message of the Scriptures as a whole. In order to do this, he draws out thematic categories in terms of their unity and diversity. Moreover, he allows the shape of the Old and New Testaments to guide this reflection.[26] While much of Aquinas's work fixates upon systematic and philosophical study, discussions such as this show that Aquinas was also engaged in the hermeneutics of textual analysis with an awareness of the implications of the canonical context.

Luther on Law and Gospel in Both the Law and the Gospels

As the Reformation developed, Martin Luther's teaching and preaching exerted immense influence. Part of Luther's break with the Roman Catholic Church of his day related to theological method: Where does ultimate authority reside? Besides advancing a strong theological position on the authority of all Scripture (*sola scriptura*), Luther also reevaluated his understanding of the literal sense of all the Scriptures (*sensus literalis*).[27]

---

24. Following this discussion, Aquinas revisits the analogy of the four beasts to describe the Gospels. Matthew designates Christ "principally in terms of the mystery of the Incarnation" (a man), Luke speaks of the "mystery of the passion" (a bull), Mark speaks of the "victory of the resurrection" (a lion), and John "flies to the heights of his divinity" (an eagle).

25. Quoting Jerome, Aquinas notes that "the Acts of the Apostles seems to give the bare history and to clothe the infancy of the nascent Church."

26. Aquinas makes this explicit in several places (e.g., Joshua–Kings being located among the Prophets and Revelation containing and concluding "all of Scripture").

27. Many have noted these particular features of Luther's thinking, their interrelationship, and the historical context and development they underwent throughout Luther's career. For recent scholarship that draws out the hermeneutical and biblical-theological significance of Luther's writing, see Mark D. Thompson, *A Sure Ground on Which to*

Luther's sustained consideration of the way biblical texts speak of Christ and the function of the Old Testament as Christian Scripture occurs in his lectures, sermons, letters, and prefaces to his biblical translations. One of his brief works that addresses the relationship between the Testaments is his 1525 sermon "How Christians Should Regard Moses."[28] In this reflection, Luther argues that the distinction between law and gospel is not a conceptual scheme divided between the Old and New Testaments respectively, but rather that law and gospel appear together in both Testaments. Luther begins by reflecting on the two "public sermons" from heaven: the giving of the law at Sinai and the coming of the Spirit at Pentecost. From these revelations, Luther discusses the nature of law and gospel. The law "commands and requires us to do certain things." The gospel "reverses the approach of the law" and does the opposite. The law says, "Do this, avoid that, this is what I expect of you." The gospel says, "This is what God has done for you; he has let his Son be flesh for you, has let him be put to death for your sake."[29]

As he reflects further, Luther insists that the Mosaic covenant is no longer binding.[30] Even the establishment of the Mosaic covenant was intended for the Jews, not the Gentiles. "We will regard Moses as a teacher, but we will not regard him as our lawgiver—unless he agrees with both the New Testament and the natural law."[31] Luther protests that "not one little period in Moses pertains to us" and entertains the question: "Why then do you preach about Moses if he does not pertain to us?"[32] However, rather than "sweep him under the rug," Luther maintains that Christians should "keep Moses" for three reasons. First, though the Mosaic covenant is not binding, it does contain examples of wise statues and commandments. If willingly accepted rather than adopted through coercion, these elements of the Mosaic covenant can prove edifying.[33]

Stand: The Relation of Authority and Interpretive Method in Luther's Approach to Scripture (Carlisle: Paternoster, 2004); Robert Kolb, *Luther and the Stories of God: Biblical Narratives as a Foundation for Christian Living* (Grand Rapids: Baker, 2012); Brian T. German, *Psalms of the Faithful: Luther's Early Reading of the Psalter in Canonical Context* (Bellingham: Lexham, 2017); and William M. Marsh, *Martin Luther on Reading the Bible as Christian Scripture: The Messiah in Luther's Biblical Hermeneutic and Theology*, Princeton Theological Monograph Series (Eugene: Pickwick, 2017).

28. See "How Christians Should Regard Moses," in *Luther's Works: Word and Sacrament I*, vol. 35, ed. and trans. E. Theodore Bachmann (Philadelphia: Fortress, 1960), 155–74. The citations of this work in the following discussion come from this volume. Originally delivered in August 1525 as a part of a series of sermons on Exodus, this sermon was subsequently published as a separate pamphlet and included as an orienting introduction to several volumes of collected sermons on the Old Testament.
29. Luther, "How Christians Should Regard Moses," 165.
30. Luther states provocatively, "Moses is dead. His rule ended when Christ came. He is of no further service" ("How Christians Should Regard Moses," 165). Part of Luther's motivation to forcefully argue this point is how figures in the peasants' war and some of the radical Anabaptists used the Mosaic covenant and its regulations. See the brief overview of these contextual factors in Bachmann's introduction to "How Christians Should Regard Moses," 157–59.
31. Luther, "How Christians Should Regard Moses," 157–59. In theological terms, Luther adds that Moses "has given the Jews a sign whereby they should lay hold of God when they call upon him as the God who brought them out of Egypt. The Christians have a different sign, whereby they conceive of God as the One who gave his Son, etc." (165).
32. Luther, "How Christians Should Regard Moses," 165.
33. Luther, "How Christians Should Regard Moses," 166–68.

Second, the Book of Moses contains something found nowhere else: "the promises and pledges of God about Christ."[34] Luther states that "this is the best thing" and admits that "I read Moses because such excellent and comforting promises are there recorded, by which I can find strength for my weak faith."[35] The texts Luther discusses in this section include the promise of the seed of the woman (Gen. 3:15), the blessing and promise of a descendant for Abraham (Gen. 22:18), and the expectation of a coming prophet like Moses (Deut. 18:15–16). Luther remarks, "Many are these texts in the Old Testament, which the holy apostles quoted and drew upon."[36]

Third, according to Luther the Book of Moses includes "beautiful examples of faith, of love, and of the cross, as shown in the fathers, Adam, Abel, Noah, Abraham, Isaac, Jacob, Moses, and all the rest." From these figures, "we should learn to trust in God and love him." The Book of Moses also offers "examples of the godless, how God does not pardon the un-faith of the unbelieving."[37] Luther states that these narrative examples possess a formative function and are necessary "for although I am not Cain, yet if I should act like Cain, I will receive the same punishment as Cain."[38]

For these three reasons, Luther argues that "we should not sweep Moses under the rug."[39] He also brings these interpretive principles to bear on the reading of the larger biblical context. As he notes, "The Old Testament is thus properly understood when we retain from the prophets the beautiful texts about Christ, when we take note of and thoroughly grasp the fine examples, and when we use the laws as we please to our advantage."[40] This hermeneutical guideline is likewise operative in the New Testament: "The same is true also in the gospel."[41] To illustrate this continuity, he observes that "in the account of the ten lepers, that Christ bids them go to the priest and make sacrifice (Luke 17:14) does not pertain to me. The example of their faith, however, does pertain to me; I should believe Christ, as they did." These hermeneutical distinctions are crucial because many well-meaning preachers and teachers "do not know how to preach Moses, nor how properly to regard his books."[42]

In this brief work, Luther shows a keen interest in the relationship between the theological concepts of law and gospel. He also connects these theological categories to the relationship between the Testaments. In Luther's view, there is both law and gospel in both the Law and the Gospels. The implication of this textual observation is that interpreters must

---

34. Luther, "How Christians Should Regard Moses," 168.
35. Luther, "How Christians Should Regard Moses," 169.
36. Luther, "How Christians Should Regard Moses," 169.
37. Luther gives Cain, Ishmael, Esau, the Flood generation, and Sodom and Gomorrah as examples.
38. Luther, "How Christians Should Regard Moses," 173.
39. Luther, "How Christians Should Regard Moses," 173.
40. Luther, "How Christians Should Regard Moses," 173.
41. Luther, "How Christians Should Regard Moses," 174.
42. Luther, "How Christians Should Regard Moses," 174.

think carefully about not only *what* the Scriptures say, but *how* they say what they say and *to whom* a particular command is addressed within a biblical text. As he remarks, "One must deal cleanly with the Scriptures."[43] Luther also seems to value the close connection between the events of redemptive history and the words of the biblical authors.[44]

The hermeneutical and theological issues addressed early in Luther's career in "How Christians Should Regard Moses" resonate with the concerns Luther engages in one of his last major writings: his 1543 "Treatise on the Last Words of David."[45] In this substantial work, Luther examines the christological significance of David's final poetic text in 2 Samuel 23:1–7. Luther also outlines his hermeneutical approach to reading the Old Testament and interacts with non-messianic Jewish interpretation. Luther's orienting assertion is that "we Christians have the meaning and import of the Bible because we have the New Testament, that is, Jesus Christ, who was promised in the Old Testament and who later appeared and brought with Him the light and the true meaning of Scripture."[46]

For Luther, this interpretive approach "is the all-important point on which everything depends." Luther states that "whoever does not have or want to have this Man properly and truly who is called Jesus Christ, God's Son, whom we Christians proclaim, must keep his hands off the Bible."[47] Towards the end of the treatise, after rejecting non-messianic inter-

---

43. Luther, "How Christians Should Regard Moses," 170. Luther follows this statement with a reminder of the strategic significance of genre: "From the very beginning the word has come to us in various ways. It is not enough simply to look and see whether this is God's word, whether God has said it; rather we must look and see to whom it has been spoken, whether it fits us. That makes all the difference between night and day." As an example, Luther notes that although God spoke to David (citing the Davidic covenant in 2 Samuel 7), "this does not pertain to me, nor has it been spoken to me. He can indeed speak to me if he chooses to do so. You must keep your eye on the word that applies to you, that is spoken to you" (170). These hermeneutical distinctions guard against misappropriation and harmful direct applications of the Mosaic covenant in a contemporary context (like the "enthusiasts" or the leaders of the peasants' war). Luther states that those teachers indiscriminately proclaim, "God's word, God's word" and do so "without any distinction" (171). In this context, making careful distinctions is critical, "for everything depends entirely upon it."

44. For example, after outlining the "public speeches" of God at Sinai and Pentecost at the beginning of the work, Luther comments on the speech "by the mouth" and "in the books of the holy prophets" ("How Christians Should Regard Moses," 162). At the end of the work, Luther distinguishes between Moses as a person (which he sometimes uses as a way of referring to the Mosaic covenant) and "his books" (to "preach Moses" and "properly regard his books") (174).

45. See "Treatise on the Last Words of David: 2 Samuel 23:1–7," in *Luther's Works*, vol. 15, trans. Martin H. Bertram (St Louis: Concordia, 1972), 265–352. The citation of this work comes from this volume. Marsh notes in particular the strategic significance of this treatise for Luther's understanding of "the Messiah in the OT and Christ as the sensus literalis of Scripture." See Marsh, Luther on Reading the Bible, 162–92. Noting that this treatise is often understood as polemical and grouped with Luther's other anti-Semitic writings, Marsh maintains that the prefaces to Luther's biblical translations provide the necessary historical context for this significant work. Marsh details the content of the prefaces (28–99) and also synthesizes the hermeneutical implications of these remarks for Luther's approach to Christ as the literal sense of Scripture (100–61). The prefaces span Luther's career as a biblical interpreter/preacher and so provide a particularly instructive line of sight into Luther's biblical-theological development. Luther's reflection in this treatise, then, demonstrates his enduring concern for these hermeneutical areas.

46. Luther, "Last Words of David," 268. Here Luther cites John 5:46 and Luke 24:44–45.

47. Luther, "Last Words of David," 268.

pretations, Luther reiterates that "the letter harmonizes readily with the New Testament, and it is certain that Jesus Christ is Lord over all. To Him Scripture must bear witness, for it is given solely for His sake."[48] Luther's purpose in writing is so that his reflection will equip others to "diligently seek and find the Lord Jesus in the Hebrew Old Testament."[49] This goal is possible, according to Luther, because God "lets Himself be found there very readily, especially in the Psalter and in Isaiah."[50]

These brief historical snapshots from the early church, the medieval period, and the Reformation illustrate the enduring concern for various elements of the biblical-theological task. Irenaeus brings figural reading and the storyline of the two-testament biblical canon to bear on his teaching and defends the "order and connection" of the Scriptures. In strategic works, Aquinas allows the shape of the biblical literature to guide his articulation of the theological message of the Bible. Throughout his ministry, Luther reflects broadly on the proper use of the Old Testament as Christian Scripture and specifically on the way Christ is presented in the literal sense of individual Old Testament texts. These examples are illustrative but not isolated. Approaching the history of interpretation in this way, we might add many more premodern examples of preachers and teachers who grappled with some facet of biblical theology.[51]

The Rise of Biblical Theology as an Independent Discipline

The remainder of this survey will orient us to the significant changes that have transpired within the field of biblical and theological studies in the modern era. The advent of the "modern era" (approximately the eighteenth through mid-twentieth centuries) has many facets worth exploring. The broad intellectual currents that swept through Europe impacted the study of the Bible within both academic and church contexts. The European Enlightenment celebrated reason, science, and human ingenuity as the keys to a flourishing society. Broadly speaking, faith in God was replaced by faith in reason. General trust in

---

48. Luther, "Last Words of David," 343.
49. Luther, "Last Words of David," 344.
50. Luther, "Last Words of David," 343. Luther restates this notion as his conclusion: "Then we will again find and recognize our dear Lord and Savior clearly and distinctly in Scripture. To Him, together with the Father and the Holy Spirit, be glory and honor in eternity. Amen" (352).
51. For example, we might examine the hermeneutical and theological focus of the fourth-century theologians who contributed to the discussions that led to the Nicene (325 AD) and Nicene-Constantinople creeds (381 AD). Athanasius, Basil the Great, Gregory of Nyssa, and Gregory of Nazianzus each engaged the theological task with an awareness of the influence the "biblical idiom" has on readers. We could also examine the entire structure of biblical scholarship embedded in the medieval education system, the monastic emphasis on scribal production and piety, and the proliferation of translations and translational techniques that surface at the rise of the Reformation. In other words, our quest for historical precursors to and resources for a contemporary "big picture" biblical theology offers an embarrassment of riches. For a possible way to incorporate this aspect of the history of interpretation into a study of biblical theology, see the assignment examples and primary sources mentioned in "Case Study 3" in chapter twenty-two.

divine providence was replaced by specific trust in human progress. This intellectual context produced several challenges to the central tenets of Christianity.[52]

During this period, the rejection of the church's worldview replaced a "hermeneutic of trust" with a "hermeneutic of suspicion."[53] In this cultural atmosphere, divergence from Christian beliefs and traditional assumptions was construed as movement away from intellectual darkness. This resulted in a shift away from the Bible as an authoritative guide for faith and practice. This period also prompted growing skepticism regarding the concept of revelation due to the Enlightenment's emphasis upon objectivity, empirical knowledge, and scientific reasoning.[54]

This type of mentality affected the discipline of biblical studies. Removed from its privileged position, biblical literature was now studied alongside other ancient literature and apart from any type of faith claim. The historical-critical method viewed the writings of the New Testament, for example, in the same way it viewed every other ancient document. For these scholars, too, the theory of evolution helped explain the rise and development of religions within ancient cultures (progressing from primitive beliefs to complex systems). Both in terms of method and confessional stance, this approach transformed the study of the New Testament into a sort of history of religions rather than a specific study of the New Testament canon.

It was also during this time period that biblical theology emerged as a discrete academic discipline. One of the benchmarks of this development was the 1787 lecture given by the German theologian J. P. Gabler, entitled "An Oration on the Proper Distinction between Biblical and Dogmatic Theology and the Specific Objectives of Each."[55] Though Gabler was not the inventor of the distinction mentioned in his lecture's title, his address nevertheless

---

52. This summary is, of course, only a snapshot of this historical period. For a survey of the broader factors of this time period, see the wide-ranging analysis in John D. Woodbridge and Frank A. James III, *Church History: Volume Two: From Pre-Reformation to the Present Day* (Grand Rapids: Zondervan, 2013), 315–562. See also Matthew Barrett's focus on the shift in the doctrine of Scripture in this same period in *God's Word Alone: The Authority of Scripture* (Grand Rapids: Zondervan, 2016), 76–114. For a contemporary defense of "criticism" as a sound interpretive approach, see John Barton, *The Nature of Biblical Criticism* (Louisville: Westminster John Knox, 2007). Conversely, for a direct engagement and strong critique of the modern period's ongoing influence in contemporary biblical studies, see Carter, *Interpreting Scripture with the Great Tradition*, 3–126. In *The Death of Scripture and the Rise of Biblical Studies* (Oxford: Oxford University Press, 2010), Michael Legaspi also discusses the antecedent factors that led to a distinction between "the scriptural Bible" and "the academic Bible" in the modern period.
53. For these categories in relation to the history of interpretation, see Kevin J. Vanhoozer, *Is There a Meaning in this Text? The Bible, The Reader, and the Morality of Literary Knowledge* (Grand Rapids: Zondervan, 1998), 25–29; and Jeannine K. Brown, *Scripture as Communication: Introducing Biblical Hermeneutics* (Grand Rapids: Baker, 2007), 57–78.
54. As an illustration of this mindset, observe Immanuel Kant's characterization of the Age of Reason's impulse: "Enlightenment is man's release from his self-incurred tutelage. Tutelage is man's inability to make use of his understanding without direction from another. Self-incurred is this tutelage when its cause lies not in lack of reason but in lack of resolution and courage to use it without direction from another. *Sapere aude!* 'Have courage to use your own reason!'—that is the motto of enlightenment." See "What Is Enlightenment?" in *The Enlightenment: A Sourcebook and Reader*, ed. Paul Hyland (London: Routledge, 2003), 54.
55. Gabler gave this address as his inaugural lecture at the University of Altdorf in Nuremberg, Germany on March 30, 1787. The text of his address can be found in John Sandys-Wunsch and Laurence Eldredge, "J. P. Gabler and

summarized and signaled a new approach to the academic study of the Bible. Gabler attempted to "establish methodological clarity respecting the subject matter of Biblical Theology."[56] Because, in many ways, dogmatics held intellectual sway during that time, Gabler wanted to take back the normative nature of biblical theology by making the assured results of the latter discipline the necessary requirements to even begin engaging the former discipline. In this way, Gabler distinguished "pure" biblical theology from "true" biblical theology. Whereas pure biblical theology involved the descriptive task of discerning what the biblical authors said in their historically conditioned context, true biblical theology involved the prescriptive task of culling universal truths from the biblical data. These timeless truths would then form the foundation for dogmatic reflection.[57]

Following the trend summarized in Gabler's address, universities and seminaries began to separate Old Testament studies from New Testament scholarship, and biblical exegesis from theological studies. Accordingly, biblical scholars and theologians were encouraged to think of their respective fields as immune from the constraints and unique challenges of other disciplines. This move towards increased specialization was a hallmark of the modern period's quest for objective viewpoints and unbiased analysis. This scenario is also significant because it "not only reflected the growing complexity of the discipline, but far more importantly the growing conviction that the historical discontinuities between the testaments defied all attempts to maintain a traditional canonical unity."[58]

A paradigmatic articulation of this position in the field of New Testament theology was given by William Wrede in his 1897 address entitled, "The Task and Methods of 'New Testament Theology.'"[59] By presupposing the "strictly historical character of New Testament theology," Wrede sought to carry out the implications of Gabler's approach and deepen the distinction between biblical and dogmatic theology.[60] Rather than take a confessional stance,

---

the Distinction between Biblical and Dogmatic Theology: Translation, Commentary, and Discussion of His Originality," *Scottish Journal of Theology* 33 (1980): 133–58.

56. Childs, *Biblical Theology*, 4.

57. See Sandys-Wunsch and Eldredge, "Gabler and the Distinction," 137–44. For a recent critical evaluation of the significance and reception history of Gabler's address for the field of biblical studies, see Mark W. Elliott, "The Pure and the True Gabler: Questioning a Received Image in the History of Biblical Theology," in *Biblical Theology: Past, Present, and Future*, ed. Mark W. Elliott and Carey Walsh (Eugene: Cascade, 2016), 3–17. Elliott emphasizes that Gabler pursued methodological distinction because he "aimed to free practical dogmatics (in preaching and catechizing) from a proof-texting way of using the Bible, but he also wanted to go further, by allowing biblical concepts, hermeneutically re-cast to inform dogmatics" (5). Because Gabler avoids a purely descriptive approach, Elliott concludes that "it is to be doubted that Gabler can be held responsible for the Religionsgeschichtliche Schule" (5).

58. Childs, *Biblical Theology*, 5.

59. Wrede delivered this address originally at a faculty session for the University of Breslau, Germany (now Wrocław, Poland). This essay appears in Robert Morgan, ed. and trans., *The Nature of New Testament Theology: The Contribution of William Wrede and Adolf Schlatter* (Eugene: Wipf and Stock, 1973), 68–116. Morgan introduces Wrede's lecture, provides the full text, and brings Wrede into dialogue with the work of Adolf Schlatter.

60. Because Gabler still argued for the role of biblical theology identifying the timeless truth that connects directly to the work of systematic theology, Wrede saw the need to absolutize the distinction by considering the task of

Wrede argues scholars must be "guided by a pure disinterested concern for knowledge."[61] Wrede avers confidently that "no New Testament writing was born with the predicate 'canonical' attached." Rather, "the statement that a writing is canonical signifies in the first place only that *it was pronounced* canonical *afterwards* by authorities of the second-to-fourth-century church, in some cases only after all kinds of hesitation and disagreement."[62] According to Wrede, any privileging of the boundaries of the biblical canon is arbitrary and driven by overtly imported theological concerns. Indeed, the biblical books should "be seen not as canonical but simply as early Christian writings."[63] For Wrede, this scenario demands that scholars view the New Testament exclusively in the purview of a broad history of religions paradigm.[64] The work of biblical theology, then, has only a tangential relationship to theological disciplines and no organic connection to the church.[65]

Consequently, during the modern period the study of biblical theology was pursued as a wholly independent discipline that worked with primarily historical categories. In this approach to biblical studies, the "diversity" of the biblical writings is assumed and any "unity" of the biblical literature must necessarily be a theological construct. As Scobie summarizes, this led to "the *division* of biblical theology (into OT and NT theology), the *decline* of biblical theology (as it was absorbed by the history of religion), and finally the virtual *demise* of biblical theology."[66]

---

biblical theology in a truly independent, historically focused manner. Wrede makes this historical connection explicit by discussing Gabler's address as an orientation to his further developed proposals (see "Task and Methods," 68–69). On the relationship between the disciplines, Wrede starts with the assumption that the notion of inspiration is "untenable." Consequently, biblical theology "has to investigate something from given documents—if not an external thing, still something intellectual. It tries to grasp it as objectively, correctly and sharply as possible. That is all. How the systematic theologian gets on with its results and deals with them—that is his own affair. Like every other real science, New Testament theology has its goal simply in itself, and is totally indifferent to all dogma and systematic theology" (69).

61. Wrede, "Tasks and Methods," 70.
62. Wrede, "Tasks and Methods," 70–71. Emphasis added.
63. Wrede, "Tasks and Methods," 71.
64. Wrede concludes his address, for instance, by arguing that "the name New Testament theology is wrong in both its terms. The New Testament is not concerned merely with theology, but is in fact far more concerned with religion." Accordingly, "the appropriate name for the subject-matter is: early Christian history of religion, or rather: the history of early Christian religion and theology. If anyone protests that this is no longer a New Testament theology, that is a strange objection. The name is obviously controlled by the subject-matter, not vice versa" ("Tasks and Methods," 116).
65. See Wrede, "Tasks and Methods," 70–73. On this point, Wrede concludes that "the questions and needs of the churches can be a legitimate influence only in a limited sense—and probably least of all in the biblical field. On the whole it is not within the historical researcher's power to serve the church through his work. The theologian who obeys the historical object as his master is not in a position to serve the church through his properly scientific-historical work, even if he were personally interested in doing so" (73).
66. Charles H. H. Scobie, *The Ways of Our God: An Approach to Biblical Theology* (Grand Rapids: Eerdmans, 2003), 6. The brief survey given here focuses on the rise of the scientific method and the historical-critical approach to biblical interpretation. Another alternative during the modern period was Pietism, which favored the religious experience of faith in Christ over the systematic study of the church's theological formulations. These approaches to

Contemporary Approaches to Biblical Theology

After discussing the definition and history of biblical theology as a practice and as a discipline, we can now consider some of the issues and unique considerations that emerge when doing biblical theology. A network of interrelated issues arises when we seek to understand the big picture of the Bible. In what follows, we will survey a selection of influential and representative biblical-theological works and also consider two major ways of categorizing contemporary approaches to the discipline. We will not address every biblical theology project that has recently been published, but rather try to give a sense of some of the major decisions that these contemporary approaches make as they go about the biblical-theological endeavor. We will also navigate some of the swirling diversity of literature within the field.

In 1968, Old Testament scholar James Barr delivered a series of lectures at Birmingham University on the discipline of biblical theology. Later published as *The Concept of Biblical Theology: An Old Testament Perspective*, this volume critically evaluates a host of works on biblical studies and Old and New Testament theology.[67] One of Barr's controlling concepts of the discipline is that biblical theology is "essentially a *contrastive* notion" and "never derived directly from the Bible, as if, given the Bible, it was obvious that the study of it was biblical theology."[68] Rather, this form of study "came to be used in contrast with various *other* modes of studying the Bible that already existed" and thus "does not have clear independent contours of its own: it depends for its existence upon that with which it is contrasted."[69]

Accordingly, Barr seeks to appropriate the legacy and central insights of the modern period's emphasis on historical-critical analysis. For Barr, the discipline of biblical theology "has clarity only when it is understood to mean theology as it existed or was thought or believed within the time, languages and cultures of the Bible itself."[70] In the study of

---

the interpretive endeavor are two ends of the same spectrum. On this alternative and its role in the modern era, see John Sailhamer, *Introduction to Old Testament Theology: A Canonical Approach* (Grand Rapids: Zondervan, 1995), 118–22; Ebeling, "Meaning," 213–17; and Mark W. Elliott, "Pietism," in *New Dictionary of Theology: Historical and Systematic*, ed. Martin Davie, et al (Downers Grove: InterVarsity, 2016), 676–77.

67. James Barr, *The Concept of Biblical Theology: An Old Testament Perspective* (London: SCM, 1999). Particularly useful for accessing Barr's understanding of the discipline is his first chapter entitled, "Definitions: The Many Faces of Biblical Theology" (1–17). For other entry points into Barr's take on the discipline, see the various articles collected in his *Bible and Interpretation: The Collected Essays of James Barr, Volume I: Interpretation and Theology*, ed. John Barton (Oxford: Oxford University Press, 2013).

68. Barr, *Concept of Biblical Theology*, 5.

69. Barr, *Concept of Biblical Theology*, 5. The disciplines Barr focuses on as a contrast to biblical theology are doctrinal theology (systematic theology), non-theological study of the Bible, history of religion, philosophical theology, and "the interpretation of *parts* of the Bible as distinct from the larger complexes taken as *wholes*." Barr draws on these contrasts throughout his work (see, for example, 468–96; and 605–7).

70. Barr, *Concept of Biblical Theology*, 4. Connected to his understanding of biblical theology as "contrastive," Barr clarifies that "only so can its difference from doctrinal theology, from later interpretation, and from later views about the Bible be maintained." Moreover, "what was thought about the Bible by Irenaeus or by Calvin is thus something quite other than biblical theology as here understood."

biblical theology, "what we are looking for is a 'theology' that existed back there and then" and a careful analysis of "biblical times and cultures."[71] Maintaining this insight means that the concept of biblical theology "as a descriptive discipline, describing the theology that was there in biblical times" should take priority over a concept that involves "normative authority, personal commitment," and contemporary interpretation and application.[72] While articulating the priority of historical and descriptive concerns, one of Barr's primary aims is to demonstrate "something of the many-sided character that attaches to the idea of biblical theology" and the clear "complexity of motives, issues and contrasts which have affected the various strands of biblical theology in modern times."[73]

Another influential work from the twentieth century is *Biblical Theology: Old and New Testaments* by Geerhardus Vos. Vos taught at Princeton Theological Seminary from 1893 until 1932. This volume, published the year before he died, represents his approach to biblical theology.[74] Vos utilizes an explicitly historical framework but also includes evangelical commitments about divine revelation, inspiration, and providence. Particularly important for Vos is the way history relates to revelation. Vos defines biblical theology as "that branch of Exegetical Theology which deals with the process of the self-revelation of God deposited in the Bible."[75] For Vos, the notion of progressive revelation in history is a required and foundational assumption. The concept of revelation is understood to be "a divine activity, not a finished product of that activity."[76] To explain the "historic progressiveness of the revelation-process," Vos states that revelation "has not completed itself in one exhaustive act, but unfolded itself in a long series of successive acts."[77] Pressing further, Vos argues for

71. Barr, *Concept of Biblical Theology*, 4. Barr presses further, noting that "if we specify Old or New Testament, then I would prefer to treat these as two sets of times and cultures—which is, incidentally, one reason for doubts about the possibility of one 'pan-biblical theology'." In Barr's view, a "pan-biblical theology" would need to reconstruct a "continuum including both Old and New Testament as one 'time' and culture, or else to think of this as a two-part theology which somehow comprised two separate times and cultures" (5). This synthetic reach is the type of analysis Barr seeks to deconstruct.
72. Barr, *Concept of Biblical Theology*, 6. This distinction informs Barr's position that biblical theology should be understood "in contrast with doctrinal theology." For Barr here, this particular point is crucial: "In many ways this differentiation, as I shall argue, remains the most important today."
73. Barr, *Concept of Biblical Theology*, 17. Barr reiterates this conclusion at several points throughout his book (e.g., 312–44; 452–67; and 605–7).
74. See Geerhardus Vos, *Biblical Theology: Old and New Testaments* (Grand Rapids: Eerdmans, 1948). This volume represents the culmination of the vision for biblical theology that Vos articulated in his inaugural address at Princeton Theological Seminary in 1894. See "The Idea of Biblical Theology as a Science and as a Theological Discipline," in *Redemptive History and Biblical Interpretation: The Shorter Writings of Geerhardus Vos*, ed. Richard B. Gaffin Jr. (Phillipsburg: P&R, 2001), 3–24.
75. Vos, *Biblical Theology*, 5.
76. Vos, *Biblical Theology*, 5. Vos also characterizes revelation here as "a noun of action." For Vos, the nature and method of biblical-theological work must "naturally have to keep in close touch with, and so far as possible reproduce, the features of the divine work itself."
77. Vos, *Biblical Theology*, 5. Vos also here connects the revelation-process to the events in redemptive history: "Revelation is the interpretation of redemption; it must, therefore, unfold itself in installments as redemption does."

the "actual embodiment of revelation in history."[78] He clarifies by making the connection explicit: "The process of revelation is not only concomitant with history, but it becomes incarnate in history." In this scenario, it is "the facts of history themselves" that acquire "revealing significance." Accordingly, Vos urges, "We must place act-revelation by the side of word-revelation."[79]

For Vos, the acts of redemptive history are the means by which God reveals himself, and the structure of a biblical theology runs along the revelation found in the unfolding of redemptive history. A more suitable name for this type of study, Vos suggests, would be the "History of Special Revelation, which precisely describes the subject matter of this discipline."[80] Whereas systematic theology "takes the Bible as a completed whole and endeavors to exhibit its total teaching in an orderly, systematic form," biblical theology in contrast "deals with the material from the historical standpoint, seeking to exhibit the organic growth or development of the truths of Special Revelation from the primitive pre-redemptive Special Revelation given in Eden to the close of the New Testament canon."[81] Accordingly, Vos traces both "pre-redemptive" and "redemptive special revelation" by describing and analyzing the historically progressing "stages" of redemptive history. He structures his study by the "Mosaic epoch," the "Prophetic epoch," and the "new dispensation" of the events surrounding Jesus recorded in the New Testament.[82] Vos ends his study by delineating both the present and future aspects of the kingdom of God.[83]

---

78. Vos, *Biblical Theology*, 6.
79. Vos, *Biblical Theology*, 6–7. Identifying the locus of revelation in the "great outstanding acts of redemption," Vos clarifies here that redemption and revelation coincide in redemptive history. However, Vos also notes that these "two-sided acts" did not take place primarily for the purpose of revelation." Rather, "their revelatory character is secondary" (7). Relating these two concepts, Vos argues that "act-revelations are never entirely left to speak for themselves; they are preceded and followed by word-revelation. The usual order is: first word, then the fact, then again the interpretive word. The Old Testament brings the predictive preparatory word, the Gospels record the redemptive-revelatory fact, the Epistles supply the subsequent, final interpretation."
80. Vos, *Biblical Theology*, v.
81. Vos, *Biblical Theology*, v–vi. One implication of this distinction is that biblical theology "occupies a position between Exegesis and Systematic Theology in the encyclopedia of theological disciplines." He also argues that biblical theology is not "more biblical" than systematic theology (v). See also the way Vos later characterizes these tasks in "Idea of Biblical Theology," 15–16. There, Vos argues that "in Biblical Theology the principle is one of historical, in Systematic it is one of logical construction. Biblical Theology draws a line of development. Systematic Theology draws a circle." This illustration draws on Vos's historical approach to biblical studies and also his understanding of the logical analytic categories that systematic theology uses in presenting theological meaning.
82. Within each major section, Vos periodizes smaller segments of redemptive history in a similar way. For example, the "Noachian revelation and the development leading up to it" (*Biblical Theology*, 45–55), the "period between Noah and the great patriarchs" (56–65), the "revelation in the patriarchal period" (66–99), and "revelation in the period of Moses" (100–82). Each redemptive-historical stage is connected to the next via an emphasis on both progressive revelation and God's providential progress of redemptive history. At the beginning of section two, for example, Vos states, "Next to Mosaism, Prophetism marks an epochal onward movement in Old Testament revelation" and also notes that "revelation follows events" (185).
83. See Vos, *Biblical Theology*, 372–402.

As the discipline of biblical theology sought to navigate the relationship between history, theology, and interpretive approaches, the work of Brevard Childs marked an important development. In his 1992 *Biblical Theology of the Old and New Testaments*, Childs articulates a "canonical approach" to the discipline. Drawing on previous studies in historical-criticism, Old and New Testament scholarship, and the history of interpretation, Childs argues that a proper understanding of the final form of the biblical canon is necessary for a proper articulation of the Bible's overall theological message.[84] For Childs, "the hermeneutical issues of Biblical Theology involved far more than simply joining together the critical study of the Old Testament with that of the New Testament."[85] Rather, "everything turned on how one understood the material which was being described."[86] As Childs understands it, biblical theology is "by definition theological reflection on both the Old and New Testament" and assumes that "the Christian Bible consists of a theological unity formed by the canonical union of the two testaments."[87] As Childs observes, this way of understanding the nature of biblical theology requires a multifaceted view of both the process and product of canon formation.

In this vein, Childs argues that "the lengthy process of the development of the literature leading up to the final stage of canonization involved a profoundly hermeneutical activity on the part of the tradents."[88] For the purpose of biblical theology, "the term canon points to the received, collected, and interpreted material of the church and thus establishes the theological context in which the tradition continues to function authoritatively for today."[89] This recognition of the controlling function of the canonical context fleshes out his understanding of the primary task of biblical theology: "At the heart of the problem of Biblical Theology lies the issue of doing full justice to the subtle canonical relationship of the two testaments within the one Christian Bible."[90] The christological focus of this approach is also necessary for Childs. As he concludes, "both testaments make a discrete witness to Jesus Christ which must be

---

84. The major works preceding his comprehensive *Biblical Theology of the Old and New Testaments* include *Biblical Theology in Crisis* (Philadelphia: Westminster, 1970); *Introduction to the Old Testament as Christian Scripture* (Philadelphia: Fortress, 1979); *The New Testament as Canon: An Introduction* (Philadelphia: Fortress, 1984); and *Old Testament Theology in a Canonical Context* (Philadelphia: Fortress, 1985). His final book focuses on the Pauline Epistles as a coherent collection: *The Church's Guide for Reading Paul: The Canonical Shaping of the Pauline Corpus* (Grand Rapids: Eerdmans, 2008). For a comprehensive description and analysis of Childs's entire corpus, see Daniel R. Driver, *Brevard Childs, Biblical Theologian: For the Church's One Bible*, Forschungen zum Alten Testament 2.46 (Tübingen: Mohr Siebeck, 2010). Driver seeks to identify the inner logic of Childs's canonical approach and also helpfully highlights the strategic notion of "canon-consciousness" as a linchpin in Childs's project as a whole (see 1–11, 137–59; note also Childs, *Biblical Theology*, 70–71).
85. Childs, *Biblical Theology*, xv.
86. Childs, *Biblical Theology*, xv.
87. Childs, *Biblical Theology*, 55.
88. Childs, *Biblical Theology*, 70. Childs expands this statement here by stating that "because the traditions were received as religiously authoritative, they were transmitted in such a way as to maintain a normative function for subsequent generations of believers within a community of faith."
89. Childs, *Biblical Theology*, 71.
90. Childs, *Biblical Theology*, 78.

heard, both separately and in concert."[91] Accordingly, in his biblical theology Childs includes historical investigation (e.g., the growth of biblical traditions), biblical-theological analysis (e.g., the effect of the canonical shape of a book on its message), and dogmatic reflection (e.g., the theological witness of both Testaments to God's being).[92]

One further issue we might note in this brief survey relates to way that the results of biblical-theological study might be presented. Charles H. H. Scobie's 2003 volume, *The Ways of Our God: An Approach to Biblical Theology* represents a distinctly thematic approach to the presentation of biblical theology. Scobie outlines an "intermediate biblical theology" that draws on the historical study of the Bible, but also seeks "to go beyond them and move from analysis to synthesis."[93] Arguing that an organizing principle is not only arbitrary but "goes to the heart of the understanding of the nature of [biblical theology]," Scobie's presentation is "multi-thematic."[94] If the final form of the Scriptures is understood to be a unified whole, an "essential part of this enterprise" will involve discerning "the basic *patterns* inherent in Scripture."[95]

Recognizing the dangers of this type of study, Scobie maintains that "so far as is humanly possible, the structure employed should be the one that arises out of the biblical material itself."[96] Scobie's "sketch" of biblical theology includes the major themes of God's order, God's servant, God's people, and God's way. Each of these major themes includes a cluster of subthemes that expand the broader category in terms of unity and diversity. Further, Scobie maintains that major biblical-theological themes should be developed along the

---

91. Childs, *Biblical Theology*, 78. This notion of the "discrete witness" of both Testaments to Jesus Christ is one of the primary means by which Childs argues for the necessary relationship between biblical studies and theological analysis. The move from "witness to subject matter" (see 80–94) requires historical research, textual analysis, and theological reflection. Significantly, Childs argues that "after the task of biblical theological reflection has begun in which the original integrity of both testaments has been respected, there is an important function of hearing the whole of Christian Scripture in light of the full reality of God in Jesus Christ." In relation to the theological disciplines, Childs insists that there is "a legitimate place for a move from a fully developed Christian theological reflection back to the biblical texts of both testaments" (87). For this reason, Childs urges "biblical scholars to be more systematic, and systematic theologians to be more biblical, and to get on with the task" (89).
92. Accordingly, the main sections of *Biblical Theology of the Old and New Testaments* after the prolegomena and method sections are "The Discrete Witness of the Old Testament" (95–208), "The Discrete Witness of the New Testament" (209–322), "Theological Reflection on the Christian Bible" (349–716), and a brief conclusion entitled, "A Holistic Reading of Christian Scripture" (719–27).
93. Scobie, *Ways of Our God,* 47. He notes further that "a true [biblical theology] seeks to go beyond a merely historical approach and to offer an understanding of the biblical material seen as a canonical whole" (85). Seeing biblical theology as this kind of "bridge" discipline also relates to Scobie's concern to connect the academic study of the Bible to the context of the churches (see ix–x, and 46–49). As he states, "If the church's norm is indeed to be found in its canonical Scriptures, then they must illuminate and direct every aspect of the church's faith and life: its theology, preaching, teaching, devotion, ethical reflection, and Christian action" (48). He also cautions, "Great care is needed, however, to distinguish between discovering and applying biblical norms to contemporary situations, and reading back contemporary social, economic, and political programs into Scripture" (48–49).
94. Scobie, *Ways of Our God,* 81.
95. Scobie, *Ways of Our God,* 81.
96. Scobie, *Ways of Our God,* 81.

pattern of proclamation and promise (rooted in the Old Testament portrayal) and fulfillment and consummation (rooted in the New Testament portrayal).[97]

A Spectrum of Biblical Theology Approaches

Alongside these major contemporary works of biblical theology, there have also been several recent attempts to categorize and map the diverse methods, assumptions, and procedures utilized within the discipline. In their recent work, *Understanding Biblical Theology: A Comparison of Theory and Practice*, Edward Klink and Darian Lockett construct a spectrum of approaches to the task of biblical theology.[98] Noting the varied directions that have been pursued under the rubric of "biblical theology," Klink and Lockett seek to find ways to get a handle on this wide-ranging diversity. They begin by noting the "nexus of issues" that surface in biblical-theological studies. They list five major issues that show up with regularity in biblical theology:

- What is the relationship between the Old Testament and the New Testament?
- How do we make sense of both the historical diversity and theological unity that we find in biblical literature?
- What is the scope, and what are the sources of biblical theology?
- What is the proper subject matter of biblical theology?
- What is the proper context for doing biblical theology: the academy or the church?

These are some of the key enduring questions that attend the study of the Scriptures as a whole. When you ask these types of questions, you engage in some way in the task of biblical theology. Depending on how you answer these questions, you will have a different approach to biblical interpretation and biblical theology.

The five major "types" of biblical theology that Klink and Lockett develop represent different answers to this set of questions. In particular, the spectrum they envision moves from overtly *historical* approaches to overtly *theological* approaches. This history–theology spectrum, then, is the line upon which they plot these different proposals. As Klink and Lockett explain, "Using a spectrum balanced on either end by history and theology, five types of biblical theology are plotted between these poles, as more

97. Scobie unpacks the ways he develops major biblical-theological themes in *Ways of Our God, 81–102.*
98. Edward W. Klink and Darian R. Lockett, *Understanding Biblical Theology: A Comparison of Theory and Practice* (Grand Rapids: Zondervan, 2012). There are several thorough surveys of the history of the discipline and the nature of contemporary approaches that emphasize various focal points. For example, see T. Desmond Alexander and Brian S. Rosner, eds,. *New Dictionary of Biblical Theology* (Downers Grove: InterVarsity, 2000); Scott J. Hafemann, ed., *Biblical Theology: Retrospect & Prospect* (Downers Grove: InterVarsity, 2002); and James K. Mead, *Biblical Theology: Issues, Methods, and Themes* (Louisville: Westminster John Knox, 2007). While many others could be listed here, these works provide wide-ranging overviews of the field and supplement the discussion offered here.

or less 'theological' or 'historical' in concern and practice."[99] As they suggest, seeing this spectrum of positions in relationship to one another can provide a starting point for the study of the discipline. The various approaches here show "some of the central issues attending to the task of biblical theology along with a practical consideration of some of the more visible thinkers working in the area."[100]

In what follows, we will briefly summarize each of the five types of biblical theology (BT) referenced by Klink and Lockett and then reflect on the value of this history–theology spectrum for understanding the field of biblical theology.

BT1: Biblical Theology as Historical Description

This approach to biblical theology is the most historical. As Klink and Lockett observe, "the task of BT1 is to affirm the exegetical or descriptive nature of biblical theology and deny the theological or normative nature of biblical theology."[101] Key components of this approach include a clear focus on historical background information and the time periods in which the biblical events occurred. Consequently, there is a strong historical diversity envisioned between the Testaments. This is a purely descriptive understanding of the discipline of biblical theology that is located squarely within an academic setting.[102]

BT2: Biblical Theology as History of Redemption

This approach to biblical theology is historical as well, but is undergirded by theological presuppositions about God's providential involvement in history and the inspiration of the Scriptures. As Klink and Lockett observe, "the task of BT2 is to discern the historical progression of God's work of redemption through an inductive analysis of key themes developing through both discrete corpora and the whole of Scripture."[103] Major themes like glory, kingdom, or covenant, "constitute the theological connecting fibers between the Old and New Testaments, and these themes necessarily run along a historical trajectory, giving fundamental structure to the theology of the Bible."[104] In this approach, there is a descriptive element that requires historical and academic analysis, but there is also a prescriptive element requiring belief and a clear connection to the life of the churches.[105]

---

99. Klink and Lockett, *Understanding Biblical Theology*, 20.
100. Klink and Lockett, *Understanding Biblical Theology*, 183. On the articulation and evaluation of these five "types," see also Darian Lockett, "Some Ways of 'Doing' Biblical Theology: Assessments and a Proposal," in *Biblical Theology: Past, Present, and Future*, eds. Mark W. Elliot and Carey Walsh (Eugene: Cascade, 2016), 91–107.
101. Klink and Lockett, *Understanding Biblical Theology*, 31.
102. Klink and Lockett give James Barr as an example of BT1 (*Understanding Biblical Theology*, 43–55).
103. Klink and Lockett, *Understanding Biblical Theology*, 61.
104. Klink and Lockett, *Understanding Biblical Theology*, 61.
105. They give D. A. Carson as an example of BT2 (*Understanding Biblical Theology*, 77–89).

BT3: Biblical Theology as Worldview-Story

This approach to biblical theology emphasizes the worldview or story-world that the biblical authors operate within. Depending on the interpreter, this worldview or story-world is accessed by reconstructing the social world of the biblical authors or conceptualizing the thought-world of the biblical authors as they composed their texts. As Klink and Lockett observe, "using the category of narrative to broker a balance between history and theology, the task of BT3 directs readers to understand the individual episodes or passages of Scripture in light of its overarching storyline. Instead of progressing from the smallest bits and pieces of the narrative to the larger whole, BT3 starts with the larger narrative portions of text through which individual units are read."[106]

BT4: Biblical Theology as Canonical Approach

This approach to biblical theology argues that the concept of "canon" is what conjoins the historical and theological dimensions of the biblical-theological task. As Klink and Lockett observe, "the task of BT4 is to affirm the exegetical form and function of the canon for biblical theology, embracing both the descriptive (historical) and prescriptive (theological) nature of Scripture and its confessional community."[107] Here, there is a focus on the final form of the canonical text and its value for the process of interpretation. The canon, then, forms the bridge between exegesis and biblical theology. The canon also must function within the context of a believing community.[108]

BT5: Biblical Theology as Theological Construction

This approach to biblical theology is the most theological. Here, there is a clear concern for the present, prescriptive theological task of biblical theology. Generally, in this approach there is an aversion to any type of historical-critical reading of the Scriptures and an insistence that biblical interpretation should be done within the context of the church community rather than solely within the academy. As Klink and Lockett observe, "the task of BT5 is to affirm the integrated nature of biblical theology as a theological, hermeneutical, and exegetical discipline with overriding theological concerns, incorporating biblical scholarship into the larger enterprise of Christian theology."[109]

Summary of the History–Theology Spectrum of Approaches

This history–theology spectrum helps us see the unwieldy landscape of contemporary biblical theology a little more clearly. Briefly considering this spectrum reveals several lines

---

106. Klink and Lockett, *Understanding Biblical Theology*, 95. They give N. T. Wright as an example of BT3 (109–22).
107. Klink and Lockett, *Understanding Biblical Theology*, 128.
108. They give Brevard Childs as an example of BT4 (*Understanding Biblical Theology*, 141–53).
109. Klink and Lockett, *Understanding Biblical Theology*, 159. They give Francis Watson as an example of BT5 (169–82).

of continuity and discontinuity. In this survey, perhaps the most important fault line to make note of occurs between the first and second approaches. In fact, by noting the similarities and differences between "Biblical Theology as Historical Description" (BT1) and "Biblical Theology as History of Redemption" (BT2), you can perceive the theological issues at stake in the methodological discussion of biblical theology.

In this manner, the approach of BT2 represents an anchoring position for most evangelicals engaged in the task of biblical theology. Evangelical biblical theology, broadly speaking, is a discipline that accepts the value of seeking the meaning of the biblical texts on their own terms. By "evangelical," we mean an approach to biblical theology that is confessional. A confessional or evangelical approach to biblical theology maintains a series of theological commitments about the biblical text and basic tenets of theological method. A central reason for this orienting point of departure is because BT2 includes affirmations of God's providence, a high view of Scripture, and the importance of seeing the unity of the Scriptures in addition to recognizing their diversity.

The third and fourth "types" of biblical theology emphasize the importance of the narratives and worldview of the biblical authors (BT3) and also the context of the biblical canon (BT4). The fifth and final approach (BT5) focuses more on the theological task and is most closely associated with the discipline of systematic theology and the theological interpretation of Scripture.

Thus, in some ways, both ends of the history–theology spectrum fall outside of what most evangelicals consider to be the main task of biblical theology: namely, the study of the whole Bible on its own terms. On the one hand, BT1 is not biblical theology in this sense because it takes a purely historical and descriptive approach to both interpretation and the broader context of the biblical writings (i.e., closer to a *history of religions*). On the other hand, BT5 is not biblical theology in this sense because it focuses directly on the theological task (i.e., closer to *theological interpretation* or *systematic theology*). Recognizing these broad observations allows us to see that the bulk of evangelical approaches to biblical theology fall in between these inner poles of the spectrum.

To reiterate the strategic insight this spectrum provides, we see the biggest shift when we move from BT1 to BT2. There is a methodological "Grand Canyon" between BT1 and BT2. However, once evangelical presuppositions about the nature of God's involvement in history (redemptive history) and the nature of Scripture (inspiration) are operative, the lines of continuity begin to coalesce. There are differences between evangelical approaches to biblical theology to be sure, but they are often intramural. In other words, once an interpreter accepts the foundation of evangelical presuppositions about God and Scripture, the distance and differences between these approaches typically look more like "rivers and ravines" rather than a "Grand Canyon."

BT2, BT3, and BT4 present the evangelical interpreter with a range of ways to grapple with the big picture of the Bible. Within a confessional approach, these three areas emphasize redemptive history, the storyline of the Bible, narrative, canon, and the interpretive tools necessary to access these big picture areas. BT5 is also a reminder of the organic and natural methodological relationship between biblical theology and systematic theology, as well as systematic theology's relationship to exegesis in theological interpretation. As full-scale approaches, however, each of these areas contain significant differences and tensions that still require examination and careful consideration. Accordingly, this spectrum of approaches maps both points of unity and diversity within contemporary evangelical approaches to biblical theology.

A Series of Hermeneutical Choices

The move from a purely historical approach to biblical theology to one that allows for theological presuppositions about the nature of Scripture and God's providence to comprise part of one's theological method is significant. The history–theology spectrum highlights this important *theological* dimension to biblical theology. There is also value to thinking further about the nature of the *hermeneutical* dimensions that are involved in evangelical approaches to biblical theology.

One of the elements that strongly unifies the broad variety of evangelical approaches to biblical theology is the firm rejection of a thoroughgoing historical-critical approach to biblical interpretation. Most evangelicals utilize critical tools at various points in their exegetical or theological method, but roundly (and rightly) reject the tenets of historical criticism as a foundational approach to biblical interpretation. However, there is still a great deal of intramural diversity within evangelical biblical theologies. Often, these differences lie not in their ultimate theological convictions, but in the realm of theological method and hermeneutics.

In a work that seeks to summarize and analyze the crucial decisions that have to be made in the discipline of biblical theology, John Sailhamer articulates in *Introduction to Old Testament Theology* four hermeneutical choices for biblical theology.[110] This set of four choices has considerable explanatory power in its own right, but can also function as a helpful complement to the spectrum of biblical theology approaches discussed above. In what follows, we will summarize the four major choices described by Sailhamer and then reflect on their value for understanding the field of biblical theology.

Choice 1: Text or Event

This first hermeneutical choice relates to the object of study in biblical theology. As Sailhamer poses, "Does an OT theology focus its attention on the scriptural text of the OT itself, or is the text primarily a witness to the act of God's self-revelation in the events

---

110. Sailhamer's book *Introduction to Old Testament Theology: A Canonical Approach* is specifically about Old Testament theology, but the bulk of his discussion of these choices considers the entire field of hermeneutics, history of interpretation, and the field of biblical theology as a discipline in its own right.

recorded by Scripture?"[111] In other words, is the focus of interpretation the biblical event itself, or the account of that biblical event in the text of Scripture?

This particular question is designed to help the reader think carefully about both aspects required for the interpretation of the biblical narrative. The Bible is indeed about the events of redemptive history, but the Bible also narrates and interprets those events. This hermeneutical insight is not designed to drive a wedge between these two realities, but to enable us to see them with clarity and reckon with their interpretive significance.

Evangelicals affirm that Scripture is God's inspired word, that the events it records really happened, and that its accounts of these events are historically reliable. Thus, for evangelicals, the issue at hand in reading biblical narratives is not primarily an *apologetic* one, but rather an *interpretive* one. Historical investigation, in other words, is necessary but not sufficient to accomplish the hermeneutical task of understanding a biblical author's portrayal of an event in redemptive history. Given what we believe and affirm about the Scriptures, how do we interpret these narratives? From this vantage, the "text or event" question is particularly relevant. Sailhamer explains, "The issue we are attempting to raise here is simply that of our commitment to an inspired *written* Word of God as the locus of God's special revelation. For the Christian today we must again raise the question: Where does the locus of God's special revelation lie? Does it lie in the meaning of historical events provided by the Scriptures or does it lie in the meaning we ourselves attach to the events of Israel's history?"[112]

Though Sailhamer's approach here is unique in how it highlights the critical significance of this hermeneutical decision, this way of addressing the relationship between historical events, narrative portrayal, the locus of revelation, and the implications for characterizing the object of a reader's analysis draws on a well-established line of inquiry in biblical and theological studies.[113] As mentioned above, this issue is specifically related to the under-

---

111. Sailhamer, *Introduction to Old Testament Theology*, 36. Sailhamer also pursues this question directly in his "Cosmic Maps, Prophecy Charts, and the Hollywood Movie: A Biblical Realist Looks at the Eclipse of Old Testament Narrative," *Criswell Theological Review* 7.2 (1994): 65–81; idem, "Johann August Ernesti: The Role of History in Biblical Interpretation," *Journal of the Evangelical Theological Society* 44.2 (2001): 193–206; and *The Meaning of the Pentateuch: Revelation, Composition and Interpretation* (Downers Grove: InterVarsity, 2009), 100–148.

112. Sailhamer, *Introduction to Old Testament Theology*, 42.

113. For example, in the early twentieth century Anglican philosopher (and eventual Archbishop of Canterbury) William Temple posed, "At once the question arises whether the Bible is supposed to be itself the revelation, or to be the record of the revelation. Is the revelation in the book or in the events which the book records?" See his *Nature, Man and God* (London: Macmillan, 1934), 308. Temple also states that "the typical locus of revelation is not the mind of the seer but the historical event. And if the revelation is essentially an event or fact, then it can be perfectly definite, although it neither is nor can be exhaustively represented in propositions" (318). In his classic work in the history of interpretation, Hans Frei also identifies this particular interpretive issue as the center of many wide-ranging shifts in the hermeneutical approaches of the modern period. See his *The Eclipse of Biblical Narrative: A Study in Eighteenth and Nineteenth Century Hermeneutics* (New Haven: Yale University Press, 1974), esp. 1–65. In his interaction with "salvation history" approaches to the locus of revelation, Childs homes in on this distinction

standing of narrative. This profoundly hermeneutical decision is urgently significant for both biblical readers and theologians because the majority of texts in the Bible are narratives. Further, because biblical theology is concerned with understanding the "big picture" or the "story" of Scripture, biblical narratives will always have a central place in any articulation of that storyline. Thus, thinking carefully about the nature of narrative is of critical importance.[114]

Choice 2: Canon or Criticism

This hermeneutical choice relates specifically to the means by which we access the text of Scripture. Do we accept the final canonical form of the text, or seek to describe or reconstruct previous stages of the text using various text-critical tools? As Sailhamer explains, "modern biblical scholarship has given us more than one way to view the Scriptures. We can view them in terms of how they have come down to us by means of tradition, or we can view them in terms of the various stages of growth they underwent before they arrived at their present form. In other words we can take the Scriptures at face value as we now have them (canon), or we can apply the various methods of biblical criticism to attempt to 'reconstruct' an earlier form of these texts (criticism)."[115]

The "canon" option here "accepts the canonical text at face value" and approaches the text "as it is."[116] Conversely, the "criticism" option uses text-critical tools to "reconstruct an earlier version of the Scriptures. Such an earlier, reconstructed version—whether of the

---

as well. For Childs, one of the "serious" problems with using salvation-history as an exclusive interpretive grid is that "the appeal to a *Heilsgeschichte* found the theological continuity between the testaments to lie in events behind the text, and it required a process of critical reconstruction to extract the real theological data from the biblical text" (*Biblical Theology*, 18). "Yet," Childs responds, "the vehicle for the witness to God's redemptive will is most frequently found in the biblical text itself and the interpretation of the Scripture is central to the disclosure of this divine purpose" (18). Finally, as he concludes in a recent introduction to his biblical theology approach, D. A. Carson states that "above all, salvation history provides the locus in which God has disclosed himself in events and in the words that explain them. As salvation history is the framework of the Bible's storyline, so it is the locus of the revelation of the living God, the Lord of history." See "A Biblical-Theological Overview of the Bible," in *NIV Biblical Theology Study Bible*, ed. D. A. Carson (Grand Rapids: Zondervan, 2018), 2325–27. Cf. also the survey and analysis of Stephen B. Chapman, "Reclaiming Inspiration for the Bible," in *Canon and Biblical Interpretation, ed. Craig Bartholomew* et al., Scripture and Hermeneutics Series 7 (Grand Rapids: Zondervan, 2006), 167–206. For our point here, Chapman observes, "No one in evangelical scholarship perceived as early or as perceptively as John Sailhamer how increased awareness of the biblical canon might helpfully reorient evangelical hermeneutics, especially in its thinking about history" (182; see also Chapman's critical interaction at 195–96).

114. Sailhamer sounds this caution: "While professing to be text-centered in their approach, evangelical biblical theologians sometimes treat the text of Scripture as a means of getting at what they perceive to be the *real* locus of God's revelation—the events in the history of Israel or the religious ideals that lie behind the text. In doing so they fail to appreciate the implications of their own orthodox view of Scripture as divine revelation" (*Introduction to Old Testament Theology*, 37).

115. Sailhamer, *Introduction to Old Testament Theology*, 86.

116. Sailhamer, *Introduction to Old Testament Theology*, 112.

text or the event—then becomes the locus of divine revelation."[117] This decision affects both the way an interpreter perceives the object of study and also the tools used to analyze that object of study. For example, if a text-critical approach is taken, the type of tools used may include form, source, or tradition criticism. Moreover, if the object of study is the final form of the canon, then the critical tools used may include compositional, redactional, or text-linguistic analysis.[118]

Choice 3: Confessional or Descriptive

This choice asks how one's faith commitments relate to the task of biblical theology. In doing biblical theology, "what role does our own personal faith play in shaping and in forming it?"[119]

A descriptive approach would *rule out* theological presuppositions whereas a confessional approach would seek to *build upon* a series of theological presuppositions in the pursuit of a biblical theology. As Sailhamer notes, "according to the descriptive approach, the task of OT theology is merely to describe the content of what the OT meant to its original readers. It leaves to the systematic theologian the question of what the OT means today."[120] Conversely, "according to the confessional approach, the task of OT theology is to define the message of the OT within the context of one's own personal faith. The task of OT theology is thus not merely to describe the meaning of the text but also to stand under its authority."[121]

Choice 4: Diachronic or Synchronic

The final choice Sailhamer mentions moves from the study of the biblical texts to the presentation of biblical theology. As he explains, "the question to which we now turn is a structural one. Specifically, what kind of structure should an OT theology have? How should we present it? Do we develop a theology that attempts to understand and explain the OT as a whole, or should our aim be an understanding only of its parts sequentially arranged throughout the OT itself?"[122] For Sailhamer, the purpose of one's theological presentation determines which type of structure may be most suitable or fitting.

The two general ways of presenting theology follow either a diachronic or a synchronic mode of presentation. A "diachronic" (*through time*) presentation explores theological development across history or a temporal sequence, whereas a "synchronic" (*within time*)

---

117. Sailhamer, *Introduction to Old Testament Theology*, 113.
118. Sailhamer, *Introduction to Old Testament Theology*, 102–3.
119. Sailhamer, *Introduction to Old Testament Theology*, 115.
120. Sailhamer, *Introduction to Old Testament Theology*, 157.
121. Sailhamer, *Introduction to Old Testament Theology*, 170.
122. Sailhamer, *Introduction to Old Testament Theology*, 184.

presentation logically or synthetically considers relationships within a particular theological system or pattern of associations (in other words, "systematically"). Biblical theology presentations have typically embraced some sort of "diachronic" mode of progression. In particular, when a theme is developed in biblical theology, there is usually a clear attempt to demonstrate a chronological progression of the theme *through time* ("diachronic").

Another way to understand the relationship between these two broad ways of presenting material is that a synchronic presentation usually arranges its components as part of a *system* whereas a diachronic presentation usually arranges its components as part of a *sequence*. As Sailhamer notes regarding Old Testament theology, "the term diachronic is taken to represent any view that includes the notion that an OT theology should present itself as an unfolding of the central theological message of the OT. In a diachronic approach, each element of the OT's theology is viewed distinctly and discreetly within a sequence rather than within a total system."[123] Conversely, a synchronic presentation is systematic insofar as it involves "an attempt to give a comprehensive arrangement of the material of the OT around a single idea, or set of ideas."[124]

Summary of the Series of Hermeneutical Choices

Sailhamer's series of four hermeneutical choices yields several benefits for the evaluation of biblical theology and its variety of approaches. First, these choices reveal the interchangeability of certain components within a given approach. This tool of analysis helps navigate some of the continuity and discontinuity between various biblical-theological proposals. Second, this series of choices elucidates the nature of the hermeneutical dimension of biblical theology. Using these choices can help expose the prominence of underlying *hermeneutical* issues in different biblical-theological approaches and proposals. Third, the "diachronic or synchronic" choice provides a category for relating the various ways that different studies present material. Finally, Sailhamer's series of hermeneutical choices is compatible with other understandings of the field of biblical theology. In particular, these hermeneutical choices can complement the biblical theology approaches described in Klink and Lockett's history–theology spectrum.

Making Sense of the Methodological Mosaic

In tandem, these two ways of surveying and processing contemporary approaches to the discipline of biblical theology can provide explanatory power when you seek to distinguish different streams of thought. For example, oftentimes the key difference between

---

123. Sailhamer, *Introduction to Old Testament Theology*, 185.
124. Sailhamer, *Introduction to Old Testament Theology*, 189. See also the discussion of diachronic and synchronic modes of presentation in chapter eleven.

Chapter 1 — Defining Biblical Theology 49

biblical-theological approaches lies in how they receptively utilize both history and historical progression in relation to narrative texts and the canonical context. Significant in this regard is the relationship between a historical-critical approach to biblical theology (BT1) and an evangelical approach (BT2).

Sailhamer's series of hermeneutical choices can help explain some of these differences from another angle. The "confessional or descriptive" choice is similar to the move from BT1 to BT2. However, the "text or event" choice provides additional insight regarding how one approaches the nature of narrative. There has been a recent resurgence of interest in the analysis and utilization of the Bible's overarching storyline. We might inquire, in light of the "text or event" choice, how this storyline is being approached. Is there a difference between a storyline, a chronology, or a salvation history? How do the biblical texts relate to the articulation of this overarching storyline or meta-narrative? So, as the history–theology spectrum of approaches highlights, the way one relates history to theology has important consequences. As the series of hermeneutical choices also highlights, the way one relates history to the nature of narratives and biblical texts has important consequences as well.

Furthermore, within a distinctly confessional approach to biblical theology, often the theological conviction that Christ is supreme in all things informs the hermeneutical conviction that the Scriptures are all about Christ. Recognizing both the theological *and* hermeneutical nature of this particular question helps us grapple with these issues in the fullest way possible. We want to consider not only *that* the whole Bible is about Christ, but also *how* the whole Bible is about Christ. While raising the question does not automatically identify the right answer, it does steer us to consider this all-important issue from multiple angles.

Boldness and Humility in the Study of Biblical Theology

This survey of the history of biblical theology and contemporary approaches to the discipline should perhaps evoke two responses: initial despair and enduring encouragement. Initially, a survey like this can produce a sense of overwhelming despair at the diversity present among those who study the Bible on both a small and large scale. Even among evangelicals, there are many approaches flying under the banner of biblical theology that oftentimes seem to be doing very different things in very different ways while pursuing very different objects of study. The volume you hold now describes and participates in this unity and diversity as well.

Upon continuing reflection, or perhaps from a different angle, this same survey can also produce a sense of enduring encouragement. First, though there are indeed many approaches to biblical theology, the history–theology spectrum of approaches and the series of hermeneutical choices outlined above demonstrate that there are also several strong lines of continuity running through these approaches to biblical theology and the study of the Bible in general. Second, for evangelicals, the clarion call to reject a historical-critical approach as an orienting framework and accept bedrock theological presuppositions about the providential involvement of God in the world and the inspiration of the Scriptures is a unifying factor that should not be taken lightly.

In fact, these theological presuppositions generate a shared framework that renders many of the differences among contemporary approaches to "whole Bible" theology intramural. To be sure, these differences are significant and must be articulated with clarity, wisdom, and methodological rigor. There is enduring encouragement here, though, for those of us engaged in this methodological discussion. Recognizing these aspects allows us to navigate the details of the discipline of biblical theology with both boldness and humility.

In the following chapters, we will outline a framework for doing biblical theology that seeks to take this discussion of the definition and discipline of biblical theology into account.

Discussion Questions

1. What is the definition of "biblical theology" and what are some of the primary ways you might unpack this working definition?

2. What is the relationship between exegesis, biblical theology, and systematic theology?

3. Describe how Irenaeus's use of the "rule of faith" serves as an example of biblical-theological study before the modern era.

4. Describe the impact that the modern era had on biblical studies in general and the discipline of biblical theology in particular. How have the concerns of the modern era shaped some of the dimensions of the discipline of biblical theology?

5. Compare and contrast Klink and Lockett's "spectrum of biblical theology approaches" and Sailhamer's "series of hermeneutical choices." What does each of these analytical tools provide on their own, and how do they complement one another?

Resources for Further Study

Alexander, T. Desmond and Brian Rosner, eds. *New Dictionary of Biblical Theology.* Downers Grove: InterVarsity, 2000.

Bartholomew, Craig, et al, eds. *Out of Egypt: Biblical Theology and Biblical Interpretation.* Grand Rapids: Zondervan, 2004.

Emerson, Matthew Y. *The Story of Scripture: An Introduction to Biblical Theology.* Nashville: B&H, 2017.

Hafemann, Scott J., ed. *Biblical Theology: Retrospect & Prospect.* Downers Grove: InterVarsity, 2002.

Mead, James K. *Biblical Theology: Issues, Methods, and Themes.* Louisville: WJK, 2007.

CHAPTER 2

THE BIBLE'S OVERARCHING SHAPE

IN CHAPTER ONE, WE LAID THE GROUNDWORK for understanding the discipline of biblical theology. Now that we have discussed the history of the discipline and various contemporary evangelical approaches to biblical theology, we can proceed to some of the aspects that will help you begin doing biblical theology in your own study. In this chapter, we will consider the Bible's overarching shape. First, we will contemplate a framework for biblical theology. Then, we will develop a set of tools particularly suited to the biblical-theological task. We will use these tools throughout the biblical-theological studies that appear later in the book.

A Framework for Biblical Theology: The Canon, the Covenants, and the Christ

A valuable starting point for doing biblical theology is establishing a comprehensive framework. The building blocks of a solid framework for doing biblical theology can be grouped into three categories: the canon; the covenants; and the Christ.[1]

Relating the Canon, the Covenants, and the Christ

As exhibited in chapter one, there are a variety of approaches to biblical theology. The approach taken here focuses on and directly relates the canon, the covenants, and the Christ. The Scriptures were composed, gathered, and circulated in such a way that they are

---

1. In this chapter, we examine the first two components of this framework for biblical theology (the canon and the covenants), and in chapter three, we discuss the third (the Christ). A recent work that also connects these broad themes and focuses on the distinctly theological implications of these areas of emphasis is Matthew Barrett, *Canon, Covenant and Christology: Rethinking Jesus and the Scriptures of Israel* (Downers Grove: InterVarsity, 2020).

able to communicate God's revelation of his saving message for future generations. This canonical context, then, is where we encounter the biblical writings. Moreover, a grand storyline arises from the many narratives comprising this canonical collection. The heartbeat of this storyline can be heard in the biblical covenants. Both the canonical collection and the biblical covenants point to Jesus as the Christ. These three interconnected categories—the canon, the covenants, and the Christ—structure our attempt to capture the crucial components of biblical theology.

The heart of the biblical theologian's task is to explore these three categories and their interrelationship. As we will demonstrate in the following chapters, these important areas of emphasis are interwoven throughout the Scriptures and encompass many of the main features of the Bible. This approach resonates with several recent trends in evangelical scholarship on biblical theology, especially those that stress the importance of textual features, the storyline of the Bible as a whole, and the strategic function of the biblical canon.

In this chapter, we will use the canonical context, the grand storyline of the Bible, the prominent role that the covenants play in that story, and the overarching focus on Christ as orienting positions from which to view and understand the entire Bible. Once we consider this framework, we will focus on tools that help us understand and articulate this big picture of the Bible. These tools will help you read individual passages well and present biblical-theological themes cogently.

The Importance of Having a Big Picture Framework

The biblical theologian asks, "What is the big picture of the Bible?" The immediate follow-up question is, "How do the many parts of the Bible relate to the larger textual whole?" How a reader understands the textual whole affects how he or she understands the parts comprising the text. A reader experiences the structural framework of a text, even when it is not overtly stated. For instance, you might never think about the design of a staircase or the practical value of its placement within a building. Yet, you still benefit from its existence and ability to get you to the next floor. In similar fashion, when we read a text, we often walk through the textual hallways, climb the structural stairs, and peer out the storied windows that its author has placed in our paths. We reap the benefits of this authorial handiwork as we understand the basic meaning of the work.

A "big picture" approach summarizes the message of the Bible and explains not only the *most* parts, but also the *most important* parts.[2] This dual distinction is important for identifying and distilling central themes in the Scriptures as well as determining how you describe

---

2. John Sailhamer uses these phrases to examine the "big idea" of the Pentateuch. As he argues, "The best (most valid) big idea is the one that explains the most and the most important parts of the Pentateuch . . . Our big idea not only should help us understand (quantitatively) most of what is in the Pentateuch, but also it should help us discover (qualitatively) what is most important to the author" (*Meaning of the Pentateuch*, 152–53).

and characterize the biblical material. The goal is to utilize categories that are broad enough to capture the diverse material found throughout the biblical collection, but also specific enough to communicate the meaning and message of the Bible clearly and effectively.

Biblical Theology as Reading and Rereading

The hard work of biblical theology involves articulating broad themes and also discerning how individual texts, groups of texts, biblical books, and groups of biblical books intersect. Maintaining a creative tension between these two tasks is one of the most challenging and rewarding aspects of the discipline of biblical theology.[3] Accordingly, this hermeneutical circle works not only on a small scale (passage-level analysis), but also on a medium scale (book-level analysis) and large scale (grouping-level analysis). We must *read* and *reread* the Bible. Especially for biblical texts, to understand and articulate the big picture is not an end in and of itself. The big picture or structural framework of a biblical book or the Bible as a whole does not replace the reading of the text, but rather serves as an informative guide to aid in future readings and rereadings.

Tools for Doing Big Picture Biblical Theology

Once you have a biblical theology framework in place, you can use the tools of biblical theology, referred to here as BT Tools, more effectively. Against the background of the canon, the covenants, and the Christ, we can take a deeper dive into each of these areas.

BT Tool: The Canonical Context

Our primary goal in biblical theology is to grapple with the Bible's big picture and understand the grand storyline of the Bible. The two-testament canon of the Old and New Testament Scriptures provides guidance for this task. Readers of the canon encounter individual documents as parts of a developed whole. The concept of canon, then, forms the basis of understanding for the church's reading of Scripture. In other words, the canon functions as the foundation of the church's engagement with God's Word to his people and the necessary context for "whole Bible" interpretation. This canonical reality faces every reader of the Bible and should have a direct impact on every biblical theologian.

Defining the Canon of Scripture

Reflecting on a few definitional questions can provide a helpful orientation to the importance of the canonical context for the task of biblical theology. Although debates concerning the formation of the canon and the etymology of relevant terms are more at home

---

3. As Childs notes, "There is need for a discipline that will attempt to retain and develop a picture of the whole, and that will have a responsibility to synthesize as well as analyze" (*Biblical Theology in Crisis*, 92).

in a different area of research, some of the key features from this discussion offer helpful insight for the study of biblical theology.[4]

Canon. Borrowed from the ancient Greek *kanōn* ("measuring stick, ruler"), the English term *canon* has two broad senses. First, canon can refer to a rule, norm, or guide. Derived from its literal Greek meaning, this usage of canon denotes an authoritative "rule" or "standard" used to judge or appraise something (e.g., "rule of law," or "rule of faith"). Second, the term canon can refer to a list or catalog. More specifically, the word often references an authoritative list of items (e.g., people, tables of measurements, important texts), thereby maintaining its first sense of "norm" or "rule." One of the reasons you might call some sort of list a "canon" is because you understand it to be an authoritative listing or gathering of those things. Along these lines, we can think of a canon as an authoritative collection of highly regarded literature.

Scripture. The English word *scripture* comes from the Latin *scriptura*, which simply means "writings." In certain contexts, the term scripture means "sacred writings." In this sense, scriptures are writings that have been deemed authoritative or are considered normative by a particular group of people. In translations of the New Testament, the term scripture is used to translate the Greek word *graphē* along these lines. For example, Paul reminds Timothy that he has known the "sacred writings" from childhood and declares that "all Scripture is breathed out by God" (2 Tim. 3:15–16). Within this context, we see that the word "Scripture" references written documents understood to be authoritative. This authority comes directly from God himself ("breathed out by God"). Paul emphasizes both the textual reality of the Scriptures (i.e., they are literary documents that have authors) and also the theological reality of the Scriptures (i.e., they find their ultimate origin in God).

Canon of Scripture. The phrase *canon of Scripture*, then, refers to an authoritative collection of authoritative writings. In other words, both the individual documents within the collection as well as the collection itself are considered authoritative and divinely inspired. In this sense, while we can distinguish between canon and scripture, we should not totally divorce these concepts. Because the notion of authority is organically connected to the concept of canon, we can call the writings that comprise the biblical collection "canonical." This affirms the authority of a scriptural text both in and of itself, and also due to its inclusion within an authoritative collection.

---

4. For an extended discussion of the formation and function of the biblical canon from a variety of angles, see Ched Spellman, *Toward a Canon-Conscious Reading of the Bible: Exploring the History and Hermeneutics of the Biblical Canon* (Sheffield: Sheffield Phoenix, 2014), 8–141; F. F. Bruce, *The Canon of Scripture* (Downers Grove: InterVarsity, 1988); Michael J. Kruger, *Canon Revisited: Establishing the Origins and Authority of the New Testament Books* (Wheaton: Crossway, 2012); and Edmon L. Gallagher and John D. Meade, *The Biblical Canon Lists from Early Christianity: Texts and Analysis* (Oxford: Oxford University Press, 2017).

During the fourth century, some Christians began to label the collection of Old and New Testament writings a canon. For example, as one writer from this period urged his readers, "Let us examine the canon of truth, I mean the divine Scriptures."[5] In so doing, the earliest churches recognized both the *authority* and *interconnectedness* of these writings.

Bible. Around this time, the church also began calling the canon the Bible. The word *Bible* means "books," so naming the canonical collection the "Bible" meant calling it something like the "Book of books." Recognizing this aspect of the term Bible is helpful because it highlights the related notions of unity and diversity. The Bible is both a *unified* work (i.e., a collection conceived of as a single "book") but also a *diverse* compilation (i.e., a single collection that contains many different books).

Additionally, calling this collection of books a "canon" ascribes authority and reverence to the Bible. The earliest churches confessed that these writings were authoritative and that the collection also carried the cumulative weight of their combined witness to God's special revelation. Theologically, then, when we use these terms to describe the Bible, we confess that this collection as a whole is God's special revelation to his people.

The Basic Shape of the Canon as a Two-Testament Witness to the Christ

One of the chief "big picture" questions that arise in the study of biblical theology is the relationship between the Testaments. This particular question emerges as readers encounter the biblical writings within a two-testament collection. This canonical reality directly impacts the way we understand the big picture of the Bible.

This juxtaposition of the Old Testament and the New Testament raises the question: What is the relationship between these two diverse collections that now sit side-by-side in the Christian canon? This canonical question can be approached from a number of different angles. Historically, the Christian canon forms as a two-testament collection. This is a significant point to consider in its own right. Theologically, the issue of the relationship between the Testaments is caught up in the confession of Jesus as Lord and Christ.[6] Hermeneutically, this question acknowledges the many interconnections that exist between the texts of both Testaments. It also prompts consideration of how reading a biblical book within the context of a broader collection affects the reader's understanding of both the message of that book and also the broader collection itself.

Because the relationship between the Testaments is connected to the unity and diversity of the Christian Bible at its highest structural level, this discussion features into several biblical-theological areas of study and research. Historically, theologically, and

---

5. See Isidore of Pelusium, *Epistles*, 4.11. Here the "canon of truth" is in an appositional position to "the divine Scripture." For this text and reference, see Bruce Metzger, *The Canon of the New Testament: Its Origin, Development, and Significance* (Oxford: Clarendon, 1987), 293n12.
6. On this christological issue, see the discussion in chapter three.

hermeneutically, then, the basic shape of the Christian canon as a two-testament collection of writings must be reckoned with when studying and presenting the message of the Bible from beginning to end.

The Biblical Collections within the Biblical Collection

An important initial step to understanding the Bible as a whole is to see it as a collection of carefully connected collections. The Old Testament, also known as the Hebrew Bible, is the name for the collection of the three groupings of books: the Law, the Prophets, and the Writings. The New Testament is the name for the collection of the groupings of the Gospels, the book of Acts, two major collections of letters, and the book of Revelation.

With this basic literary and canonical category of "collection" in place, a reader or interpreter is better equipped to discern the big picture of the Bible. Though it is perhaps easy to conceive of biblical books independent of the collections where they are located, this conceptual re-orientation can have a significant effect on our ability to articulate the message of the Bible and navigate both its unity and diversity.

The Grouping of the Groupings

One of the striking features of the canonical collection is its relative stability. While Christian communities have ordered and interpreted the biblical texts in different ways, when compared to the sheer randomness that is possible, there are several clear lines of continuity and distinct patterns that emerge when the biblical books are collected together.

For example, there are twenty-four possible ways to order the four Gospels. However, the biblical manuscript evidence reveals two general orderings of these texts: the more frequent Matthew–Mark–Luke–John; and the less frequent Matthew–John–Luke–Mark. When we consider groupings influenced not only by canonical considerations but also by compositional considerations (i.e. the "books" are part of a single "book"), the numbers are even more striking. For instance, there are 120 possible ways to order Genesis, Exodus, Leviticus, Numbers, and Deuteronomy. However, because these five books comprise the Book of Moses, or Pentateuch, they almost always appear in this ordered sequence in manuscripts and lists of books. The same holds true for Hosea through Malachi. There are 479,001,600 possible ways to sequence these twelve books, but within manuscripts of the Book of the Twelve there are only a handful of significant orderings of these works.

These brief examples should suffice to illustrate that while there are variations in how the books of the biblical canon are ordered, there are nevertheless historically demonstrable and readily discernible patterns of stability that can be detected across the collection.

Very early in the formation of the New Testament, the writings of the apostles were circulated in groups. As this process took place, those circulating these documents were concerned about the preservation of the content of these writings as well as the order in which they were arranged. As was the case with the Hebrew Bible, the New Testament groupings were constructed with a level of consistency that allowed a rough order of reading to be established. To give a few broad examples, the Gospels were naturally read first, as they contained the "beginning of the Gospel of Jesus Christ" (Mark 1:1), and the book of Revelation was situated at the end due to its preoccupation with the "end of days." Paul's Letters and the Catholic Epistles were likewise read in light of the historical framework provided by the book of Acts. Accordingly, when the individual groupings of the New Testament books begin circulating together, and when later lists of the New Testament books emerged, they tended to follow this broad conceptual arrangement.

The Role of the Believing Community

The presence of a received canon in the history of the church shows that a community existed that consciously preserved and gathered together the writings they viewed as authoritative Scripture. In other words, the churches not only received and treasured the biblical writings, they also handed them down to later generations in a way that would maintain their compositional shape and extend their literary legacy. In fact, the concept of canon implies that these authoritative writings were collected for the purpose of preserving them for future generations of readers.

A community guided by the message of the prophets and apostles gathered their respective writings into collections and groupings. Members from this community then passed along these Scriptures in these groupings within an authoritative canon. Because of their location within this canonical collection, each of the individual biblical writings could more easily reach a broader readership.

The canonical context, then, serves as the church's guide for reading all of its Scriptures.[7] In this sense, the canonical collection compensates for the reality that "we are not prophets or apostles."[8] Though communities of believers can no longer be guided by the actual hands of the prophets and apostles, they can be guided by their handiwork.

---

7. The notion of the canonical context as a guide for the church echoes Brevard Childs's discussion of the way Paul's letter collection serves as the "church's guide for reading Paul." See Childs, *Reading Paul*.

8. Childs uses the phrase "we are neither prophets nor apostles" in *Biblical Theology*, 381: "We are neither prophets nor Apostles. The function of the church's canon is to recognize this distinction. The Christian church does not have the same unmediated access to God's revelation as did the Apostles, but rather God's revelation is mediated through their authoritative witness, namely through Scripture." On this issue, see also Childs, *Biblical Theology in Crisis*, 99–114. Christopher Seitz exposits and develops this idea at length in *Character of Christian Scripture*, 93–114. Cf. Seitz, "The Canonical Approach and Theological Interpretation," in *Canon and Biblical Interpretation*, ed. Craig Bartholomew et al., Scripture and Hermeneutics Series 7 (Grand Rapids: Zondervan, 2006), 99: "A canonical approach insists the inspired witness is building a bridge to us which is sure and which has our seasons in mind. We are not prophets or apostles, but the canon appreciates this reality with all its witnessing majesty, as we are brought fully into the range of the Holy Spirit's work by virtue of the canon's shape and character as witness."

Using the Canonical Context as a BT Tool

A key takeaway from this discussion is that the "canon" and "canonical context" are *already* forms of biblical theology. Because the shape of the canon is hermeneutically and theologically significant, the canonical context helps us understand how individual books relate to one another. This broader context can also help us grapple with the grouping of the groupings, relate the Old Testament to the New Testament, and perceive how the biblical books collectively contribute to a unified theological message. The task of the biblical theologian, then, is to discern the meaning found in the canonical context and take it into account when considering the message of the Bible as a whole.

BT Tool: The Grand Storyline of the Bible

Another major tool of biblical theology is a working knowledge of the grand storyline of the Bible. Being able to recognize and articulate the story found in the Scriptures is crucial for understanding how the Bible fits together as a whole. One of the means by which the biblical canon shapes the expectations of its readers is the way that it frames the biblical meta-narrative and situates the prophetic and apostolic discourse in the larger storyline.

The Many Narratives of the Bible (the Stories)

Readers of the Bible will immediately encounter a disproportionately large portion of narrative texts. The Bible is a book brimming with narrative. In this respect, a majority of biblical texts are either narratives or directly connected to narrative sections that influence the setting and interpretation of those non-narrative portions. The predominance of narrative in the biblical collection has a profound effect on the shape of the collection as a whole.

One of the immediately noticeable features of biblical narratives is that they are realistic historical narratives. This genre choice made by the biblical authors entails that one of the most prominent things the Bible does is tell stories. During most of your time reading the Bible, you will experience some sort of story. Sometimes the story is cosmic, like when God speaks the world into existence in Genesis 1. Sometimes the story is mundane, like when the tabernacle designs are delivered in Exodus 26. Sometimes the story is dramatic, like when Paul proclaims the gospel as a prisoner during a shipwreck on his journey to see the Emperor in Rome (Acts 27). Sometimes the story is relatively static, like when Paul preaches under house arrest after he finally arrives in Rome (Acts 28).

The many narratives found throughout the Bible come in all different shapes and sizes, with different theological purposes and textual strategies. Nevertheless, every major grouping within the biblical canon includes significant segments of narrative. This scenario must be reckoned with as we consider the Bible's overarching shape. In this regard, a focus on the storyline of Scripture in biblical theology is an emphasis that follows directly from the sheer number of narratives in the biblical collection.

The Mega-Narrative of the Bible (the Grand Storyline)

When gathered together into a collection, the biblical narratives generate an overarching *mega-narrative* that begins in Genesis and ends in Revelation. Because the biblical writers often composed their books in light of other biblical narratives (especially the Book of Moses), a basic coherence in worldview and theological framework runs through the biblical texts. Directly related to the Genesis-to-Revelation storyline that biblical theology seeks to capture, there are also a series of thematic and intertextual connections between Genesis 1–3 and Revelation 21–22. The first and last chapters of the grand storyline of the biblical canon furnish bookends for what God is doing in the world. In the beginning, God creates the heavens and the earth. In the end, he creates a new heaven and a new earth.

The history of redemption is set within this biblical-theological framework. The task of the biblical theologian is to highlight the way each textual *part* contributes to this storied *whole*. The shape of the narratives found within the biblical canon are sufficient to produce a grand narrative storyline or mega-narrative that situates readers as they travel through each literary corpus and from one grouping to the next within the larger collection.

This hermeneutical reading strategy arises from the fact that these many biblical narratives have been gathered together *in just this way* and have been associated with one another within the context of a canonical collection. This location within a collection not only enables readers to perceive the connections between books, but also allows them to see each book as part of the grand narrative storyline that spans the two-testament collection.

It is difficult to overestimate the effect that the canonical context has on our ability to access and understand the overarching biblical mega-narrative. The many narratives of the Bible do not unfold and intersect like a single piece of cloth. Rather they form an overarching storyline when woven together *within the same collection*. The narrative storyline that emerges is coherent but also complex. The big story of the Bible begins and then reaches its final destination, but it does not always take the same route or move in a straight line. As Dempster observes, "the larger Story is not one-dimensional. And although the Bible is a coherent Story, it is a sprawling one, a sort of ramshackle narrative with many stops and starts, dead ends and detours, and any number of high and low points. Often it is only the perspective gained from a later point in the story that enables one to see the overall shape of the narrative."[9] The end goal of biblical theology at this point is not to flatten out these contours but rather to make sense of the textual topography that the biblical mega-narrative lays out before us within the scope of the biblical canon.[10]

---

9. See Stephen Dempster, "Review of *God's Glory in Salvation through Judgment*" in *9Marks Journal* (January–February 2011): 46. Available at https://9marks.org/review/gods-glory-salvation-through-judgment/. See also Dempster's discussion of the nature of narrative in *Dominion and Dynasty*, 15–43.

10. Cf. Richard Bauckham, "Reading Scripture as a Coherent Story," in *The Art of Reading Scripture*, eds. Ellen F. Davis and Richard B. Hays (Grand Rapids: Eerdmans, 2003), 38–53. Note also Christopher Seitz's caution about

The Meta-Narrative of The Bible (the Story That Explains All Other Stories)

As noted above, because of the biblical canon, the *many* narratives of the Bible contribute to a *mega-narrative*. This grand storyline generates a series of assumptions about who God is, who we are, and how we are to respond as a result. In other words, the biblical narratives make claims upon their readers. As a mega-narrative, the biblical narratives also collectively generate a *meta-narrative* that makes a series of claims about the nature of reality. The biblical narratives claim not only that "all the world's a stage," but also that all the world's on *its* stage.

The term "meta-narrative" entered intellectual discourse by way of Jean-Francois Lyotard's oft-quoted characterization of postmodernity as "incredulity toward metanarrative."[11] Though Lyotard has a technical understanding of what a meta-narrative is, biblical scholars have used the term "to refer to the overall story told by the Christian Scriptures, which is not totalizing or oppressive, and which makes possible the 'redemptive-historical' level of biblical interpretation."[12] Thus, most uses of the term meta-narrative in biblical studies reference the overarching storyline of the Bible when viewed as a whole (i.e., the "mega-narrative").[13] However, it is also instructive to observe the distinction between the storyline itself, the assumptions required to understand the message of that storyline,

---

characterizing the Bible too directly as a single unbroken narrative in his chapter "The Strange Old Book: The Limits of Narrative" in *The Elder Testament: Canon, Theology, Trinity* (Waco: Baylor University Press, 2018), 71–84. Noting that the biblical canon contains a mix of genres, different biblical books contain different types of narratives, and the narratives themselves often do not proceed in strictly "one-event-right-after-the-next" fashion (features Bauckham also notes at length), Seitz argues that we should seek to "make sense of a biblical text on the terms of its own givenness, and account for what genuinely makes the text what it is, and also appreciate just what an unusual thing it is as it does its work of narrating" (76). In sounding these cautions, Seitz seeks to balance the "economic and ontological dimensions at work in the testimony of Israel's Scriptures" (72).

11. See *The Postmodern Condition: A Report on Knowledge* (Minneapolis: University of Minnesota Press, 1984), xxiv.
12. Albert Wolters, "Metanarrative," in *Dictionary for Theological Interpretation of the Bible*, ed. Kevin J. Vanhoozer (Grand Rapids: Baker, 2005), 506–7. Wolters briefly notes the positive and negative connotations of the word. See also Wolters's related entry on "Worldview" in the same volume.
13. For more on this distinction between "meta-narrative" and "mega-narrative," see Horton, *Christian Faith*, 14–19. Horton analyzes the origins and function of the term meta-narrative within modern and postmodern contexts and also connects this discussion to the task of systematic theology. Horton draws on Merold Westphal's analysis of this topic in *Overcoming Onto-Theology: Toward a Postmodern Christian Faith* (New York: Fordham University Press, 2001), xi–xvi. One of Westphal's key insights is that Christianity's "mega-narrative" is a first-order reflection rather than a second-order reflection. As Westphal argues, "in philosophical discourse, 'meta' signifies a difference of level and not primarily of size. A metanarrative is a metadiscourse in the sense of being a second-level discourse not directly about the world but about a first-level discourse" (xiii). Accordingly, while Christianity is a "big story" (a "*mega*narrative"), "the story that begins with 'Let there be light' and ends with the 'Hallelujah Chorus' under the baton of the angel Gabriel is not a *meta*narrative." Rather, "the recital of the *Heilsgeschichte* in creeds and in sermons, in lessons and in songs, as well as its enactment in sacraments, belongs to first-order Christian discourse. It is kerygma, not apologetics" (xiii). Bauckham analyzes these categories as well in "Reading Scripture," 45–53. Bauckham uses the phrase "nonmodern metanarrative" to nuance the effect of the biblical story and contrast the "meta-metanarratives" of modernity.

and also the presuppositions that inform how its worldview is communicated through the many narratives that comprise the grand storyline of the Bible as a whole.

For example, we can observe that the stories recounted in the biblical canon encourage a certain view of the world, one in which readers are implicated as part of the "real world" those narratives generate.[14] *In The Eclipse of Biblical Narrative*, Hans Frei argues that this type of mindset was predominant before the rise of the modern period. According to Frei's analysis, pre-critical interpreters held that the Bible contained "all those stories which together went into the making of a single storied or historical sequence."[15] For them, "the real world" was formed "by the sequence told by the biblical stories."[16] By using figural interpretation, these interpreters made sense of the biblical stories "by weaving them together into a common narrative referring to a single history and its patterns of meaning."[17] The biblical reader, in turn, was "to see his disposition, his actions and passions, the shape of his own life as well as that of his era's events as figures of that storied world."[18]

In the study of biblical theology, it is helpful to keep in mind the relationship between the many narratives of the Bible, the way these narratives intersect within the canonical collection to form a grand storyline (the mega-narrative), and the worldview this storyline assumes and pressures readers to adopt (the meta-narrative). The many stories of the Bible comprise the grand storyline of the Bible, and the biblical authors claim this grand storyline is the story that explains all other stories.

---

14. Cf. Eric Auerbach's classic observation about the way biblical narrative functions differently than other ancient literature: "The Bible's claim to truth is not only far more urgent than Homer's, it is tyrannical—it excludes all other claims. The world of the Scripture stories is not satisfied with claiming to be a historically true reality—it insists that it is the only real world, is destined for autocracy." See *Mimesis: The Representation of Reality in Western Literature* (Princeton: Princeton University Press, 1953), 14–15. Auerbach concludes his point by noting that "the Scripture stories do not, like Homer's, court our favor, they do not flatter us that they may please us and enchant us—they seek to subject us, and if we refuse to be subjected we are rebels" (15). Similarly, Michael B. Shepherd, writes that "the biblical authors are in the business of world making, and they insist that theirs is the only real world." See *The Textual World of the Bible*, Studies in Biblical Literature 156 (New York: Peter Lang, 2013), 1. Shepherd also argues that it is the "rendering of the present arrangement of the Scriptures that establishes the framework of the real world into which the reader must fit" (2).

15. Frei, *Eclipse*, 1.

16. Frei, *Eclipse*, 1. In this regard, Jeannine Brown observes that the "biblical authors both assume and contribute to the meta-narrative of Scripture because they are convinced that they are participants in the biblical story." For readers, "we may speak of entering the world of the text as a way of allowing its normative story to shape us" (*Scripture as Communication*, 46).

17. Frei, *Eclipse*, 2.

18. Frei, *Eclipse*, 3. Cf. Meir Sternberg's critical interaction with Frei's central claims about narrative and history in *The Poetics of Biblical Narrative: Ideological Literature and the Drama of Reading* (Bloomington: Indiana University Press, 1985), 81–83. Sailhamer summarizes this effect of the biblical meta-narrative: "The OT narratives record real historical events that provide the framework for the early history of the world and of humanity, and it is precisely that history that envelops the history of the New Testament, the church, and the modern world. Moreover, it is that history that will culminate in the return of Christ. In this sense, real history is that history recorded in the text of Scripture and that text is the focal point of divine revelation" (*Introduction to Old Testament Theology*, 37). He notes here as well that "the pre-critical view is, in fact, virtually the same as that of modern evangelicalism."

Narration and Interpretation within the Storyline

In light of this focus on the storyline of the Bible and its importance for biblical theology, we can note here a uniquely relevant feature of narrative texts. The narratives found in the biblical canon not only *narrate* the events they recount, but also *interpret* them. Biblical narratives are a combination of story and significance, of text and event, of revelatory deeds and revelatory words. Within these narrative books, theological arguments are made by the authors about God's person and character.

For the purpose of biblical theology, it is particularly significant that there are many biblical narratives, that they have been strategically collected, and that they narrate and interpret God's work in the world. At distinctive points in the narrative flow of the Old and New Testament collections, there are reflective summaries of redemptive history. These notable passages demonstrate that later biblical writers understood their past not only in light of an oral history, but also in light of specific accounts found in previously written biblical texts.

When a prophet, such as Hosea for example, recounts the exodus, often their account echoes the literary presentation of this event found in the book of Exodus. Even within the Pentateuch itself, there are several accounts of a single event that build upon and interpret one another. To give one example, Exodus 19–24 describes the giving of the Ten Commandments (or Decalogue, "ten words") and the Book of the Covenant. In Deuteronomy 5, this scene and these words are reiterated and interpreted for a new generation of Israelites. So, even within the same biblical book, events that are initially narrated become subsequently recounted and interpreted. This pattern of narration and interpretation is a notable aspect of narratives in general, and an especially crucial feature to observe regarding the biblical narratives in particular.[19]

As you make use of the biblical storyline in the study of biblical theology, it is imperative to take this textual and authorial feature into account. The biblical authors have already sought to present and interpret the meaning and significance of redemptive history for future generations of readers. As members of that group of future readers, our primary task is to discern what the biblical authors have given to us in their texts. These interpretive summaries of redemptive history can inform the way we summarize and interpret that same redemptive history. In this way, the biblical *writers* provide guidance for biblical *readers* in understanding the nature and significance of the overarching storyline of the biblical narratives.

---

19. Significant examples of a biblical figure or writer recounting Israel's history in light of its previous portrayal in Israel's Scriptures include Nehemiah 9:5–37; Psalms 78; 105–106; and Hebrews 11. For a close reading of many of these types of textual examples, see Shepherd, *Textual World*, 5–86. Shepherd identifies biblical-theological summaries from the Law (Deut. 6:20–25; 11:1–17; 26:5–9), the Prophets (Josh. 24:1–15; Judg. 2:1–5; 6:7–10; 10:11–16; 1 Sam. 12:6–17; Jer. 2:1–13; Ezek. 20; Amos 2:6–3:2; Mic. 6:1–8), the Writings (Pss. 78; 105–106; 135–136; Neh. 9), and the New Testament (Acts 7; 13:13–41; Heb. 11). Though these passages have often been understood in terms of tradition history or "salvation history" (*Heilsgeschichte*), Shepherd argues that these texts present themselves as exegetical in nature.

In particular, as we make our way through the grand storyline of the Bible, we will make special note of the narrations of the final speeches given by major figures at the end of their life. These "famous last words" often include a summary of redemptive history, interpretation of God's past actions, commentary on the people's covenant relationship, and a word of exhortation for a future generation.

- Last words of Jacob (Genesis 49)
- Last words of Moses (Deuteronomy 27–33)
- Last words of Joshua (Joshua 23–24)
- Last words of Samuel (1 Samuel 12–13)
- Last words of David (2 Samuel 23:1–7; 1 Kings 2)
- Last words of the author of Kings (2 Kings 17 and 25)
- Last words of Stephen (Acts 6–7)
- Last words of Paul (Acts 20 and 28)
- Last words of Jesus (Matthew 28; Luke 24; Acts 1; Revelation 22)

There are many speeches in the narratives of the storyline that are significant, but the speeches listed above are particularly significant in their narration and interpretation of redemptive history as it is unfolds across the biblical canon.

The Covenants as the Textual and Theological Heartbeat of the Bible's Storyline

The grand storyline of the Bible, supplied by the canonical context, tells a consistent and coherent story of God's purposes in the world and among his people. Recognizing this small-scale and large-scale textual feature of the biblical canon, we can ask: Is there anything that helps characterize the focus of the many narratives of the Bible, the mega-narrative of the Bible, and the patterns that make up the meta-narrative of the Bible? Indeed there is. A prominent and recurring thread that runs throughout the story of the Scriptures is the story of the covenants. The biblical covenants are major signposts in the story that the Scriptures tell.

Why select the covenants for special attention within the flow of redemptive history? Why should we spend more time directly considering the biblical covenants? The answer to this question draws upon the previously established points about the nature of narrative. As readers we focus on the major covenants in the biblical storyline because the biblical authors themselves focused on the biblical covenants as they composed and shaped how the biblical storyline was presented in their texts and in their books.

In fact, the only reason biblical readers are able to detect the strategic importance of the covenants for God's purposes in the world is because of the strategic role they play in biblical texts. The biblical authors "slow down" redemptive history at just these points and provide both a narration and interpretation of the establishment of these covenant relationships at just these moments in redemptive history at just these textual locations. When we focus on the covenants, the story they tell, and the implications they inevitably bear for the nature of God and his purposes in the world, we are seeking to follow the lead of the biblical authors themselves.

What is a biblical covenant? We can define a covenant here simply and broadly as *a relationship based on a promise.*[20] More specifically, a biblical covenant is a relationship in the biblical storyline between God and a group of his created people that is based on a spoken promise. These covenant relationships usually include the formal expectation of blessings for obedience and curses for disobedience.

As you make your way through the grand storyline of the Bible, you will encounter six major covenants or covenant relationships.

- Covenant with Adam (Gen. 1–3, esp. 1:26–31; 2:15–17)
- Covenant with Noah (Gen. 6–9, esp. 8:20–9:17)
- Covenant with Abraham (Gen. 12–22, esp. 12:1–7; 15:1–21)
- Covenant with Moses and Israel (Exod. 19–24)
- Covenant with David (2 Sam. 7, esp. 7:8–17; 1 Chron. 17)
- The New Covenant (Deut. 30:6–10; Jer. 31:31–35; Ezek. 36:22–32; Heb. 8–10)

How Do the Biblical Covenants Help with the Reading of Scripture?

The biblical covenants can provide a theological framework that affects and enhances your reading of Scripture. When you read a given passage of Scripture, you can ask, "What biblical covenant is in the foreground of this text?" Additionally, you can ask, "Is there a biblical covenant in the background of this text that elucidates its broader context?" Asking these questions will help you understand where the passage you are studying fits in the larger storyline of God's redemptive purposes. There are several features of the biblical covenants that aid readers in the biblical-theological process.

---

20. This definition is a working definition designed to provide a starting point for readers as they approach these strategic points in the biblical storyline and in strategic textual locations in the biblical canon. Scholars from a variety of disciplines note the diversity of the concept in parallel historical contexts but also some of the main lines of continuity in the primary covenant relationships portrayed in biblical texts. For example, Timothy Ward observes that "as Scripture develops, it becomes clear that the primary form in which God works for the redemption of humanity from the curse of sin and death is through his establishment of the covenant. A covenant of course, is at heart a relationship established by means of the uttering of a promise." See *Words of Life: Scripture as the Living and Active Word of God* (Downers Grove: InterVarsity, 2009), 22. Similarly, Thomas Schreiner defines a biblical covenant as "a chosen relationship in which two parties make binding promises to each other." See *Covenant and God's Purpose for the World*, Short Studies in Biblical Theology (Wheaton: Crossway, 2017), 13. Part of Schreiner's instinct to define covenant broadly stems from his recognition that there is a range of diversity in how major and minor covenant relationships are portrayed in the Scriptures, that a given specific definition of "covenant" drawn from a particular historical context might not fit each or any instance, and that the term covenant is not always used even when the concept of a covenant relationship is clearly in view. See his methodological overview in *Covenant*, 13–18.

The covenants are embedded. A primary feature of the biblical covenants is that they are embedded in the text of Scripture. The scope and sequence of the biblical covenants emerges out of the canonical texts themselves. In this way, you could say that a canonical framework is also a covenantal framework. Utilizing the covenants portrayed in the biblical narratives also emphasizes the sufficiency of Scripture to provide both the content and the structure of our theological understanding of the Bible.

Our understanding of a "covenant" is drawn from the various depictions of covenant relationships found in the biblical texts themselves, rather than from the surrounding cultures and nations that were present during the history of Israel. The canon, then, set limits for the range of interpretive possibilities. The canon also provides the fullest context in which the covenants are interpreted. This anchoring textual context puts readers in a prime position to read each of the covenant narratives in light of the others and see any historical, textual, and theological development between them.

The covenants are interconnected. All six of the major biblical covenants are interconnected and exist in a relationship that can be recognized by readers of the biblical canon. As we note the content and structure of the covenants, we strive to observe and discern textual features of the narratives. The connections between passages oftentimes relate to how their authors portray and structure the covenant narratives in addition to the actual covenant situation itself. Many of the most strategic intertextual connections within the Scriptures involve either the biblical covenants themselves or the narratives in which the biblical covenants are portrayed. This sequence is important because every text of Scripture bears on these covenants and the story they tell. Together, they illuminate the whole of the Scriptures. This is one way of articulating the Bible's big picture that helps connect and give coherence to the canon while at the same time allowing for diversity and direct lines of development.

The covenants are directive. Because of these textual and theological features, the covenants are signposts that direct readers through sections of the biblical canon and also portions of the Bible's grand storyline. They also direct readers to focus on the all-important relationship between God and his people. Oftentimes, a biblical writer will appeal to one or more of these covenants in order to communicate his message.

For example, in prophetic literature the prophets frequently use elements of the Mosaic covenant, the Davidic covenant, and the new covenant to convey their message. The prophets set up the idea of the need for complete obedience to the Lord. To drive home their emphasis upon the need for repentance and obedience, the prophets often keep the Mosaic covenant and its stipulations in the foreground. However, the fact of the matter is that the people do not obey these stipulations. Consequently, the prophets appeal to the hope of the Davidic covenant in the background. As the situation worsens through the sustained lack of repentance and obedience, the prophets use the failure of the Mosaic covenant (due to the people's lack of faith) to point to the need for the new covenant, the measure of hope. This particular sequence captures the thematic trajectory of several prophetic books.

For the New Testament writers, the biblical covenants are the means by which they tell the story of Jesus as the Christ. For instance, during the first Lord's Supper when Jesus says "this cup that is poured out for you is the new covenant in my blood" (Luke 22:20; cf. 1 Cor. 11:25) it is no wonder that mention of the forgiveness of sins follows, because one of the promises of the new covenant is the forgiveness of sins (Matt. 26:28; Jer. 31:31–34). When reading the Old and New Testaments, the "story of the Bible" is often a way of speaking about the "story of the covenants." The way the covenants build upon one another also implies an important sense of progression and development as readers make their way through the biblical collection from beginning to end.[21]

The covenants are comprehensive. The eschatological vision of the Scriptures can be perceived and interpreted by means of this sequence of covenants. The biblical covenants function as an interpretive grid for seeing how God is at work in his cosmic plan and his eternal purposes. It is no wonder, then, that we can say that the promises of God are "yes" in Christ (2 Cor. 1:20). The central promises of God expressed in the Scriptures are directly related to God's presence witnessed in the benefits of the covenants. If the covenants are embedded in the biblical narratives, intertextually interconnected to one another, and theologically directive in their vision of God's expectation for relationship with him, then they are also comprehensive.

For these reasons, a working knowledge of the biblical covenants will greatly benefit the biblical theologian seeking to grasp and articulate the big picture of the Bible. Knowing the biblical covenants themselves, the narratives that portray them, and the story they are connected to will equip readers to find their way in the Word and in the world. Keep your eyes on the covenants and you will gain a line of sight into who God is and what God does.

BT Tool: The Web of Textual Connections

Another area of biblical-theological study involves observing and analyzing the web of textual connections found within the Bible. There are three broad types of textual

---

21. The literary and theological development between the covenants provides one of the most fruitful lines of inquiry in the biblical-theological task. The critical importance of reckoning with the covenants and their interrelations can be seen in the way that the covenants function in different traditions and theological systems that seek to make sense of the message of the entire Bible. See, for instance, the prominent but varied role of the covenants in the following approaches: O. Palmer Robertson, *The Christ of the Covenants* (Philipsburg: P&R, 1987); Craig A. Blaising and Darrell L. Bock, *Progressive Dispensationalism* (Grand Rapids: Baker, 1993); and Peter J. Gentry and Stephen J. Wellum, *Kingdom through Covenant: A Biblical-Theological Understanding of the Covenants* (Wheaton: Crossway, 2018). While recognizing the very real differences in these representative works (and the implications for theological formulation and interpretation of texts), each of these approaches argue for the particular prominence of the covenants, their organic relationship, and their strategic importance for how the message of the Bible fits together. In light of this scenario, our modest point here is not to arrive at a particular conclusion (or articulation of the way the covenants function) but to argue for the urgent necessity of this particular exegetical, biblical-theological, and systematic area of study.

connections in the biblical canon. These include textual connections *within* biblical books (biblical inner-textuality), textual connections *between* books (biblical inter-textuality), and *canonical* connections *between* books (canonical con-textuality). There are many wide-ranging issues that go into each of these levels of investigation.[22] Here, we will note a few of the central features of each these three types of analysis and note the strategic function that these areas of study have for the study of biblical theology.

Textual Connections within Biblical Books (Biblical Innertextuality)

As readers of the entire Bible, we need to understand the way biblical theology relates to the exegesis and interpretation of individual biblical passages. In addition to interpreting the words, sentences, and phrases of a passage, we also want to be aware of the proper context necessary to understand the meaning of that passage. The close reading of a particular passage is best complemented by an understanding of its surrounding literary context (i.e., paragraphs, larger sections, and blocks of discourse). The reader ultimately aims to see how a particular passage functions in light of the book in which it appears.

The goal here is to notice any textual connections that an author makes within a single biblical book. This level analysis is *innertextual*, as it analyzes the relationship between the various parts of a particular text within the scope of the work itself. This approach to exegesis or close reading emphasizes book-level meaning as the proper context in which an individual passage functions. An author's textual intention is seen most fully at the book level of composition. In other words, while it is often appropriate to focus on an individual section or a portion of a biblical book for a given study, project, or sermon, the meaning of that passage or section is governed and guided by the meaning of the book as a whole.

To give just one quick example, consider the biblical books whose message would be characterized very differently without taking into account their beginning or end. When reading Jonah 1–3, it would be possible to surmise that the reason Jonah flees to Tarshish is because he fears that the people of Nineveh will *fail* to listen and repent. In Jonah 4, however, this interpretation is ruled out as Jonah explicitly states that he fled because he feared that the people of Nineveh would *in fact* listen and repent. Because of his knowledge of

---

22. For an extended discussion of biblical intertextuality from a variety of angles, see Spellman, *Toward a Canon-Conscious Reading,* 142–83; Sailhamer, *Introduction to Old Testament Theology,* 200–15; Michael B. Shepherd, *Text in the Middle,* Studies in Biblical Literature 162 (New York: Peter Lang, 2014); G. K. Beale and D. A. Carson, eds., *Commentary on the New Testament Use of the Old Testament* (Grand Rapids: Baker, 2007); G. K. Beale, *Handbook on the New Testament Use of the Old Testament: Exegesis and Interpretation* (Grand Rapids: Baker, 2012); and Abner Chou, *The Hermeneutics of the Biblical Writers: Learning to Interpret Scripture from the Prophets and Apostles* (Grand Rapids: Kregel, 2018). These works engage many of the key questions and challenges that arise from this area of study. The specific issue of the New Testament's use of the Old Testament is well-established in the field of biblical studies. The works noted here from Beale and Carson survey and represent some of the main hermeneutical and methodological options for addressing this particular question.

God's character, Jonah knows the Lord would relent and deliver them (Jonah 4:1–3). This leads to an articulation of the theme of the book as a whole: God's sovereign freedom to execute judgment and extend mercy. This theme resonates with the broader context of the Book of the Twelve and connects with the character of God developed in strategic texts in the Pentateuch (e.g., Exodus 34). Only a book-level reading of Jonah's narrative as a whole is capable of discerning this aspect of the author's theological purpose and perceiving the book's connection to broader biblical-theological themes.

This simple hermeneutical guideline allows a biblical author to direct our focus when we seek to reflect upon his purpose in writing or summarize the theological message of his book. This way of keeping the book-level meaning in view also prepares us for any biblical-theological analysis that involves the relationship between the messages of two or more biblical books.

Textual Connections between Biblical Books (Biblical Intertextuality)

A further level of analysis notes textual connections *between* biblical books. This type of analysis is *intertextual*, as it studies the relationship between two or more texts. More specifically, biblical intertextuality is the study of the relationship between two or more biblical texts. Further, biblical intertextuality focuses on the connections that are a part of a biblical author's textual intention. For the purpose of biblical theology, we can first consider the types of intertextual connections themselves and the main categories of intertextual connections that we find within the biblical literature, and then consider some of the implications this area of study has for biblical theology.

Types of Intertextual Connections

Biblical quotations. A biblical quotation occurs when an author directly cites another biblical text. Usually, this intertextual connection is acknowledged by the author in some way, and possesses precise verbal and often thematic parallels to the referenced text. A quotation is the most direct form of intertextual connection. With a quotation, a reader will readily discern that a text is being referenced from another literary location.

Biblical allusions. A biblical allusion occurs when an author makes an indirect reference to another biblical text. Allusions are not as formal as direct quotations but are nevertheless discernible to those who are familiar with the text or group of texts that are being referenced. Some of the most common ways the biblical authors allude to other biblical texts include using verbal, thematic, and structural parallels from the text being alluded to in their own composition. So, in order for readers to detect a biblical allusion, they must be able to recognize the words, themes, or structural similarities between the two texts.

Biblical echoes. A biblical echo occurs when an author makes a subtle reference to a concept or poetic image from another biblical text. Sometimes a particular concept or literary element can encompass several biblical texts. This type of intertextual connection can happen on either a small or large scale. For example, an author might describe a narrative scene in ways that evoke the setting or plot of a narrative scene from another biblical work. An author might structure a section of his book in order to mirror the structure of another biblical book. He might also adopt a similar compositional strategy that echoes the same discernible strategy of another biblical text. The category of an intertextual echo recognizes that authors often make subtle and creative uses of other biblical texts that do not neatly fit into the categories of biblical quotation or allusion.

To give an example of each of these types of intertextual connections in close proximity, we can briefly consider the first chapter of Mark's Gospel. After a direct opening ("The beginning of the gospel of Jesus Christ, the Son of God," Mark 1:1), Mark uses a *quotation* from Mal. 3:1 and Isa. 40:3. He introduces the blended quotation by saying, "As it is written in Isaiah the prophet" (Mark 1:2). Following the conclusion of his brief baptism account, Mark describes how a voice from heaven declares, "You are my beloved Son; with you I am well pleased" (1:11). Here, Mark makes an *allusion* to Psalm 2, as the words recorded in this declaration from the Father indirectly reference the words of this psalm. The opening chapter of Mark's Gospel ends with the temptation account where Jesus "was in the wilderness forty days, being tempted by Satan" (1:13). Unlike the temptation accounts of Matthew and Luke, Mark adds the unique detail that while he was in the wilderness Jesus "was with the wild animals, and the angels were ministering to him" (1:13). This detail is a possible *echo* of several biblical narratives that describe Israel being tested in the wilderness where there were also wild animals (e.g. Deut. 7–8, esp. 7:22 and 8:15; Ezek. 34:5).

These three main types of intertextual connections can equip you to see what a biblical author is doing in a biblical text. While Mark's opening stretch of narrative will make sense even if you overlook these references, reckoning with the presence of these connections is like restoring the intertextual electricity to a messianic floodlight that illuminates the person and work of Jesus as the Christ.

Discerning Intertextual Connections

After this brief reflection on the three main types of intertextual connections, we can consider some of the steps you might take when interpreting an intertextual reference and analyzing its implications for biblical theology.

- First, as you read, ask: *Is there an intertext?* For each type of intertextual connection, a reader's familiarity with the referenced text will be significant. For quotations, a reader of a text like Mark 1:2–3 will readily realize that another text is being cited. For allusions, a reader will need to be familiar with the intertext in order to recognize its indirect reference. For echoes, you will need to be a careful reader of the first passage but also a careful reader of the text the author is echoing.

- Second, once you discern that an author has indeed utilized another biblical text, ask: *What is the intertext?* This step involves identifying the biblical text the author is drawing upon. Once this identification is made, you will need to become familiar with that text within its textual context. This task involves understanding that passage in relation to the broader message of the biblical book where it is found.

- Third, once you have identified the presence of an intertext and also the original textual location of that intertext, ask: *How is the intertext presented?* How has the author introduced this intertextual connection to the passage you are reading? Does it come in the form of a direct quotation, an indirect allusion, or a more subtle echo? In biblical intertextuality, this question provides some of the orienting clues for understanding the author's purpose in using the referenced biblical text.

- Fourth, once these basic questions have been answered, you can now ask: *What effect does the intertextual connection have on the passage*? Now that you have considered *how* the author has introduced this intertextual connection into the passage you are reading, you are now better prepared to ask *why* the author has made this connection. This question represents the heart of the study of biblical intertextuality and also interfaces with the way that this type of study informs the task of biblical theology. If an author has woven an intertextual connection into the fabric of his text, then a close reading of that passage will need to include intertextual analysis.

Sometimes an intertextual reference supports the author's argument; sometimes it serves as a point of contrast or an illustration. Sometimes it is simple; sometimes it is complex. Sometimes it is difficult to discern exactly what a biblical author intended in the use of an intertextual link. The intertextual practice of the biblical authors is diverse but consistent. If they have utilized another biblical text, you can be certain that they have a reason (a "textual intention"), and our role as readers is to discern that purpose in their writing. This last step of intertextual analysis returns to the point of departure and asks what impact the intertextual payload made when it entered the atmosphere of the passage at hand.

Intertextuality within a Canonical Context

Old Testament use of the Old Testament. While at first it may seem that the possibilities for intertextual connections are endless, there are several clearly discernible patterns established by the biblical authors. The canonical context can guide readers as they observe and analyze these textual connections. Chief among these is the prominence of the Pentateuch in the intertextual references of the biblical authors. References to individual texts, themes, or poetic images that come from Genesis, Exodus, Leviticus, Numbers, or

Deuteronomy frequently appear throughout the literature of the Old Testament. Both the prophets and poets of Israel take their bearings from the theological themes and narrative world of the Pentateuch. Subsequent biblical writers and leaders of Israel meditate on the Law of Moses day and night, and this practice is reflected in their writings.[23] There are of course many other techniques that the Old Testament writers employ, but the intertextual use of the Book of Moses is a central one.

New Testament use of the Old Testament. The same intertextual strategy occurs in the New Testament. The New Testament authors continue the practice of using older texts in the canon to tell their stories and give meaning to their writings. Sometimes it is said that the New Testament writers are doing something brand new in their use of Old Testament texts. However, they are actually adopting a pattern that they have seen developed and employed within the Old Testament collection. In this sense, the New Testament's use of the Old Testament is preceded by the Old Testament's use of the Old Testament. The continuance of this pattern is another way we can affirm the unity of the entire Bible. The New Testament authors follow the Old Testament authors in their use of other biblical texts and application of the intended meaning of those preceding texts in their own writings.

In the Gospels, Jesus argues that his story was anticipated in the Old Testament and that Moses and the Prophets built a path that directly led to him. Moreover, the New Testament writers enlist a large cast of supporting characters from Old Testament narratives in portraying their messianic protagonist. The worldview of the New Testament writers is aligned with the textual world of the Old Testament. When a New Testament writer wants to make a theological point, illustrate an argument, or utilize a metaphor, they most often draw on the images and narratives developed in the Old Testament.

If you read the Scriptures, you will encounter biblical intertextuality. Further, quite often the intertextual links that occur in a given passage include references to other major sections of the canonical collection. Indeed, the study of biblical intertextuality is closely related to exegesis (close reading), innertextuality, and the canonical context of multiple biblical passages. Accordingly, intertextuality is one of the most challenging and rewarding features of the biblical-theological task.

---

23. For example, see Joshua 1:7–8; Psalm 1:2; Malachi 4:4, etc. Cf. Stephen G. Dempster, "Canon and Old Testament Interpretation," in *Hearing the Old Testament: Listening for God's Address*, ed. Craig G. Bartholomew and David H. J. Beldman (Grand Rapids: Eerdmans, 2012), 169: "When prophets began to record their words to preserve them as evidence of their truthfulness, many of their condemnations are comprehensible only with the assumption of a body of earlier, authoritative texts—the Torah—and many of their promises are clothed with the language of previous descriptions of pivotal events in Israel's early history." To illustrate, Dempster points to Hosea's use of the "ten words" (Hos. 4:1–3), the covenant (1:9), and the exodus image (1:10–11) from the Pentateuch in his prophetic discourse.

Canonical Connections between Biblical Books (Canonical Contextuality)

In addition to book-level meaning in the study of innertextuality and the relationship between two or more biblical texts in the study of biblical intertextuality, we can also note the significance of the canonical connections between biblical books within the collection. This level of analysis is called *canonical contextuality*, as it considers the effect of the *canonical context* on the reading of an individual book. Here we ask: What impact does it make to juxtapose *just these specific works* in *just this fashion*.

Because part of the biblical-theological task is to consider the theological message of the Bible as a whole, to trace central themes across the canon, and to reflect upon the relationship between the Testaments, this question of canonical contextuality is a significant one. Several scholars use this or related concepts to discuss how book-ordering and the canonical context in general impacts the interpretive task. Sailhamer defines biblical "con-textuality" as "the notion of the effect on meaning of the relative position of a biblical book within a prescribed order of reading."[24] Greg Goswell speaks of contextuality as a "para-textual" element of Scripture.[25] Hendrik J. Koorevaar engages this topic in terms of a work's broad "macrostructure."[26] David Trobisch investigates the "redactional frame" of the "canonical edition" of the New Testament.[27] These notions are in some ways complementary and each seeks to take into account a given work's broader textual context and spatial relationship to other literary entities.

The phrase "canonical contextuality" has the benefit of emphasizing the notion of context. Contextuality is the study of a writing's textual or literary context.[28] Where an indi-

---

24. Sailhamer, *Introduction to Old Testament Theology*, 213. Cf. Childs's concern "to deal seriously with the effect which the shape of the canonical collection has on the individual parts. At times the larger corpus exerts a major influence by establishing a different context from that of a single composition" (*New Testament as Canon*, 52).

25. Goswell has analyzed the ordering of collections as a meaningful example of partatextuality in a consistent stream of articles for over a decade. For example, see "The Order of the Books in the Hebrew Bible," *Journal of the Evangelical Theological Society* 51.4 (2008): 673–88; and Goswell, "The Johannine Corpus and the Unity of the New Testament Canon," *Journal of the Evangelical Theological Society* 61.4 (2018): 717–33. While not necessarily arguing for any particular model for the formation of these orderings, the underlying presupposition of these many studies is that "biblical book order is of hermeneutical import, for where a book is placed in relation to other canonical books generates expectations of what the book may be about" ("Johannine Corpus," 718). He notes further that, "the order of the biblical books serves to guide how these texts are to be read. In particular, books placed in apposition or put in the same canonical grouping are viewed as conversation partners, whose interaction takes priority over other possible intra-canonical links" (718).

26. For example, see Hendrik J. Koorevaar, "The Torah Model as Original Macrostructure of the Hebrew Canon: A Critical Evaluation" *Zeitschrift für die Alttestamentliche Wissenschaft* 122 (2010): 65–80.

27. David Trobisch, *The First Edition of the New Testament* (Oxford: Oxford University Press, 2000), 3. Trobisch argues that "when editors publish material they guide readers to interpret it in a specific way by setting certain signals within a redactional frame" (45).

28. Cf. Gerald T. Sheppard, "Canon Criticism: The Proposal of Brevard Childs and an Assessment for Evangelical Hermeneutics," *Studia Biblica et Theologica* 4 (1974): 13: "To the degree that historical-grammatical or historical-critical exegesis is successful in reviving a 'lost' historical context, it effectively de-canonizes the literature by putting it in some other context than the canonical.

vidual writing is positioned in relation to other writings in a collection (either materially or conceptually) has significant hermeneutical ramifications. In this sense, the broad context of a given writing involves all of the writings within its textual proximity.[29] This type of study seeks to uncover the "semantic effect of a book's relative position" within the biblical canon.[30] In this sense, "context" is now "context within the literary shape of the final form of the canon."[31] Any time a physical or conceptual reading sequence has been established, the study of contextuality is both possible and worth pursuing.[32]

Mere Contextuality

The level of analysis that observes these contextual effects without dealing with the issue of intention can be described as mere contextuality. Mere contextuality is the effect that arises in the mind of the reader when certain writings are seen in relation to other writings. This level of analysis focuses on the connections produced by a broader literary context. Moreover, studies of mere contextuality are not necessarily concerned with how individual writings come to be included in a collection, associated with certain groupings, or positioned in a specific manner. Instead, their focus is deliberately on the result of that placement or location. The main concern of mere contextuality is the meaning generated by the juxtaposition of these writings rather than how they became ordered or grouped together in such a way. In sum, the goal of mere contextuality is to observe the meaningful effect that an order of reading has on our understanding of the biblical books.

Meant Contextuality

Whereas mere contextuality restricts itself to analyzing the effect that the broader context of the biblical collection has on an individual writing without recourse to intention, there are also ways to ask whether the shape of the biblical canon has been intended in some way. This analysis moves from mere contextuality to meant contextuality. The concept of canonical shaping and canon-consciousness among the biblical authors allows for the possibility of an intended contextuality. Indeed, the location of a particular text among a collected group of writings demonstrates that someone has already deemed these works

---

29. Cf. Greg Goswell, "The Order of the Books of the New Testament," *Journal of the Evangelical Theological Society* 53.2 (2010): 225: "Readerly habit views enjambment as a clue that significant relations are to be discerned between a particular book and its neighbors in the library of canonical books."

30. Sailhamer, *Introduction to Old Testament Theology*, 213. Cf. Joseph Blenkinsopp, *Prophecy and Canon: A Contribution to the Study of Jewish Origins* (Notre Dame: Notre Dame University Press, 1977), 11: "Redaction study also must take account of the canon as context. The reason is, of course, that canon implies a positive attempt to give form, structure and meaning to traditional material by placing it in a particular context."

31. Christopher Seitz, *Prophecy and Hermeneutics* (Grand Rapids: Baker, 2007), 179.

32. For an extended discussion of the concept of "canonical contextuality" including a delineation of the notions of "mere contextuality" and "meant contextuality," see Spellman, *Toward a Canon-Conscious Reading*, 101–41.

to be connected in some way.[33] In some cases, at least, the order of reading itself represents an interpretive move. To give a standard example, the position of the Law and the Gospels at the beginning of the Old Testament and New Testament, respectively, indicates their perceived foundational role.

On one hand, the study of mere contextuality can help us recognize the often unacknowledged impact that sequence and ordering have on us as readers. On the other hand, the study of meant contextuality can help us be mindful of how the content of the biblical writings and the direction of the biblical authors themselves have shaped the very canonical context through which we access and read the Scriptures. For the purpose of biblical theology, we can note that the shape of individual books, their relationship to other biblical books as part of canonical groupings, and their ordering within larger sections of the canonical collection can and do have an impact on a reader's understanding of the message of the Bible as a whole. At the very least, the question of book ordering is worth considering when describing the message of a particular section of the canon or a particular grouping within the Old or New Testaments.[34]

In this regard, the ordering of biblical books within the canon can be a useful tool for analysis. Observing this feature of the canonical context also recognizes the multifaceted nature of the biblical canon itself. When we define the Bible, there are historical, theological, and hermeneutical dimensions to this understanding. The ordering of biblical books, their relationship to one another within groupings, the groupings of those groupings, and any effects this might have on the Bible's overarching theological message are all of interest to the biblical theologian.

To illustrate the types of textual connections we have discussed in this section, we can briefly consider the gospel of Matthew. As part of an innertextual study, you might ask how the quotation of Isaiah 7 and Matthew's explanation of the word Immanuel ("which means, God with us") to explain Jesus's birth in Matthew 1:23 relates to Jesus's promise to the disciples in Matthew 28:20: "behold, I am with you always, to the end of the age." These words about the presence of God in Christ are some of the first and last words we encounter in Matthew's narrative. As part of an intertextual study, you might ask how Matthew's mention of the "son of David, son of Abraham" (Matt. 1:1) connect to the Old Testament narratives about David, Abraham, and the covenant promises made to them. As a part of the study of canonical contextuality, you might ask how the gospel of Matthew relates to the other three Gospels, or fittingly begins the New Testament. You might also ask how Matthew serves to connect the New Testament as a whole to the Old Testament in both general

---

33. Cf. John Barton, *Holy Writings, Sacred Text: The Canon in Early Christianity* (Louisville: Westminster John Knox, 1997), 34: "Collecting books together is potentially an interpretive process."
34. For an example of some of the ways the canonical collection might shape our understanding of the message and grand storyline of the Bible, see the development of the "Story of Scripture" in chapters five through ten.

and specific ways. These quick illustrations should suffice to demonstrate the immediate relevance of each of these levels of analysis to big picture biblical theology and also their organic interconnection.[35]

Becoming a Biblical Theologian by Developing a Canon-Consciousness

We conclude this discussion of biblical-theological tools with a closing reflection on how the discipline of biblical theology draws upon these tools within a coherent framework that emphasizes the canon, the covenants, and the Christ.

A chief skill of the biblical theologian is to develop a robust canon-consciousness. The wide-ranging literary texts, contexts, meanings, and messages found within the biblical literature are bound together by a reader's sense of the big picture of the canonical context. What is more, a focus on this canonical context also means a reader will encounter directly the grand storyline that flows from the many narratives found within the biblical collection. The story of the biblical covenants features prominently in this grand storyline. Further, because these features are found in biblical texts, the web of textual connections both within and between books in the biblical collection will shape our understanding of the message of the Bible as a whole. Collectively, then, the biblical canon guides its readers through the biblical material by limiting and generating meaning. In turn, one of the central goals of biblical theology is to enable readers to discern and accept this hermeneutical and theological guidance.[36]

The tools introduced and outlined in this chapter are used in subsequent chapters in this book. In chapter three, we discuss some of the issues involved in seeing that the whole Bible is about Christ. In chapter four, we examine some of the theological commitments we make about Scripture that enable us to approach biblical theology in the way that we have. In chapters five through ten, we will consider the story of Scripture from beginning to end. In chapters eleven through twenty, we will survey several central themes that appear throughout the Bible. In these studies, we will make use of the biblical-theological tools discussed in this chapter. These studies are not exhaustive but serve as an invitation to doing biblical theology along these lines.

---

35. To the point, in the first example, the innertextual connection relating to the presence of God in Christ (at the beginning and end of the book) is communicated in Matthew 1 by an intertextual quotation and explication of Isaiah 7. In the second example, the intertextual allusion to the "son of David" is one of the "themes" that tie Matthew's gospel together, as he uses the "son of David" title in strategic ways throughout the rest of the Gospel. Finally, in the last example, the way the book of Matthew relates to other biblical books depends partly on the way that it draws upon the Old Testament (intertextuality) and partly on the way that it is internally ordered (innertextuality).

36. For a further reflection along these lines, see Ched Spellman, "The Scribe Who Has Become a Disciple: Identifying and Becoming the Ideal Reader of the Biblical Canon," *Themelios* 41.1 (2016): 37–51.

Discussion Questions

1. What is the purpose and strategic significance of having a "framework" for biblical theology? How do the canon, the covenants, and the Christ relate to one another to provide a helpful framework for the study of the whole Bible on its own terms?

2. What is the "canonical context" and how would you describe its significance in general and as a "BT Tool" in particular?

3. What is the relationship between the many narratives, the mega-narrative, and the meta-narrative of the Bible? How do these concepts inform the study of biblical theology?

4. What is the difference between "mere contextuality" and "meant contextuality"? How do these areas of study relate to the biblical storyline and the analysis of textual connections?

5. How would you describe the strategic significance of the biblical covenants for the study of biblical theology? How does the study of the biblical covenants relate to the "BT Tools" mentioned in this chapter?

Resources for Further Study

Beale, G. K. and D. A. Carson. *Commentary on the New Testament Use of the Old Testament.* Grand Rapids: Baker, 2007.

Dempster, Stephen. *Dominion and Dynasty: A Theology of the Hebrew Bible.* Downers Grove: InterVarsity, 2003.

Kruger, Michael J. *Canon Revisited: Establishing the Origins and Authority of the New Testament Books.* Wheaton: Crossway, 2012.

Seitz, Christopher R. *The Character of Christian Scripture: The Significance of a Two-Testament Bible.* Grand Rapids: Baker, 2011.

Spellman, Ched. *Toward a Canon-Conscious Reading of the Bible: Exploring the History and Hermeneutics of the Canon.* Sheffield: Sheffield-Phoenix, 2014.

CHAPTER 3

THE BIBLE'S OVERARCHING GOAL

IN CHAPTER ONE, WE CONSIDERED THE NATURE and definition of biblical theology as a discipline. We also considered several approaches to the task of biblical theology. In chapter two, we outlined a specific approach to biblical theology that took as its orienting framework the canonical context of the Bible, the narrative flow of the biblical storyline, and the strategic place of the biblical covenants in that storyline. We also discussed several tools that are necessary for the accomplishment of the biblical-theological task and its analysis of this type of big picture biblical theology. In chapter three, we move to consider the final part of our framework for biblical theology. The culminating feature of this biblical-theological framework is its conviction that one of the main purposes of Scripture is to display Jesus Christ.

There are many disciplines and subdisciplines that have tackled this particular theological question. In this chapter, we will consider the unique contribution that biblical theology as a discipline can make to this important topic. Accordingly, our analysis in this chapter will draw on the foundation established in chapters one and two.

Theological Considerations: The Gospel as the Glory of God in Christ

One of the motivating factors in seeing Christ in all of Scripture is the theological conviction that Jesus is the apex of the self-revelation of God. In Christ, we both experience redemption and receive revelation of God's inner life. The glory of God as revealed in the person and work of Christ is at the core of the gospel message. This christological reality, then, informs our grasp of the message of the Scriptures as a whole. An evangelical approach to biblical theology operates within this foundational commitment. Indeed, a *Christian* biblical theology must be relentless in its pursuit to discern and articulate the obvious and subtle ways Christ impacts the biblical-theological task and shapes its message.

In 2 Corinthians 4, Paul provides a particularly striking description of the gospel message. Paul initially laments that "the god of this world has blinded the minds of the unbelievers" and has kept them from "seeing the light of the gospel of the glory of Christ, who is the image of God" (2 Cor. 4:4). He then continues, "For what we proclaim is not ourselves, but Jesus Christ as Lord, with ourselves as your servants for Jesus' sake. For God, who said, "Let light shine out of darkness," has shone in our hearts to give the light of the knowledge of the glory of God in the face of Jesus Christ" (4:4–5).

In this masterful articulation of the gospel message, Paul makes theologically loaded statements about what God is doing in the world and who Jesus is, and connects it all to the grand storyline of the biblical canon. At the heart of the story of the biblical covenants is the bedrock conviction that the God of creation is the God of the covenants. This is the God who meets you when you are gripped by this gospel. With the darkness and light imagery of the Genesis creation account in view, the light of the gospel is contrasted to the darkness of unbelief. God speaks, "Let light shine out of the darkness" (2 Cor. 4:6). In the beginning, God *spoke* and darkness was dispelled by the presence of light. Because of Christ's redemptive work in the present, God speaks again in the gospel proclamation to "give the light of the knowledge of the glory of God in the face of Jesus Christ" (4:6). This is a breathtaking claim. Knowledge of Jesus as the Christ gained through the gospel message brings salvation, knowledge, and fellowship with God himself. This theological formulation, of course, is in line with Paul's understanding of the person of Jesus and the significance of his atoning work. Paul's description of the "the gospel of the glory of Christ, who is the image of God" (2 Cor. 4:4) is a particularly helpful orientation to the questions of this chapter.

As is clear from passages like this one, seeing the light of Christ in the gospel is a theological focus of the New Testament message. So, we can begin by examining this direct assertion: The whole Bible is about Jesus. The pivotal follow-up question is this: *how* is the whole Bible about Jesus? There seem to be some really helpful ways to answer this question but also some really unhelpful ways to answer this question. In this chapter, we discuss some of the textual and hermeneutical considerations that inform this simple but profound question: "Is the entire Bible about Jesus?"

Textual Considerations

The Relationship between the Testaments

Our current question relates directly to the broader issue of the relationship between the Old Testament and the New Testament within the Christian canon. When thinking about this particular question, we could think about a series of concerns that are intimately related to this line of inquiry. These include questions such as: What does it mean to read the Old Testament as Christian Scripture? What is the *nature* of the relationship between the two Testaments? Is this a literary relationship, a historical development, a narrative storyline connection, or is this simply a theological confession? These are all options, but for those who would seek to simply say, "yes," it must be recognized that none of these options are "givens." In other words, oftentimes when we describe the Testaments as two parts of a unified whole, we are making a series of hermeneutically significant assumptions whether we realize it or not.

As we have discussed in chapters one and two, depending on your understanding of the nature of Scripture and the proper way to study it, you may come to one of several different conclusions about the way the Testaments relate to one another. As mentioned previously, though there are diverse approaches to biblical theology, the relationship between the Testaments is at the heart of the biblical-theological task. Any approach to biblical theology that neglects this issue fails to engage one of the areas of emphasis that gives the discipline its distinctive identity.

The Gospel as a Story That Takes Two Testaments to Tell

In light of our discussion in this chapter, we note that the question of the relationship between the Testaments is a profoundly confessional and christological issue. Indeed, a critical component of a confessional approach to the study of the Bible includes a commitment to grapple with this question about the relationship between the Testaments. In particular, the set of convictions about Jesus and his relationship to the Scriptures and the covenants commits you to an understanding of the Bible as a two-testament collection that is ultimately unified in its witness to Jesus as the Christ. Moreover, the assumption that the Old Testament is a unified whole is also learned from a close reading of the New Testament. Here, we see the relationship between a focus on Jesus as the Christ and a commitment to whole Bible theology.

This issue is central for the study of biblical theology because it is central for the biblical authors themselves. In other words, the biblical authors are consistently considering the textual and theological relationship between the old covenant and the new covenant, between the Book of Moses and the Prophets, and between the Old Testament and the words of Jesus. The biblical canon provides guidance for the task of understanding how the relationship between the Testaments relates to the person and work of Jesus as the promised Christ. Further, even long after the resurrection, the biblical canon is *still* the church's guide for understanding Jesus as the coming son of David. In this regard, the gospel is still a story that takes two Testaments to tell.[1] This will be the case, "until he comes" (1 Cor. 11:26).

---

1. Seitz speaks of the depiction of Israel's history within the shape of the Book of the Twelve as a "story that takes two Testaments to tell" in *Prophecy and Hermeneutics*, 242.

To give one brief example of the way confessional statements about the Christ seamlessly interplay with biblical-theological themes in biblical texts, consider the majestic opening lines of the Letter to the Hebrews. The writer says:

> Long ago, at many times and in many ways, God spoke to our fathers by the prophets, but in these last days he has spoken to us by his Son, whom he appointed the heir of all things, through whom also he created the world. He is the radiance of the glory of God and the exact imprint of his nature, and he upholds the universe by the word of his power. After making purification for sins, he sat down at the right hand of the Majesty on high, having become as much superior to angels as the name he has inherited is more excellent than theirs. (Heb. 1:1–4)

In these few words, the writer masterfully pulls together many of the threads that the discipline of biblical theology seeks to explicate: the textual and theological relationship between the Testaments; the nature of redemptive history; the grand storyline of the Bible; the person and work of Christ as the fulfillment of Scripture and the story of the covenants; and the relationship between the past, present, and future words and actions of God. The same God who spoke "long ago" speaks "in these last days." The time of "our fathers" is connected to "us." The revelation "by the prophets" is connected to the revelation "by his Son." Of course, the Letter to the Hebrews itself addresses these themes in a powerful and unique way throughout the rest of its "word of exhortation." We can simply note that the writer demonstrates that the question of the relationship between the Testaments, the notion of unity and diversity, the story of the covenants, and the confession that Christ is the overarching goal of the Scriptures are all topics that are inextricably linked.

Our point of departure here can draw upon and develop the orienting framework for biblical theology that we discussed in chapter two—the canon, the covenants, and the Christ. In particular, what is the relationship between the canon, the covenants, and the Christ? One of the strengths of articulating the big picture of the Bible within the scope of this framework is the organic and interrelated nature of these elements. Considering the question "How does the whole Bible point to Christ?" serves as an apt illustration of the interrelated nature of these elements. In short, not only do the canon and the covenants point to Christ, but Christ himself points to the canon and the covenants.

The Canon Points to Christ

First, we consider how the Scriptures as a whole point to Christ. More specifically, how individual texts speak about the person and work of Christ, and how those texts are part of a broader mosaic that finds its fullest shape in the books of the canonical collection. This collection of Scripture as a whole provides a portrait of the work of God through Christ in redemptive history. The design of this canonical collection enables readers to perceive this message about the person and work of Jesus as the Christ with clarity and force.

The First Words of the Resurrected Christ (Luke 24)

In Luke 24, Jesus directs two of his disciples to consider the Scriptures as a whole in order to understand his messianic role and his work of redemption. Here, Jesus helps these disciples see his own glory displayed in all the Scriptures. On the road from Jerusalem to Emmaus, two disciples were reflecting upon the recent dramatic events of the crucifixion and burial of Jesus. Luke notes that these two disciples were reeling from disappointment and unmet expectations ("they stood still, looking sad," 24:17). As they walk along the way, "Jesus himself drew near" and began walking with them, though "their eyes were kept from recognizing him" (24:16–17). Jesus asks them about what they were discussing before he had joined them. They respond, "Are you the only visitor to Jerusalem who does not know the things that have happened there in these days?" (Luke 24:18). In the most striking case of embodied dramatic irony in all of history, these two disciples ask this question to the only one who did know the full extent of what had indeed taken place in Jerusalem. With the deft enquiry of a master teacher, Jesus queries, "What things?"

The disciples respond by summarizing the events of the last few days with a focus on the identity of Jesus as they have understood him: "Concerning Jesus of Nazareth, a man who was a prophet mighty in deed and word before God and all the people, and how our chief priest and rulers delivered him up to be condemned to death, and crucified" (Luke 24:19–20). After these details comes the disappointment: "But we had hoped that he was the one to redeem Israel." So too comes the despair: "Yes, and besides all this, it is now the third day since these things happened" (24:21). And then comes the confusion: "Moreover, some women of our company amazed us. They were at the tomb early in the morning, and when they did not find his body, they came back saying that they had even seen a vision of angels, who said that he was alive. Some of those who were with us went to the tomb and found it just as the women had said, but him they did not see" (24:22–24).

At this point, Jesus engages the conversation with force. He says to them, "O foolish ones, and slow of heart to believe all that the prophets have spoken! Was it not necessary that the Christ should suffer these things and enter into his glory?" (Luke 24:25–26). After Jesus makes this forceful and programmatic statement, Luke then provides a summary editorial comment that captures the scope and sequence of the textual journey that Jesus leads these disciples on as they journey along the path. Luke writes, "And beginning with Moses and all the Prophets, he interpreted to them in all the Scriptures the things concerning himself" (24:27). Later, when Jesus appears again to his gathered group of disciples, he again articulates this way of understanding the witness of the Old Testament. As he says,

"These are my words that I spoke to you while I was still with you, that everything written about me in the Law of Moses and the Prophets and the Psalms must be fulfilled" (24:44).

The Prophets, the Lord, and the Apostles (2 Peter 3)

In his second letter, Peter encourages his readers to pursue holiness and reject false teaching by remembering the reality of the coming day of the Lord. He does this by developing the theme of the reality of the past judgment of the flood and the promise of future judgment. Prior to these reminders, he mentions the basis for this hope and authority. He writes, "This is now the second letter that I am writing to you, beloved. In both of them I am stirring up your sincere mind by way of reminder, that you should remember the predictions of the holy prophets and the commandment of the Lord and Savior through your apostles" (2 Peter 3:1–2). Peter's statements here are helpful because they represent the shape of a two-Testament witness to Jesus as Lord, surrounded by the prophets on one side and the apostles on the other.

The Gospel Accords with the Law, the Prophets, and the Psalms (1 Corinthians 15 and Acts)

This broad understanding of the way the Scriptures as a whole point to Jesus as the Christ is confirmed in the preaching of the apostles. As Paul directly proclaims in a classic formulation in 1 Corinthians, "For I delivered to you as of first importance what I also received: that Christ died for our sins *in accordance with the Scriptures*, that he was buried, that he was raised on the third day *in accordance with the Scriptures*, and that he appeared to Cephas, then to the twelve" (15:4–5). Significantly, Paul puts forth the death and resurrection of Christ as happening "in accordance with the Scriptures" understood from the perspective of the entire collection. Rather than provide an exposition of particular passages (which he does with ease elsewhere), Paul here calls forth the textual testimony of the Scriptures as a unified witness to the risen Christ.

Paul not only consistently preaches about Jesus as the Christ from specific Old Testament texts, but also from the Old Testament as a whole. For example, in Acts 13 Paul proclaims the gospel in the synagogue "after the reading from the Law and the Prophets" (13:15). In his discussion of Israel's history, he also quotes several psalms, thus basing his preaching in this instance on the Law, the Prophets, and the Psalms. When Paul is brought before the governor in Acts 24, he asserts that his belief in God and faith in Christ (his adherence to "the Way") is founded upon "everything laid down by the Law and written in the Prophets" (24:14).

Finally, the last image we see of Paul in the book of Acts is of him "proclaiming the kingdom of God and teaching about the Lord Jesus Christ with all boldness and without hindrance" (24:31). Luke recounts that the great numbers that came to hear Paul during his house arrest in Rome heard a gospel rooted in the witness of the Old Testament: "From morning till evening he expounded to them, testifying to the kingdom of God and trying to convince them about Jesus both from the Law of Moses and from the Prophets" (Acts 28:24).

Christ Points to the Canon

Not only does the canon as a whole point to Christ, but Christ himself points to the canon. More specifically, we not only see the biblical authors consistently speak about Jesus as the Christ, but we also see Jesus identify himself as the Messiah and articulate his person and work in messianic terms by drawing directly on biblical texts. Highlighting the way Jesus utilizes individual Scriptures and also the way Jesus refers to the Scriptures as a whole coheres with the pattern established by the biblical authors.

In Luke's gospel, Jesus begins and ends his ministry as the Messiah by pointing to the biblical canon and making biblical-theological connections. In Luke 4, as Jesus returns "in the power of the Spirit" to Galilee, he comes to Nazareth and enters the synagogue "as was his custom" (4:16). As he stands up to read, he takes the "scroll of the prophet Isaiah, unrolls the scroll, and finds the place where it is written, 'The Spirit of the Lord is upon me, because he has anointed me'" (4:17–18). After reading this quotation from Isaiah 61:1–2, Jesus "rolled up the scroll and gave it back to the attendant and sat down. And the eyes of all in the synagogue were fixed on him" (4:20). Luke recounts that Jesus said to them, "Today this Scripture has been fulfilled in your hearing" (4:21). In dramatic and unmistakable fashion, Jesus makes clear that he understands his ministry to be marked by the presence of the Spirit, messianic in its orientation, and the fulfillment of the prophetic hope found in the Scriptures.

One of the first acts of Jesus's ministry in Luke's gospel is his reading and explanation of Scripture. Fittingly, then, one of the last acts of Jesus's ministry in Luke's gospel also involves his reflection and explanation of the Scriptures as a whole. Here we simply emphasize that it is Jesus himself who points to the biblical canon as a guide to a proper understanding of his identity as the Messiah. In Luke 24:27, Luke summarizes the substance of what Jesus teaches the two disciples on the road to Emmaus ("beginning with Moses and all the Prophets"). Then, in Luke 24:44, Luke records the actual articulation of this scope and sequence by Jesus himself ("everything written about me in the Law of Moses and the Prophets and the Psalms"). In other words, Jesus seems to know and interact with the Hebrew Bible *in its entirety* and *as an entirety.*[2]

---

2. Sailhamer uses these phrases in his comment about the Bible of Jesus (*Meaning of the Pentateuch*, 210). He argues later that "the Tanak was, for the most part, the only Bible that Jesus and the early church acknowledged as Scripture (cf. 2 Tim. 3:15). The early first-century church . . . did not yet have the completed NT, but they did have the OT, and it was their NT" (606).

The strategic importance of this moment at the culmination of Luke's gospel can scarcely be overemphasized for the contours of biblical theology. Here the resurrected Christ himself chooses to articulate the person and work of the resurrected Christ using the guidance provided by the shape of the biblical canon.

In a significant passage in John's gospel, Jesus develops a lengthy discussion concerning the ones who bear witness on his behalf. He speaks of his own testimony (John 5:30–31), the testimony of John the Baptist (5:32–35), his own works (5:36), the testimony of the Father (5:37–38), and then the testimony of the Scriptures (5:39). Jesus states directly, "You search the Scriptures because you think that in them you have eternal life; and it is they that bear witness about me, yet you refuse to come to me that you may have life" (5:39–40). After establishing in general that *the Scriptures* (as a whole) testify about him, Jesus specifies more directly regarding the testimony of the Book of Moses. He concludes this section of his dialogue by stating, "Do not think that I will accuse you to the Father. There is one who accuses you: Moses, on whom you have set your hope. For if you believed Moses, you would believe me; for he wrote of me. But if you do not believe his writings, how will you believe my words?" (5:45–47).

For our purposes, these last few lines are hermeneutically significant for several reasons. Here Jesus once again *points to the canon.* The Book of Moses *testifies* about the identity of Jesus. Belief involves perceiving what Moses wrote about Jesus in his book. There is a clear textual focus here as well. Jesus says, "for he [Moses] wrote of me," and then follows this up with a comment about "his writings." In other words, Jesus seems to refer to the *Book of Moses* rather than a legal code, the Mosaic covenant, or some sort of oral tradition. Finally, notice too how Jesus's comments at this point conclude an extended discourse about an entire body of testimony and evidence regarding the truth and trustworthiness of Jesus in his role as the Son sent from the Father to do the work of redemption. In this scope of redemptive history, Jesus places the words of Moses ("his writings") alongside of his own words ("how will you believe my words"). This *theological* and *hermeneutical* move lays the foundation for a later collection that will include a book of Moses's words and also a book of Jesus's words.

The Covenants Point to Christ

As developed in chapter two, one of the distinctive features of the Bible as a whole is the overarching storyline that emerges from the many narratives found within the canonical collections. At the center of this storyline is the story of the covenants. Through their strategic location and prominence in biblical texts, the biblical storyline, and the canonical collection, these covenants form a major component of the big picture of the Bible.

One of the clearest christological convictions of the New Testament writers is that the story of the covenants points to Jesus as the Christ. The gospel of Matthew states this in a particularly memorable way. Matthew begins, "The book of the genealogy of Jesus Christ, the son of David, the son of Abraham" (1:1). For Matthew, to begin an account of Jesus as the Christ entails remembering the Davidic and Abrahamic covenants. In Luke's gospel, the angel announces the birth of Jesus in terms of these same covenants. Jesus "will be great and will be called the Son of the Most High. And the Lord God will give to him the throne of his father David, and he will reign over the house of Jacob forever, and of his kingdom there will be no end" (Luke 1:32–33).

When Paul speaks of the gospel, the good news, he has in mind the message that he constantly proclaims. For Paul, the gospel is a story that takes two Testaments to tell. Accordingly, in order to be a proclaimer of the gospel, you must also be a reader of the Scriptures. When Paul provides programmatic articulations of the gospel, he often mentions its connection to the prophetic fulfillment of the Davidic covenant.

For example, the Letter to the Romans begins with Paul saying that he is "set apart for the gospel of God, which he promised beforehand through his prophets in the holy Scriptures, concerning his Son" (Rom. 1:1–2). Paul specifies further that this Son was "descended from David according to the flesh and was declared to be the Son of God in power according to the Spirit of holiness by his resurrection from the dead" (1:3–4). This son of David, who is also the Son of God, is the one Paul identifies as "Jesus Christ our Lord" (1:5). On the basis of the gospel message of this Messiah, Paul has received his "grace and apostleship to bring about the obedience of faith for the sake of his name among all the nations, including you who are called to belong to Jesus Christ" (1:6).

In 2 Timothy, Paul writes, "Remember Jesus Christ, risen from the dead, the offspring of David, as preached in my gospel, for which I am suffering, bound with chains as a criminal. But the word of God is not bound! Therefore I endure everything for the sake of the elect, that they also may obtain the salvation that is in Christ Jesus with eternal glory" (2 Tim. 2:8–10). In a remarkably compact way, Paul demonstrates that this gospel is one that takes two Testaments to tell and two Testaments to remember. The confession that Jesus is the Christ draws together an entire network of biblical-theological threads. Unpacking this title with the phrases "risen from the dead" and "offspring of David" both fills out this messianic portrait and confirms the direction of our intertextual and theological reflection. Remembering Jesus in this way requires us to remember both the canon and the covenants.

The writer of Hebrews, too, relentlessly draws out the implications of the work of Jesus as the Christ in relation to the covenants. The writer summarizes, "as it is, Christ has obtained a ministry that is as much more excellent than the old as the covenant he mediates is better, since it is enacted on better promises. For if the first covenant had been faultless, there would have been no occasion to look for a second" (Heb. 8:6–7).

This very brief survey represents the perspective of both Old and New Testament authors who see the covenants as part of a connected story and connect that story to the story of the Christ.

Christ Points to the Covenants

The same relationship between Christ and the canon exists between Christ and the covenants. The covenants not only point to Jesus as the Christ, but Christ himself also points explicitly to these same covenants as he articulates his person and work as the Son of God and the promised Messiah.

Just as the writer of Hebrews advances, Jesus points to the promise of the new covenant being fulfilled in his death. In Luke's portrayal of the Last Supper, Jesus directly makes this biblical-theological connection. As Luke records, Jesus "took bread, and when he had given thanks, he broke it and gave it to them, saying, 'This is my body, which is given for you. Do this in remembrance of me.' And likewise the cup after they had eaten, saying, 'This cup that is poured out for you is the new covenant in my blood.' But behold, the hand of him who betrays me is with me on the table" (Luke 22:19–21).[3] On the eve of this crucial moment in Jesus's life and all of redemptive history, he openly draws attention to the story of the covenants as the means of interpreting the meaning of his impending death.

The way Jesus highlights the Davidic covenant is perhaps the most strategic example of this pattern. The hope that the blessings of the covenants might be fulfilled is expressed throughout important Old Testament texts. These theologically loaded passages often center on the coming son of David who would establish an eternal kingdom of God and bring about the obedience of the people. The biblical writers consistently characterize Jesus as the son of David through a variety of literary strategies (quotations, allusions, echoes, imagery, etc.). The point we are making here, though, is that these biblical authors are following the lead of Jesus himself.

In Matthew 22, Jesus is involved in a series of dialogues centered on theological arguments and biblical interpretation. As Matthew notes, at this juncture "the Pharisees went and plotted how to entangle him in his words" (22:15). Thus, in this section, there is a close focus on how Jesus answers their questions and the concepts he prompts his audience to consider. Jesus addresses a politically loaded question about paying taxes (22:16–22), a theologically complex question about marriage in the resurrection (22:23–33), and finally a textual question about the greatest commandment (22:34–40). Regarding this last question, Jesus responds by quoting from Deuteronomy 6:5 ("You shall love the Lord your God") and Leviticus 19:18 ("You shall love your neighbor"). Further highlighting that he was making a point not only about particular laws, but also about the interpretation of the Mosaic covenant in light of the prophetic witness, Jesus adds, "On these two commandments depend all the Law and the Prophets" (Matt. 22:40).

---

3. In Matthew 26:28, Jesus says, "for this is my blood of the covenant, which is poured out for many for the forgiveness of sins." In Mark 14:24, he says, "This is my blood of the covenant, which is poured out for many."

After he quotes these passages and refers to the Law and the Prophets in response to this line of questioning, Jesus brings up a prominent psalm in a question of his own. Matthew notes that "while the Pharisees were gathered together," Jesus asked them this question: "What do you think about the Christ? Whose son is he?" (Matt. 22:41–42). When he asks the Pharisees this question, Jesus tests not only their Scripture memory, but also their reading strategy.

After the Pharisees correctly answer that the Christ is the son of David, Jesus proceeds with a textual question about Psalm 110: "How is it then that David, in the Spirit, calls him Lord?" In Psalm 110, David begins by saying, "The Lord said to my Lord, 'Sit at my right hand, until I put your enemies under your feet'" (110:1). In light of the psalm's opening line, Jesus asks, "If then David calls him Lord, how is he his son?" (Matt. 22:45). Jesus's simple question about the identity of the person speaking and the one being spoken about in this text stumps the Pharisees, and this type of interpretive riddle has left plenty of readers silent since that day in Jerusalem.

There is much to contemplate about the point Jesus makes in this discussion with the Jewish leaders and his messianic understanding of Psalm 110. For our purpose here, Jesus directs attention specifically to the identity of the Christ as the son of David in the context of a discussion of Scripture taking place within view of the canon as a whole.

This section of Matthew, then, provides an example of Jesus engaging a wide range of political, theological, and hermeneutical issues by interpreting individual texts specifically but also within the scope of the entire Hebrew Bible. This sequence of scenes is thus an illuminating example of Jesus pointing to the canon and the covenants as a way of communicating and revealing his messianic identity and redemptive purpose.

The Last Words of the Resurrected Christ (Revelation 22)

As a final example of the interrelatedness of the biblical-theological categories of the canon, the covenants, and the Christ, we can consider the closing orientation that the book of Revelation provides for a biblical theology framework.

The New Testament begins and ends with Jesus. This emphasis is usually appreciated. What is easier to miss is the number of texts involved. Alongside the affirmation of the supremacy of Jesus as the Christ, there is a remarkable and relentless focus on written texts. Matthew begins his work by mentioning, "the book of the genealogies of Jesus, the Christ, son of David, son of Abraham" (Matt. 1:1). This "book" refers to the genealogy and narrative that follows in the gospel of Matthew and also alludes to the "book of the generations of Adam" (Gen. 5:1). These are the very first words we read in the New Testament.

Some of the last words we read in the New Testament are the final words of the resurrected Christ to the churches. In Revelation 22 Jesus says, "I, Jesus, have sent my angel to testify to you about these things for the churches. I am the root and the descendant of David, the bright morning star" (22:16).

Several things stand out about these words. First, Jesus's words here about the angel testifying to John "for the churches" draws us back to Revelation 2–3 where seven letters are composed to be sent to the seven churches. Here Jesus references an earlier portion of the book of Revelation, which becomes a part of the New Testament collection. In this way, *Christ himself points to the canon.*

Second, after mentioning these letters (and this book of Revelation), Jesus reminds John and, by extension, believing readers of his identity. Remember, these are the last words that Jesus speaks to the churches in the New Testament. This position gives them a clear sense of urgency. What will this final word be that the resurrected Christ will leave the fledgling churches? What could sustain them until he comes? He says, "I am the root and the descendant of David, the bright morning star" (Rev. 22:16).

The very first book of the Bible spoke of a coming ruler who would come from the tribe of Judah and rule with righteousness (Gen. 49:8–12). This same promise forms the basis of the vision of what is to come at the beginning of the John's vision in Revelation. As John records, "And one of the elders said to me, 'Weep no more; behold, the Lion of the tribe of Judah, the Root of David, has conquered, so that he can open the scroll and its seven seals'" (Rev. 5:5). Standing at the end of the vision and the end of the book, Jesus echoes the words of this covenant promise. His final message to the churches is this: *I am the son of David. And I am coming soon. So, hold on, my covenant promises are still good.* In this way, *Christ himself points to the covenants.*

Why would the resurrected Christ do this? Why would John and Matthew do this as biblical authors? Why is this the first and last thing we hear about in the New Testament? Could there really be something so powerful in these biblical texts?

Biblical theology contributes the resources to answer these types of questions. In particular, the setting of the canon and the story of the covenants are necessary for Jesus's words to make sense. More pointedly, we might say that Jesus's words *only* make sense in light of these textual and theological realities. The biblical-theological significance of this concluding statement is that it makes the case that the biblical canon and the covenant story *still* point to the resurrected Lord. Matthew, John, and Jesus are all pointing to some of the *oldest* and most *enduring* promises mentioned in the Law, the Prophets, the Writings, the Gospels, Acts, the Epistles, and Revelation.

Believing readers still await the coming of the son of David. The New Testament writers from beginning (Matt. 1:1) to end (Rev. 22:16) confirm and expand that expectation to mean that believing readers anticipate the coming of the resurrected son of David. As Paul says, "Remember Jesus Christ, risen from the dead, offspring of David" (2 Tim. 2:8). The gospel is a story that takes two Testaments to tell. The biblical canon equips the churches to endure until the end and respond to the promise of his coming with the believing response, "Amen. Come, Lord Jesus!" (Rev. 22:20).

Hermeneutical Considerations: How Is the Whole Bible about Christ?

Thinking about the relationship between the canon, the covenants, and the Christ is helpful as we consider how the Bible fits together. This biblical reflection also has a distinctly hermeneutical component. In other words, the biblical theology framework of the canon and the covenants impacts how we understand the whole Bible as a book that is ultimately about Christ. Here we return to the confession and question that began this chapter. The whole Bible is about Christ, but *how* is the whole Bible about Christ?

Following the Guidance of the Biblical Authors

The approach taken above leans into the orienting framework of biblical theology to grapple with this question. A guiding framework does not answer every question about every text, nor is it designed to do so. Rather, this framework is intended to function as a guide for reading. In fact, because the pillars of this framework attempt to summarize both individual passages and clear lines of textual development within the biblical canon—the canon and the covenants point to Christ; Christ points to the canon and the covenants—this guidance can serve in a way that is mindful of how the biblical authors speak of these topics as well.

In terms of interpretive practice, or as part of a broader hermeneutical approach to reading biblical texts, this biblical theology framework can resonate quite strongly. What would this look like? How might a *reader* seek to "find Jesus in all of Scripture" in actual practice? If the whole Bible is about Christ, we might ask, how is a particular passage about him? To put the matter in other terms, did Jesus read the Bible *christologically*? This last question is particularly forceful in light of this christological confession: Jesus says the entirety of the Scriptures (the whole) testify about him, so as I read individual passages in that collection (the parts), how do I relate the two when it does not seem obvious?

The strength of having a biblical-theological framework is that it allows you to be guided by the *contours* and *pacing* of the biblical literature. If the relationship between the canon, the covenants, and the Christ that we have discussed is broadly sound, then this framework can serve a guiding and governing function.

At any point in the biblical canon, you can ask a simple series of questions to help you discern how a text speaks about Christ:

- What does this text say?
- Where is this text located within its *book*?
- Where is this text located within the *canon*?
  - » Which part of the grand storyline am I in?
  - » What time is it within the scope of redemptive history?

- Does this text mention any biblical *covenants*?
  - » If yes, focus on these.
  - » If no, does the book mention any biblical covenants?

These simple questions provide an orienting framework within which to pursue the christological question. This is a starting point you can work from as you read and reread biblical texts and think carefully about what these texts say about Jesus as the Christ.

Part of the strategy here involves reading individual texts within the scope of book-level meaning. A relentless focus on an author's textual intention, not only in individual passages but also in larger sections and across entire books, is critically important. With this book-level focus, seeing the way the whole Bible is about Christ will be a much more organic task. Indeed, many rich messianic passages are seen most clearly when viewed against the backdrop of book's entire message. When removed from their literary location within an author's textual mosaic, these passages can sometimes appear to be shards of isolated case studies rather than the brilliant centerpieces they are. It is much easier to resort to prooftexting or making arbitrary connections to Christ when only a few phrases or a single passage is in view. Oftentimes, simply widening the scope of your analysis to the broader paragraph or larger discourse section can provide enough textual context to see the connections that are part of the author's purpose.

Two hermeneutical statements can begin to capture the conviction of the New Testament authors. For them, Jesus both *fulfills* and *fills out* the Scriptures. This twofold way of phrasing this phenomenon describes the relationship between Christ and the Bible at both the textual and canonical level.

Jesus Fulfills the Scriptures

An underlying assumption of the biblical authors, and thus an approach to biblical theology that takes its cues from the biblical authors, is that *Jesus fulfills the Scriptures.*

In fact, one of the biblical-theological patterns that emerge from reading the Scriptures as a whole is a movement from promise to fulfillment. This *promise–fulfillment* pattern is a hermeneutically and theologically significant feature to keep in mind. It is important to not unevenly apply the notion of promise–fulfillment as a rigid scheme such that the Old Testament is primarily understood to contain only promise whereas the New Testament contains only fulfillment. This pattern informs the question of the relationship between the Old Testament and New Testament, but it is also a pattern that is already fully established within the composition and development of the Old Testament itself.

Further, this promise–fulfillment pattern helps readers recognize a feature of redemptive history and the nature of biblical texts that the biblical authors expound in their own writings. Finally, the promise–fulfillment pattern frequently centers on the person and work of Jesus as the promised Messiah, the coming one of prophetic promises.

This assumption that Jesus fulfills the Scriptures surfaces with remarkable clarity in the opening section of Matthew's gospel. After an intertextually loaded opening chapter that draws on the shape of the Hebrew Bible as a whole, Matthew develops a distinct pattern of interpreting events in the life of Jesus with passages of Scripture. Matthew signals this intention by pausing the flow of the narrative, drawing attention to a specific intertextual reference or asserting the fulfillment of a prophetic Scripture, and then supplying a quotation of the relevant biblical text.[4] This use of fulfillment quotations is a particularly prominent and sustained example of this christological assumption held by the New Testament writers.

This fulfillment formula pattern surfaces again in the passion narrative in John 19. Here, John utilizes Psalms 22 and 34 along with Zechariah 12:10. In each case, John prefaces his biblical reference with an introductory formula that identifies the quoted text as "Scripture."[5] By quoting these passages, John asserts in striking fashion that specific details of Jesus's crucifixion scene correspond to the scene of suffering depicted in Psalm 22. That other details of the Psalm correspond to John's crucifixion account further highlights his interest in showing a connection between the two texts. In John's account Jesus's thirst (John 19:28/Ps. 22:15), his pierced hands and feet (John 19:23/Ps. 22:16), and his preserved bones (John 19:33/Ps. 22:17) all resonate with the psalmist's depiction. Through these intertexts, John allows the quoted context of Psalm 22 to reverberate in his own narrative composition.

Because of their initial and final locations in the fourfold Gospel corpus, these sections of Matthew and John respectively bookend one of the overarching themes of the gospel proclamation; namely, that Jesus represents the fulfillment of Scripture. An attentive reader of the New Testament Gospels is thus encouraged to view the four Gospels in light of key Old Testament quotations.

Jesus Fills Out the Scriptures

The notion that Jesus fulfills the Scriptures is important, but also raises an interpretive tension in some instances. The idea of fulfillment works in a natural and almost straightforward way alongside the notion of predictive prophecy. Predictive prophecy denotes when one text predicts a future event or situation, and a later text describes an individual or situation that meets those expectations. Many prophetic messianic texts work in this manner as they predict some aspect of the person or work of the coming Messiah. Other texts, though, do not openly seem to be future-looking or predictive, but rather simply describe the life of David or other biblical figures. In these cases, a New Testament writer will reference this

---

4. The specific connections alluded to in this paragraph are Matthew 1:22–23/Isaiah 7:14; Matthew 2:5–6/Micah 5:2; Matthew 2:15/Hosea 11:1; Matthew 2:17–18/Jeremiah 31:15; Matthew 2:23/Isaiah 11:1; and Matthew 4:14–15/Isaiah 9:1–2.
5. The exact texts are John 19:24 (Ps. 22:18), 19:36 (Exod. 12:46; Num. 9:12; and Ps. 34:20), and 19:37 (Zech. 12:10).

text and say that Scripture has been fulfilled by Jesus. This scenario raises the question: How can Jesus fulfill texts that do not seem to be predictive prophecies about the Messiah?

An important way to answer this question is to recognize that the biblical writers anticipate the Messiah in multiple ways. Sometimes they *predict* the future of the Messiah, but other times they *prefigure* the person of the Messiah and the nature of his future work of redemption. In this way, Jesus directly fulfills predictive prophecies about the Messiah, but he also *fills out* the messianic portrayal found in other texts.

One of the ways that interpreters have sought to make sense of this particular way that Jesus fills out the Old Testament is by characterizing these instances as "typological connections." Typology is a way of viewing past events, persons, and institutions as types or patterns of the future. The three major elements of a typological relationship are correspondence, escalation, and replacement.[6] For example, a historical figure could be seen as a type that corresponds to a later antitype. This antitype is greater than and replaces the type that prefigured it, having fulfilled what the original type anticipated. The type is a shadow of the reality that the antitype embodies. This approach assumes a high view of God's providential working in all of history, for the type actually prefigures the later antitype.

We can illustrate this approach in John's gospel. In his crucifixion account, John quotes specific psalms that include details about the life of David. One way to explain the manner in which John is using these biographical details is to recognize that John employs a typological interpretation of David's life. In this model, David is viewed as a type of the coming Messiah. Thus, John can appropriate the details of David's life in his portrayal of Jesus as the Messiah from David's line. David's deeds and words become highly predictive of the one whom he prefigures. As a young man, David was a shepherd adept at caring for his flock and defending his sheep from harmful predators (1 Sam. 16:11; 17:34–37). In God's providence he became the anointed successor to King Saul as a "man after God's own heart" (16:12–13; cf. 13:14). As the king of Israel, David defeated God's enemies and united the nation in worship and obedience to Yahweh. He also paved the way for his son, Solomon, to build the temple where the Lord would dwell among his people.

By employing these significant details from David's life in their expectation and exposition of the Messiah, the biblical writers treat David as a paradigmatic figure, a type of

---

6. This understanding of typology might be classified as "traditional typology." For proponents of this view, see Leonhard Goppelt, *Typos: The Typological Interpretation of the Old Testament in the New*, trans. Donald H. Madwig (Grand Rapids: Eerdmans, 1982), esp. 17–19. Others view typology more in terms of analogy and reject the escalation between the type and antitype. Paul Hoskins provides a helpful delineation of these two "concepts" of typology in *Jesus as the Fulfillment of the Temple in the Gospel of John* (Milton Keynes: Paternoster, 2006), 18–36. Note also D. A. Carson's perspective that typology is "based on a perception of patterns of continuity across the sweep of salvation history" in his "John and the Johannine Epistles," in *It is Written: Scripture Citing Scripture*, ed. D. A. Carson and H. G. M. Williamson (Cambridge: Cambridge University Press, 1988), 249. Along these lines, see also G. K. Beale's discussion of typology in *Handbook on the New Testament Use of the Old Testament*, 55–93.

the one who is to come. David's life becomes a pattern that anticipates fulfillment in one coming after him. Accordingly, the roles David served in as a shepherd and king provide striking images when applied to a figure who will be like David. The coming one will be like David in that he will be the King and the Shepherd. The other side of this picture is that David also suffered and went through physical trials. Because the Psalms are filled with poetic expressions of these struggles, they are uniquely relevant for the writers of the Gospels. For John, certain psalms strikingly demonstrate that Jesus is the Messiah and that his death fills out a pattern found in the suffering of David.[7] This type of pattern helps explain why John used these Davidic psalms to illuminate the passion narrative.[8]

Narrative Typology and Intertextual Typology

More specifically in this case, John seems to employ a form of intertextual typology in relating the suffering of David to the suffering of the Christ.[9] The connections are intertextual because John utilizes previous biblical texts to generate a corresponding relationship. The use of quotations and allusions is the manner by which John connects two narrative figures. The connections are typological because of the theological nature of the relationship between David and Christ. John seems to present a typological relationship rooted in intertextual connections.

Further, the term intertextual typology implies that this presentation is a feature of the compositional strategy of both the Old Testament and New Testament author. Both the type and the antitype are embedded by their respective authors into the narratives in which they appear. What is more, the reason an individual, event, or institution is given typological significance is due to their portrayal by a biblical author. Accordingly, if an author intentionally uses a kind of narrative typology where he portrays an individual, event, or institution as a kind of future-oriented pattern, then this textual strategy itself becomes the basis for a subsequent author's perception and appropriation of that individual, event, or institution as future-looking and meaningful in this manner.[10]

---

7. Cf. Paul M. Hoskins, *That Scripture Might Be Fulfilled: Typology and the Death of Christ* (Longwood: Xulon Press, 2009), 54: "Jesus shows that he is the true King of Israel, because he faithfully suffers like David and even more than David. For those with eyes to see, Jesus suffers and dies as the true Son of David." Hoskins highlights the importance of John's typological understanding of the life of David in understanding John's use of the Psalms. As he notes, "Part of God's plan for David's life was for David to suffer and for David to write about his suffering in such a way as to anticipate specific aspects of the suffering of Jesus, the Christ" (55).

8. Carson makes this point about the Psalms in "John and the Johannine Epistles," 249: "The Davidic typology that surfaces repeatedly in the NT may well stand behind some of the Psalm quotations in the FG [fourth Gospel]."

9. Because typology has received negative connotations in the history of interpretation, those who hold that it remains a helpful interpretive principle usually modify the term in some way. Those wanting to regain the typology developed by interpreters such as Goppelt sometimes opt for "traditional" typology. The choice of "intertextual" typology in this instance seeks to combine the insights of traditional typology with the intentional focus on an author's textual intention and a broader literary context provided by the terms narrative typology and intertextual typology.

10. Sailhamer discusses the notion of "narrative typology" in *The Pentateuch as Narrative: A Biblical-Theological Commentary*, Library of Biblical Interpretation (Grand Rapids: Zondervan, 1992), 37–44. Part of this authorial

Understood in this way, typological interpretation is less a method of a reader than a strategy of an author. As a reader, you are seeking to understand a typological relationship based on the guidance of the biblical author rather than your own perception or reconstruction of salvation history. This way of understanding the Bible's two-testament witness to Jesus as the Christ requires a central role for the textual intention of the biblical authors, a commitment to the divine inspiration of the Scriptures, and also a high view of God's providence in history.[11]

Hence, it is in the writings of the Old Testament that David is cast as a paradigmatic figure for the Messiah, the coming king of Israel. The origin of this expectation stems from the Lord's promise to David that one of his descendants will be God's son and will inherit an eternal kingdom. This promise to David is picked up by later writers who build an expectation for this coming Son of David in terms of David's life. From a book-level perspective, the biblical portrayal of David *prefigures* and *foreshadows* the life of Jesus as the Christ. Two of the most prominent Davidic images used in prophetic literature are the ones John uses in his text; namely, the good king and the good shepherd (e.g., Ezek. 34:20–24; 37:24–28; John 10:1–30). John therefore does not create these associations, but rather picks up and fills out what the Old Testament authors have already done in their portrayal of David.

---

technique involves the way "earlier events foreshadow and anticipate later events. Later events are written to remind the reader of past narratives" (37). "By means of this technique," Sailhamer notes, "the author develops central themes and continually draws them to the reader's attention" (37). The examples he gives from the Pentateuch include the way the account of Abraham and Sarah in Genesis 12:10–20 foreshadows Genesis 41–Exodus 12; the way the spread of sin in Genesis 1–11 foreshadows the defilement of the camp in Leviticus 11–16; and how the exodus account foreshadows the Balaam narratives in Numbers 23–24. Part of this clearly established strategy (and in relation to the use of poetry in the Pentateuch) is "an eschatological reading of . . . historical narratives." The author, then, cares deeply about the "inherent relationship between the past and the future. That which happened to God's people in the past portends of future events. To say it another way, the past is seen as a lesson for the future" (37). See also Sailhamer, "The Canonical Approach to the OT: Its Effect on Understanding Prophecy," *Journal of the Evangelical Theological Society* 30.3 (1987): 307–15. He states more broadly that the biblical authors "see the historical narratives they recount as fundamentally a picture, or foreshadowing, of the future. We might even say they understand their texts as 'types' or 'typologies' of the future" (307).

11. On these features of this discussion, see the method and examples provided by Peter J. Link Jr. and Matthew Y. Emerson, "Searching for the Second Adam: Typological Connections between Adam, Joseph, Mordecai, and Daniel," *Southern Baptist Journal of Theology* 21.1 (2017): 123–44. Link and Emerson examine the ways "typology exists within the OT as an act of writing and not merely a way of reading" (125). They delineate the connection and distinction between typological reading and typological writing and argue for the strategic significance of the latter. See also Joshua Philpot's discussion of approaches that foreground the author's intention in the study of typological connections in "See the True and Better Adam: Typology and Human Origins," *Bulletin of Ecclesial Theology* 5.2 (2018): 79–103. Taking a complementary approach, Seth D. Postell directly associates typology with the compositional strategies of both Old Testament and New Testament authors. See "The Old Testament in the Old Testament" and "Typology in the Old Testament" in *The Moody Handbook of Messianic Prophecy*, ed. Michael Rydelnik and Edwin Blum (Chicago: Moody Publishers, 2019), 103–117; and 161–75. Cf. Seitz's emphasis on the role of the canonical context and the theological category of providence in the use of figural interpretation in the wide-ranging essays in *Figured Out: Typology and Providence in Christian Scripture* (Louisville: Westminster John Knox, 2001).

In this way, John's appropriation of Davidic typology is exegetical in nature. By connecting the life and death of Jesus to the expectation of the messianic, Davidic shepherd-king, John picks up on the messianic trajectory of the Hebrew Scriptures. In this approach, both the Old Testament and New Testament writers play a significant role in the portrayal of these narrative figures. The resulting overall witness of both Testaments is that Jesus both corresponds to and surpasses David who prefigures him. Jesus not only bears an analogical family resemblance to David, but also refashions the prophetic imagery and fills it out. Whereas David was a flawed man after God's own heart, Jesus is the perfect man who is God's own Son.

Avoiding Arbitrary Ways of Seeing Christ in All of Scripture

This approach to recognizing that the whole Bible is about Christ is not the only way to address this question. It also does not necessarily exclude other exegetical techniques or interpretive practices. However, this way of understanding the nature of the biblical canon and the role of its texts, authors, and meaning does seek to diverge from approaches that employ arbitrary or surface-level ways of seeing Christ in all of Scripture.

For example, one way of artificially producing a christological interpretation of a particular passage would be to use an overtly allegorical method that focuses on surface-level verbal or thematic connections. Here, a reader who is convinced that the whole Bible is about Christ could strive to interpret each biblical passage and every given detail as christological. This method puts considerable pressure on the interpreter to visualize every passage in light of later theological concepts developed in the New Testament. As an all-encompassing method, this form of allegory stresses unity at the cost of distinction and the diversity of the texts themselves. This method also strains the exegetical integrity of the initial passage under examination, as its christological content may be unclear to the reader or only tangentially connected to the verbal meaning of the passage.

Two common examples of this technique include the association of the color red with the blood of Christ, and the association of any prominent perpendicular shape with the cross of Christ. Regarding the former example, the "scarlet cord" tied by Rahab to her window in the Jericho story (Josh. 2:17–20) becomes construed as a direct reference to the blood of Jesus. Regarding the latter example, Moses's outstretched arms as he stands to part the waters is taken as a perpendicular image that resembles the cross of Christ. Similarly, the perpendicular arrangement of the camps around the tabernacle becomes a connection to the cross. In all of these examples, though, the connection to Christ is arbitrary and based on a surface-level parallel (i.e., the color red or the perpendicular shape of the cross). Ironically, though, these particular examples are found in scriptural locations that are rife with rich theological messages that are integrally connected to the Bible's portrayal of Jesus as the Christ. Making only surface-level and arbitrary links actually ends up short-circuiting a more brilliant connection.

Should You Make a Beeline for the Cross?

As we have seen, this issue is important to keep in mind when interpreting biblical texts. It is also helpful to remember when presenting the meaning of a passage in a lesson, sermon, or devotional context. Convinced that the whole Bible is about Christ, sometimes a reader might seek to quickly move from the passage being read to its christological sense, or simply *speed up* the storyline to get to Christ. This raises the question in another way: If the whole Bible is about Christ, should we look for Christ in every passage and make him the focus of every sermon in the same fashion?

In 1859, Charles H. Spurgeon preached a sermon called "Christ Precious to Believers." In this sermon, Spurgeon includes an anecdote from a Welsh minister. In this anecdote, a young preacher gives a sermon and receives feedback from an older minister. The older minister critiques his "very poor sermon" not because of his explanation of the text, which he found very good, but rather because "there was no Christ in it." The younger preacher answers that, "Christ was not in the text; we are not to be preaching Christ always, we must preach what is in the text." The older minister responds, "Don't you know, young man, that from every town, and every village, and every little hamlet in England, wherever it may be, there is a road to London?" After the young preacher agrees, the older minister concludes:

> And so from every text in Scripture, there is a road to the metropolis of the Scriptures, that is Christ. And my dear brother, your business is when you get to a text, to say, 'Now what is the road to Christ?' and then preach a sermon, running along the road towards the great metropolis—Christ. And . . . I have never yet found a text that had not got a road to Christ in it, and if I ever do find one that has not a road to Christ in it, I will make one; I will go over hedge and ditch but I would get at my Master, for the sermon cannot do any good unless there is a savour of Christ in it.[12]

Spurgeon's anecdote is a vibrant illustration which, in typical Spurgeon fashion, clearly communicates the powerful impact of preaching Christ. However, while the above anecdote is helpful, it is also susceptible to misuse. There is both warrant and motivation to preach Christ "from every text in Scripture." The issue, however, is not theological (i.e., that Christ is worthy to be preached and the goal of Scripture) but hermeneutical: *How* is Christ to be understood and proclaimed "from every text in Scripture" that does justice to every text in Scripture?

In Spurgeon's illustration, the Scriptures are envisioned as a network of towns, villages, and hamlets scattered across England. They are disconnected from one another, but all have

---

12. For the text of this sermon, see Charles Spurgeon, "Christ Precious to Believers," The Spurgeon Archive, Midwestern Baptist Theological Seminary, http://archive.spurgeon.org/sermons/0242.php.

a road that leads to the central metropolis of the country: London. In the same way, each text of Scripture has a "road toward the great metropolis—Christ." When you encounter a text in this approach, you must eventually run toward the great christological metropolis. Most pointedly, this method is applied to every passage and every sermon: "I have never yet found a text that had not got a road to Christ in it, and if I ever do find one that has not a road to Christ in it, I will make one."

Sometimes this hermeneutical and homiletical technique is paraphrased and attributed to Spurgeon as, "I take my text and make a beeline for the cross." When used without careful reflection, this phrase can become a hermeneutical principle that influences the way a reader reads and a preacher preaches. The modest point we can make here relates to the contribution of biblical theology to this particular issue of reading and preaching. Before we can ask how the whole Bible points to Jesus, we must ask how the whole Bible fits together. Knowing what the Bible as a whole is about and how it fits together is an inestimably valuable aid for seeing how it all leads to Jesus as the Christ.

Pursuing Exegetical and Homiletical Patience

The biblical authors have laid out a textual journey for their readers to follow. Our goal as biblical theologians is to follow these authors and ask what they are up to. How has an author directed us to think a certain way or to interpret an event, a concept, or a theme? In other words, the Spurgeon illustration actually turns out to be useful, if thought out a little further. In this scenario, it is not that every text has a special dedicated road that leads only to Christ. Rather, every text is part of a complex but orderly system of roads that ultimately leads to Christ. Further, those roads are often interconnected. Just as the towns, villages, and hamlets of England possess roads that lead to London, they also have roads that connect to one another. The key difference here is that the paths of the Scriptures are not simply byways for vagabond travelers, but are more like roads that have been plotted on a carefully designed roadmap that we have access to. This textual transportation system consists of books, groupings, two Testaments, and a narrative storyline signposted by a series of covenants. The final part of the Spurgeon illustration, then, is where the biblical theologian would get off the train.

For the biblical theologian, the role of the reader is never to *make* a path to Christ, but always to *follow* the path to Christ that the biblical authors have laid down. This route requires patience, but only the patience necessary to get you to the text. Once you are there, your journey awaits. There you will find the biblical author waiting, by the Spirit revealing God in Christ to you. The grand storyline of the Bible and its network of covenant promises and expectations find their end in Christ. This path is long and winding, but will lead you to your destination. This line is not as the crow flies, but is the one where the cross lies. Taking a canonical line to the cross may not be straight or fast, but it's true.

The discipline of biblical theology aims to navigate this balance of unity and diversity. The gospel of Jesus Christ is to be proclaimed from all of the Scriptures. The gospel according to Genesis will have a different shape, tone, and feel than the gospel according to Galatians. This sensitivity to the details of the biblical texts, the theological developments of the biblical storyline, and the unity of God's work in the divine plan of redemption will ably equip us to reckon with the gospel wherever we might find ourselves in our travels to and fro across the literary landscape of the biblical canon.

Discussion Questions

1. How does the study of biblical theology inform the question: "Is the whole Bible about the Christ?"

2. Describe and explain the specific ways in which the biblical theology framework of the canon, the covenants, and the Christ helps us answer the question about Christ in all of Scriptures.

3. What is the relationship between *narrative typology* and *intertextual typology*? How do these concepts help us think about Jesus as the fulfillment of Scripture?

4. Analyze and reflect upon both the value and caution in the advice to "make a bee-line for the cross" in every sermon you preach. How does the discipline of biblical theology inform this issue?

5. Describe and explain the guidance Jesus's own words provide in Luke 24 and Revelation 22 when asking how the whole Bible is about Christ.

Resources for Further Study

Alexander, T. Desmond. *The Servant King: The Bible's Portrait of the Messiah.* Vancouver: Regent, 1998.

Goldsworthy, Graeme. *Preaching the Whole Bible as Christian Scripture: The Application of Biblical Theology to Expository Preaching.* Grand Rapids: Eerdmans, 2000.

Hoskins, Paul M. *That Scripture Might Be Fulfilled: Typology and the Death of Christ.* Longwood: Xulon Press, 2009.

Rydelnik, Michael and Edwin Blum, eds. *The Moody Handbook of Messianic Prophecy: Studies and Expositions of the Messiah in the Old Testament.* Chicago: Moody, 2019.

Sailhamer, John. "The Messiah and the Hebrew Bible." *Journal of the Evangelical Theological Society* 44.1 (March 2001): 5–23.

CHAPTER 4

THE BIBLE'S THEOLOGICAL CHARACTERISTICS

THE DISCIPLINE OF BIBLICAL THEOLOGY relies upon a particular view of the Bible. John Frame rightly observes, "The idea that God communicates with human beings in personal words pervades all of Scripture and is central to every doctrine of Scripture."[1] If we are to know God rightly, we must understand who he is by means of the revelation he has given us in Scripture. Like anything we describe in life, Scripture has its own set of characteristics and qualities. And in defining the discipline of biblical theology as we have in previous chapters, we are assuming some inherent realities that are attributable to Scripture.

These characteristics are essential to observe going forward as we describe the storyline, key themes, and applicability of biblical theology to the life of the church and the academy. Our aim is to look at what Scripture says about Scripture and defend these claims by means of "the Bible's own worldview, its own epistemology, and its own values."[2] Our aim here, therefore, is not to provide an apology for the veracity of Scripture, but to demonstrate the qualities of Scripture described within Scripture itself.[3] Each attribute, therefore, will be

---

1. John M. Frame, *The Doctrine of the Word of God*, A Theology of Lordship Volume 4 (Philipsburg: P&R, 2010), 6.
2. Frame, *The Word of God*, 7.
3. Frame does raise the important—though tangential for our purposes—point that if one proceeds from Christian presuppositions to Christian conclusions, "how can these arguments be persuasive to a non-Christian?" Additionally, "how can he avoid the charge of vicious circularity?" He goes on to argue, "circular argument of a kind is unavoidable when we argue for an ultimate standard of truth. One who believes that human reason is the ultimate standard can argue that view only by appealing to reason. One who believes that the Bible is the ultimate standard can argue only by appealing to the Bible. Since all positions partake equally of circularity at this level, it cannot be a point of criticism against any of them. *Narrowly* circular arguments, like 'the Bible is God's Word, because it is God's Word' can hardly

spoken of with Scriptural warrant and proceed in a logical manner, with successive qualities building on the previous ones.

Inspired

Many books are spoken of as "inspiring," igniting political movements, leading someone to change careers, or helping a person adjust to a particular circumstance in life. While some may find the Bible to be inspiring in this sense, the emphasis on "inspiration" carries a much different connotation. Specifically, when one refers to the Bible as an inspired book, they are stating that, although written by human authors, the Bible has divine origins. More specifically, Matthew Barrett claims, "The inspiration of Scripture refers to that act whereby the Holy Spirit came upon the authors of Scripture, causing them to write exactly what God intended, while simultaneously preserving each author's style and personality. This supernatural work of the Holy Spirit upon the human authors means that the author's words are God's words and therefore are reliable, trustworthy, and authoritative."[4]

This definition is seen most clearly in two biblical passages: 2 Timothy 3:16–17 and 2 Peter 1:20–21. The first text states, "All Scripture is breathed out by God [Greek: *theopneustos*; inspired] and profitable for teaching, for reproof, for correction, and for training in righteousness, that the man of God may be complete, equipped for every good work." God's words are breathed out, coming from him to us.[5] Scripture is profitable, therefore, not because we are reading a story about someone's individual religious experience, but rather because we are reading a text that God himself has authored through human agents. As such, this definition indicates there are "divine and human aspects to Scripture, though the former is primary."[6] One could say that God works in a way that is compatible or concursive with God using ordinary minds to write down his words.[7] As Warfield claims, concursive involvement means,

---

be persuasive. But more *broadly* circular arguments can be. An example of a more broadly circular argument might be 'The Bible is God's Word, because it makes the following claims, makes the following predictions that have been fulfilled, presents these credible accounts of miracles, is supported by these archaeological discoveries, etc.' Now this argument is as circular as the last if, in the final analysis, the criteria for evaluating its claims, its predictions, its accounts of miracles, and the data of archaeology are criteria based on a biblical worldview and epistemology. But it is a broader argument in the sense that it presents more data to the non-Christian and challenges him to consider it seriously. God created our minds to think within the Christian circle: hearing God's Word obediently and interpreting our experience by means of that Word. That is the only legitimate way to think, and we cannot abandon it to please the unbeliever. A good psychologist will not abandon reality as he perceives it to communicate with a delusional patient; so must it be with apologists. In the final analysis, saving knowledge of God comes supernaturally. We can be brought from one circle to another only by God's supernatural grace." John M. Frame, "Presuppositional Apologetics," *Frame-Poythress.org*, May 23, 2012, https://frame-poythress.org/presuppositional-apologetics/.

4.   Barrett, *God's Word Alone*, 229.
5.   Some refer to this concept as "spiration" to avoid confusion. See, for example, David S. Dockery, *Christian Scripture: An Evangelical Perspective on Inspiration, Authority, and Interpretation* (Eugene: Wipf and Stock, 2004), 41.
6.   Barrett, *God's Word Alone*, 229.
7.   These terms are most often used under the heading of divine providence and human responsibility. For an excellent articulation and defense of how divine sovereignty and (compatibilist) human freedom relate to the inspiration of

"the whole of Scripture is the product of divine activities which enter it, however, not by su-perseding the activities of the human authors, but confluently with them; so that the Scrip-tures are the joint product of divine and human activities, both of which penetrate them at every point."[8] God uses ordinary means to bring about his divine Word.

This is also seen in 2 Peter 1:20–21, which states, "knowing this first of all, that no prophecy of Scripture comes from someone's own interpretation. For no prophecy was ever produced by the will of man, but men spoke from God as they were carried along by the Holy Spirit." Read straightforwardly, one can see that Scripture—specifically Old Testament prophecy, though applying to all of Scripture—is not the product of mere man. Rather, men spoke and wrote as they were directed by the Holy Spirit to do his work and articulate the spoken and written revelation of God.[9] This is why so often, especially in the Old Testa-ment, the biblical authors declare God's words by saying, "Thus says the Lord." The words they spoke and wrote were God's, not merely dictated to them, but coming through them in such a way as to not obliterate human personality or their unique writing style.[10]

This understanding—contrary to other views regarding the authoring of Scripture—is known as *verbal plenary inspiration*.[11] By verbal inspiration, one means that the words of Scripture, and not only the ideas of the biblical writers, are God's Word (see Matt. 7:24–28; Mark 8:38; 13:31; John 3:34; 5:47; 6:63; 8:47; 14:10, 24; 17:8; Acts 15:15; 1 Cor. 2:13; 1 Tim. 4:6; 2 Tim. 1:13; 2 Peter 3:2; Rev. 1:3; 19:9; 21:5; 22:6–10, 18–19). Plenary inspiration refers to the fact that everything in Scripture is God's Word (Prov. 30:5).[12] We do not, therefore, restrict the meaning of inspiration to the thoughts or ideas of the biblical authors; rather we affirm every word of Scripture as God-breathed and thus profitable in myriad ways. Thus, we con-clude with Hamilton, "The inspiration of the Holy Spirit results in written communication

Scripture, see Stephen J. Wellum, "The Importance of the Nature of Divine Sovereignty for Our View of Scripture," *Southern Baptist Journal of Theology* 4.2 (2000): 76–91.

8. Benjamin B. Warfield, "The Divine and Human in the Bible," in *Selected Shorter Writings of Benjamin B. Warfield*, ed. John E. Meeter, 2 vols. (Philipsburg: P&R, 2001), 2:547. See also Herman Bavinck, *Reformed Dogmatics*, trans. John Bolt, 4 vols. (Grand Rapids: Baker, 2011), 1:432–43; Scott R. Swain, *Trinity, Revelation, and Reading: A Theological Introduction to the Bible and Its Interpretation* (New York: T&T Clark, 2011), 67.

9. Warfield elaborates on this passage: "The Spirit is not to be conceived as standing outside of the human powers employed for the effect in view, ready to supplement any inadequacies they [the human authors] may show and to supply any defects they may manifest, but as working confluently in, with and by them, elevating them, directing them, controlling them, energizing them, so that, as his instruments, they rise above themselves and under his inspiration do his work and reach his aim. The product, therefore, which is attained by their means is his product through them." Benjamin B. Warfield, *Revelation and Inspiration* (Grand Rapids: Baker, 2003), 27.

10. There are some instances of literal dictation, such as when God dictated the words of the law to Moses (e.g., Exod. 34:27; cf. Jer. 36:4; Rev. 2–3).

11. For a succinct articulation of alternative views of inspiration, see Barrett, *God's Word Alone*, 224–26; Robert L. Plummer, *40 Questions About Interpreting the Bible* (Grand Rapids: Kregel, 2011), 31–32.

12. John M. Frame, *Systematic Theology: An Introduction to Christian Belief* (Philipsburg: P&R, 2013), 596.

that is totally true and trustworthy."[13] The concept of inspiration is foundational as it relates to the doctrine of Scripture, and proper understanding of this doctrine directly affects our understanding of the other qualities of Scripture.

Inerrant

Perhaps the quality of Scripture most closely associated to inspiration is that of inerrancy. The doctrine of inerrancy naturally flows out of the doctrine of inspiration. If God has breathed out his Word by means of human authors, it would follow that this Word is without errors, recognizing that God does not lie, deceive, mislead, or err (Titus 1:2).[14] Thus, the doctrine of Scripture is closely linked to the doctrine of God.

In terms of definition, inerrancy refers to the fact that Scripture is without error in everything the biblical authors assert. More specifically, Feinberg maintains, "When all facts are known, the Scriptures in their original autographs and properly interpreted will be shown to be wholly true in everything they affirm, whether that has to do with doctrine or morality or with the social, physical, or life sciences."[15] We have a true word from God, containing no mistakes, depicting truth, and thus one can proclaim, "When the Bible speaks, God speaks."[16]

Several points should be noted. First, though we do not have the original autographs (i.e., the original manuscript of a biblical document), we can have confidence we possess an inerrant text because of the discipline of textual criticism. Scripture as "breathed out by

---

13. James M. Hamilton Jr., "Still *Sola Scriptura:* An Evangelical Perspective on Scripture," in *The Sacred Text: Excavating the Texts, Exploring the Interpretations, and Engaging the Theologies of the Christian Scriptures*, ed. Michael F. Bird and Michael W. Pahl, Gorgias Précis Portfolios 7 (Piscataway: Gorgias, 2010), 217.
14. For a thorough response to recent challenges of the doctrine of inerrancy, see G. K. Beale, *The Erosion of Inerrancy in Evangelicalism: Responding to New Challenges to Biblical Authority* (Wheaton: Crossway, 2008).
15. Paul Feinberg, "The Meaning of Inerrancy," in *Inerrancy*, ed. Norman L. Geisler (Grand Rapids: Zondervan, 1980), 293. For an even lengthier definition, one can look to "A Short Statement" in the *Chicago Statement of Biblical Inerrancy* (http://www.bible-researcher.com/chicago1.html):
    1. God, who is Himself Truth and speaks truth only, has inspired Holy Scripture in order thereby to reveal Himself to lost mankind through Jesus Christ as Creator and Lord, Redeemer and Judge. Holy Scripture is God's witness to Himself.
    2. Holy Scripture, being God's own Word, written by men prepared and superintended by His Spirit, is of infallible divine authority in all matters upon which it touches: it is to be believed, as God's instruction, in all that it affirms: obeyed, as God's command, in all that it requires; embraced, as God's pledge, in all that it promises.
    3. The Holy Spirit, Scripture's divine Author, both authenticates it to us by His inward witness and opens our minds to understand its meaning.
    4. Being wholly and verbally God-given, Scripture is without error or fault in all its teaching, no less in what it states about God's acts in creation, about the events of world history, and about its own literary origins under God, than in its witness to God"s saving grace in individual lives.
    5. The authority of Scripture is inescapably impaired if this total divine inerrancy is in any way limited or disregarded, or made relative to a view of truth contrary to the Bible's own; and such lapses bring serious loss to both the individual and the Church.
16. R. Albert Mohler, "When the Bible Speaks, God Speaks: The Classical Doctrine of Biblical Inerrancy," in *Five Views on Biblical Inerrancy* (Grand Rapids: Zondervan, 2013), 58.

God" (2 Tim. 3:16) refers to the words contained in the document of Scripture itself. We do not possess these original documents, but this should not lead to skepticism of ancient manuscripts and modern translations. We can affirm this point because many biblical figures such as Solomon (1 Kings 2:3; cf. Deut. 17:18), the men of King Hezekiah (Prov. 25:1), Ezra (Ezra 7:14; Neh. 8:8), Jesus (Luke 4:16–21), Paul (Col. 4:16; 2 Tim. 3:16; 4:13), and the apostles (Luke 4:16–21; John 5:39; Acts 17:2, 11; 18:28; 2 Tim. 3:15–16) all relied on copies of Scripture, and treated them as canonical and authoritative.[17] Also, the discipline of textual criticism—the process of analyzing ancient manuscripts and ascertaining the original wording of a text—grants confidence that we possess the original biblical text God gave us. While tedious, textual criticism yields high accuracy in our translations, and where there are manuscript disagreements, they are insignificant matters (e.g., spelling, inclusion or exclusion of a definite article), not key doctrinal distinctions.[18]

Second, Scripture is true in all that it affirms, but Scripture does not exhaustively address all matters in life. Therefore, whatever Scripture addresses, whether it be doctrine, ethics, history, or geography, its assertions are true.[19] While not serving as a chemistry textbook, Scripture does provide the grounding and foundation for every area of life, knowing that "from Him, and through Him, and to Him are all things, to Him be glory forevermore" (Rom. 11:36). Therefore, we use all the linguistic and exegetical tools at our disposal, allowing Scripture to interpret Scripture, and affirm the total truthfulness of all that Scripture declares.[20]

Finally, passages such as 2 Timothy 3:16–17 and 2 Peter 1:20–21 contain Scripture's testimony about itself. These key texts for the doctrine of inspiration also direct us to belief in Scripture's inerrancy. The use of the phrase "Thus says the Lord" in the Old Testament, as well as attestation of New Testament references to the Old Testament as given by God (e.g., Acts 4:25 citing Ps. 2:1–2; Heb. 3:7 citing Ps. 95:7–11; Rom. 9:15–17 citing Exod. 9:16; 33:19) are clear indications of an understanding of the Word of God as inerrant. Paul also directly refers to the word the Thessalonians received from him and his fellow workers to be "the Word of God" (1 Thess. 2:13). Thus, as Mohler asserts, "the Bible consistently and relentlessly claims to be nothing less than the perfect Word of the perfect God who breathed out its very words."[21]

---

17. Barrett, *God's Word Alone*, 266.
18. For a brief introduction about textual criticism, see Jason S. DeRouchie, *How to Understand and Apply the Old Testament: Twelve Steps from Exegesis to Theology* (Phillipsburg: P&R, 2017), 128–56; Andrew David Naselli, *How to Understand and Apply the New Testament: Twelve Steps from Exegesis to Theology* (Phillipsburg: P&R, 2017), 36–49. For further study see Stanley E. Porter and Andrew W. Pitts, *Fundamentals of New Testament Textual Criticism* (Grand Rapids: Eerdmans, 2015); Emanuel Tov, *Textual Criticism of the Hebrew Bible*, 3rd ed. (Minneapolis: Fortress, 2011).
19. This understanding is *contra* "limited inerrancy" which asserts that Scripture is inerrant only in matters of salvation. See Frame, *Doctrine of the Word of God*, 167–69.
20. For more on this last point as it relates to biblical interpretation and inerrancy, see J. I. Packer, "Infallible Scripture and the Role of Hermeneutics," in *Scripture and Truth*, ed. D. A. Carson and John D. Woodbridge (Grand Rapids: Baker, 1992), 321–56 (see 349–53); Plummer, *40 Questions*, 41–45.
21. Mohler, "When the Bible Speaks," 37.

Infallible

If inerrancy means that Scripture is without error in everything the biblical authors assert, infallibility refers to the fact that Scripture is incapable of erring or failing, and thus it serves as a safe and reliable guide.[22] While quite similar in terms of definition, these two concepts refer respectively to the reality of truthfulness (inerrancy) and the incapability of any failings in what is said (infallibility). There are no errors in the biblical text because there can be no errors in divine speech.

The Psalmist tells us, "For the word of the Lord is upright, and all his work is done in faithfulness" (Ps. 33:4). The Hebrew word "upright" (*yashar*) connotes something that is straight (i.e., no deviation from the standard or norm) or morally good, and often parallels the concept of "faithfulness," particularly in all of God's creation work. In linking God's Word to his character and his work, it is clear—especially in light of the clear teaching of inspiration and inerrancy—the Bible is incapable of erring since God, perfect in all his ways, is incapable of erring.

Clear

While many in our modern milieu seek to deny certainty in interpretation, alleging that a text derives meaning from a reader's response to it within a particular context and community and thus a text's meaning can change,[23] the clear affirmation of Scripture is that God's words are clear and comprehensible. Thompson helpfully defines clarity, also referred to as perspicuity,[24] as "that quality of Scripture which, arising from the fact that it is ultimately God's effective communicative act, ensures its meaning is accessible, when viewed in the context of the canonical whole, and is accessible to all who come to it in faith and dependent upon the Holy Spirit."[25]

---

22. Frame recognizes that the term "infallible" is a modal term. Thus, "It deals not merely with the presence of error, but with the *capability*, the *possibility* of error." See *Doctrine of the Word of God*, 168. This is important to note as some theologians assert that the term "infallible" is weaker than "inerrant," even allowing for the possibility of errors in an infallible text. See, for example, Jack B. Rogers and Donald K. McKim, *The Authority and Interpretation of the Bible: An Historical Approach* (San Francisco: Harper & Row, 1979) which espouses the following thesis: the Bible is authoritative in matters of faith and conduct, but it is not infallible when it comes to historical or scientific details. Further, they assert, the doctrine of inerrancy is an innovation of the nineteenth century. Rogers and McKim argue that the Princeton theologians of the nineteenth and early twentieth centuries, most notably B. B. Warfield, created the doctrine of inerrancy, which teaches that the Bible is entirely without error in all that it affirms. For a direct response to this work see John D. Woodbridge, *Biblical Authority: A Critique of the Rogers/McKim Proposal* (Grand Rapids: Zondervan, 1982).
23. See, for example, Stanley Fish, *Is There a Text in This Class? The Authority of Interpretive Communities* (Cambridge: Harvard University Press, 1980).
24. The term perspicuity was used in past decades to describe this attribute of Scripture. However, the terms "clarity" and "perspicuity" are virtual synonyms, and the former is used more often in present-day vernacular.
25. Mark Thompson, *A Clear and Present Word: The Clarity of Scripture* (Downers Grove: InterVarsity, 2006), 169–70; see also his, "The Generous Gift of a Gracious Father: Toward a Theological Account of the Clarity of Scripture," in *The Enduring Authority of the Christian Scriptures*, ed. D. A. Carson (Grand Rapids: Eerdmans, 2016), 617–18. A similar definition is as follows: "Scripture is the written word of the living Word, God's communicative act, and the Spirit who

This definition calls attention to God's own character and works, as well as Scripture's self-testimony regarding the clarity of its overarching message. First, it must be understood that the Creator God is a communicative God. God has breathed out words in his determination to be known by his people. God, who authors Scripture by means of inspired human authors, is a God of order (1 Cor. 14:33), and is perfectly true and pure in his character. As such, he cannot lie or deceive or fail to keep a promise, since that would be a violation of his own nature (Num. 23:19, Heb. 6:18). He is a faithful and covenant-keeping God (Jer. 33:14–22). And this God, who is perfectly pure and trustworthy, has given us an orderly account of his work of redemption throughout history in a textual witness (Josh. 1:8; Ps. 1:1–3; cf. Luke 24:27, 44–45).[26] Scripture, as authored by God, has an order, substance, and key message that is conceptually attainable, by his grace.

While objections will arise regarding this doctrine due to the multiplicity of interpretations one can find on various passages of Scripture, this is not the result of some defect in either the character of God or the text itself.[27] By affirming the truth of Scripture's clarity, one is not saying that all texts are equally clear or overly simple, or that there is no longer any need for teaching or commentary on Scripture.[28] Rather, "when viewed in the context of the canonical whole" and "dependent on the Holy Spirit," the message of Scripture, especially the message of the *euangelion* (Greek for "good news" or "gospel"), is accessible and able to be understood.[29] This is so because God communicates both to and though fallen but epistemologically competent people (2 Tim. 2:7).

Scripture testifies to this character of God, and in doing so gives ample affirmation of its own clarity. The biblical texts call for the private and public proclamation of Scripture to children (Deut. 6:6–7) and churches (Acts 20:26–28; 1 Tim. 4:13; 2 Tim. 3:16–4:5), indicating that the Word of God is understandable to ordinary, average people.[30] Scripture

---

authored it chooses to continue to speak most directly through it. Therefore, we are right to trust that God in Scripture has spoken and continues to speak sufficiently clearly for us to base our saving knowledge of him and of ourselves, and our beliefs and our actions on the content of Scripture alone, without ultimately validating our understanding of these things or our confidence in them by appeal to any individual or institution." See Ward, *Words of Life*, 126–27. See also Gregg R. Allison, *The Baker Compact Dictionary of Theological Terms* (Grand Rapids: Baker, 2016), 162–63.

26. For further thoughts on the textual nature of Scripture, see Stephen G. Dempster, *Dominion and Dynasty: A Biblical Theology of the Hebrew Bible*, New Studies in Biblical Theology 15 (Downers Grove: InterVarsity, 2003).

27. Thompson, "Generous Gift," 618. See also Kevin J. Vanhoozer, *Biblical Authority after Babel: Retrieving the Solas in the Spirit of Mere Protestant Christianity* (Grand Rapids: Brazos, 2016).

28. Concerning this final point, Ward observes, "Expository biblical preaching in fact assumes rather than denies the clarity of Scripture. An expository preacher takes it that his sermon can be judged as either a faithful or an unfaithful exposition of Scripture by his hearers, as they discern for themselves whether his teaching is or is not warranted by his biblical text." Ward, *Words of Life*, 121.

29. Thompson, "Generous Gift," 618. One can say that, as finite beings, while we may not know all truth exhaustively, we can know truth truly as contained in God's Word.

30. Note that many of Paul's letters were written to entire churches filled with people who obviously did not serve as pastors or teachers (1 Cor. 1:1–2; 2 Cor. 1:1; Gal. 1:1; Eph. 1:1; Phil. 1:1; Col. 1:1–2; 1 Thess. 1:1; 2 Thess. 1:1).

is not distant and helplessly opaque (Deut. 30:11–14; cf. Rom. 10:8–13); instead it assures us that by reading and hearing its words the simple will be made wise (Ps. 19:7). When dealing with hearers understanding Scripture, Jesus always assumes that the blame for misunderstanding any teaching of Scripture lies not with the Scriptures themselves, but rather those who misunderstand or fail to accept what is written (Matt. 9:13; 12:3–5; 19:4; 21:42; 22:29–31; John 3:10). This certainly implies that Scripture is understandable, and this is the very heart of Jesus's critique. One could also note the cognizant way the New Testament authors use, rely upon, and interpret Scripture.[31] While some may say that only the New Testament authors were inspired by the Spirit, these men wrote for audiences across time with the confidence that both the Old and New Testament would be understood.

In summarizing this concept of clarity, Grudem helpfully offers seven caveats. He maintains "Scripture affirms that it is able to be understood but (1) not all at once, (2) not without effort, (3) not without ordinary means, (4) not without the reader's willingness to obey it, (5) not without the help of the Holy Spirit, (6) not without human misunderstanding, and (7) never completely."[32] Thus, as redeemed people with Spirit-empowered effort, time, a humble and submissive attitude, and the realization that we will never fully arrive at perfect and complete comprehension, we affirm Scripture's clarity.

Necessary

We have seen thus far that Scripture is inspired, inerrant, infallible, and clear. These truths lead one to understand that the Bible is also necessary in two distinct yet connected ways. First, as Allison maintains, the Word of God is "essential for knowing the way of salvation, for progressing in holiness, and for discerning God's will."[33] No one can be saved apart from the proclamation of God's Word concerning Jesus Christ (Rom. 10:13–17; cf. John 14:6; Acts 4:12), and we cannot live or grow spiritually apart from Scripture (Matt. 4:4).

Underlying this understanding of necessity is a second aspect, namely that God revealed himself. Indeed, God could have provided truth to his people in an ongoing fashion by other means, but one could say that God provides a written Word by way of *necessitas ex hypothesi dispositionis* ("necessity on account of a hypothesis of disposition").[34] Muller

---

31. For an incisive analysis of the New Testament authors' use of Old Testament Scripture as the basis for their interpretations, particularly of Christ's person and work, see Beale, *New Testament Use of the Old Testament*; Beale, ed., *The Right Doctrine from the Wrong Texts? Essays on the Use of the Old Testament in the New* (Grand Rapids: Baker, 1994). For a commentary that focuses solely on the way in which New Testament authors allude to the Old Testament Scriptures, see Beale and Carson, *Commentary on the New Testament*.

32. Wayne Grudem, "The Perspicuity of Scripture," *Themelios* 34.3 (2009): 291.

33. Allison, *Baker Compact Dictionary of Theological Themes*, 145.

34. Graham A. Cole, "Why a Book? Why This Book? Why the Particular Order within This Book? Some Theological Reflections on the Canon," in *The Enduring Authority of the Christian Scriptures*, ed. D. A. Carson (Grand Rapids: Eerdmans, 2016), 469.

explains this concept as "a necessity brought about or conditioned by a previous contingent act or event so that the necessity itself arises out of contingent circumstances; thus, conditional necessity."[35] In other words, having decided to reveal himself, God inspires a Word, and thus "provides for its preservation, which as a consequence requires writing and a canon."[36] While oral tradition is beneficial, the written Word protects against egregious error and brings about unity amongst those who claim Christ as Lord (John 17:20–21).

Sufficient

Closely related to the concept of necessity is the sufficiency of Scripture. Although as Christians we affirm that God reveals himself to us in natural revelation by means of creation (Ps. 19:1; Acts 14:16–17; Rom. 1:18–24) and conscience (Rom. 2:12–16), we also say this form of revelation is insufficient to save us or guide us to all truth. We need revelation that offers sufficient content for faith and practice, and Scripture serves as such a resource, offering a comprehensive guide for the Christian life.

According to Barrett, the sufficiency of Scripture entails that all things necessary for "God's glory, salvation, and the Christian life" are given to God's people in Scripture. Implicit here for Barrett is that although nothing should be added to the Bible, this does not preclude the inward illumination of the Spirit or natural revelation.[37] God has not revealed all things to us (Deut. 29:29), but what he has revealed equips us for every good work (2 Tim. 3:16–17). Scripture is "particular" in its sufficiency insofar that it will not address every detail about the physical sciences, politics, plumbing, lawn care, or other fields of practice or information. Yet, Scripture is also "general" in its sufficiency insofar that it points us toward doing all things for his glory (1 Cor. 10:31; Col. 3:17).[38]

Two important challenges to the concept of sufficiency are raised by Roman Catholicism and some branches of charismatic theology. Roman Catholic theology espouses the belief

---

35. Richard A. Muller, *Dictionary of Latin and Greek Theological Terms: Drawn Principally from Protestant Scholastic Theology* (Grand Rapids: Baker, 1986), 200.
36. Cole, "Some Theological Reflections on Canon," 469n44.
37. Barrett, *God's Word Alone*, 335–39. See also Chapter 1.6 of the Westminster Confession, which offers a cogent definition of this topic: "The whole counsel of God concerning all things necessary for his own glory, man's salvation, faith and life, is either expressly set down in Scripture, or by good and necessary consequence may be deduced from Scripture: unto which nothing at any time is to be added, whether by new revelations of the Spirit, or traditions of men (2 Tim. 3:15–17; Gal. 1:8–9; 2 Thess. 2:2). Nevertheless, we acknowledge the inward illumination of the Spirit of God to be necessary for the saving understanding of such things as are revealed in the Word (John 6:45; 1 Cor. 2:9–12) and that there are some circumstances concerning the worship of God, and government of the church, common to human actions and societies, which are to be ordered by the light of nature, and Christian prudence, according to the general rules of the Word, which are always to be observed (1 Cor. 11:13–14; 14:26, 40)."
38. See Frame, *Doctrine of the Word of God*, 225–28. See also Kevin J. Vanhoozer, "May We Go Beyond What Is Written After All? The Pattern of Theological Authority and the Problem of Doctrinal Development," in *The Enduring Authority of the Christian Scriptures*, ed. D. A. Carson (Grand Rapids: Eerdmans, 2016), 759–61.

that Scripture and tradition are two sources of revelation from God equal in authority.[39] This differs from a Protestant doctrine of sufficiency, which is tightly linked to the concept of *sola Scriptura* (i.e., Scripture alone is our final authority). While we greatly value tradition and the teaching of those who have come before us, we in no way view its authority on the same level as that of Scripture. A second challenge comes from some branches of charismatic theology. Most charismatics would affirm that the canon is closed and that any "new revelation" is not on par with Scripture.[40] However, functionally the reception of direct revelation from the Lord that cannot be questioned by outside sources sounds in many ways like new revelation from God. If that is the case, then it is difficult not to put such direct revelation on the same level with Scripture.[41] Some have done extensive and helpful work in clarifying these matters, asserting that modern-day prophecies and tongues differ from biblical prophecy and inscripturated revelation.[42] Nevertheless, it seems more clarity is needed.[43]

Authoritative

Taking into account the truth that God's Word is inspired, inerrant, infallible, clear, necessary, comprehensive, and sufficient, one must see that Scripture stands authoritatively over our lives as image-bearers of God. These doctrines are of little value if we do not obey God's Word (John 14:15; James 1:22–25). The authority of Scripture means that all the words in Scripture are God's words, and thereby direct us towards what we can and cannot do as beings made in God's image. As such, the Scriptures are authoritative in such a way that to disbelieve or disobey any word of Scripture is to disbelieve or disobey God.[44]

---

39. For a more detailed analysis of this teaching, see Gregg R. Allison, *Roman Catholic Theology and Practice: An Evangelical Assessment* (Wheaton: Crossway, 2014), 71–116; Gregg R. Allison and Chris Castaldo, *The Unfinished Reformation: What Unites and Divides Catholics and Protestants after 500 Years* (Grand Rapids: Zondervan, 2016) 67–72.

40. See for example Sam Storms, *Practicing the Power: Welcoming the Gifts of the Holy Spirit in Your Life* (Grand Rapids: Zondervan, 2017).

41. See J. I. Packer, *Keep in Step with the Spirit: Finding Fullness in Our Walk with God* (Grand Rapids: Baker, 2005), 156; Thomas R. Schreiner, *Spiritual Gifts: What They Are and Why They Matter* (Nashville: B&H Academic, 2018), 11. Both of these authors have excellent tone and humility in dealing with issues regarding charismatic theology in a biblical manner.

42. See Wayne A. Grudem, *The Gift of Prophecy in the New Testament and Today*, rev. ed. (Wheaton: Crossway, 2000).

43. Schreiner argues that New Testament prophecy is not mixed with error, but is infallible and inerrant. He differentiates between what some call prophecy today and the concept of "impressions," which should not be received with the same level authority as Old or New Testament prophecy. See Schreiner, *Spiritual Gifts*, 101–22. John Frame also engages briefly with this argument, offering helpful commentary on how we can better nuance our language when speaking of "revelation" from God. In his descriptions, Frame seems to lean more toward language like "divine assistance in the application of Scripture" and argues that that kind of language can be demonstrated scripturally. See Frame, *Doctrine of the Word of God*, 233–36. It should be clarified that charismatic theology does not necessarily rule out the sufficiency of Scripture; the question is rather one of definition and consistency.

44. Ward maintains, "The authority of Scripture is dependent entirely on the authority of God, and comes about only because of what God has chosen to do in the way he authored Scripture, and because of what he continues to do in presenting himself to us through Scripture as a God we can know and trust." Ward, *Words of Life*, 128. For an

Thus, the authority of Scripture finds its basis in its author, the Creator God, who possesses all authority. Authority, or God's right to rule, is fundamental to his nature. MacArthur and Mayhue rightly highlight the authority of God: "God's authority becomes obvious and unquestionable when one considers three facts. First, God created the heavens, the earth, and all that exists therein (Genesis 1–2). Second, God owns the earth, all it contains, and those who dwell in it (Ps. 24:1). Third, in the end God will consume it all, just as he declared (2 Peter 3:10)."[45] No authority is over God; rather, all authority exists because of him (Rom. 13:1). All power belongs to God (Ps. 62:11); in his hand is all power and might (2 Chron. 20:6); none can stay his hand (Dan. 4:35); and he works all things according to the counsel of his will (Eph. 1:11).

In authoring Scripture, God granted divine authority to be meted out in revelatory form, and the authors and recipients of his Word understood this to be so. What the Old Testament writers recorded was revelation from God (Deut. 18:18; 2 Sam. 23:2; Isa. 59:21; Zech. 7:12). The Old Testament writers wrote at God's direction (Deut. 31:24–26; Jer. 30:1–2), with the result that this book bears divine authority (2 Tim. 3:16–17; cf. Matt. 15:4; 22:43; Acts 4:25–26; 13:34–35). Jesus saw God as the ultimate source of Scripture and the Holy Spirit as its ultimate author (Matt. 15:4; 22:43). He emphasized the importance of every word (Matt. 5:18; Mark 12:24–27), believed the Scriptures had to be fulfilled because they were the Word of God (Matt. 26:52–54; Luke 24:44; John 10:35), and placed himself under the authority of the Old Testament (Matt. 4:4, 7, 10; Luke 24:25–26). Likewise, the apostles claimed that their message was not their own, but God's authoritative Word (1 Cor. 14:37; Gal. 1:11–12; 1 Thess. 2:13; 1 Peter 1:23–25; Rev. 22:18–19) as was the teaching of Jesus (Luke 5:1; 8:21). And as apostles, what they taught and wrote had the authority of Jesus (John 16:13; Acts 1:1–2; 2:42; Rom. 1:1; 1 Cor. 14:37; Eph. 2:20, 29; 2 Peter 3:2). In at least two places the New Testament Scriptures are also placed on the same level as the Old Testament, and thus possess the same authority (1 Tim. 5:18, 2 Peter 3:15–16).[46]

As an authoritative revelation from God, Scripture is meant not merely to inform—though it certainly does that—but to affect (James 1:22–25). The Holy Spirit uses God's authoritative Word to save and sanctify, effectively accomplishing the purpose for which it was sent (Isa. 55:10–11).[47] Reading and studying the text of Scripture, we must place our-

erudite study of the relationship between the authority of God and the authority of Scripture, see Peter F. Jensen, "God and the Bible," in *The Enduring Authority of the Christian Scriptures*, ed. D. A. Carson (Grand Rapids: Eerdmans, 2016), 477–96.

45. John MacArthur and Richard Mayhue, eds., *Biblical Doctrine: A Systematic Summary of Bible Truth* (Wheaton: Crossway, 2017), 101.

46. For a summary of these points, see Herman Bavinck, *Reformed Dogmatics: Abridged in One Volume*, ed. John Bolt (Grand Rapids: Baker, 2011), 90–96.

47. Barrett argues, "God's written Word is not merely a revelation (though it's certainly not less), but a *communication*. His words don't just convey information; they do something. To borrow from speech-act theory, with any given

selves under its revealed truth in full submission. We must also use all of the interpretive tools at our disposal to ensure that we understand rightly and respond in proper fashion to God's authoritative, revelatory Word.[48]

God, the Bible's Theological Characteristics, and Biblical Theology

God and his revelatory Word are inextricably linked. Throughout this chapter, we have seen how God's character affects the way in which we receive his Word. God, who does not lie or deceive, mislead or err, but only speaks the truth, has revealed himself in a book that is in keeping with his character. Our God is transcendent, immanent, glorious, eternal, omnipresent, omniscient, omnipotent, sovereign, perfect, self-existent, unchanging, holy, righteous, loving, good, gracious, merciful, and covenant-keeping.[49] In his perfect and pure

---

utterance, there is not only a *locution* (words spoken) but an *illocution* (the action performed by words) as well as a *perlocution* (the consequence or effect of the performed words) . . . God's spoken and written Word does the same" (*God's Word Alone*, 305). For further thoughts on speech-act theory, see J. L. Austin, *How to Do Things with Words* (Cambridge: Harvard University Press, 1962); Brown, *Scripture as Communication*; John R. Searle, *Speech Acts: An Essay in the Philosophy of Language* (Cambridge: Cambridge University Press, 1969); Kevin J. Vanhoozer, *Morality of Literary Knowledge*, 201–80.

48. The authority of Scripture *qua* Scripture has been demonstrated in biblical and theological fashion throughout this chapter. An inspired, inerrant, infallible word given by God to humanity holds us to account before our Creator. We are under his authority by means of his Word. We must also take note of two additional points: First. we are always growing in our interpretation of Scripture; Second, we are always considering our application of Scripture. First, as regards interpretation, Doriani notes, "Since Scripture has God's very authority, interpreters should be humble and open to correction. To read the Bible is not to dissect a lifeless text—mere marks on a page. We come to it humbly, expecting to learn. Since we know our minds are finite and (worse) prone to self-interested distortion, we expect to be corrected when we read the Bible. We study Scripture closely to know the personal God by hearing his Word." Daniel M. Doriani, "A Redemptive-Historical Model," in *Four Views on Moving Beyond the Bible to Theology*, ed. Gary T. Meadors (Grand Rapids: Zondervan, 2009), 77. Again, this does not detract from the implicit authority of God's Word, but it does entail serious study so as to rightly come under that authoritative Word. Related to this, the way in which the application of authoritative Scripture is to be done is a complex and crucial area of study. While there is nothing new under the sun, cultural challenges do change with the growth of new technologies, for example. It is imperative, therefore, under this category of the authority of Scripture, that one gives careful consideration to its ethical and moral application in all of life. For further thoughts on applying Scripture, see Doriani, *Putting the Truth to Work: The Theory and Practice of Biblical Application* (Phillipsburg: P&R, 2001). For a study focusing on the appropriation of the "solas" to engage in biblical interpretation as a means of coming under the authority of Scripture, see Vanhoozer, *Biblical Authority after Babel*. There are also a number of outstanding works dedicated to biblical ethics. One would be well served by looking at John S. Feinberg and Paul D. Feinberg, *Ethics for a Brave New World*, 2nd ed. (Wheaton: Crossway, 2010); John M. Frame, *The Doctrine of the Christian Life*, A Theology of Lordship 3 (Phillipsburg: P&R, 2008); David W. Jones, *An Introduction to Biblical Ethics*, B&H Studies in Biblical Ethics (Nashville: B&H, 2013).

49. Many works articulate and biblically defend this view of God, including Stephen Charnock, *Discourses Upon the Existence and Attributes of God* (Grand Rapids: Baker, 1979); John S. Feinberg, *No One Like Him: The Doctrine of God*, Foundations of Evangelical Theology (Wheaton: Crossway, 2001); John M. Frame, *The Doctrine of God*, A Theology of Lordship 2 (Phillipsburg: P&R, 2002); Mark Jones, *God Is: A Devotional Guide to the Attributes of God* (Wheaton: Crossway, 2017); Bruce A. Ware, *God's Greater Glory: The Exalted God of Scripture and the Christian Faith* (Wheaton: Crossway, 2004).

character, he has provided and preserved for us a sure word from him, by which we know him and seek to live in submission to him.[50]

This vision of God and Scripture, as revealed within Scripture, gives way to a particular approach to biblical theology. Biblical theology is a textual study with a textual basis. As Hamilton states, "Rather than try to go behind the text to get at what really happened, as though the text is mere propaganda, we are trying to understand what the biblical authors have written."[51] God inspired authors who wrote down his words, and we know not only what earlier authors wrote down, but also how later authors interpreted those earlier writings. This assumes that Scripture is not merely an anthology of disparate texts that contain various narratives and laws, but rather a work that is mutually interpretive. In other words, later authors (e.g., prophets, psalmists, Jesus, apostles) read, interpreted, and expounded upon what earlier authors (e.g., Moses) wrote in an exegetically responsible, Spirit-inspired manner.[52] Thus, the study of biblical theology must be done in such a way so as to focus on the intertextual and literary features of the text for the sake of understanding authorial intent.[53] This kind of approach adheres to the literary and textual features of Scripture, takes seriously the claim that Scripture is a Word from God that we must rightly understand, interpret, and apply in its various levels of context (e.g., passage, chapter, book, Testament, canon), and best coheres with the kind of character Scripture possesses as the Word of the Lord.

---

50. Concerning the preservation of the canonical books, Krueger rightly maintains, "To state the obvious, the church cannot respond (positively or negatively) to a book of which it has no knowledge. Christ's promise that his sheep will respond to his voice pertains only to books that have had their voice *actually heard* by the sheep (John 10:27). If God intended to give a canon to his corporate church—and not just to an isolated congregation for a limited period of time—then we have every reason to believe that he would providentially preserve these books and expose them to the church so that, through the Holy Spirit, it can rightly recognize them as canonical . . . If God did not bring about the condition of corporate exposure to the church, then we would have no basis for thinking that the complete canon could actually be known" (*Canon Revisited*, 94–95).

51. James M. Hamilton, *With the Clouds of Heaven: The Book of Daniel in Biblical Theology*, New Studies in Biblical Theology 32 (Downers Grove: InterVarsity, 2014), 21.

52. One could—rightly in our estimation—infer from this that the apostles, for example, serve as exemplary exegetes from whom we should learn in terms of our own biblical interpretation. This stance is *contra* Richard N. Longenecker, *Biblical Exegesis in the Apostolic Period*, rev. ed. (Grand Rapids: Eerdmans, 1999). Instead, it follows along the lines of Hamilton, *With the Clouds of Heaven*, 21–30; Thomas R. Schreiner, *New Testament Theology: Magnifying God in Christ* (Grand Rapids: Baker, 2008).

53. For a work that focuses on biblical literature from a canonical, generic, and linguistic perspective, see Andreas J. Köstenberger and Richard Duane Patterson, *Invitation to Biblical Interpretation: Exploring the Hermeneutical Triad of History, Literature, and Theology* (Grand Rapids: Kregel, 2011), 151–688.

Discussion Questions

1. Why is a proper doctrine of Scripture so crucial as one considers the discipline of biblical theology?

2. Which attribute of Scripture is most likely to be rejected in our present culture? Why?

3. Define inspiration, inerrancy, and infallibility. What makes these three attributes so foundational for all the other attributes of Scripture seen in this chapter?

4. Why is Scripture necessary in the lives of humanity?

5. In what ways is it difficult to apply the authority of Scripture? Are there areas of your life you need to submit more readily to God's authoritative Word?

THE BIBLE'S GRAND STORYLINE

CHAPTER 5

THE STORY OF THE LAW

HAVING COMPLETED OUR DISCUSSION of the discipline of biblical theology in chapters one through four, in chapters five through ten we will consider the outline of the grand storyline of the Bible. In these chapters we will examine both the basic structure of each major grouping of the canon and some of the canonical considerations that might impact the way we understand the shape of the narrative storyline that appears in these groupings.[1] Accordingly, the focus of these chapters is the narration and interpretation of redemptive history that the biblical authors provide in their narratives.

The Shape of the Law

The first five books of the Bible are the foundation for the rest of the Scriptures. While many readers are accustomed to studying these books as five individual units, in the Hebrew Bible the books of Genesis, Exodus, Leviticus, Numbers, and Deuteronomy form one work, sometimes called the Pentateuch (i.e. five books) or simply the Book of Moses. The Pentateuch was meant to be read as a whole, with each of its five parts connected to and building upon the others. The five books of Moses are really five narrative components of the one Book of Moses.

Another common name for the Pentateuch is the Law or Torah, the latter of these names derived from the Hebrew word meaning "instruction." This characterization of the book

---

1. As a complement to this reflective outline of the grand storyline of the Bible, see the works cited in the initial sections of chapters five through ten, the discussion of the nature of narrative in general and the biblical storyline in particular in chapter three, and also the lists of the major orderings of the Old Testament and New Testament provided in the appendix on canonical orderings. On the narrative focus in these chapters, see the clarifying discussion in the introduction.

121

clues readers into the fact that the Pentateuch is not just a series of laws or legal stipulations, but rather as a whole is meant to instruct readers on how to live and have life with God. In other words, though there are "laws" in the Law, it would be a grave and glib mistake to characterize the Pentateuch solely as a law book or the "constitution" of ancient Israel. Indeed, part of the purpose of the "story of the Law" is to recount and provide an interpretation of the Mosaic covenant and its stipulations. In other words, the Law (Pentateuch) provides an interpretation of the Law (Mosaic covenant) along with its selection of laws (legal requirements). These simple but crucial distinctions are important to establish clearly when studying the Pentateuch and the "story of the Law."

The Pentateuch is known for its many laws, but it also contains other many other literary elements. This includes poems ("Then Moses and the people of Israel sang this song to the Lord," Exod. 15:1); genealogies ("This is the book of the generations of Adam," Gen. 5:1); collections of laws ("Now these are the rules that you shall set before them," Exod. 21:1); census lists ("Take a census of all the congregation of the people of Israel," Num. 26:4); building instructions ("Exactly as I show you concerning the pattern of the tabernacle . . . so you shall make it," Exod. 25:9); and travel logs ("These are the stages of the people of Israel, when they went out of the land of Egypt," Num. 33:1).

As a skillful literary artist, Moses has drawn together these diverse literary elements into a coherent narrative framework. Within the Book of Moses, each type of document serves an intelligently designed function and contributes to its overall message. The end product of this textual work is a masterfully composed Mosaic mosaic of literary elements.

The grand storyline of the Bible encourages readers to recognize that the Scriptures provide a cohesive and interconnected account of God's dealing with his people and the world. Through the grandeur of its scope and the provocative implications of its direct statements, the Pentateuch generates and grounds this grand storyline of the Bible. The opening narratives of the Pentateuch set the conceptual parameters for the many narratives that follow in the biblical canon. At no point do later biblical authors work outside of the textual and theological framework generated by the Book of Moses.

The narrative of the Pentateuch itself has a definite shape. There are three broad movements to consider: Genesis beginning the book; the Exodus–Leviticus–Numbers sequence in the middle; and the speeches of Deuteronomy concluding the book. This broad structural framework of the Pentateuch helps readers see what its message is all about.

The Story of the Law

Moving through Redemptive History with Moses

The basic chronology of the Pentateuch provides a structural framework. The Pentateuch "recounts a single story that begins with the creation of the world and the preparation of the land and ends with the postponement of the possession of that land. A central theme of the Pentateuch is the inhabitable land that God has prepared for his creatures."[2] This is the most basic way that we can understand the Pentateuch as one book: It is telling one story. This story is a sometimes winding, sometimes wonderful, sometimes disturbing, sometimes beautiful story, but one story nonetheless.

We often take the simple narrative sequence of a historical text for granted, but we need to recognize this element as an important window into the author's purpose in writing. The major narrative sections of the Pentateuch tell a discernable story. This narrative storyline is the backbone of the Pentateuch and moves the reader through time and redemptive history. The narrative skeleton the author provides is then fleshed out with other literary elements that provide further theological interpretation of what God is doing in the world and in the life of his people.

In the Beginning . . . (Genesis)

The early history of the world (primeval history) is recounted in Genesis 1–11. The pattern found in Genesis 1–11 provides a picture of what God is really like and what human beings are really like. As readers, we see the gracious pattern of the creator God and also the sinful pattern of humanity. This part of the story is a wide-angle lens perspective on a sequence of events that have worldwide effects. These chapters quickly move from the creation of the world, humanity, and the land (Gen. 1–2), to the effects of sin and exile from the land (Gen. 3–4). The effects of sin spread, wickedness fills the earth, and God sends judgment through a worldwide flood (Gen. 5–9). These patterns repeat after the flood beginning with Noah and his family. Eventually, the people seek to build a tower to the heavens, and God scatters them into divergent languages and directions (Gen. 10–11).

The lives of the fathers (patriarchal history, Gen. 12–50) zooms in on one of Noah's descendants, Abram, and his family. At this point, the Lord calls Abram (later renamed Abraham) and gives him the promise of a new land (Gen. 12–25). This call of Abraham and the promise that the Lord gives him changes the lives of this family and shapes the course of redemptive history. The rest of Genesis follows the lives of Abraham's family as this promise is passed along to his descendants. Isaac, Jacob, and Esau (Gen. 25–36) each enter into the story, and the promise to Abraham is repeated at several points (15:18–21; 26:3; 28:13). Genesis ends with a clear focus on Joseph as he is abandoned to slavery in Egypt, protected by the Lord, rises to power, and protects and delivers his family through his integrity and wisdom (Gen. 37–50). As Genesis closes, the family that began with the call of Abraham now consists of a caravan headed to Egypt under the leadership of Jacob and Joseph.

---

2. Sailhamer, *Meaning of the Pentateuch*, 242.

Failure and Faithfulness at Sinai (Exodus–Leviticus–Numbers)

The next major arc in the storyline begins where Genesis ends. In Exodus 1 we find the people of Israel in Egypt, but now Joseph is only a distant memory and the people are under oppression. The Lord reveals himself to Moses and displays his power through signs and wonders. After a series of increasingly deadly plagues against Egypt and Pharaoh, the Israelites are able to depart from Egypt (Exod. 3–13). After Pharaoh and his army chase after the Israelites in order to re-capture them, the Lord again demonstrates his power over the created order by causing the waters of the sea to part and dry land to appear, thus allowing the Israelites to cross and escape. Witnessing the judgment of Egypt and the salvation of Israel, the people celebrate (Exod. 15), and then continue their journey toward Mount Sinai.

When the Israelites arrive at the foot of the Mount Sinai, the narrative progress essentially stops. The time spent at Mount Sinai extends from Exodus 20 through Numbers 10. There are two primary events that happen at Sinai. First, the Lord reveals the words of the covenant to Moses on the mountain, and second the people breach the covenant in the valley. As Moses receives the first and second commandments (Exod. 20), the people create a golden calf that shatters these very commandments. When Moses comes down the mountain the first time to witness this breach of covenant, he burns with anger and breaks the tablets that the Lord had written the words of the covenant upon (Exod. 32). Moses's actions here represent the burning anger of the Lord and the failure of the newly established Mosaic covenant.[3]

After facing the judgment of the Lord, Moses intercedes for the people and the Lord calls Moses back to the mountain to rewrite the tablets (Exod. 33–34). The Lord gives Moses those same words again but also continues to reveal himself. The Lord declares, "The Lord, the Lord, a God merciful and gracious, slow to anger, and abounding in steadfast love and faithfulness, keeping steadfast love for thousands, forgiving iniquity and transgression and sin, but who will by no means clear the guilty" (Exod. 34:6–7). This characterization of the Lord becomes the heart of the covenant relationship between God and his people. It will encourage and convict both Israel and the nations.

After many other laws and instructions are given to order the nation and curtail the sinful tendencies of the people, the time comes for the Israelites to leave Sinai. This part of the story reports the wilderness wanderings, explains why Israel did not immediately enter

---

3. The narrative account of Israel's time at Mount Sinai are interspersed across Exodus, Leviticus, and Numbers with the actual details of the laws, instructions, and collections of legal material that Moses records and strategically arranges. For an extended discussion of the textual issues involved in interpreting these narratives, see T. Desmond Alexander, *From Paradise to the Promised Land: An Introduction to the Pentateuch*, 3rd ed. (Grand Rapids: Baker, 2012), 209–74; Dempster, *Dominion and Dynasty*, 93–116; Sailhamer, *Meaning of the Pentateuch*, 283–415; James M. Todd III, *Sinai and the Saints: Reading Old Covenant Laws for the New Covenant Community* (Downers Grove: InterVarsity, 2017), 11–88; and Joshua E. Williams, "The Message of the Pentateuch," *Southwestern Journal of Theology* 52.1 (2009): 2–16.

the land of promise, and recounts the shift from the first generation of Israelites who came out of Egypt to the second generation that enters the land.[4] The censuses taken at the beginning (Num. 1–2) and end (Num. 26) of the book of Numbers articulate this somber note, highlighting the hope and expectation of the new generation about to cross into the land while also remembering the generation that fell away in the wilderness.

At first, it seems that the order established by the laws and lessons of Sinai had their effect. When Israel leaves Sinai, everything happens as planned. The nation proceeds in orderly fashion just as the Lord had commanded Moses (Num. 10:13). The rumbles of the people's grumbles, however, follow close behind. The gnawing discontent begins at the edges of the camp and moves quickly to the center of the people's leadership. First, the people on the outskirts of the camp complain about their misfortunes and the anger of the Lord burns against them (Num. 11:1–3). Next, the people's hunger causes them to bemoan their lack of Egyptian meat and dissatisfaction with the manna the Lord had provided (Num. 11:4–10). Soon after this, Miriam and Aaron bring a complaint against Moses and his leadership (Num. 12).

This pattern of creeping discontent culminates in the nationwide refusal of Israel to follow God's command to enter the land after the spies return with their report of opposition in the land (Num. 13–14). Though spared from immediate destruction, the Lord decrees that this generation of Israel will not enter the land of promise (14:20–38). The generation that saw the signs and wonders in Egypt, received the most direct revelation from the Lord in redemptive history, and formed a nation of God's own people, also become a symbol of nationwide disobedience and a lack of faith in God's promise to save.

It was the best of times. It was the worst of times.

Famous Last Words of Moses (Deuteronomy)

After the first post-exodus generation passes away in the wilderness, the Israelites approach the promised land. Before they enter the land, Moses gathers the people and proclaims the word of the Lord to them for the last time. The book of Deuteronomy represents Moses's final words to the second generation of Israelites as they are on the threshold of the land. This lengthy speech provides a concluding commentary on the Lord, the people, and the covenant promises of the Pentateuch's storyline.[5] Moses exhorts the younger generation to trust and obey the Lord in light of the failures of the older generation. In this assessment, Moses provides a prophetic critique of Israel's past and Israel's future. The hope of the people's blessing in the land of promise is conditioned on their obedience to the Lord.

---

4. Additionally, there is also a geographical movement throughout the book as the people journey from the Sinai wilderness (see Num. 10:12) to the Kadesh region (13:26; 20:1) and end on the plains of Moab (21:10–20; 22:1; and 36:13).
5. This setting and basic understanding of Deuteronomy can be seen in the opening of the book: "These are the words that Moses spoke to all Israel beyond the Jordan in the wilderness. . . . Beyond the Jordan, in the land of Moab, Moses undertook to explain this law" (Deut. 1:1, 5).

Moses first recounts parts of the nation's recent history and rehearses the giving of the Law at Sinai (Deut. 1–11). He continues his sermon by providing instructions for the life of Israel when they enter the land of promise (chapters 12–26). He then proclaims and explains the nature of the curses for disobedience and the blessings for obedience that are central to Israel's covenant relationship with the Lord (chapters 27–30). Next, Moses exhorts the people and commissions Joshua as the successor that the Lord has chosen to lead the people after he dies (chapter 31). The Pentateuch concludes with the Song of Moses (chapter 32), the Blessing of Moses (chapter 33), and an account of the death of Moses (chapter 34).

These blocks of narrative tell the basic story of the Pentateuch. The story of the Law provides a narration and interpretation of God's dealing with the world in general (Gen. 1–11) and God's dealing with Israel in particular (Gen. 12–Deut.). Within the storyline of the Pentateuch there are several notable features about the shape of the "story of the Law."

The God of Creation Is the God of the Covenants

Genesis provides a two-part orientation to the grand biblical storyline. Part of the big picture of the Pentateuch is that the *God of creation* is the *God of the covenants*. Not only does God speak, he speaks good things. Not only does he speak the world directly into existence, he speaks directly to his people.

God creates the heavens and the earth and therefore has dominion over what and whom he has created. God also creates the nation of Israel through his covenants and therefore rules over them as well. The Genesis 1–11 narratives stress the totality of humanity. This scope informs both the history of Abraham and the history of Moses and Israel. The one who called the universe into being is the one who called Abraham. This same voice that calls Abraham to journey to the land of promise is the one Moses hears calling from the burning bush. Exodus 3:15 makes this explicit: "Thus you shall say to the sons of Israel, 'The Lord, the God of your fathers, the God of Abraham, the God of Isaac, and the God of Jacob, has sent me to you.' This is my name forever, and this is my memorial-name to all generations" (NASB).

The theme of creation is foundational for much of the biblical and prophetic understanding of the world. God's status as creator of the heavens and the earth is one of the most important characterizations of Israel's God. The words that begin the Hebrew Bible portray God as creator of the universe and are stunning in scope: "In the beginning God created the heavens and the earth" (Gen. 1:1).

The two divine activities of God *saying* and *seeing* are strategically stressed as the story of the Bible begins. There is also an emphasis on the sequence and order of this account. God carefully crafts and fashions creation, preparing the world in general and the land in particular for his people. What was once uninhabitable becomes habitable.

God calls forth the world with the power of his words. In the beginning, God speaks and light emanates (Gen. 1:3), expanses move into place (1:6), dry land materializes (1:9), vegetation begins to grow (1:11), the sun and moon are given purpose (1:14), the waters begin to teem with sea creatures and birds begin to soar above the earth (1:20), land animals populate the fields (1:24), and a special creature is made in God's own image and given dominion over all these things (1:26–30).

God then gives his commentary on this litany of creative speech acts. He surveys "all that he had made" and makes a comprehensive evaluation of the effect of his words: "it was very good" (Gen. 1:31). Not only does he speak, but he speaks good things. When God speaks, it is always an aptly spoken word. So, in the beginning, the voice of the Lord creates the universe.

This creation account that begins the book of Genesis is the foundation of the biblical portrait of God's character and purpose for his people.[6] The God of Israel is creator of the heavens and the earth, and he is good. These traits are what distinguish the God of Israel from the false gods of the nations throughout biblical history. As Jonah declares when asked to identify himself, "I am a Hebrew, and I fear the Lord, the God of heaven, who made the sea and the dry land" (Jonah 1:9). The author of Hebrews notes this confession as well, stating that "by faith we understand that the universe was created by the word of God, so that what is seen was not made out of things that are visible" (Heb. 11:3).

Blessings for Obedience: Worship and Obey

Before the fall into sin recounted in Genesis 3, a snapshot of the purpose of mankind on the earth is provided in Genesis 2. Adam and Eve are placed in the garden to serve God and enjoy his presence. They were brought into being to worship and obey their creator.

This purpose can be seen in the primary directive given to Adam: "The Lord God took the man and put him in the garden of Eden to work it and keep it" (Gen. 2:15). The Hebrew verbs in Genesis 2:15 translated as "work" and "keep" are elsewhere used to describe the worship of Israel, specifically the priestly "service" and "guarding" of the tabernacle.[7] By using these terms, the author shows that one of mankind's created purposes involves worship and obedience to the Lord by keeping his commands and guarding the covenant relationship God has entered into with humanity. This idea is confirmed in the following

---

6. A particularly striking example of the effect of this theology of creation is the way Israel's six-day work week is patterned after the shape of the six-day creation account in the "ten words" in Exodus 20:8–11: "Remember the Sabbath day, to keep it holy. Six days you shall labor, and do all your work, but the seventh day is a Sabbath to the Lord your God. On it you shall not do any work, you, or your son, or your daughter, your male servant, or your female servant, or your livestock, or the sojourner who is within your gates. For in six days the Lord made heaven and earth, the sea, and all that is in them, and rested on the seventh day. Therefore the Lord blessed the Sabbath day and made it holy." Cf. also Exod. 15:10–12; Pss. 8:3–4; 86:7–10; and Isa. 43:1–3.

7. E.g. Num. 3:7–8; 8:25–26; 18:5–6, 1 Chron 23:32; and Ezek. 44:14.

verse where Adam is given a commandment from God that he is to obey (2:16).[8] They were to be God's people, and the Lord was to be their God.

This purpose is the foundational element of the various covenant relationships that occur in subsequent biblical narratives. The garden of Eden was intended to be the place where God met with his people. The later Old Testament institutions of the tabernacle and temple serve a similar worship-oriented function. The garden, the tabernacle, and the temple are all means by which God is present among his people. A series of intertextual references and allusions span the biblical narratives recounting the creation of the garden (Gen. 1–2), the construction of the tabernacle (Exod. 25–40), and the building of the temple (2 Chron. 3–5).[9] Thus, the scene in the garden in Genesis 2 serves as a theological blueprint for humanity's ultimate created purpose: To worship and obey the Lord in the good place that he has provided.

With the clear literary and theological relationship between Genesis 1 and 2, the author directly connects the creation account with the accounts of the covenants. He does this for two main reasons: "First, he intends to draw a line connecting the God of the fathers and the God of the Sinai covenant with the God who created the world. Second, he intends to show that the call of the patriarchs and the Sinai covenant have as their ultimate goal the reestablishment of God's original purpose in Creation. In a word, the biblical covenants are marked off as the way to a new Creation."[10]

Curses for Disobedience: Sin, Serpents, Seed

This initial covenant relationship is broken and complicated when Adam and Eve's lack of trust in God's words cause them to eat of the tree that will give them their own "knowledge of good and evil." This moment in the storyline provides a snapshot of the first sin and also an archetype of every sin. The man and the woman here question the goodness of the Lord's provision by disregarding his words. The serpent's opening assault comes in hermeneutical terms: "Did God actually say . . ." (Gen. 3:1). Indeed, this is at its root a theological and hermeneutical crisis: How will the words of the Lord be interpreted?

---

8. On the significance of this scene, Williams notes these verbs are "associated with worship and keeping the Law, respectively. Therefore, the narrative portrays humans as priestly monarchs who are intended to rule while worshiping and obeying the Lord God" ("Message of the Pentateuch," 7–8). On this covenantal emphasis in Genesis 2, see also Sailhamer, *Pentateuch as Narrative*, 100–2; and Gordon J. Wenham, *Genesis 1-15*, Word Biblical Commentary 1 (Nashville: Thomas Nelson, 1987), 66–67.
9. On this connection, see T. Desmond Alexander, *From Eden to the New Jerusalem: An Introduction to Biblical Theology* (Grand Rapids: Kregel, 2008), 13–73; idem, *The City of God and the Goal of Creation*, Short Studies in Biblical Theology (Wheaton: Crossway, 2018); and G. K. Beale, *The Book of the Revelation*, New International Greek Testament Commentary (Grand Rapids: Eerdmans, 1999), 1110–12.
10. Sailhamer, *Pentateuch as Narrative*, 81.

This brief dialogue directly brings the words of God into conflict with the words of the serpent. The dramatic tension in the narrative builds as the woman must decide: Whose words carry more weight?[11] Whose account of reality will prevail? Which "textual world" being projected is the real one? The textual world where the Lord's commands and blessings are abundant, or the one where those same commands are oppressive? This is the heart of this interpretive and theological crisis. Does God get to speak for himself and interpret his own words, or does the serpent get to assign motives to the Creator's designs?

The serpent's boldest assertion involves his theological interpretation of God's purpose in creation and covenant. He tells the woman, "For God knows that when you eat of it your eyes will be opened, and you will be like God, knowing good and evil" (Gen. 3:5).

The tragic irony is that the man and the woman were *already* "like God" because they were created in his image. What is more, they already had *knowledge* of "good" and "not good" because God had spoken to them and given them both the categories of good and evil and also the means to distinguish between the two: namely, the guidance of his words.[12]

For readers of Genesis 1–2, the actions of the woman at this point are fraught with significance. God is the one who *sees* the finished work of creation and *says* what is good. Here the woman *sees* that the tree is "good for food," "a delight to the eyes," and that the "tree was to be desired to make one wise" (Gen. 3:6). After so much deliberation, the actual act is described in strikingly simple terms: "she took of its fruit and ate, and she also gave some to her husband who was with her, and he ate" (3:6).

This breach of covenant has immediate horizontal and vertical consequences. There is a relational rift between the man and the woman. They immediately seek to distance themselves from one another. Whereas before, "the man and his wife were both naked and were not ashamed" (Gen. 2:25), now they seek to cover themselves (3:7). Whereas before they walked with the Lord in the garden, now "the man and his wife hid themselves from the presence of the Lord God among the trees of the garden" (3:8).[13]

In addition to these relational consequences, the Lord also declares several formal consequences of this breach of covenant. There are blessings for obedience to the Lord, but

---

11. Note the directness of the contrast. The woman recounts that God said "lest you die," and the serpent says to the woman, "You will not surely die" (Gen. 3:4).

12. For example, the Lord is the one who brings the animals to the man to show him that he is in fact alone. The Lord is the one who gives both positive and negative commands. The Lord is the one who explains to the man and the woman the categories of "knowledge of good and evil." The serpent does not provide new revelation; he simply introduces an alternative hermeneutical grid through which to interpret the words and actions of God.

13. The extent of the relational breakdown affected by the presence of sin is quickly conveyed by this initial dialogue in Genesis 3:8–13. In response to God's call, the man says, "I heard the sound of you in the garden, and I was afraid, because I was naked, and I hid myself." God responds, "Who told you were naked? Have you eaten of the tree of which I commanded you not to eat?" The man responds by passing culpability to the woman: "The woman whom you gave to be with me, she gave me fruit of the tree, and I ate." Likewise, when the Lord asks the woman, "What is this that you have done?" The woman replies, "The serpent deceived me, and I ate."

curses for disobedience. For the serpent (Gen. 3:14–15), the woman (3:16), and the man (3:17–19), God declares that there will be ongoing and permanent changes in their relationships with the world, each other, and God himself. The man and the woman are also exiled from the land that God created for them. This exile concludes this initial scene, and here we see the pattern of disobedience begin. Here lies the heart of the human condition.

In the midst of the curses that result from the sins of the man and the woman, there is a "seed" of hope that will grow as the story of the Law continues. As God tells the serpent, "I will put enmity between you and the woman, and between your offspring and her offspring" (Gen. 3:15). This image of hostility between the descendants of the serpent and the descendants of the woman is used by later biblical authors to describe the enemies of the Lord and the people of God.[14] After this broad comment regarding Adam and Eve's progeny, a single descendant is mentioned: "He shall bruise your head, and you shall bruise his heel" (3:15).

At this point in the narrative, the identity of this descendant ("seed") who will bruise or crush the head of the serpent is unclear. However, for Adam and Eve, life is not over. Childbearing will be painful, but will continue (Gen. 3:16). Eve's name signifies the endurance of life after the curse ("because she was the mother of all living," 3:20). She will soon bear children "with the help of the Lord" (4:1). The serpent and sin have had a devastating effect, but the serpent's curse has been meted out as well. And, one day, the Lord has also said, the seed of the woman would crush the head of the serpent. Even in exile, a seed of hope accompanied those who sojourned east of Eden.

Genesis 1–3 sets the pattern that plays out for the rest of the biblical storyline. In Genesis 4, there is murder in the heart of Cain. In Genesis 5 we see the spread of sin and death. We also see glimmers of hope as well; Abel offered an acceptable sacrifice, and Enoch "walked" with God. This movement helps explain the situation in effect as Genesis 6 opens. Wickedness is widespread, yet there are a few who still fear the Lord.

One of the reasons why the beginning of the Bible's storyline is so important is because it contains the pattern that helps explains the rest of the stories that we find in the grand storyline of the Bible. As Adam and Eve leave Eden, the storyline of the Bible focuses on returning to this place. This return relates not only to coming back to the physical location of the garden and the land, though the specific locations that God chooses to dwell with his people are always significant throughout the story. Rather, what Genesis 1–3 provides is a narration and interpretation of the beginning of all things, the heart of life's purpose, the

---

14. For example, see the imagery in texts like Numbers 24:17; Habakkuk 3:14; Micah 7:14–20; Psalms 68:21–22; 72:4–9; and Romans 16:20. Cf. James Hamilton, "The Skull Crushing Seed of the Woman: Inner-Biblical Interpretation of Genesis 3:15," *Scottish Journal of Theology* 10.2 (2016): 30–54. Hamilton provides a "catalog of the intertextual use of the theme of the smashing of the skulls of the enemies of God" (31) along with a discussion of the interpretive choices to be made and a messianic interpretation of these texts that draw upon the themes and imagery of Genesis 3:15.

reason why God's purpose in the world is often thwarted, and also the means by which God is going to one day make all things new.

Reason for Despair: Moses's Prophetic Pessimism

As mentioned above, the story of the Law comes to a close with the people of Israel on the brink of entering into the land of promise. The book of Deuteronomy functions like a commentary on the exodus event, the giving of the law, and the law's role in Israel's life. Perhaps a surprising aspect of Moses's final word of exhortation to Israel is its tone. In his reflection on the nation's recent history and prospects for moving forward, Moses has an overall negative tone (see especially Deut. 27–31). What explains Moses's prophetic pessimism here at the pinnacle of the Pentateuch?

These final words from Moses provide both a retrospective interpretation of the Mosaic covenant and a prospective warning for the people as they enter the land of promise. In short, the Mosaic covenant has failed to bring about the obedience of the people. The failure of the Mosaic covenant becomes evident throughout the rest of Israel's history. The Book of Moses delivers this very perspective for its readers. According to Moses, the primary cause of the failure of this covenant is not a flaw in the system, but rather the heart problem of the people. Moses gains this insight through divine revelation and from personal experience. This knowledge explains Moses's prophetic pessimism pertaining to the people here at the pinnacle of the Pentateuch. He knows this heart condition is a human condition.

This perspective influences the shape of the Pentateuch as a whole which begins with an account of the fall of the first people God created (Gen. 1–3) and ends with Moses's somber reflection on this same pattern at work in the first nation God created (Deut. 27–31). Moses's final words thus provide a remarkable level of cohesion for the story of the Law and also prepare the way for the story that follows. The prophetic history will follow the contours of Moses's prophetic vision that he delivers in this final speech.

Moses begins by articulating the high standard of God's covenant with the nation, saying, "This day you have become the people of the Lord your God. You shall therefore obey the voice of the Lord your God, keeping his commandments and his statutes, which I command you today" (Deut. 27:9–10). He then articulates the curses for disobedience (27:11–26), briefly states the blessings for obedience (28:1–14), and then finally returns to emphasize and more fully develop the curses for disobedience (28:15–68).

When the people enter the land, Moses insists they must serve the Lord and listen to his word. The warning is clear and direct: "If you will not obey the voice of the Lord your God or be careful to do all his commandments and his statutes that I command you today, then all these curses shall come upon you and overtake you" (Deut. 28:15). Moses now allows his hearers to see further into the prophetic vision, as they see further down the road of disobedience in the land. Defeat will come: "The Lord will cause you to be defeated before your enemies" (28:25). The kingdom will be lost: "The Lord will bring you and your king whom you set over you to a nation that neither you nor your fathers have known. And there you shall serve other gods of wood and stone. And you shall become a horror, a proverb, and a byword among all the peoples where the Lord will lead you away" (28:36–37). Possession of the land of promise will be lost: "You shall father sons and daughters, but they shall not be yours, for they shall go into captivity" (28:41). All pride and dignity will be a thing of the past: "The sojourner who is among you shall rise higher and higher above you, and you shall come down lower and lower. He shall lend to you, and you shall not lend to him. He shall be the head, and you shall be the tail" (28:43–44).

Moses culminates this prophetic vision with covenantal language and the image of a predatory eagle. He grimly conveys, "All these curses shall come upon you and pursue you and overtake you till you are destroyed, because you did not obey the voice of the Lord your God, to keep his commandments and his statutes that he commanded you" (Deut. 28:45). The bitter consequence of not serving the Lord is that Israel will now serve their enemies. The Lord will "bring a nation against you from far away, from the end of the earth, swooping down like the eagle" (28:49). After a grim picture of what exile would be like, Moses states that "the Lord will scatter you among all peoples . . . and among these nations you shall find no respite" (28:64).

When Moses finishes the Pentateuch, he also notes, "Take this Book of the Law and put it by the side of the ark of the covenant of the Lord your God, that it may be there for a witness against you. For I know how rebellious and stubborn you are. Behold, even today while I am yet alive with you, you have been rebellious against the Lord. How much more after my death!" (Deut. 31:26–27). Thus, many of Moses's final words are prophetic judgments that indict the people for their prior lack of obedience and express skepticism that they will be able to follow the commands and demands of the Mosaic covenant in the future.

Reason for Hope: Holding Out for a New Covenant and a Coming Messiah

This is a grave set of warnings indeed, but this is not the only emphasis Moses sounds in his closing words. In the midst of his vision of the future, Moses includes the possibility of future repentance after the disaster of exile. In a remarkable passage Moses says:

> When all these things come upon you, the blessing and the curse, which I have set before you, and you call them to mind among all the nations where the Lord your God has driven you, and return to the Lord your God, you and your children, and obey his voice in all that I command you today, with all your heart and with all your soul, then the Lord your God will restore your fortunes and have mercy on you, and he will gather you again from all the peoples where the Lord your God has scattered you. (Deut. 30:1–3)

Even if the people are scattered all over the earth, "from there the Lord God will gather you, and from there he will take you" (30:4). The land that is lost will be regained: "And the Lord your God will bring you into the land that your fathers possessed, that you may possess it" (30:4). Those rebellious hearts will return to the Lord because of God's sovereign work: "And the Lord your God will circumcise your heart and the heart of your offspring, so that you will love the Lord your God with all your heart and with all your soul, that you may live. . . . And you shall again obey the voice of the Lord and keep all his commandments that I command you today" (30:6–8).

Moses concludes this brief glimpse of future restoration by exhorting the people. As he urges:

> See, I have set before you today life and good, death and evil. If you obey the commandments of the Lord your God that I command you today, by loving the Lord your God, by walking in his ways, and by keeping his commandments and his statutes and his rules, then you shall live and multiply, and the Lord your God will bless you in the land that you are entering to take possession of it. But if your heart turns away, and you will not hear, but are drawn away to worship other gods and serve them, I declare to you today, that you shall surely perish. (Deut. 30:16–18)

Moses summarizes the function of this entire section by emphasizing the seriousness and urgency of his comments ("choose life, that you and your offspring may live," 30:19). He also makes an explicitly backward-and-forward looking connection by reminding the post-exodus generation that the land they are about to enter is the land promised to Abraham, Isaac, and Jacob.[15]

With the explicit reference to the promise to Abraham, Moses indicates that this hope for the future worship and obedience of the people is not a generic hope. Rather, it is tied to specific promises that we find at strategic places in the story of the Pentateuch. In other words, we can ask: Where does this hope originate? Where can we find out more information about the content of this hope? As we see from the story of the Pentateuch, the ability of the people to follow the law and maintain obedience from a willing heart is an insufficient place to put our hope. In fact, this is the theme explicitly articulated by a pessimistic Moses at the climax of the Pentateuch. In his book-length closing speech, Moses argues that the Mosaic covenant has failed to bring about the obedience that the Lord requires in the hearts of the people. What hope is there for the second generation? For the reader of the Pentateuch?

---

15. As Moses declares, "I call heaven and earth to witness against you today, that I have set before you life and death, blessing and curse. Therefore choose life, that you and your offspring may live, loving the Lord your God, obeying his voice and holding fast to him, for he is your life and length of days, that you may dwell in the land that the Lord swore to your fathers, to Abraham, to Isaac, and to Jacob, to give them" (Deut. 30:19–20).

Reading and rereading the story of the Pentateuch as a whole highlights that the pattern that Moses identifies on the plains of Moab began in Eden. This pattern is a primal one. So too, the hope that Moses anticipates has its roots in that same garden.

The forward momentum of this narrative progression is a primary way that the Pentateuch functions. Throughout this sweeping narrative storyline, though, there are strategically placed poetic sections that provide reflective commentary on the story. These carefully arranged and strategically composed poems function like windows into the meaning of the Pentateuch's purpose and also offer a glimpse into the author's meaning. Within these poems, we find a cluster of images that profile the promises that bind the major themes of the Pentateuch together.[16] Within these poetic compositions, an individual is described who will one day defeat God's enemies and bring about blessing for the people rather than despair. A future hope is promised, and the proof is in the poetry. A brief survey of these textual locations can orient us to this aspect of the story and the message of the Pentateuch.

The Seed of the Woman

As mentioned above, after the man and the woman fall into sin in Genesis 3, God explains the curse and its consequences. It was the worst of times. But in the midst of these curses for disobedience, God includes a seed of hope. He tells the serpent that there will be "enmity" between his descendants and the descendants of the woman. And then God speaks of a specific descendant: "He shall bruise you on the head, and you shall bruise him on the heel" (Gen. 3:15). God then continues listing out the consequences for the man and the woman. However, here in Genesis 3:15, there is a hint of hope for humanity. Who is this seed of the woman who will crush the head of the serpent?

This language of crushing the head of the serpent also gave later readers a way of speaking of the hope that one day God would defeat his enemies. Here at the origin of humankind's greatest foe, the threat of unforgiven sin, is the promise that one might come who could crush the head of even this monster. Who is the seed? Where is this descendant? When will he come? To answer that question, we must keep reading the Book of Moses. This "seed" will eventually flower into a fully developed messianic nerve center that will run straight through the Old Testament Scriptures. We are now heavily invested in what happens to this descendent. We want to know what becomes of the offspring of the woman.

This developing expectation of a coming descendent explains the "extraordinary emphasis on genealogy" in the Pentateuch.[17] This is why the biblical authors take pains to trace

---

16. On the strategic use of poetry and narrative in the Pentateuch as well as the complementary theme of hope in the book, see Sailhamer, *Pentateuch as Narrative*, 35–37; Shepherd, *Textual World*, 15–16; and Williams, "Message of the Pentateuch," 14–16.

17. On this point, see Stephen G. Dempster, "The Servant of the Lord," in *Central Themes in Biblical Theology: Mapping Unity in Diversity*, eds. Scott J. Hafemann and Paul R. House (Grand Rapids: Baker, 2007), 137: "This focus on

this lineage. This is why the "book of the generations" of Adam, Noah, and so on, is so important. Through shaping the narrative in this way, the author has enabled us as readers to keep our eyes trained on the seed. We are watching a promise of redemption unfold before our eyes. Everything rides on what happens to this line. The narratives and genealogies that follow Genesis 3 serve to connect these poetic promises to each other. The author has taken out his narrative telescope and focused in on the descendant ("seed").

The Son of Abraham

Later in Genesis 12, the narrative focuses on the "seed of Abraham." Here we hear of a promise to Abraham that his descendants will be numerous. The Lord says to Abraham, "I will make of you a great nation, and I will bless you and make your name great, so that you will be a blessing. I will bless those who bless you, and him who dishonors you I will curse, and in you all the families of the earth shall be blessed" (Gen. 12:2–3). The Lord also tells Abraham, "To your offspring I will give this land" (12:7). Through the storyline, the *seed of the woman* is now connected to the *seed of Abraham.* Now we have a little more information. The line of promise will go through Abraham. In Genesis 15, this particular promise is highlighted. Abraham has faith in the promise that God will give him a line of descendants (15:1–6).

Many of the narratives and genealogies of Genesis show the continuance of the line of Abraham, Isaac, and Jacob. The narrative tension of this part of the storyline emerges when this line of descent is jeopardized in some way. This tension is what makes the offering of Isaac so critical, the famine in the land so pressing, and Joseph's time in Egypt so dramatic. These narratives address many different aspects of God's relationship with these people and teach a variety of theological realities about God. They also show that through divine providence and often in spite of the actions of God's people, the promise of a coming descendant still approaches its fulfillment. These narratives demonstrate that God continues to make a way for the promise to Abraham, Isaac, and Jacob to persist.

The Lion from the Tribe of Judah

This promise is directly repeated to Abraham, Isaac, and Jacob. As Jacob gives his final blessing in Genesis 49, he gathers his family together to declare what will take place "in days to come" (49:1). He gives a special blessing to one of his sons, Judah (49:8–12). From Judah, a ruler will come who will bring about the obedience of the people and establish a

---

descendants explains the extraordinary emphasis on genealogy in Genesis. It is not just a backward-looking device that traces the roots of a people; it functions to create anticipation for a future descendant. This is why Eve is so happy when she gives birth to Seth after the death of Abel (Gen. 4:25), and why Seth's genealogy (Gen. 5:1–32), in contrast to Cain's, focuses on life, concluding with the birth of a son, Noah, who is regarded as a signal of hope for the future (Gen. 5:29)."

kingdom. As Jacob says, this descendant will be like a lion: "he crouched as a lion and as a lioness; who dares rouse him? The scepter shall not depart from Judah, nor the ruler's staff from between his feet, until tribute comes to him; and to him shall be the obedience of the peoples" (49:9–10). Now, the expectation of a coming one includes a focus on a descendant who will come from the lineage of Judah. We are now looking for a lion from the tribe of Judah, a ruler from Judah who will one day bring peace to the land and the people.

The Coming One's New Exodus

We might ask at this point: Do these lines of expectation go together? In fact, before we leave the Book of Moses, there are texts that draw these lines of expectation together. For example, in Numbers 24 the prophet Balaam tries to curse Israel, but ends up blessing the people instead. At the end of the wilderness wanderings, the nation of Israel grows large again and a local king named Balak hires Balaam to curse Israel (Num. 22). This situation parallels the beginning of the book of Exodus where the Pharaoh seeks to suppress and oppress Israel because they had grown into a large nation (Exod. 1).

In Balaam's discourse and blessing (Num. 23–24), he speaks of Israel in general, but then begins to speak of a specific king from Israel who rules over an exalted kingdom. In this section, other texts from the Pentateuch are utilized to speak of this coming one:

- 24:8: "God brings him out of Egypt" (an allusion to the exodus narrative).
- 24:8: "He shall eat up the nations, his adversaries, and shall break their bones in pieces and pierce them through with his arrows" (an allusion to the seed of the woman in Gen. 3:15).
- 24:9: "He crouched, he lay down like a lion and like a lioness; who will rouse him up?" (an allusion to Jacob's promise to Judah, Gen. 49:8–12).
- 24:9: "Blessed are those who bless you, and cursed are those who curse you" (an allusion to the promise to Abraham, Gen. 12).

By alluding to previous texts in the Pentateuch, this passage develops the theme of the coming one. This passage directly connects the promise of a redeemer who will crush the head of God's enemies (Gen. 3:15) to the coming ruler from Judah who will reign over God's people (49:8–12), and the descendent ("seed") who will bring blessing to Israel and to the nations (Gen. 12). Further, this description of the coming one is developed in the context of what will happen in "the days to come" (Num. 24:14, 17). The arrival of this coming one is also set within the imagery of a "new exodus" ("God brings him out of Egypt," 24:8).

In the poetry of the Pentateuch, the triumph of the Lord over his enemies is related to the triumph of a coming king from the line of Judah. This cluster of images is frequently utilized by the later prophets and poets of Israel as they express enduring hope in God's future work among the people and future sending of the messiah.[18]

The Coming One's New Covenant

From the viewpoint of the Pentateuch as a whole, the big picture of Pentateuch, we find out that the seed of the woman who will crush the head of the serpent and deal with humanity's greatest enemy will also be the son of Abraham through whom all the nations of the earth will be blessed. This figure will be the lion that will come from the tribe of Judah, rule with righteousness, bring about the obedience of the peoples, and establish a kingdom for the Lord. For ancient readers of the Book of Moses, these covenant promises shaped their expectations about what God was going to do in the future. When all else was falling apart, these promises provided a measure of hope. One day this coming one would set all things right.

Within the context of the failure of the Mosaic covenant, this hope persisted for the readers of the Pentateuch. Keep trusting in the Lord's words, because God is still working to fulfill the promises of his coming presence and the blessings for obedience. We discover that this coming one will circumcise the hearts of the people and enable them to love the Lord with all their heart and soul (Deut. 30:1–10). As the narratives of the Hebrew Bible progress, the hope in this promise continues. A big part of the message of the Pentateuch is to worship and obey the Lord, trust in his promises, and hold out hope for the coming one. The failure of the Mosaic covenant (reason for despair) and the hope in the coming descendant (reason for hope) are two major features of the story of the Pentateuch.

Keeping an Eye on the Storyline and the Promised Line

The story of the Book of Moses provides both reason for despair and also reason for hope. It was the best of times. It was the worst of times.

Moses's final words at the pinnacle of the Pentateuch produce a theological dynamic that forms the backdrop for the entire prophetic history. This dual emphasis is given a large amount of textual real estate in the closing portion of the story of the Law. The people are about to enter into the land of promise, but Moses here gives his comprehensive and somber word of exhortation. This textual feature has an impact for readers trying to understand this portion of the Bible's grand storyline.

To revisit its hermeneutical and theological significance, Moses's prophetic speech has a remarkable scope. He reaches back to the promises of the patriarchs in Genesis and reflects on the rescue of the people from Egypt. He provides commentary on the giving of the law,

---

18. On this topic, see the biblical texts surveyed and discussed in T. D. Alexander, *The Servant King: The Bible's Portrait of the Messiah* (Vancouver: Regent, 1998); Michael Rydelnik, *The Messianic Hope: Is the Hebrew Bible Really Messianic?* (Nashville: B&H, 2010); and John Sailhamer, "The Messiah and the Hebrew Bible," *Journal of the Evangelical Theological Society* 44.1 (2001): 5–23.

the establishment of the Mosaic covenant, and its failure at Sinai and in the wilderness. Moses exhorts the current generation to learn the lessons of the first generation, anticipates the entry into the land, and envisions the establishment of the people in the land. He also foresees the sustained rebellion of the nation, details the eventual disaster of exile, and then holds out hope of a return from exile after genuine repentance.

In light of these textual and theological features, there is little wonder why the prophets and poets of Israel return to the Book of Moses with relentless regularity.

Discussion Questions

1. As you consider the story of the Law, what elements of the biblical-theological framework of the canon, the covenants, and the Christ do you see developed?

2. How many of the major biblical covenants are mentioned or developed in the Pentateuch?

3. Describe and explain the biblical-theological significance of Genesis 1–3 for the biblical storyline.

4. Describe and explain the biblical-theological significance of Moses's final speech for the biblical storyline.

5. In what ways is the Story of the Pentateuch a "story of despair" and in what ways is it also a "story of hope"?

Resources for Further Study

Alexander, T. Desmond. *From Paradise to the Promised Land: An Introduction to the Pentateuch*. Grand Rapids: Baker, 2012.

Blackburn, W. Ross. *The God Who Makes Himself Known: The Missionary Heart of the Book of Exodus*. Downers Grove: InterVarsity, 2012.

Chen, Kevin S. *The Messianic Vision of the Pentateuch*. Downers Grove: InterVarsity, 2019.

Morales, L. Michael. *Who Shall Ascend the Mountain of the Lord? A Biblical Theology of the Book of Leviticus*. Downers Grove: InterVarsity, 2015.

Sailhamer, John. *The Meaning of the Pentateuch: Revelation, Composition and Interpretation*. Downers Grove: IVP, 2009.

CHAPTER 6

The Story of the Prophets

The Shape of the Prophets

THE SECOND MAJOR SECTION of the Old Testament is the Prophets. The books of Joshua, Judges, 1 and 2 Samuel, and 1 and 2 Kings form the first sweeping movement of this section. These books are sometimes called the "historical books" of the Old Testament because they are historical in nature. However, in the Hebrew Bible, they are grouped with the Prophets and sometimes called the Former Prophets. They thus provide the prophetic history of the people of Israel and God's dealing with them.

The second movement of the Prophets includes the three major prophetic books of Isaiah, Jeremiah, and Ezekiel alongside the Book of the Twelve. These books are sometimes characterized as the "Latter Prophets" or the "writing prophets." These prophetic books are set within the storyline told by the prophetic history and often provide theological commentary on those events. Collectively, these biblical books continue the story of God's dealings with his people as they look back to previous promises and look forward to future deliverance. They also contain the revelation of God as he pronounces words of both salvation and judgment through his prophets.

One of the key features of the Prophets as a major section of the Hebrew Scriptures is its clear and consistent connection to the Book of Moses. Joshua through 2 Kings continues the narrative storyline of the Pentateuch. In particular, the Former Prophets support and illustrate the basic message of the book of Deuteronomy. In both literary and theological terms, the prophetic history acts as a continuation of the story that leaves off in Deuteronomy. What is more, the prophetic history as a whole does something similar to what the Pentateuch as a whole does: it looks back on Israel's history and provides both warning and hope for future generations of readers. Together, these two major sections form the core of the Hebrew Scriptures as the Law and the Prophets.

Another important feature of this section is the unity of books typically separated into multiple parts in English translations. For example, 1 Samuel and 2 Samuel comprise the single book of Samuel, and 1 Kings and 2 Kings comprise the single book of Kings. Moreover, what are sometimes known as the twelve "Minor Prophets" (Hosea through Malachi) constitute the unified Book of the Twelve. In this way, the writing Prophets as a group consist of four major prophetic books of relatively equal length with a similar scope and sequence. Noting these textual and book-level features will help you see the guidance that the canonical context provides as you read these books and encounter the story of the Prophets.[1]

The Story of the Prophets

The story of the Prophets narrates and interprets Israel's rise and fall. The prophetic history of Joshua, Judges, Samuel, and Kings continues the narrative of Israel's history as they occupy the land, establish a kingdom, and then descend into exile. The writing prophets of Isaiah, Jeremiah, Ezekiel, and the Book of the Twelve are situated within this prophetic history and provide prophetic reflection and commentary on God's character and relationship with his people as they turn toward exile.

The overarching purpose of the prophetic history and the prophetic commentary is first to explain the Babylonian captivity, and second to hold out hope for a return from exile. Two of the dominant themes that show up throughout the storyline of the Prophets are the Lord's faithfulness to the covenant (he keeps and graciously renews it) and the people's failure to keep the covenant (they break and continually neglect it).

In this collection of books, we see Israel enter the land (Joshua), experience exile within the land (Judges), gain a king (Samuel), and finally lose the kingdom (Kings).

Entering the Land (Joshua)

The narrative storyline of the book of Joshua focuses on Israel's entry into Canaan and their conquest of the land. Following this successful conquest, Joshua distributes the land into territories, renews the covenant with the people, and offers a prophetic word about Israel's role in the land.

---

1. For an extended discussion of the canonical shape of the Prophets as well as key features of these narratives, see Stephen B. Chapman, *The Law and the Prophets: A Study in Old Testament Canon Formation* (Grand Rapids: Baker, 2019); Christopher Seitz, *The Goodly Fellowship of the Prophets: The Achievement of Association in Canon Formation* (Grand Rapids: Baker, 2009); and Stephen Dempster, "The Prophets, the Canon and a Canonical Approach: No Empty Word," in *Canon and Biblical Interpretation*, ed. Craig Bartholomew et al., Scripture and Hermeneutics Series 7 (Grand Rapids: Zondervan, 2006), 293–329.

Within the context of the Hebrew Bible, Joshua represents a clear continuation of the story of the Pentateuch. After Moses dies, the Lord tells Joshua, "Moses my servant is dead. Now therefore arise, go over this Jordan, you and all this people, into the land that I am giving to them, to the people of Israel" (Josh. 1:2). Creating a clear literary and theological line of continuity between these two eras of Israel's history, the Lord assures Joshua, "Just as I was with Moses, so I will be with you. I will not leave you or forsake you" (1:5).

The Lord next echoes the commission Joshua receives at the end of Deuteronomy: "Be strong and courageous, for you shall cause this people to inherit the land that I swore to their fathers to give them. Only be strong and very courageous, being careful to do according to all the law that Moses my servant commanded you. Do not turn from it to the right hand or to the left, that you may have good success wherever you go" (Josh. 1:7). If Israel is to have success in the land, they must worship and obey God in the land. They must keep the covenant and follow the law. Israel's guide for understanding the Mosaic covenant is the Book of Moses. As the Lord says, "This Book of the Law shall not depart from your mouth, but you shall meditate on it day and night, so that you may be careful to do according to all that is written in it. For then you will make your way prosperous, and then you will have good success" (1:8). The primary covenant blessings that result from this form of obedience in the land of promise will be the presence of the Lord himself among the people. As God says to Joshua, "Do not be frightened, and do not be dismayed, for the Lord your God is with you wherever you go" (1:9).

With these words, the Lord connects the story of the Prophets to the story of the Law in a particularly direct and strategic way. In this series of statements, the opening of Joshua alludes to the beginning of the Pentateuch (the promise to Abraham), the middle of the Pentateuch (the Mosaic covenant), the end of the Pentateuch (the commission of Joshua by Moses) and also the entire Pentateuch itself (this "Book of the Law"). These literary and theological links are significant ways to see the storyline continue as we move into this next major section of the Old Testament. The people are about to cross the Jordan River into the land. For those with eyes to see, the flow of redemptive history continues. Despite recent and distant failure, the story of the covenants continues to be told. The land of promise awaits and teems with blessing and curse. Jericho and Ai. Rahab and Achan. Mount Ebal and Mount Gerizim. By the end, Joshua and the author of the book demand: Choose!

After these opening words, Israel enters the land (Josh. 1–5) and then completes the conquest of the land by battling, driving away, and destroying the people living in the land (Josh. 6–12). While there are many dramatic narratives in the book of Joshua, the longest section is actually devoted to the details surrounding the distribution of the land (Josh. 13–22). The narrative progress simply stops as the author recounts the way the land is distributed among the people of Israel as the nation gains control of the region.

After the nation has settled in the land and Joshua has grown old, he gathers the leaders of the nation and gives a farewell speech to Israel's leaders and people to reaffirm their commitment to the covenant (Josh. 23–24).[2] After the flurry of activity in the first part of the book and the distribution of the land in the second part of the book, this last section provides a retrospective analysis of this important moment in the storyline. Indeed, Joshua's last words provide a commentary on the people's status in the land of promise. This is an important moment. The people have entered the land of promise. They have followed the guidance of the Book of Moses, for the most part, and they have experienced initial rest in the land. It was the best of times.

The speech Joshua gives in Joshua 23–24 strongly echoes the speech Moses gave at the end of his life. Just as the beginning of the book of Joshua resonated with the Book of Moses, so too the somber tone of Joshua's last words echo the prophetic pessimism that marked Moses's final words at the pinnacle of the Pentateuch (Deut. 27–31). If the people trust and obey the Lord, they will receive rest and blessing in the land, but if they reject the word of the Lord they will experience hardship and lose possession of the land. As Joshua urges, "Be very strong to keep and to do all that is written in the Book of the Law of Moses, turning aside from it neither to the right hand nor to the left" (Josh. 23:6). The Israelites are not to mix with the nations around them or "make mention of the names of their gods" but rather "cling to the Lord your God" (23:8). Joshua warns them, "Be very careful, therefore, to love the Lord your God" (23:11). The Lord fights for them, but if they reject the Lord and turn to the gods of the nations, those very nations will become a "snare and a trap" for Israel (23:12). Exile will come as the nation perishes "from off this good ground that the Lord your God has given you" (23:13).

Joshua then repeats this position in explicitly covenantal terms. Noting his impending death, he insists that "not one word has failed of all the good things that the Lord your God promised concerning you" (23:14). These good things are the blessings for obedience and rest in the land that they have experienced. On the basis of these fulfilled promises, Joshua maintains the people should also firmly believe in the promises of judgment for disobedience.[3]

---

2. This speech occurs "a long time afterward, when the Lord had given rest to Israel from all their surrounding enemies, and Joshua was old and well advanced in years" (Josh. 23:1). This scenario is similar to Jacob at the end of Genesis gathering his twelve sons at the end of his life (Gen. 49) and Moses gathering the people at the end of his life (Deut. 27–31).

3. Joshua makes this connection directly: "But just as all the good things that the Lord your God promised concerning you have been fulfilled for you, so the Lord will bring upon you all the evil things, until he has destroyed you from off this good land that the Lord your God has given you, if you transgress the covenant of the Lord your God, which he commanded you, and go and serve other gods and bow down to them. Then the anger of the Lord will be kindled against you, and you shall perish quickly from off the good land that he has given to you" (23:15–16).

Joshua next gathers all the tribes together for a final speech and word of exhortation. Joshua recounts a word from the Lord, echoing the way the book began. In this instance, Joshua relays the Lord's words as God recounts redemptive history beginning with Abraham, the promise of the land and descendants, and the growth of that family into the nation that went down to Egypt (Josh. 24:2–4). The Lord notes, "I sent Moses and Aaron, and I plagued Egypt with what I did in the midst of it, and afterward I brought you out" (24:5). Next the Lord says, "I brought your fathers out of Egypt" and recounts the deliverance at the Red Sea (24:6). He says, "Your eyes saw what I did in Egypt. And you lived in the wilderness a long time" (24:7). These wilderness wanderings include the blessings from Balaam (24:9–10). At this point, the Lord summarizes the events described in the book of Joshua from the crossing of the Jordan River to the fall of Jericho and the battles with the Amorites (24:11–12). He encapsulates this entire conquest by saying, "I gave you a land" (24:13).

Next, Joshua directly addresses the people, saying, "Now therefore fear the Lord and serve him in sincerity and in faithfulness" (24:14). The Israelites are to "put away" the gods they served in Egypt and serve the Lord. In his final speech, Moses proclaimed, "See, I have set before you today life and good, death and evil" and urged the people to, "choose life" (Deut. 30:15, 19). So too Joshua urges the people, "If it is evil in your eyes to serve the Lord, choose this day whom you will serve, whether the gods your fathers served in the region beyond the River, or the gods of the Amorites in whose land you dwell. But as for me and my house, we will serve the Lord" (24:15).

The people respond positively, confessing their allegiance to the Lord and affirming God's providential work on their behalf. They assert, "We also will serve the Lord, for he is our God" (Josh. 24:18). Instead of optimism, however, Joshua articulates prophetic pessimism about the people's ability to keep the covenant in the land. As he somberly counters, "You are not able to serve the Lord, for he is a holy God. He is a jealous God; he will not forgive your transgressions or your sins" (24:19). Joshua continues by explaining, "If you forsake the Lord and serve foreign gods, then he will turn and do you harm and consume you, after having done you good" (24:20). A dialogue then ensues. The people object, "No, but we will serve the Lord." To this, Joshua counters again, "You are witness against yourselves that you have chosen the Lord, to serve him" (24:22). After affirming these commitments, Joshua "wrote these words in the Book of the Law of God" and made a memorial stone as a "witness" to the commitment that the people had made (24:25–28).

It was the best of times, so why this word of warning?

Though the book of Joshua seems to present the fulfillment of the promises of the covenant, there are clear hints toward the end of the book that the conquest did not entirely fulfill these covenant promises. There is still a heart problem lurking in the shadows. The context of Joshua's words, too, points in this direction. The land has been conquered, but not all of it. There is still more work to be done. Joshua is about to be gone, but the work of guarding the covenant and keeping the land must continue. This is true physically but also spiritually. Israel is in the land of promise, but will they be able to keep it?

One of the final comments of the book is also subtly foreboding: "Israel served the Lord all the days of Joshua, and all the days of the elders who outlived Joshua and had known all the work that the Lord did for Israel" (Josh. 24:31). Joshua's final words forcefully raise the question about the future obedience of the people. This note prompts concern for the reader. Israel served the Lord "all the days of Joshua" and during the lives of the elders who were with Joshua who "had known all the work that the Lord did for Israel."[4] But what about the next generation? Did this next generation grow up and forget what the Lord had done? As these generations pass, the stone of remembrance stands as a witness against the people regarding the certainty of God's promise of judgment for covenant disloyalty.

Here at the end of Joshua, there is a reason for despair but also a reason for hope. In this closing section, two memorials are mentioned: A stone and some bones. The stone is a reminder of the curses for disobedience, but the bones are a reminder of the blessings of obedience. The last words of Joseph in the book of Genesis are about these very bones. Before he dies, Joseph speaks to his brothers about the promise that God had made in the past and the work that God will do in the future. As he says, "I am about to die, but God will visit you and bring you up out of this land to the land that he swore to Abraham, to Isaac, and to Jacob" (Gen. 50:24). Here Joseph anticipates the exodus from Egypt and makes his brothers swear that they will carry his body into the land of promise. He insists, "God will surely visit you, and you shall carry up my bones from here" (50:25).

Years later, when Israel actually makes their exodus, among the wide-angle panoramic of the people leaving Egypt, this small detail is brought into focus: "Moses took the bones of Joseph with him, for Joseph had made the sons of Israel solemnly swear, saying, 'God will surely visit you, and you shall carry up my bones with you from here'" (Exod. 13:19). In light of these narrative details, the final link in this story arc sums up the significance of this part of the Prophets: "As for the bones of Joseph, which the people of Israel brought up from Egypt, they buried them at Shechem, in the piece of land that Jacob bought from the sons of Hamor the father of Shechem for a hundred pieces of money. It became an inheritance of the descendants of Joseph" (Josh. 24:32).

If these bones could talk, they would probably tell the story that was told to them. Joseph himself anticipates the story of the Prophets, and his bones bear witness to its continuation. The story continues. Joseph's faith stands as part of the dual witness here at the end of Joshua. A stone and some bones. Both are part of the story of redemption and the message of the covenants: Blessings for obedience and curses for disobedience.

---

4. The final note of the book that Eleazar has died (Josh. 24:33) intensifies this scenario as well. If Joshua and Eleazar are now gone, who is left who knows, fears, and serves the Lord?

Exile in the Land (Judges)

The story of Judges begins with the people asking for the Lord's guidance after Joshua dies. The Lord directs the tribe of Judah to lead the conquest of the remaining nations still in the land (Judg. 1:1–26). The other tribes, however, "did not drive out completely" these inhabitants from the regions where they settled.[5] A messenger from the Lord immediately appears and reminds the people why this incomplete conquest is a breach of the covenant.[6] Anchoring his message in the story of the Pentateuch, the messenger says on behalf of the Lord, "I brought you up from Egypt and brought you into the land that I swore to your fathers. I said, 'I will never break my covenant with you, and you shall make no covenant with the inhabitants of this land; you shall break down their altars.' But you have not obeyed my voice. What is this you have done? So now I say, I will not drive them out before you, but they shall become thorns in your sides, and their gods shall be a snare to you" (2:1–4).

At the end of the book of Joshua, there was a lingering question about the obedience of the people after the death of Joshua. There were portions of the land that still needed to be consolidated, and the covenant needed to be maintained as the years continued. Here, the author of Judges answers this lingering question. The death of Joshua is recounted again but with the addition of an ominous epilogue: "And there arose another generation after them who did not know the Lord or the work that he had done for Israel" (Judg. 2:10).

The book of Judges recounts this time in Israel's history after the leadership of Joshua had passed. Israel was without a strong leader like Moses or Joshua. The people had gained the land but lost their leader. The lack of consistent leadership becomes a dominant theme in the book. The book of Judges as a whole anticipates the recurring pattern of disobedience that carries on through the rest of the prophetic history. The author summarizes this distinct pattern that develops in Israel's history at the beginning of the narrative (Judg. 2:11–23).

A Recurring Pattern: Tracing the Downward Spiral of Unfaithfulness (Judg. 2:11–23)

1. **Israel turns away from God.** As the author notes, "The people of Israel did what was evil in the sight of the Lord and served the Baals. And they abandoned the Lord, the God of their fathers, who had brought them out of the land of Egypt" (Judg. 2:11). Notice the near constant use of the story of the Pentateuch to identify the God of Israel. The theological heart of this disobedience involved a breach of covenant loyalty: "They went after other gods, from among the gods of the peoples who were

---

5. The phrase "did not drive out" is repeated in this section (see 1:27, 28, 29, 30, 31, 32, 33).
6. Note the connection between the angel of the Lord here (Judg. 2:1–5) and the captain of the Lord's hosts that met Joshua at the beginning of the conquest of the land (Josh. 5:13–15). It was the best of times, it was the worst of times.

around them, and bowed down to them. And they provoked the Lord to anger. They abandoned the Lord and served the Baals and the Ashtaroth" (2:12–13).[7]

2. **God sends an adversary against Israel.** "So the anger of the Lord was kindled against Israel, and he gave them over to plunderers, who plundered them. And he sold them into the hand of their surrounding enemies, so that they could no longer withstand their enemies" (Judg. 2:14). This situation was "as the Lord had warned, and as the Lord had sworn to them" (2:15).[8]

3. **Israel calls out to God for help, and God raises up a judge who delivers them.** In the midst of their oppression, the Israelites cry out to the Lord. For example, in the first instance of this pattern in the book, the people are being oppressed by the king of Mesopotamia (Judg. 3:8). The author notes, "But when the people of Israel cried out to the Lord, the Lord raised up a deliverer for the people of Israel, who saved them."[9] As the author summarizes, "The Lord raised up judges, who saved them out of the hand of those who plundered them" (2:16). In one sense, the rule of the judges foreshadows the rule of the future kings of Israel. Within the storyline, these judges rule over the nation until the kingdom of Israel is established. These judges provided protection from both the physical and spiritual enemies of Israel. They sought to guard the people's national relationship with the land and also their covenantal relationship with the Lord.[10]

4. **After the judge dies, the people turn away from God again.** Though the details change, the underlying pattern endures throughout the book. After God delivers the people, there is peaceful rule as long as the judge lives. The author notes, though, that the people "soon turned aside from the way in which their fathers had walked, who had obeyed the commandments of the Lord, and they did not do so. Whenever the Lord raised up judges for them, the Lord was with the judge, and he saved them from the hand of their enemies all the days of the judge" (Judg. 2:17–18). "But whenever the judge died," however, "they turned back and were more corrupt than their fathers, going after other gods, serving them and bowing down to them" (2:19).[11]

---

7. This part of the pattern typically begins with the statement that Israel "did evil in the eyes of the Lord" (Judg. 3:7, 12; 4:1; 6:1; 10:6; 13:1).
8. The author adds here, "And they were in terrible distress" (Judg. 2:15). See also 2:14; 3:8, 12; 4:2; 6:1; 10:7; 13:1.
9. See Judg. 3:9, 15; 4:3; 6:6, 7; 10:10.
10. See Judg. 2:16, 18; 8:23; 11:2. The successful judge is one that acknowledges that the Lord is the one who ultimately judges Israel, and the judges rule by the power of God's Spirit.
11. The Lord makes the covenant breach explicit by saying, "Because this people have transgressed my covenant that I commanded their fathers and have not obeyed my voice, I will no longer drive out before them any of the nations

The result of this breach of covenant is that "the anger of the Lord was kindled against Israel" (2:20). The author summarizes, "So the Lord left those nations, not driving them out quickly" (2:23).

Because of the way the author chooses to begin this part of the narrative, the story of Judges has a clear shape and rhythm that builds toward a somber conclusion. This recurring pattern that the author so clearly recounts traces a downward spiral of disobedience and unfaithfulness. As one narrative leads into the next, one era of Israel's history touches the next, and one account connects to the next, this pattern helps us see a literary continuity and tragic theological line of continuity between these accounts. Part of what resonates is a downward spiral of disobedience that descends into the disaster depicted in the final scenes of the book.

There are twelve judges mentioned in the book of Judges: six "major judges" who receive an extended narrative account, and six "minor judges" who receive a more brief account. This feature shows that this narrative storyline does not represent an exhaustive account of this time period. Rather, the author has selected certain events in order to provide a snapshot of this era.

For example, few details are given about the judge Othniel (Judg. 3:7–11), but this narrative sets the pattern of the book clearly. The accounts after Othniel develop various aspects of this pattern. The story of Ehud, a left-handed man who defeats the king of Moab, highlights the unexpected ways God uses the judges to deliver the people from the nations who oppress them (3:12–30). Deborah's victory over the king of Canaan also shows how the judges led the nation when its military leaders hesitated and its people refused to go to war (4:1–24).[12]

The call and rule of Gideon in Judges 6–8 is a particularly instructive example of the promise and pattern of the book. Gideon serves the Lord, relies on the Lord's strength, leads the people with a zeal for the purity of worship, and reminds the people that God is their sole ruler. He declares, "I will not rule over you, and my son will not rule over you; the Lord will rule over you" (Judg. 8:22–23). However, Gideon also makes key mistakes, such as allowing the people to make a golden Ephod that eventually becomes a snare of idolatry for the nation's worship of the Lord (8:24–27). Gideon's son Abimelech directly contrasts his father in his narrative (9:1–57). Whereas Gideon said, *the Lord* is your King, Abimelech whispers, I am your king (9:1–2). Abimelech conspires to kill his brothers, but Jotham escapes

---

that Joshua left when he died, in order to test Israel by them, whether they will take care to walk in the way of the Lord as their fathers did, or not" (Judg. 2:20–22).

12. Deborah's account is the only one in the book to include a poetic reflection, which highlights the unexpected nature of Deborah's involvement and victory, the refusal of many of the leaders of Israel to participate, and the role that Jael plays in finishing the conflict by executing Sisera (Judg. 5:1–31).

and prophesies against him. Eventually, Abimelech's three-year reign ends in civil war and instability, just as the curses of Jotham anticipated would come to pass (9:57).

The story of Gideon and Abimelech illustrates the message of Judges. Gideon's success exemplifies the type of leader Israel needs, but his failure also demonstrates the core of the problem: the heart of the people and their leaders. Neither the people nor the leaders of Israel have the ability to worship and obey God with a fully devoted heart. The pattern is not uniform but continues to spiral downward as the alternating cycle of faithfulness and disobedience intensifies.

After its account of the judges, the final scenes of the book of Judges are the most disturbing (Judg. 17:1–21:25). There is a shift in these narratives from an external crisis (the surrounding nations) to an internal crisis (the people themselves). Israel becomes her own worst enemy.

The two narrative sequences at the end of the book encapsulate the depth of Israel's depravity. In the first (Judg. 17–18), the rank idolatry and spiritual disorder rife in the land are put on display. Idolatry is thought to be what pleases the Lord within the context of a household and even an entire tribe. In the second (Judg. 19–21), the moral corruption and stunning lack of godly leadership becomes painfully apparent. A traveling Levite and his concubine decide to stay the night in the Benjaminite city of Gibeah at the house of an old man. That evening, the Benjaminite men of the city surround the house seeking to assault the Levite. The old man of the house offers these strangers his defenseless daughter and the Levite's concubine instead. When the mob refuses, the Levite forces his concubine to go to the group of Benjaminites, who brutally assault her until the morning when she dies on the doorstep. When the Levite returns to his home, he dismembers his concubine and sends her body parts to each of the twelve tribes (19:27–30). This action sets off a civil war, as the other tribes demand to know how the tribe of Benjamin did this evil act (20:1–48). War ensues and the tribe of Benjamin is defeated. The narrative ends with a disturbing account of how the elders schemed to deal with the fallout from this civil war, including kidnapping women in order to repopulate the tribe of Benjamin (21:1–24).

Through the effect of this narrative pattern, the author of Judges conveys to the reader the depth of Israel's sin and their great need for a godly leader. The people are in the land, but they have no king and behave like the nations they were supposed to drive out of the land. The holy people have turned into a heinous people. Having entered the land, the people now experience exile within the land. After they enter the land, the Israelites struggle with the nations who serve other gods and engage in morally depraved practices. By the end of this part of the storyline, however, the Israelites struggle with themselves as they are now the ones who serve other gods and engage in morally depraved practices. The nations continually encroach their borders and the people act like a nation that has forgotten the Lord. Israel has become virtually indistinguishable from the nations that surround them.

The last words of the book of Judges draw these themes together and serve as an interpretive summary of this era in Israel's history: "In those days there was no king in Israel. Everyone did what was right in his own eyes" (21:25).[13]

It was the worst of times. It was the worst of times.

Gaining a King (Samuel)

The book of Samuel opens in the time of the judges and closes in the time of the kings. The pressing question implied by the last scenes of the book of Judges is, can a king save us? The book of Samuel carries the storyline along by connecting these two eras in Israel's history while providing a prophetic analysis of this period of redemptive history. Kingship in Israel is a solution to the disarray of the time of the judges. Samuel's narrative provides a historical and theological evaluation of this all-important transition.

There are three main figures in the book of Samuel, each of whom represent an important moment in the history of Israel. Samuel serves as the last judge of Israel (1 Sam. 1–12), Saul serves as the first king of Israel (1 Sam. 13–31), and David is anointed and serves as the first Davidic king of Israel (2 Sam. 1–24).

The book of Samuel opens with the story of Hannah praying to the Lord for a son. After the treachery and barbarism occurring at the close of Judges, the opening of Samuel is like an antidote to the theological disease that spreads like gangrene through Israel. Hannah cries out to the Lord for a child and receives a son. In response, Hannah dedicates her son to the service of the Lord in the temple at Shiloh and offers a prayer of worship and thanksgiving (1 Sam. 1–2). The author of Judges notes that, "In those days there was no king in Israel. Everyone did what was right in his own eyes" (Judg. 21:25). By contrast, Hannah acknowledges, that "the Lord is a God of knowledge, and by him actions are weighed" (1 Sam. 2:3). Further, Hannah concludes her prayer by focusing on the hope of a future king: "The Lord will judge the ends of the earth; he will give strength to his king and exalt the horn of his anointed" (2:3). Here, in a kingless nation that has forgotten their God, Hannah envisions a good king who serves the Lord. Thus, in a remarkable way, Hannah's song connects the preceding story of Judges to the coming story of Samuel.[14]

---

13. This phrase serves as a structural marker in the last section of Judges, helping readers see the way these narratives are designed to function within the flow of the book. See Judges 17:6 ("In those days there was no king in Israel. Everyone did what was right in his own eyes"), 18:1 ("In those days there was no king in Israel. And in those days the tribe of the people of Dan was seeking . . ."), and 19:1 ("In those days, when there was no king in Israel, a certain Levite . . .").

14. The theological and literary significance of Hannah's song (1 Sam. 2:1–10) is difficult to overestimate. Her song sets the tone and initiates the refrain that will develop as the book progresses. Further, Hannah's song, along with David's lament for Saul (2 Sam. 1:17–27), and David's final reflective song at the end of the book (22:1–23:7) all serve to focus our attention on the theme of God's faithfulness in the past and God's future work through a coming king.

As Samuel serves the Lord and leads Israel as a judge, he helps the nation defeat the Philistines, regain the ark of the covenant, and spark a revival among the people (1 Sam. 3–7). The transition of Israel into a kingdom begins when the people demand a king and Samuel selects Saul (1 Sam. 8–12).[15]

Samuel's last words to the people echo a consistent theme in the prophetic history. In his old age Samuel addresses "all Israel" (1 Sam. 12:1), saying "The Lord is witness, who appointed Moses and Aaron and brought your fathers up out of the land of Egypt" (12:6). Samuel then recalls key moments in redemptive history, including the story of Jacob and the sons of Israel going to Egypt, the exodus from Egypt, and the entry into the land (12:7–8). He then recounts several of the episodes from Judges and how Israel was unfaithful, experienced oppression, cried out to the Lord, and then received deliverance through the judges (12:9–11). Samuel includes himself in this pattern, and notes the irony that the people demanded a king to reign over them "when the Lord your God was your king" (12:12).

After this rehearsal of redemptive history, Samuel emphasizes the heart of the covenant relationship to the people. Having a king in the land will go well, if the people worship and obey the Lord. As he declares, "If you will fear the Lord and serve him and obey his voice and not rebel against the commandment of the Lord, and if both you and the king who reigns over you will follow the Lord your God, it will be well" (1 Sam. 12:14). Conversely, Samuel insists, "If you will not obey the voice of the Lord, but rebel against the commandment of the Lord, then the hand of the Lord will be against you and your king" (12:15).

After the people consider the weight of Samuel's words and see the thunder and rain sent by Lord, they become greatly afraid and express sorrow. Samuel maintains, though, "Do not be afraid; You have done all this evil. Yet do not turn aside from following the Lord, but serve the Lord with all your heart. And do not turn aside after empty things that cannot profit or deliver, for they are empty" (1 Sam. 12:20–21). Samuel also reiterates that "the Lord will not forsake his people, for his great name's sake, because it has pleased the Lord to make you a people for himself" (12:22).

Samuel's last words echo Moses and Joshua's last words. Before Israel entered the land, after they entered the land, and now as they demand a king, the heart of the covenant relationship between God and his people remains: Worship and obey. The fact that the people now have a king will not save them, unless that king is one who fears the Lord and follows his ways. As Samuel concludes, "Only fear the Lord and serve him faithfully with all your heart. For consider what great things he has done for you" (1 Sam .12:24). Foreshadowing

15. When the people demand a king, Samuel conveys a prophetic warning from the Lord. In Samuel's initial dialogue with the Lord, the Lord makes clear the covenant breach involved in a request for a king: "Obey the voice of the people in all that they say to you, for they have not rejected you, but they have rejected me from being king over them. According to all the deeds that they have done, from the day I brought them up out of Egypt even to this day, forsaking me and serving other gods, so they are also doing to you" (1 Sam. 8:7–8).

the following narratives, Samuel adds, "But if you still do wickedly, you shall be swept away, both you and your king" (12:25). As Samuel anticipates in his farewell speech, Saul quickly fails as the faithful king of God's people (1 Sam. 13–14). The kingdom is not immediately taken from Saul, but David is anointed the next king of Israel. In 1 Samuel 15–31, each event plays some part in the fall of Saul and the rise of David.

After the death of Saul and Jonathan at the hands of the Philistines (1 Sam. 31), the storyline focuses on the consolidation of the kingdom of Israel under David in Jerusalem (2 Sam. 1–6). When David seeks to build a temple in Jerusalem for the Lord, the Lord responds by saying that David will not be the one to accomplish this task (2 Sam. 7). Rather, one of David's sons will build this temple. David wanted to build a "house" (temple) for the Lord, but the Lord will instead build a "house" (dynasty) for David (7:10–11).

The next words of this promise echo the poetic promises of the Pentateuch and shape the expectations about God's future work through a "son of David" who would rule God's people with justice and righteousness. The Lord says that after David dies, "I will raise up your offspring after you, who shall come from your body, and I will establish his kingdom. He shall build a house for my name, and I will establish the throne of his kingdom forever. I will be to him a father, and he shall be to me a son" (1 Sam. 7:12–14).[16] Significantly, in light of the prophetic history's account of the downward spiral of disobedience in the time of the judges and the fall of Saul, the Lord includes a word of warning about the nature of this covenant relationship with David and his line. As the Lord notes, "When he commits iniquity, I will discipline him with the rod of men, with the stripes of the sons of men, but my steadfast love will not depart from him, as I took it from Saul, whom I put away from before you" (7:14–15).[17]

This statement looks backward but also anticipates the narrative of the book of Kings, which describes the long succession of Davidic kings that follow Solomon's initial rise and devastatingly fast downfall. The promise of an eternal kingdom and a son of David will remain secure in spite of the failure of any given individual in that lineage. As the Lord declares, "Your house and your kingdom shall be made sure forever before me. Your throne shall be established forever" (2 Sam. 7:16).

After the strategic significance of the covenant with David, the rest of David's story includes the slow decline of the house of David due to his sins and covenant disloyalty (2 Sam. 8–20).[18] David's last words and acts as king are a mix of repentance and confession for sin and hope in the promises that God had made to him and his house (2 Sam. 21–24).

---

16. See also the discussion in chapter seven of this promise to David portrayed in 1 Chronicles 17.
17. The mention of the descendant's sin and discipline by the Lord is one of the key differences between the account of the promise to David in 2 Samuel 7 and the one in 1 Chronicles 17.
18. Some of the most prominent failures in David's life in the latter part of his reign that the author highlights include his sin against Bathsheba and his murder of Uriah (2 Sam. 11–12), and the military census David takes (2 Sam. 24).

Losing the Kingdom (Kings)

The book of Kings moves from the death of David straight through to the Babylonian exile. This post-David history of Israel covers around 350 years. The looming large-scale military threats to Israel are Assyria and Babylon. The book of Kings is thus a carefully crafted narrative about a long period of time. The chronological framework is an intentional strategy. The author of Kings quickly takes us from one king to the next. He slows down on a king in some instances and speeds up the narrative in other cases. What could explain these shifts in focus?

As the last book in the prophetic history, Kings functions as the conclusion to this sequence of books in the Prophets. The book is written from the perspective of Israel in exile (2 Kings 24–25). The author gives a historical and theological explanation for the exile. Positioned in this way, this book encapsulates the message of the prophetic history as a whole. How did this happen? Does the reality of the exile mean that the word of God has failed? The author looks backwards but also forward. He provides a retrospective commentary on Israel's history, but also offers a prospective answer to these questions: Where do we go from here? Can the people return from exile? Is this even possible? Is there anything in the history of redemption that can reveal the path of return?

The book of Kings contains accounts of both kings and prophets, but more pointedly their combative interactions. Much of the story is about the prophets and their contentious interactions with the kings of Judah and Israel. In this fast-paced narrative, it is when a prophet declares a word of judgment against a disobedient king that the narrative pace often slows down long enough to overhear long stretches of discourse.[19] Further, the section that describes Elijah and Elisha's ministry comes at the center of the book, serving as a transition from the extended development of Solomon's reign that *precedes* this section, and the sequence of kings that *follow*. Even the shape of the book, then, is designed to highlight this near-constant interaction between Israel's kings and God's word spoken by God's prophets.

In this light, the author of Kings not only composes a history, but does so with a clearly defined literary strategy. Part of the theological purpose of the book of Kings relates to the fulfillment of prophetic promises in redemptive history. The author argues that the words spoken by the prophets have been fulfilled. The word of the prophet *always* stands, even when the prophet is powerless or passes away before that word is fulfilled. The author's strategy allows the reader to see word-upon-word spoken and word-upon-word fulfilled.[20]

---

19. For example, note the extended dialogue between Ahab, Jehoshaphat, the group of false prophets, and the prophet Micaiah in 1 Kings 22. Further, the amount of space devoted to Ahab's reign and his interaction with the prophet Elijah is significant (1 Kings 16–22).
20. For example, in 1 Kings 16:34, the author notes that when Hiel the Bethelite built Jericho, "he laid its foundations with the loss of Abiram his firstborn, and set up its gates with the loss of his youngest son Segub, *according to the word of the Lord*, which he spoke by Joshua the son of Nun" (Josh. 6:26). Elijah predicts Jezebel's death in 1 Kings 21:17–24 ("the dogs shall eat Jezebel within the bounds of Jezreel") and this is precisely what happens in

This pattern of fulfilled promises happens on a small scale throughout the book, but also on a large scale as the author summarizes and explains the history of Israel as a whole. Towards the end of the book of Kings, the author provides two prophetic obituaries for Israel and Judah. These are the "last words" of the author of the book of Kings.

The Fall of Israel to Assyria (2 Kings 17:7–23) and Judah to Babylon (2 Kings 24–25)

After describing the fall of Samaria to the king of Assyria, the author directly states, "this occurred because the people of Israel had sinned against the Lord their God, who had brought them up out of the land of Egypt from under the hand of Pharaoh king of Egypt, and had feared other gods and walked in the customs of the nations whom the Lord drove out before the people of Israel, and in the customs that the kings of Israel had practiced" (2 Kings 17:7–8). The author states further that the people "did secretly against the Lord their God things that were not right" (17:9). These things included building alternate places of worship in their towns, setting up idols to other gods throughout the land, and sacrificing at these places just "as the nations did whom the Lord carried away before them" (17:11).[21] Moving to the theological message of the prophetic history, the author notes, "Yet the Lord warned Israel and Judah by every prophet and every seer, saying, 'Turn from your evil ways and keep my commandments and my statutes, in accordance with all the Law that I commanded your fathers, and that I sent to you by my servants the prophets'" (17:13).

Despite this long line of prophets, Israel and Judah "would not listen, but were stubborn, as their fathers had been, who did not believe in the Lord their God" (2 Kings 17:14). The author describes the sustained wicked actions of the Northern Kingdom, including their construction of two golden calf idols and sacrificial offerings to Baal. He then notes that only Judah remained (17:18). Even Judah, though, "did not keep the commandments of the Lord their God, but walked in the customs that Israel had introduced" (17:19). The author summarizes this indictment by noting that Israel did not depart from the sins of Jeroboam "until the Lord removed Israel from out of his sight, as he had spoken by all his servants the prophets." So, the author concludes, "Israel was exiled from their own land to Assyria until this day" (17:23).

Similarly, in the final days of Judah the Babylonian king Nebuchadnezzar gains authority over the kings of Judah (2 Kings 24:1–7), invades Jerusalem (24:10–17), and begins taking groups of people and officials captive to Babylon. Finally, Nebuchadnezzar and his army lay

---

2 Kings 10:31–37 ("This happened according to the word of the Lord which he spoke to Elijah"). When Jeroboam sets up a false altar, a "man of God" tells him that "this is the sign that the Lord has spoken: Behold, the altar shall be torn down, and the ashes that are upon it shall be poured out" (1 Kings 13:1–3). Many years later, Josiah purges the land of alters. When he destroys Jeroboam's alter, the author notes that this happened "according to the word of the Lord which the man of God proclaimed, who had predicted these things" (2 Kings 23:14).

21.   The author is even more direct when he says, "And they did wicked things, provoking the Lord to anger, and they served idols, of which the Lord had said to them, 'You shall not do this'" (1 Kings 17:11–12).

siege to Jerusalem, destroy the city, desecrate the temple, and execute the leading officials (25:1–21). As the author comments, "So Judah was taken into exile out of its land" (25:21).

Reason for Despair: Words of Judgment Have and Will Come to Pass

The author of Kings is not the first to come up with these standards by which he evaluates the people of Israel and their leaders. He functions as a prophetic author, giving a word of exhortation while narrating and interpreting redemptive history for future generations of readers. In fact, on this point the author of Kings stands in a long line of prophetic authors who make the same assessment. The measuring stick here is the Book of Moses. The last words of the author of Kings demonstrate the fulfillment of prophetic words first spoken not by the author, but by Moses in his final speech to the people before they entered the land of promise in Deuteronomy 27–31. There, Moses said that if the people forsook the Lord and served other gods that they would lose the land and go into exile. If they repented and trusted in the Lord, then they would be blessed and regain the land. Moses's last words reverberate throughout the prophetic history. Joshua's last words in Joshua 23–24 after the people have entered the land echo Moses's last words in Deuteronomy. Samuel's last words (1 Sam. 12) and David's last words (2 Sam. 22–23; 1 Kings 2:1–9) about the need for an obedient king also resonate with this perspective. The argument of the book of Kings is that this is exactly what has happened to Israel. The judgment of the Lord in exile is thus explained, and God is justified in his judgment.

The exile is the tragic amen to the warnings of the prophetic history.

Reason for Hope: Words of Blessings Have and Will Come to Pass

Despair, therefore, is justified. But, what about hope? Another facet of the author's message in Kings is the positive side of promise and fulfillment. The message of the prophets also includes an element of future hope. A measure of this hope is for the present time. If the king and the people will worship and obey God in the land, then the Lord will prosper them, dwell among them, and give them rest.

The author of Kings demonstrates that if Israel repents, then God will rescue them. He does this by giving examples of bad kings, like Jeroboam who forsakes God and reaps the consequences, and also good kings, like Hezekiah who repents and sees God deliver Judah from the Assyrians. The point is that peace in the land and with God requires repentance and trust.

The standard for kings is also found in the Pentateuch. They were to guard the temple (Deut. 12:8–14) and lead the people in worship of the one true and living God (Deut. 6). Good kings were also to mediate on the Law of the Lord and lead the people to do the same (17:14–20). They were to listen to the words of the prophets (18:15–22). They were to follow the first commandment to have no other gods before the Lord (5:7) and also the second commandment to make no graven images to use in worship (5:8). These are the criteria by which the author of Kings evaluates the reign of each king. This explains why some kings get more textual real estate than others. The author is interested in whether or not a particular king *affirmed* or *transgressed* the covenant relationship and expectations required of the leaders by the people.

Good kings slowed the descent into exile and the bad kings of Israel accelerated this descent.[22] The good kings in Israel's history were able to bring about times of rest and blessing in Israel's history (e.g., the early part of Solomon and Josiah's reigns). However, even the best kings were unable to stop the downward spiral toward the inevitability of exile.[23] If there is a message of hope in the prophetic history, it is explicitly not located in the ability of the people to observe the demands of the Mosaic covenant. Indeed, part of the theological purpose of these books is to illustrate Moses's prophetic pessimism about the people's ability to keep the covenant. There is a dim measure of hope in these books in the realization that when the people are obedient, blessings follow. However, the overshadowing realization is that the consistent pattern of the people's disobedience and inability to maintain covenant loyalty repeats on a small and large scale.

The reasons for despair are very clear when reading about the nation's descent into exile. We see this emphasis very clearly as readers. But what about the promise to David? Has God's word failed? Because the theological purpose of Kings and the prophetic history is that the word spoken by the prophets stands, this will include all of those words. The prophets have spoken words of judgment, but also words about the hope of salvation. These promises about the hope of future salvation coalesce around the promise to David. When will the son of David come? When will the kingdom arrive that will never depart? When will a descendant of David rule with righteousness and bring about the obedience of the people? A close reader of the story of the Law and the Prophets might very well ask: Is this even possible? As the narrative storyline of the prophetic history closes with the chains of Babylon's ruling power, we might rightly ask: Is the coming one still coming?

The Son of David and the Sons of David

As the book of Kings opens, David has grown old, Solomon has established his transition to the throne, and David gives Solomon a final charge before he dies (1 Kings 2:1–9). In this final speech to Solomon, David draws upon the story of the Law and the Prophets as he

---

22. This pattern in Kings is similar to the pattern developed in the book of Judges.
23. For example, Jehoiakim rips the scroll of the prophet to shreds and burns it out of blatant rebellion (see Jer. 36 and 2 Kings 23:34–24:5). He is considered one of the worst kings and becomes the first king of Judah to experience exile in Babylon. By contrast, Josiah rediscovers the Book of Moses because he was restoring the Temple. When he hears the words of the law, he rips his clothes in repentance (see 2 Kings 22–23). Josiah is considered one of the "best" kings, but sadly he cannot stop the slide into exile (2 Kings 23:24–27).

articulates both blessings for obedience and the consequences for disobedience to the Lord and his covenant. Much like Moses had urged Joshua, David tells Solomon, "Be strong, and show yourself a man, and keep the charge of the Lord your God, walking in his ways and keeping his statutes, his commandments, his rules, and his testimonies, as it is written in the Law of Moses, that you may prosper in all that you do and wherever you turn" (2:2–3). David next connects this exhortation to a reminder of the promises God made concerning one of his descendants: "If your sons pay close attention to their way, to walk before me in faithfulness with all their heart and with all their soul, you shall not lack a man on the throne of Israel" (2:4).

Solomon believes he is the promised descendant of David (1 Kings 2:24; 5:19), consolidates his kingdom, and asks for wisdom (1 Kings 3–5). As Solomon builds the temple, the Lord comes to Solomon and affirms that Solomon is the promised "son of David" *as long as* he maintains obedience to the Lord. The Lord tells Solomon directly, "Concerning this house that you are building, if you walk in my statutes and obey my rules and keep all my commandments and walk in them, then I will establish my word with you, which I spoke to David your father. And I will dwell among the children of Israel and will not forsake my people Israel" (6:12–13).

When Solomon dedicates the temple, he declares that the promises to David have been fulfilled (1 Kings 8:12–21). Referring to the building of the temple among the people, Solomon proclaims, "Blessed be the Lord, the God of Israel, who with his hand has fulfilled what he promised with his mouth to David my father . . . Now the Lord has fulfilled his promise that he has made. For I have risen in the place of David my father, and sit on the throne of Israel, as the Lord promised, and I have built the house for the name of the Lord, the God of Israel" (1 Kings 8:15, 20).

In many ways, Solomon is the ideal wise king. He functions as a prophet who speaks directly to the Lord and seeks divine wisdom. He functions as a priest who builds, guards, and helps officiate the work of the temple. He functions as a king who consolidates the kingdom, provides rest for the people, and proclaims the name of the Lord to the nations. It was the best of times, and Solomon seems like the best candidate for the fulfillment of the "coming one" promises that we have seen in the whole course of redemptive history.

After the dedication of the temple, the Lord appears to Solomon to confirm the divine presence in the temple. He also reiterates Solomon's weighty task: "As for you, if you will walk before me, as David your father walked, with integrity of heart and uprightness, doing according to all that I have commanded you, and keeping my statutes and my rules, then I will establish your royal throne over Israel forever, as I promised David your father" (1 Kings 9:4–5). However, the Lord continues, "If you turn aside from following me, you or your children, and do not keep my commandments and my statutes that I have set before you, but go and serve other gods and worship them, then I will cut off Israel from the land that I have given them, and the house that I have consecrated for my name I will cast out of my sight . . . and this house will become a heap of ruins" (9:6–8).[24] In these warnings, the Lord outlines the treasure of obedience, but also the steep and deadly cost of disobedience.

Solomon and his reign represented the golden days of Israel's kingdom and the reign of a descendant of David. But nothing gold can stay. After the height of his success (1 Kings 10), Solomon falls to the depths of idolatry and involvement with other nations lead his heart astray (11:1–13).[25] The Lord "raised up an adversary against Solomon" (11:14), and this marked the end of Solomon's possible fulfillment of the promises to David. The author of Kings draws out the significance of Solomon's breach of covenant: "And the Lord was angry with Solomon, because his heart had turned away from the Lord, the God of Israel, who had appeared to him twice and had commanded him concerning this thing, that he should not go after other gods. But he did not keep what the Lord commanded" (11:9–10). The verdict is swift and devastating as the Lord makes two things clear at this point: The promise he made in his covenant with David is still secure, but Solomon will not be the one to bring about its fulfillment.[26]

The wisdom of Solomon had established the kingdom and produced rest and blessing for the people. The folly of Solomon and the foolishness of his son Rehoboam cause the fragmentation of the kingdom, as well as the loss of the nation's wealth and blessing (1 Kings 12). The divided kingdom will become a breeding ground for idolatry, unrest, and social injustice as the kings of the Northern and Southern Kingdoms lose their grip on the land of promise and the people careen toward the exile. It was the worst of times.

---

24. The Lord draws out the implications of this for the covenantal relationship as well by drawing on the story of the Pentateuch: "Then they will say, 'Because they abandoned the Lord their God who brought their fathers out of the land of Egypt and laid hold on other gods and worshiped them and served them. Therefore the Lord has brought all this disaster on them'" (1 Kings 9:9).

25. One of the points of the author's portrayal of Solomon's downfall seems to relate directly to Solomon's breach of the expectations of an Israelite king outlined in Deuteronomy 17:14–20. The grandiose description of Solomon's great wealth in 1 Kings 10 includes direct violations of these guidelines. For example, "he must not acquire many horses for himself or cause the people to return to Egypt in order to acquire many horses, since the Lord has said to you, 'You shall never return that way again'" (Deut. 17:16; see 1 Kings 10:26–29, esp. v. 28: "And Solomon's import of horses was from Egypt"). Further, "nor shall he acquire for himself excessive silver and gold" (Deut. 17:17; see 1 Kings 10:14–22, esp. v. 21: "All King Solomon's drinking vessels were of gold. None were of silver; silver was not considered anything in the days of Solomon"). Finally, "And he shall not acquire many wives for himself, lest his heart turn away" (Deut. 17:17; See 1 Kings 11:1–8, esp. v. 4: "For when Solomon was old his wives turned away his heart after other gods, and his heart was not wholly true to the Lord his God, as was the heart of David his father"). Thus, when Solomon's downfall is depicted in 1 Kings 11, the author demonstrates that this is not a new "plot twist" that enters the story for the first time here, but rather the re-entry of a pattern that is all too familiar to the people of Israel and readers of the Pentateuch. The very résumé of evidence that seemed to indicate his favor from the Lord was, in reality, Exhibit A in the author's indictment of Solomon's covenant disloyalty.

26. As the Lord says to Solomon, "Since this has been your practice and you have not kept my covenant and my statutes that I have commanded you, I will surely tear the kingdom from you and will give it to your servant. Yet for the sake of David your father I will not do it in your days, but I will tear it out of the hand of your son. However, I will not tear away all the kingdom, but I will give one tribe to your son, for the sake of David my servant and for the sake of Jerusalem that I have chosen" (1 Kings 11:11–13).

Are You the One, or Should We Look for Another?

After showing that Solomon is not the promised son of David, the author of Kings focuses upon each successive king and asks the question: Is this ruler the promised descendant of David? For each new king of Israel, the reader can ask: How does he act? Does he serve the Lord, or turn to idols? Does he listen to the word of the prophets, or does he assault them? Does he worship and obey God?

As the author moves from one king to the next, from the Northern Kingdom to the Southern Kingdom, from generation to generation, the answer continues to be, "no!" Even the best kings fall short of the standard articulated by the Lord in the charge to David. The worst kings illustrate the need for a good king. The good kings illustrate the need for a great king. What is more, even the best of these kings are only a shadow of the ruler promised in the Davidic covenant. No king of Israel or Judah can prevent the beast of Babylon from devouring the nation. By the end of the book, exile ceases to be a hypothetical feature of the prophetic warnings and becomes a settled feature indicative of everyday life.

A "Son of David" Rising from the Ashes of Exile

An important detail to note about the book of Kings is where it ends. The land is lost, the temple is destroyed, and those who have survived are in exile, but there is an interesting comment about what happens to the king of Judah in Babylon. The book ends in the darkness of the exile with the former king Jehoiachin, a descendant of David, in chains. As the narrative closes, though, the author indicates that perhaps dawn is coming.

The last words of the book recount how during Jehoiachin's thirty-seventh year in exile, the king of Babylon "graciously freed Jehoiachin king of Judah from prison" (2 Kings 25:27). Going a step further, the Babylonian king "spoke kindly to him and gave him a seat above the seats of the kings who were with him in Babylon" (25:28). As a result, thirty-seven years after being imprisoned, "Jehoiachin put off his prison garments" (25:29). Jehoiachin does not return to his own land or receive any level of authority, but he does receive the care and provision he needs to survive: "And every day of his life he dined regularly at the king's table, and for his allowance, a regular allowance was given him by the king, according to his daily needs, as long as he lived" (25:29–30).

There is only the faintest glimmer here, but a careful reader will note the significance of a ruler from the line of David surviving the exile. A feeble exiled ruler from the house of David has thrown off his prison garments and is now eating at the Babylonian king's table. Could the line of David endure? Might the son of David still come?

In the structure of the book of Kings, you can see the movement from wisdom to folly, from the heights of the kingdom to the depths of exile, and from stability on all sides to disaster everywhere. To illustrate this, contrast the confidence of Solomon as he ascends the throne with the humiliation of Jehoiachin as he emerges from prison in Babylon. Can you imagine Jehoiachin standing up from that table and proclaiming that he is the fulfill-ment of the soaring prophetic vision of the Davidic covenant? The roaring furnace of God's promise is now but a flicker.

But how far that little candle throws its beams!

Keeping an Eye on the Storyline and the Promised Line

By way of summary, we can say that the story of the Prophets provides a narration and interpretation of Israel's rise and fall. In this collection of books, we see Israel enter the land (Joshua), experience exile within the land (Judges), gain a king (Samuel), and finally lose the kingdom (Kings). The overarching purpose of the prophetic history and its commentary is first to explain the exile and Babylonian captivity, and second to hold out hope for a return from exile.

Throughout the storyline of the Prophets, the theological emphasis is on the Lord's faith-fulness to the covenant (he keeps it and graciously renews it) and the people's failure to keep the covenant (they break it and continually neglect it). As the prophetic books convey their message, they draw on the history of Israel depicted in the Book of Moses. They also continue to develop the theological reasons for despair and hope that are initially found in the story of the Law. The themes of the nature of the covenants, God's rule through his kingdom, and the promises connected to the coming ruler from the line of David are particularly prominent in the story of the Prophets. The prophetic history continues the account of redemptive history and also develops the hope of redemption articulated in this storyline.

Discussion Questions

1. As you consider the story of the Prophets, what elements of the biblical-theological framework of the canon, the covenants, and the Christ do you see developed?

2. What is the significance in considering Joshua, Judges, Samuel, and Kings as the "prophetic history" and not only the "historical books" of the Old Testament? How would you characterize the overall "prophetic" message of these books when understood as a coherent collection?

3. List and describe at least two textual and theological connections between each book in the prophetic history (Joshua, Judges, Samuel, Kings). Are there similar connections between this sequence of books and the Pentateuch?

4. Explain the significance of the promise to David (the Davidic covenant in 2 Samuel 7). Where else in the prophetic history (before and after) are connections made to this promise? Why is this particular promise significant?

5. Reflect on the way that the concept of exile functions in these books. How is it treated in Kings, and how is it anticipated in Joshua, Judges, and Samuel?

Resources for Further Study

Bodner, Keith. *The Theology of the Book of Kings.* Cambridge: Cambridge University Press, 2019.

Chapman, Stephen B. *The Law and the Prophets: A Study in Old Testament Canon Formation.* Grand Rapids: Baker, 2020.

Seitz, Christopher R. *The Goodly Fellowship of the Prophets: The Achievement of Association in Canon Formation.* Grand Rapids: Baker, 2009.

Shead, Andrew G. *A Mouth Full of Fire: The Word of God in the Words of Jeremiah.* Downers Grove: InterVarsity, 2012.

Shepherd, Michael B. *The Textual World of the Bible.* New York: Peter Lang, 2013.

CHAPTER 7

THE STORY OF THE WRITINGS

The Shape of the Writings

THE FINAL MAJOR GROUPING in the Old Testament is the Writings. This major section is a diverse but coherent grouping of poetic texts, brief narratives, and lengthy histories. The sequence of the books in the Writings has a different flow than the sequence in the Prophets. For example, there is no grand "prophetic history" or tightly connected Book of the Twelve. However, within the framework provided by Psalms and Chronicles, the individual books of the Writings find their place. There are several textual and theological patterns in the Writings worth noting that are maintained even within the various arrangements found in the manuscripts of this collection.

In relation to the Law and the Prophets, the Writings represent a shift from *prophetic* commentary to *poetic* commentary. Many of the books in this collection contain poetic reflections on Israel's life before, during, and after the exile. In fact, one of the features of this collection is its broad scope and far-sighted theological outlook. Toward the end of the Writings, the narratives of Esther, Daniel, Ezra–Nehemiah, and Chronicles return to the narrative storyline and collectively function as the conclusion to the Hebrew Bible.

Within the shape of the Writings, the books of Psalms and Chronicles have a unique role. The book of Psalms usually appears at the beginning of the Writings. In most orderings, Chronicles comes last in the Writings grouping and thus concludes the entire Hebrew Bible as well. In the one ordering of canonical books where Chronicles appears first among the Writings, it is immediately followed by the book of Psalms. In all the major canonical orderings, then, Chronicles and Psalms seem to function together as either the head of the Writings or as the bookends of this grouping. These two books therefore set the literary and theological tone for the big picture of this section of the Old Testament.

There are also two books in the Writings that are actually intentionally shaped collections of smaller texts. The book of Psalms gathers together 150 individual poetic texts (i.e., psalms) ranging from the time of Moses (Ps. 90) to the ages of David (Ps. 23) and Solomon (Ps. 72), and then finally to the exile (Ps. 137). Similarly, the book of Proverbs contains several distinct collections of wise sayings (i.e., proverbs), many of which are attributed to Solomon. Some of these collections were gathered together later in Israel's history (e.g., Prov. 25:1) and include adages penned by non-Solomonic sages (see 30:1; 31:1). Both of these books gather together individual texts into coherent collections that possess a distinct shape and have been designed for future generations of readers.

The books of Lamentations, Esther, Daniel, Ezra–Nehemiah, and Chronicles appear in close proximity to each another in most orderings. These books in particular revisit the setting and theological interpretation of the exile found in the closing moments of the prophetic history in the book of Kings. Since this sequence of books occurs at the end of the Writings, and therefore at the close of the Old Testament as a whole, these books seem to continue the storyline that abruptly ends at the conclusion the prophetic history.

When we carefully consider this cluster of books in the Writings, the themes of exile and return from exile emerge. The authors of these biblical texts contemplate the nature of this return from exile, but also look beyond the return and evaluate the prophetic promises of a new covenant in light of this post-exilic situation. While each of these books offers their own coherent narrative, together they provide a condensed and sequenced storyline at the close of the Writings.[1]

The Story of the Writings

The narratives of Esther, Daniel, Ezra–Nehemiah, and Chronicles dramatically conclude the storyline of the Writings and the Old Testament as a whole. These books each reflect on the purposes of God in redemptive history as Israel experiences judgment and then returns from exile. This particularly unique collection also includes reflections upon the eras of Israel's life before the exile. As mentioned above, this occurs most often in the Writings through poetic reflection (e.g., Psalms and Proverbs). However, there are a few

---

1. For an extended discussion of the canonical shape of the Writings as well as key features of these narratives, see the essays in Julius Steinberg and Timothy J. Stone with Rachel Stone, eds., *The Shape of the Writings*, Siphrut 16 (Winona Lake: Eisenbrauns, 2015); Timothy J. Stone, *The Compilational History of the Megilloth: Canon, Contoured Intertextuality and Meaning in the Writings*, Forschungen zum Alten Testament 2.59 (Tübingen: Mohr Siebeck, 2013); Michael B. Shepherd, *Daniel in the Context of the Hebrew Bible*, Studies in Biblical Literature 123 (New York: Peter Lang, 2009); Peter H. W. Lau and Greg Goswell, *Unceasing Kindness: A Biblical Theology of Ruth*, New Studies in Biblical Theology 41 (Downers Grove: InterVarsity, 2016); John Sailhamer, *First and Second Chronicles* (Chicago: Moody, 1983).

examples of narratives set within the earlier periods of Israel's history (Job and Ruth). These narratives interconnect with multiple time periods in Israel's history (before, during, and after the exile). Located within a collection of Writings that concludes the Hebrew Bible, these texts overlap settings and textual contexts from the Law and the Prophets.

Remembering a Time before the Exile (Job and Ruth)

One of the unique books appearing toward the beginning of the Writings collection is the book of Job. This book gives an account of a man who is tested by God in suffering (Job 1–2), engages in extended dialogue with several companions about the character of God (Job 3–37), and then hears from God out of a whirlwind (Job 38–40). The book of Job opens by providing the basic historical setting for the subsequent dialogue: "There was a man in the land of Uz whose name was Job, and that man was blameless and upright, one who feared God and turned away from evil" (1:1). The setting of the book seems to be from a time much like the historical setting of the account of Abraham, Isaac, and Jacob in Genesis. As part of the Writings, Job begins with a brief narrative framework centered on a wide-ranging theological examination of the fear of the Lord, the presence of the Lord in suffering, and whether suffering is always (or ever) the result of divine judgment. The book of Job does this primarily through back-and-forth dialogue between Job and the other main figures in the account.

This book set in time of Genesis is complemented by another brief narrative at the beginning of the Writings set in the time of Judges. The book of Ruth connects with clear themes from the story of the prophetic history as well as the other works in the Writings. Ruth begins by locating its setting in one of the darkest times in Israel's history: "In the days when the judges ruled there was a famine in the land, and a man of Bethlehem in Judah went to sojourn in the country of Moab, he and his wife and his two sons" (Ruth 1:1). Once this family arrives in Moab, though, this man dies and leaves his wife Naomi a widow. After some time, Naomi's two sons die as well and she decides to return to the land of Israel. The wife of one of her sons, Ruth, decides to accompany her to Israel, pledging her loyalty to Naomi and her God (1:16).[2] Naomi's return causes a stir among the women of the town, but Naomi expresses her sorrow saying, "Do not call me Naomi; call me Mara, for the Almighty has dealt very bitterly with me. I went away full, and the Lord has brought me back empty. Why call me Naomi, when the Lord has testified against me and the Almighty has brought calamity upon me?" (1:20–21).

Through the kindness and integrity of Boaz (the Benjaminite landowner and distant relative of Naomi), Ruth and her mother-in-law are able to receive provision in their new

---

2. As Ruth declares, "Do not urge me to leave you or to return from following you. For where you go I will go, and where you lodge I will lodge. Your people shall be my people, and your God my God" (Ruth 1:16).

home. Boaz eventually redeems Ruth by purchasing her inheritance and marrying her (Ruth 4:13).[3] Ruth and Boaz then conceive and give birth to a son. By the end of the narrative, Naomi's expression of bitterness has turned into an expression of blessing. The hunger and death at the beginning of the story are connected to the provision and new life at the end of the story. As the women of the town exclaim, "Blessed be the Lord, who has not left you this day without a redeemer, and may his name be renowned in Israel! He shall be to you a restorer of life and a nourisher of your old age, for your daughter-in-law who loves you, who is more to you than seven sons, has given birth to him" (4:14–15).

The grandchild on Naomi's lap is further identified by the author: "They named him Obed. He was the father of Jesse, the father of David" (4:17). Ruth then concludes with a ten-generation genealogy of this child ("Now these are the generations of," 4:18). The final word of the book is the name "David" (4:21). While the book of Ruth conveys a clear message about God's providence in general, the mention of David here clearly highlights God's specific providence in fulfilling a specific promise regarding the house and line of David. Positioned in the Writings but with a direct link to the time of Judges, Ruth works to connect groups of biblical texts, profiles of promise, and several biblical theological themes.[4]

Remembering the Sorrow of Exile (Lamentations)

After the structural pause in the narrative storyline of the Hebrew Bible that includes the Latter Prophets and the first part of the Writings, the book of Lamentations signals a return to the dominant theme of exile. Encountering Lamentations positions readers squarely within the broken city of Jerusalem. Standing at ground zero, readers are confronted again with the social and theological disaster of exile.

As the book of Lamentations opens, the prophetic poet exclaims, "How lonely sits the city that was full of people! How like a widow has she become, she who was great among the nations! She who was a princess among the provinces has become a slave" (Lam. 1:1). Directing focus quickly on the cause of this pain, the writer observes, "Judah has gone into exile because of affliction and hard servitude; she dwells now among the nations, but finds no resting place; her pursuers have all overtaken her in the midst of her distress" (1:3).

---

3. After Boaz's acts as the "kinsman-redeemer" of Ruth (4:7–10), the people directly connect his actions to the biblical storyline. As they state, "We are witnesses. May the Lord make the woman, who is coming into your house, like Rachel and Leah, who together built up the house of Israel. May you act worthily in Ephrathah and be renowned in Bethlehem, and may your house be like the house of Perez, whom Tamar bore to Judah, because of the offspring that the Lord will give you by this young woman" (4:11–12). The reference to Tamar, Perez, and Judah (Genesis 38) along with the mention of Perez in the concluding genealogy, provide a connecting link to the time of Genesis and give the book of Ruth a remarkably wide textual, historical, and theological scope.

4. To give one example, the strong connection to the time of the book of Judges and the prophetic history is obvious from the beginning of the book (Ruth 1:1). The genealogy that ends the book that is focused on David (Ruth 4:18–21) is also a strong connection to Genesis (e.g., Genesis 5) and Chronicles (e.g., 1 Chronicles 1–9), two biblical books that strategically utilize genealogies.

Like the Psalms, the poetry of Lamentations expresses dismay at what the Lord has done in judgment, but also continued hope in that same Lord. As the writer insists, "this I call to mind, and therefore I have hope: The steadfast love of the Lord never ceases; his mercies never come to an end; they are new every morning; great is your faithfulness" (Lam. 3:21–23). There is an enduring hope in the character and faithfulness of the Lord at the heart of Lamentations, but it shines forth in the context of the darkness of God's rendered judgment and the sting of exposed unfaithfulness among the people. Those who trust in the Lord's promise articulated in the center of the book must wait "quietly for the salvation of the Lord" (3:26). This historical and theological dynamic captures the tone of the latter part of the "story of the Writings."

At this point in the Writings, the book of Lamentations plays a strategic role in raising interpretive tensions about the fall of Jerusalem, the judgment of the Lord, and the reality of the exile that each of the following books address in their own way. In particular, the closing lines of Lamentations 5 raise questions that loom large in Daniel, Esther, Ezra–Nehemiah, and Chronicles. The poet asks God, "Why do you forget us forever, why do you forsake us for so many days?" (Lam. 5:20).

Enduring the Exile (Esther and Daniel)

After the emotional reminder of the events of the exile in Lamentations, the stories of Daniel and Esther in the courts of Babylon and Persia respectively pick up on this theme.

The book of Daniel recounts events and visions experienced by Daniel from his arrival in Babylon (Dan. 1:1) through the reign of King Cyrus of Persia (10:1). Daniel thus witnesses the fall of Babylon and the rise of Persia while he is in exile. Part of the message of the book of Daniel is that even though Israel is in exile, it is still possible to worship and obey God. As the narrative portrays, Daniel serves the Lord, interprets the dreams of the king, and reads the Scriptures. His friends also refuse to bow to the idols of Babylon, and Daniel defies an order to cease praying to his God (Dan. 1–6, 9). Daniel's visions and interpretations of prophecy point readers to future hope beyond exile and encourage individual and corporate faithfulness among the people (Dan. 7–12).

In particular, two accounts in the book of Daniel help provide cohesion to this part of the story of the Writings. In the time of Babylonian captivity, Daniel sees a vision of a future deliverer. In Daniel 7, Daniel envisions God as "the Ancient of Days" seated on a throne of power (7:9). This throne was on fire and surrounded by thousands upon ten thousands of the heavenly host. These heavenly beings were assembled as a court of judgment with their books opened wide (7:10). Connected to this scene is a vision of a "son of man" who approaches the Ancient of Days. As Daniel describes, "behold, with the clouds of heaven there came one like a son of man, and he came to the Ancient of Days and was presented before him" (7:13). To this son of man is given "dominion and glory and a kingdom, that all peoples, nations, and languages should serve him." This authority has a global scope and also a never-ending duration: "his dominion is an everlasting dominion, which shall not pass away, and his kingdom that shall not be destroyed" (7:14).

After Persia conquers Babylon, Daniel sees a vision of a future departure from captivity.[5] In Daniel 9, we see Daniel reflect upon the historical and theological dimensions of the exile. Meditating upon the book of Jeremiah, Daniel reads that the exile in Babylon will last seventy years (Dan. 9:1–2; cf. Jer. 25:11; 29:10).[6] He then prays to "the great and awesome God, who keeps covenant and steadfast love with those who love him and keep his commandments" (9:4). Daniel also acknowledges the theological lesson of the exile and the message of the prophetic history: "We have sinned and done wrong and acted wickedly and rebelled, turning aside from your commandments and rules. We have not listened to your servants the prophets, who spoke in your name to our kings, our princes, and our fathers, and to all the people of the land" (9:5–6).[7]

As Daniel finishes his prayer, he is answered by the angel Gabriel with a message about Israel's eventual departure from Babylon as well as the extended nature of this return, the actions of the messiah, and the future work of God among the people (Dan. 9:20–27). The people will leave Babylon and return to Jerusalem, but the coming of the anointed one still lies in the future (9:25). Even as they return to the land, then, the people will still need to trust in these visions of the future work of God in a coming messiah and a coming kingdom.

Similar to the exilic setting of the book of Daniel, the book of Esther takes place in the courts of Persia and narrates the story of Esther and her relative Mordecai. Esther is a Jewish woman who becomes the queen of the Persian king Ahasuerus (Esther 1–2). Mordecai is identified as a Jew from the tribe of Benjamin "who had been carried away from Jerusalem among the captives carried away with Jeconiah king of Judah, whom Nebuchadnezzar king of Babylon had carried away" (2:5–6).

Through their positions in the Persian courts, Esther and Mordecai are able to thwart a plot by one of the king's high-ranking officials to destroy the Jewish people in the Persian

---

5. The setting for this scene is "the first year of Darius the son of Ahasuerus, by descent a Mede, who was made king over the realm of the Chaldeans—in the first year of his reign" (Dan. 9:1).

6. As this scene opens, Daniel notes, "I, Daniel, perceived in the books the number of years that, according to the word of the Lord to Jeremiah the prophet, must pass before the end of the desolations of Jerusalem, namely, seventy years" (9:2).

7. Daniel repeats this basic premise several times in his prayer in Daniel 9:3–19. He includes several appeals to the standards of blessings for obedience and curses for disobedience that are "written in the Law of Moses the servant of God" (9:11, 13). He also appeals to the story of the exodus in articulating the foundational faithfulness of the Lord and the unfaithfulness of the people: "And now, O Lord our God, who brought your people out of the land of Egypt with a mighty hand, and have made a name for yourself, as at this day, we have sinned, we have done wickedly" (9:15). Daniel's appeal to the Lord for forgiveness, mercy, and deliverance are then based on the character of the Lord ("because of your great mercy," 9:18).

kingdom (Esther 3–9).[8] This adversary of the Jewish people is identified as "Haman the Agagite, the son of Hammedatha" (3:1).[9] In a dramatic and ironic turn, Haman himself is hanged on the very gallows he had prepared for Mordecai (7:7–10). The king says to Esther, "Behold, I have given Esther the house of Haman, and they have hanged him on the gallows, because he intended to lay hands on the Jews" (8:7).[10]

By the authority of queen Esther and Mordecai, the Jews actually defeat those who had intended to destroy them (Esther 9). The Feast of Purim is then inaugurated to commemorate "the days on which the Jews got relief from their enemies, and as the month that had been turned for them from sorrow into gladness and from mourning into a holiday" (9:22). In terms of the storyline of the Old Testament, the books of Daniel and Esther both recount the endurance and survival of the Jewish people during the time of the exile.

Remembering the Return from Exile (Ezra–Nehemiah)

The Ezra–Nehemiah narrative tells the story of Israel's winding road back from exile and covers about a century of time (from around 539 to 433 BC). The decree of Cyrus, king of Persia, allows a large group of exiles led by Zerubbabel (the civic leader) and Joshua the priest (the religious leader) to return to the land of Israel. The book of Ezra opens by emphasizing that the return from exile occurred so that "the word of the Lord by the mouth of Jeremiah might be fulfilled" (Ezra 1:1). The Lord, the author insists, "stirred up the spirit of Cyrus king of Persia, so that he made a proclamation throughout all his kingdom and also put it in writing" (1:1). Thus, this last stretch of narrative in the Old Testament begins with the confident assertion that what has taken place fulfills prophecy due to the work of God's providential Spirit.

The beginning of Ezra includes the decree of Cyrus as a historical summary of what is about to happen and also as an indication that God's prophetic word is being fulfilled through this written document. Cyrus decrees:

The Lord, the God of heaven, has given me all the kingdoms of the earth, and he has charged me to build him a house at Jerusalem, which is in Judah. Whoever is among you of

---

8. The threat to the Jewish people is highlighted by the author ("as they had made known to him the people of Mordecai, Haman sought to destroy all the Jews, the people of Mordecai, throughout the whole kingdom of Ahasuerus," Esther 3:6) and by Haman himself ("There is a certain people scattered abroad and dispersed among the peoples in all the provinces of your kingdom. Their laws are different from those of every other people, and they do not keep the king's laws, so that it is not to the king's profit to tolerate them. If it please the king, let it be decreed that they be destroyed," 3:8–9).

9. Haman is identified by the author as "Haman the Agagite" several times (see Esther 3:10; 8:3; 8:5; 9:24).

10. The references to the Babylonian exile locate Esther within the historical and theological context of the latter part of the story of the Writings. Another feature of the books in the Writings is how they echo portions of the Law and the Prophets. For example, the lineages of Mordecai and Haman respectively connect to the prophetic history. In 1 Samuel 15:1–3, Saul fails to destroy Agag, king of the Amalekites, against the command of the Lord. The conflict between the Benjaminite king Saul and Agag parallels the conflict between the Benjaminite Mordecai and Haman the Agagite.

all his people, may his God be with him, and let him go up to Jerusalem, which is in Judah, and rebuild the house of the Lord, the God of Israel—he is the God who is in Jerusalem. And let each survivor, in whatever place he sojourns, be assisted by the men of his place with silver and gold, with goods and with beasts, besides freewill offerings for the house of God that is in Jerusalem (Ezra 1:2–4).

After recording this decree, Ezra recounts the actual return from Babylon. First, Ezra 1–6 describes the restoration of the Jerusalem temple. While local adversaries initially oppose the rebuilding project, the prophets Haggai and Zechariah come and encourage the people to continue (5:1–2) and they finally finish the temple and observe the Passover in the land (6:19–22). Once the temple is restored, next it is the people who require restoration (Ezra 7–10). The scribe Ezra leads another group of exiles to Jerusalem from Babylon and seeks to reform the people. He exhorts the people with the Law of Moses (7:6–10) and helps them establish worship in the temple and observe the Law (Ezra 8). Ezra then confronts the pervasive problem of intermarriage with the local non-Jewish peoples before leading the Jews in confession and reconciliation with God (Ezra 9–10).

After Ezra's religious reforms, the walls of Jerusalem now need restoration. The Jewish official Nehemiah arrives in Jerusalem with another group of exiles to rebuild the city fortifications (Neh. 1–2). Like with the reconstruction of the temple, local adversaries again oppose this rebuilding project, but Nehemiah encourages the people to keep working (chapters 3–7). Once the walls are rebuilt, the people again require restoration. Ezra and Nehemiah lead the Jews in the public reading of the Law of Moses, corporate repentance, and a communal commitment to the covenant (chapters 8–10). The people resettle Jerusalem and the surrounding land (chapter 11), the wall is dedicated and worship in the temple is organized (chapter 12), and there is great joy among the people.

It was the best of times, once again.

However, as time passes the people systematically neglect each of the recently restored religious practices: the purity of the temple worship is compromised (Neh. 13:4–9), the support of the priesthood through tithes diminishes (13:10–14), and the people fail to observe the Sabbath (13:15–22) and again engage in mixed marriages with the surrounding nations (13:23–30). The patterns of covenant disloyalty that resulted in the exile surface again even after the return from Babylon. The people returned to the land, but they brought back their heart problem with them as well. The prophetic fervor witnessed in Ezra 1 fades into the spiritual brokenness of Nehemiah 13. Nehemiah's final words in the book are a cry of desperation and lament (13:31).

It was the worst of times, once again.

Finishing the Story (Chronicles)

The book of Chronicles explores a historical spectrum that goes from Adam (1 Chron. 1:1) to Exile (2 Chron. 36). Positioned in the Writings after Ezra–Nehemiah and at the

conclusion of the entire Hebrew Bible, this narrative is uniquely suited and situated to conclude the storyline of the Hebrew Scriptures. This position allows Chronicles to function
as a kind of narrative commentary on the prophetic history and the nature of future hope
after the return from exile.

What does the author of Chronicles (also known as the Chronicler) choose to focus
on? There are several distinctive features of the story of Chronicles. Its narrative has a clear
concentration on David and his covenant promise with God. This literary and theological
focus on David and the promises of the Davidic covenant helps explain the overarching
purpose of the book.

Accordingly, Chronicles also details how each king maintains the temple and follows
the Law of Moses. Whereas the book of Kings bounces back and forth between the kings of
Israel and Judah, the Chronicler has a laser focus on the kings of Judah and the Southern
Kingdom. Chronicles also offers no extended account of the ministry of the prophets Elijah
and Elisha. One compelling explanation for these omissions is the book's emphasis upon
David, his sons, and the Davidic covenant.

Chronicles starts with a lengthy series of genealogies. This allows the author of Chronicles to situate his story about David and his descendants within the context of world history. From the beginning to the end of Chronicles, the story of David and his promised
seed remains significant by any standard of measurement. Beginning with "the generations
of Adam" (1 Chron. 1:1), 1 Chronicles 1–3 spans the ancient history of Israel, including
the sons of Noah and Abraham, the children of Israel, and then the line of David. Next,
1 Chronicles 4–7 charts the families descended from Israel starting with Judah. The house
of Saul is listed next (1 Chronicles 8), and then the author significantly notes the families
that returned from the exile (9:1–34) before concluding these genealogies with a brief repeat
of Saul's lineage (9:35–44).

What do these genealogical lines achieve? Beginning Chronicles with this genealogy
provides a historical timeline extending from the first human being (Adam) to the return
from exile. As the author summarizes, "so all Israel was recorded in genealogies, and these
are written in the Book of the Kings of Israel." He then recounts the exile, anticipating
where the book's story will end: "Judah was taken into exile in Babylon because of their
breach of faith" (1 Chron. 9:1). Going even further, the author describes the return from
exile and the events reported in the book of Ezra–Nehemiah: "Now the first to dwell again
in their possessions in their cities were Israel, the priests, the Levites, and the temple servants. And some of the people of Judah, Benjamin, Ephraim, and Manasseh lived in Jerusalem" (9:2–3). These comments are very significant because the author will conclude his
story before the return from exile. Why might this be?

After recounting the exile and the postexilic return of the people, the Chronicler
catalogs Saul's lineage again before beginning the narrative in the middle of a raging

battle that ends with the death of Saul (1 Chron. 10).[11] After Saul dies, "all Israel" gathers to anoint David as their king (11:1–3). The Lord says to David, "You shall be shepherd of my people Israel, and you shall be prince over my people Israel" (11:2). The opening of the book and the way it transitions into the narrative sequence implies that the story of the world in general and the story of redemption in particular are intimately connected to David and his line.

The Chronicler not only draws on Israel's history but also on Israel's Scriptures. The way the Hebrew Bible ends echoes the way it begins. The book of Genesis is one of the places in the Old Testament where genealogies play a strategic narrative function. In Genesis 5:1, the author states, "This is the book of the generations of Adam." This genealogy demonstrates the passage of time in redemptive history, but also connects the story of Adam (5:1) to the story of Noah (5:32) within the Pentateuch. This genealogy also helps the reader track the "seed of the woman" mentioned in Genesis 3:15. Genealogies also connect the accounts of Noah and Abraham historically, textually, and theologically (Gen. 10–11). The promise to Abraham is repeated in narratives about his son Isaac and grandson Jacob. Additionally, Jacob's sons are later listed and blessed in a strategic final passage of the book (Gen. 49).

In Genesis, the emphasis on genealogy not only serves as a way to move through history; it is also a way to move through redemptive history. The biblical authors use genealogies to guide readers towards the promises related directly to the seed of the woman, the son of Abraham, and the lion from the tribe of Judah. Accordingly, the textual prominence of these genealogies at the beginning of Chronicles, combined with its subsequent focus on David and the Davidic covenant, makes this book one of the most overtly messianic works in the Hebrew Bible.

---

11. The narrative proper in Chronicles begins "in the middle of things" (*in media res*). The curtains of the story open to reveal the helter-skelter of a desperate retreat following a clear military defeat: "Now the Philistines fought against Israel, and the men of Israel fled before the Philistines and fell slain on Mount Gilboa" (1 Chron. 10:1). The story telescopes quickly as the men of Israel and the sons of Jonathan and Saul fall (10:2) and the Philistines pursue Saul (10:3). The Philistine archers find and wound Saul, and the first bit of dialogue in Chronicles we hear is the king of Israel commanding his armor-bearer to kill him with his sword (10:4). After the armor-bearer refuses from great fear, Saul falls on his own sword and the first summary statement of the book provides a comprehensive and startling obituary of the first anointed king of Israel and the death of his dynasty: "Thus Saul died; he and his three sons and all his house died together" (10:6). It is difficult to think of a more dramatic way to begin a biblical narrative account. The theological obituary that follows is equally devastating: "So Saul died for his breach of faith. He broke faith with the Lord in that he did not keep the command of the Lord, and also consulted a medium, seeking guidance. He did not seek guidance from the Lord" (10:13–14). These are canon-conscious comments that assume knowledge of the narratives of the prophetic history. Further, the next statement strategically transitions from the prophetic history to the laser focus on David that will dominate the rest of the book and bring the reader's perspective back to the horizon of the postexilic story of the Writings: "Therefore the Lord put him to death and turned the kingdom over to David the son of Jesse" (10:14).

In this account of Israel's history, David's reign receives the most textual real estate (1 Chron. 11–29). After Solomon builds the temple, establishes the kingdom, but then falls away at the end of his reign because of his folly (2 Chron. 1–9), the narrative pace quickens considerably. In both David and Solomon's accounts their mistakes are acknowledged, but there is also an emphasis on how each king prefigures aspects of the coming king who will be like them, but will surpass them.[12]

A Tale of Two Covenants (1 Chronicles 16–17)

At an important point in his reign, David seeks to restore the worship of the Lord by bringing the ark of the covenant back to Jerusalem (1 Chron. 16:1–6). Here, David functions as the worship leader of Israel, enabling the people to worship and obey the Lord in the land. While doing this, David offers a psalm of thanks that immediately connects Israel's praise to the participation of the nations in the worship of the Lord: "Oh give thanks to the Lord; call upon his name; make known his deeds among the peoples" (16:8). David's words here anticipate the vision of Isaiah 12: "Give thanks to the Lord, call upon his name, make known his deeds among the peoples, proclaim that his name is exalted" (Isa. 12:4).[13]

This emphasis in David's words regarding the nations connects to God's covenant with Abraham. As David pronounces, "Remember his covenant forever, the word that he commanded, for a thousand generations, the covenant that he made with Abraham, his sworn promise to Isaac, which he confirmed to Jacob as a statute, to Israel as an everlasting covenant" (1 Chron. 16:15–17).[14] This comment is followed by further reflection on the worship of the nations (16:23–34) and salvation from the nations (16:35–36). The connection between the nations and the covenant with Abraham is a natural one, as this covenant includes implications for the nations (Gen. 12:3).

This setting of worship and obedience alongside this reminder of God's covenant with Abraham is the textual and theological context for God's covenant with David in 1 Chronicles 17. In this part of the story, David plans to build a house (temple) for the Lord, but the Lord reveals his plan to build a house (lineage) for David.

---

12. Two of the most striking omissions in David's account are his sin against Bathsheba (2 Sam. 11) and the mention of wrongdoing in God's promise to David regarding his descendant in 1 Chronicles 17 (cf. 2 Sam. 7:14). Because it seems that the author expects readers to be familiar with the book of Kings, the author is not hiding these features of David and Solomon. Rather, he seems to be highlighting those aspects of their reigns that represent what the future "son of David" (messianic king) will be like.
13. In Isaiah 12:3–6 these words are introduced by, "With joy you will draw water from the wells of salvation. And you will say in that day" and are followed by, "Sing praises to the Lord, for he has done gloriously; let this be made known in all the earth. Shout, and sing for joy, O inhabitant of Zion, for great in your midst is the Holy One of Israel."
14. David includes the content of this covenant as, "To you I will give the land of Canaan, as your portion for an inheritance" (16:18).

As the Lord makes this covenant with David, he comments on several key eras in redemptive history. Anticipating the reign and work of Solomon, the Lord says to David (through Nathan the prophet), "It is not you who will build me a house to dwell in" (17:4). The Lord reasons, "For I have not lived in a house since the day I brought up Israel to this day, but I have gone from tent to tent and from dwelling to dwelling. In all places where I have moved with all Israel, did I speak a word with any of the judges of Israel, whom I commanded to shepherd my people, saying, 'Why have you not built me a house of cedar?'" (17:5–6). Here the Lord connects his presence with the people since the exodus from Egypt ("brought up"), the wilderness wanderings ("from tent to tent"), and the time of Joshua and Judges after entering the land ("any of the judges of Israel"). Continuing through the story of the Prophets (the book of Samuel in particular) the Lord comments, "I took you from the pasture, from following the sheep, to be prince over my people Israel" (17:7–8).

The Lord then says to David, "I will make for you a name, like the name of the great ones of the earth. I will appoint a place for my people Israel and will plant them, that they may dwell in their own place and be disturbed no more" (1 Chron. 17:8–9).[15] The Lord specifies, "I declare to you that the Lord will build you a house" (17:10) and promises that when David dies, "I will raise up your offspring after you, one of your own sons, and I will establish his kingdom. He shall build a house for me, and I will establish his throne forever" (17:11–12). Even more significant, the Lord proclaims regarding David's son, "I will be to him a father, and he shall be to me a son. I will not take my steadfast love from him, as I took it from him who was before you, but I will confirm him in my house and in my kingdom forever, and his throne shall be established forever" (17:13–14).

David first responds to this promise with humility: "Who am I, O Lord God, and what is my house, that you have brought me thus far?" (1 Chron. 17:16). David soon transitions, though, to express faith in God's promise: "Now, O Lord, let the word that you have spoken concerning your servant and concerning his house be established forever, and do as you have spoken" (17:23). This response becomes a model for later generations of readers as they encounter the story of David and the promises concerning one of his future descendants.

As mentioned above, in 1 Chronicles 16–17, the promise to David and God's plan for the nation of Israel in particular is closely connected to the promise to Abraham and God's plan for the nations in general. A reader of the story of the Law, the Prophets, and the Writings is positioned to see these historical, literary, and theological threads interwoven

---

15. This comment is followed by another reference to the time of the judges (1 Chron. 17:9–10). Note also the way the covenantal language of planting, putting, and dwelling in relation to God creating a place for his people to live in fellowship with him echoes the Genesis creation narratives: "And the Lord God planted a garden in Eden, in the east, and there he put the man whom he had formed" (Gen. 2:8; cf. 2:15).

through these covenant promises. This particular profile of promises echo throughout the storyline of Scripture: The son of David is coming, and this makes all the difference.

The sequences of victories that David experiences immediately after this covenant is made allow him to defeat the nations surrounding Israel, consolidate the safety of the nation, establish rest, and confirm that he has received the blessings of obedience to the covenant.[16] As the author notes, "the Lord gave victory to David wherever he went" (1 Chron. 18:13).

After Solomon's reign, the folly of Rehoboam causes the division of the kingdom (2 Chron. 11–12). Some of the kings of Judah demonstrate faithfulness to the covenant by guarding the temple or following the requirements of the Law of Moses. These kings receive extended reflection by the author of Chronicles as he associates their reigns with the time of David or even Moses.[17] However, most of the kings of Judah continue the downward descent toward deportation. Here again, the author typically notes these kings did evil in the sight of the Lord and *did not* walk in the ways of their father David.[18] This pattern further confirms that part of the author's purpose in this story as a whole is to connect the hope of future godly leadership to the promises of the Davidic covenant.

The Gospel according to Chronicles: A Story of Despair, A Story of Hope

The final moments of Chronicles draw together these strands of theological interpretation and conclude the story of the Writings. As the Chronicler summarizes, "The Lord, the God of their fathers, sent persistently to them by his messengers, because he had compassion on his people and on his dwelling place. But they kept mocking the messengers of God, despising his words and scoffing at his prophets, until the wrath of the Lord rose against his people, until there was no remedy" (2 Chron. 36:15–16). The author then recounts the Babylonian exile, the rise of Persia, and the decree of the Persian king Cyrus that allows Israel to return to the land (36:20–23).[19] Whereas Ezra–Nehemiah includes the entire decree and recalls the details of the return, the Chronicler does something unique and quite dramatic. At the beginning of Chronicles, we hear of a time after Cyrus's decree (1 Chron.

---

16. These nations include the Philistines (1 Chron. 18:1), Moabites (18:2), Arameans (18:3–11), Edomites (18:12–13), and Ammonites (19:1–20:3).

17. For example, the Chronicler devotes extended time to Jehoshaphat and notes that "The Lord was with Jehoshaphat, because he walked in the earlier ways of his father David" (2 Chron. 17:3; 20:32; Cf. 34:1–3, 14; 35:18, 24–27).

18. For example, the Chronicler notes that Jehoram, the son of Jehoshaphat "did what was evil in the sight of the Lord" because he walked not in the way of David but "walked in the way of the kings of Israel, as the house of Ahab had done" (2 Chron. 21:6). The Chronicler also notes, though, that "the Lord was not willing to destroy the house of David, because of the covenant that he had made with David, since he had promised to give a lamp to him and to his sons forever" (21:7).

19. See 2 Chronicles 36:20–21: "He took into exile in Babylon those who had escaped from the sword, and they became servants to him and to his sons until the establishment of the kingdom of Persia, to fulfill the word of the Lord by the mouth of Jeremiah, until the land had enjoyed its Sabbaths. All the days that it lay desolate it kept Sabbath, to fulfill seventy years." The Chronicler's mention of Jeremiah's prophecy also connects the narrative of Chronicles to the discussion of this prophetic text in the book of Ezra–Nehemiah (Ezra 1) and the book of Daniel (Dan. 9).

9:1–3). But here, at the end of the book, the author stops short of recounting the return from exile. In fact, the story ends halfway through Cyrus's decree that captive Israel may return to the land to rebuild the temple. The last words of the story of the Writings thus ring out with messianic urgency: "Whoever is among you of all his people, may the Lord his God be with him. Let him go up" (2 Chron. 36:23).

As noted earlier, a full version of Cyrus's decree is provided in Ezra 1, including the sentence the Chronicler works from here: "Whoever is among you of all his people, may his God be with him, and let him go up to Jerusalem, which is in Judah, and rebuild the house of the Lord, the God of Israel—he is the God who is in Jerusalem" (Ezra 1:1). In a striking literary move, the Chronicler begins his narrative "in the middle of things" (i.e., the battle at Mt. Gilboa in 1 Chron. 10:1) and ends his narrative "in the middle of things" (i.e., halfway through an official decree in 2 Chron. 36:23). These subtle features give his story a feeling of urgency and a sense of being part of a larger story from beginning to end. The narrative of Chronicles simultaneously feels complete while pointing beyond itself in both directions. *On its own terms*, in other words, the narrative asks not to be read *on its own*.

As a result of his strategy of selection, the Chronicler provides a tightly focused look back to David. However, it is important to note that this emphasis on David within the context of the Writings is not simply a historically informative account. Rather, at this point in Israel's history and within this section of Israel's Scriptures, this look back to David also serves as a way to *look forward* to the *son of David* who is to come. David is dead and gone. Exile has come (Lamentations). The people have survived the exile (Esther and Daniel) and have returned to the land, but the patterns of disobedience that afflicted them before the exile resurface even after their return (Ezra–Nehemiah).

As noted in Ezra–Nehemiah, the return from exile was not as glorious as the people hoped it would be. By the end of both Ezra and Nehemiah, the people still incline toward sinful word and deed. This disappointing situation perhaps prompted the theologically loaded question, "Was the return from exile in Ezra–Nehemiah the fulfillment of the prophetic messianic promises?" By shaping his book in this way and ending it where he does, the Chronicler answers, "Not Yet!" Indeed, by its literary and theological focus on David and the promise of a coming son of David, Chronicles seems to hold out a measure of hope that one is still coming who will not only bring the people back to their land, but will also transform the people's hearts.

The call to rebuild the temple at the end of Chronicles can be heard as a note of messianic expectation: Perhaps the good king of Israel who will crush the head of the serpent, deal with the heart problem of the people, and lead them in worship and obedience to the Lord will one day arrive in Jerusalem.

Chronicles leaves us looking for a son of David who will fulfill these promises and fill out this prophetic vision about God's eternal king and God's eternal kingdom.

Keeping an Eye on the Storyline and the Promised Line

As we noted above, the shape of the Writings is unique as it contains a rich diversity of genres and theological themes. However, we also see how Esther, Daniel, Ezra–Nehemiah, and Chronicles together provide a narrative sequence that dramatically concludes the storyline of the Old Testament as a whole. Each of these books reflect upon the purposes of God in redemptive history as Israel experiences judgment and then returns from exile.

Within the Writings, the story of the Law and the Prophets provides an orienting focus. Many of the most prominent biblical-theological themes in the Writings expand upon or articulate the implications of ancient covenantal promises. As the Law and the Prophets narrate and interpret the exodus from Egypt and the Mosaic covenant, the Writings narrate and interpret the Babylonian exile and postexilic return to Israel. The Writings thus pick up where the prophetic history left off and continue to develop the biblical-theological themes of God's faithfulness, the people's unfaithfulness, the blessing of the covenant, the reality of judgment, and the hope of salvation centered on a coming messiah. In this way, the story of the Law, the Prophets, and the Writings as a whole witness to God's person and work on their own terms and also prepare readers for the continuation of the grand storyline of the Bible in the Gospels.

Discussion Questions

1. As you consider the story of the Writings, what elements of the biblical-theological framework of the canon, the covenants, and the Christ do you see developed?

2. Reflect on the way that the concept of "exile" functions in these books. How is it treated in Lamentations, Esther, Daniel, Ezra–Nehemiah, and Chronicles?

3. In what ways is Chronicles a fitting conclusion to the Old Testament as a whole?

4. List and describe some of the biblical-theological themes that the narrative books of the Writings develop. How do these themes relate to the non-narrative books in the Writings?

5. What are some of the connections that the narrative books in the Writings make to the narrative books of the Law and the Prophets?

Resources for Further Study

Lau, Peter H. W. and Greg Goswell, *Unceasing Kindness: A Biblical Theology of Ruth*. Downers Grove: InterVarsity, 2016.

Sailhamer, John. *First and Second Chronicles*. Chicago: Moody, 1983.

Shepherd, Michael B. *Daniel in the Context of the Hebrew Bible*. New York: Peter Lang, 2009.

Steinberg, Julius and Timothy J. Stone, eds. *The Shape of the Writings*. Winona Lake: Eisenbrauns, 2015.

Webb, Barry G. *Five Festal Garments: Christian Reflections on The Song of Songs, Ruth, Lamentations, Ecclesiastes and Esther*. Downers Grove: InterVarsity, 2000.

CHAPTER 8

THE STORY OF THE GOSPELS

The Shape of the Gospels

THE NEW TESTAMENT BEGINS with the story of Jesus. In dramatic fashion, the Gospel writers identify Jesus and then narrate his life, ministry, and death. Readers are immediately forced to reckon alongside various characters in these narratives with the question, "Who is this man?"

As mentioned in chapter two, the Gospels were composed, quickly gathered together, and circulated as a fourfold grouping. The most well-established order of these four books is Matthew–Mark–Luke–John, although a few later manuscript groupings order them Matthew–John–Luke–Mark, perhaps to keep Matthew and John together at the front as apostles and Luke and Mark afterwards as "servants of the word" (cf. Luke 1:2). Collectively, these four books shape the way the story and identity of Jesus the Messiah is understood.

As the first major part of the New Testament, the fourfold Gospel collection represents both a continuation of the story of redemptive history as well as a story of new beginnings. Mark announces the "beginning of the gospel of Jesus Christ" (Mark 1:1). Luke compiles his account of "the things accomplished among us" by drawing on "those who from the beginning were eyewitnesses and servants of the word" (Luke 1:2). Reaching back to eternity past, John reveals what took place "in the beginning" (John 1:1). As the Gospel writers present and interpret Jesus as the Messiah, they intentionally situate their accounts in line with the contours of the Old Testament. Indeed, "without the Old Testament the New Testament is simply a brute fact appearing as it were out of nowhere, a climax without a plot."[1]

---

1. Dempster, "Canon and Old Testament Interpretation," 160. Dempster also adds here, "Likewise, without the New Testament the Old Testament is a plot without a climax."

Even in the way they shape their narratives, the Gospel writers exhibit canon-consciousness regarding their location in the narrative world generated by the shape of Old Testament texts. In this sense, the Gospels are "like theologies of the Hebrew Scriptures in story form."[2] As multifaceted and introductory narratives firmly grounded in a well-established textual plotline, the Gospels are uniquely suited and well-situated to be the first word readers experience as they open the New Testament collection.[3]

The Story of the Gospels

The story of the Gospels is at once an easy yet also challenging part of the grand storyline of the Bible to tell. Initially, we can observe that the story of the Gospels is relatively straightforward and simple. This part of the story describes and interprets the birth, life, ministry, death, resurrection, and ascension of Jesus the Christ. While the Gospels cover the span of a single generation and focus upon a single person, the burden of the entire biblical storyline is designed to help readers see how this is the very moment the story reaches its apex. Accordingly, the events of the life of Jesus can be summarized and narrated relatively quickly. Their significance and theological depth, though, require careful and extended reflection.

When Peter preaches the gospel message to those gathered at the house of Cornelius in Acts 10, he outlines the essential story of the Gospels. As he tells them, "You yourselves know what happened throughout all Judea, beginning from Galilee after the baptism that John proclaimed: how God anointed Jesus of Nazareth with the Holy Spirit and with power" (Acts 10:37–38). He then summarizes Jesus's ministry: "He went about doing good and healing all who were oppressed by the devil, for God was with him. And we are witnesses of all that he did both in the country of the Jews and in Jerusalem" (10:38–39). Peter next connects their ministry to Jesus's death, resurrection, and commission of the disciples to preach the gospel: "They put him to death by hanging him on a tree, but God raised him on the third day and made him to appear, not to all the people but to us who had been chosen by God as witnesses, who ate and drank with him after he rose from the dead" (10:39–40). Peter concludes this summary by noting that Jesus commanded the apostles to preach and

---

2. Shepherd, *Textual World*, 83.
3. For an extended discussion of the canonical shape of the Gospels as well as key features of these narratives from a variety of angles, see Francis Watson, *The Fourfold Gospel: A Theological Reading of the New Testament Portraits of Jesus* (Grand Rapids: Eerdmans, 2016); Richard B. Hays, *Echoes of Scripture in the Gospels* (Waco: Baylor, 2016); Jonathan T. Pennington, *Reading the Gospels Wisely: A Narrative and Theological Introduction* (Grand Rapids: Baker, 2012); C. E. Hill, *Who Chose the Gospels? Probing the Great Gospel Conspiracy* (Oxford: Oxford University Press, 2010); Richard Bauckham, ed., *The Gospels for All Christians: Rethinking the Gospel Audiences* (Grand Rapids: Eerdmans, 1998); Brevard Childs, "The One Gospel in Four Witnesses," in *The Rule of Faith: Scripture, Canon, and Creed in a Critical Age*, ed. Ephrain Radner and George Sumner (Harrisburg: Morehouse, 1998), 51–62; and Spellman, *Toward a Canon-Conscious Reading*, 71–80.

testify "that he is the one appointed by God to be judge of the living and the dead" (10:42). "To him," Peter insists, "all the prophets bear witness that everyone who believes in him receives forgiveness of sins through his name" (10:43).

Peter's sermon shares many similarities with the basic shape of the Gospel narratives. Each of the Gospels includes their own account of this basic outline of Jesus's ministry, teaching, death, and resurrection. Although each of the Gospels possesses distinctive features unique to their respective narratives, all four examine the full scope of Jesus's teaching ministry while focusing a large amount of attention and textual detail on the final days of Jesus's life in Jerusalem and the circumstances and immediate effects of his death and resurrection. These textual and theological features make the Gospel narratives complementary in relationship to one another, yet distinct in relationship to other contemporary literature.

The titles associated with these narratives also convey an immediate sense of unity and diversity. There is unity (the *one gospel message*) and also diversity (*according to . . .*). Accordingly, as the New Testament opens and the grand storyline of the Bible continues, so do many of the major biblical-theological themes developed across the canon. The storyline not only slows down at this point; it repeats four times at this exact moment in redemptive history. Within the shape of the canonical collection, in other words, this repetition is unique and communicates that the apex of the storyline is located here. This four-times underlined account of redemption is what makes biblical history *redemptive* history.

Now that we have considered the outline of the events advanced by the story of the Gospels, we can briefly explore some of the ways each book provides a unique vantage point from which to view this all-important moment of redemptive history.

Jesus as the Son of David (Matthew)

"Now the Birth of Jesus Christ Took Place in This Way"

Where does the gospel of Matthew actually begin? In Matthew 1:18, Matthew recounts, "Now the birth of Jesus Christ took place in this way." At this point, Matthew begins the story of how Mary and Joseph discover her pregnancy, how Joseph plans to divorce Mary quietly, the angel of the Lord's message to him, and the eventual birth and naming of Jesus (Matt. 1:18–24). From here, Matthew's narrative continues with the visit of the wise men from the east (2:1–12), the family's escape to Egypt from Herod (2:13–18), and their return to Nazareth years later (2:19–23). The next scenes in the story explore the ministry of John the Baptist and the beginning of Jesus's ministry as John baptizes him in the Jordan River (3:1–17). This account of Jesus's birth and his earliest years with his family are followed by Matthew's lengthy account of Jesus's ministry following his baptism by John. The opening of the actual story, though, does not begin until after an important section that influences how we understand these opening scenes and the story of the Gospels as a whole.

There is no narrative action in the first seventeen verses of Matthew. The narrative proper does not begin until Matt 1:18. In fact, every single word of Matthew 1:1–17 represents an allusive non-narrative element. What, then, is the purpose of this opening section in Matthew 1:1–17? Why is it here?

The Book of the Genealogy of Jesus Christ (Matt. 1:1)

The first words of the Gospel—"The book of the genealogy of Jesus Christ"—signal that Matthew is about to provide an account of Jesus's lineage. This comment prepares the reader for the genealogy that comes in the following verses as well as the brief birth narrative that follows this genealogy. These words also allude to the first genealogy of Genesis 5, which opens with these words: "This is the book of the generations of Adam" (Gen 5:1). As mentioned in our discussion of the story of the Law, one of the functions of the genealogies in Genesis is to focus our attention on the seed of the woman who would one day crush the head of the serpent (Gen. 3:15). As the story of redemptive history continues throughout the Prophets and the Writings, this hope in a coming descendant becomes more prominent and connects to an entire profile of promises about God's future work on behalf of his people.

By characterizing this Gospel narrative as a "book of genealogy," Matthew signals that he is telling a story that has its roots in a garden and a long trajectory of growth from the soil of the Hebrew Scriptures. By calling Jesus the Christ, Matthew also directly associates Jesus with the expectations concerning the Messiah. In other words, Matthew's gospel will be a "book" like many others, but also a book like no one has ever seen before. Each component looks forward and backward. The book of the genealogy anticipates Matthew's forthcoming narrative and echoes the genesis of the biblical storyline. The birth of "Jesus" will be described in the next section of Matthew's narrative; the "Christ" has been described throughout Matthew's Scriptures.

The Son of David, the Son of Abraham

After mentioning Jesus as "the Christ," Matthew expands upon this notion by identifying Jesus as "the son of David, the son of Abraham" (Matt. 1:1). These references are not simply historical observations, but textual and theological ones as well. The reason Matthew mentions the *son* of David and *son* of Abraham is because he is referring to the Davidic and Abrahamic covenants. The allusion to the Genesis 5 genealogy already emphasizes a coming descendant, and now Matthew connects two other prominent Old Testament promises that relate to this coming descendant. These references are also out of chronological order, mostly likely because the Davidic covenant helps explain the meaning of the title, "Christ."

The covenantal overtones of these few phrases in the opening sentence of the New Testament are explosive and majestic. The first words encountered by readers of the New

Testament point to its narratives whose main focus is the "seed of the woman," the "seed of Abraham," and the "seed of David." These phrases call up entire narrative storylines that narrate and interpret the covenant promises God makes with Abraham and David. Telling the story of Jesus thus requires telling the story of the covenants.

Abraham to David to the Exile to the Christ (Matt. 1:2–17)

After this orienting first line, Matthew provides a brief, structured genealogy in 1:2–17. This genealogy moves first from Abraham to David (1:2–6), then from David to the exile (1:7–11), and finally from the exile to Jesus (1:12–16).

The way this genealogy is structured emphasizes both David and the exile. After the mention of "son of David" in 1:1, the kingship of David is stressed at his first mention in the list: "Jesse the father of David the king" (1:6). Jechoniah and his brothers are also mentioned as those who were present "at the time of the deportation to Babylon" (1:11). Accordingly, the next sequence begins with the comment, "And after the deportation to Babylon" (1:12). After Matthew's genealogy ends with "Joseph the husband of Mary, of whom Jesus was born, who is called Christ" (1:16), he provides a statement that summarizes the generations listed and again highlights David and the exile: "So all the generations from Abraham to David were fourteen generations, and from David to the deportation to Babylon fourteen generations, and from the deportation to Babylon to the Christ fourteen generations" (1:17).

This genealogy at the beginning of Matthew functions as a structural echo of the opening of Chronicles. The book of Chronicles is the only other biblical work where a genealogy features so prominently at its beginning.[4] This structural parallel to Chronicles introduces the notions of exile, return from exile, and the hope of a coming "son of David" into the beginning of Matthew's narrative. By using the phrase, "book of the genealogies," in Matthew 1:1, Matthew alludes to the *first* book of the Hebrew Bible. By including a wide-ranging genealogy that emphasizes the role of David and the exile as an opening section, Matthew alludes to one of the *last* books of the Hebrew Bible. This genealogy, then, not only references Israel's *historical* past, but also communicates a network of *textual* and *theological* connections with the story of the Law, the Prophets, and the Writings.

By beginning his gospel in this intentionally intertextual fashion, Matthew implies that the proper context within which to read his message about Jesus is the Hebrew Bible as a whole. Taking seriously the possibility that Matt 1:1 ("book of the genealogies") and 1:2–17 (genealogy and exile) refer not only to historical realities but also textual entities, we can say that Matthew gives his readers a canon-conscious summary of the entire Hebrew Bible. If asked how much of the Hebrew Bible is necessary to understand the story of Jesus, Matthew

---

4. Genealogies feature prominently in Genesis which is referenced in Matthew 1:1. A genealogy serves a strategic function at the *end* of the book of Ruth as well (mentioning Perez and ending with David).

here responds, "All of it!" Matthew not only urges his readers to remember biblical history, but also to read biblical texts.

The hope of redemptive history and the promises of the covenant story are wrapped up in the one who is called by these names and is from this line of descent. This story of redemptive history is a story of both despair and hope. By bringing up the history of Israel, the specter of exile thus looms large over the opening of the gospel of Matthew. In many ways, this is a dark and somber way to begin a story of "good news." Matthew provides a structured reminder of the long and winding road from the generations of Adam to the story of Abraham, from the life of David to the disaster of exile, from the return from Babylon to the lingering failure of the Mosaic covenant to deal with the heart problem of the people. Israel's greatest enemy is still undefeated as the curtain rises on story of the New Testament.

With the darkness of this past, we are able to see the brightness of the angel of the Lord's words: "Joseph, son of David, do not fear to take Mary as your wife, for that which is conceived in her is from the Holy Spirit. She will bear a son, and you shall call his name Jesus, *for he will save his people from their sins*" (Matt. 1:20–21). The presence of this son of David will mean the presence of God himself (i.e., Immanuel, "God with us," 1:23). The forgiveness of sins is a characteristic feature of the blessings of the new covenant (Matt. 26:28; Jer. 31:31–34). After this reminder of the exile and the failure of the old covenant, the announcement of the arrival of the forgiveness of sins with the coming of Jesus is good news indeed.

Later in the narrative, John the Baptist sends word to Jesus from prison asking, "Are you the one who is to come, or shall we look for another?" (Matt. 11:3). The Chronicler had put each successive heir to the Davidic throne before the eyes of the reader and essentially asked, "Are you the one or should we look for another?" The book of Chronicles answers this query for the reader: No, they were not the ones, and you *should* look for another ("let him go up!" 2 Chron. 36:23). By beginning in the way that he does, Matthew takes up the Chronicler's question and answers firmly, "Look no further, the son of David we have been looking for walks among us."[5]

---

5. After the concentrated emphasis on Jesus as the "son of David" in Matthew 1, the other location in the book where there is repeated use of this title is when Jesus enters Jerusalem (21:1–17). The way Matthew uses Psalm 22 to inform his portrayal of the crucifixion scene in Matthew 27 is also significant here. Further, during Jesus's ministry, several people come up to him, cry out to him for healing, appeal to his mercy, and identify him as the son of David (e.g., 9:27; 12:23; 15:22; 20:30–31). Thus, Jesus as the "son of David" shows up at strategic thematic and structural locations throughout Matthew's narrative. Note also Jesus's comments in Matthew 12:42 (in a discussion about "signs"): "The queen of the South will rise up at the judgment with this generation and condemn it, for she came from the ends of the earth to hear the wisdom of Solomon, and behold, something greater than Solomon is here."

Jesus as the Son of God (Mark)

Mark's Gospel is the shortest within the four Gospel collection. One of the distinctive aspects of Mark is its geographical structure that follows Jesus as he teaches and minsters to the crowds and the disciples. After Jesus's baptism and temptation in the wilderness (Mark 1:1–13), he teaches and ministers around the area of Galilee (Mark 1–8). After Peter's confession that Jesus is the Christ near Caesarea Philippi (8:27–30), Jesus begins teaching his disciples more directly about his impending death (8:31–33). Jesus then travels toward Jerusalem while he continues his teaching ministry (Mark 9–10) and, after his initial entry into the city, the remainder of the Gospel narrative takes place in Jerusalem during the final week of Jesus's life (Mark 11–16).

In a sense, Mark is a fast-paced Gospel of "action." It does not include many elements mentioned by the other Gospel narratives, and one of its key transitional words is the adverb "immediately."[6] However, it is important to note that Mark's breakneck pace is intentional and his condensed selection of narrative material generates some unique theological and literary effects. On a large scale, the basic structure of Mark allows us to see a connection between the preaching of Peter and the apostles.[7] Further, in this brief narrative considerable textual space is devoted to the final week in Jerusalem. This emphasis on the cross and the significance of Christ's death is stressed by Mark's compositional shape. On a small scale, there are also places where Mark speeds up and slows down the narrative pace. For example, Mark quickly summarizes the baptism and temptation of Jesus in 1:9–13, but then provides a detailed account of a single day in Jesus's life of ministry in 1:16–45. This textual feature provides a dynamic reading experience, but also allows readers to understand all of the individual activities of Jesus's ministry (a "day in the life") in light of the theological meaning of his baptism and temptation (e.g., "this is my beloved son").[8]

A further aspect that Mark develops through his narrative pacing is his focus on Jesus's identity. In several strategic places, individuals directly ask about the identity of Jesus. After Jesus rebukes an unclean spirit, the people say, "What is this? A new teaching with authority! He commands even the unclean spirits and they obey him" (1:27). Mark notes that "at once his fame spread everywhere throughout all the surrounding region of Galilee" (1:28). After Jesus forgives a man's sins, a group of scribes wonder, "Why does this man speak like that? . . . Who can forgive sins but God alone?" (2:7). After Jesus calms the storm, the disciples fear greatly and say to one another, "Who then is this, that even the wind and

---

6. The word "immediately" transitions many narrative scenes in Mark's narrative. See, for example, 1:10, 12, 18, 20, 21, 23, 29, 30, and 42.
7. For instance, see the outline of Peter's summary of Jesus's preaching ministry in his sermon in Acts 10:36–43.
8. Two extended discourse sections in Mark include the series of parables in 4:1–34 and the speech about the end of days in 13:1–37. Both of these sections also exhibit a future-looking orientation (i.e., the coming kingdom).

the sea obey him?" (4:41).[9] Mark's fast-paced narrative, thus, allows this particular question about the identity of Jesus to linger throughout the story: This Jesus, whose son is he?

Mark opens his book with a remarkably straightforward declaration about its contents and the identity of Jesus: "The beginning of the gospel of Jesus Christ, the Son of God" (Mark 1:1). The beginning, middle, and end of the gospel of Mark all directly reiterate this confession of Jesus as the Son of God. Several verses later, while John baptizes Jesus a voice from heaven declares, "You are my beloved Son; with you I am well pleased" (1:11). Significantly, these words proclaimed by the Father are an intertextual allusion to Psalm 2. So, very quickly in the opening scenes of the narrative, Mark connects the confession of Jesus as the Son of God to the messianic promises of a coming one from Psalm 2.[10]

Toward the middle of the narrative, Mark recounts the transfiguration of Jesus on the mountain (9:2–13). At this point, the disciples again hear a voice from heaven say, "This is my beloved Son; listen to him" (9:7). Finally, at the end of the Gospel, after the crucified Jesus "uttered a loud cry and breathed his last," Mark recalls that "when the centurion, who stood facing him, saw that in this way he breathed his last, he said, 'Truly this man was the Son of God!'" (15:37–39). Here, significantly, the confession of Jesus as the son of God is expressly associated with his death on the cross. In fact, Mark takes care to specify that the Gentile centurion stands facing Jesus on the cross when he makes his statement ("who stood facing him").

In Mark's Gospel, Mark himself at the beginning of the narrative, God the Father at the baptism and transfiguration of Jesus, and a Roman centurion at the foot of the cross make the direct confession that Jesus is the Son of God. This clear emphasis on the identity of Jesus alongside a presentation of his words and actions forces a reader of Mark's narrative to consider the questions raised throughout the story in a direct way. Who is this man? How will you respond?

The Journey toward Jerusalem (Luke)

The gospel of Luke is the longest of the four Gospels and most comprehensive in scope. Luke begins with the birth narratives of Jesus and John the Baptist (Luke 1–2) and ends with the ascension of the resurrected Jesus into heaven (Luke 24). One of the key structural features of Luke's gospel is his clear narrative focus on the final journey to Jerusalem (9:51–19:28). While each of the Gospels describe this event, Luke uses the journey to Jerusalem as a geographical, textual, and theological framework for Jesus's teachings about the

---

9. Further, when Jesus returns to his hometown, the people say, "Where did this man get these things? What is this wisdom given to him?" They take offense at him, reasoning, "Is not this the carpenter, the son of Mary and brother of James and Joses and Judas and Simon? And are not his sisters here with us?" (6:2–3). Note, too, how the following discussion of John the Baptist relates directly to the identity of Jesus (6:14–20).
10. See Psalm 2:7–9: "I will tell of the decree: The Lord said to me, 'You are my Son; today I have begotten you. Ask of me, and I will make the nations your heritage, and the ends of the earth your possession. You shall break them with a rod of iron and dash them in pieces like a potter's vessel.'"

significance of his death and resurrection, the task of discipleship, and the future work of God that will endure among his disciples as they continue to walk this path.

The journey begins in Luke 9. In the transfiguration account in Luke 9:28–36, when Moses and Elijah appear and speak to Jesus, they talk "of his departure, which he was about to accomplish at Jerusalem" (9:31). On the next day, after healing a boy, Jesus anticipates his impending death: "Let these words sink into your ears: The Son of Man is about to be delivered into the hands of men" (9:45). Luke notes later that "When the days drew near for him to be taken up, he set his face to go to Jerusalem" (9:51). Luke mentions that the Samaritans did not receive Jesus and his disciples because they knew that "his face was set toward Jerusalem" (9:53).

From this point onward, Luke consistently draws attention to the fact that Jesus is "on the way" or "on the road" toward Jerusalem.[11] Many of the discussions about the cost and nature of discipleship in Luke's gospel occur in this section of the narrative as Jesus journeys toward Jerusalem.[12] Toward the beginning of this final trip, Luke recounts a series of exchanges that highlight what it takes to follow Jesus. "As they were going along the road," someone comes up to Jesus and declares, "I will follow you wherever you go" (9:57). Jesus responds by saying, "Foxes have holes, and birds of the air have nests, but the Son of Man has nowhere to lay his head" (9:58). Jesus calls others to join him on this path of discipleship. He tells someone on the path, "Follow me," but this person responds, "Lord, let me first go and bury my father" (9:59). Jesus reorients his focus, saying, "Leave the dead to bury their own dead. But as for you, go and proclaim the Kingdom of God" (9:60). After a similar exchange, Jesus emphasizes again, "No one who puts his hand to the plow and looks back is fit for the kingdom of God" (9:62). This series of exchanges at the beginning of the journey to Jerusalem capture the themes that Jesus will develop and reiterate as he continues along this path.

As the narrative progresses, Jesus continues his ministry but does so with a relentless focus on the destination of his journey. As Luke notes, "He went on his way through towns and villages, teaching and journeying toward Jerusalem" (13:22).[13] Jesus even laments over Jerusalem, saying, "O Jerusalem, Jerusalem, the city that kills the prophets and stones those who are sent to it! How often would I have gathered your children together as a hen gathers her brood under her wings, and you were not willing! Behold, your house is forsaken. And I tell you, you will not see me until you say, 'Blessed is he who comes in the name of the Lord!'" (13:34–35).

---

11. See Luke 9:57 ("As they were going along the road"); 10:38 ("Now as they went on their way"); 17:11 ("On the way to Jerusalem he was passing along between Samaria and Galilee"); 19:11 ("As they heard these things, he proceeded to tell a parable, because he was near to Jerusalem").

12. Many parables unique to Luke are also found within this section (e.g., the parable of the lost sheep, the lost coin, and the lost son in Luke 15).

13. Note that the disciples are sent away and return from their mission while the journey to Jerusalem is still ongoing (Luke 10:1–24).

When Jesus finally arrives at Jerusalem, he weeps over the city (19:41). He then proclaims a word of prophetic judgment, saying, "Would that you, even you, had known on this day the things that make for peace! But now they are hidden from your eyes. For the days will come upon you, when your enemies will set up a barricade around you and surround you and hem you in on every side and tear you down to the ground, you and your children within you. And they will not leave one stone upon another in you, because you did not know the time of your visitation" (19:42–44). Upon entering Jerusalem, Jesus continues to teach and preach the gospel, warn of coming judgment, and call the people to repent, arguing that the kingdom of God is near (Luke 20–22). Jesus is then arrested, put on trial, crucified, and buried (Luke 23–24). Luke's textual and theological focus on the journey toward Jerusalem magnifies Jesus's teaching about his own death and resurrection in a unique way.

The journey *toward* Jerusalem in Luke's gospel is echoed after the resurrection in the journey *away* from Jerusalem on the road to Emmaus (Luke 24:13–35).[14] Just as the journey toward Jerusalem emphasizes the meaning of Jesus's coming death, the journey away from Jerusalem emphasizes the expansive meaning of Jesus's death and resurrection. As Jesus declares to the two disciples, "Was it not necessary that the Christ should suffer these things and enter into his glory?" (24:26). Like his journey toward Jerusalem, Jesus explains on the road to Emmaus who he is and what he has done in light of the Scriptures. As Luke recounts, "And beginning with Moses and all the Prophets, he interpreted to them in all the Scriptures the things concerning himself" (24:27).[15]

The journey toward Jerusalem and toward the cross in Luke's gospel also anticipates the journey away from Jerusalem in the story of Acts. Jesus himself foreshadows this next movement of redemptive history in his final words to the disciples: "These are my words that I spoke to you while I was still with you, that everything written about me in the Law of Moses and the Prophets and the Psalms must be fulfilled" (Luke 24:44). Luke notes that Jesus then "opened their minds to understand the Scriptures" (24:45). In this remarkable moment, Jesus argues that the story of the Law, the Prophets, and the Writings anticipates and is fulfilled in the story of the Gospels.

What is more, Jesus also here outlines the next part of the storyline for his disciples. As he explains, "Thus it is written, that the Christ should suffer and on the third day rise from the dead, and that repentance for the forgiveness of sins should be proclaimed in his name to all nations, beginning from Jerusalem" (24:46–47). Jesus next anticipates the coming of the Holy Spirit and the opening of the story of Acts: "You are witnesses of these things. And

---

14. Luke sets the scene by noting, "That very day two of them were going to a village named Emmaus, about seven miles from Jerusalem, and they were talking with each other about all these things that had happened" (24:13–14).
15. For a theological and hermeneutical reflection on this passage, see chapter three.

behold, I am sending the promise of my Father upon you. But stay in the city until you are clothed with power from on high" (24:48–49).

The words of the resurrected Christ here shape our understanding of the task of discipleship, the mission of the churches, the nature of the gospel, the Trinitarian character of God's action in the world, and the flow of redemptive history. Part of the reason we are able to see this movement with such clarity is because of the way that Luke has shaped and structured his narrative. He has allowed us as readers to follow along with Jesus as he journeys toward Jerusalem, teaches the disciples about the true nature of discipleship, and speaks of the path to becoming a true disciples.

The Death of the Davidic Shepherd-King (John)

The gospel of John starts by quickly establishing the divine person and work of Jesus. As John writes, "In the beginning was the Word, and the Word was with God, and the Word was God. He was in the beginning with God" (John 1:1–2). John here alludes to the creation narrative of Genesis 1. By doing so, John connects the story of the Gospel to the story of the Law in the most majestic way possible. This story John tells (or rather continues) begins before the foundation of the world. John's biblical-theological prologue prepares for his thickly theological account of the incarnation: "And the Word became flesh and dwelt among us, and we have seen his glory, glory as of the only Son from the Father, full of grace and truth" (John 1:14). As with the other Gospels, following his orienting reflection John refers to "the Word who became flesh" simply as "Jesus" for the rest of his Gospel. The reader must decide what they will make of Jesus.

John articulates his literary purpose along these same lines at the end of his narrative. He writes, "Now Jesus did many other signs in the presence of the disciples, which are not written in this book; but these are written so that you may believe that Jesus is the Christ, the Son of God, and that by believing you may have life in his name" (John 20:30–31). Similar to Matthew's purpose expressed in Matthew 1:1, John here mentions writing a "book" designed to convince readers that Jesus is "the Christ, the Son of God." Although he never uses the Davidic title in the same way Matthew, Mark, and Luke do, John draws on significant Davidic texts and images in his portrayal of Jesus as the messianic King of Israel. In fact, the center of John's presentation of the death of Jesus as the fulfillment of the Scriptures lies in identifying him as the true and better David. Accordingly, one critical component of John's strategy in his Gospel entails demonstrating that Jesus is the Davidic shepherd-king of Israel whose suffering and death fulfills the Scriptures.

In his account of Jesus's crucifixion, John makes clear references to Davidic Old Testament texts and images. In addition to direct citations of the Davidic psalms, John also alludes to two important images: the Davidic king and the Davidic shepherd.

Jesus as the Davidic King

At the beginning of his crucifixion narrative, John portrays Jesus as the Davidic King. In 19:17–22 John highlights the title given to Jesus during his crucifixion. After Jesus carries his cross to Golgotha, he is crucified between two other men (19:17–18). There, Pilate writes an inscription and places it upon the cross that reads, "Jesus of Nazareth, the King of the Jews" (19:19). John notes that many Jews read the inscription because the cross was near the city and the sign was written in three languages (Hebrew, Greek, and Latin). Because the title was so prominent, the chief priests ask Pilate not to write "King of the Jews" since Jesus had only claimed that, "I am the King of the Jews" (19:21).[16] Pilate responds to this inquiry by invoking his perceived final authority: "What I have written I have written" (19:22).[17]

Before the crucifixion, John highlights the conversation that takes place between Jesus and Pilate regarding Jesus's status as king. After the Jews bring their prisoner to him, Pilate questions Jesus's kingship by asking, "Are you the King of the Jews?" (18:33). From this point until the actual crucifixion, John carefully traces the way Pilate consistently raises this issue with the Jews and Jesus himself. In these exchanges, the nature of Jesus's kingdom is outlined. After questioning Pilate's motivation for asking about his kingship (18:34), Jesus reveals that his kingdom is otherworldly. If his kingdom was of this world, his servants would be fighting so that Jesus would not be handed over to the Jews. As it is, his kingdom is "not from the world" (18:36).

Pilate recognizes the significance of Jesus's claims and asks, "So you are a king?" Jesus responds, "You say correctly that I am a king" (18:37, NASB). Alluding to his messianic mission, Jesus conveys that "For this purpose I was born and for this purpose I have come into the world—to bear witness to the truth." (18:37). After hearing this, Pilate again offers the Jews a chance to release their "king" (18:39). Rather than release their "lawful" king, the Jews choose to free the robber Barabbas. In a scene fraught with irony, the soldiers then scourge and mock their Jewish prisoner. Because of Jesus's alleged royalty, the soldiers twist together a crown of thorns and give him a purple robe, sarcastically hailing him as "King of the Jews!" (19:3).[18] Rather than bowing before him, they bring him blows.

After the Jews insist that Pilate execute this man, Pilate engages Jesus in further dialogue. Though Pilate positions himself as the superior ruler, Jesus undermines Pilate's authority and asserts his own. When Jesus does not answer the governor's question regarding where he is from, Pilate stresses his power: "Do you not know that I have authority to release you and authority to crucify you?" (19:10). Jesus reverses his logic by asserting that Pilate

---

16. By drawing out this discourse, John allows for emphatic repetition of the title, "King of the Jews."

17. Pilate's confident statement is ironic in light of Jesus's denial of Pilate's authority in 19:11 and John's assertion that the judicial process facilitated by Pilate actually fulfills Scripture "written" long before (cf. Acts 4:27–28).

18. These words highlight the irony of the scene, as the soldiers pronounce in derision what should be on the lips of the Jews in devotion.

"would have no authority" over him unless it had been given from above (19:11). Pilate responds by trying again to release him, but the Jews argue that releasing an imposter king would make Pilate no friend of Caesar (19:12). Despite the politically expedient argument of the Jews, John's narrative still focuses on the debate over Jesus's kingship. Sitting down on his "judgment seat," Pilate exclaims "Behold, your King!" and asks once more, "Shall I crucify your King?" The chief priests then solidify their theological treason by answering, "We have no king but Caesar" (19:14–15). Thus, the man identified as the King of the Jews by a pagan Gentile ruler is crucified by his own people. In his account of Jesus before Pilate, John illustrates the way the true king of Israel "came to his own, and his own people did not receive him" (1:10).

There are two other important places in the Gospel where John applies the expectation of a coming king to Jesus. In the account of Jesus calling his disciples in 1:43–51, John highlights the messianic expectation of a coming one foretold in the "Law and also the prophets" (1:45). After Jesus tells Nathaniel that he saw him under the fig tree, Nathaniel exclaims, "Rabbi, you are the Son of God! You are the King of Israel!" (1:49). This reference to the King of Israel clearly demonstrates that a significant aspect of messianic expectation included the anticipation of a coming king.

John revisits this expectation in his account of Jesus's entry into Jerusalem in chapter 12. After Mary anoints him in Bethany, Jesus enters Jerusalem. Hearing of his arrival, a large crowd comes out to meet him armed with palm branches and the words of Psalm 118. They cry out, "Hosanna! Blessed is he who comes in the name of the Lord, even the King of Israel!" (12:13). This declaration of the people connects the words of Psalm 118:26 with expectations concerning the coming King of Israel. In John's account, the "one who comes in the name of the Lord" is the coming king. John immediately follows these words with the detail that Jesus rides upon a young donkey into city. This image parallels the portrayal of the coming king of Israel found in Zechariah 9:9–10. By noting this connection, John identifies Jesus as the king featured in Zechariah's prophecy. John's account here is brief but significant, for it keeps the kingship of Jesus in front of the reader.

Jesus as the Davidic Shepherd
After Jesus is crucified and pierced by the soldier's spear, John notes how this fulfills the Scripture that says, "They will look on him whom they have pierced" (John 19:37). John's reference to Zechariah 12:10 here resonates not only with his earlier emphasis on the Davidic kingship in John 18, but also with his use of Davidic shepherd imagery. The "pierced one" of Zechariah's prophetic vision is associated with both a king and a shepherd. In Zechariah 9, Zechariah describes the Lord saving Israel as "the flock of His people" (9:16). Because of false dreams and vain comfort, the people will "wander like sheep" who are afflicted "because there is no shepherd" (Zech. 10:2). Those shepherding Israel have angered

the Lord of Hosts because they have neglected "his flock, the house of Judah" (10:3). As the good shepherd, the Lord will "whistle" and gather his redeemed sheep, the ones he scattered in order to gather to himself again (10:8–12). Using this shepherd imagery, the Lord directs Zechariah to "pasture the flock doomed to slaughter" (11:4). Zechariah thus represents the Lord as the shepherd of the people, but his guidance is rejected. In a reversal of the imagery of the good shepherd, the Lord then directs Zechariah to embody the "foolish shepherd" who will "not care for the perishing, seek the scattered, heal the broken, or sustain the one standing" (11:15–16). This "worthless shepherd" not only leaves the sheep, but is also incapable of guiding and protecting the flock (11:17).

In this context, the Lord describes to Zechariah a day when Jerusalem will be attacked (Zech. 12:1–5) but will ultimately be delivered by the Lord (12:6–9). On that day, the Lord will set about to "destroy all the nations that come against Jerusalem" (12:9). In the midst of this restoration, the house of David and the people of Jerusalem will mourn their sin and idolatry (12:11–14). Those who speak false prophecies will also grieve and be ashamed of their deceptive visions (13:1–6). Though the people will recognize their depravity, the Lord will nevertheless pour out on them "a Spirit of grace and pleas for mercy" that will enable them to look "on me, on him whom they have pierced" (12:10). They will mourn and bitterly weep over this pierced one "as one mourns for an only child" (12:10). This pierced one resembles the shepherd struck down in Zechariah 13:7. There the Lord declares, "Awake, O sword, against my Shepherd" and orders, "Strike the Shepherd that the sheep may be scattered" (13:7). These words echo the words of Zechariah 10:9–10 and show how they will be accomplished. The Lord will scatter the sheep by striking the shepherd. This event will cause them to call on his name, and he will answer them (13:9). Thus, though the shepherd is struck down and the sheep scatter, the Lord will enable the people to "look on him" with mourning and repentance, resulting in their eventual and ultimate redemption.[19]

In a broad sense, the shepherd imagery utilized in Zechariah 9–13 resonates with John's narrative. In John 10:1–30, John gives sustained attention to Jesus's teaching that he is the good shepherd. In the first part of the chapter, Jesus outlines how a shepherd protects his sheep from strangers, thieves, and robbers. In this "figure of speech" (John 10:6), the contrast between the shepherd and other people is striking. The sheep follow only the voice of the shepherd, and only the shepherd knows them and guides them to safety (10:3–4). After painting this pastoral scene, Jesus makes direct use of this imagery. He asserts that he is "the door of the sheep" (10:7) in that those who enter through him will be saved (10:9). The sheep will find rest and shelter in him as they go in and out to find pasture. Carrying the metaphor further, Jesus states he is not only the door of the sheep, but also the guardian of that door.

---

19. Ultimate redemption is implied in 13:9: "I will say, 'They are my people,' And they will say, 'The Lord is my God.'" This is the language of covenant promises.

Bringing this metaphor to a climax, Jesus declares, "I am the good shepherd" (10:11). He then expounds his role as that figure. The good shepherd lays down his life "for the sheep" (10:11). Rather than fleeing at the sight of danger like a hired hand (10:12–13), the "good shepherd" is concerned about his sheep and says, "I know my own and my own know me" (10:14). This good shepherd knows and is known by the Father (10:15). Because the shepherd lays down his life and takes it up again for the sake of the sheep, the Father loves him (10:17). The shepherd also has the task of bringing in the "other sheep" who are "not of this fold." The goal of the shepherd's mission is to form "one flock" that has "one shepherd" (10:16).

John confirms the messianic nature of this shepherd imagery in 10:22–30. After Jesus's words incur a division among the Jews (10:19–21), they gather around Jesus and ask, "How long will you keep us in suspense? If you are the Christ, tell us plainly" (10:24). Jesus responds, "I told you, and you did not believe" (10:25). To explain this unbelief, Jesus again casts himself as the shepherd. The Jews did not believe because they were not of his sheep. The sheep hear his voice, he knows them, and they follow him (10:27). The sheep are given to him by the Father and are eternally secure in the shepherd's hand (10:28–30). Thus, Jesus responds to the question concerning the identity of the Christ by essentially reasserting that he is the good shepherd. Jesus implies that when he told the Jews that he was the good shepherd, he was in fact telling them he was the Christ. The reason why Jesus's logic makes sense is because shepherd imagery is part of the messianic tapestry developed in the prophets of the Hebrew Bible.[20]

Thus, when Jesus speaks of himself as the good shepherd, he draws upon a strong messianic image from the Old Testament. A close reader of the Hebrew Bible will note that Jesus's quotation of Zechariah 12:10 upon the cross in John's gospel combines these messianic pastoral images with the messianic kingship images of the trial in John 18. The piercing passage is particularly appropriate for John at this point in his narrative, since both the shepherd and king images are prominent in that portion of Zechariah. As we have seen above, the same images are also prominent throughout John's narrative.[21] The immediate connection John makes in John 19:37 regards the specific detail of Jesus's pierced side. Though there is some ambiguity in Zechariah 12:10 regarding the identity of the figure who is pierced,[22] there is no ambiguity for John: the pierced one whom Israel looks upon is Jesus the Christ.

---

20. In addition to the aforementioned texts in Zechariah, the book of Ezekiel contains some of the most developed shepherd imagery connected to messianic expectation. In Ezekiel 34 and 37, the coming Messiah is cast as a Davidic shepherd-king who will restore the hopes of Israel. In this eschatological vision, Israel will live in the land, David will rule over them forever, and the Lord will dwell in their midst forever, having made an everlasting covenant of peace with them (34:25–28). The coming rule of this Davidic shepherd-king will be the fulfillment and culmination of the promises made in the biblical covenants.

21. Piercing (Zech. 12:10/John 19:37) and striking (Zech. 13:7/John 19:3) imagery are also present in both contexts.

22. Identifying the "pierced one" of Zechariah 12:10 is a notoriously difficult interpretive issue. For our purposes, it is enough to note that the pierced one is closely associated with the messianic images of its surrounding context (i.e., king and shepherd).

By quoting these words, John identifies Jesus as the promised one of messianic prophecy. By connecting the piercing of Jesus to the "pierced one" of Zechariah's prophecy, John ends his crucifixion narrative by demonstrating that Jesus is the Davidic shepherd-king who is being struck down in order to gather his scattered people.

The Death of the Davidic Shepherd-King Fulfills the Scriptures

In the midst of these two vibrant Davidic images that coalesce in the crucifixion narrative, John demonstrates that the details of Jesus's crucifixion fulfill specific Davidic psalms.

The first detail concerns what happens to Jesus's clothes in 19:23–25. After the soldiers crucify Jesus, they divide his outer garments amongst themselves. John notes that Jesus's tunic was seamless, "woven in one piece" (19:23). Instead of tearing it, they "cast lots for it" (19:24). John records that the soldiers "did these things" in order "to fulfill the Scripture." He then quotes Psalm 22:18: "They divided my outer garments among them, and for my clothing they cast lots." In a striking way, John asserts that this specific element of Jesus's crucifixion corresponds to the scene depicted in Psalm 22. Several other specific details in Psalm 22 correspond to John's crucifixion account and further highlight his interest in demonstrating this intertextual connection. These include Jesus's thirst (John 19:28/Ps. 22:15), his pierced hands and feet (John 19:23/Ps. 22:16), and his preserved bones (John 19:33/Ps. 22:17).

Further resonance can be found between Psalm 69 and Jesus's thirst on the cross. After Jesus entrusts his mother Mary to "the disciple whom he loved" (19:25b–27), he exclaims, "I am thirsty." John records that Jesus knew that "all things had already been accomplished" and spoke these words in order "to fulfill the Scripture" (19:28). Jesus's indication of his thirst matches the details of the scene presented in Psalm 69. There the psalmist writes, "They gave me poison for food, and for my thirst they gave me sour wine to drink" (Ps. 69:21). Accordingly, John recounts that "a jar full of sour wine stood there" (19:29). The soldiers take a sponge full of this sour wine and lift it to Jesus's mouth using a branch of hyssop. After receiving the sour wine, Jesus says, "It is finished!" and, bowing his head, gives up his spirit (19:30). By recording Jesus's statement, "I am thirsty," John makes a thematic allusion to Psalm 69.[23] By referencing this text alongside Psalm 22, John asserts that what Jesus "finished" on the cross was completely in line with "the Scriptures." Indeed, this accomplished work *fulfills* the Scriptures and *fills out* the messianic vision of these psalms down to the seemingly trivial details concerning the disposal of garments and distribution of sour wine.

---

23. John has already cited Psalm 69 twice before in his Gospel (2:17; 15:25), and the Synoptic Gospels utilize this Psalm in their crucifixion accounts. These considerations strengthen the probability that John has Psalm 69 in view here.

The final detail relates to Jesus's bones remaining unbroken (19:31–36). John recounts that the Jews wanted the bodies taken down from the crosses because it was the day of preparation and the Sabbath was drawing near (19:31). However, when the soldiers came to break Jesus's legs, "they saw that he was already dead" and did not break any of his bones (19:32–33). Perhaps to guarantee Jesus was truly dead, one of the soldiers "pierced his side with a spear," which immediately caused blood and water to flow from his body (19:34). John asserts one last time that these things came to pass to fulfill Scripture. In addition to the piercing of Jesus's side fulfilling Zechariah 12:10, John asserts that the preservation of Jesus's bones fulfilled the Scripture that, "Not one of his bones will be broken" (19:36). This statement has strong Passover connotations in connection with Exodus 12:46 and Numbers 9:12, and also relates to John's conviction that Jesus fulfills and replaces the role of the Passover lamb.

Additionally, these words resonate with Psalm 34:20. In Psalm 34 David reflects on the Lord's deliverance of the righteous by saying, "He keeps all his bones, not one of them is broken" (34:20). This reflection made by David in the midst of his suffering is filled out in the details of what happens to Jesus on the cross. In this way, John demonstrates that even the details of Jesus's passion go according to plan. By referencing the Psalms, John interprets a scene of seemingly meaningless brutality. Rather than merely an execution planned by indignant religious leaders and carried out by a complicit Roman government, John demonstrates that the death of Israel's Messiah falls within the design of divine providence. Even its smallest details have been prefigured in the words of the Davidic Psalms. John's scene does not depict abandonment, but rather fulfillment. Additionally, the Passover connections point to the saving nature of Jesus's sacrificial death, while the Davidic connections stress that the Lord has not abandoned his Messiah, even as he is murdered.

By highlighting the king and shepherd motifs, John employs two of the most significant Davidic images available to him from the Hebrew Scriptures. John writes his Gospel so that the reader might believe that Jesus is the Christ (John 20:30–31). In other words, the Son of God is also the Son of David. This emphasis also has an implication for the fourfold Gospel collection. John's portrayal of Jesus as the Davidic messiah connects with Matthew's clear emphasis on Jesus as the "Son of David" (Matt. 1:1). Matthew focuses on the Davidic title "Son of David" and primarily uses allusions in his references to the Psalms in his crucifixion account (Matthew 27). Conversely, John chooses to focus on Davidic images in his narrative rather than the Davidic title, but makes direct quotations of the Davidic Psalms in his passion account (John 19). John also uses explicit fulfillment language in reference to the manner in which David's life anticipates and prefigures the life of Jesus the Messiah.

Rather than pitting these two compositional strategies against each another, one might view them in a more interconnected way. Matthew raises the "Son of David" question in a striking manner and consistently keeps before the reader the question, "Could this be the Son of David?" (Matt. 12:23). Matthew raises the David issue by directing focus upon the title, and John picks up on this motif and fills out the rest of the picture by ending his Gospel with a flurry of kingly discourse. Whereas Matthew addresses the question, "Could this be the Son of David?" John asks, "Is this the King of Israel?" Both authors answer in the affirmative and demonstrate that this Son of David is in fact the King of Israel. The emphasis on and development of Jesus as the Davidic Messiah is thus one of the textual and thematic elements that draw the Gospels as a whole together.

The Master Teacher's Lesson about Himself

After considering this brief profile of these distinctive Gospels, we can also ponder the multifaceted manner in which the Gospel writers portray Jesus as a master teacher. Among the Gospels, one of the strong lines of textual and theological continuity is the central place of Jesus's words and the strategic function of his teachings in each narrative. "In the beginning was the Word," John begins, and the "Word became flesh and dwelt among us" (John 1:1, 14). The Word also *spoke* among us! In the Gospels we behold his glory by reading and hearing his words.[24] Matthew incorporates large blocks of Jesus's discourse at strategic locations in his writing (e.g., Matthew 5–7). While Mark typically focuses on Jesus's actions, he also highlights a series of Jesus's parables on the kingdom (Mark 4) and Jesus's discussion of the end of days (Mark 13). Luke's extensive account of Jesus's final journey to Jerusalem is dominated by teaching, parables, and proclamations (Luke 9–19). John also provides a lengthy account of Jesus's theological conversations and prayers (John 14–17). In these ways, all the Gospel writers strategically showcase the fact that Jesus is a master teacher whose words embody divine wisdom and carry unparalleled weight.

The characterization of Jesus as a master teacher, then, represents both a common theological theme in the Gospels as well as a clear facet of each writer's compositional strategy. Jesus brings out of the storehouses words old and new (Matt. 13:52) as he fulfills and fills out messianic expectations. Jesus speaks both his own words and the words of the Old Testament Scriptures. His opening gospel declaration is, "the time is fulfilled, and the kingdom of God is at hand; repent and believe in the gospel" (Mark 1:15). In the vein of the prophets, Jesus's

---

24. Along these lines, there is an interesting connection in the opening moments of John's gospel where Jesus the Christ is connected to Jesus the teacher. The final words of the prologue emphasize revelation and state that "no one has ever seen God; the only God, who is at the Father's side, he has made him known" (John 1:18). What immediately follows is an account of dialogue between the Jewish leaders and John the Baptist regarding the identity of the Messiah ("Who are you? . . . I am not the Christ," 1:19–28). In response to Jesus's first words in the narrative ("What are you seeking?"), they say, "Rabbi, where are you staying?" John here adds the editorial translation of the Aramaic word Rabbi, "which means teacher" (1:38). After this, Andrew tells his brother Simon Peter about Jesus, saying, "We have found the Messiah." John again provides the editorial translation for the word Messiah, "which means Christ" (1:41). In this manner, John identifies the Word who became flesh as the Messiah who will teach them about himself, and thereby reveal knowledge of the only God.

message about the kingdom includes pronouncements of both salvation and judgment. In Luke's gospel, Jesus begins his ministry by unrolling the scroll of Isaiah and declaring its fulfillment (Luke 4:16–30; Isa. 61:1–2). He then continues to "preach the good news of the kingdom of God" because as Luke states, Jesus "was sent for this purpose" (Luke 4:43).

Though we might develop this theme in many directions, an important aspect to highlight is that one of the distinct patterns in Jesus's teaching concerns himself. Common refrains in the Gospels include, "Whose son is he?" and, "Who is this man?" Many answers are given to these questions, but the burden of the Gospel writers is to show that Jesus provides the definitive answer to these queries. As he journeys toward Jerusalem just before the crucifixion, Jesus explains, "The Son of Man must suffer many things and be rejected by the elders and chief priests and scribes, and be killed, and on the third day be raised" (Luke 9:22). As he journeys away from Jerusalem after the resurrection, Jesus once again explains that "these are my words that I spoke to you while I was still with you, that everything written about me in the Law of Moses and the Prophets and the Psalms must be fulfilled" (24:44). In other words, the first one to produce a post-resurrection "biblical theology of the messiah" is the resurrected Christ himself.

Keeping an Eye on the Storyline and the Promised Line

The fourfold Gospel collection begins and ends with the mention of a "book" about Jesus the Christ (Matt. 1:1; John 20:30–31). In our consideration of the story of the Gospels, we briefly explored how each Gospel writer paints a portrait of Jesus's life, ministry, death, and resurrection that reveals distinct but complementary angles for us to behold as we seek to understand the depth and beauty of the gospel message. Part of the purpose of these books is to continue and culminate a larger story, as well as anticipate a new chapter in this story.

While reflecting on how each Gospel bears its own distinctive shape, situates itself within a fourfold Gospel collection, and captures a strategic selection of Jesus's words and deeds, it is difficult to improve upon the sentiment expressed in the last words of John's gospel: "Now there are also many other things that Jesus did. Were every one of them to be written, I suppose that the world itself could not contain the books that would be written" (John 21:25).

Discussion Questions

1. As you consider the story of the Gospels, what elements of the biblical-theological framework of the canon, the covenants, and the Christ do you see developed?

2. What about the story of the Gospels makes it one of the easiest yet most challenging parts of the grand storyline of the Bible to tell?

3. List and describe at least two distinctive structural or theological aspects from each Gospel account. How do these distinctive angles on the person and work of Jesus complement one another?

4. Discuss the ways in which each Gospel individually positions itself in relation to the texts, themes, and narrative storyline of the Old Testament. Consider further how the fourfold Gospel corpus does this as a collection.

5. Discuss the ways in which the Gospels (individually or as a fourfold Gospel corpus) anticipate or connect to the story of Acts, the New Testament letter collections, and the book of Revelation.

Resources for Further Study

Emerson, Matthew Y. *Christ and the New Creation: A Canonical Approach to the Theology of the New Testament.* Eugene: Wipf & Stock, 2013.

Hays, Richard B. *Echoes of Scripture in the Gospels.* Waco: Baylor University Press, 2016.

Hill, C. E. *Who Chose the Gospels? Probing the Great Gospel Conspiracy.* Oxford: Oxford University Press, 2010.

Pennington, Jonathan T. *Reading the Gospels Wisely: A Narrative and Theological Introduction.* Grand Rapids: Baker, 2012.

Watson, Francis. *The Fourfold Gospel: A Theological Reading of the New Testament Portraits of Jesus.* Grand Rapids: Eerdmans, 2016.

CHAPTER 9

THE STORY OF ACTS AND THE LETTERS

The Shape of Acts and the Letters

THE BOOK OF ACTS provides a remarkable level of cohesion for the shape of the New Testament. Luke's narrative begins with clear ties to the story of the Gospels in general and the text of the gospel of Luke in particular (Luke 1:1–4; Acts 1:1–8). This clear literary and theological link with the Gospels creates a natural next step for reading the New Testament collection.

An important situation to note, however, is that although Acts has strong associations with the Gospels, the manuscript evidence indicates that the book of Acts never circulated as single-volume unit with Luke (i.e., Luke–Acts). In fact, Acts is most often linked with and circulated alongside the New Testament letters of James, 1–2 Peter, 1–3 John, and Jude. Accordingly, both the gospel of Luke and the books of Acts have complementary but distinct purposes. Luke likely composed his Gospel before he wrote the book of Acts as a closely related narrative with its own compositional purpose. In this scenario, Luke writes Acts with a broad awareness of both the Old Testament Scriptures and the burgeoning collection of the New Testament writings. Written with this canon-conscious outlook, the book of Acts is particularly well-suited to help us see the shape and flow of the New Testament canon.

As the letters of the New Testament were written, they quickly began circulating in groupings. Paul's Letters represent one of the earliest collections to form and function in an authoritative way for the earliest churches. The thirteen Letters of Paul, along with Hebrews, form a major section of the New Testament. The other major letter collection, known as the Catholic Epistles, consists of James, 1–2 Peter, 1–3 John, and Jude.

There are two primary positions these letter groupings take within the ordering traditions. In English translations of the New Testament, Acts is followed by Paul's Letters (Romans through Philemon), Hebrews, and finally the Catholic Epistles. In many important

205

early manuscripts, though, Acts is followed by the Catholic Epistles, and then the collection of Paul's Letters. While this difference obviously impacts the flow of the New Testament to some extent, Acts maintains an orienting function in both of these major ordering traditions. Indeed, the story of Acts connects to the story of the Gospels, carries on its storyline through the initial years of the earliest churches, and introduces the authors, recipients, and social settings behind the letter correspondences encountered in the rest of the New Testament collection.

Thus, while there is some diversity in the organization of this part of the New Testament canon, the coherence of Acts followed by these two corpora of New Testament epistles cannot be overestimated.[1]

The Story of Acts and the Letters

On the heels of the four Gospel narratives, the book of Acts continues the storyline of the New Testament. As the Gospels directly connect to the storyline of the Old Testament, so too Acts directly connects to the narrative storyline of the Gospels. As Luke writes, his Gospel had "dealt with all that Jesus began to do and teach" (Acts 1:1). The book of Acts begins immediately after the resurrection, with the resurrected Jesus teaching the disciples for forty days about the kingdom of God and his identity as the suffering messiah (1:4–5).

After Jesus announces the imminent coming of the Holy Spirit, the disciples ask, "Lord, will you at this time restore the kingdom to Israel?" (1:6). Rather than chastise them or simply say "no," Jesus responds by explaining the next steps in redemptive history. He tells them, "It is not for you to know times or seasons that the Father has fixed by his own authority. But you will receive power when the Holy Spirit has come upon you, and you will be my witnesses in Jerusalem and in all Judea and Samaria, and to the end of the earth" (1:7–8). With these words, Jesus elucidates how the promises about the kingdom will work themselves out during this present time in redemptive history. The coming of the Holy Spirit will empower the disciples and those who hear their message to join this community bearing witness to Jesus as the Christ who brings about the salvation of both Jews and Gentiles.

---

1. For an extended discussion of the canonical shape of Acts and the two major letter collections of the New Testament, as well as key features of these biblical books from a variety of angles, see Alan J. Thompson, *The Acts of the Risen Lord Jesus: Luke's Account of God's Unfolding Plan* (Downers Grove: InterVarsity, 2011); Greg Goswell, "The Place of the Book of Acts in Reading the NT," *Journal of the Evangelical Theological Society* 59.1 (2016): 67–82; Darian R. Lockett, *Letters from the Pillar Apostles: The Formation of the Catholic Epistles as a Canonical Collection* (Eugene: Pickwick, 2017); David R. Nienhuis and Robert W. Wall, *Reading the Epistles of James, Peter, John, and Jude as Scripture: The Shaping and Shape of a Canonical Collection* (Grand Rapids: Eerdmans, 2013); Childs, *Reading Paul*; David Trobisch, *Paul's Letter Collection: Tracing the Origins* (Minneapolis: Fortress, 1994); Brian S. Rosner, *Paul and the Law: Keeping the Commandments of God* (Downers Grove: InterVarsity, 2013); and Thomas R. Schreiner, *Paul, Apostle of God's Glory in Christ: A Pauline Theology*, 2nd ed. (Downers Grove: InterVarsity, 2020).

The shape of the book of Acts is designed to demonstrate the fulfillment of Jesus's final words before his ascension. Beginning with Jesus's words in Acts 1:8, Luke provides a sequence of important summary statements that trace the progress of this promise as the Spirit empowers believers to make disciples of Christ.[2]

From a broad view, the structure of the book starts with a focus upon Jerusalem (Acts 1–7), and then transitions to its surrounding geographical regions (chapters 8–15) before following Paul on his multiple missionary journeys that eventually end in Rome (chapters 16–28). In each major section, Luke describes the geographical progress of the preached word of God. For example, in Acts 6, Luke observes that "the word of God continued to increase, and the number of the disciples multiplied greatly in *Jerusalem*, and a great many of the priests became obedient to the faith" (6:7). As believers spread away from Jerusalem after Stephen is martyred (8:1) and Saul meets Jesus on the road to Damascus (9:1–19), Luke observes, "So the church throughout *all Judea and Galilee and Samaria* had peace and was being built up. And walking in the fear of the Lord and in the comfort of the Holy Spirit, it multiplied" (9:31). Finally, during his work in Ephesus Paul resolves to continue his trip and "also see *Rome*" (19:21). Luke also notes here that "the word of the Lord continued to increase and prevail mightily" (19:20). Paul's final journey takes him to Rome, where he testifies and preaches the gospel message to both Jews and Gentiles (28:28–31; cf. 23:11).

These summary statements capture the main themes of Acts. The churches are unified as the gospel spreads by the power of the Spirit and the boldness of the apostles from Jerusalem to Judea and Samaria and the ends of the earth (represented by Antioch and Rome). This growth crosses geographic, ethnic, and redemptive-historical boundaries. By so clearly structuring his narrative around this progress of the word through strategic summaries and narrative pacing, Luke clearly connects Acts to the structural focus of the gospel of Luke. In Luke 9–19, Luke emphasizes the journey *to* Jerusalem; in Acts 1–28, Luke emphasizes the journey *from* Jerusalem.

This literary connection has theological implications as well. The disciples proclaim the word of the gospel message everywhere with boldness because of the work Christ accomplished on the cross. They do this through the power of the Holy Spirit who the resurrected Christ sent from the right hand of the Father (2:32). They do this on the basis of the new covenant as the community of God made up of Jewish and Gentile believers in Jesus as the Christ (chapter 15). They do this in light of the *finished* work of God in Christ (i.e., the kingdom that has come) and the *future* work of God in Christ (i.e., the kingdom that is to come).

One of the prominent features of the book of Acts is the number of speeches it contains. In these speeches, we hear the apostles interpret the resurrection and ascension of Christ. Moreover, just as the Gospels narrate and interpret the coming of the Son, the speeches in

---

2. Some of the strategic summary statements include Acts 2:41, 47; 4:4; 11:21; and 12:24.

Acts narrate and interpret the coming of the Spirit. Collectively then, the Gospels and Acts provide the biblical-theological framework within which to understand the location that the churches occupy in redemptive history (expanded upon by the New Testament letters) until the return of Jesus at the end of days (expanded upon by the book of Revelation).

The speeches of Acts serve a hermeneutical and theological purpose in the context of its larger narrative. They function as interpretive guides to its narrative events. Luke strategically locates speeches at critical moments in the storyline of the book. New phases in the history of the church are often directly explained or reflected upon by an apostle in an extended speech or dialogue.

The content of these speeches also connect the Bible's grand storyline directly to the death and resurrection of Jesus the Messiah. They show how that storyline directly impacts those who hear this message. In other words, the speeches are examples of the process of biblical theology as the biblical storyline, intertextual references, and theological assertions about God's character and purpose in history are brought to bear on the message of the gospel and its call for faith and repentance. The speeches of Acts also illustrate the unity of the gospel message and the diversity of its many applications. Different speakers deliver speeches to different audiences (both Jewish and Gentile) with different emphases and major themes, but with the same shape of the gospel, the same group of biblical texts as the basis of authority, and the same overarching understanding of redemptive history at work in each speech.

Peter Interprets the Coming of the Spirit (Acts 2)

After the Spirit arrives on Pentecost, Peter gives a sermon that interprets and clarifies what has taken place. When the Spirit comes, there is the sound of a rushing wind, a visible display of fire, and a verbal proclamation of the gospel message in many different languages (2:2–4). Peter explains that this coming of the Spirit fulfills the "last days" vision of Joel 2:28–32. The presence of the Spirit and the prophesying of God's people signify that the day of the Lord has come. Peter quotes this passage from Joel, which ends with the statement, "And it shall come to pass that everyone who calls upon the name of the Lord shall be saved" (Joel 2:31; cf. Acts 2:21).

After citing Joel 2:28–32 about the presence of the Spirit "in the last days," Peter directly connects this vision to the coming of Jesus. The day of the Lord is the day of the Lord Jesus. As Peter declares, "Men of Israel, hear these words: Jesus of Nazareth, a man attested to you by God with mighty works and wonders and signs that God did through him in your midst, as you yourselves know—this Jesus, delivered up according to the definite plan and foreknowledge of God, you crucified and killed by the hands of lawless men" (Acts 2:22–23). Connecting the crucifixion to the resurrection, Peter notes that "God raised him up, loosing the pangs of death, because it was not possible for him to be held by it" (2:24).

To illustrate the fittingness of this connection, Peter quotes Psalm 16:8–11 and shows how this text establishes Jesus as the true son of David. Because of the Davidic covenant, David writes prophetically about a messiah who would rule over an eternal kingdom. As Peter maintains, David "foresaw and spoke about the resurrection of the Christ, that he was not abandoned to Hades, nor did his flesh see corruption" (2:31). Peter then directly identifies the messianic figure of the Davidic covenant as the resurrected Jesus: "This Jesus God raised up, and of that we are all witnesses" (2:32).

What Peter says next is one of the most significant statements in the entire book of Acts for helping us see how God is at work in this era of redemptive history. How does the work of Christ in the Gospels relate to the work of the Spirit in Acts? Peter explains, "Being therefore exalted at the right hand of God, and having received from the Father the promise of the Holy Spirit, he has poured out this that you yourselves are seeing and hearing" (2:33). The work of the Spirit among the churches as the word progresses cannot be seen apart from the risen Christ at the right hand of the Father. Peter's explanation here helps illuminate the transition from the old covenant to the new covenant, the relationship between the Old Testament and the New Testament, and also the unified actions of the Father, Son, and the Spirit in the economy of salvation, the work of redemption, the spread of the gospel, and the growth of the churches.

Peter ends his sermon by quoting Psalm 110:1 and reiterates that he speaks not of David, but of the *son of David*, the messiah described in the story of the covenants (2:34–35). The fulfillment of these promises in Christ did not happen by chance or as a historically inevitable occurrence. Rather, Peter insists, redemptive history is ordered and guided by divine providence from beginning to end. As he proclaims, "Let all the house of Israel therefore know for certain that God has made him both Lord and Christ, this Jesus whom you crucified" (2:36).

Stephen Interprets Redemptive History (Acts 6–7)

Another strategic speech is that of Stephen in Acts 6–7. There Stephen defends himself against charges that he spoke "blasphemous words against Moses and God" (6:11). The false witnesses that charged Stephen claimed, "This man never ceases to speak words against this holy place and the law" (6:13). Their basis for this charge is that Stephen said that "Jesus of Nazareth will destroy this place and will change the customs that Moses delivered to us" (6:14). In his defense, Stephen argues that he does not speak against the temple or the Mosaic covenant. Rather, his message is that these institutions were designed to serve a purpose for a time, and because the new covenant has been inaugurated by the coming of the Son and the Spirit (Acts 2), the old covenant institutions and authorities are no longer binding. They have served their purpose. Stephen's speech in chapter 7 is the longest speech in Acts and utilizes large swaths of redemptive history and biblical-theological themes to make its point.

After the high priest asks, "Are these things so?" (7:1), Stephen responds with a wide-ranging treatment of redemptive history. Stephen traces how God dealt with Abraham (7:2–8), Joseph (7:9–16), Moses (7:17–44), Joshua (7:45), David (7:45–46), and Solomon (7:47). In each account, Stephen highlights that God appeared to these people apart from the location of the temple. Abraham met God "when he was in Mesopotamia" (7:2). Joseph was sold into Egypt "but God was with him" (7:9). The Lord spoke to Moses in the burning bush (7:30) and gave him the law on Mount Sinai (7:38). The tabernacle moved with the people through the wilderness and into the land (7:44–45). Solomon built the temple, but as Stephen concludes at the climax of his speech, "Yet the Most High does not dwell in houses made by hands" (7:48).

Notable in this speech too is the attention and textual space given to Moses (7:17–44). Stephen was charged with blaspheming the Mosaic covenant and the temple, so this dictates the focus of his survey of redemptive history. From the perspective provided by the Law and the Prophets, the Mosaic covenant was unable to produce obedience in the hearts of the people (as the golden calf incident immediately demonstrates). Stephen reasons that God has required the same response at every point in redemptive history: worship and obedience to God's spoken word. With the coming of the "righteous one" and the Spirit (7:52–53), the temple and the Mosaic covenant should be understood according to their intended purpose: as pointers to the coming Christ and new covenant.

After this canon-conscious survey of Israel's history in relation to the temple, Stephen adopts the tone and content of the biblical prophets. Having summarized, synthesized, quoted, and echoed the biblical writings, Stephen now imitates the biblical writers.[3] He chides the Jewish leaders, "You stick-necked people, uncircumcised in heart and ears, you always resist the Holy Spirit. As your fathers did, so do you" (7:51). Stephen then protests, "Which of the prophets did your fathers not persecute? And they killed those who announced beforehand the coming of the Righteous One, whom you have now betrayed and murdered, you who received the law as delivered by angels and did not keep it" (7:52–53).

The response to Stephen's speech is swift and devastating. Enraged at his words, the Jewish leaders take Stephen outside the city and murder him by stoning (7:54, 57–58). "Full of the Holy Spirit," Stephen gazes into heaven and sees "the glory of God, and Jesus standing at the right hand of God" (7:55).[4] The final words of Stephen's speech provide a harsh warning and judgment. The final words of his life express shocking kindness and

---

3. Aside from the fact that the historical account that Stephen provides here is clearly influenced by the narratives of the Hebrew Bible, Stephen also cites several Old Testament texts directly: Gen. 12:1 (7:3); Gen. 12:7 (7:5); Gen. 15:13 (7:6); Exod. 1:8 (7:18); Exod. 2:13–15 (7:28–29); Exod. 3:1 (7:30); Exod. 3:5–7 (7:32–34); Deut. 18:15 (7:37); Exod. 32:1 (7:40); Amos 5:25–27 (7:42–43); Isa. 66:1–2 (7:49–50).

4. Stephen responds to this vision by saying, "Behold, I see the heavens opened, and the Son of Man standing at the right hand of God" (7:56).

mercy: "Falling to his knees he cried out with a loud voice, 'Lord, do not hold this sin against them'" (7:60).[5]

The Apostles Interpret the Gospel in the New Covenant (Acts 15)

Another important set of speeches occurs at the gathering in Jerusalem in Acts 15. In many ways, the council at Jerusalem and the dialogue that takes place there together represent a major structural moment in the shape of the book. Many of the central themes of the book are directly addressed there and connected to the grand storyline of the Bible. These include the relationships between Antioch and Jerusalem, the Jews and the Gentiles, the old covenant and the new covenant, and the observance of Jewish customs and the mission to the Gentiles.

After returning from their initial mission of preaching among the Gentiles, Paul and Barnabas return to Antioch to report to the gathered church "all that God had done with them, and how he had opened a door of faith to the Gentiles" (14:27). Around this time, though, a group of men from Judea spread the teaching that Gentile believers must be circumcised "according to the custom of Moses" in order to receive salvation (15:1). Paul and Barnabas object to this teaching, debate this Judean group, and decide to travel to Jerusalem to address this issue formally (15:2–3).[6]

After much debate in Jerusalem among the apostles and elders (15:6), Peter addresses the group by recounting his experience preaching the gospel to the house of Cornelius in Acts 10–11. As he says, "Brothers, you know that in the early days God made a choice among you, that by my mouth the Gentiles should hear the word of the gospel and believe" (15:7). Peter testifies that this salvation did in fact go to the Gentiles: "And God, who knows the heart, bore witness to them, by giving them the Holy Spirit just as he did to us, and he made no distinction between us and them, having cleansed their hearts by faith" (15:8). In his statement, Peter connects the scene portrayed in Acts 10–11 among the Gentiles to the scene in Acts 2–3 among the Jews in Jerusalem. Next, Peter shifts his reflection from the new covenant to the old covenant and its effectiveness in redemptive history: "Now,

---

5. These final words echo Jesus's words from the cross: Jesus says, "Father, forgive them, for they know not what they do" (Luke 23:34). The words that Stephen speaks as he is being stoned ("Lord Jesus, receive my spirit") also echo the words of Jesus after he is being crucified ("Father, into your hands I commit my spirit," Luke 23:46).

6. Luke notes that Paul and Barnabas "had no small dissension and debate with them" and that those at Antioch appointed a group to go to the apostles and elders at Jerusalem to discuss this question (15:2). On the way to Jerusalem, Paul and Barnabas report "in detail the conversion of the Gentiles" in the regions they passed through. This report brought "great joy to all the brothers" (15:3). Similarly, Luke notes as they entered Jerusalem, Paul and Barnabas were "welcomed by the church and the apostles and the elders, and they declared all that God had done with them" (15:4). Significantly, then, Luke seems to suggest that the mission to the Gentiles and the glad acceptance of this mission is not the minority position, but rather the consensus of the earliest churches. In this respect, the position of "some believers who belonged to the party of the Pharisees" represents a significant theological question that lingers in light of redemptive historical realities (i.e., the established old covenant institutions), but should probably not be seen as the enthusiastic consensus at this gathering.

therefore, why are you putting God to the test by placing a yoke on the neck of the disciples that neither our fathers nor we have been able to bear?" (5:10). Peter then articulates a cumulative and normative account of faith and belief for both Jews and Gentiles in the new covenant. As he declares, "We believe that we will be saved through the grace of the Lord Jesus, just as they will" (5:11).

Immediately following Peter's description of the conversion of the Gentiles and the normative nature of faith in Christ, Paul and Barnabas recount the "signs and wonders God had done through them among the Gentiles" (5:12). This summary essentially chronicles their missionary journey recorded by Luke in Acts 13–14. After Paul and Barnabas finish speaking, James mentions again Peter's testimony about how God has "visited the Gentiles" and has taken "from them a people for his name" (15:14). James insists, "with this the words of the prophets agree" (15:15). James then quotes Amos 9:11–12, which envisions a future time when God will "rebuild the tent of David that has fallen" so that "the remnant of mankind may seek the Lord, and all the Gentiles who are called by my name" (15:16–17). By citing this passage from Amos, James combines the expectation of a coming messiah with the inclusion of the Gentiles in God's plan of salvation.

As James concludes, "My judgment is that we should not trouble those of the Gentiles who turn to God" (5:19). In their letter to the believers in Antioch, James and the Jerusalem apostles include an exhortation to abstain from sexual immorality and food associated in any way with the practice of idolatry (i.e., was sacrificed to idols, strangled, or contained blood). They summarize this discussion in a letter and send it with Paul and Barnabas as they return to Antioch. When those at Antioch read the letter, "they rejoiced because of its encouragement" (15:31).

The discussion of the Jews, the Gentiles, and the gospel at this council in Jerusalem is a place in the book of Acts where the story of the Law, the Prophets, the Writings, and the Gospels are all shown to comprise one grand storyline. Peter, Paul, and James draw on various parts of this storyline as they argue that God's plan of redemption is seen clearly as the one gospel of Jesus Christ is believed and proclaimed by both Jews and Gentiles.

Paul Equips and Envisions Future Generations (Acts 20)

What about the time after the apostles? In Acts 20 Paul gives a farewell address to the leaders of the church at Ephesus. Paul begins by reminding the Ephesians how he had served them even in the midst of trials. Even then, he notes, "I did not shrink from declaring to you anything that was profitable, and teaching you in public and from house to house, testifying both to Jews and to Greeks of repentance toward God and of faith in our Lord Jesus Christ" (20:20–21).

After this reminder of his past ministry, Paul anticipates the uncertainty of his immediate future (20:22–23). He will suffer much in his preaching ministry, and none of the

Ephesians will see him again (20:25). After insisting that, "I did not shrink from declaring to you the whole counsel of God" (20:27), Paul envisions a time after his departure: "Pay careful attention to yourselves and to all the flock, in which the Holy Spirit has made you overseers, to care for the church of God, which he obtained with his own blood" (20:28). Though false teachers will come who will twist the truth (20:29–30), Paul declares that the gospel that he preached will equip them to defend the people of God and guard the gospel message. Paul concludes by commending the Ephesians "to God and to the word of his grace, which is able to build you up and to give you the inheritance among all those who are sanctified" (20:32) before departing with sorrowful final exchanges.

Paul's final address to the Ephesians is significant for several reasons. His speech represents one of Paul's final sustained interactions with the churches established on his missionary journeys. In the rest of Acts, much of Paul's story will involve his arrest and defense before government officials on his path to Rome. For the story of Acts, too, Paul emphasizes the nature of the Gospel of Jesus Christ for both Jews and Gentiles. Paul has preached the "whole counsel of God" (20:27) and this is sufficient for the churches to establish themselves, to build themselves up in the faith, and to defend themselves against false teaching. Paul also envisions a time after his departure. He will leave them, but the gospel of Jesus Christ will remain with them. Further, Paul envisions a broader horizon as well, as he insists that the gospel of Jesus Christ will ensure their inheritance among "all those who are sanctified" (20:32).

In this way, just as Peter's speech in Acts 2 asserted the continuity in God's plan between the old covenant and the new covenant, between the coming of the Son and the coming of the Spirit, so too does Paul's speech in Acts 20 asserts the continuity in the function of the gospel to establish the people of God in the new covenant before and after the time of the apostles. Paul assures the Ephesians that the gospel that has established and given them life in his presence will continue to do so after his departure. Even if he ends up in chains.

The Gospel Goes to Rome and Beyond (Acts 28)

The story of Acts ends with Paul in Rome under house arrest (28:16). Luke ends his narrative with Paul bound in Rome but "proclaiming the kingdom of God and teaching about the Lord Jesus Christ with all boldness and without hindrance" (28:31). When Paul first arrives in Rome, he explains to the local leaders the path that lead him there (28:17–22). They allow him time to speak, and a large group comes to hear Paul deliver his message. Paul's speech to this group is the final speech in the book of Acts.

"From morning until evening," Luke recounts, Paul testifies to them about the kingdom and tries to convince them about the gospel message of Jesus "both from the Law of Moses and from the Prophets" (28:23). Luke notes that "some were convinced by what he said, but others disbelieved" (28:24). For many of these people, the point of decisive disagreement arose when Paul spoke of the role of the Gentiles in the plan of God. Paul insists that to resist this truth is to resist God's purpose and design for his people. If the Jews harden their hearts to the message of the gospel, then they will not receive salvation but will see it go to another people. This was true in the past (Paul cites Isa. 6:9–10 as an example; Acts 28:25–27) and remains true in the present. As Paul concludes, "Let it be known to you that this salvation of God has been sent to the Gentiles; they will listen" (28:28).

Here, at the end of the story of Acts, Paul proclaims the message of the kingdom of God and the gospel of Jesus Christ with boldness in Rome. Collectively, the speeches of Acts help readers orient themselves in redemptive history and press forward upon that same storyline. The disciples of Jesus have gone from Jerusalem, to Judea and Samaria, and now to Rome. Here we see the fulfillment of Jesus's promise in Acts 1:8 and also the anticipation that this word about the kingdom of God and the gospel of Jesus Christ will continue. The message of Acts is designed to convince readers that though Paul is under house arrest in Rome, the gospel message will continue across geographic, ethnic, and temporal boundaries.

Reading the Letters in Light of the Story of Acts

The story of Acts connects to the story of the Gospels while providing the historical, textual, and theological framework for reading the letters that follow in the New Testament canon. After the narrative framework provided by Acts, the Catholic Epistles and Paul's Letters are naturally understood to be the correspondence between the churches mentioned in Acts and their apostolic leaders. The epistle genre represents a significant portion of the New Testament canon and has an important effect on readers.

Structurally, the interconnections between the narratives and letters of the New Testament are similar to the ones at work between the prophetic history and the Latter Prophets in the Old Testament. Though there are bits of historical information in the Catholic Epistles and Paul's Letters, the narrative flow of the New Testament is essentially put on hold. After a strong narrative beginning, the New Testament epistles move in many different directions with multiple apostles writing letters to a variety of churches in divergent geographic locations. An illustration of this diverse range of locations and recipients can be found in Peter's address in 1 Peter 1:1: "To those who reside as aliens, scattered throughout Pontus, Galatia, Cappadocia, Asia, and Bithynia." Similarly, James writes "to the twelve tribes who are dispersed abroad" (James 1:1). Paul also addresses a broad audience when he writes in Galatians 1:1–2, "Paul . . . and all the brothers who are with me, to the churches of Galatia."

In light of the narrative framework previously established in the Gospels and Acts, readers can view the letters of the New Testament as a literary dialogue penned by the figures introduced in the historical accounts of the earlier groupings. The New Testament Epistles function as a kind of interactive commentary on the person and work of Jesus as the Christ, the nature and rhythm of the Christian life, the importance of the believing community, and the shape of future hope in God's plan for the world and his people. Even as the apostles speak to specific issues in specific churches at specific locations, they speak with a broad authority, envision a broad audience for their message, and expect a broad circulation for their letters.

Part of the function of these two major letter collections is to preserve and pass along this apostolic dialogue for future generations of readers. In writing these letters, the biblical authors seek to communicate their teaching and mediate their presence. Paul, for example, frequently foregrounds this mediating quality of his written correspondence. For instance, in 2 Corinthians Paul writes, "I do not want to appear to be frightening you with my let-ters. For they say, 'his letters are weighty and strong, but his bodily presence is weak, and his speech of no account.' Let such a person understand that what we say by letter when absent, we do when present" (2 Cor. 10:9–11).[7] Even when the apostles are alive and active among the churches, their letters already begin to function as an authoritative guide for the apostolic understanding of the gospel message.

Keeping an Eye on the Storyline and the Promised Line

The writings of the apostles guide and govern the churches even after the apostles are no longer present because of distance, detainment, or death. Both Paul and Peter anticipate their inevitable departure, but also insist that their teaching and the truth of the gospel message will endure (2 Tim. 4:6–8; 2 Peter 1:12–15).

As Paul writes from prison, "*Remember* Jesus Christ, risen from the dead, the offspring of David, as preached in my gospel, for which I am suffering, bound with chains as a crim-inal. But the word of God is not bound! Therefore I endure everything for the sake of the elect, that they also may obtain the salvation that is in Christ Jesus with eternal glory" (2 Tim. 2:8–10). And as Peter writes toward the end of his life, "This is now the second letter that I am writing to you, beloved. In both of them I am stirring up your sincere mind *by way of reminder*, that you should remember the predictions of the holy prophets and the commandment of the Lord and Savior through your apostles . . . But according to his promise we are waiting for new heavens and a new earth in which righteousness dwells" (2 Peter 3:1–2, 13).

This perspective is both retrospective and prospective. Rooted in the reality of gospel message that is connected to the story of the Law, the Prophets, the Writings, the Gospels, and Acts, the churches are equipped to endure until the risen Christ returns. The means by

---

7. See also 2 Cor. 3:1–3, Gal. 6:11, and 2 Peter 3:15–16 (cf. too 2 John 1:2).

which the churches will persevere to the end will be to remember both old words and new words. Paul and Peter each point to the shape of a gospel that takes two Testaments to tell: Jesus, the Christ; Son of David, risen from the dead; predicted by the prophets, proclaimed through the apostles. Between the advents, the churches press on to maturity and press on to the end alongside of these exhortations provided by the engaging and ordered collection of New Testament Epistles.

Discussion Questions

1. As you consider the story of Acts and the New Testament Letters, what elements of the biblical-theological framework of the canon, the covenants, and the Christ do you see developed?

2. How does the book of Acts continue the story of the Gospels and prepare you for what comes next in the letter collections of the New Testament?

3. What role do the speeches play in the book of Acts? Describe and reflect upon some of the textual and theological connections that exist between the speeches themselves and between the speeches and the rest of the book.

4. Reflect on the narrative emphasis on the "journey to Jerusalem" in Luke and the emphasis of Jesus's words in Acts 1:8. What are some of the historical, textual, and theological implications of this connection?

5. In Acts 1–2 how do Jesus and Peter explain the relationship between the coming of the Son and the coming of the Spirit in God's plan of redemption? What biblical-theological themes connect to these explanations?

Resources for Further Study

Childs, Brevard S. *The Church's Guide for Reading Paul: The Canonical Shaping of the Pauline Corpus*. Grand Rapids: Eerdmans, 2008.

Lockett, Darian R. *Letters from the Pillar Apostles: The Formation of the Catholic Epistles as a Canonical Collection*. Eugene: Pickwick, 2017.

Rosner, Brian S. *Paul and the Law: Keeping the Commandments of God*. Downers Grove: InterVarsity, 2013.

Schreiner, Thomas R. *Paul, Apostle of God's Glory in Christ: A Pauline Theology*. Second Edition. Downers Grove: InterVarsity, 2020.

Thompson, Alan J. *The Acts of the Risen Lord Jesus: Luke's Account of God's Unfolding Plan*. Downers Grove: InterVarsity, 2011.

CHAPTER 10

THE STORY OF REVELATION

The Shape of Revelation

THE STORY OF THE NEW TESTAMENT begins with the Gospel collection and its four diverse yet complementary accounts of the coming of the Son. The book of Acts continues this narrative storyline by providing an account of the coming of the Spirit and the growth of the churches. The New Testament Epistles provide two distinct collections of apostolic teaching and dialogue about the nature of the gospel and the life of the churches.

Though at first it may seem disconnected from the story of the New Testament, it is important to recognize that the book of Revelation (also known as the Apocalypse of John) strategically picks up the narrative that began with the Gospels and Acts. After the structural pause represented by the Catholic Epistles and Paul's Letters, Revelation provides a multilayered narrative that connects the earliest churches to the end of days. Because John's Apocalypse is technically an epistle as well, it is fitting that it appears alongside these letter collections in the broader New Testament collection. This apocalyptic letter serves a crucial canonical function. The beginning of the book contains seven letters to seven churches, mirroring the middle section of the New Testament canon. These seven letters structurally and thematically bind the book of Revelation to the rest of the New Testament writings.

An element that strengthens the connection between Revelation and the rest of the New Testament Epistles is that each of its seven letters to the churches has a clear structure, highlighting that they were composed as distinguishable letters for distinct churches. Each of the seven letters includes a greeting to the church's leader, a description of Christ, words of commendation or criticism, a warning or exhortation, and a promise for those who persevere.[1]

Accordingly, after two major collections of epistles, Revelation begins with a carefully crafted letter collection. Readers of the New Testament will be familiar with such a sequence of letters by an author to a number of churches. The Muratorian Fragment, an early canon list, connects the seven letters in Revelation 2–3 to the Pauline Corpus. In the middle of a discussion concerning Paul's Epistles, the Muratorian Fragment reads, "For John also in the Apocalypse, though he writes to seven churches, nevertheless speaks to all."[2] What is more, John "speaks to all" in one literary location, namely, his *book* of Revelation. These seven letters to the seven churches could be read by everyone because each one was received and passed along within this embedded letter collection. This structural feature of Revelation echoes and anticipates the shape of the New Testament collection.

After the epistolary interlude of this letter section, Revelation 4 picks up the narrative thread and John's vision carries it into the eschatological horizon of a new heaven and a new earth (Revelation 21–22). Because of these textual features, John's Apocalypse is the exclamation point of the biblical storyline. Here redemptive history culminates in the vision John recounts in the final chapters of his book. The *Revelation* of Jesus Christ functions as the fitting canonical counterpart to the *Gospel* of Jesus Christ. The overarching narrative framework of the New Testament provides the believing community with a narration and interpretation of its origin (Gospels), expansion (Acts), and eschaton (Revelation).

The Story of Revelation

Though its enigmatic symbols, visions, and prophecies have perplexed interpreters throughout church history, a number of Revelation's features indicate the unity of the work as a whole.[3] One of the best ways to see the unity of the book is through a close reading of its beginning and ending. The prologue and epilogue provide readers with important clues for understanding the content that lies between them. There are many innertextual

1. To give two examples, each of these brief "letters to the churches" begin with the phrase "to the angel of the church of . . . write" (Rev. 2:1, 8, 12, 18; 3:1, 7, 14) and end with a form of the phrase, "He who has an ear, let him hear what the Spirit says to the churches" (2:7, 11, 17, 29; 3:6, 13, 22).
2. For this translation, see Metzger, *Canon of the New Testament*, 307.
3. For an extended discussion of the canonical shape of Revelation as well as some of its textual features from a variety of angles see Richard Bauckham, *The Theology of the Book of Revelation* (Cambridge: Cambridge University Press, 1993); William J. Dumbrell, *The End of the Beginning: Revelation 21-22 and the Old Testament* (Homebush West: Lancer, 1985); Alexander, *New Jerusalem*, 9–73; Külli Tõniste, *The Ending of the Canon: A Canonical and Intertextual Reading of Revelation 21-22*, Library of New Testament Studies 526 (London: Bloomsbury, 2016); Matthew Y. Emerson, *Christ and the New Creation: A Canonical Approach to the Theology of the New Testament* (Eugene: Wipf and Stock, 2013), 142–66; G. K. Beale, *John's Use of the Old Testament in Revelation*, Library of New Testament Studies 166 (London: Bloomsbury, 2015); and Brian J. Tabb, *All Things New: Revelation as Canonical Capstone* (Downers Grove: InterVarsity, 2019). The analysis of Revelation in this chapter also draws at various points on Spellman, *Toward a Canon-Conscious Reading*, 139–40, 225–34. Used by permission.

connections between Revelation 1 and 22 that serve as clear bookends for the work and help bind its various textual threads together. Revelation 1 contains a prologue (1:1–3), an epistolary introduction (1:4–6), and the beginning of the book's narrative sequence (1:9–20). The final chapter concludes the narrative begun in the first chapter (22:1–5), and contains an epistolary epilogue alongside a sequence of closing editorial comments (22:10–20) and a benediction (22:21). These similarities provide an initial sense of cohesion for the complex content of the rest of the book.[4]

The prologue of Revelation 1:1–3 serves an important function in alerting the readers to the subsequent content of "this book." The book's subject matter is the "revelation of Jesus Christ." This revelation has its ultimate source in God ("which God gave him") and its purpose is "to show to his servants the things that must soon take place" (1:1). Further, this revelatory vision of the future is mediated through God's angel who communicates the message to God's bond servant. John in turn bears witness to the word of God and testimony of Jesus Christ (1:2). John is identified here as a faithful and comprehensive witness who testifies concerning everything that he sees.

Though there is much debate regarding the exact chronological sequence of the events described in the book, John gives a definite shape to the narrative as a whole that helps readers access its message. The narrative begins on earth with John located on the island of Patmos. Though the bulk of the book recounts his eschatological vision, a straightforward historical narrative frames the book. After greeting his readers (1:4–7), John tells his story in the first-person perspective: "I, John, your brother . . ." (1:9).

This brief narrative sequence that begins the book is crucial for understanding the shape of Revelation as a whole. The apocalyptic events and visions that occur throughout the bulk of the book are set within this narrative framework. John provides the setting for his narrative by recounting that he was on the "island called Patmos" because of the "word of God and the testimony of Jesus" (1:9). More specifically, John was "in the Spirit on the Lord's day" (1:10) when he hears behind him a voice that he soon realizes comes from the risen Christ (1:12–16).

After Jesus commands him to write what he sees in a book, John describes the dramatic scene that followed: "When I saw him, I fell at his feet as though dead" (1:17).[5] What happens next sets the tone for the rest of the book and essentially begins the "revelation of Jesus." Jesus places his right hand on John and begins to speak. After comforting John and commanding him again to write (1:17–19), Jesus explains the vision that John beholds and

---

4. Note also the emphasis on reading and writing a "book" in the opening and closing sections of Revelation (1:3, 17; 22:7, 10, 18–19).

5. A prophet falling at the feet of a heavenly being is a common theme in the literature of the Old Testament (see especially Dan. 8:15–27; 10:5–20; Ezek. 1:28; 2:1).

dictates seven letters for John to send to the seven churches of Asia Minor. This extended section of dialogue concludes the first scene of the book.

After this first scene (chapters 1–3), John is ushered by the Spirit into the throne room of heaven where he sees an extended series of visions (chapters 4–16). A clear pattern in this section of the vision is the use of the number seven. The action of God's end-time judgment is displayed in the opening of seven seals (6:1–8:5), the sounding of the seven trumpets (8:6–11:19), the sequence of seven significant events (12:1–14:20), and the outpouring of seven bowls (15:1–16:21). John is then carried away by the Spirit into the wilderness where he envisions a great struggle between the Lamb and his enemies. After this struggle Christ returns in triumph, reigns for a thousand years, and then metes out cosmic judgment (chapters 17–20). Finally, John witnesses the creation of a new heaven and a new earth, and receives by the Spirit a vision of the heavenly Jerusalem (chapters 21–22). Though these narrative sections obviously require much exegetical effort and analysis, the point here is that they have a clear sense of forward momentum through time and are presented in an overarching narrative framework provided by Revelation 1 and Revelation 22.[6]

The narrative sequence of John's reception of these eschatological visions concludes in Revelation 22:6 following the completion of the final vision of cosmic re-creation. Here, the angel assures John (and the readers) that "these words are trustworthy and true," arguing for the authenticity and credibility of the previous prophetic visions.[7] Following this angelic discourse, an editorial comment recounts the main purpose of the Apocalypse in a way that echoes the introduction: "The Lord, the God of the spirits of the prophets, has sent his angel to show his servants what must soon take place."[8] After this comment and Jesus's words in 22:7, John makes one final editorial statement that seeks to ensure the genuine nature of his writing and demonstrate that his account is based on sound eyewitness testimony. He confesses, "I, John, am the one who heard and saw these things" (22:8).[9]

In 22:16, Jesus makes a succinct statement that sums up the structure of the first three chapters: "I, Jesus, have sent my angel to testify to you about these things for the churches." John then ends the book with a salutation typical of the other New Testament Epistles.[10] These words also resonate with John's epistolary greeting in 1:4. There is thus literary cohesion between the various editorial and narrative features of the beginning and ending of the book.

---

6. The broad outline of the narrative given here utilizes the references to John being transported "in the Spirit" as indications of scene transition.

7. The speaker in Revelation 22:6 is identified later as "one of the seven angels who had the seven bowls full of the seven plagues" (22:9).

8. Note the verbal links with the prologue of Revelation 1:1–3.

9. John's editorial comments in chapter 22 counterpart his authorial introductions in Revelation 1:4, 9. John makes similar statements in his Gospel and 1 John with a similar "eyewitness" formula (e.g., John 19:35, 1 John 1:1–4).

10. In the benediction, John says, "The grace of the Lord Jesus be with you all. Amen." Paul usually ends his letters with a similar benediction (e.g., Rom. 16:20; 1 Cor. 16:23; 2 Cor. 13:14).

Revelation as a Fitting Conclusion to the Grand Storyline

One of the important points to make about the book of Revelation is its basic narrative framework. Here at the end of the New Testament collection, we receive a final revelation from the resurrected Christ. The book has a narrative framework that includes a commission from Jesus to one of his apostles, letters to seven churches, allusions to the beginning of all things, and a vision of the end of all things. Revelation is situated at the close of the New Testament canon to provide a remarkably cohesive account of the past, present, and future work of God in the world and how believers should function in light of this all-encompassing vision of reality.

One of the clear ways Revelation helps us see the coherence of the grand storyline of the Bible as a whole is the way that it ends. As mentioned in the story of the Law in chapter five, the narratives of Genesis 1–3 are of critical importance for the biblical storyline and the resulting biblical meta-narrative (i.e., worldview). Important themes mentioned here are developed throughout the Old and New Testaments.

Genesis begins with the creation of the heavens and the earth (Gen. 1:1) and Revelation ends with the creation of a *new* heaven and a *new* earth. In the final chapters of his book, John explores how the work of God in the risen Christ brings about the renewal of all creation, the restoration of God's original purpose for humanity, and the enduring promise of a coming redeemer. Each of these themes is supported by verbal, thematic, or structural links to significant texts from the Hebrew Bible. In particular, through a network of intertextual allusions to the narratives of Genesis 1–3, John creates in Revelation 21–22 a book-length bookend for the biblical canon and storyline.

Renewed Creation

After the judgment at the great white throne (20:11–15), John recounts, "Then I saw a new heaven and a new earth" (21:1). Next, John sees "the holy city, new Jerusalem, coming down out of heaven from God, prepared as a bride adorned for her husband" (21:2). After this creative event, "a loud voice from the throne" provides an interpretation of what John has just seen which emphasizes the incredible effect the divine presence has on the worship of God's people (21:3–4).

In the following paragraph this "loud voice from the throne" makes a summary pronouncement over this new creation: "Behold, I am making all things new." John is again commanded to "Write this down, for these words are trustworthy and true" (21:5). God then tells John with a note of finality, "It is done. I am the Alpha and the Omega, the beginning and the end." Thus ends the sequence of creative actions in these last chapters of Revelation. The remainder of Revelation 21 describes and explains the new creation that takes place in 21:1–5. After proclaiming the completion of the new creation, God offers blessings for those who believe and overcome and curses for those who are cowardly and do not believe (21:7). After beholding God fashion the new creation, John gets a guided tour of the new Jerusalem (21:10–27), including the river of the water of life and the tree of life (22:1–2). The pastoral imagery and heavenly vision of Revelation 21:1–22:5 is set within the framework of God's creative activity.

This theme of creation is foundational for much of the biblical and prophetic understanding of the world. God as creator of the heavens and the earth is one of the most important characterizations of Israel's God. Accordingly, the idea of a *new* creation is just as important and builds upon the theology of God as creator. Just as in the Genesis account, "he who was seated on the throne" in Revelation 21:5 speaks and *all things* are made new: "Behold, I am making all things new."

Renewed Worship

Continuing the parallel with the creation narratives, Revelation 21 displays a scene that essentially fills out the original purpose of creation. Before the fall into sin described in Genesis 3, a snapshot of the purpose of mankind on the earth is provided in Genesis 2. Adam and Eve are placed in the garden to serve God, enjoy his presence, and worship and obey their creator. The scene in Genesis 2 indicates humanity's created purpose. As mentioned in chapter five, the verbs in Genesis 2:15 translated as "work" and "keep" are elsewhere used to describe the worship of Israel, specifically the priestly "service" and "guarding" of the tabernacle.[11]

By using these terms, the author of Genesis shows that one of humanity's created purposes is to worship and obey the Lord by keeping his commands and guarding his covenant relationship with them. They were to be God's people, and the Lord was to be their God. This purpose is the foundational element of the various covenant relationships that occur in subsequent biblical narratives. The garden of Eden was intended to be the place where God met with his people. The later Old Testament institutions of the tabernacle and the temple were intended to serve a similar worship-oriented function. The garden, the tabernacle, and the temple are all means by which God could be present among his people.

In his account of the eschatological recreation in Revelation 21–22, John makes use of all three of these sacred locations. After beholding the new heaven and earth (21:1), John sees "the holy city, new Jerusalem, coming down out of heaven from God" (21:2). The covenantal overtones are indicated by the use of marriage imagery. The holy city has been "prepared as a bride adorned for her husband" (21:2).[12] The new Jerusalem represents God's divine presence. The portrayal of the new Jerusalem in Revelation 21:10–21 draws on prophetic descriptions

---

11. E.g., Num. 3:7–8; 8:25–26; 18:5–6, 1 Chron. 23:32; Ezek. 44:14.
12. Note the connection between a marriage at the beginning of the Bible (Genesis 2) and a marriage at the end of the Bible (Revelation 19, 21). Isaiah 61:10 and 62:5 pick up the marriage imagery as well.

of the future temple.[13] The details of this description reveal that the city has been constructed with the most precious of materials. Everything in the new Jerusalem demonstrates its exceeding value and worth. However, the rarity and worth of the city is ultimately derived from the one who dwells there: God himself. The brilliance of the city is rightly seen only in relation to its most profound characteristic, namely "the glory of God" (21:11).

That the portrayal and purpose of the holy city points to God's divine presence with his people is confirmed by references to the tabernacle and the temple after this description of the new Jerusalem. In Revelation 21:3, John hears a voice say, "Behold, the tabernacle of God is among men" (NASB). This voice provides another expression of covenantal relationship by saying that "He will dwell with them, and they will be his people, and God himself will be with them as their God" (21:3).[14] After the description of the city (21:10–21), John notes the absence of a temple in its midst: "I saw no temple in the city." John explains that the divine presence removes the need for a temple. He reasons, "for its temple is the Lord God the Almighty and the Lamb" (21:22).

The new Jerusalem also no longer needs the light of the sun or the moon, "for the glory of God gives it light, and its lamp is the Lamb" (21:23). This detail regarding the obsolete function of the sun and the moon indicates that the new creation far surpasses the old creation. Whereas before the sun and moon lit up the world of humankind, the Lamb who was slain for them now performs that function. This is a profound fulfillment of what John says in the prologue of his Gospel: "The true light, which gives light to everyone, was coming into the world" (John 1:9). This light illumines not only Israel, but also the nations who will walk "by its light" and the kings of the earth who will "bring their glory into it" (21:24). The illumination of the divine presence reorders the way the universe works.[15]

Renewed Eden

Another striking element of this new creation is the removal of sin and the reversal of the curse. In Revelation 22, John is shown the "river of the water of life, bright as crystal, flowing from the throne of God and of the Lamb through the middle of the street of the city" (22:1–2). Alongside this crystal-clear river is "the tree of life" that bears twelve kinds of fruit which it yields every month.[16] This idyllic scene strongly echoes the picture of the garden of Eden in Genesis 2. However, this new garden is altogether different, for here

---

13. The details John records regarding the holy city are imbued with imagery from Ezekiel 40–48.
14. Cf. the wording of John 1:14: "And the Word became flesh, and dwelt among us, and we saw His glory, glory as of the only begotten from the Father, full of grace and truth."
15. For instance, "In the daytime (for there will be no night there) its gates will never be closed" (Rev. 21:25). The details given here parallel the scene in Isaiah 60:19ff.
16. Though Ezekiel mentions "many trees" in his vision (Ezek. 47:7), the "tree of life" in Revelation 22:2 likely originates in the Genesis creation narratives (Gen. 2:9).

there is no serpent lurking in the shadows.[17] The leaves of this tree of life no longer recall transgression, but are "for the healing of the nations" (22:2). Whereas Genesis 3 recounts the consequences of disobedience among the trees in the garden, on this day "there will no longer be any curse" (Rev. 22:3, NASB). The eschatological garden will be the throne room of God and the Lamb, and "his servants will worship him" (22:3).

This reversal of the effects of the curse is anticipated in Revelation 21:4–5. Acknowledging the pain and suffering that has taken place between the garden of Eden and the new Jerusalem, the voice tells John that God "will wipe away every tear from their eyes" and "death shall be no more, neither shall there be mourning, nor crying, nor pain anymore, for the former things have passed away" (21:4).[18] This scene paints a picture of the fulfillment of the new covenant. Sins have been forgiven, pain is no more, and the curse has been reversed. In short, paradise has been restored.

Renewed Promise

A final connection between Revelation 21–22 and Genesis 1–3 involves the identification of the one who accomplishes this redemption. Revelation makes clear that the work of the Lamb is the sole reason God's people are able to experience his presence in this new creation. In chapter 1 the Lamb is the one who has "has freed us from our sins by his blood" (Rev. 1:5). John's vision also reveals that this *Lamb* of God is also the *Lion* of Judah. John recounts in Revelation 5:5 that Jesus is "the Lion that is from the tribe of Judah, the Root of David."

These references to "the Lion of Judah" and "the Root of David" are clear thematic allusions to messianic texts of the Old Testament.[19] Later, in Revelation 22:16, Jesus declares, "I am the root and the descendent of David, the bright morning star."[20] This characterization of Jesus strongly resonates with the expectations found in the story of the Hebrew Bible concerning the coming Davidic king. The anticipation of a coming king from the tribe of Judah who will crush God's enemies, rule in power, and receive

---

17. In Revelation 12:9, John identifies "the great dragon" who was thrown down out of heaven as "the serpent of old who is called the devil and Satan, who deceives the whole world." This same "serpent of old" is bound for a thousand years in 20:2, and then in 20:10 is thrown into the lake of fire to be "tormented day and night forever and ever." Thus, readers of Revelation will know at this point in the book why there is no serpent found in this eschatological garden.

18. The statement of the reversal of the curse also "fills out" the prophetic vision of Isa 65:19–25.

19. The "lion of Judah" phrase is drawn from Genesis 49:9, and the "root of David" comes from Isa. 11:1, 10 (cf. Paul's use of this text in Rom. 15:12). These images are further utilized in Jeremiah 11:10; 23:5; 33:15; Zechariah 3:8.

20. Revelation 22:16, in particular, makes an important intertextual reference to one of these messianic passages. Here Jesus identifies himself as the "bright morning star." In Numbers 24:17, Balaam says that "A star shall come forth from Jacob, A scepter shall rise from Israel, And shall crush through the forehead of Moab, and tear down all the sons of Sheth" (NASB). In the latter part of Revelation, the Davidic messiah conquers the enemies of God, thus fulfilling the picture hinted in the Numbers passage. Cf. also 2 Peter 1:19.

the obedience of the people stems from promises of the Pentateuch (e.g., Gen. 49:8–10; Num. 24:7–9).[21]

This kingly promise is later joined with God's covenant promise to David in 2 Samuel 7. The coming king of the Pentateuch will be a son of David. In the story of the Law, the Prophets, and the Writings, the eschatological King of Israel comes from David's seed. Accordingly, in the Hebrew Bible, when the coming king is mentioned, the eschatological son of David is usually in view, or at least lurking nearby.[22]

Keeping an Eye on the Storyline and the Promised Line

By strategically identifying Jesus as the son of David, John adopts an important biblical image. One of the purposes of the vision of Revelation is to "fill out" this prophetic portrayal of Jesus as the reigning Davidic king. As the voices in the heavenly court proclaim in Revelation 11:15, John's vision anticipates the moment when "the kingdom of the world has become the kingdom of our Lord and of his Christ, and he shall reign forever and ever."

Just as John's gospel showed how Jesus's crucifixion filled out the scene of the suffering servant of Psalm 22, here John's Apocalypse shows how Jesus's exaltation fills out the scene of the reigning son of Psalm 2.

Just as the focus on Jesus as the Christ ties the book of Revelation to the rest of the New Testament, so too this emphasis binds it to the story of the Old Testament. Indeed, the revelation of Jesus as the prophesied Davidic Messiah might be "the canonical integrating element within the whole of the OT and the NT."[23] Only in this coming king is the hope of a new creation and a new life made a reality.

---

21. As mentioned in chapter five, the promise of a redeemer begins even as the curse is being pronounced in Genesis 3:15. The future-oriented perspective of the kingly blessing in Genesis 49 is drawn from the "end of days" perspective of Jacob's blessing (49:1).
22. See these themes developed in chapters five through seven.
23. See Sailhamer, *Meaning of the Pentateuch*, 461.

Discussion Questions

1. As you consider the story of Revelation, what elements of the biblical-theological framework of the canon, the covenants, and the Christ do you see developed?

2. List and discuss the emphasis on reading and writing in Revelation. What is the significance of this textual focus on texts?

3. What are some of the central ways in which the major vision that John sees relates to the rest of the book of Revelation as a whole (i.e., the opening and closing sections, and the letters to the churches)?

4. What aspects of the book of Revelation connect to the shape of the New Testament canon?

5. Describe ways in which the book of Revelation functions as a fitting conclusion to biblical canon and the grand storyline of the Bible.

Resources for Further Study

Bauckham, Richard. *The Theology of the Book of Revelation*. Cambridge: Cambridge University Press, 1993.

Beale, G. K. *John's Use of the Old Testament in Revelation*. London: T&T Clark, 2015.

Dumbrell, William J. *The End of the Beginning: Revelation 21-22 and the Old Testament*. Homebush West, NSW: Lancer, 1985.

Tabb, Brian J. *All Things New: Revelation as Canonical Capstone*. Downers Grove: InterVarsity, 2019.

Tõniste, Külli. *The Ending of the Canon: A Canonical and Intertextual Reading of Revelation 21-22*. London: T&T Clark, 2016.

SECTION 3

THE BIBLE'S SIGNIFICANT THEMES

CHAPTER 11

TOOLS FOR ORGANIZING AND PRESENTING BIBLICAL THEOLOGY

IN SECTION ONE, WE DISCUSSED several foundational elements crucial for under-standing the Bible's overarching shape and message. In section two, we surveyed the grand storyline of the Bible as it unfolds across the Old and New Testament collections. These are important ways of accessing and analyzing the message of the Bible as a whole on its own terms. In section three, we shift from analyzing the Bible's theology to organizing and presenting the Bible's theology. This section of the book will highlight the key themes that emerge in the overall study of Scripture as well as explore the tools that help us discern and develop these themes.

Central Themes in Biblical Theology

The *central theme tool* involves tracing a biblical-theological theme across the entire scope of the canon. While recognizing that anything that appears in biblical literature is important and worthy of further study, there are nevertheless certain themes that are es-pecially strategic and pervasive. These themes enable us to see interconnections between the Law, the Prophets, the Writings, the Gospels, Acts, the Letters, and Revelation. When a theme shows up in a strategic or pervasive way in each of these groupings, we can confi-dently classify it as a *central theme*. In other words, this type of theme is central to the mes-sage and textual intention of the biblical authors who have written their books with specific purposes in mind.

These themes help the reader recognize what merits the greatest amount of attention in the Scriptures. The goal of this type of study is to explore the development of these themes across the canon and observe how each theme progresses at different points in the grand storyline of the Bible. Initially, though, it is important to define what a central theme is, identify the criteria for selecting a central theme, and discern the purpose of these themes for both biblical authors and readers.

Is Tracing a Central Theme across the Canon Still Considered Biblical Theology?

Many evangelical approaches to biblical theology emphasize the importance of a "whole Bible" theology. One way to achieve this is to trace central themes across the canon. One might ask, however, whether tracing a theological theme within a book, across a corpus, and ultimately throughout the entire canon is still distinctly *biblical theology*? Or, at this point, have we moved into the realm of systematic theology or "pan-biblical" theology?[1]

The crucial issue seems not to be whether one develops a central theme, but rather the method by which one develops and presents that theme. A methodologically solid thematic approach develops a theme as it organically unfolds across the canon. A central theme that is developed with careful attention given to the literary and canonical features of the biblical writings qualifies as a biblical theology "tool" that can showcase a textual and intertextual reality. Part of the task of biblical theology is to function as a guide for reading. Central themes are part of that task insofar as they highlight for readers in an ordered and clear way the main lines of emphasis that occur throughout the Bible.

Further, it is possible to trace a central theme across the canon while maintaining clear distinctions between exegesis (close reading), biblical theology, and systematic theology. In other words, when you trace a central theme, you are doing something different than exegeting an individual passage. However, because these central themes are developed through analysis of intertextual connections, the shape of canonical collections, and the theological emphases of biblical authors within their own discrete writings, these central themes are textually and theologically anchored by the contours of Bible's literary landscape. Moreover, because this type of analysis notes, traces, and organizes these textual features across books, corpora, and testaments, it has a synchronic aspect to its practice.

Conceiving of biblical theology as only a "bridge discipline" that links exegesis to systematic theology is probably too rigid. However, tracing central biblical-theological themes across the Old and New Testaments (with all of the unity and diversity entailed in this study) seems to provide a *bridging* element that *blends* both diachronic and synchronic elements.

---

1. For a survey of the range of opinion on this particular question, see Klink and Lockett, *Understanding Biblical Theology*, 67–73. For James Barr's critique of "whole Bible" theologies, see *Concept of Biblical Theology*, 4–14. Barr identifies this type of analysis as pan-biblical as opposed to biblical theology because he understands biblical theology as a primarily historical and descriptive task (see also the discussion of Barr's perspective in chapter one).

Why "across the Canon" Rather Than Only "through History"?

When you trace a central theme, you are making a decision about the way you will organize the results of your biblical-theological study. One key difference between the discrete disciplines of systematic theology and biblical theology is their mode of presentation. Typically, systematic theologies develop logically in relation to some sort of "synchronic" structure (*within time*). Biblical theology presentations instead typically utilize some sort of "diachronic" progression (*through time*). In particular, when a theme is developed in biblical theology, there is usually a clear attempt to demonstrate a temporal or chronological progression of the theme *through time* ("diachronic"). This way of presenting biblical theology themes resonates with the hallmark of most biblical theology approaches rooted in historical development.[2]

For evangelicals with a strong belief in divine providence and a high view of Scripture, this historical emphasis focuses on salvation history or redemptive history. In this manner, a central theme is traced "through time" or "through redemptive history." Klink and Lockett summarize this emphasis: "While insisting on a 'whole-Bible theology,' the way to discern this development is through tracing the major themes and overarching structural ideas through the whole of Scripture. Crucially, however, these themes and structural ideas are only discernable as they develop chronologically."[3]

A particularly helpful articulation of this clear attention to historical progression as the primary organizing principle of biblical theology is D. A. Carson's approach to the discipline. As the editor of the NIV Biblical Theology Study Bible, Carson outlines his emphasis on salvation history in "A Biblical-Theological Overview of the Bible."[4] For Carson, biblical theology studies "keep one eye focused on the passage of time—i.e., on where any biblical document or theme is located in what is often called 'salvation history' (the history of redemption). God did not choose to disclose everything in one moment of spectacular revelation. Rather, he chose to disclose himself and his purposes progressively, through events and words spread across many centuries, climaxing in his Son, Jesus Christ."[5]

---

2. Cf. also the discussion of the terms diachronic and synchronic in chapter one.

3. Klink and Lockett, *Understanding Biblical Theology*, 59. More fully, they note that "the task of BT2 is to discern the historical progression of God's work of redemption through an inductive analysis of key themes developing through both discrete corpora and the whole of Scripture. Major themes such as covenant and kingdom constitute the theological connecting fibers between the Old and New Testaments, and these themes necessarily run along a historical trajectory, giving fundamental structure to the theology of the Bible" (61). For Lockett's interaction and critique of this particular aspect of salvation-oriented approaches, see Darian Lockett, "Limitations of a Purely Salvation-Historical Approach to Biblical Theology," *Horizons in Biblical Theology* 39.2 (2017): 211–31.

4. D. A. Carson, "Biblical-Theological Overview." For other entry points to Carson's biblical-theological method, see his "Systematic Theology and Biblical Theology"; "Current Issues in Biblical Theology: A New Testament Perspective," *Bulletin for Biblical Research* 5 (1995): 17–41; and "Biblical Theology," in *Dictionary of Biblical Criticism and Interpretation*, ed. Stanley E. Porter (London: Routledge, 2007), 35–41.

5. Carson, "Biblical-Theological Overview," 2325.

Carson summarizes the shape of salvation history as creation, fall, redemption, and consumption. As he says, "That is the entire story, painted with the broadest brush."[6] After discussing how this salvation history could be deepened and utilized, Carson concludes, "Above all, salvation history provides the locus in which God has disclosed himself in events and in the words that explain them. As salvation history is the framework of the Bible's storyline, so it is the locus of the revelation of the living God, the Lord of history."[7]

While noting the value of biblical-theological work produced along these lines, there are also several reasons to speak of tracing a central theme across the canon rather than only through history.

- **The canon provides the resources to perceive both the historical and theological development of a central theme through time.** In other words, tracing a theme *across the canon* satisfies the criteria that often drive an interpreter towards either a reconstructed historical setting or a reconstructed salvation history. Because of the way the canon is ordered, if a theme emerges at different or multiple points across the spectrum of the collection, it will in fact be presented in the context of different periods of redemptive history. Thus, the narrative flow and canonical context of the biblical collection seems to serve as an adequate and sufficient ordering principle for the diachronic development of central themes in biblical theology.
- **The canon provides a narrative context that includes a forward momentum.** Within the canonical collection, the many biblical narratives influence the perception and shape of the biblical storyline. Redemptive history is generated from the shape of these canonical narratives. Accordingly, if the development of a central theme takes its cues from this unfolding storyline, this organic development is a direct result of the inter-connected narratives and ordered collections found in the canon itself. The use of a storyline in biblical theology is well-established among evangelicals. The point being made here is that this forward-moving grand storyline is a direct product of reading and studying *just these texts* in *just this collection*.
- **The canon provides both a narration and interpretation of redemptive history.** Because the biblical authors both narrate and interpret the history of redemption, their many narratives collected and intertextually connected in the biblical canon can serve as a natural and logical means by which a central theme can organically unfold. This orienting focus allows an interpreter to make full use of the nature of narrative and an author's textual intention in the development of a biblical theme.

---

6. Carson, "Biblical-Theological Overview," 2326.
7. Carson, "Biblical-Theological Overview," 2327.

- **The canon guards the enduring relevance of the Old Testament as Christian Scripture.** Sometimes, when the categories of progressive revelation and historical progression are stressed as the primary means of development, it can become difficult to maintain or articulate the enduring relevance of Old Testament texts. Once an Old Testament theme or concept reaches fulfilment in the new covenant or is developed by a New Testament author, what then is its enduring value? Developing a theme or concept by using canonical categories rather than only historical ones helps demonstrate the theological and hermeneutical value of earlier texts in the canon even though the development of that theme or concept will continue in subsequent locations in the biblical canon.

Why Central Themes Rather Than a Center?

In the field of evangelical biblical theology, there is a longstanding general consensus that the articulation of a "center" or single organizing theme that integrates all the others is not a feasible pursuit or a helpful endeavor. Rather than pinpoint a *single center* to organize the produce of biblical theology, the more fruitful way forward is to articulate a *collection* of *central* biblical-theological themes that capture major swaths of the theological message found across the Bible.

In relation to Old Testament theology, Sailhamer notes that "problems arise primarily when one takes the position that the whole of OT must be fit into a single idea or concept and then narrows that concept to such an extent that it begins to distort the biblical material."[8] He also observes that "although this suggestion falls short of the goal of finding a single theme, it goes a long way toward unifying the theological message of the OT and at the same time of easing the pressure of having to fit all of the OT around a single theme."[9] In relation to New Testament theology, Carson observes, "the pursuit of the center is chimerical." According to Carson, "We will make better progress by pursuing clusters of broadly common themes which may not be common to all NT books."[10] Further, while

---

8. Sailhamer, *Introduction to Old Testament Theology*, 193. He notes further that "it is possible to arrange the theology of the OT around a single idea or cluster of themes without insisting that everything in the OT conform precisely to that idea or those themes" (193). "The purpose of structure," Sailhamer insists, "is to enhance our understanding of the material, not distort that material" (193).
9. Sailhamer, *Introduction to Old Testament Theology*, 21.
10. D. A. Carson, "New Testament Theology," in *Dictionary of the Later New Testament and Its Developments*, ed. Ralph Martin and Peter Davids (Downers Grove: InterVarsity, 1997), 811. Cf. Gerhard Hasel's comment reflecting on his analysis of the New Testament theology produced in the first part of the twentieth century: "The richness of the NT testimonies can be grasped by such a multiplex approach as is commensurate with the nature of the NT. This multiplex approach with the multitrack treatment of longitudinal themes frees the Biblical theologian from the notion of an artificial and forced unilinear approach determined by a single structuring concept, whether it is covenant, communion, kingdom of God, or something else, to which all NT testimonies, thoughts, and concepts are made to refer or are forced to fit." See *New Testament Theology: Basic Issues in the Current Debate* (Grand Rapids: Eerdmans, 1978), 217.

many minor themes are present in various books, "the points of connection from corpus to corpus must be delineated" through the "major themes." For, "although it seems wise to avoid committing oneself to one disputable center, inevitably the texts themselves will force a hierarchializing of unifying themes."[11]

Similarly, Paul House argues that "we should give up arguing that one theme and one theme only is the central theme of the Bible and highlight major themes that allow other ideas as subpoints."[12] At the same time, House continues, "we must acknowledge that salvation history, covenant, creation and messiah are necessarily broad themes that require elaboration and schematization. *Any* theme that links much of the Bible must be broad and must not be rejected for being broad. A broad theme is not the canon's only theme; it is a centering theme." With this in mind, House explains, "as long as the major theme is clearly discernible in several parts of the canon, as long as it is charted alongside other major themes, as long as it is treated as an important part of a whole instead of being the whole, then it should be welcomed, used and critiqued."[13]

In the end, a collection of themes better captures what we find within a collection of diverse yet unified biblical writings. Within the framework of the canon, the covenants, and the Christ, we find several central themes that the biblical authors themselves introduce and develop. Accordingly, when detecting and studying these central themes, the goal is to use as many textual features as possible in our analysis. This approach to the shape and analysis of the Bible highlights the remarkable level of coherence that the biblical canon possesses as a collection on its own terms.

After considering some of these orienting matters, we can now focus on a few practical aspects regarding the study of central themes. First, we will address some of the issues to consider when *perceiving* and then *presenting* a central theme.

Perceiving a Central Theme

In developing a central theme, the first step is to *perceive* the central theme itself. In order to do this, you must have a general understanding of the criteria for discerning a

---

11. Carson, "New Testament Theology," 811.
12. Paul R. House, "Biblical Theology and the Wholeness of Scripture: Steps Toward a Program for the Future," in *Biblical Theology: Retrospect and Prospect*, ed. Scott J. Hafemann (Downers Grove: InterVarsity, 2002), 276.
13. House, "Wholeness of Scripture," 276. In the end, for House, "unitary biblical theology should include canonical synthesis of major themes. After intertextual exegetical work has been done in book-by-book canonical order for the purpose of identifying and utilizing major themes it is necessary to produce clear treatments of major themes as they emerge from the whole of Scripture" (277). House illustrates this approach to central themes in his essay, "The Day of the Lord," in *Central Themes in Biblical Theology*, ed. Scott J. Hafemann and Paul R. House (Grand Rapids: Baker, 2007), 179–224. On this theme, House concludes that "this subject plays a strategic role not just in the proclamation of the gospel, its most important role, but also in the construction of a unity paradigm for biblical theology" (224). He also notes that the presentation of the day of the Lord theme is "an interesting example of unity within a normal and understandable level of diversity" (224).

central theme, including what a central theme is, and what makes a theme "central" for the study of biblical theology.

- A central theme is a theme that *shows up* and *develops* across the canon. A central theme shows up multiple times at strategic *moments* in the Bible's grand storyline and at strategic *locations* in the biblical canon. In this way, the canon and the covenants can help identify and shape what the central themes of the biblical canon are, as well as the content and nature of these central themes.
- A central theme will *interface* with several other major and minor themes.[14] As noted above, a central theme will have several textual connections with a variety of biblical passages throughout the canon. These textual connections are often the means by which you can see the theological development of a theme as multiple biblical authors take up a topic as part of their own purposes in writing.
- A central theme is one that is *central for the biblical authors themselves*. Thus, one of the controlling criteria for identifying a central theme is the textual intention of the biblical authors. Is this theme central for multiple biblical authors across the biblical canon? If the answer to this question is yes, then you are on firm ground for identifying this as one of the central biblical themes that tie the canonical material together.[15]

Presenting a Central Theme

As a biblical theologian, after you *perceive* a central theme, you must then *present* it in some fashion. Once you have *perceived* a central theme through careful analysis, how do you then *present* that theme with clarity?

To present a central theme, you will need to first utilize the big picture framework for biblical theology. The canon, the covenants, and the Christ are the contours that can guide your understanding and articulation of the major themes of the biblical canon. Ideally, you will pursue your central theme in light of a working knowledge of the entire biblical canon.

- You'll need to identify the major passages that inform the central theme.
- You'll need to situate those passages in relation to the meaning and message of the books within which they appear.

---

14. Cf. Elmer A. Martens, "Tackling Old Testament Theology," *Journal of the Evangelical Theological Society* 20 (1997): 123–32: "Biblical theology investigates the themes presented in Scripture and defines their inter-relationships. Biblical theology is an attempt to get to the theological heart of the Bible" (123).
15. Cf. Alexander, *New Jerusalem*, 11: "Biblical scholarship as a whole has not articulated clearly the major themes that run throughout Scripture. Since these themes were an integral part of the thought world of the biblical authors, an appreciation of them may significantly alter our reading of individual books."

- You'll need to reckon with the way your central theme develops. This means paying special attention to how its distinctive treatment in each book interfaces with its treatment in other books and major canonical groupings.[16] Here you're asking: Is there any theological development as we move across the canon from Genesis to Revelation? From the Law to the Prophets? From before the exile to after the exile? From before the resurrection to after the resurrection? From Paul's letters to Peter's letters?
- You'll also need to ask how your central theme fits into the grand storyline of the Bible in its broadest scope: from creation to new creation (Genesis 1–3 to Revelation 21–22).

As you make your way through these steps, you'll be looking for verbal, thematic, and structural links between your passage and other biblical passages. Any intertextual quotations, allusions, or echoes in these passages represent the organic pathways given by the biblical authors to help readers see the intended connections that they make with other parts of the canonical collection.

What does *perceiving* and *presenting* a central theme as a biblical theologian mean? A biblical-theological approach both guides and governs the task of discerning and developing a central theme. You are looking for the ways that the biblical texts and authors, alongside the canonical context and the storyline of the Bible as a whole, impact and inform a particular theme. The study of central themes provides, too, a helpful case study of the blended approach that should oftentimes be taken when studying the entire Bible.

Tools for Tracing Central Themes

The Word/Concept Tool

When tracing a central biblical-theological theme, there are several methodological reminders or "tools" worth reflecting upon. One of these is the *word/concept tool*. The word/concept tool identifies where a given term or concept appears. This tool is a reminder that there is not a one-to-one correspondence between biblical words and biblical concepts. In other words, there are often *other words* that can be used even when the same concept is still in view.

The word/concept tool is a particularly important guard against the limitations of superficial word studies. As Rosner notes, "word studies alone are a shaky foundation upon which to base theology."[17] The reason for this scenario is the simple reality that an author

---

16. Cf. House, "Wholeness of Scripture," 269: "From the reading of sacred texts I am convinced that the Bible is a connected, canonical, theological whole. This emphasis on canonical wholeness leads me to believe that it is possible to use the shape of the canon as a structuring device for biblical theology." House notes further here that "the canonical order of books is a particularly attractive option because it can be viewed as an inherent part of the text."

17. Brian S. Rosner, "Biblical Theology," in *New Dictionary of Biblical Theology*, ed. T. Desmond Alexander and Brian S. Rosner (Downers Grove: InterVarsity, 2000), 6.

can use multiple terms and expressions to articulate and develop a single concept. While multiple biblical authors may use similar words and phrases to develop a single theme or concept, they may also utilize unique words and phrases. As a result, "concepts rather than words are a surer footing on which to base thematic study such as that involved in biblical-theological synthesis."[18]

Without the word/concept tool, a reader might neglect biblical passages that are relevant to the development of a central theme. This tool also highlights the necessarily interpretive component of even the seemingly straightforward task of identifying the appropriate passages for the study of a particular topic or theme.[19]

The caution of the word/concept tool is instructive to note as well. On the one hand, if a term or phrase does not appear frequently, but the concept does appear in many places and qualifies as a significant theme (e.g., "image of God"), you will need to think carefully about how those terms relate to the broader concept and then how the meaning of those biblical passages and books relate to one another. On the other hand, if a term or phrase does appear frequently (e.g., "glory"), it is still necessary to carefully observe how the term is used in each instance. Does the term possess the same meaning when used in Exodus and Isaiah as it does in Proverbs and Psalms? Does the term used in Matthew have the same sense in Romans and Revelation? This attention to the textual context of a particular term or phrase will help guard against funneling the formal results of a wide-ranging biblical-theological study back into a single use of a particular word.[20] Such a practice often asks biblical words to shoulder a weight they were never meant to bear.

---

18. Rosner, "Biblical Theology," 6. Rosner also notes that "in most cases the concept is in fact far bigger than the words normally used to refer to it, even when the words in question appear frequently" (6). Sometimes, though, "concepts have a relatively slim lexical base and yet can lay no less a claim to be of central importance" (7).

19. For a good example of the word/concept theme in action, see Stephen Dempster's development of the "Servant of the Lord" as a central theme in "Servant of the Lord," 128–78. As Dempster notes, the Servant of the Lord theme is a "dominant subject in only a few passages, yet is one of the major underlying concepts of the biblical message" (128). The word/concept tool enables Dempster to trace this theme across the two-testament canon. As he notes, "if one leans on linguistic evidence alone, the Servant theme does not seem to be as prominent in the New Testament as in the Old. But one should be wary of this type of analysis" because the concept of Jesus as the Servant of the Lord is a significant feature of New Testament Christology (134). In sum, "the concept of servant may be present even without the explicit wording" (135).

20. This phenomenon has been characterized as an "illegitimate totality transfer." Moisés Silva explains that this is "a somewhat awkward phrase intended to stress the simple fact that any one instance of a word will not bear all the meanings possible for that word." See *Biblical Words and Their Meaning: An Introduction to Lexical Semantics* (Grand Rapids: Zondervan, 1994), 25. He cautions that it is all too easy "to comment on the broad meanings of a word at the risk of obscuring its specific function in a given text" (26). Carson characterizes this mistake as an "unwarranted adoption of an expanded semantic field" involving the "supposition that the meaning of a word in a specific context is much broader than the context itself allows and may bring with it the word's entire semantic range." See *Exegetical Fallacies* (Grand Rapids: Baker, 1996), 60. Biblical theologians should keep this caution ever in mind when tracing a theme across the canon.

Accordingly, the word/concept tool reminds you to think carefully about how you analyze and synthesize both words *and* concepts. This type of reflective study remains critical not only when your central theme includes key words that frequently appear in biblical literature, but also when it includes terms that are far less frequent.

The Unity/Diversity Tool

Another methodological reminder is the *unity/diversity tool*. The unity/diversity tool involves recognizing how a central theme is presented across the canon in *connected* yet *different* ways. In other words, you must note where there is *continuity* and *discontinuity* with the central theme you are studying. There is both unity and diversity within the canonical collection. Grappling with this textual and theological reality is at the heart of the biblical theology endeavor. Accordingly, it is imperative to keep this dynamic in mind when presenting a central theme.[21]

The terms "Bible" and "canon" are both collective nouns that call us to conceptualize the Scriptures as a collection of individual writings that, simultaneously, constitute a composite whole. The notion of unity and diversity, then, is embedded in the very concept and creation of the biblical canon. The Book of the Twelve, the book of Psalms, the book of Proverbs, and the fourfold Gospels are all examples of this canonical phenomenon.

At this point, we can see the impact of the definitional decisions discussed in chapter one. If you take a purely historical approach that sees the historical distance between texts or the Testaments as too high a hurdle to overcome, then the notion of unity will seem unobtainable. In this approach, the Old Testament is rendered "a collection of many testimonies of faith from around a thousand years of the history of ancient Israel" which "has no unitary theology, nor can it."[22] Here the controlling category is diversity.

On the other hand, a theologian might affirm the theological unity of the Scriptures in such a way that the literary diversity of the biblical texts is muted or downplayed. Here, a narrative text might be analyzed alongside a poetic text or an epistle with no sense of the

---

21. Cf. Carson, "Current Issues in Biblical Theology." One of Carson's conclusions is that the most useful type of biblical-theological studies are those "that stress the distinctiveness of individual biblical corpora, while pressing toward a 'gesamtbiblische Theologie' [whole-Bible theology]" (17).

22. Erhard Gerstenberger, *Theologies in the Old Testament* (London: T&T Clark, 2001), 1. Gerstenberger's position illustrates the connection between one's view of the biblical canon and their approach to biblical theology. Because of Gerstenberger's understanding of the nature of the biblical canon (i.e., fragmented and incapable of organic unity) his understanding of biblical theology is built upon this foundation (likewise fragmented and incapable of organic unity). After the above quotation, he articulates, "The unitary belief in God, which we constantly want to emphasize . . . does not lie in the [Old Testament] texts themselves, even in the collected writings or the canon, but solely in our perspective." He says further, "The Old Testament cannot of itself offer any unitary theological or ethical view, since it is a conglomerate of experiences of faith from very different social situations." From Gerstenberger's perspective, the fact that these testimonies are "very fragmentary" and have been "edited and manipulated very heavily before coming down to us" is what frees us as readers from having to seek any type of overarching unity (1–2).

differing tone, perspective, or emphases articulated by different authors writing at different points in redemptive history. Here the controlling category is unity.

The concept of canon helps navigate and balance unity and diversity. The goal of interpreters is to grapple with this unity and diversity within the canonical collection. For example, it is significant that the Old Testament was never re-edited or re-assembled on a large scale by the earliest churches. Rather than discard it, harmonize it with recent events, or modify its contents in some other way, the churches by and large opted to preserve the contours of the individual books and groupings of the Hebrew Bible. This textual and canonical reality had a historical, theological, and hermeneutical impact on the earliest churches.

Similarly, when it came to collecting the Gospels, the churches on the whole rejected both Marcion's option (to select only one Gospel out of many) and Tatian's option (to harmonize all the Gospels into one). Rather, the consensus of the earliest churches produced the established practice of receiving the fourfold Gospel corpus of Matthew, Mark, Luke, and John. A fourfold Gospel collection, they insisted, is superior to either a single Gospel or a composite Gospel. This canonical reality commits the interpretive community that treasures these canonical texts to grapple with the relationship between unity and diversity. Why are the Gospels so similar? Why are they so different? This is not simply an issue of critical inquiry or trivial pursuit, but a question prompted by the canonical text we have received.

Tracing a central theme across the canon will involve highlighting the overarching coherence and unity of a theme while also noting how each author, book, grouping, or testament uniquely contributes to it. For evangelicals who believe in the unity of Scripture for theological reasons, the methodological reminder about unity/diversity is one of the most important tools in the interpretive tool chest. The broad canonical context, the biblical authors' shaping of their books, and intertextual connections between books will help direct and preserve distinct lines of continuity and discontinuity. In fact, this particular aspect of tracing central themes may be one of the most distinctive contributions of biblical theology to both the academic study of the Bible and the function of the Scriptures as the Word of God for the churches.

The Strategic Selection Tool

A final practical tool to consider is the *strategic selection tool*. When presenting a central theme, you must decide where to *summarize* and where to *analyze*. This is more than a trivial "tip for success" for presenting biblical theology. Rather, the strategic selection tool involves skillfully discerning what is most important to present about a particular topic, text, or theological statement in order to communicate these ideas clearly.

The strategic selection tool seems like it should come at the end of the process as purely a matter of presentation, but this task is, at its core, hermeneutical. It is an interpretive and translational task that requires prior small-scale and large-scale study. The biblical theologian must possess a working knowledge of the project and audience at hand, but also the relevant source materials (e.g., the biblical text, the theological theme, the way it all fits together). Herein lies the challenge and excitement of biblical theology for the interpreter, teacher, or minister. You must say everything at once. You must also omit things out of necessity in such a way that nothing of ultimate importance is ever left out.

You must decide where to *speed up* and where to *slow down*. When you choose to summarize large sections of text or broad thematic developments across a group of books (i.e., speed up), you must make sure your formulations resonate or fit with the meaning and contours of those passages. When you choose to focus on a particular text or thematic strand within a book or section of the canon (i.e., slow down), you must keep an eye on the broader context and avoid comprehensive formulations that exclude other major developments of the theme in other parts of the canon.

Selecting Themes to Include in a Study of Biblical Theology

Range of Possible Themes

Once you decide to pursue the study of a central theme in biblical theology, you will have to choose which theme or set of themes you want to investigate. If you take the approach to studying central themes in biblical theology outlined above, there will be a *large* but *limited* number of central themes to be examined. This is because a central theme must conform to the qualifying criteria described above and also fit into the compositional strategy of the biblical authors. These controls thus guide and govern the perception, presentation, and selection of central themes in biblical theology. Accordingly, there is an abundant but not unlimited number of central themes a reader of the biblical canon might discern and delineate.

A brief survey of the themes featured in relatively recent works of biblical theology will illustrate this scenario. After an analysis of both Testaments in his *Biblical Theology of the Old and New Testaments*, Brevard Childs provides an extensive section entitled "Theological Reflection on the Christian Bible." Childs treats ten themes in this section: the identity of God; God as Creator; covenant, election, people of God; Christ the Lord; reconciliation with God; Law and Gospel; humanity: old and new; biblical faith; God's kingdom and rule; and finally a discussion of ethics and "the shape of the obedient life" in both testaments.[23]

Taking a thematic approach, Charles Scobie organizes the central themes of biblical theology around the framework of God's Order; God's Servant; God's People; and God's Way. Within these four major headings, Scobie explores other central themes, including: the Spirit; the Messiah; the Son of Man; glory; the nations; land and city; worship; and

---

23. Childs, *Biblical Theology*, 349–716.

God's commandments. For Scobie then, broad thematic categories encompass and order the collection of central themes and subthemes.[24]

In the volume *Central Themes in Biblical Theology: Mapping Unity in Diversity*, Scott Hafemann and Paul House curate a collection of essays on seven central themes. These themes include: the covenant relationship; the commands of God; the atonement; the servant of the Lord; the day of the Lord; the people of God; and the history of redemption.[25] Another important work in evangelical theology, the *New Dictionary of Biblical Theology*, covers a wide range of biblical theological themes.[26] Some of these themes are substantial and require long entries, such as the entries for covenant, mission, Jesus Christ, and the kingdom of God. Others are minor and fairly technical, such as the entries for light, mountains, or water.

Taking the bookends of Genesis 1–3 and Revelation 21–22 as his orienting framework, T. D. Alexander develops six major themes across the canon in his book *From Eden to the New Jerusalem*: the presence of God; the sovereignty of God; the devil and the presence of evil; the sacrificial lamb and the concept of redemption; the tree of life the concept of holiness and wholeness; and finally the people of God and the concept of future hope.[27]

As a further example, the *NIV Biblical Theology Study Bible* from Zondervan includes a section of brief articles on various central themes ranging from glory and creation to the people of God and shalom.[28] Other recent biblical theology studies combine two or more central themes as a way of framing the scope of their investigation and analysis.[29]

---

24. Scobie, *Ways of Our God*, 93–99.
25. Scott J. Hafemann and Paul R. House, eds., *Central Themes in Biblical Theology: Mapping Unity in Diversity* (Grand Rapids: Baker, 2007).
26. T. Desmond Alexander and Brian S. Rosner, eds., *New Dictionary of Biblical Theology* (Downers Grove: InterVarsity, 2000). Cf. also the range of central themes represented in the New Studies in Biblical Theology series from InterVarsity Press. One of the stated areas of focus for the series is "the delineation of a biblical theme across all or part of the biblical corpora." Recent volumes have included the themes of preaching in the New Testament; death and the afterlife; circumcision; the land promise; prayer; repentance; the image of God; and the ascension of Christ.
27. Alexander, *New Jerusalem*.
28. D. A. Carson, ed., *NIV Biblical Theology Study Bible* (Grand Rapids: Zondervan, 2015), 2328–82. Other examples include: sin; covenant; law; temple; priest; sacrifice; exile and exodus; kingdom; sonship; city of God; prophets and prophecy; death and resurrection; wisdom; holiness; justice; wrath; love and grace; the gospel; worship; mission; and the consummation.
29. For example, note the combination of central themes in these recent volumes: Graeme Goldsworthy, *The Son of God and the New Creation*, Short Studies in Biblical Theology (Wheaton: Crossway, 2016); T. Desmond Alexander, *The City of God and the Goal of Creation*, Short Studies in Biblical Theology (Wheaton: Crossway, 2018); and Patrick Schreiner, *The Kingdom of God and the Glory of the Cross*, Short Studies in Biblical Theology (Wheaton: Crossway, 2018). Several recent full-scale biblical theologies also make a sustained argument about the *presence* and *relationship* of two or more central themes in their understanding of the Bible's overall message. For example, Gentry and Wellum combine and relate the central themes of kingdom and covenant in *Kingdom through Covenant*. James Hamilton likewise combines and relates the central themes of glory, salvation, judgment, and the sacrificial work of Christ on the cross in *God's Glory in Salvation through Judgment: A Biblical Theology* (Wheaton: Crossway, 2010).

On the one hand, there is considerable diversity in this quick survey of biblical theology studies of central themes. The number, content, and development of these themes differ in each of these major studies. On the other hand, there is also considerable overlap. Just from this very brief snapshot, you can see several recurring areas of emphasis and themes that surface in very different theological traditions and approaches. This, in fact, would be another argument that a particular concept or theme might qualify for a theme that is genuinely central to what the biblical canon is about at the perspective of the whole. The nuance and diversity within this survey of themes, too, highlights the practical value in recognizing a wide but ordered collection of central themes.

Further, with methodological precision we can recognize that tracing a central theme involves organizing and presenting the results of biblical-theological study as well as a feature of biblical theology proper. This acknowledgement should relieve some of the pressure of interpreters and readers as they approach the biblical-theological task. Tracing a central theme is one instrument in the tool chest of a reader as he or she seeks to grasp the big picture of the Bible.

Themes Included in This Volume

In light of this orienting discussion, we can briefly consider the themes that appear in the following section of this volume. These themes are not the *only* themes that could be pursued in biblical theology, but they are each *central* in some way. In other words, they meet the criteria discussed above. For example, they show up and develop across the canon, and they are central not only for biblical readers but also for the biblical writers.

- God and His Glory (chapter 12)
- Kingdom (chapter 13)
- Covenant (chapter 14)
- Temple and Priesthood (chapter 15)
- Worship (chapter 16)
- Messiah and Atonement (chapter 17)
- Salvation and Judgment (chapter 18)
- The Holy Spirit (chapter 19)
- Mission (chapter 20)

In a broad sense, these particular themes aim to examine aspects of the biblical-theological foundation that deepen our understanding of the grand storyline of the Bible. These themes provide a starting point for a study of how the Bible guides and governs the way we speak and think about what God is doing in the world. These themes also unfold *theo*-logically by thinking about God first, and all things in relation to God afterward; a theo-logic the biblical storyline engenders as well.

We begin with a reflection on God and his glory. In his sovereign plan, God creates and establishes a kingdom that includes relationship with his people through covenant. The temple and the priesthood represent a way for the sinful people of Israel to maintain their relationship with God through repentance and worship. These themes inform the concept of atonement and also the Messiah who will ultimately bring about this salvation. The person and work of Jesus as the Christ is seen fully in light of both divine judgment and salvation. The person and work of the Holy Spirit also illuminates the means by which God in Christ redeems and sustains a people for himself. Finally, the theme of God's mission connects who God is, what God does, and how God calls us to respond. The people of God strive to join in this mission as they reach people with the gospel, make disciples, and proclaim the good news that the rule of God has come in Jesus Christ. The orienting purpose found in this storyline, in these themes, and in this mission is sufficient for the Christian life until he comes.

As mentioned above, this particular collection of central themes is not exhaustive, but rather representative of the biblical-theological riches found in the Bible's diverse but unified message. Recognizing this modest claim also relates to the importance of using the "tracing of central themes" as a biblical theology tool alongside the other instruments of analysis we have discussed as part of the discipline (e.g., canonical context, grand storyline, and textual connections). As you read and reread the Scriptures within the context of the canon, certain central themes will appear, intersect, and develop. Studying the way the biblical authors direct our attention to these themes helps us appreciate the depth and design of God's sovereign plan revealed in the Scriptures.

Discussion Questions

1. What makes a theme a "central" theme?

2. Discuss the role that the study of central themes plays in the discipline of biblical theology: Why is this type of study debated? What unique function does this biblical-theological study have? What cautions are necessary?

3. Discuss the reasons why a central theme can be traced "across the canon" as well as "through history." What historical, hermeneutical, and theological dimensions are involved in this distinction?

4. Describe and discuss the "tools" that are necessary to use when studying a biblical-theological theme.

5. Reflect upon the lines of continuity and discontinuity in evangelical treatments of central themes in the Scriptures. As you survey the field of biblical theology, what themes surface repeatedly? Which themes continue to relate to one another, and what conclusions might be drawn from these patterns of association?

Resources for Further Study

Alexander, T. Desmond. *From Eden to the New Jerusalem: An Introduction to Biblical Theology*. Grand Rapids: Kregel Academic, 2009.

Alexander, T. Desmond and Brian Rosner, eds. *New Dictionary of Biblical Theology*. Downers Grove: InterVarsity, 2000.

Gladd, Benjamin L. *From Adam and Israel to the Church: A Biblical Theology of the People of God*. Downers Grove: InterVarsity, 2019.

Hafemann, Scott J., and Paul R. House, eds. *Central Themes in Biblical Theology: Mapping Unity in Diversity*. Grand Rapids: Baker Academic, 2007.

Scobie, Charles H. *The Ways of Our God: An Approach to Biblical Theology*. Grand Rapids: Eerdmans, 2003.

CHAPTER 12

GOD AND HIS GLORY

BIBLICAL THEOLOGY IS THE STUDY of the whole Bible on its own terms. And at its most fundamental level, "the subject matter of biblical theology is the *Bible's* understanding of *God's* character and purposes."[1] The Bible is a story preeminently about one main character: the triune God.[2] The triune God is a relational being, in both an immanent and an economic sense. Eternally, the triune God has existed in relationship to himself as the Father, Son, and Holy Spirit, loving, rejoicing, and delighting in intra-Trinitarian community.[3] The Bible also has one main plot: the display of God's glory in creation amongst a people who will reflect that glory and dwell with him forever.[4] Wellum and Gentry observe, "Scripture

---

1. Scott J. Hafemann, "The Covenant Relationship," in *Central Themes in Biblical Theology: Mapping Unity in Diversity,* eds. Scott Hafemann and Paul House (Grand Rapids: Baker, 2007), 20. See also G. L. Bray, "God," in *New Dictionary of Biblical Theology*, eds. T. Desmond Alexander and Brian S. Rosner (Downers Grove: InterVarsity, 2000), 511–21, who maintains, "The ultimate author and principle subject of the Bible [is God]" (511).

2. For specific works related to God as Trinity, see Robert Letham, *The Holy Trinity: In Scripture, History, Theology, and Worship* (Phillipsburg: P&R, 2004); Michael Reeves, *Delighting in the Trinity: An Introduction to the Christian Faith* (Downers Grove: InterVarsity, 2012); Fred Sanders, *The Deep Things of God: How the Trinity Changes Everything* (Wheaton: Crossway, 2010); Sanders, *The Triune God*, New Studies in Dogmatics (Grand Rapids: Zondervan, 2016).

3. For more on this concept, see Reeves, *Delighting in the Trinity*.

4. Recognizing God as creator is fundamental to understanding who he is as well as the work he has done and continues to do by means of his providence. While this is beyond the purview of this volume, it is important to recognize that while Christian theologians recognize God as creator, there has been much debate about the timing of the creation act and whether there is a young earth, old earth, or if God created by means of evolution. A survey of each view can be seen in J. B. Stump, ed., *Four Views on Creation, Evolution, and Intelligent Design* (Grand Rapids: Zondervan, 2017). For a helpful explanation of the views that tends toward old-earth creationism, see Kenneth D. Keathley and Mark F. Rooker, *40 Questions about Creation and Evolution* (Grand Rapids: Kregel, 2014). For an explanation and refutation of theistic evolution, see J. P. Moreland et al., eds., *Theistic Evolution: A Scientific, Philosophical, and Theological Critique* (Grand Rapids: Zondervan, 2017). For

confronts us with the sovereign, supernatural God; the one who is personal yet transcendent—the triune God—who demands all of our attention, love, obedience, and devotion. The God of Scripture is central to everything."[5] The doctrine of God seen throughout the canon would have to consider his character, attributes, and works.[6] This would far surpass the focus and scope of this chapter.[7] As such, this chapter will attend to one central attribute and feature that God possesses: glory.[8] The glory of God, as we will see, shapes the whole of the grand narrative of Scripture.[9]

Both the Old and New Testament use glory as a designator for God, referring to him as the "Glory of Israel" (1 Sam. 15:29), the "King of glory" (Ps. 24:8–10), the "God of glory" (Ps. 29:3; cf. Acts 7:2), and the "Father of glory" (Eph. 1:17).[10] Scripture amply uses the term, but glory must be defined to have any real theological emphasis. In terms of the vocabulary of "glory," the Old Testament uses words such Hebrew words as *kabod* (weight, majesty), *tiph'arah* (beauty), *hod* (splendor), *hadar* (majesty), and *tsebi* (beauty). *Kabod* is the most commonly used of these terms, and possesses the literal meaning of

---

support of young-earth creationism, see John MacArthur, *The Battle for the Beginning: Creation, Evolution, and the Bible* (Nashville: Thomas Nelson, 2012).

5. Gentry and Wellum, *Kingdom through Covenant*, 654.
6. For a succinct summary of these points, see Bray, "God," 511–21.
7. See, for example, the length of works such as Feinberg, *No One Like Him*; Frame, *Doctrine of God*.
8. Schreiner avers, "The word 'glory' is used broadly [throughout Scripture] to capture the supremacy of God." See *New Testament Theology*, 126. As such, God does what he does for his glory, and thus his glory is a central facet of his character, which is why there is a repeated call for his people to live for his glory (1 Cor. 10:31; Col. 3:17) (see 126–28). See also Christopher W. Morgan, "Toward a Theology of the Glory of God," in Christopher W. Morgan and Robert A. Peterson, eds., *The Glory of God*, Theology in Community 2 (Wheaton: Crossway, 2010), 153–88 (see 157–59).
9. Morgan maintains, "In a way that is consistent but by no means uniform, every major section of Scripture addresses the subject of the glory of God: Law, Prophets, Writings, Gospels, Acts, Pauline Epistles, General Epistles, and Revelation. Every major doctrine is also significantly related to it: revelation, God, humanity, sin, Christ, salvation, the church, and eschatology" ("Glory of God," 155). Morgan goes on to give a sampling of Scripture dealing with the glory of God, demonstrating that, even if it is not the "center" of Scripture, it certainly constitutes as a major theme: God's glory is revealed through creation (Gen. 1; Ps 19:1–2; Rom. 1:18–25); identified with humans being created in God's image (Gen. 1–2; Ps. 8:3–5; 1 Cor. 11:7); linked with the Exodus (Exod. 3; 13:31; 16:10; 24:9–18; 34:29); linked to light/shining (Exod. 3; 13:31; 16:10; 24:9–18; 34:29; Lev. 3:9–23; Isa. 60:1–3; 60:19; Ezek. 1:28; 10:4; 43:2; Luke 2:9; 2 Cor .3:7; 4:4–6; Heb. 1:3; Rev. 18:1; 21:11–23); linked to the Sabbath (Exod. 19 and 24); fills the tabernacle (Exod. 40:34; cf. Lev. 9:6, 23; Num. 14:21; 16:19, 42; 20:6); fills the temple (1 Kings 8:11); fills the earth (Num. 14:20–23; Ps. 8:1; 19:1–2; Isa. 6:3); identified with his people, Israel (Isa. 40:5; 43:6–7; 60:1); identified with Christ—including his incarnation (John 1:1–18; Heb. 1:3), birth narrative (Luke 2:9, 14, 32), miracles (John 2:11; 11:38–44), transfiguration (Matt. 17:1–13; Mark 9:2–13; Luke 9:28–36; 2 Peter 1:16–21), suffering and crucifixion (Luke 24:26; John 7:39; 12:16, 23–28; 13:31–32; 17:1–5; 21:19; Rom. 3:25–26; 1 Peter 1:10–11), resurrection/exaltation (Acts 3:13–15; Rom. 6:4; Phil. 2:5–11; Heb. 2:5–9; 1 Peter 1:21; Rev. 5:12–13), ascension (Acts 1; 1 Tim. 3:16), reign (Acts 7:55–56), and coming victory (Matt. 16:27; 19:28; 24:30; 25:31; Mark 8:38; 10:37; 13:26; Luke 9:26; 21:27; Rom. 8:21; 2 Thess. 1:6–9; Titus 2:13); identified with the Holy Spirit (1 Peter 4:14; cf. John 16:14; Eph. 1:13–14); identified with the church (Eph. 1:22–23; 3:20–21; 5:22–29); and manifested in the new creation (Isa. 66; Rom. 8:18–27; Rev. 21–22). See ibid., 155–56.
10. David VanDrunen, *God's Glory Alone: The Majestic Heart of Christian Faith and Life*, Five Solas Series (Grand Rapids: Zondervan, 2015), 44–45.

weightiness or heaviness (1 Sam. 4:18). The figurative use of *kabod* is far more frequent and conveys the ideas of abundance and wealth (Gen. 31:1; Isa. 61:6), splendor (Gen. 45:13; 1 Chron. 29:28; Isa. 22:18; Ezek. 31:18; Hag. 2:3, 9), and honor (Gen. 34:19; 1 Sam. 9:6; Ps. 112:9; Prov. 29:23; Jer. 48:18).[11] Within these biblical contexts, *kabod* is used to describe a number of items on a human level. However, Gaffin maintains, "Glory is preeminently a divine quality; ultimately only God has glory."[12] Glory, in this sense, exists only derivatively amongst humanity; God will not share his glory with another (Isa. 42:8; 48:9–11; cf. 1 Chron. 29:11–12).

With this background in mind, glory conveys the substantive and manifest reality of who God is. Hamilton defines the glory of God as "the weight of the majestic goodness of who God is, and the resulting name, or reputation, that he gains from his revelation of himself as Creator, Sustainer, Judge, and Redeemer, perfect in justice and mercy, lovingkindness and truth."[13] Similarly, Morgan defines the glory of God as "God's manifestation of his person, presence, and/or works, especially his power, judgment, and salvation."[14] Likewise, Jonathan Edwards sees God's glory as central and notes that all things in creation are done for his glory:

> It appears that all that is ever spoken of in the Scripture as an ultimate end of God's works is included in that one phrase, *the glory of God* . . . In the creature's knowing, esteeming, loving, rejoicing in, and praising God, the glory of God is both *exhibited* and *acknowledged*; his fullness is *received* and *returned*. Here is both an *emanation* and *remanation*. The refulgence shines upon and into the creature, and is reflected back to the luminary. The beams of glory come from God, are something of God, and are refunded back again to their original. So that the whole is *of* God, and *in* God, and *to* God; and he is the beginning, and the middle, and the end.[15]

---

11. Richard B. Gaffin Jr., "Glory," in *New Dictionary of Biblical Theology*, eds. T. Desmond Alexander and Brian S. Rosner (Downers Grove: InterVarsity, 2000), 507–8. See also C. J. Collins, "*Kabod*," in *New International Dictionary of Old Testament Theology and Exegesis*, ed. Willem VanGemeren (Grand Rapids: Zondervan, 2012), 2:577–87.

12. Gaffin, "Glory," 508.

13. Hamilton, *God's Glory in Salvation*, 56.

14. Morgan, "Glory of God," 157. See also Sverre Aalen, "*Doxa*," in *New International Dictionary of New Testament Theology*, ed. Colin Brown (Grand Rapids, Zondervan, 1971), 2:44–48; Frame, *Systematic Theology*, 400; Wayne A. Grudem, *Systematic Theology: An Introduction to Biblical Doctrine* (Grand Rapids: Zondervan, 1994), 220–21; Kevin J. Vanhoozer, *Faith Speaking Understanding: Performing the Drama of Doctrine* (Louisville: Westminster John Knox, 2014), 76.

15. Jonathan Edwards, "A Dissertation Concerning the End for Which God Created the World," in *The Works of Jonathan Edwards: Volume 8*, ed. Paul Ramsey (New Haven: Yale University Press, 1989), 526–27.

Beginning with the Pentateuch, this glory will be traced across the canon as we note the contours of how God displays the greatness of who he is,[16] as well as its role as the canonical foundation for the rest of the Old Testament as well as the New Testament.[17]

God and His Glory in the Law

God is. The Bible makes no apologetic case for the existence of God, nor does it get into speculative discussions of any kind. It states that in the beginning, the majestic, intrinsically glorious, self-existent, self-sufficient, Trinitarian God created the heavens and the earth (Gen. 1:1–2:25; cf. John 1:1–4; Col. 1:15–20; Heb. 1:1–4). Since there was nothing in existence before God made the universe, he created out of nothing, displaying his power and wisdom. God is thus distinct from his creation (i.e., transcendent), though, as we will see, he also chooses to be involved with his creation (i.e., immanent).

Man and woman were created in God's image to reflect his glory and exercise dominion over the face of the earth (Gen. 1:26–28). God blesses Adam and Eve, who are to function as his vice-regents,[18] and places them in a garden where they will experience blessing and God's presence, provided they obey God's command to not eat from one particular tree in the garden (2:15–17). They, however, succumb to temptation, rebel, and eat from the tree of the knowledge of good and evil (3:1–7), grasping after their own glory in self-sufficiency and pride. Essentially, they act as "glory thieves."[19] While the prospect of death—along with other negative results of the fall—is clarified as a consequence of their error (3:8–19), rebellion and disobedience ensue with the outcome of exile from their garden paradise (3:23–24).

If the story ended there, it would be a rather morbid conclusion; however, there is hope to be seen in this passage, as well as God's gracious character. House affirms this fact and asserts, "With the consequences of sin clearly stated and with a long-term promise of the serpent's defeat in place, God acts in mercy to sustain the fallen couple. God clothes them (3:21). The Lord also removes them from the garden to protect them from eating of the tree of life, which had not been forbidden previously, so that they will not live forever in a sinful

---

16. There appears to be a movement in Scripture from the more limited and local manifestations of God's glory to Old Testament Israel toward the universal and eschatological goal of God's glory filling the whole world. See Hamilton, *God's Glory in Salvation*, 106, 116, 268–69, 343, 483. Beale concurs, stating, "I contend that goal of the New Testament storyline is God's glory, and that the main stepping stone to that goal is Christ's establishment of an eschatological new-creation kingdom and its expansion." G. K. Beale, *A New Testament Biblical Theology: The Unfolding of the Old Testament in the New* (Grand Rapids: Baker, 2011), 16. Note that Beale's conception of the Old Testament storyline is quite similar and highlights the centrality of God's glory.

17. On the overall message and key themes of the Pentateuch receiving attention in later sections of Scripture, see Alexander, *Promised Land*, 113–314; Sailhamer, *Meaning of the Pentateuch*, 243–56.

18. For a more detailed understanding of man acting as God's vice-regent in the Garden, see Dempster, *Dominion and Dynasty*, 59–62.

19. I have heard this phrase used by Paul Tripp in numerous articles, books, and sermons.

condition (3:22–24). Not even their sin can separate them from God's concern for and commitment to the well-being of the people he has created."[20]

Beyond what is mentioned here, God also pronounces the *protoevangelion* in Genesis 3:15, promising that a seed of the woman—namely, Jesus Christ (Gal. 3:16)—would one day crush the head of the serpent, Satan. Thus, Calvin also asserts that, for Adam, a "solemn excommunication" was administered by the Lord, not to cut him off from all hope of salvation, but rather to motivate him to seek new assistance elsewhere. Calvin continues, "From the moment in which he became alienated from God, it was necessary that he should recover life by the death of Christ, by whose life he then lived."[21] God, therefore, demonstrates his justice and grace, showing that sin is a grotesque affront to his holiness, while also providing for humanity in both a temporal and eternal fashion.[22] The rest of the biblical story revolves around the glorification of God by means of the eventual restoration of the relationship between God and humanity.

After the exile of Adam and Eve, God manifests his wrath toward the pervasive sin of humanity by means of a global flood (Gen. 6–8). He also scatters the peoples of the earth in response to their idolatrous intentions of making a name (i.e., glory) for themselves (chapter 11). Then, God makes a covenant with a man named Abram and promises to give him a land, make him into a nation of numerous descendants, and bless him as well as the nations of the earth (12:1–3). In so doing, God brings about the beginnings of the reversal of the curse seen in Genesis 3.[23] This nation will be a blessing to all nations, such that the earth will be filled with the knowledge of the glory of the Lord (Hab. 2:14) with humanity receiving and reflecting his glory as his image-bearers.

The nation mentioned in the Abrahamic covenant is Israel who, in the beginning of the book of Exodus, is in captivity in Egypt. God repeatedly declares that he will act on behalf of Israel through various signs and, ultimately, that his name, power, and glory would be known by both Israel and Egypt (Exod. 6:7–8; 7:5; 8:10, 22; 9:14, 29; 10:2; 14:4, 18).[24] God

---

20. Paul R. House, *Old Testament Theology* (Downers Grove: InterVarsity, 1998), 66.

21. John Calvin, *Commentaries on the First Book of Moses, Called Genesis*, trans. John King, vol. 1 (Grand Rapids: Eerdmans, 1948), 184.

22. Roy E. Knuteson, *Calling the Church to Discipline: A Scriptural Guide for the Church That Dares to Discipline* (Nashville: Action Press, 1977). He states, "Discipline is God's business. How graphically this is seen in the beginning years of human history. Adam and his wife Eve were driven from the Paradise of God and cherubim with a flaming sword guarded the way to the tree of life (Gen. 3:24). A loving Creator thus excluded the first couple by disciplinary action. We must realize that if He had allowed them access to the Tree of Life, after spiritual death had begun its awful toll; our first parents would have lived endlessly in aging and weakening bodies. This discipline of exclusion was for their own good . . . Divine discipline has always been exercised as a means of grace; it is the evidence of love and a tangible sign that God really cares" (21–22). Thus, God is glorified in rendering both judgment and mercy.

23. For more on the connection between Genesis 3:14–19 and Genesis 12:1–3 see James Hamilton, "The Seed of the Woman and the Blessing of Abraham," *Tyndale Bulletin* 58.2 (2007): 253–73.

24. This theme is pervasive in the Old Testament. Beyond these texts, see Exod 16:12; 29:46; 31:13; Deut. 29:5; 1 Kings 20:13, 28; Isa. 45:3; 49:23, 26; 60:16; Jer. 9:24; 24:7; Ezek 5:13; 6:7, 10, 13, 14; 7:4, 9, 27; 11:10, 12; 12:15, 16, 20; 13:14, 21, 23;

raises up the pharaoh for this very purpose (Exod. 9:16; cf. Rom. 9:17). At the crossing of the Red Sea, Israel appears to be trapped. Longman notes, "Pharaoh will think that the Israelites have foolishly trapped themselves, but God tells Moses that he has other plans in mind: 'I will harden Pharaoh's heart and he will pursue them, and I will get glory over Pharaoh and all his host, and the Egyptians shall know that I am the Lord (Exod. 14:4).'"[25] In his divine sovereignty, God ushers Israel out of Egypt and the nation recognizes the unique power and authority of Yahweh, praising him for his glory in triumph over enemies, declaring there is no god like him, awesome in glorious deeds (15:1–21).

Journeying from Egypt, God's glory is then seen in the pillar of cloud and pillar of fire that lead Israel through the wilderness. God thus displays his presence, protection, and provision for his people (13:21; 14:19–20; 16:10; cf. 24:15–18).[26] God also leads his people and shows his glory in the provision of food (16:7). His glory appears in the cloud of presence (16:10)[27] and he declares that Israel would know that he is the Lord their God through his provision of manna and quail (16:11–12). After a time of travel, the people come to the foot of Mount Sinai, where God declares that Israel is a unique nation with whom he will enter into covenant relationship (Exod. 19:1–6). He reminds them of his redeeming work, how he glorified himself by removing them from Egypt and safeguarded them as his people (19:4). Based on this gracious and redemptive work, God calls his people to "obey my voice and keep my covenant" (19:5). If they do this, they will be a treasured possession among all peoples, a kingdom of priests, and a holy nation (19:5–6). In other words, as descendants of Abraham, the whole nation is called to function as priestly mediators of God's word and presence, living as an example of holiness to the idolatrous nations. God is establishing a kingdom through his covenants amongst a people (Israel) in a particular place (the land he promises to them). Even after they later organize as a nation with a king to rule and be God's representative to them, Israel must still live in conformity to God's moral statutes so that all the peoples of the earth may know that he is God and there is no other (1 Kings 8:60). As Eichrodt maintains, in keeping with his perfect and glorious nature, God is "the jealous God, who will admit no derogation from his majesty."[28]

14:8; 15:7; 16:62; 17:21, 24; 20:12, 20, 38, 42, 44; 20:48; 22:16, 22; 24:27; 25:5, 7, 11, 17; 26:6, 14; 28:22, 23, 26; 29:6, 9, 21; 30:8, 19, 25, 26; 32:15; 33:29; 34:27, 30; 35:4, 9, 12, 15; 36:11, 23, 36, 38; 37:6, 13, 14, 28; 38:23; 39:6, 7, 22, 28; Joel 3:17.

25. Tremper Longman III, "The Glory of God in the Old Testament," in *The Glory of God*, ed. Christopher W. Morgan and Robert A. Peterson, Theology in Community 2 (Wheaton: Crossway, 2010), 50. Longman continues, "What do we learn about God's glory from this account? . . . God's glory was displayed by shattering the pretentious glory of Egypt and its Pharaoh by the dramatic means of separating the sea to allow the Israelites to go through to safety and to close it in judgment on the Egyptians. God's saving and judging actions thus demonstrate his glory with the result that the Israelites worship him" (50–51).

26. See Longman, "Glory of God," 53–54.

27. For further detail on God's glory as seen in the pillars of cloud and fire in the wilderness wanderings, see VanDrunen, *God's Glory Alone*, 43–59.

28. Walter Eichrodt, *Theology of the Old Testament*, 2 vols. (Philadelphia: Westminster, 1961), 1:44.

God makes this covenant with Israel, and Israel agrees to it (Exod. 24:1–18). It is also during this time that Israel observes the visible manifestation of the glory of the Lord as a thick cloud and devouring fire (24:15–17). God instructs Moses concerning the moral precepts of the law, as well as the cultic rites that would set them apart as a holy nation. Israel would build a tabernacle, the dwelling place of the glory of God, as well as consecrate priests and offer sacrifices. When they do this obediently and consistently, God promises to dwell with them and sanctify that place by his glory (29:38–44). He would dwell among the people and manifest his presence in a unique way, and they would know that he is Yahweh, their God, who brought them out of Egypt (29:45–46). This is the aim of God's work in creation after the fall; namely, that he would display his glory and dwell amongst a kingdom of covenantal people who would receive and reflect that glory and make it known to the ends of the earth (cf. Lev. 26:11–13; 2 Cor. 6:16–18; Rev. 21:3).

After the golden calf incident (an event where Israel gives glory to an idol, not to God; Exod. 32:1–35) Moses pleads with God to accompany Israel to the promised land, since his presence with them is what distinguished them from the rest of the nations (33:1–6, 12–16). At this time, Moses meets with God outside the camp in the tent of meeting (33:7–11), and having found favor with God, he reverses the people's idolatrous desires and requests God to show him his glory (33:17–23). The Lord graciously responds to Moses's request to see his glory, saying "I will make all my goodness pass before you and will proclaim before you my name '[Yahweh]'" (33:19). Thus, as Hamilton maintains, "when Moses asks to see God's *glory*, God responds that he will show him his *goodness* and proclaims his *name*. This means that God's glory is seen in his goodness, and the proclamation of his name reveals Yahweh's goodness, which is his glory."[29] Furthermore, there is a visible manifestation of what seems to be the intense light of God's glory that Moses himself reflects (33:21–23, 29–35). Lister comments concerning the revealing of this glory, "In affirming his commitment to be redemptively present with his people and uphold the promise of dwelling among them, the Lord gives Moses a glimpse of what is to come when his redemptive mission will be complete . . . it is a glorious episode pointing to the finalization of the Lord's redemptive agenda when Yahweh will finally pull his hand back to reveal his unmediated presence to all the redeemed."[30] We will see the unfolding of this glory as we progress through

---

29. Hamilton, *God's Glory in Salvation*, 103–4. Gaffin agrees and elaborates: "The interchangeableness or close association in this passage of God's glory and his presence/face, his goodness, his name, and his radiance, both veiled and unveiled, and the fact that Moses both does and may not yet see the Lord's face, indicates that God's glory is his manifest presence, which, without further mediation, will destroy his creatures, but which admits of mediated expressions involving the most intimate fellowship with him" ("Glory," 508).

30. J. Ryan Lister, *The Presence of God: Its Place in the Storyline of Scripture and the Story of Our Lives* (Wheaton: Crossway, 2015), 199. One can note throughout the biblical storyline that the dwelling place of God and the glory of God are intricately related, with glory describing the manifestation of God's presence (Exod. 16:7, 10; 25:8; 29:43; 40:34; 1 Kings 8:11; Pss. 26:8; 63:2; Isa. 35:2; 40:5; 57:15; 58:8; 59:19; 60:1–2; 66:18; Zech. 2:10–11).

Scripture, but here we see its specific manifestation to Moses, and the real focus appears to be on the name, character, and goodness of God. While God is not obligated to do so, he nevertheless displays his glory to Moses in grace and mercy (33:19).

Moses once again ascends Mount Sinai. When God descends, he reveals his goodness, shows his glory, and proclaims his name before Moses, declaring, "The Lord, the Lord, a God merciful and gracious, slow to anger, and abounding in steadfast love and faithfulness, keeping steadfast love for thousands, forgiving iniquity and transgression and sin, but who will by no means clear the guilty, visiting the iniquity of the fathers on the children and the children's children to the third and fourth generation" (Exod. 34:6–7). This declaration of God's glory and character is a paradigm seen throughout Scripture (Num. 14:18; Deut. 5:9–11; 7:9–10; 2 Chron. 30:9; Neh. 9:17, 31–32; Pss. 86:15; 103:8; 111:4; 145:8; Isa. 63:7; Jer. 32:18; Hos. 2:19–20; Joel 2:13; Jonah 4:2; Mic. 7:18; Nah. 1:2–3). God's self-description displays his greatness and goodness in both showing mercy and upholding his righteous standard. In this declaration of his infinitely worthy name, God announces his goodness as seen in his mercy and wrath toward sin, demonstrating that he is Judge and Redeemer.

God also gives detailed instructions concerning how to build the tabernacle (Exod. 25–31), the place where God would dwell with and make his presence known among his people (29:43). As one ventured into the tabernacle, gradations of holiness increased with each successive section.[31] The glorious cloud of God's presence settles on the tabernacle, and God's glory resides there so that the people respond with worship (40:34–38). This is an early indication that God's glory will someday fill the earth (Num. 14:21; cf. Hab. 2:14).

God and His Glory in the Prophets

The prevalent theme of glory continues in the prophetic books. 1 Samuel 4–5 show the connection of the glory and the presence of God to the ark of the covenant. When Israel is defeated in battle and Eli's sons are killed, the Philistines seize the ark as their plunder. This news sends Eli's daughter-in-law into premature labor. Dying in childbirth, she names the child Ichabod (meaning "no glory"), stating that the glory of God had departed from Israel (4:21–22). The next chapter depicts the negative consequences brought upon the Philistines when they bring the ark into their camp. The image of Dagon, the Philistine god, is found prostrated before the ark, and the people are afflicted with diseases (5:1–12). The story, thus, shows a close connection between the ark and God's glory and presence.

---

31. Longman observes, "The structure of the tabernacle represents this [increasing gradations of holiness as one draws nearer to the ark of the covenant, the footstool of his royal throne; 1 Chron. 28:2] also by virtue of the ascending value of the metals (bronze, silver, gold, pure gold) as one moves from the bases of the poles for the curtains of the court-yard in toward the Most Holy Place. Increasing holiness is also evidenced by the increasing difficulty of access as one moved from outside the camp (the realm of Gentiles and the unclean) to inside the camp (ritually clean Israelites), to the tabernacle area, where one had to be accompanied by Levites consecrated for service, to the Most Holy Place, accessible only to the high priest and to him only once a year (Leviticus 16)." Longman, "Glory of God," 54.

Later in the Prophets, one sees that much like the tabernacle at the end of Exodus, God also dwells in the Jerusalem temple (1 Kings 8:10–11). Again, the reader can perceive the connection between God's glory and his presence among his people. The worship of God is rendered, therefore, in a specific location by means of the cultic rites expressed in the Law.

In the Latter Prophets especially, glory focuses more on the future of the new creation and the coming Messiah. Gaffin observes:

> In the latter part of Isaiah, for example, the prophet foretells the coming and activity of the Lord's anointed servant (42:1–4; 49:1–12; 52:13–53:12; the NT explicitly applies such passages to Jesus, as the Christ; e.g., Matt. 12:18–21; Luke 2:32; 2 Cor. 6:2; Acts 3:13). . . . This future revelation of messianically mediated glory will mean not only the full, eschatological restoration of Israel (Isa. 58:8; 60:1–2, 19; 62:2–3), but will be universal (66:18), including the salvation of the nations (59:19) . . . This prophetic expectation of the final, saving revelation of the divine glory through the messianic servant is expressed most comprehensively in the hope that "the earth will be filled with the knowledge of the glory of the Lord, as the waters cover the sea" (Hab. 2:14).[32]

Among the prophets, the book of Isaiah in particular depicts God as glorious. Longman summarizes this book, "Isaiah was, in the first place, a prophet of judgment. Israel had put its confidence in other nations and in false gods. But these nations and gods had no glory; only God has glory. God will destroy the nations' and gods' pretensions to glory and will assert his own. Isaiah envisions salvation beyond the judgment. The refined remnant will emerge from the judgment with a new affirmation of the glory of God."[33]

Isaiah 6 is a well-known passage wherein the glory of God is put on display. In Isaiah's vision of the throne room of God, the seraphim proclaim, "Holy, holy, holy is the Lord of hosts; the whole earth is full of his glory" (Isa. 6:3).[34] A close relationship exists between "holiness" and "glory." Holiness is understood as an inward characteristic, an essential divine attribute that denotes his transcendence and purity.[35] Glory is the outward manifestation of that holiness, the radiant outshining splendor of God's presence.[36] Thus, in Isaiah 6:3, the reference to

---

32. Gaffin, "Glory," 508–9.

33. Longman, "Glory of God," 70.

34. Robin Routledge argues for the centrality of the glory of God throughout the book of Isaiah, with chapter six serving as a definitive component of his thesis in "Is There a Narrative Substructure Underlying the Book of Isaiah?" *Tyndale Bulletin* 55.2 (2004): 183–204.

35. Routledge, "Narrative Substructure," 194. See also J. A. Naudé, "*Qadosh*," in *New International Dictionary of Old Testament Theology and Exegesis*, ed. Willem VanGemeren (Grand Rapids: Zondervan, 2012), 3:877–87.

36. Routledge, "Narrative Substructure," 194.

the glory of God filling the earth is not separate from its ascription of holiness, but is a corollary of it.[37]

The prophet continues and later states that God will work for the remnant of his people. He will be their "crown of glory" (28:5), and they will see the glory and majesty of God (35:1–2; 40:3–5). A future eschatological glory will be experienced when God, acting as divine warrior, decisively and definitively defeats sin (60:1–3).[38]

The prophet Jeremiah bemoans the fact that Israel has "changed their glory for that which does not profit" (Jer. 2:11). Certainly, the glory they forfeited for the sake of their worship of empty idols that offer no spiritual profit is God's glory (2:12–13). This is especially egregious since God created humanity for the glory of his name (see Isa. 43:6–7).[39] Ezekiel speaks a great deal about the glory of God in his visions of the heavenly throne room (Ezekiel 1), the departure of God's glory from the temple due to Israel's ongoing idolatry, rebellion, and sin (chapters 9–11), and the future day when God's glory will once again fill the temple (chapters 40–48). The glory of God is closely connected to his presence among his people, which is removed during the exile but restored in the postexilic eschatological temple (Ezek. 43:2–5; cf. 44:4).[40]

The prophet Haggai states, "For thus says the Lord of hosts: Yet once more, in a little while, I will shake the heavens and the earth and the sea and the dry land. And I will shake all nations, so that the treasures of all nations shall come in, and I will fill this house with glory, says the Lord of hosts . . . The latter glory of this house shall be greater than the former, says the Lord of hosts. And in this place I will give peace, declares the Lord of hosts" (2:6–7, 9). Haggai calls for the people to set their sights on "something much greater than a new temple their own hands would build. They needed to look for the promised Savior of all nations and for the new heavens and new earth that he would bring. Only through these gifts, the OT prophets indicate, would God's greater glory come to bless Israel and all the world (cf. Heb. 12:25–29)."[41]

In the Book of the Twelve, the glory of God is treated extensively in Hosea, Habakkuk, and Zechariah. Similarly to Isaiah and Jeremiah, Hosea pronounces destruction due to Israel's idolatry and glorification of false gods (Hos. 10:5–6). Habakkuk predicts a future day when

---

37. The significance of the holiness of God for Isaiah in relationship to his glory is also seen in the description of God as the "Holy One." This expression occurs 30 times in the Old Testament, of which 25 are in the book of Isaiah (1:4; 5:16, 19, 24; 10:17, 20; 12:6; 17:17; 29:19, 23; 30:11, 12, 15; 31:1; 37:23 [= 2 Kings 19:22]; 40:25; 41:14, 16, 20; 43:3, 14–15; 45:11; 47:4; 48:17; 49:7; 54:5; 55:5; 57:17; 60:9, 14). See also Routledge, "Narrative Substructure," 194.
38. See John Oswalt, *The Book of Isaiah. Chapters 40-66*, New International Commentary on the Old Testament (Grand Rapids: Eerdmans, 1998), 462–64.
39. For more on this, see chapter sixteen on the topic of worship.
40. VanDrunen, *God's Glory Alone*, 67. See also Thomas R. Schreiner, *The King in His Beauty: A Biblical Theology of the Old and New Testaments* (Grand Rapids: Baker, 2013), 372–74.
41. VanDrunen, *God's Glory Alone*, 69.

"the earth will be filled with the knowledge of the glory of the Lord as the waters cover the sea (Hab. 2:14). However, the wicked will only experience shame since they refuse to delight in God's glory (2:16). Zechariah describes a vision with a hope-filled message that God himself "will be to her a wall of fire all around" and he will "be the glory in her midst" (Zech. 2:5).[42]

God and His Glory in the Writings

The theme of God and his glory pervades the Psalms, so our analysis must be selective. The book of Psalms reminds us that there is hope for those who delight in and submit to God and his kingship. Psalm 3 depicts the time when David fled from Absalom. David cries out that the number of enemies he has is great (3:1–2), but proclaims that God is "a shield about me, my glory, and the lifter of my head" (3:3). Thus, God's glory is displayed in the salvation and protection he provides. Psalm 8 parades the glory of God in creation, including humanity as the image-bearers of God, evoking praise from his people.[43] Psalm 24 portrays God as the king of glory, strong and mighty in battle. God's victory is displayed and his glory is manifested as he enters through the gates of Jerusalem (24:7–10).

Psalm 26 also speaks of dealing with one's enemies. The psalmist states that he loves the habitation of God's house, the place where his glory dwells (26:8). Here, God's glory is associated with his dwelling place, the temple. Psalm 29 commands the people of God to ascribe glory to the Lord due to his name (29:1–2). Throughout the psalm, God's glory is depicted as a primal force of nature, such that all in his temple cry "Glory!" (29:9). This connection between God's glory and the temple is crucial, as the temple is both the place where his glory dwells and where he receives glory from his people as they worship. Psalm 57 describes when David fled Saul in the cave of Adullam (1 Sam. 22:1–5). While making his case before God for deliverance, he concludes by saying, "Be exalted, O God, among the heavens! Let your glory be over all the earth" (Ps. 57:5, 11). In his cry for deliverance, David calls for God to be glorified in his worship, confident that he will save him from defeat.

Later in the Writings, Daniel reminds us of the promise of God's universal kingdom reigning over all rival kingdoms. Specifically, Daniel 7 points to the coming glory of "the son of man," whom, we are told, will be given dominion, glory, and a kingdom (Dan. 7:13–14).[44] This son, as will be seen, is the focus of New Testament glory. He is the one who will receive all things from the Ancient of Days and reign over an eternal kingdom.

Likewise, Chronicles speaks of the purposes of God throughout Israel's history, affirming God's universal kingship through a Davidic king. Longman notes regarding this

---

42. Longman, "Glory of God," 75–76.
43. Longman observes, "As high and dignified a view of humanity this psalm presents, it is clear from the fact that God 'crowned them' that human glory is derivative and dependent on divine glory." See "Glory of God," 63.
44. Longman, "Glory of God," 77. The New Testament quotes this passage often (Matt. 24:30; Mark 13:26; 14:62; Luke 21:27; Rev. 21:13) in reference to Jesus of Nazareth as the Messiah.

final book of the Writings, "While Chronicles, like Kings, speaks of the glory cloud descending on the temple before Solomon's dedicatory prayer and at the entry of the ark into the temple (2 Chron. 5:14), the Chronicler also alerts the reader to the manifestation of God's glory right after the prayer (2 Chron. 7:1–3). He also speaks of the worshipful response of the priests at the manifestation of his glory (2 Chron. 7:3)."[45] In this brief overview, biblical themes are evident and cohesive with the whole of Scripture.

God and His Glory in the Gospels

The New Testament declares that God and Christ possess the divine glory (i.e., *doxa*) referenced in the Old Testament. They share the Deity's perfect nature, yet each has individual glory as well. The texts speak of God's glory and Christ's glory. The two work in perfect harmony. Christ glorifies God by his words and actions, God is pleased to have Christ represent him so effectively, and all the while the Holy Spirit glorifies Father and Son.[46]

In the Gospels, the glory of God is preeminently focused on and in Jesus the Messiah. In the birth narratives, the glory of the Lord appears to shepherds in the angelic pronouncement of Jesus's arrival (Luke 2:9). This evokes praise from a host of angels, who exalt God, saying, "Glory to God in the highest," and this glory is manifested in the birth of the Messiah (2:14). In keeping with Old Testament promises, the infant Jesus is described as "a light for revelation to the Gentiles and for glory to your people Israel" (2:32; cf. Isa. 46:13; 49:6). He is with God, and is God, with "glory as the only Son from the Father" (John 1:14). In Jesus's earthly ministry his messianic glory is highlighted in his teaching (Matt. 7:28–29), miracles (John 2:11; 11:4, 40), casting out of demons (Matt. 12:22–28), healing (Matt. 9:2–8; 15:30–31; John 11:1–16), transfiguration (Matt. 17:1–8; Luke 9:28–36), and death and resurrection (John 3:14; 12:32, 34; 17:1–5). Gaffin maintains, "By this impending glorification, the now incarnate Word-Son will be invested with the glory he has shared eternally with the Father. This will happen so that he, in turn, may share his glory with believers, 'that they may be one as we are one' (17:22; cf. v. 24a)."[47]

Summarizing the use of glory in Matthew and Mark, one can note that this term points to the character of God, the praise of God by his people, his eschatological glory described as the second coming, and Jesus as the means by which people encounter God's glory on earth.[48] Luke depicts the transfiguration as a moment of immense glory. Here the disciples see Moses,

---

45. Longman, "Glory of God," 60. See also Raymond Dillard, *2 Chronicles*, Word Biblical Commentary 15 (Dallas: Thomas Nelson, 1987), 56–57; Schreiner, *King in His Beauty*, 171.
46. Richard Melick declares, "This shared glory demonstrates the deity of Christ." See his "The Glory of God in the Synoptic Gospels, Acts, and the General Epistles," in *The Glory of God*, eds. Christopher W. Morgan and Robert A. Peterson, Theology in Community 2 (Wheaton: Crossway, 2010), 105.
47. Gaffin, "Glory," 509.
48. Melick, "Glory of God," 83.

Elijah, and Jesus "in glory" (Luke 9:29–32; cf. Matt. 17:1–8; Mark 9:2–8).[49] The transfiguration reveals the glory continually but not openly possessed by Jesus. In other words, Jesus's
eschatological glory was not just a future reality; it could also manifest under unique circumstances during his life on earth.[50] And in this transfigured state, Jesus discusses with Moses
and Elijah his "departure" or "exodus." This apparently refers to Christ's death and resurrection, and it certainly draws the reader back to Israel's exodus from Egypt (Exod. 1–12), as well
as the coming "new exodus" (Isa. 11:11–16; 35:10; 40:1–31; 41:17–18, 22–23; 49:9–11; 51:9–11).
As such, maintains Schreiner, this moment reminds us that the work of Christ will bring
about an inaugurated new reality: "The new exodus promised in Isaiah and the new creation
anticipated therein will become a reality only through Jesus' exodus at the cross."[51]

Glory terminology is observed forty-two times in the gospel of John, with twenty-five
references in chapters 1–12, and seventeen references in chapters 13–21.[52] Both sections
are saturated with references to glory, a key theme in the book. The book begins with John
stating, "And the Word became flesh and dwelt [i.e., tabernacled] among us, and we have
seen his glory, glory as of the only Son from the Father, full of grace and truth" (1:14).
This verse connects the glory of Jesus with previous manifestations of God's presence in
the tabernacle and temple. Jesus, as the new temple (2:21), manifests the glory of God (cf.
Exod. 40:34–35; 1 Kings 8:10–11; 2 Chron. 5:13–14; 7:1–2; Hag. 2:7; Ezek. 10:4; 43:5; 44:4).
This glory is displayed in Jesus's incarnation, specifically in his signs (2:11; 9:3–4; 11:4, 40),
as well as his death on the cross (12:23, 28; 13:31–32; 17:1, 4–5). Moreover, John speaks of
Jesus's glory as that which was observed by the prophet Isaiah (John 12:41; cf. Isa. 6:1–3).[53]

John also depicts the glorification of the Son by the Spirit. Carson states regarding John
16:14–15 and the glory of the Holy Spirit, "Just as the Son by his ministry on earth brought
glory to his Father (7:18; 17:4), so the Paraclete by his ministry brings glory to Jesus: that is
his central aim. His means is the unfolding of Jesus' person and work."[54] The ministry of the
Spirit and his spreading of God's glory are clearly seen in the writing of the early church.

---

49. Melick observes that this is the first time "glory" in the Synoptic Gospels is applied to humans (Moses and Elijah).
    Their glory, he notes, "is derived from their situation after death. Visible glory evidences their relationship with
    God." Melick, "Glory of God," 88. See also Robert H. Stein, *Luke*, New American Commentary 24 (Nashville:
    Broadman, 1992) who notes regarding the lack of attribution of glory to Moses and Elijah in Matthew and Mark,
    "By this addition Luke emphasized that Moses and Elijah brought with them the glorious splendor that came from
    their presence with God" (284).

50. J. A. Dennis, "Glory," in *Dictionary of Jesus and the Gospels*, 2nd ed., eds. Joel B. Green, Jeannine K. Brown, and
    Nicholas Perrin (Downers Grove: InterVarsity, 2013), 314.

51. Schreiner, *New Testament Theology*, 270. See also Lister, *Presence of God*, 259–60.

52. For further analysis of "glory" in John, see W. Robert Cook, "The 'Glory' Motif in the Johannine Corpus," *Journal
    of the Evangelical Theological Society* 27.3 (1984): 291–97.

53. See Andreas J. Köstenberger, *A Theology of John's Gospel and Letters*, Biblical Theology of the New Testament
    (Grand Rapids: Zondervan, 2009), 294–95.

54. D. A. Carson, *The Gospel according to John*, Pillar New Testament Commentary (Grand Rapids: Eerdmans, 1991),
    541.

God and His Glory in Acts and the Letters

The book of Acts connects the glory of God in the Old Testament to the glory of the risen Christ (cf. Acts 3:12–26). The continuation of Jesus's ministry through the Spirit-empowered apostles—the witnesses to his resurrection—seems to inform the prominent occurance of miracles and messages produced in the "name" of Jesus in Acts.[55] Jesus receives glory in what is said and done by his followers. The sermons in Acts (2:14–36; 3:11–26; 10:34–43) also point to this reality, focusing on how humanity has sinned in numerous ways, including killing the Messiah. The people are told how God raised Jesus up and then are called to repent and receive the forgiveness of God.[56] As the Word of God spreads (6:7; 12:24; 19:20), salvation comes to both Jews and Gentiles. In this way, virtually the entire book of Acts is a testament to God's glory manifested in the spread of the gospel.

Paul's usage of glory within his writings is rather extensive.[57] This term is explicit in Paul's pronouncement of the gospel, referring to this good news as "the light of the gospel of the glory of Christ" and the "light of the knowledge of the glory of God in the face of Christ" (2 Cor. 4:4, 6). For Paul, the same God who spoke light into existence at creation (Gen. 1:3) has shone in our hearts to display Christ's new creation glory. This is why New Testament authors often focus their attention on Jesus Christ as the one in whom glory resides.[58] Since the fall of humanity, Paul observes, we have all sinned and fallen short of God's glory (Rom. 3:2). However, before the foundations of the world, the triune God has been bringing about the plan of redemption to the praise of God's glory (Eph. 1:3–14). God has revealed himself in Christ, who, in his death and resurrection, has inaugurated the new covenant, which far supersedes the old covenant in glory (2 Cor. 3:1–4:6).[59]

---

55. See Acts 2:38; 3:6, 16; 4:7, 10, 12, 17, 18, 30; 5:28, 40, 41; 8:12, 16; 9:14, 15, 16, 21, 27, 28; 10:43, 48; 15:17; 16:18; 19:5, 13, 17; 21:13; 22:16.
56. For further analysis of this point, see James M. Hamilton, "The Center of Biblical Theology in Acts: Deliverance and Damnation Display the Divine," *Themelios* 33.3 (2008): 40.
57. Much of this paragraph is based on Gaffin, "Glory," 507–9.
58. Gaffin avers, "In the Old Testament, then, glory is preeminently the manifestation-mode of who God is in the fullness of his self-revelation as creator and savior. Against that broad background and with reference to the creation of light in Genesis 1 and to God's glory that Paul finds implicit there, 2 Corinthians 4:4–6 affirms that divine glory has found its focused manifestation and, as we will see ever more clearly from the immediate and broader context of his teaching, its full and final manifestation in Jesus Christ as Lord. Further, the glory-manifestation that Christ is specifies the content of Paul's gospel." See Richard B. Gaffin Jr., "The Glory of God in Paul's Epistles," in *The Glory of God*, ed. Christopher W. Morgan and Robert A. Peterson, Theology in Community 2 (Wheaton: Crossway, 2010), 131. For a detailed analysis of Christ's glory in 2 Corinthians, see Matthew Y. Emerson and Christopher W. Morgan, "The Glory of God in 2 Corinthians," *Southern Baptist Journal of Theology* 19. 3 (2015): 21–39.
59. Gaffin elaborates, "The status of Christ as 'the Lord of glory' was veiled in his crucifixion (1 Cor. 2:8), but has been openly revealed in his resurrection. Rewarded with life for his obedience to death (Phil. 2:6–9), he has been 'vindicated by the Spirit . . . taken up in glory' (1 Tim. 3:16). The resurrection gives him an unprecedented relationship with the Holy Spirit; 'raised in glory' (1 Cor. 15:43), as the 'last Adam' he has become a 'life-giving Spirit' (1 Cor. 15:45; cf. 2 Cor. 3:17)." See "Glory," 510.

Christ is the head of the church (Eph. 1:22–23; 5:23; Col. 1:18), and through the church the manifold wisdom of God is made known to the rulers and authorities in heavenly places (Eph. 3:10). In this way, Paul states, God is glorified through his church as they seek to do all things for his glory (1 Cor. 10:31). God's glory is a central theme in Paul's theology because the "gospel of the glory of Christ" (2 Cor. 4:4) is at the center of his theology. Jesus, in his person and work, is glorious. The fact that Jesus is in us stands as "the hope of glory" (Col. 1:27), and someday every knee will bow "in heaven and on earth and under the earth, and every tongue confess that Jesus Christ is Lord, to the glory of God the Father" (Phil. 2:10–11; cf. Isa. 45:23; 1 Cor. 15:20–28).

In Hebrews, writes Gaffin, "the eternal glory which is ascribed to God in the closing doxology (13:21) is at the outset predicated of the Son as 'the radiance of God's glory and the exact representation of his being' (1:3)."[60] Hamilton likewise acknowledges, "The glory of God is clearly the gravitational center of the theology of Hebrews."[61] Jesus's glory exceeds that of the angels (1:7–14; 2:7, 9), Moses (3:3), the post-conquest rest Joshua gave Israel (3:7–4:10), the high priests (5:1–10), the old covenant (8:1–13), and the Old Testament sacrificial system (10:1–18). The prologue of Hebrews is the paramount expression in the book of God's glory revealed in Christ (1:1–4). As the "radiance" of God's glory, Jesus brings the divine attributes of the Father into the realm of humanity, manifesting the person and presence of God (Luke 9:32; John 1:14; 2:11; 17:5; Rom. 8:17; 1 Cor. 2:8; Phil. 3:21; 2 Thess. 2:14).[62] Citing Psalm 8:4–6, Hebrews 2:7–9 shows how the God-man reveals the Father's glory to us. While being made for a little while lower than the angels, Jesus atoned for sin and through his work brings many sons to glory (Heb. 2:10). Hebrews 13:21, much like other doxologies (Rom. 11:36; 16:27; Gal. 1:3–5; Eph. 3:20–21; Phil. 4:20; 1 Tim. 1:17; 2 Tim. 4:18; 2 Peter 3:18; Jude 25; Rev. 1:4–6; 5:13; 7:12),[63] attributes glory to God through Christ forever and ever. Although the supremacy of

---

60. Gaffin, "Glory," 510.
61. Hamilton, *God's Glory in Salvation*, 515. Hamilton goes on to argue on the next page that the opening prologue of Hebrews is chiastic and highlights the centrality of God's glory in Christ:
1:1–2a, The Son contrasted with the prophets
    1:2b, The Son as messianic heir
        1:2c, The Son's creative work
            1:3a–b, The Son as the radiance of God's glory and ruler
        1:3c, The Son's redemptive work
    1:3d, The Son as messianic king
1:4, The Son contrasted with angels
See also Daniel J. Ebert, "The Chiastic Structure of the Prologue to Hebrews," *Trinity Journal* 13 (1992): 163–79.
62. The term "radiance" (Greek: *apaugasma*) occurs nowhere else in New Testament literature, and only once in the Septuagint (Wis. 7:26). William L. Lane, *Hebrews 1-8*, Word Biblical Commentary 47A (Grand Rapids: Zondervan, 2015), 13.
63. These texts contain mainly doxologies to God the Father, though there are several directly attributable to God the Son. Schreiner observes, "Doxologies that are clearly directed to Jesus Christ seldom occur in the New Testament, though 2 Tim. 4:18 and Rev. 1:5–6 are doxologies to Christ. A doxology to Christ constitutes another way that the letter is framed, for we already saw in 1:2 that Peter identified Jesus Christ as God and Savior. Doxologies, of

Jesus has been exalted throughout the entire book, the author sees fit to point one last time to the praiseworthy nature and character of God as seen in Christ.

First Peter emphasizes the glory of Christ and the glory we will receive upon his return (1:7; 4:13; 5:1, 4). God the Father gave Jesus glory in his resurrection and enthronement (1:21), and at our resurrection we too will be glorified. We live, serve, and speak in the strength that God supplies for his glory (4:11), knowing he will one day call us to his "eternal glory in Christ" (5:10).

Second Peter 1:16–18 refers to the transfiguration scene depicted in the Synoptic Gospels (Matt. 17:1–8; Mark 9:2–8; Luke 9:28–36). Its emphasis, notes Schreiner, is on "God's imprimatur of approval upon his Son. The Son received honor and glory from the Father. The Father signified his approval with a divine voice that came from heaven itself (cf. Dan. 4:31; Rev. 11:12; 16:1)." He is the embodiment of the prophesied Messiah. Schreiner continues, "The words spoken demonstrated that God was pleased with his Son, Jesus . . . He then described God as 'the Majestic Glory' (*tēs megaloprepous doxēs*). Sirach speaks of "the glory of his voice" (Sir. 17:3). In v. 17 the Greek word for 'majestic' differs from the word used for Christ in v. 17, but the idea is the same. Peter implied that the majesty of the one and only God was shared by his Son. Furthermore, the glory that belongs to God also belongs to Jesus, for the Son received glory from the Father, the one who is majestic in glory."[64] The event of the transfiguration, understood as a manifestation of the coming of the kingdom (cf. Matt. 16:28–17:13; Mark 9:1–13; Luke 9:27–36), is significant as Peter recalls this moment in anticipation of Christ's glory when he returns (cf. 2 Peter 3:1–13).[65]

God and His Glory in Revelation

In the final book of Scripture, the glory of God is starkly displayed. In its doxologies alone we see the glory of God lifted up in the praise of the Father and the Son (Rev. 1:6; 4:11; 5:12–13; 7:12; 19:1). John indicates the overarching structure of Revelation by using the phrase "in the Spirit" near the beginning of its major sections (1:10; 4:2; 17:3; 21:10).[66] This sets the stage for how we view God's glory throughout the book.

---

course, are only directed to God himself, and so the deity of Jesus Christ is communicated in the doxology. Glory should be attributed to Christ because the salvation and perseverance of believers is ultimately his work, and the one who does the work deserves the glory." Thomas R. Schreiner, *1, 2 Peter, Jude*, New American Commentary 37 (Nashville: B&H, 2003), 401–2.

64. Schreiner, *1, 2 Peter, Jude*, 314–15.
65. Schreiner, *1, 2 Peter, Jude*, 316.
66. James M. Hamilton, *Revelation: The Spirit Speaks to the Churches*, Preaching the Word (Wheaton: Crossway, 2012), 21. Hamilton labels these sections as follows: Jesus and the Letters (1:9–3:22), The Throne and the Judgments (4:1–16:21), The Harlot, the King, and the Bride (17:1–22:9), and The Apocalyptic Prophecy's Epistolary Closing (22:10–21) (see 21–27). For a similar approach to the structure of the book, see Daniel L. Akin, *Exalting Jesus in Revelation*, Christ-Centered Exposition Commentary (Nashville: B&H, 2016); Grant R. Osborne, *Revelation*, Baker Exegetical Commentary on the New Testament (Grand Rapids: Baker, 2002).

Glory terminology in the Apocalypse references both God the Father and God the Son. Revelation 1:4–6 sets the stage well: "Grace to you and peace from him who is and who was and who is to come, and from the seven spirits who are before his throne, and from Jesus Christ the faithful witness, the firstborn of the dead, and the ruler of kings on earth. To him who loves us and has freed us from our sins by his blood and made us a kingdom, priests to his God and Father, to him be glory and dominion forever and ever. Amen." A Trinitarian introduction gives way to focusing on Jesus, the Son of Man who will come on the clouds (cf. Dan. 7:13), the first and the last, who is alive forevermore and has the keys of death and Hades (Rev. 1:17–18). Jesus is exclusively worthy of all worship, not earthly rulers.[67]

In the throne room scene, both God the Father and the Son receive glory in worship. The twenty-four elders and the four living creatures ascribe glory, honor, thanks, and power to the Father and declare he is worthy of all these things as the Creator and Sustainer of the universe (4:9–11). In this scene, a scroll is presented that no one is able to open. However, John is told that the Lion of the tribe of Judah has conquered and can open the scroll. John sees this one as "a Lamb standing, as though it had been slain" (5:6) who is also worshipped by the elders and living creatures: "Worthy are you to take the scroll and to open its seals, for you were slain, and by your blood you ransomed people for God from every tribe and language and people and nation, and you have made them a kingdom and priests to our God, and they shall reign on the earth" (5:9–10). Innumerable angels take up the cry, "Worthy is the Lamb who was slain, to receive power and wealth and wisdom and might and honor and glory and blessing!" (5:12) Finally, every creature in heaven, on earth, and under the earth proclaim, "To him who sits on the throne and to the Lamb, be blessing and honor and glory and might forever and ever!" (5:13; cf. Phil. 2:10–11) While the world is depicted as rejecting God and the gospel message, these verses describe the unadulterated worship of God who is worthy.[68]

Similar to Revelation 4–5, the reader later sees worship rendered to the Lamb by a great multitude. Together with the elders and four living creatures that ascribe "Blessing and glory and wisdom and thanksgiving and honor and power and might to God forever and ever" (7:12). This worship is rendered again because of Christ's redeeming work (cf. 7:14). Later in the book, survivors of an immense earthquake give glory to God (11:13). In Revelation 14 a

---

67. Commenting on Revelation 1:6, Osborne observes that the terms "glory" and "dominion" stand in "decided contrast to the imperial cult—only God and Christ, not Caesar, has dominion and is worthy of 'glory.'" Osborne, *Revelation*, 67.

68. Köstenberger observes that in this context glory is ascribed to the Lamb that was slain, drawing attention to the crucifixion of Jesus, prophesied of in the Old Testament (Isa. 52:13–53:12). "This draws attention to the fact that the cross is the center of John's glory theology, not only in the Gospel, but also in the Apocalypse. It is the salvific mission of the Lamb of God as the one who took away the sin of the world (John 1:29, 36) that is the source of glory and honor and blessing, in a direct reversal of the world's judgment." See "The Glory of God in John's Gospel and Revelation," in *The Glory of God*, ed. Christopher W. Morgan and Robert A. Peterson, Theology in Community 2 (Wheaton: Crossway, 2010), 107–26 (quote on 122).

call is made for all to "Fear God and give him glory" (14:7), which is followed by a prediction of God being glorified by all people (15:4). A later vision depicts the sanctuary "filled with smoke from the glory of God and from his power" (15:8), an image reminiscent of God's glory in the tabernacle and temple (Exod.40:34–35; 1 Kings 8:10–12; Isa. 6:1–4).[69]

Toward the end of the book, we see a heavenly multitude again praise God, declaring that "salvation and glory and power" belong to him because of his just judgments and the institution of the marriage supper of the Lamb (Rev. 19:1–2, 6–8). The new Jerusalem, observed from the vantage point of a great high mountain (cf. Isa. 2:2–3; 4:1–5; 25:6–26:2; Ezek. 40:1–2; Mic. 4:1–2), is illumined only by God's glory, with no need of the sun or moon (Rev. 21:10–11, 22; cf. Isa. 58:8; 60:1–2, 19; Ezek. 43:1–12), and the people there will bring into it "the glory and honor of the nations" (Rev. 21:26; Isa. 60:3–5). The radiance of the new Jerusalem evinces the infinite and eternal glory surrounding where God will dwell with his people (Rev. 21:3; Lev. 26:11–12; Ezek. 37:26–28; Zech. 2:10–11).[70]

From beginning to end, Scripture reveals a glorious God worthy of all adoration and praise.[71] God perfectly possesses his divine attributes—e.g., omniscience, omnipotence, omnipresence, aseity, immutability, love, holiness, justice, wrath, grace—and he displays the greatness of his glory for all to see. The weight of the majestic goodness of who God is renders a particular response from his creation, namely worship. How great is our God.

---

69. See Osborne, *Revelation*, 571.
70. Beale compares the glory of God throughout redemptive history to the New Jerusalem, "The theme of God's intimate presence dwelling fully and permanently with his people, briefly developed in vv. 1–8, is introduced again in v 11 and runs throughout 21:11–22:5. 'The city, the holy Jerusalem' is further described in v 11 as 'having the glory of God.' The temple in Israel was the temporary place where God's glory (presence) dwelled. But in the new creation God's presence will not be limited to a temple structure, with the people outside the structure, but the people themselves will be both the city and the temple in which God's presence resides (so 21:2–3, 12–14). In the light of the clear allusions to Isaiah 40–66 in 21:1–22:5 (e.g., 21:1–2, 4–5, 19–21, 23–26; 22:5), the reference to 'the glory of God' here must derive from Isa. 58:8 and 60:1–2, 19, which prophetically portray 'the glory of the Lord' residing in the latter-day Jerusalem. 'The glory of God' is the presence of God himself." See G. K. Beale, *The Book of Revelation: A Commentary on the Greek Text*, New International Greek Testament Commentary (Grand Rapids: Eerdmans, 1999), 1066.
71. Beale avers, "The glory of God is the uppermost goal even within the storyline, since every aspect of the consummated new-creational reign is designed to display the divine glory complete in contrast to the partial manifestation of it on earth during preconsummation history (see Num. 14:21; Rev. 21:1–22:5). . . . God's glory should be seen as the major point of the storyline, since it is the ultimate goal, and new-creational kingship and its expansion are the main means toward achieving that goal." Beale, *New Testament Biblical Theology*, 182–83.

Discussion Questions

1. While all of God's attributes are worth studying and discussing, why would it be helpful to focus on God's glory in relation to his other attributes?

2. When we say "the glory of God" what are we referring to? How should we describe this attribute he possesses?

3. What is the relationship between the glory of God and idolatry? Look specifically at the section dealing with Jeremiah 2.

4. What Old Testament passage or set of passages most informed and/or impacted your thinking on this topic? Why?

5. What New Testament passage or set of passages most informed and/or impacted your thinking on this topic? Why?

Resources for Further Study

Bray, Gerald L. *The Doctrine of God.* Contours of Christian Theology. Downers Grove: InterVarsity, 1993.

Feinberg, John S. *No One Like Him: The Doctrine of God.* Foundations of Evangelical Theology. Wheaton: Crossway, 2006.

Frame, John M. *The Doctrine of God.* A Theology of Lordship 2. Phillipsburg: P&R, 2002.

Morgan, Christopher W., and Robert A. Peterson. *The Glory of God.* Theology in Community 2. Wheaton: Crossway, 2010.

VanDrunen, David. *God's Glory Alone: The Majestic Heart of Christian Faith and Life.* Grand Rapids: Zondervan, 2015.

CHAPTER 13

KINGDOM

THE KINGDOM OF GOD is one of the grandest themes of Scripture, but perhaps also one of the most misunderstood. Some think the kingdom of God refers to the church or the nation of Israel. Others think the concept denotes God's general sovereignty or the future reality of the new heaven and new earth. The kingdom of God has been widely studied and debated in recent years with a growing consensus regarding its definition.[1] While the concept of the kingdom is multifaceted, it is crucial to uphold a definition that fits with the entirety of Scripture.[2]

The Bible is the story of God's glory, as seen in the previous chapter. The Trinitarian God is the main character of all history and has created and redeemed a people to put his glory on display (Ps. 19:1; Isa. 43:7; Eph. 1:3–14). As such, the kingdom of God is "first and foremost a statement about God—who he is (king) and what he does (reign)."[3] The realm in which God's glory is supremely displayed is referred to as his kingdom, which is "God's

---

1. For data on the amount of research done on this topic, see Leslaw Chrupcala, *The Kingdom of God: A Bibliography of 20th Century Research* (Jerusalem: Franciscan, 2007). A brief historical survey can be found in Stephen Nichols, "The Kingdom of God: The Kingdom in Historical and Contemporary Perspectives," in *The Kingdom of God*, eds. Christopher W. Morgan and Robert A. Peterson, Theology in Community 4 (Wheaton: Crossway, 2012), 25–48.

2. For broad details concerning the kingdom of God, see Blaising and Bock, *Progressive Dispensationalism*; John Bright, *The Kingdom of God: The Biblical Concept and Its Meaning for the Church* (Nashville: Abingdon, 1953); Gentry and Wellum, *Kingdom through Covenant*; Graeme Goldsworthy, *The Goldsworthy Trilogy* (Carlisle: Paternoster, 2000); George Eldon Ladd, *A Theology of the New Testament* (Grand Rapids: Eerdmans, 1993); Russell D. Moore, *The Kingdom of Christ: The New Evangelical Perspective* (Wheaton: Crossway, 2004); Christopher W. Morgan and Robert A. Peterson, eds., *The Kingdom of God*, Theology in Community 4 (Wheaton: Crossway, 2012); Schreiner, *King in His Beauty*.

3. Jeremy R. Treat, *The Crucified King: Atonement and Kingdom in Biblical and Systematic Theology* (Grand Rapids: Zondervan, 2014), 41.

people in God's place under God's rule and reign."[4] Certainly "kingdom" language can be used to convey the activity of God exercising his sovereignty over all things (Deut. 2:5, 9, 30; 4:19; 29:25–26; 32:8; Isa. 45:5–7). Most often, however, God's kingdom refers to his particular activity of exercising authority over his subjects who, out of their faith in and love for him, serve only him.[5] One could thus identify the kingdom of God as his universal reign and eternal dominion, as God's rule over the nation of Israel (theocracy, Davidic kingship) inaugurated in the person and work of Christ. God's kingdom is an inaugurated and growing reality for the church (i.e., citizens of the kingdom), and an eschatological expectation in which all the promises of God for salvation are fulfilled.[6] Thus, one can see that the kingdom denotes God's status as king, and while he does use human kings, God himself will arise as king to set right what human sin has made wrong.[7]

To understand how this kingdom presents itself in Scripture, one must note that the specific outworking of the kingdom within redemptive history is linked to the covenants given by God to his people.[8] The term "covenant" (Hebrew: *berith*; Greek: *diathēkē*) designates an enduring agreement that establishes a defined relationship between two parties. A covenant involves a "solemn, binding obligation to specified stipulations on the part of at least one of the parties toward the other, which is taken by oath under threat of divine curse and ratified by a visual ritual."[9] While a covenant can refer to various agreements between humans (e.g., Gen. 21:22–24; 1 Sam. 18:3; 1 Kings 5:1–12; 2 Kings 11:17; Ezek. 16:8; Mal. 2:14), the

---

4. Goldsworthy, *Goldsworthy Trilogy*, 54. See also Patrick Schreiner who states "The kingdom is the King's power over the King's people in the King's place" (*Kingdom of God*, 18).
5. See Bruce K. Waltke, "The Kingdom of God in the Old Testament: Definitions and Story," in *The Kingdom of God*, ed. Christopher W. Morgan and Robert A. Peterson, Theology in Community 4 (Wheaton: Crossway, 2012), 49–50. Ladd also observes, "The kingdom is primarily the dynamic reign or kingly rule of God, and derivatively, the sphere in which the rule is experienced." See *Theology of the New Testament,* 109. The key components one should keep in mind are that God's kingdom are his inaugurated and inbreaking rule in the midst of people, and a reign over a realm, all of which will be consummated at the end of history.
6. Gregg R. Allison, *Sojourners and Strangers: The Doctrine of the Church* (Wheaton: Crossway, 2012), 89–100. See also Allison, "The Kingdom and the Church," in *The Kingdom of God*, ed. Christopher W. Morgan and Robert A. Peterson, Theology in Community 4 (Wheaton: Crossway, 2012), 187; Blaising and Bock, *Progressive Dispensationalism*, 232–83; George Eldon Ladd, *The Presence of the Future: The Eschatology of Biblical Realism* (Grand Rapids: Eerdmans, 1974), 205.
7. This idea is what Beale refers to as "the story of the movement toward the new-creational kingdom." See *New Testament Biblical Theology*, 171.
8. This concept is dealt with in detail in Gentry and Wellum, *Kingdom through Covenant*, 591–601. The authors summarize what they mean by kingdom in the following five points: God is Creator and sovereign Ruler over the universe; God's reign is rejected at the fall and thus God must act in a saving way; God's kingdom is revealed and comes about through covenants; Old Testament promises, hopes, and expectations about the kingdom are declared by the prophets; As the New Testament begins one sees the inauguration and eventual consummation of the kingdom through the life, death, resurrection, ascension, and return of Jesus the Messiah. See also Hafemann, "Covenant Relationship," 27. More will be said about the concept of covenant in chapter fourteen.
9. See Daniel C. Lane, "The Meaning and Use of the Old Testament Term for 'Covenant': With Some Implications for Dispensational and Covenant Theology" (PhD Diss., Trinity International University, 2000), 314.

concept of covenant applies predominantly to divine-human commitments.[10] In terms of ecclesiology and discussions pertaining to the people of God, it is necessary to rightly understand the nature of the kingdom and the covenants so as to see how the New Testament church is distinct from Old Testament Israel. This distinction is most demonstrably shown in the final covenant discussed in Scripture, which is known as the new covenant.

In one sense, God has always been exercising his kingdom power and sovereignty over all things (Deut. 2:5, 9, 30; 4:19; 29:25–26; 32:8; 2 Kings 19:15; Pss. 29:10; 145; Isa. 6:5; Jer. 46:18). In another sense, God exercises particular kingly authority over those in covenant relationship with him. Out of faith in and love for him, God's people serve him as kingdom subjects (Exod. 15:18; Num. 23:21; Deut. 33:5; Isa. 43:15). With these kingdom subjects God makes covenants which give them a mandate for creation (Adamic covenant; Gen. 1:26; 2:15–17; cf. Hos. 6:7), deliver them from his wrath (Noahic covenant; Gen. 9:8–13), establish them with a land (Abrahamic covenant; Gen. 12:1–3), reveal to them the law (Mosaic covenant; Exod. 19:3–6), and provide them a king (Davidic covenant; 2 Sam. 7:8–16). These covenants culminate in the salvation and transformation of those kingdom subjects and ultimately all peoples (new covenant; Jer. 31:31–34; Ezek. 36:25–27).

The storyline of the Old Testament revolves around the call of Israel as God's chosen nation of kingly priests (Exod. 19:5–6) manifesting God's glory to the nations. However, Israel failed in this charge. By God's grace, through the progression of the covenants and ultimately through the coming messianic king, God's particular kingdom Israel breaks into creation to have restorative impact on the more general, universal kingdom of God.[11] One must be careful to note the progression of these covenants and the position of each covenantal passage within the redemptive story that unfolds across the canon of Scripture when considering how the kingdom manifests itself in the world. Thus, the kingdom of God, denoting his rule and reign over a people in a particular place, is a central motif to the biblical storyline and crucial for rightly understanding how God relates to his people.

The Kingdom in the Law

Like the term "Trinity," the phrase "kingdom of God" does not appear in the Old Testament. However, this in no way takes away from the fact that the concept is frequently alluded to throughout its pages. The Old Testament conceives of God as creator, the sovereign one over the kings and kingdoms of this world, and the one who enters into covenant with his people. In this manner, the kingdom of God is "the very heart of the message of the Hebrew Scriptures."[12]

---

10. P. R. Williamson, "Covenant," in *New Dictionary of Biblical Theology*, ed. T. Desmond Alexander and Brian S. Rosner (Downers Grove: InterVarsity, 2000), 420.
11. This summary was derived mainly from Waltke, "Kingdom of God."
12. Graeme Goldsworthy, "Kingdom of God," in *New Dictionary of Biblical Theology*, eds. T. Desmond Alexander and Brian S. Rosner (Downers Grove: InterVarsity, 2000 [615-20]), 618. See also Scobie, *Ways of Our God*, 106–7.

One first observes God's kingly presence in his creation of the cosmos. While a number of passages describe God as creator, Genesis 1 addresses crucial details at the very beginning of our Bible. The first chapter of Genesis presents God in all his power, majesty, and transcendence as he speaks the universe into existence. There is a definite rhythm to the six days of creation, wherein God speaks authoritatively and the various facets of the cosmos come into existence. First, light and darkness appears (1:3–5), then the heavens (1:6–8), the earth, sea, and vegetation (1:9–13), the sun, moon, and stars (1:14–19), the sea creatures and birds of the air (1:20–23), and finally the beasts of the earth and man and woman as his image-bearers (1:24–31). Throughout the creation account, a constant refrain runs as God classifies his creative work as "good" (1:4, 10, 12, 18, 21, 25, 31). Genesis 1 thus shows God to be intrinsically glorious as Lord over all, demonstrating his greatness and goodness in an extrinsic way.[13] In creation, God displays his glory, power, and existence in the cosmos (cf. Ps. 19:1; Rom. 1:18–20).

The climax of creation occurs when God forms man from the dust of the ground and woman from the rib of man (Gen. 2:7–22). One must understand that human beings are both distinct from and dependent on God, but that does not negate their uniqueness in the created order. Made in the image and likeness of God, humanity possesses a distinctive role before God in his world (1:26–27). Thus, God's people (Adam and Eve) live in covenant relationship with him and dwell in God's place (Eden) under God's sovereign rule.[14]

However, the fall disrupts this idyllic kingdom setting in Eden. In Adam and Eve's rebellion against God (3:1–7) they disrupt their communion with God (3:8–10) and suffer the consequences (3:11–19). This act of sin is rebellion against God's absolute claim to lordship and rule, a claim our God makes over all of creation as the eternal King of kings.[15] From the time of this rebellion onwards, Scripture displays a God who is still sovereign over all, who works all things according to the counsel of his will (Eph. 1:11), and who will bring about a new creational kingdom through the work of a coming one (cf. Gen. 3:15).[16] This kingdom

---

13. Goldsworthy rightly observes "Because God is the creator of all, he is the sole ruler to whom allegiance is owed by all his creatures (Gen. 14:19, 22; Exod. 20:11; Deut. 32:6; 2 Kings 19:15; Job 38:1–42:6; Isa. 37:16; 40:12–28; 42:5; 43:15; 45:1–18). A number of Psalms celebrate the kingship of Yahweh on the basis of his being the creator (Pss. 93:1; 96:4–10; 104:1–35; 136:1–9)." See "Kingdom of God," 618.
14. Gentry helpfully elucidates the relationship between the image of God, covenant, and kingdom: "The relationship between Gen 2:8–17 and Gen 1:26–27 is significant. Gen 2:8–17 explains the relationship between 'likeness' and 'image' in the covenant relationship between man and God. Only when the father-son relationship is nurtured through worship, fellowship, and obedient love will humankind appropriately and properly reflect and represent to the world the kind of kingship and rule intrinsic to God himself. Kingship is affected through covenant relationship." Peter J. Gentry, "Kingdom through Covenant: Humanity as the Divine Image," *Southern Baptist Journal of Theology* 12.1 (2008): 39.
15. Goldsworthy, "Kingdom of God," 618.
16. See William J. Dumbrell, "Genesis 2:1-17: A Foreshadowing of the New Creation," in *Biblical Theology: Retrospect and Prospect*, ed. Scott J. Hafemann (Downers Grove: InterVarsity, 2002), 56–57.

will both exclude in judgment and include in salvation (cf. Gen. 6:5–9:17), depending on one's posture toward God as King (cf. Ps. 2:1–12).

The details of this kingdom are fleshed out further in God's covenant with Abram. Here God promises a land for Abram's descendants—who will be as numerous as the sands of the sea and the stars of the sky—and that the nations of the earth would be blessed through Abram and this people (Gen. 12:1–3; cf. 15:1–21; 17:1–14; 22:15–19). As God begins his covenantal work with humanity that will extend toward a new creational kingdom, one can observe that God is providing the means necessary for humanity to overcome the consequences rendered in the curse.[17]

At the end of Genesis, God's people are in Egypt and eventually are enslaved there. God works through Moses to bring about their redemption through ten plagues that eventually overcome Pharaoh. At Sinai, Abraham's descendants, the nation of Israel, are constituted as a theocratic nation that will operate as a kingdom of priests and a holy nation with God as their king, the one who has redeemed Israel with sovereign power (Exod 19:1–6). The people are to live as faithful representatives of God, displaying his holiness and serving as a light to the nations. While subjugated to wandering in the wilderness for decades due to their willful rebellion, Israel eventually enters Canaan, the land God had promised them.

In the Law, we see God as the creator and sovereign ruler over all things (Genesis 1) and humanity as his vice-regents ordained to exercise dominion and expand the borders of the garden until the glory of God covers the earth (Gen. 1:26–28; 9:6–7; Hab. 2:14). As sovereign king, God acts in judgment at the fall (Gen. 3), but promises redemption (3:15). God's covenant with Abraham initiates God's plan to bring renewal from the curse (12:1–9; cf. 22:17–18; 49:10). In Israel, we see God's kingdom rule, which eventually is exercised through the kingly line.

The Kingdom in the Prophets

As king of all, God institutes judges and then kings to reign over Israel in accordance with his commands. As Goldsworthy observes, "The rule of the Davidic kings is representative of the rule of God over his kingdom."[18] This is most demonstrable in the covenant God makes with David, promising him an everlasting dynasty (2 Sam. 7:4–16; 1 Chron. 17:3–14).[19] The Davidic line is a crucial component of God's salvation project. As God progressively fulfills his promises he makes clear that the redemptive promises once associated

---

17. Hamilton avers, "The promise of seed to Abraham guarantees that the cursed difficulty in childbirth and conflict between the genders will be overcome. The conflict between the seed of the serpent will also be resolved by the seed of Abraham, in whom all of the nations will be blessed. And the curse on the land is answered by the promise of land, where the collective seed of Abraham will become a great nation." See *God's Glory in Salvation*, 82. See also Hamilton, "Seed of the Woman."
18. Goldsworthy, "Kingdom of God," 619.
19. See Dempster, "The Servant of the Lord," 150–51.

with Adam and his seed (Gen. 3:15) and Abraham (Gen. 12:1–3) are now connected with David and his offspring. God will establish his eternal kingdom through a son from the line of David (2 Sam. 7:12–13; cf. Gen. 49:10).[20] This seems to climax with Solomon and his construction of the temple, after which we see the division of the Northern and Southern kingdoms and the eventual decline of Israel and its kings, all the way to the point of exile.[21]

Tension arises in the Old Testament between God's sovereign rule and the actual happenings within the kingdom of Israel. In speech and writing, the prophets call Israel to faithfulness and a lifestyle aligned with the purposes and patterns of God's kingdom. Many prophets spoke regarding the impending destruction of Israel and Judah, but also a coming renewal. Often the prophets connect the hope of restoration to the expectation of a future rule and reign of God. The overall pattern of this renewal follows earlier biblical patterns: a new exodus; a new covenant; a new entry into the land; a new Jerusalem with a new temple; and a new Davidic king who will rule forever in a perfect and glorious kingdom.[22] The Israelite kings—especially David—were "typological anticipations of the ideal messianic king to come."[23] God promises David a descendant who will reign forever (2 Sam. 7; cf. Dan. 7:14) Thus, one can observe that despite the ups and downs in Israel's history, through Abraham and David God promises a renewed and everlasting kingdom (Ezek. 36–37) with a new covenant (Jer. 31) and a new creation (Isa. 65:17–25). This is why, for example, Isaiah says that he can wait for God and the fullness of his reign (Isa. 8:17). The Lord will reign over all definitively and manifestly (Isa. 24:23) and the kingdom will belong to the Lord (Obad. 21). God's rule will be experienced by Israel as well as the rest of the world.[24]

Other prophets, such as Zephaniah, also speak of God as King by linking his kingdom to the day of the Lord.[25] The day of the Lord is a frequent theme in the prophets (Isa. 2:6–22; 13:1–22; 22:1–25; 24:1–23; 34:1–17; Jer. 25:30–38; 46:1–12; Ezek. 7:1–27; 38:1–39:29; Joel 1:1–20; 2:1–11, 28–32; 3:1–21; Amos 5:16–27; Obad. 1–21; Nah. 1:1–15; Hab. 3:1–16; Zeph. 1:1–18; 2:1–15; 3:8–13; Zech. 12:1–9; 14:1–15; Mal. 3:1–5; 4:1–3), and denotes judgment against God's enemies as well as salvation for his people (Zeph. 3:11–13). On the day of the Lord, God will clear away the enemies of Israel and be in their midst as king so Israel will never again have

---

20. See Lister, *Presence of God*, 211.
21. Lister maintains, "God's redemptive purposes find expression in the installation of David as covenant king. In response to the predicament set forth in the Judges narrative—i.e., Israel's descent into apostasy facilitated by a lack of covenant leadership—Yahweh raises up a new Israelite ruler. David's rule, from a canonical standpoint, however, is the exception and not the norm. For this reason, the Davidic narrative stands as a light shining between Israel's dark history in Judges and the ensuing darkness of Kings and Chronicles." See *Presence of God*, 209.
22. Goldsworthy, "Kingdom of God," 619.
23. Beale, *New Testament Biblical Theology*, 893.
24. See Scobie, *Ways of Our God*, 121–22.
25. For more on this connection, see Craig Blaising, "A Case for the Pretribulation Rapture," in *The Rapture: Pretribulation, Prewrath, or Posttribulation*, ed. Stanley N. Gundry (Grand Rapids: Zondervan, 2010), 25–73; House, "The Day of the Lord," 207–13.

to fear evil (3:14–15). God will be king and his people will dwell in security as he rejoices over them (3:16–17). This future is certain for God's people; he will do it.[26]

Finally, it is clear from the Prophets that a major focus of the kingdom of God is the coming messianic king. God's initial promise to David includes an eternal kingdom (2 Sam. 7:16) that will be free from strife (Isa. 9:6–7; 11:1–10). After God's people have been raised, they will be governed by a coming Davidic ruler (Ezek. 37:1–28; Zech. 9–14). The Lord will give his kingdom to this chosen one (Pss. 2 and 110). And, ironically, this Son of Man will redeem his people by being cut off (Dan. 9:24–27; cf. Isa. 53:1–12). God will do a great work in and through the death and resurrected (Ps. 16:9–11) reign of this coming king.[27]

The Kingdom in the Writings

In Psalms, kingship typically refers to the office in general (33:16), including foreign rulers (2:2, 10; 45:9; 76:12) and the kings of Israel (2:6; 21:1, 7; 45:11; 89:18), as well as God's divine kingship (5:2; 10:16; 24:7–10; 29:10; 44:4; 47:2, 6–7; 48:2; 68:24; 74:12; 84:3).[28] In the latter two books of the Psalter, however, there is a reduced emphasis on the Israelite kings. Instead, one observes increased usage of terms such as "servant" (132:10; 144:10) and "anointed one" (105:15; 132:10, 17). This change of emphasis in the last two books of the Psalter points the reader beyond mere human kings to the coming messianic king (cf. Gen. 49:10; Num. 24:17; 2 Sam. 7:1–17) who is anointed by God, functions as his servant, and ushers in his eschatological kingdom. These references in the Psalms, Wilson maintains, "would have been increasingly understood eschatologically as hopeful anticipation of the Davidic descendant who would—as YHWH's anointed servant—establish God's direct rule over all humanity in the kingdom of God."[29] Ultimately, this paves the way for Jesus's self-understanding of his role as messianic king and suffering servant whose life, death, and resurrection inaugurate the kingdom of God.

Daniel details an apocalyptic vision of the kingdom of God. God's kingdom will demolish all rival human kingdoms and be a universal and eternal reality (2:31–45; 7:1–28). God's kingdom is also mentioned in the humbling of Belshazzar, who is reminded that God "rules the kingdom of mankind and sets over it whom he will" (5:21) while being told that his own kingdom will be taken away (5:26). In chapter 6, after Daniel is unjustly accused and cast to the lions, Darius sees how Daniel's God delivers him and declares that he is "the living God, enduring forever; his kingdom shall never be destroyed, and his dominion shall

---

26. See Schreiner, *King in His Beauty*, 414–15.
27. House, *Old Testament Theology*, 509.
28. Gerald H. Wilson, "Psalms and Psalter: Paradigm for Biblical Theology," in *Biblical Theology: Retrospect and Prospect*, ed. Scott J. Hafemann (Downers Grove: InterVarsity, 2002), 107.
29. Wilson "Psalms and Psalter," 108–9.

be to the end" (6:26). Ultimately, the son of man, a human figure who receives and restores God's kingdom, will usher in the kingdom of God (7:13–14).

In Ezra–Nehemiah the foundations are laid for the inauguration of the kingdom that will be seen in the New Testament. Israel returns to the land, rebuilds Jerusalem and its wall, and erects a new temple. However, many of the promises given by the prophets—especially Isaiah, Jeremiah, and Ezekiel—have still not come to full fruition.[30] Ezra and Nehemiah remind the people of the beauty and coming fullness of God's kingdom by "provoking, preserving, and adding to the hope for a glorious eschatological restoration when the Messiah would reign."[31]

In summary, the Old Testament presents the kingdom of God as the means of bringing about redemption, victory over evil, forgiveness of sins, and a new exodus.[32] It is an established reality, but also described in its coming fullness at a future time. God's kingdom will reign over all others (Dan. 2:44) and, as we will see, Jesus's exorcisms (Matt. 12:28–29), best-known prayer (Matt. 6:9–13), and work on the cross (Col. 2:13–15) all demonstrate his defeat of the "ruler of this world" (John 12:31). God's kingdom will also come to put an end to sin (Dan. 9:24) by means of a messianic king who delivers his people again through a new exodus, resulting not only in a new land, but in a new heaven and a new earth (Isa. 52:11–12; 65:17).

The Kingdom in the Gospels

When one comes to the teachings of the New Testament, the content on the kingdom of God is immense and quite detailed. This is important, as the theme of the kingdom contributes in many ways to the overarching storyline of Scripture. There are about one hundred references to the kingdom in the Synoptic Gospels.[33] There are two references in John (John 3:3, 5; 18:36), six in Acts, and eight in Paul's Letters. In keeping with the teaching of the Old

---

30. See J. G. McConville, "Ezra-Nehemiah and the Fulfillment of Prophecy," *Vetus Testamentum* 36 (1986): 205–24.
31. James M. Hamilton Jr., *Exalting Jesus in Ezra and Nehemiah*, Christ-Centered Exposition Commentary (Nashville: B&H, 2014), xii.
32. See Treat, *Crucified King*, 43–45. Jonathan Lunde gives a more exhaustive list for the coming of the kingdom in the Old Testament: "the judgment of Israel's enemies (e.g., Isa. 9:4–7; 1:1–9; 16:5; 32:1–5, 14–20; 42:1–9; 61:1–3; Jer. 30:21–22; 33:15–26; Ezek. 37:21–25; Joel 3:2, 12–13; Amos 9:11; Zech. 3:8; 6:12–13; 9:9–10); the return of the exiles (e.g., Isa 11:1, 10–16; Mic. 4:6–8); the renewal of the land (e.g., Amos 9:13–15); the rebuilding of the temple (e.g., Ezek. 43:1–7); the coming of the Messiah (e.g., Ezek. 37:21–25); the establishment of a New Covenant (Jer. 31:31–34); the outpouring of the Spirit (e.g., Joel 2:28–29); the healing and purification of the people (e.g., Isa. 62:1–3; Jer. 33:6–8); and the inclusion of the nations in the blessings of the kingdom (e.g., Zech. 8:20–23)." Jonathan Lunde, *Following Jesus, the Servant King: A Biblical Theology of Covenantal Discipleship*, Biblical Theology for Life (Grand Rapids: Zondervan, 2010), 49.
33. See Robert W. Yarbrough, "The Kingdom of God in the New Testament: Matthew and Revelation," in *The Kingdom of God*, eds. Christopher W. Morgan and Robert A. Peterson, Theology in Community 4 (Wheaton: Crossway, 2012), 99–100.

Testament, one must be careful to maintain the tension of a kingdom that is already but also not yet.[34]

The kingdom's arrival is the supernatural and sovereign work of God who brings about its inauguration in "the fullness of time" (Gal. 4:4–5).[35] Jesus Christ, God incarnate, comes to earth as king to rule in such a way as to usher in "a new kingdom and new creation where the eschatological objectives of God reach their culmination."[36] Jesus of Nazareth is the bringer and embodiment of the kingdom of God. Jesus begins his ministry with the message, "Repent, for the kingdom of heaven is at hand" (Matt. 4:17). Schreiner observes, "The coming of the kingdom that Jesus proclaimed designated something new, a time when God's enemies would be demonstrably defeated and the righteous would be visibly blessed."[37] In other words, Jesus as the Son of Man (Matt. 10:23; 24:27, 37; 25:31; Mark 13:26; 14:62; Luke 17:22, 30; 18:8; 21:36; John 1:51; cf. Dan. 7:13–14) exercised his kingly authority (Matt. 9:6) over all the brokenness in the world by healing disease (Matt. 8:1–13), casting out demons (Matt. 8:14–17), calming the sea (Matt. 8:23–27), forgiving sins (Matt 9:1–8), raising the dead and alleviating long-term anguish (Matt 9:18–26), and giving sight to the blind and speech to the mute (Matt. 9:27–34). Jesus disarms and triumphs over the powers and works and kingdom of darkness, a work that will culminate in his crucifixion and resurrection (Col. 2:13–15).[38]

This kingdom was misunderstood even by the likes of John the Baptist. He sends messengers to ask Jesus, "Are you the one who is to come, or shall we look for another?" (Matt. 11:3). As Schreiner contends, "John the Baptist voiced doubts about Jesus, presumably because he languished in prison, and his expectations regarding the kingdom were not realized. We can think back to the words of his father, Zechariah, anticipating salvation,

---

34. Scobie observes, "Thus, while the reign of God is inaugurated with the Christ event, the NT also looks forward to the final consummation of all things; as well as the 'already,' there is also a 'not yet.' The NT maintains this distinction between 'this age' and 'the age to come' (Matt. 12:32; Mark 10:30; Luke 20:34–35; Eph. 1:21), but its characteristic position is that believers now live in the *overlap of the ages*. They are those 'on whom the ends of the ages have come' (1 Cor. 10:11); though still living in 'the present evil age' (Gal. 1:4), they have also 'tasted . . . the powers of the age to come' (Heb. 6:5). In one sense they are already living in 'the last days' (Acts 2:17; 2 Tim. 3:1; Heb. 1:2; 1 Peter 1:20; 1 John 2:18), but in another sense the (final, apocalyptic) 'last day' still lies in the future (Matt. 13:39; 28:20; James 5:3; 1 Peter 1:5)." See *Ways of Our God*, 141. See also Ladd, *Theology of the New Testament*, 54–102.
35. Ladd, *Presence of the Future*, 193; Schreiner, *King in His Beauty*, 456.
36. Lister, *Presence of God*, 286. Beale agrees with this assessment: "These pivotal events of Christ's life, trials, death, and resurrection are eschatological in particular because they launched the beginning of the new creation and kingdom" (*New Testament Biblical Theology*, 19).
37. Schreiner, *New Testament Theology*, 53–54. Goldsworthy also maintains, while upholding the nuance of each of the Gospels, that this proclamation of Jesus is central to his coming. Simply put, "Jesus is declared to be the bringer of the kingdom through his life (which includes his miracles and his teachings), his death and his resurrection." Goldsworthy, "Kingdom of God," 616.
38. Hamilton, *God's Glory in Salvation*, 370. See also Craig A. Evans, "Inaugurating the Kingdom of God and Defeating the Kingdom of Satan," *Bulletin for Biblical Research* 15 (2005):49–75.

'from our enemies and from the hand of all who hate us' (Luke 1:71)."[39] Seemingly, John the Baptist anticipated a socio-political kingdom wherein the Messiah would defeat Rome and bring his people out of oppression. In response, Jesus tells the messengers, "Go and tell John what you hear and see: the blind receive their sight and the lame walk, lepers are cleansed and the deaf hear, and the dead are raised up, and the poor have good news preached to them. And blessed is the one who is not offended by me" (Matt. 11:4–6).

Christ is, in effect, reminding John of the Prophets and the way they spoke of the Messiah and the kingdom of God. This coming Messiah would heal the blind, deaf, mute, and lame, and save God's people (Isa. 35:1–10; cf. 29:18; 40:9; 42:6–7; 52:7; 58:6; 61:1–2; 65:17–25; cf. Luke 4:18–19). The promises of Isaiah have reached their climax and fulfillment in the kingdom of Christ. Lister comments, "Through his teachings and ministry, Jesus clarifies that his fulfillment comes in cosmic terms including, and even surpassing, the limited perceptions of Israel's own nationalistic messianic assumptions. Christ, therefore, comes to save not predominantly from external oppression but from the bondage of sin in order to reconcile a people to the eternal joy of God's relational and eschatological presence."[40]

Throughout the gospel of Matthew the kingdom of God (or heaven)[41] is a key theme.[42] Jesus is immediately identified as the son of David (1:1; cf. 1:20), which reminds the reader of the Davidic covenant (2 Sam. 7:4–17; 1 Chron. 17:3–15) and the context of kingship. Jesus is perceived to be a king (Matt. 2:1–2) in keeping with Old Testament prophecy (2:6; cf. Mic. 5:2). He proclaims the gospel of the kingdom (4:23), and notes who will partake of the kingdom (5:3, 10, 19; 6:33; 7:21; 18:3–4; 19:14) and who will not (7:21; 19:23–24; 21:43; 23:13). God requires child-like faith in the person and work of Christ to enter his kingdom; self-righteousness and self-sufficiency will avail no one. By casting out demons and performing various miracles, Jesus demonstrates that in him the kingdom has come near (9:35; 12:28). Many of the parables Matthew records also give further information regarding the inauguration and growth of God's kingdom (13:24, 31, 33, 44–47; 18:23; 20:1; 22:2; 25:1). Jesus states his disciples have been granted knowledge of the "mysteries" of the kingdom of heaven (13:11).[43] The irony of many of Jesus's parables is how they excoriate those who

---

39. Schreiner, *New Testament Theology*, 56.
40. Lister, *Presence of God*, 293. See also Schreiner, *New Testament Theology*, 56.
41. For more on the usage of "kingdom of heaven" in Matthew's gospel, see Jonathan T. Pennington, *Heaven and Earth in the Gospel of Matthew*, Supplements to Novum Testamentum 126 (Leiden: Brill, 2007); Pennington, "The Kingdom of Heaven in the Gospel of Matthew," *Southern Baptist Journal of Theology* 12.1 (2008): 44–51.
42. Portions of this summary are derived from Goldsworthy, "Kingdom of God," 616.
43. Ladd explains the concept of "mystery" against the backdrop of Daniel 2. "Mystery" in that context, Ladd asserts, refers to a divine revelation about matters pertaining to the future work of God, hidden generally from human understanding, but revealed to a prophet and made known to God's people at the proper time. While most expected God's kingdom to come with power and force over all people in one event, Jesus's kingdom comes first in an inaugurated manner, will grow, and will be consummated at his second coming. Ladd, *Presence of the Future*, 223–42. See also Beale, *New Testament Biblical Theology*, 432–33.

assume they are in right standing with God (5:20; 8:12; 21:31, 43; 23:13). This is especially the case as Jesus tells the parable of the sower, quoting from Isaiah 6 and making the point that these parables will have a hardening effect on some, which will lead to judgment. Some, however, will hear and believe Jesus's words (Matt. 13:1–17).[44]

Two other key texts in Matthew connect the concept of the kingdom to the church (16:13–19; 18:15–20). These passages have a close linguistic connection, particularly in their use of the term *ekklēsia* ("church")[45] as well as the appearance of the concepts of "binding" and "loosing." As a community of citizens of the inaugurated, but not yet consummated kingdom of God, the church aims to live corporately as loyal subjects of the king. Regarding Matthew 16:16–19, a key text for rightly understanding the church's relationship to the kingdom, Allison argues "Specifically, the church is the instrument through which entrance into the kingdom is granted, as the church has been entrusted with and employs 'the keys of the kingdom of heaven' (v. 19)."[46] These keys pertain to the gospel and humanity's response to it. As the community of the kingdom, the church provides entrance into the kingdom through the proclamation of the gospel, and its newly born citizens live as kingdom people under the sovereignty of the king. God has allowed the church to exercise the authority of the keys not only concerning admission into the church, but also, if needs be, removal from the church (Matt. 18:15–20).[47] This relationship between the kingdom of God and the church assumes a regenerate people exercising the authority of the keys of the kingdom.

The gospel of Mark, with its more action-oriented and fast-paced feel, also focuses on the kingdom of God as evidenced in Jesus's earthly ministry. Indeed, it is a central theme

---

44. For more on this point see Douglas S. McComiskey, "Exile and the Purpose of Jesus' Parables (Mark 4:10–12; Matt. 13:10–17; Luke 8:9–10)," *Journal of the Evangelical Theological Society* 51.1 (2008): 59.

45. Due to its rare usage of *ekklēsia*, some have doubted the centrality of the church in the gospel of Matthew. Two works that argue for the authenticity and the contextual and cultural fittingness of this term include, Edmund P. Clowney, "The Biblical Theology of the Church," in *The Church in the Bible and the World: An International Study*, ed. D. A. Carson (Grand Rapids: Baker, 1987), 16–27; Benjamin L. Merkle, "The Meaning of *ekklēsia* in Matthew 16:18 and 18:17," *Bibliotheca Sacra* 167.667 (2010): 281–91.

46. Allison, "Kingdom and the Church," 189. For further exegetical details and warrant for this interpretation regarding Matthew 16:16–29 and 18:15–20 as it relates to this topic, see Jeremy M. Kimble, *That His Spirit May Be Saved: Church Discipline as a Means to Repentance and Perseverance* (Eugene: Wipf and Stock, 2013), 37–47.

47. Carson demonstrates the conceptual connection between Matthew 16:19 and 18:18 by saying, "If the church, Messiah's eschatological people already gathered now, has to exercise the ministry of the keys, if it must bind and loose, then clearly one aspect of that will be the discipline of those who profess to constitute it. Thus the two passages are tightly joined: 18:18 is a special application of 16:19. Again, if we may judge from Paul's ministry, this discipline is a special function of apostles, but also of elders and even of the whole church (1 Cor. 5:1–13; 2 Cor. 13:10; Titus 2:15; 3:10–11)—an inescapable part of following Jesus during this age of the inaugurated kingdom and of the proleptic gathering of Messiah's people. The church of Jesus Christ is more than an audience. It is a group with confessional standards, one of which (viz., 'Jesus is the Christ') here precipitates Jesus' remarks regarding the keys. The continuity of the church depends as much on discipline as on truth. Indeed, faithful promulgation of the latter both entails and presupposes the former." D. A. Carson, "Matthew," in *The Expositor's Bible Commentary*, rev. ed. (Grand Rapids: Zondervan, 2010), 425.

of the Gospel (Mark 1:1–15).[48] As Goldsworthy summarizes, "Like Matthew, Mark sees the kingdom in the miracles. Jesus exercises his dominion in nature, over people, over sickness, and over the powers of darkness."[49] Mark also clearly teaches that, ironically, the kingdom comes only through the death and resurrection of Christ (8:31–9:1; 9:30–32; 10:32–34; 15:16–20). Jesus bore God's wrath so that his people would enjoy salvation and believe in and submit to the risen King of kings.[50]

In Luke's gospel, Jesus is designated as the Son of the Most High, Son of David, and ruler over the house of Jacob (Luke 1:30–33). Like Matthew, Luke speaks of the baptism of Jesus, highlighting the Father's words, "You are my beloved Son, with you I am well pleased" (3:22; cf. Matt. 3:17). The first part of this saying cites Ps. 2:7 and refers to Jesus as the ruler of the kings of the earth, linking him directly to the kingdom of God.[51] Jesus is the prophesied messianic king who would establish God's kingdom in his life, death, and resurrection. Luke (and Acts) also links the gospel to the kingdom of God (4:43; 8:1; 16:16; Acts 8:4) and binds the good news of Jesus's work on earth to the concept of God's rule and reign over a people.

The kingdom of God is mentioned only five times in the gospel of John (3:3, 5; 18:36). However, Jesus as the messianic king and Lord of creation is a prominent theme in John's writings.[52] In fact, Schreiner notes, "the stated purpose of this Gospel is that people believe that Jesus is the Christ and God's Son (20:30–31), and this plays a central role in the Johannine Epistles as well (1 John 2:22–23; 3:23; 4:2, 14–15; 5:1, 5, 6, 9–13; 2 John 7, 9). Hence, the purpose of the Gospel and the Epistles is seeing and believing that Jesus is the true king and God's Son, and when one sees who he truly is, then one will believe in him."[53] Thus, the kingdom of God is directly tied to both the person and work of Christ. Goldsworthy also notes, "John's distinctive teaching links perception of and entrance into the kingdom to the miracle of birth from above (John 3:3, 5)."[54] One also observes at the trial of Jesus a reference to the kingdom, which at that time was characterized not by force of power but sacrifice (18:36).

Thus, in the Gospels we see John and Jesus announcing the coming of the kingdom (Matt. 3:2; 4:17). The kingdom is present in an inaugurated sense in Jesus's first coming (Matt. 12:28; 13:31–33; Luke 4:16–30; cf. Ps. 103:19). The signs Jesus performs and salvation

---

48. See Mark L. Strauss, *Four Portraits, One Jesus: An Introduction to Jesus and the Gospels* (Grand Rapids: Zondervan, 2007), 199.
49. Goldsworthy, "Kingdom of God," 616.
50. Schreiner, *King in His Beauty*, 462–63.
51. For further details on the quotation from the Old Testament and its significance, see Beale and Carson, *Commentary on the New Testament*, 280–81.
52. This brings to mind the "word/concept tool" described in chapter eleven.
53. Schreiner, *King in His Beauty*, 504.
54. Goldsworthy, "Kingdom of God," 616.

he brings are all part of the inauguration of the kingdom. Yet, Jesus also prays for the kingdom to come (Matt. 6:10), and speaks of coming into his kingdom one day (Mark 14:61–62). In effect, Christ inaugurates his kingship and his kingdom at his first coming by means of his person and work, disarming the rulers, authorities, and powers of evil in the world (Col. 2:15) and establishing a people who submit to him as Lord and are called to participate in his kingdom.

The Kingdom in Acts and the Letters

In Acts, the kingdom of God is presented as a central message in the apostles' gospel proclamation (Acts 1:3; 8:12; 14:22; 19:8; 20:25; 28:23, 31). As Jesus preached the gospel of the kingdom, so too the apostles proclaim the realities of Jesus's kingly rule and reign. The advent of the church is seen at Pentecost in Acts 2, and God advances his kingdom primarily through the church, though it must be noted that the church is not identical to the kingdom.[55] And this advancement occurs through making disciples of king Jesus by means of gospel proclamation (Acts 1:8; cf. Matt. 28:18–20). Acts, therefore, testifies to this inaugurated but not yet consummated kingdom, focusing on both its present and future aspects while speaking of the kingdom as an ongoing theme in the preaching of the apostles (Acts 28:30–31).

The concept of "kingdom" is, surprisingly, not a prominent theme in Paul's writings. However, when the term is used (fourteen times in his writings), it functions as a crucial component of his theology. Paul addresses Jesus as the second Adam who perfectly obeyed the Father in all ways (Rom. 5:12–21; 1 Cor. 15:22) and is presently seated at the right hand of God (Rom. 8:34; Eph. 1:20; Col. 3:1; Heb. 1:3; 8:1; 10:12; 12:2), before whom all knees will someday bow (Phil. 2:9–11).[56] Thus, Paul speaks of God's kingdom in a future sense and highlights the final destruction of demonic powers and death, Christ handing the kingdom over to the Father, and God being all in all (1 Cor. 15:24–28). Paul also warns that "the unrighteous will not inherit the kingdom of God" (1 Cor. 6:9–10; cf. 15:24, 50; Gal. 5:21; Eph. 5:5; 1 Thess. 2:12; 2 Thess. 1:5; 2 Tim. 4:1, 18). The day of judgment will arrive, Jesus will defeat his enemies, and his everlasting kingdom will be consummated in the new heaven and new earth (Rev. 21–22).

---

55. Treat maintains, "The kingdom is a more comprehensive notion of God's eschatological reign over the earth, whereas the church is the people of the king between the already and not yet of the kingdom. Yet, just as they are distinct, the church and the kingdom are also inseparable. The church is a sign of the kingdom, a display to this present evil age of the proleptic reality of God's reign in the age to come. In short, the church is distinct from the kingdom of God but central to its advancement." Treat, *Crucified King*, 244. As such, salvation is a prerequisite to church membership; church members are representative members of the kingdom of God. This is due to the relationship between the church and the kingdom of God presently. For more on this point, see Jeremy M. Kimble, *40 Questions About Church Membership and Discipline* (Grand Rapids: Kregel, 2017), 39–43.
56. For more on Christ's already/not yet reign and the eventual restoration of the vice-regency of humanity, see Dan G. McCartney, "'Ecce Homo': The Coming of the Kingdom as the Restoration of Human Viceregency," *Westminster Theological Journal* 56.1 (1994): 1–21.

While future-oriented, the kingdom is also a present reality for Paul. For example, Paul progressively unfolds a distinct picture of the inaugurated aspects of God's kingdom in Col. 1:12–14, 15–20, and 2:13–15. Here Paul highlights the beauty of salvation wherein God has "delivered us from the domain of darkness and transferred us to the kingdom of his beloved Son" (Col. 1:13). The gospel of the kingdom is the present power of God unto salvation (Rom. 1:16; cf. 1 Cor. 1:18). This salvation occurs on both a personal and cosmic level through the work of Christ on the cross (Col. 1:15–20). Finally, it is by God's redemptive work in Christ that the demonic powers are decisively defeated.[57] In summary, the Spirit, the gospel, and the concept of inheritance all intimate an already but not yet approach to the kingdom of God in the writings of Paul.[58]

The author of Hebrews reminds readers that we have received "a kingdom that cannot be shaken," and we should thus offer God sincere worship with "reverence and awe" (Heb. 12:28). Christ has been offered up as a once-for-all sacrifice for our salvation and sanctification (10:14), but the book of Hebrews strikes the tension of an already/not yet kingdom dynamic. In several warnings, the readers are urged not to neglect their great salvation (2:1–4), but to encourage each other so they are not hardened by the deceitfulness of sin (3:12–4:13). They must put away apathy so as to obtain the promise as they continue to persevere in their faith (5:11–6:12). They must continue to hold fast to the confession of faith and run the race with faithful endurance (10:19–12:3). Indeed, Schreiner observes, "Homiletical warnings permeate the letter, demonstrating that believers inhabit the period between the already and the not yet. Salvation in that sense is eschatological, and believers await its consummation, and hence they are called, to believe, obey, and endure in the interval."[59] This inaugurated but not yet consummated nature of the kingdom demonstrates that believers are in Christ, have the firstfruits of the Spirit, and are called and empowered to persevere in their faith (cf. Phil. 2:12–13).

The Kingdom in Revelation

In observing key texts from Revelation regarding the kingdom of God, it is important to make several observations. First, in Revelation God's people are made into a "kingdom of priests" by means of Christ's atoning work (1:5–6). This atoning work yields a lion-like victory through lamb-like means (5:5–6). By the blood of Christ's cross, people from all tribes and nations are freed from sin to live as citizens of God's kingdom, proclaim the gospel of the

57. Treat, *Crucified King*, 118–19.
58. Schreiner, *King in His Beauty*, 560–61. Goldsworthy also maintains, "While the present, earthly expressions of the kingdom are imperfect, the gathering is described as having been raised with Christ to sit with him in heavenly places (Eph. 2:5–6), and as having come to Mt. Zion (Heb. 12:22–24). Thus the resurrection and ascension of Jesus, and the sending of the Holy Spirit, inaugurates an overlap of the ages. While believers belong through faith to the kingdom of God and the new age, they are living in the old age, and will do so until Christ returns." See "Kingdom of God," 620.
59. Schreiner, *New Testament Theology*, 111.

kingdom, and await its future fulfillment (5:9–10). In an inaugurated sense, Christ's work has rendered Satan defeated (12:10–11) although his final defeat is yet to come (20:1–10).[60]

Goldsworthy observes that in terms of the trajectory of the kingdom seen in Revelation:

> God's people are made a kingdom who will reign on earth (Rev. 5:10). The kingdom of the world will become the kingdom of God (11:15). Christ will return as King of kings and Lord of lords, slaying all enemies aligned against him (Rev. 19:11–21). The returning King will set up a millennial kingdom on earth, during which the saints will reign with him for 1,000 years (Rev. 20:1–6). Satan will be released at the end of this period for one final rebellion, but he will be overthrown and eternally judged, along with all who did not believe in him as Lord and Savior (Rev. 20:7–15). The final vision is of the new heaven and earth with a New Jerusalem let down from heaven to earth (21:1–4). The kingdom of God is finally seen to be located in the new creation, inhabited only by people whose names are written in the Lamb's book of life (21:27).[61]

God will eternally dwell with and reign over all his people with perfect love and justice in the new heavens and new earth (Rev. 21–22). This is the eschatological hope for which we wait with eager longing along with all of creation (Rom. 8:19–25).

The kingdom of God is God's people in God's place under God's rule. Specifically, it is the rule of God expressed presently in his saving power (of all nations) by means of Christ's atoning work and the ministry of the Holy Spirit. In the future, the consummation of the kingdom of God is seen as the fulfillment of all of God's promises to his people and his direct, divine rule over all creation.

It is crucial as believers to neither over-realize nor under-realize our expectations of the kingdom of God. We can succumb to neither naïve utopianism nor withdrawal and cultural apathy. Jesus is the rightful ruler of the cosmos, but his kingdom is not yet fully consummated. We seek first his kingdom (Matt. 6:33) with a present and future focus. The kingdom continues to grow and permeate the present world (Matt. 13:31–33) as people come to faith in Christ and are indwelt by the Spirit, and one day God will dwell with us in a new heavens and new earth where he will be our God and we will be His people (Rev. 21:1–4). He is and will be King of all. Yarbrough reminds us that God is not a local deity limited in the scope of his rule and reign. Instead, the theme of the kingdom of God reminds us that "While 'kingdom' is of special interest to those who know and bow to the King, 'kingdom' is relevant to every creature on the earth and every square inch of this world's domains."[62] May his kingdom come.

---

60. See Treat, *Crucified King*, 126–27.
61. Goldsworthy, "Kingdom of God," 617.
62. Yarbrough, "Kingdom of God," 104–5.

Discussion Questions

1. What is the kingdom of God? Give a succinct, biblically warranted definition.

2. Describe how the kingdom of God is both already and not yet.

3. How does our understanding of the kingdom of God affect the way we conceive of the people of God (i.e., Israel and the church) across the testaments?

4. What Old Testament passage or set of passages most informed and/or impacted your thinking on this topic? Why?

5. What New Testament passage or set of passages most informed and/or impacted your thinking on this topic? Why?

Resources for Further Study

Ladd, George Eldon. *The Presence of the Future: The Eschatology of Biblical Realism*. Grand Rapids: Eerdmans, 1974.

Moore, Russell D. *The Kingdom of Christ: The New Evangelical Perspective*. Wheaton: Crossway, 2004.

Morgan, Christopher W., and Robert A. Peterson, eds., *The Kingdom of God*. Theology in Community 4. Wheaton: Crossway, 2012.

Schreiner, Patrick. *The Kingdom of God and the Glory of the Cross*. Short Studies in Biblical Theology. Wheaton: Crossway, 2018.

Treat, Jeremy R. *The Crucified King: Atonement and Kingdom in Biblical and Systematic Theology*. Grand Rapids: Zondervan, 2014.

CHAPTER 14

COVENANT

ETERNALLY, OUR GOD HAS EXISTED in relationship to himself as Father, Son, and Holy Spirit, loving, rejoicing, and delighting in intra-Trinitarian community.[1] God delights infinitely in what is infinitely delightful; namely, himself existing as the three persons of the Trinity.[2] And God's love, joy, and delight do not stop there; God also created and relates to his creation, especially humanity. There are a myriad of means by which God relates to us as human beings, but one specific—and biblically thematic—way in which God enters into relationship with people is by means of covenant.

Covenant is one of the most important themes in biblical theology.[3] The concept exists at significant points in the Bible's storyline and functions as the theological adhesive that binds promise to fulfillment. If one wishes to understand how the Scriptures fit together from beginning to end—particularly in how the New Testament relates to the Old

---

1. For more on this concept, see Reeves, *Delighting in the Trinity*. See also the discussion of God and his glory in chapter twelve.
2. For greater detail on this point, especially the Father's delight in the Son, and the Spirit as the link of love between the two, see John Piper, *The Pleasures of God: Meditations on God's Delight in Being God*, rev. ed. (Sisters: Multnomah, 2000), 25–46.
3. Schreiner notes that many theologians have seen "covenant" as the central theme in all of Scripture. "Covenant has played a vital role in theology from the beginning. Early church fathers, such as Origen, Irenaeus, and Augustine, assigned covenant a significant place in their writings. Covenant also came to prominence among the Reformers and their successors. Johannes Oecolampadius (1482–1531), Johannes Cocceius (1609–1669), and Herman Witsius (1636–1708) advanced the importance of covenant in interpreting the Scriptures. In the modern period the importance of covenant was set forth by a number of scholars, perhaps most notably by the great Old Testament scholar Walther Eichrodt (1890–1978)." Thomas R. Schreiner, *Covenant and God's Purpose for the World*, Short Studies in Biblical Theology (Wheaton: Crossway, 2017), 11–12. More recent scholars claim the importance of covenant, but see it as a framework explaining the storyline of the Bible or as a structuring and organizing motif. See Gentry and Wellum, *Kingdom through Covenant; Horton, Christian Faith*.

Testament—it is imperative to have a good grasp on the unfolding of the covenants God makes with his people across the canon. As was stated in the previous chapter, the term "covenant" (Hebrew: *berith*; Greek: *diathēkē*) designates an enduring agreement or chosen association that establishes a defined relationship between two parties involving a "solemn, binding obligation to specified stipulations on the part of at least one of the parties toward the other, which is taken by oath, usually under threat of divine curse, and ratified by a visual ritual."[4] God is omnipresent, but demonstrates a particular kind of relational presence that is covenantal in nature.[5]

Multiple covenants are given in Scripture (Gen. 21:24–32; 26:14–33; 31:17–55; Josh. 9:3–27; 1 Sam. 18:3–4; 20:8, 16–17; 2 Sam. 3:12–13, 21; 5:3; 21:1–9; 1 Kings 5:12; 15:18–20), but several of these stand out as prominent, as they are repeated, given by God, and ultimately impact not just one individual, but God's people as a whole. There is also a certain kind of progression visible in the covenants as one navigates the biblical storyline. In this way, biblical covenants form the "backbone" of Scripture and give a certain shape to its narrative.[6] By tracing this theme throughout the canon, one can observe how God makes covenants with Adam, Noah, Abraham, Moses, David, and then finally establishes the new covenant. Understanding whom the covenants are for, what promises are connected to them, and when these promises will come to fruition are key to rightly comprehending the unfolding plan of God's redemptive work.

Covenant in the Law

Although the Bible does not explicitly mention a covenant until Gen 6:18, many believe that God first made a covenant with Adam.[7] Schreiner provides helpful argumentation for this assertion.[8] First, the word "covenant" does not have to be present for a covenant to exist, as the concept and general pattern of a covenant communicates the same idea. One example of this phenomena is when God enters into a covenant with David in 2 Samuel 7 (see also 1 Chron. 17). The word "covenant" is not used to describe the promise the Lord made to David. However, subsequent biblical writers who reflect upon God's promise to

---

4. See Lane, "Old Testament Term for 'Covenant'," 314. As such, a covenant is a particular kind of relationship in which two parties make binding promises to each other.

5. Lister, *Presence of God*, 52. Frame also avers, "God is not merely present in the world; he is *covenantally* present. He is *with* his creatures to bless and to judge them in accordance with the terms of the covenant. See *Doctrine of God*, 94.

6. See Blaising and Bock, *Progressive Dispensationalism*, 128–211; Gentry and Wellum, *Kingdom through Covenant*, 21–37.

7. There has been scholarly debate over whether the relationship God had with Adam and Eve was indeed covenantal. For example, see Paul R. Williamson, *Sealed with an Oath: Covenant in God's Unfolding Purpose* (Downers Grove: InterVarsity, 2007), 52–58, 69–76. Contra Williamson, strong arguments defending a covenantal relationship include William J. Dumbrell, *Covenant and Creation: An Old Testament Covenantal Theology* (Carlisle: Paternoster, 1984), 15–26; Gentry and Wellum, *Kingdom through Covenant*, 177–222; Meredith G. Kline, *Kingdom Prologue: Genesis Foundations for a Covenantal Worldview* (Overland Park: Two Age, 2000), 82–103.

8. Regarding the following points, see Schreiner, *Covenant*, 20–23.

David specifically call it a covenant (Pss. 89:3, 28, 34, 39; 132:12; Jer. 33:21). It is apparent, then, that the concept of covenant may be present when the word is entirely lacking.

Second, we have textual evidence for a covenant at creation with Adam in Hos. 6:7. The interpretation is disputed,[9] but a reference to a covenant with Adam seems to be the most likely reading.[10] In Hosea 6, God refers to Israel who, like Adam, violates the covenant he set up for them and thus must deal with the consequences.

Third, as with other covenants, there are certain elements present in the creation narrative that lead the reader toward seeing this relationship as covenantal in nature. The creation narrative presents two partners: God and humanity. As covenant Lord, God gave the stipulation that Adam and Eve refuse to eat from the "tree of the knowledge of good and evil" (Gen. 2:17; 3:3, 11). Furthermore, conditional curses for disobedience and blessings for obedience were given, key components in later covenants. If Adam and Eve disobeyed, they would die (2:17; 3:3), but if they obeyed they would then enjoy life with God. These are all consistent elements of biblical covenants.

Finally, the parallel between Adam and Christ enunciated in Romans 5:12–19 and 1 Corinthians 15:21–22 supports an Adamic covenantal relationship. Both Adam and Christ function as representatives of those who belong to them. In other words, they serve as heads of their respective covenants. Therefore, sin, death, and condemnation belong to all human beings by virtue of their covenant connection to Adam, whereas grace, righteousness, and life belong to all those united to Jesus Christ. The covenantal and representational role of Adam is clear in the biblical storyline.

Seeing the warrant for a covenant with Adam, further details must be shown regarding what this covenant actually is. God created all things and the pinnacle of his creation is the creation of man and woman in his image (Gen. 1:26–27). As God's image-bearers, Adam and Eve are granted the capacity to relate to God and one another and function as vice-regents called to exercise dominion over the earth (1:28).[11] They would manage God's creation under his lordship and thus were not completely autonomous in their stewardship. The Lord put Adam and Eve in the garden "to work it and keep it," and commanded them

---

9. Williamson, *Sealed with an Oath*, 55.

10. For further support, see John A. Davies, *A Royal Priesthood: Literary and Intertextual Perspectives on an Image of Israel in Exodus 19.6*, Journal for the Study of the Old Testament Supplement Series 395 (London: T&T Clark, 2004), 202–3.

11. More will be said regarding the details of the image of God in chapter fifteen. For our purposes in this chapter, it is sufficient to say that God creates humanity in his image, and it is because of this unique status that he covenants with them. For more on this topic generally, see Anthony A. Hoekema, *Created in God's Image* (Grand Rapids: Eerdmans, 1986); John F. Kilner, *Dignity and Destiny: Humanity in the Image of God* (Grand Rapids: Eerdmans, 2015); Richard Lints, *Identity and Idolatry: The Image of God and Its Inversion*, New Studies in Biblical Theology 36 (Downers Grove: InterVarsity, 2015).

to eat from any tree except the "tree of the knowledge of good and evil" for the day they ate of that tree, they would "surely die" (2:15–17).

One can see covenant curses and blessings pronounced within the text of Genesis 2. The tree of life is also there, suggesting that perhaps after some time (though the text is not explicit about this), Adam and Eve would be able to partake and live with God in right relationship forever (Gen. 2:9; cf. 3:22–24; Rev. 22:2, 14, 19). Once Adam and Eve disobeyed, they came under the covenant curses. However, as Schreiner points out, "The curses of the covenant weren't limited to Adam and Eve alone; they had a universal impact."[12] As previously mentioned, Adam functioned as a covenant head, such that sin, death, and condemnation spread to all of humanity and even impacted the creation itself (Rom. 8:18–25).

Adam and Eve were made in God's image to rule the world on his behalf. They were to represent God on earth and display his holiness and goodness in the way they lived and exercised dominion. Their rebellion and its concomitant results demonstrate that humanity and creation need redemption.[13] Scripture is clear: our greatest plight is standing before God as condemned sinners. Yet even in these early stages, there is hope. Subsequent to the breaking of the covenant and the fall, God promised that an offspring from the woman would eventually come and crush the head of the serpent (Gen. 3:15). While the first Adam brought about sin, condemnation, and death, a new Adam is needed who will bring about righteousness, justification, and life (Rom. 5:12–19; 1 Cor. 15:21–22).[14] The covenantal structure of Scripture points in this very direction.

The next covenant found in Scripture is made with Noah. Following the fall, the narrative of Genesis depicts a world that, in many ways, is falling apart. Adam and Eve's immediate offspring, Cain, murders his brother Abel after being angered by his offering not being accepted by God (Gen. 4:1–8; cf. Heb. 11:4). Lamech displays his arrogance and flippancy toward violence (4:22–23) and death is the resounding theme for humanity (5:1–32). Genesis 6:5 aptly describes the depth of evil in the human heart: "The Lord saw that the wickedness of man was great in the earth, and that every intention of his heart was only evil continually." The earth was corrupt and full of violence, which grieved God's heart and was an affront to his holiness (6:11–13). The detrimental results of Genesis 3 are displayed in full array within these chapters and beyond.

Standing in direct distinction to this rampant wrongdoing was Noah, who "found favor in the eyes of the Lord," and was "righteous," "blameless," and one who "walked with God"

---

12. Schreiner, *Covenant*, 27.
13. See D. A. Carson, *The Gagging of God: Christianity Confronts Pluralism* (Grand Rapids: Zondervan, 2002), 215–16, who argues that "the impact of sin on human beings reaches to every facet of our existence, our will, our bodies, our emotions, our imagination, our reason, our relationships." The beginnings of sin are delineated in Genesis 3, "and many of the features of sin that will be unpacked in sordid detail in later canonical writings are already there depicted *in nuce*."
14. See Michael Scott Horton, *God of Promise: Introducing Covenant Theology* (Grand Rapids: Baker, 2006), 83–104.

(6:8–9).[15] According to God's command, Noah builds an ark and he, his family, and the animals on board are brought safely through the waters of the flood while the rest of humanity and the animals perish (6:14–7:24; cf. 1 Peter 3:20). Although God announces his covenant with Noah prior to the flood (6:18), he establishes it with Noah only after the water subsides (8:20–9:17). Once Noah, his family, and the animals exit the ark, God makes this decree: "I will never again curse the ground because of man, for the intention of man's heart is evil from his youth. Neither will I ever again strike down every living creature as I have done. While the earth remains, seedtime and harvest, cold and heat, summer and winter, day and night, shall not cease" (8:21–22; cf. 9:9–11). God pledges here that humanity would be preserved until the end of history.

This covenant highlights God's plan to preserve Noah and the others in the ark. God's covenant with Noah after the flood reaffirms his original creational intent, and in many ways sets up a parallel between Noah and Adam.[16] Thus, God solemnly promises that a "suspension of the natural order" will never again interrupt the fulfillment of humanity's creational mandate (cf. 1:26–30; cf. 9:1–7).[17] Essentially, God promises that humanity will not be "annihilated before the promises of Genesis 3:15 is realized . . . God's gracious purpose for human beings will not be frustrated."[18] In other words, though undeserved, God's grace abounds.

The sign of the Noahic covenant is seen in God's display of a "bow in the cloud" (9:12–17). As Schreiner observes, "The bow, as the sign of the covenant, represents a weapon of war (cf. Gen. 48:22; Josh. 24:12; 1 Sam. 2:4). If God unleashed his bow and let it fly, then all humanity would be destroyed. The sign of the covenant is that God has withdrawn his bow. He has put his weapons of war down and will not wipe out the human race again."[19] God's mercy is shown to a sinful and undeserving people, including Noah (Gen. 9:20–24). While humanity is

---

15. Schreiner helpfully highlights that "Noah walked with God by virtue of his faith (Heb. 11:7). Noah didn't earn or merit God's favor; he pleased God because of his faith, and his goodness testified to his trust in God." See *Covenant*, 32. This is important as we must recognize Old Testament saints were also saved by their faith, not good works.

16. There are key connections between Noah and Adam, and thus between the covenants God makes with them. Most prominently one can observe several features. Adam and Eve were blessed by God and enjoined to be fruitful and multiply (Gen. 1:28), and with Noah this command was issued afresh. The flood, in other words, did not mean the abolition of human beings; rather God blessed Noah as he had blessed Adam and Eve (9:1, 7). Adam and Eve were also given dominion over the world (1:26, 28; 2:14). God asserted this rule still existed in a fallen world and revealed that animals, birds, and fish are under the rule of human beings (9:2). God also provided food for humans by giving them fruits and vegetables to eat (1:29). Human beings are also seen as the crown of creation because they are made in the image of God (1:26). The Noahic covenant demonstrates that human beings retained God's image (9:6). See Warren Austin Gage, *The Gospel of Genesis: Studies in Protology and Eschatology* (Winona Lake: Carpenter, 1984), 16; Gentry and Wellum, *Kingdom through Covenant*, 176; J. V. Fesko, *Last Things First: Unlocking Genesis 1-3 with the Christ of Eschatology* (Fearn, Ross-shire: Mentor, 2007), 118; Schreiner, Covenant, 33–34.

17. See Williamson, "Covenant," 421–22.

18. Schreiner, *Covenant*, 31.

19. Schreiner, *Covenant*, 35.

preserved from God's rightful judgment being meted out this way every few years, the Noahic covenant does not provides redemption for humanity. However, it is a covenant by God to humanity that points toward our need for the seed of the woman to crush the head of the serpent and deliver us from sin and death, lest we face eternal judgment from God (Rom. 6:23).

Next, God makes a covenant with Abraham. Even after the covenant with Noah, humanity continues its downward spiral of sin that culminates in their attempted construction of the tower of Babel (11:1–9), which results in the confusion of languages and the scattering of people across the face of the earth. The plight of sin is still a present and pervasive reality. Humanity, it seems, is destined to continue down the path of sin and destruction. If there is to be a way forward where the serpent and his ways will finally be defeated, God will have to act and initiate that plan in his grace.[20] The Abrahamic covenant marks the beginning of God's design to initiate his redemptive plan, answering the issue of "how the earth once more becomes the dwelling place shared by God and humanity."[21]

This call of Abraham begins to bring focus to the line through which God would fulfill the promise given in Genesis 3:15.[22] God covenants with Abraham to make him into a great nation, give him a land, and bless all the nations of the earth through him (12:1–3).[23] These three promises—land, seed, and blessing—are the key components of this covenant. Concerning the land, after Abraham went out of Ur, he is told that this land would be Canaan (12:7; 13:14–17; 15:7, 16; 17:8; 22:17). Specifically, Abraham's offspring would possess the land "from the river of Egypt to the great river, the river Euphrates" (15:18). As the story

---

20. This is why, as VanGemeren observes, it is important to view the Abrahamic covenant as foundational when thinking of the remainder of the covenants. It is a clear explication of God's covenantal dealings, and the components of this covenant are embedded in the promises he makes within other covenants. Willem VanGemeren, *The Progress of Redemption: The Story of Salvation from Creation to the New Jerusalem* (Grand Rapids: Baker, 1988), 129.

21. Alexander, *New Jerusalem*, 14. See also Blaising and Bock, *Progressive Dispensationalism*, 130–40.

22. For more detail regarding how Gen 12:1–3 matches the content of the curses in 3:14–19, and thus shows how God is beginning to bring about the reversal of the curses brought about by the fall, see Hamilton, "Seed of the Woman." Wright concurs: "Abraham emerges within the structure of Genesis as the answer to the plight of all humankind. The line of disaster and of the 'curse' from Adam, through Cain, through the flood to Babel, begins to be reversed when God calls Abraham and says, 'in you shall all the families of the earth be blessed.'" N. T. Wright, *The New Testament and the People of God* (Minneapolis: Fortress, 1992), 262.

23. One should recognize the Abrahamic covenant as one covenant, but with distinctive emphases that receive further explanation throughout Genesis. The covenant highlights the nation (Israel) and the nations being blessed at various stages from Genesis 12 onward. The national dimension of God's promise is the focus of Genesis 15 where God establishes (or "cuts") a covenant with Abram (15:18). The international dimension of the promise, apparently unreferenced in Genesis 15, is alluded to in Genesis 17 (cf. 17:4–6, 16) where God announces an "everlasting covenant" (17:7): the so-called "covenant of circumcision" (Acts 7:8). At the initial time this covenant was given, there was a formal ratification of God's promise to make Abraham into a "great nation" (12:2). Thus the primary focus is on how God will work out his goal (15:1–6) in Abraham's biological "offspring," first in Isaac (21:1–7) and then the subsequently identified sons of Abraham, Isaac, and Jacob (i.e., Israel). Focus then turns to how Abraham, through the "seed" descended from him, would mediate blessing to "all peoples on earth" (12:3; cf. 22:17–18). This seems to be the main focus as greater detail is given concerning this covenant in Genesis 17 and 22. See Gentry and Wellum, *Kingdom through Covenant*, 275–80; 630–31; Williamson, "Covenant," 422–23.

of the Old Testament unfolds, it becomes apparent that Canaan is viewed as a new kind of Eden where the Lord will walk among his people (Gen. 3:8; Lev. 26:11–12; Deut. 23:14).[24] The land promise is later confirmed to Abraham's son Isaac (Gen. 26:3) and grandson Jacob (28:13–15; 35:12). Though still marked by wandering and the eventual departure from Canaan due to famine, Israel would return from slavery in Egypt once again to the land God promised (Exod. 3:13–17; 6:3–9).

Second, God promises to Abraham "seed" or offspring. God says that he will make Abraham into a "nation" (12:2) that will be "great and mighty" (18:18). Although Abraham and Sarah are old and have no children, God promises them that a mighty nation and kings would come from their line (17:7, 16). Abraham's offspring would one day be as numerous as the stars and the sand on the seashore (15:5), and his offspring would "possess the gate of his enemies" (22:17). The promise of seed is also confirmed with Isaac and Jacob (28:14; 35:11), denoting an organized political entity functioning as a kingdom under God. Ironically, Abraham and Sarah have no children when this promise is given, but Abraham believes God and this belief is counted to him as righteousness (15:6; cf. Rom. 4:3; Heb. 11:11–12), and God fulfills his word.

Finally, God promises that all the nations of the earth would be blessed through Abraham and his offspring (Gen. 12:3; cf. 18:18; 22:18; 26:4; 28:14). The blessing language here seems to pick up on the blessings God gave to Adam (1:28) and Noah (9:1), thus putting Abraham in the path of God's redemptive plan for all the peoples of the earth.[25] God's pledge of blessing is "indicative of Abraham's positive relationship with the Lord and anticipate[s] the divine presence in the midst of the nation of Israel."[26] In other words, Abraham marks the beginning of God's work with the nation of Israel and, ultimately, all the nations. The divine purposes demonstrated at creation would be realized in God's plan through the blessings brought by the offspring of Abraham not only to the people of Israel, but to all peoples.

As Abraham's covenant is mentioned several times in Genesis, one observes the initial giving of the covenant, God demonstrating his faithfulness to the covenant by walking between the cut-up animals (15:12–21), and the sign of the covenant (circumcision; 17:1–14). God's covenant with Abraham is unconditional, though one can also see some conditional elements to it, such as leaving Ur (12:1–3), a call to blamelessness (17:1), circumcision (17:9–14), doing righteousness and justice (18:19), and the sacrifice of Isaac (22:16–18). It is clear that Abraham does not always obey God's commands, and thus there is a tension between these conditional and unconditional elements of the covenant. This tension calls for an offspring

---

24. See Gordon Wenham, "Sanctuary Symbolism in the Garden of Eden Story," in *"I Studied Inscriptions from before the Flood": Ancient Near Eastern, Literary, and Linguistic Approaches to Genesis 1–11*, ed. Richard S. Hess and David Toshio Tsumara, Sources for Biblical and Theological Study 4 (Winona Lake: Eisenbrauns, 1994), 400–401.
25. Schreiner, *Covenant*, 46.
26. Alexander, *Promised Land*, 129.

of Abraham who will perfectly keep God's righteous standards and serve as the mediator of God's covenant promises. God keeps the covenant unconditionally and the offspring upholds God's righteous standards. The continuation of the covenants gives greater detail to God's call to holiness, the line of Abraham's offspring, and humanity's need for a new heart.

God established the Mosaic covenant right after a significant development anticipated in Genesis 15 had taken place: the liberation of Abraham's descendants from oppression in a foreign land (Gen. 15:13–14; cf. Exod. 2:23–24; 3:7–8, 16–22; 6:4–6; 13:5, 11; 19:4–6; 20:2). In continuity with the Abrahamic covenant—though displaying its own distinctive elements—God covenants with Israel to bring them into Canaan, bless them, and be present with them (Exod. 6:1–8; 29:45–46; cf. Lev. 26:11–13; Deut. 7:7–9; Jer. 11:2–5).[27] The focus at Sinai is less on what Israel must do to inherit the land and more on how they should conduct themselves within the land as the unique nation that God has intended them to be. This calling is only possible because God has initiated a relationship with them by grace and redeemed them as a people (Exod. 19:4; cf. 20:2). Grace precedes God's commands.

As God's "treasured possession," "kingdom of priests," and "holy nation" (Exod. 19:5–6), Israel must respond to the grace God has extended to them by keeping this covenant, submitting to its requirements (i.e., the stipulations set forth in Exod. 20–23), and thereby displaying the greatness of God's character. In this way, Israel would serve as a "God-exalting witness in the midst of the world."[28] By adhering to these and the subsequent covenant obligations given at Sinai, Israel would be manifestly different from the other nations and thus reflect God's wisdom and greatness to the surrounding peoples (cf. Deut. 4:6–8).[29] By reflecting God's holiness (Lev. 19:2), Israel would showcase a true theocracy and thus serve as God's witnesses to a watching world.

The Mosaic covenant also encompasses the means by which the divine-human relationship between Yahweh and Israel should be maintained: sacrificial worship (Lev. 1–7), particularly on the Day of Atonement (Lev. 16). This practice would ritually atone for Israel's sin by the substitution of an animal's life for that of the sinful nation and symbolically express God's forgiveness. Israel was called to obey God's covenant stipulations, but sacrifice was necessary so that Israel could have their sin atoned for and thus be holy as God is holy (Lev. 11:44). Therefore, just as the Noahic covenant guaranteed the preservation of human life on earth, so too the Mosaic covenant gave the means for the preservation of Israel, Abraham's descendants, in the land (unless they completely disobeyed the commandments of God and broke

---

27. Dempster rightly suggests, "The goal of Exodus is thus the building of the Edenic sanctuary so that the Lord can dwell with his people, just as he once was Yahweh Elohim to the first human beings." See *Dominion and Dynasty*, 100. See also John I. Durham, *Exodus*, Word Biblical Commentary 3 (Waco: Word, 1987), 21; Frank J. Gorman, *Leviticus: Divine Presence and Community*, International Theological Commentary (Grand Rapids: Eerdmans, 1997), 10.
28. DeRouchie, *Exegesis to Theology*, 404.
29. Williamson, "Covenant," 424.

covenant, in which case exile from the land was promised; Deut. 28–29). This was a crucial next stage in the fulfillment of God's promises: establishing a people in the land and a royal line through which Abraham's ultimate "seed" would eventually come (cf. Gal. 3:16).

It should also be noted, however, that even within the Pentateuch there is indication that Israel would not keep this covenant. God requires obedience and love from his people, but recognizes they will fall short of these demands. Thus, he commands Israel to "Circumcise the foreskin of your heart and be no longer stubborn" (Deut. 10:16). He knows their proclivity for idolatry and beckons Israel to worship him alone. After listing the covenant blessings and curses (Deut. 27–28) there is a declaration that these blessings and curses will in fact come upon Israel in their future (30:1). This assumes ongoing, unrepentant disobedience on the part of Israel, and God intervening eventually by means of exile from the land. While God called Israel to circumcise their hearts earlier in the book, it is now declared, "And the Lord your God will circumcise your heart and the heart of your offspring, so that you will love the Lord your God with all your heart and with all your soul, that you may live" (30:6). The Mosaic covenant, therefore, is limited in scope.[30] There is need for a future covenant wherein hearts are made new and the law is written upon them.

Covenant in the Prophets

Within the Prophets other covenants emerge, but there is also commentary on the ways in which previous covenant promises come to fruition. Under Joshua, Israel comes into possession of Canaan by conquest. Joshua reminds the people that God called Abraham as a pagan out of Ur and by his grace has worked mightily on their behalf (Josh. 24:2–3). Thus, God fulfilled his covenant promises to Israel, though they did not drive out the people completely (Josh. 21:44–45; 24:13, 18–19). The Old Testament climax of the fulfillment of the promise of land and offspring to Abraham was realized later during the reign of Solomon. "Judah and Israel were as many as the sand by the sea. They ate and drank and were happy. Solomon ruled over all the kingdoms from the Euphrates to the land of the Philistines and to the border of Egypt." (1 Kings 4:20–21). Schreiner observes that the promises made to Abraham seem to have been fulfilled in its entirety in 1 Kings 4:20–21. "During Solomon's reign Israel seemed to be on the cusp of becoming a blessing to all nations. But near the end of Solomon's reign things begin to go awry. Solomon, under the influence of his wives, turned toward the worship of idols, and a process began

---

30. As Wellum and Gentry point out, looking to Christ as the fulfillment of the Mosaic law (Matt. 5:17; Rom. 10:4), "Scripture views the 'old covenant' as temporary in God's plan, or better, as a crucial part of God's redemptive purposes, yet when that to which it points arrives, the covenant with Israel *as a whole covenant package* comes to its end and Christians are no longer under it *as a covenant*." Gentry and Wellum, *Kingdom through Covenant*, 635. See also Douglas J. Moo, "The Law of Christ as the Fulfillment of the Law of Moses," in *The Law, the Gospel, and the Modern Christian: Five Views*, ed. Wayne G. Strickland (Grand Rapids: Zondervan, 1993), 319–24.

that led to the dissolution of all Israel."[31] This again signals the need for Israel to possess a new heart so as to walk in God's ways.

The blessings of the Abrahamic covenant feature prominently in the Latter Prophets (e.g., Isa. 2:1–4; 11:10; 12:4; 19:16–25; 42:6–7; 45:22; 49:6; 52:15; 55:4–5; Jonah 1:1–4:11; Mic. 4:1–5; Zeph. 3:9–10). In many instances these promises of blessing speak of the nations coming to worship God, or of Israel returning to the land and turning from their idolatrous ways to right worship. A link, therefore, can be seen between the Abrahamic and Mosaic covenants. God's people have neither obeyed his covenant stipulations nor made his name known to the nations, and are thus removed from the land. Yet, God will accomplish his purposes and call both Israel and the nations to himself to worship, such that his glory will cover the earth as the waters cover the sea (Isa. 11:9; Hab. 2:14).

After the Mosaic covenant, the next major covenant is made with the king of Israel, David (2 Sam. 7:4–17; 1 Chron. 17:3–15).[32] David is the offspring of Adam, Abraham (Gen. 17:6, 16; 22:17–18; 35:11; cf. Num. 24:17–19), and Judah (Gen. 49:9–20), and now serves as the monarch of God's people who live under the blessings of the Abrahamic covenant and the stipulations of the Mosaic covenant. The Davidic covenant continues the trajectory of the Adamic, Mosaic, and Abrahamic covenants. God's plans for David and Israel are clearly intertwined (cf. 2 Sam. 7:8–11, 23–26). Moreover, significant parallels link David to Abraham: God promises both men a great name (Gen. 12:2; 2 Sam. 7:9); in the future both will conquer their enemies (Gen. 22:17; 2 Sam. 7:11; cf. Ps. 89:23); both have a significant relationship with God (Gen. 17:7–8; 2 Sam. 7:24; cf. Ps. 89:26); "offspring" is a key component of God's promise to them (Gen. 21:12; 2 Sam. 7:12–16); both of their descendants must keep God's laws (Gen. 18:19; 2 Sam. 7:14; cf. Ps. 89:30–32; 132:12); and both of their offspring would mediate international blessing (Gen. 22:18; Ps. 72:17).[33]

God's kingdom is being established by means of God's covenants, and here one sees the beginning (though not the culmination) of covenantal fulfillment: a human king who functions as a representative of the people to God.[34] After gaining peace in his kingdom, David intends to build a "house" (temple) for God, but God promises to build a "house" (dynasty) for David. In similar fashion to the Mosaic covenant, David is told that there will be consequences for disobedience (2 Sam. 7:14). Individual kings who transgress God's covenantal stipulations

---

31. Schreiner, *Covenant*, 45.
32. Neither 2 Samuel 7 nor 1 Chronicles 17 explicitly describe God's promise as a "covenant," but several other texts do (cf. 2 Sam. 23:5; 2 Chron. 7:18; 13:5; Ps. 89:3; Jer. 33:21).
33. Williamson, "Covenant," 425.
34. Kaiser argues that David inherits the role of Adam and Israel as "son of God" to humanity as a whole, indicating that the role of David (and ultimately the promised seed) as covenant mediator would affect the divine rule in the entire world as God intended it for humanity originally (2 Sam. 7:19). See Walter C. Kaiser Jr., "The Blessing of David: The Charter for Humanity," in *The Law and the Prophets: Oswald T. Allis Festschrift*, ed. John H. Skilton (Philadelphia: P&R, 1974), 311–14.

will not receive blessings, but insetad curses. And, as with other covenants, an unconditional aspect exists wherein God will "establish the throne of his kingdom forever" (2 Sam. 7:13, 16; cf. Jer. 33:17–22) and God's "steadfast love will not depart from him" (2 Sam. 7:15).[35] A kingly offspring of Adam, Abraham, Judah, and David will inherit an eternal kingdom.

The Davidic covenant identifies more precisely the "offspring" who will mediate international blessing: he will be a royal descendant of Adam and Abraham through David. This royal seed, already mentioned explicitly in the Pentateuch (cf. Gen. 3:15; 35:11; 49:10; Num. 24:17; cf. Gen. 38; Ruth 4:18–22), culminates in a single conquering offspring who fulfills the promise of Genesis 22:18 and the hope expressed in Psalm 72:17.[36] He would be the promised and hoped for king who would rule over all (Isa. 9:6–7; Jer. 23:5–6; Ezek. 34:23–25).[37] Even when the promise for David's offspring and the nation looks bleak, God will keep his word (Amos 9:11; Zech. 12:10–13:1). Again, like the Abrahamic covenant, this tension between God's keeping of the covenant and the condition of obedience on the human king is palpable, especially as one notes the trajectory of Israel's kings. As such, a king in David's line who will walk in perfect accordance with God's covenant demands is needed to bring fulfillment to all of God's promises.[38]

As one observes the progression of the covenants across the canon, anticipation builds toward a culminating covenant between God and his people. Persistent failure to live according to God's covenant requirements leads to the inevitable disaster of exile for both the nation and its monarchy. God, however, has not forsaken his people. His promises would be brought to fulfillment by means of the promised seed. There is a new covenant he is bringing about with his people that will serve as the culmination and fulfillment of all the covenants displayed in Scripture.[39]

While only referred to explicitly as a "new covenant" once in the Old Testament (Jer. 31:31), several other passages allude to this covenant. In several places this arrangement between God and humanity is known as the "everlasting covenant" (Isa. 55:3; 61:8; Jer. 32:40; 50:5; Ezek. 16:60; 37:26). In Isaiah, this "covenant of peace" is closely associated with the figure of "the servant" (42:6; 49:8; 54:10; 55:3; 61:8; cf. Ezek. 34:25).[40] While Jeremiah and Ezekiel use

---

35. This is shown abundantly in 1–2 Kings where the keeping of God's covenant stipulations—or lack thereof—brings about blessing and cursing, culminating eventually in the destruction of Israel by Assyria and the exile of Judah to Babylon.

36. Williamson, "Covenant," 425–26.

37. Daniel I. Block, *The Book of Ezekiel: Chapters 25-48*, New International Commentary on the Old Testament (Grand Rapids: Eerdmans, 1998), 419.

38. Dempster, *Dominion and Dynasty*, 198.

39. Terms such as "culmination" and "fulfillment" do not infer complete similarity between all of the covenants. As will be noted, while there are some similarities, there are also distinct aspects of progression and discontinuity to be seen within the promises of the new covenant.

40. Note that the Noahic covenant is also referenced in Isaiah 54:9. Comparison is made regarding the preservation of the earth to the preservation of God's people. God will have compassion on them and will make them new.

different terminology to describe this covenant, both anticipate a fundamental change taking place in the covenant community: Jeremiah speaks of internalizing the law (Jer. 31:33), and Ezekiel speaks of the removal of the heart of stone and the insertion of a heart of flesh and the Holy Spirit, resulting in radical transformation (Ezek. 36:26–27; cf. 11:18–19).

People would enter into this covenant not through their ethnicity, but through a transformed heart generated through faith.[41] Unlike Israel who existed as a "mixed community" under the Mosaic covenant (Rom. 9:6–10:4), this new covenant community will all know the Lord, "from the least of them to the greatest" (Jer. 31:34).[42] In other words, each member of this new covenant community would be regenerated, their sins forgiven by God. They would receive a new heart, fear the Lord, and walk in his ways (Jer. 32:39–42). This is a distinct point of departure from the mixed community that was Israel (Deut. 10:12–16; 30:6). For these prophets, this inner renewal would result in the ideal divine-human relationship, which this and earlier covenants express in terms of the covenant formula "I will be their God, and they will be my people."[43] Israel did not keep the old covenant, as they needed new hearts to do so. In this new covenant, all the hopes and expectations of previous covenants will attain climactic fulfillment and eschatological expression.[44] The hearts of God's people will be made new by his Spirit.

Covenant in the Writings

Various themes from these covenants are taken up in the Writings, demonstrating the way in which God would accomplish his plan.[45] Ezra–Nehemiah describes the restoration

---

41. Schreiner helpfully maintains, "In many respects the covenant with Abraham is fulfilled in the new covenant, but the covenants should not be collapsed together as if they are identical covenants, because there is discontinuity between the two as well . . . The point is that the new covenant promises regeneration to every covenant member." Schreiner, *Covenant,* 50.

42. Speaking of the New Testament church as the new covenant community, Wellum asserts that the church "is *new* in redemptive history precisely because she is the community of the *new* covenant." He continues, "the church, unlike Israel, is *new* because she is comprised of a *regenerate, believing* people rather than a 'mixed' group." See Stephen J. Wellum, "Beyond Mere Ecclesiology: The Church as God's New Covenant Community," in *The Community of Jesus: A Theology of the Church,* eds. Kendall H. Easley and Christopher W. Morgan (Nashville: B&H, 2013), 194. As such, the new covenant is not merely a renewal of previous covenants, as significant progression and discontinuity can be seen. For a brief summary of the continuity and discontinuity that exists between Israel and the church, see Kimble, *40 Questions,* 21–25.

43. Williamson, "Covenant," 426.

44. Williamson, "Covenant," 426–27.

45. Hamilton maintains that one of the tensions developed in the Writings is a kind of Old Testament "inaugurated eschatology. These books show key aspects of the new-exodus and return-from-exile prophecies being realized—such as Isaiah's prophecy of Cyrus and Jeremiah's prophecy of seventy years for Babylon. And yet it is also revealed to Daniel that there will be seventy weeks of years before all things are consummated. The nation returns from one exile but not the other. . . . These books maintain, however, that the 'not yet' prophecies will be realized. As the authors of these books re-present key aspects of the promises to David (1 Chronicles 17) and retell the narrative of Solomon's building the temple, they are reaffirming the program: God will raise up a seed of David who will rule from the restored temple, and God's glory will radiate out from Jerusalem to cover the dry lands as the waters cover the sea." Hamilton, *God's Glory in Salvation,* 323.

of Israel to the land, but also foreshadows the restoration of God's kingdom yet to come. Within that context, the reader is reminded that Abraham was called out by God and chosen to be brought into a covenant relationship (Neh. 9:6–7). Abraham was chosen, not because of anything he had done, to be in covenant and blessed by God. The theme of universal blessing within the Abrahamic covenant is also found in the Psalms, which speak of the nations worshipping God under his kingship (e.g., Pss. 22:27; 67:6–7; 96:7). This inclusion of the Gentiles fulfills the promise that through Abraham and his seed all the nations of the earth would be blessed.[46]

Psalm 72 mentions the Adamic, Abrahamic, and Davidic covenants. Attributed to Solomon, this psalm at the end of book two of the Psalter highlights God's fulfillment of his promises by means of the promised seed, a kingly descendant of David. The enemies of this king will lick the dust (72:9; cf. Gen. 3:15), the covenant to Abraham will come to fruition in the form of land (72:8) and blessing (72:10–11, 15–17), and the psalm concludes "by identifying the psalms in Book 2 as Davidic, for they will be fulfilled through a Davidic heir."[47] Recognizing how Psalm 72:17 cites Genesis 22:17–18, Alexander explains, "While the psalm's title associates it with Solomon, its contents clearly envisage a king whose reign surpasses by far that of Solomon. Indeed, this future monarch is described as ruling the entire earth, bringing deliverance to the oppressed by defeating their enemies (cf. Ps. 72:4– 14)."[48] And all of this would result in the whole earth being filled with God's glory (72:19).

Chronicles also displays God's covenant to David. In its concise summary of the Old Testament from Adam to exile,[49] Chronicles essentially repeats the Davidic covenant (1 Chron. 17:1–15; cf. 2 Sam. 7:1–17). The covenant with David promises him a dynasty that will not end as well as a seed to reign forever and bring blessing to the world. Individual kings will receive blessings or consequences based on their obedience of God's stipulations or lack thereof, but there will come a king whose throne would be established forever. Unlike Samuel, Chronicles does not focus on the sins of David and Solomon. Rather, the author focuses on their strengths, seemingly to give hope to the nation of Israel as they anticipate a future king who will reflect and even surpass all of the virtue of David and Solomon.[50] Despite the unfaithfulness of Israel's kings, God would remain faithful to his covenant (2 Chron. 21:7; 36:1–23) and bring about the promised royal offspring who would bring blessing to the nations in the form of the new covenant.

---

46. See Schreiner, *King in His Beauty*, 491.
47. Schreiner, *King in His Beauty*, 261.
48. T. Desmond Alexander, "Further Observations on the Term 'Seed' in Genesis," *Tyndale Bulletin* 48.1 (1997): 365. See also Jack Collins, "A Syntactical Note (Genesis 3:15): Is the Woman's Seed Singular or Plural?" *Tyndale Bulletin* 48.1 (1997): 142–44.
49. House, *Old Testament Theology*, 523.
50. Bruce Waltke, *An Old Testaments Theology: An Exegetical, Canonical, and Thematic Approach* (Grand Rapids: Zondervan, 2007), 760.

Covenant in the Gospels

In the New Testament we come to a time in redemptive history where the promises of God seen in the covenants come to fruition. Jesus is depicted as the anointed one (Matt. 16:13–16; 26:63–66; John 20:30–31) in the line of Adam, Abraham, Judah, and David (Matt. 1:1–17; Luke 3:23–38). Zechariah, the father of John the Baptist, proclaims that God has raised up Jesus as the Christ "to show the mercy promised to our fathers and to remember his holy covenant, the oath that he swore to our father Abraham" (Luke 1:72–73). In other words, Jesus is the one who fulfills the Abrahamic covenant as the true offspring who will bring ultimate blessing to the nations.

The Gospel writers also demonstrate that Jesus fulfilled the covenant made to David (Matt. 9:27; 15:22; 20:30–31; 21:9, 15; Mark 10:47–48; 11:10; Luke 1:27; 2:4; 18:38–39). The angel declares to Mary, "He will be great and will be called the Son of the Most High. And the Lord God will give to him the throne of his father David, and he will reign over the house of Jacob forever, and of his kingdom there will be no end" (Luke 1:31–32). Also, Zechariah praises God for the birth of Jesus, declaring that the Lord "has raised up a horn of salvation for us in the house of his servant David" (Luke 1:69).[51] Where David and his sons failed, giving in to sin, Jesus overcame temptation (Matt. 4:1–11) and walked in perfect obedience and submission to the Father (John 5:19; 17:4). He perfectly fulfilled the stipulations of the Mosaic covenant (Matt. 5:17) doing what Israel could not, and as such the Father enthroned him as the crucified, resurrected, and reigning Lord, as both David's descendant and David's Lord (Matt. 22:41–46; cf. Ps. 110:1).

In the person and work of Jesus Christ the new covenant is ratified and inaugurated, specifically in his death and resurrection (Luke 22:20; 1 Cor. 11:11–25; cf. Rom. 1:1–6). At the Last Supper with his disciples, Jesus alludes to both the forgiveness associated by Jeremiah with the new covenant (Matt. 26:28; cf. Jer. 31:34) and the blood associated with the establishment of the old (i.e., Mosaic) covenant (Luke 22:20; cf. Exod. 24:8). The Gospels, therefore, present Jesus as the climax of the covenants,[52] as the one who brings about judgment for those who refuse to repent (Matt. 8:12; 13:12–14; 21:43; 23:37–39; cf. Luke 16:19–31) and salvation for those who confess Christ as Lord, Savior, and Treasure (Matt. 11:28–30;

---

51. See Schreiner, *Covenant*, 81–82.
52. Williamson affirms this point: "Through Jesus the promises made to Abraham find their ultimate fulfillment (Matt. 1:1, 17; 3:9; 8:11–12; cf. Luke 1:55, 72–73; John 8:31–59). He is the one anticipated in the Pentateuch, and in whom the obligations of the Mosaic covenant have been both fulfilled and transcended (Matt. 3:15; 5:17–48; 9:16–17; 11:28–30). He is the royal son of David (Matt. 1:1; 3:17 [cf. Ps. 2:7]; 4:15–16 [cf. Isa. 9:1–2]; 15:22; 16:16; 21:5; 22:41–45; cf. Luke 1:69–70), who will shepherd the people of God (Matt. 2:6; 9:36; 15:29–39 [cf. Ezek. 34:11–16]; cf. John 10:1–16). He is portrayed as the remnant, the 'true Israel' through whom salvation will come to the nations (Matt. 2:15; 4:1–11; 5:13–16; 8:11; 12:18–21; 13:47; 21:42–44; 24:14; 25:31–34; 28:19; cf. Luke 2:14, 32), and in whom 'new covenant' blessings such as cleansing and forgiveness are experienced (Matt. 1:21; 8:1–4, 17; 9:1–8; 11:2–5)." Williamson, "Covenant," 427. See also Gentry and Wellum, *Kingdom through Covenant*, 651.

John 3:1–18). Thus the covenants find their fulfillment in him, and those who follow him are brought into covenant relationship with the Father.

Covenant in Acts and the Letters

Beyond Jesus's life, death, resurrection, and ascension, his disciples proclaim the truth of who he is in covenantal terms. In Acts, Peter declares on Pentecost that the Spirit is being poured out on God's people in keeping with the new covenant (Acts 2:16–21; cf. Joel 2:28–32). He also proclaims, "Let all the house of Israel therefore know for certain that God has made him both Lord and Christ, this Jesus whom you crucified" (Acts 2:36). Jesus is the anointed king at God's right hand (7:56), the Davidic Messiah who fulfills God's promises (5:42; 8:12; 9:22; 10:36; 17:3; 18:28). It is important to keep this covenantal background in mind as Jesus is referred to as "Lord" and "Christ" throughout the New Testament.

In other key passages within the Epistles, one can see the interconnectedness and fulfillment of the Adamic, Abrahamic, Davidic, and new covenants. Where Adam brought about sin, condemnation, and death, Jesus as the second Adam brought about righteousness, salvation, and life (Rom. 5:12–21; 1 Cor. 15:22). Jesus is the ultimate seed of Abraham through whom blessings come to those united to him by faith (Rom. 4:1–25; Gal. 3:1–9). As the Davidic Messiah, Schreiner notes, "Jesus, in fulfillment of Psalm 110, has now sat down (after his atoning sacrifice and resurrection) at God's right hand (Heb. 1:3; 8:1; 10:12; 12:2). He rules as a priest-king over the cosmos. He rules as the Davidic king until God places all enemies under his feet (1 Cor. 15:25). Jesus as the descendant of David is now by virtue of his resurrection also crowned as Lord (Rom. 1:3–4)."[53] As Lord, angels, authorities, and powers have been subjected to Jesus (Col. 1:15–16; 1 Peter 3:21–22).

The rest of the New Testament emphasizes the forgiveness of sins and the indwelling of the Spirit, two things only fully attainable under the new covenant (Acts 13:38–39; cf. Heb. 10:4) as the primary benefits of Jesus's death (e.g., Luke 1:77; 24:46–47; Acts 2:38; 10:43; 13:38; 26:18; Rom. 3:24–25; Eph. 1:7; Col. 1:14; Heb. 9:12, 28; 1 John 1:7; Rev. 1:5; 7:14; 12:10–11). Jews and Gentiles are saved by grace through faith in Jesus the Messiah (Eph. 2:1–22).[54] According to the New Testament writers, the new covenant is far superior to the old (i.e., the Mosaic covenant). Such is already implicit in the use of the adjective "new" in 1 Cor. 11:25 (cf. Luke 22:20), which seems to allude to Jeremiah's negative contrast of the old covenant with the new (Jer. 31:31–32). The Spirit, a key component of the new covenant,

---

53. Schreiner, *Covenant*, 84.
54. Jesus, therefore, is the one means of salvation for both Jew and Gentile (John 14:6; Acts 4:12) to be brought into the people of God by faith. However, lest one think that God is done working with Israel and that the church has "replaced" them as the people of God, there is still a future for ethnic Israel, when one day near the end of history God will save a great number of Jews through faith in Jesus (Rom. 11:25–32). For further detail see Douglas J. Moo, *The Epistle to the Romans*, New International Commentary on the New Testament (Grand Rapids: Eerdmans, 1996), 710–39.

indwells all believers (1 Cor. 3:16–17; 6:12–20; 2 Cor. 6:16–7:1), teaches us (1 John 2:20, 27; cf. John 6:45; Isa. 54:13) and empowers us for lives of godliness (Rom. 7:1–8:17). In 2 Corinthians 3 Paul explicitly contrasts the new and the old covenants, highlighting the vast inferiority of the old in comparison with the surpassing glory and permanence of the new.[55] Paul makes a similar negative comparison in his "figurative" contrast between Hagar and Sarah in Galatians 4:21–31.

The most comprehensive thoughts about the new covenant are penned by the author of Hebrews. Having noted the superiority of the new covenant (7:22), the writer elaborates his point in Hebrews 8–10 through an extended commentary on Jeremiah 31:31–34 (cf. Heb. 8:9–12; 10:16–17). Not only does Jesus exercise a permanent, perfect, and heavenly priesthood (7:23–8:6), but the covenant he mediates is established on better promises (8:6b), explained in terms of an "eternal redemption" (9:12) and "eternal inheritance" (9:15), and is secured through the blood of Christ (9:11–10:18), later described as "the blood of the eternal covenant" (13:20).[56] Like Paul, therefore, the contrast is not between something bad and something good, but between something good (but temporal) and something better (because, unlike the old covenant, the new is unbreakable and eternal).

Covenant in Revelation

While these new covenant realities are in many respects already present (cf. Heb. 9:11), it is nevertheless true that the best is still to come. In Jesus's first coming he fulfilled prophecies, inaugurated a kingdom, and brought meaning and content to the fulfillment of God's promises. The ultimate expression of God's creative and redemptive goal seen in his covenant promises awaits fulfillment in the eschatological reality of the new creation.

The book of Revelation highlights the return of king Jesus, who will bring about complete fulfillment of God's promises as he saves his people and judges his enemies. Jesus, the Lion of the tribe of Judah and the root of David, is the one found worthy to open the scroll (Rev. 5:5). He displays his might throughout Revelation as one who will not be overcome by the enemy, but who will reign as Lord and Christ forever (11:15). There is a day when his reign will be not only inaugurated but also made complete in the new creation. Every enemy will be utterly destroyed (1 Cor. 15:26), the new creation will dawn (Rev. 21:1–22:5), and God and the Lamb will reign forever.

---

55. Specifically, the differences listed in 2 Corinthians 3 include the following: the old covenant was initiated by Moses (3:8), of the letter (3:6a), kills (3:6b, 7a), engraved on stone (3:3b, 7a), glorious (3:7a) though its glory faded (3:7b, 11a, 13b), condemns men (3:9a), is being brought to an end (3:13), remains veiled to hardened minds (3:13–15), and is non-transforming (3:15). The new covenant is initiated by Christ (3:4), of the Spirit (3:6a, 18b), gives life (3:6b), engraved on hearts (3:3b; cf. Jer. 31:33), superior and ever-increasing in glory (3:8, 11b, 10, 18), brings righteousness (3:9b), bold and unveiled marking freedom (3:12–17), and transforming (3:18).
56. Williamson, "Covenant," 429.

On that day the promise to David will be fulfilled in its entirety. Every enemy will be routed, and Jesus will reign as Lord and Christ forever and ever (Rev. 11:15–19). God's covenant promises will finally and fully come to fruition for Israel and the nations as the people of God.[57] It is then that we will experience one of the great ends of God's covenant: "Behold, the dwelling place of God is with man. He will dwell with them, and they will be his people, and God himself will be with them as their God" (Rev. 21:3).[58] Every covenant finds its fulfillment in Christ as the second Adam, the blessing to all nations, the better David, and the inaugurator of the new covenant. And the progressive fulfillment of these covenants provides divine assurance that God will accomplish his purpose for creation by fully establishing his kingdom on earth.

---

57. As Carson contends, "the promise that through Abraham's seed all the nations of the earth will be blessed, gradually expanded into a major theme in the Old Testament, now bursts into the Great Commission, the mushrooming growth of the Jewish church into the Gentile world, the spreading flame reaching across the Roman Empire and beyond, in anticipation of the climactic consummation of God's promises in the new heaven and new earth." Carson, *Gagging of God*, 263.
58. In keeping with this theme of God dwelling with his people so that we can know, love, and worship him fully as the ultimate end of God's covenants with us, Hafemann contends, "The covenant formula itself reveals that the primary provision and promise of the covenant relationship is knowing God himself. Knowing God is not a means to something else, but all of God's other gifts are intended to bring his people into an ever-growing relationship with God himself." Hafemann, "The Covenant Relationship," 36.

Discussion Questions

1. What is a covenant? In what ways are covenants a crucial aspect of God's plan with humanity?

2. Name the covenants seen in Scripture? What is promised within each covenant context?

3. In what ways do we see progression within the covenants as we read through Scripture? In other words, how do the covenants build upon one another?

4. How is Jesus the fulfillment of all the covenants?

5. What covenant are we under? What is presently fulfilled within that covenant and what are we still awaiting when Jesus returns?

Resources for Further Study

Blaising, Craig A., and Darrell L. Bock. *Progressive Dispensationalism.* Grand Rapids: Baker, 1993.

Dempster, Stephen J. *Dominion and Dynasty: A Biblical Theology of the Hebrew Bible.* New Studies in Biblical Theology 15. Downers Grove: InterVarsity, 2003.

Gentry, Peter J., and Stephen J. Wellum. *Kingdom through Covenant: A Biblical-Theological Understanding of the Covenants.* 2nd ed. Wheaton: Crossway, 2018.

House, Paul R. *Old Testament Theology.* Downers Grove: InterVarsity, 1998.

Schreiner, Thomas R. *Covenant and God's Purpose for the World.* Short Studies in Biblical Theology. Wheaton: Crossway, 2017.

CHAPTER 15

TEMPLE AND PRIESTHOOD

PRIOR TO CREATION, GOD EXISTED in perfect intra-Trinitarian community. He had no lack, no needs, no wants of any kind. There was only perfect love, delight, and knowledge within the persons of the Godhead. And yet, God saw fit to create outside of himself. He made a universe that would declare his praise (Ps. 19:1) and created humanity in his image, such that he would be their God and they would be his people, worshipping, loving, knowing, and delighting in the triune God.

While God was present in all places, he chose to come near to humanity in a particular way so as to relate to them for the accomplishment of his purposes by means of the temple. The temple, as the dwelling place of God, is a key theme that permeates the whole of Scripture. Petrotta states, "The biblical authors from Moses through Ezekiel and Haggai to John of Patmos offer a vision of what the temple was to be: the locus of the presence of God."[1] Thus, the temple functions as a place where God is present in a unique way with his people.[2] And it is the priests who are vested with the stewardship of serving and protecting the temple.

---

1. A. J. Petrotta, "Temple," in *Evangelical Dictionary of Biblical Theology*, ed. Walter A. Elwell (Grand Rapids: Baker, 1996 [759–61]), 759.
2. This description should not lead the reader to think that God's presence was bound only to the temple. God is present at all points of space, but there is also a prominent motif of God's special presence with his people, and the threat of his departure should they break covenant. Horton helpfully elaborates, "The question of God's presence and absence in the covenantal drama is equivalent to the question of judgment and salvation. In other words, we meet in Scripture both an *ontological omnipresence* and a *covenantal-judicial presence* in blessing or wrath. Of course, God is omnipresent in his essence, but the primary question in the covenantal drama is whether God is present for us, and if so, where, as well as whether he is present in judgment or in grace." Michael Horton, *Christian Faith*, 255.

The Hebrew term for "priest" (kohen) occurs approximately 750 times in the Old Testament and can refer to priests of the one true God or those of other supposed gods that other nations (and sometimes also the Israelites) worshiped.[3] Priests were anointed for service (Exod. 29:7; 40:12–15; Lev. 8:12), consecrated, and set apart from the rest of the community for service (Lev. 21:6; Num. 8:14; Deut. 10:8; 1 Sam. 7:1; 1 Chron. 23:13). They had distinct access to the temple courts along with unique privileges, responsibilities, and restrictions (Exod. 28:43; 30:17–21; 40:31–32; Num. 8:7; 10:8–11; 21:1–6).[4]

As one studies the entirety of Scripture, it becomes clear that the temple comes in specific iterations (Eden, tabernacle, temple, Jesus, church, new heaven and earth), all of which are connected but distinct in certain ways, based on the heavenly temple (Heb. 8:5) and progressing toward a certain goal. Additionally, the priesthood is a pervasive theme typically connected to the place of God's presence. What begins in Eden will eventually result in the new Jerusalem. Although Adam and Eve's rebellion against God delays the project, through various phases God will eventually bring it to completion. In the end, God's people will dwell as priests in the new heaven and new earth and function as God's people in God's dwelling place.

Temple and Priesthood in the Law

Before looking specifically at the concepts of temple and priesthood, it is important to understand their connections to humanity as image-bearers. In creation, God fashioned human beings on day six as the pinnacle of all that he made (Gen. 1:26–28). Created in the image of God, humanity is given mediated authority over the other creatures and entrusted to function as stewards of all that God has created. Ample theological debate revolves around what the image of God actually is.[5] This is due to the fact that there are so few passages in Scripture that treat the topic, and none of them provide an exhaustive definition (Gen. 1:26–27; 5:1–2; 9:6–7; 1 Cor. 11:7; James 3:9–10; cf. Rom. 8:29; 2 Cor. 3:18; Eph. 4:23–24; Col. 3:10).[6] However, one must minimally affirm that an image points to the person that is "being imaged." The image serves as a representation or representative of that individual.

---

3. R. E. Averbeck, "Priest, Priesthood," in *Evangelical Dictionary of Biblical Theology,* ed. Walter A. Elwell (Grand Rapids: Baker, 1996), 632.

4. See Paul Ellingworth, "Priests," in *New Dictionary of Biblical Theology,* ed. T. Desmond Alexander and Brian S. Rosner (Downers Grove: InterVarsity, 2000[696–701]), 697.

5. For a survey of views regarding the image of God, see Gregg R. Allison, *Historical Theology: An Introduction to Christian Doctrine* (Grand Rapids: Zondervan, 2011), 321–41; Frame, *Systematic Theology,* 783–92; Hoekema, *Created in God's Image,* 11–111; Horton, *Christian Faith,* 379–406; Kilner, *Dignity and Destiny,* 85–232.

6. The various views include the functional, relational, and substantive views respectively. The functional view maintains that the image of God consists in something humans do. Primary emphasis is placed on the exercise of dominion over creation. The relational view argues that the image consists primarily in our capacity for relationship with God and other humans. And the substantive view maintains that the image of God is a particular feature of

This was true of ancient kings who would place statues, temples, and images throughout their kingdom. These edifices reminded their subjects who their ruler was—even if he did not often appear in that territory in person—and how they were to live as a result. This is also how the God-image works in God's kingdom. God puts his image-bearers in a garden and commands them to be fruitful, multiply, fill the earth, and subdue it (Gen. 1:28), all to the end that the earth would be filled with the knowledge of his glory (Hab. 2:14).

As such, it would make sense to understand image-bearing as a reality that involves relating to, representing, and reflecting God with the capacities he has given to us.[7] Adam was ontologically made a volitional, rational, and moral being to the end that "he was to reflect moral attributes such as righteousness, knowledge, holiness, justice, love, faithfulness, and integrity (for the first three attributes as part of the divine image, see Eph. 4:24; Col. 3:10), and above all he was to reflect God's glory."[8] In other words, images magnify or glorify their source. In this case, human beings were made to glorify God in every facet of their lives, testifying to the fact that "from him and through him and to him are all things" (Rom. 11:36).

This is the ontological aspect of the image of God, but one can also see that humanity is called to rule and steward as a result of being made in the divine image. Ruling, in other words, is not the essence of the image itself, but the functional aspect to which humanity is called because they are made in God's image.[9] Subsequent to creating humankind, God commands them, "Be fruitful and multiply and fill the earth and subdue it, and have dominion over the fish of the sea and over the birds of the heavens and over every living thing that moves on the earth." (Gen. 1:28) This language is kingly in nature, showing that human beings, as image-bearers of God, are to act as vice-regents, exercising God's rule in a mediated fashion to reflect and display his glory.

We are also told that God put Adam in the garden to "work it and keep it" (Gen. 2:15), which is the same call God gave to the Levitical priests to "serve" and "guard" the tabernacle (Num. 3:7–8; 8:26; 18:5–6; 1 Chron. 23:32; Ezek. 44:14). As such, Adam's stewardship is not merely a kingly rule, but also a priestly rule. He is an image-bearer, vice-regent, and priest who represents and gives witness to the rule of God. As Leeman avers, this kind of priest-king stewardship "requires him to consecrate himself to the law of the over-king, assent to the over-king's judgments, name what is clean and unclean according to the over-king, and

---

humanity not found in any animal. In other words, the image is some property uniquely characteristic of humans (e.g., intellect, emotion, will).
7. This refers to what some theologians call an "eclectic" or "dynamic" view.
8. Beale, *New Testament Biblical Theology*, 32. See also Lints, *Identity and Idolatry*, 43–77; Schreiner, *King in His Beauty*, 5–7.
9. For more on this point, see Gentry, "Kingdom through Covenant," 22–33.

guard the over-king's glory."[10] In other words, Adam as the image-bearing priest-king was to represent God, give witness to expand God's glory, and guard God's dominion.[11]

And if Adam served as a priest-king in Eden, the domain within which he resided would be sacred and viewed as a temple, which would seemingly be ever-expanding.[12] However, Adam and Eve rebel against God and thus do not "work it and keep it" as God called them to (Gen. 2:15; 3:1–7). Consequently, God banishes Adam and Eve from Eden, who continue to exist as image-bearers of God (cf. Gen. 9:5–6), but are now deeply marred by sin.[13] Defiled by their sin, they can no longer serve within a holy sanctuary (Gen. 3:24). Although total destruction is deserved and looms over every human, restoration with God is possible by means of his grace (cf. Gen. 3:15). From this point on, the biblical narrative develops how the human–divine relationship can be restored.

As one continues through the biblical narrative, one can observe the similarities between Eden and the building of altars. Beale argues that the language in Genesis 1:28 involved five elements: God's blessing; "be fruitful and multiply"; "fill the earth"; "subdue the earth"; and "rule over the earth."[14] These five elements are repeated to Israel's patriarchs and others in direct connection to the building of small sanctuaries (Gen. 12:2–3; 17:2, 7, 8, 16; 22:18; 26:3–4, 24; 28:4, 14; 35:11–12; 47:27; 48:3, 15–16; Exod. 1:7; Deut. 7:13; cf. Ps. 107:38; Isa. 51:2).[15] Beale elaborates, "the result of Abraham, Isaac, and Jacob building altars at Shechem, between Bethel and Ai, at Hebron, and near Moriah was that the terrain of Israel's future land was dotted with shrines," which ultimately leads the reader to the tabernacle (Exod. 35:30–40:38) and then the temple (1 Kings 5:1–9:9; 2 Chron. 3:1–7:22).[16]

After rescuing the Israelites from slavery in Egypt, God enters into a covenant relationship with them at Mount Sinai. One aspect of this covenant is the appraisal of the nation

---

10. Jonathan Leeman, *Don't Fire Your Church Members: The Case for Congregationalism* (Nashville: B&H, 2016), 39. See also G. K. Beale, *The Temple and the Church's Mission: A Biblical Theology of the Dwelling Place of God*, New Studies in Biblical Theology 17 (Downers Grove: InterVarsity, 2004), 70, who states, "Adam should always best be referred to as 'priest-king,' since it is only after the 'fall' that priesthood is separated from kingship."
11. Leeman, *Church Members*, 39–40.
12. Wenham concurs: "The garden of Eden is not viewed by the author of Genesis simply as a piece of Mesopotamian farmland, but as an archetypal sanctuary, that is a place where God dwells and where man should worship him. Many of the features of the garden may also be found in later sanctuaries, particularly in the tabernacle or Jerusalem temple. These parallels suggest that the garden itself is understood as a sort of sanctuary." See "Sanctuary Symbolism," 399.
13. Connecting the concepts of the image of God and priesthood by means of later linguistic links (e.g., "blessing" and "be fruitful and multiply"), Beale argues that after Adam's failure to fulfill God's mandate, God will raise up other Adam-like figures to whom he passes on his commission, until the "last Adam" arises (Gen. 1:28; 9:1, 7; 12:1–3; 17:2, 6, 8; 22:17–18; 26:3–4, 24; 28:3–4, 13–14; 35:11–12; 47:27). See *New Testament Biblical Theology*, 623–24.
14. G. K. Beale, "Eden, the Temple, and the Church's Mission in the New Creation," *Journal of the Evangelical Theological Society 48.1 (2005): 13.
15. Beale, "New Creation," 13.
16. Beale, "New Creation," 15.

and their identity as the redeemed people of God (Exod. 19:1–4). Just as Adam functioned as a priest, God calls Israel to operate as a "kingdom of priests" (Exod. 19:5–6)[17] and live as a holy people in the land God would give to them. That the entire nation is understood in priestly terms indicates that Israel was called to mediate God's holiness to the surrounding nations (cf. Isa. 61:6; 66:21).[18]

While the nation was called to live as a kingdom of priests, God installs Aaron and his descendants from the tribe of Levi to serve distinctively as the priests of Israel and oversee God's dwelling place (Exod. 28:1–29:46; Lev. 8:19–24; 21:1–22:33; Num. 3:1–39; 8:5–26; 18:1–32).[19] With the Levites assisting the priests and watching over the tabernacle, the priests performing sacrifices on behalf of the people, Aaron and his descendants are made responsible for maintaining the proper relationship of the people to the Lord in regards to key facets of the Mosaic covenant: the administration and ministry of the sanctuary, and the custody and administration of the law of Moses.[20] In this way, the priests exercise a mediatorial function between God and humanity. The ministry of priesthood focuses especially on administering and ministering in the Lord's presence (Exod. 33:14–15; Lev. 10:2) maintaining holiness and cleanness within the nation (Lev. 10:10), and atoning for sin through sacrifice (Lev. 10:17). The high priest would also atone for the sins of the nation once a year on the Day of Atonement (Lev. 16:1–34). Following these rules and procedures was a matter of survival for the nation in general (Lev. 15:31) as well as for the priests in particular (see the death of Nadab and Abihu in Leviticus 10).[21]

The priesthood would thus function such that Israel would be a distinct people amongst the nations, following the law of God with God dwelling in their midst (Lev. 11:44–45; Deut. 7:6–26). The place in which God would dwell among them would be a portable tent made extensively of gold and richly-colored fabrics. This tent Israel was called to construct was known as the tabernacle. As Peterson argues, the tabernacle "was to operate as a means by which God's presence and his rule over [his covenant people] was dramatically

---

17.   Beyond the data given to suggest Adam functioned as a priest, one can also observe Melchizedek (Gen. 14:18) and Moses's father-in-law Jethro (Exod. 2:16; 3:1) performing priestly duties prior to Israel's calling as a kingdom of priests.

18.   Averbeck maintains, "Israel was to be a 'kingdom of priests' in terms of its corporate participation in the service of worship to the Lord in the sanctuary (Exod 24:3–8) as well as in its position and ministry toward the nations roundabout them (Isa. 61:6)." Averbeck, "Priest, Priesthood," 633. See also Gentry and Wellum, *Kingdom through Covenant*, 309–24.

19.   For more on the distinction between the call of the nation of Israel to be priests and the call for individual priests, see Andrew S. Malone, *God's Mediators: A Biblical Theology of Priesthood*, New Studies in Biblical Theology 43 (Downers Grove: InterVarsity, 2017).

20.   Averbeck, "Priest, Priesthood," 634. See also Ellingworth, "Priests,"697–98, who argues that the duties of a priest include offering sacrifices on behalf of the people, seeking God's will by means of the Urim and Thummim (Exod. 28:30; Lev. 8:8; Num. 27:21; Deut. 33:8; 1 Sam. 14:41; Ezra 2:63; Neh. 7:65), and instructing the people in the law of God (Lev. 10:10; Deut. 33:8–10; Jer. 2:8; 18:18; Ezek. 22:26; 44:23; Hos. 4:6).

21.   Averbeck, "Priest, Priesthood," 634.

expressed."[22] The tent would provide separation because of God's utter holiness, as well as access to his covenant presence.

Alexander notes a number of parallels that exist between Eden and the tabernacle (and eventually the temple): the Lord walks in both places (Gen. 3:8; Lev. 26:12; Deut. 23:15; cf. 2 Sam. 7:6–7); both Eden and the tabernacle are guarded by cherubim and accessed from the east (Gen. 3:22–24; Exod. 25:18–22; 26:31–33); the terms "work" and "keep" used in God's command to care for the garden (Gen. 2:15) appear together to describe the duties of the Levites in the sanctuary (Num. 3:7–8; 8:26; 18:5–6); a connection seems to exist between the tree of life in Eden and the lampstand in the tabernacle (Gen. 2:9; 3:22; Exod. 25:31–35); a river flows out of Eden as well as out of the end-time temple in Ezekiel's vision (Gen. 2:10; Ezek. 47:1–12); and materials found in Eden are also used in the construction of the tabernacle (Gen. 2:11–12; Exod. 25:7, 11, 17, 31).[23] The ark of the covenant, which sat within the Most Holy Place, functioned as the footstool of the heavenly throne (cf. 1 Chron. 28:2). Heaven and earth were joined within the tabernacle.

Eden, thus, anticipates this theme of God's dwelling place which, as can be seen, serves as a major thread in the biblical storyline. Serving as the realm where human beings could encounter the presence of God, Eden was an earthly version or microcosm of God's heavenly dwelling/temple. As a king-priest functioning on behalf of God, Adam is called to rule in space and time over the good creation God has made, worshipping and reflecting God. Israel is now called to do the same in a land God would give them where he would dwell among them (Exod. 29:45–46). And this is all done so that God's glory would be known and extended to the ends of the earth.

After receiving the precepts of the law and instructions concerning the erection of the tabernacle (Exod. 25–31), the place where God's glory would dwell, Moses and the people begin preparations for its construction (35:4–39:43). After Israel blatantly disobeys the moral will of God and indulges in idolatry (32:1–35; the Levites alone joined Moses in avenging the Lord's honor), the text now highlights Israel's meticulous obedience to God's building instructions (Exod. 39:1, 5, 6, 21, 26, 29, 31, 32, 42, 43; 40:16, 19, 21, 23, 25, 26, 27, 29, 32). The nation demonstrates their desire to fulfill their unique calling to act as a holy nation and a royal priesthood before God. This will be the place where God will dwell with his people (25:8) and speak with Moses (25:22), and where sacrifices will be offered (29:38–43; 30:7–10).[24]

After the tabernacle is erected in the midst of Israel's camp with the ark of the covenant situated in the holy of holies, the text states, "Then the cloud covered the tent of

22. David Peterson, *Engaging with God: A Biblical Theology of Worship* (Downers Grove: InterVarsity, 2002), 36.
23. Alexander, *New Jerusalem*, 21–23. See also Beale, *Temple*, 66–80; Schreiner, *King in His Beauty*, 7–8; Wenham, "Sanctuary Symbolism," 400–401.
24. See R. J. McKelvey, "Temple," in *New Dictionary of Biblical Theology*, ed. T. D. Alexander and Brian S. Rosner (Downers Grove: InterVarsity, 2000), 806.

meeting and the glory of the Lord filled the tabernacle. And Moses was not able to enter the tent of meeting because the cloud settled on it, and the glory of the Lord filled the tabernacle" (Exod. 40:34–35).[25] God's people had built his house for him with precision, and he showed his approval of their labors and, more importantly, his desire to reside among them.[26] The tabernacle was known as the "tent of meeting" because Moses conversed with God there (e.g., Exod. 27:21; 28:43; 29:4; 40:1; Lev. 1:1; 3:2; Num. 1:1; 2:2). The tabernacle was also called the "sanctuary" (e.g., Exod. 25:8; Lev. 12:4) with the inner room of the tent known as "the Most Holy Place" (e.g., Exod. 26:33–34; Lev. 16:2). God's presence made this place holy, and there he would make his dwelling among the people (Lev. 26:11–13). Only the high priest was permitted to enter the Most Holy Place, and only once a year on the Day of Atonement (Lev. 16:1–34).

Whereas the fall had sundered the fellowship that existed between God and man, the tabernacle (and eventually the temple) demonstrates the means by which God would bring about the eventual reversal of that situation. Ironically, once God's glory comes to rest in the tabernacle, Moses, as the head and representative of the nation, is not able to enter inside (Exod. 40:35). While God had come to reside with his people, there was a threshold of holiness required if the people were to be near him. If the people would obey the decrees spoken by God in the law (see especially Lev. 11:44 and the call to be holy as God is holy), he would dwell with them as their God and do good for them. The Levitical priests would work to maintain the spiritual life of the nation, overseeing sacrifices, teaching the law, and shepherding the people toward holiness to embody the call God had given them to be a royal priesthood and a holy nation as God's presence dwelt among them in the tabernacle (Deut. 27:9–10). What God did in the tabernacle (and temple) he would eventually do in the world: fill it with his glory.[27] As such, the broader purpose of the exodus and the establishment of the law, priesthood, and the tabernacle was that God could display his glory and see a nation receive and reflect that glory.

Temple and Priesthood in the Prophets

As Israel comes into the land promised by God, the priests lead the way across the Jordan bearing the ark of the covenant (Josh. 3:6, 17; 4:15–18). They carry the ark around

---

25. The "cloud" was the same manifestation that first appeared in Exodus 12:21–22 and guided the Israelites in the wilderness (14:19–20, 24; 16:10). This was also the same cloud Israel had seen atop Mount Sinai upon their arrival (19:9, 16; 24:15–18) and at the entrance to the tent of meeting outside the camp which indicated the presence of Yahweh (33:9–10; 34:5). This cloud was the way God chose to manifest himself. He left Mount Sinai and came to dwell among his people, as he promised (33:14–17).

26. See Douglas Stuart, *Exodus*, New American Commentary 2 (Nashville, B&H, 2006), 791.

27. As Lister summarizes, "The tabernacle and its later expression in the temple are both archetypal representations of what will finally be fulfilled in the new city-temple that is the new heaven and new earth." Lister, *Presence of God*, 112.

the city of Jericho, which denotes God's presence and power to bring down its walls.[28] The Levites were scattered throughout Israel to minister and lead the people (Josh. 21:1–45). Like the nation of Israel, the priesthood experiences spiritual peaks and valleys (cf. Judg. 17:1–19:30). One example of this is the extended treatment of the priest Eli and his sons, Hophni and Phineas (1 Sam. 1:3).

While Eli led Israel as a priest for many years and shows external signs of conformity to God's law, his sons were wicked (1 Sam. 2:12–17). Eli rebukes them for their treacherous acts (2:22–25), but God puts Hophni and Phineas to death because of their wickedness. It is especially scandalous to see those in the role of priest act in this way due to their specific calling. Recognizing that Eli had not restrained his sons who blasphemed the Lord (3:11–14; 4:1–18), God ends their line as priests and calls Samuel to serve as priest after the days of Eli (3:10–14, 19–21). Under the leadership of Samuel the ark of the covenant was returned to the house of Abinadab in Kiriath-jearim (6:1–7:2) after being lost in battle to the Philistines during the days of Eli (4:1–11). When David becomes king, the ark is brought from the house of Abinadab to Jerusalem where the temple would soon be built (2 Sam. 6:1–15).

The much larger and permanent Jerusalem temple built by David's son Solomon eventually replaces the tabernacle.[29] After the construction of the temple is completed, Solomon dedicates this temple with a prayer, and the glory of the Lord fills the new sanctuary (1 Kings 8:10–11; cf. 2 Chron. 7:1–2) just as it had previously filled the tabernacle (Exod. 40:34–35). Within this context God reiterates for Solomon and the rest of Israel the need for obedience to his covenant stipulations. God promised Abraham land, offspring, and blessing (Gen. 12:1–3), called Israel to specific obedience to the law in the Mosaic covenant (Exod. 19:5–6), and promised David an everlasting dynasty and a king who would rule forever (2 Sam. 7:5–16). If they obeyed, God's presence would be with them and they would be blessed, but if they disobeyed they would suffer the consequences for breaking the covenant (1 Kings 9:1–9).

---

28. See the comments on Joshua 1:5, 9 and 6:27 to this end in David M. Howard Jr., *Joshua*, New American Commentary 5 (Nashville: B&H, 1998), 83–89, 176.

29. Like the tabernacle, the temple has direct parallels with Eden that continue to solidify the trajectory of the dwelling place of God throughout the canon. According to Beale, Eden resembles the temple in its gradation of holiness relating to its parts. He highlights how the garden surrounds the central location of Eden, which includes the river flowing out of Eden to water the garden (Gen. 2:10). Thus, he sees Eden as the pinnacle of holiness, similar to the holy of holies, both sources of physical and spiritual life, while the garden is more comparable to the Holy Place "where God's priestly servant worships God by obeying him, by cultivating and guarding." Moving outward geographically once more, Beale asserts that "the land and seas to be subdued by Adam outside the garden were roughly equivalent to the outer court." Furthermore, the theme of cherubim protection, as seen in the tabernacle, is not lost in the building of Solomon's temple. Solomon builds two wooden cherubim in the innermost part of the temple whose wings extended to the outer walls, and carves figures of cherubim, palm trees, and open flowers on the walls of the temple in the inner and outer rooms (1 Kings 6:23–32). The arboreal decorations also allude to Eden. See Beale, "New Creation," 10.

Subsequent to Solomon's reign, the Jerusalem temple became the primary location for the worship of God as pilgrims journeyed there to sing for joy to the living God (Ps. 84:1–4; cf. 42:1–4; 43:3–4; 122:1–9; Isa. 35:10). Eventually, however, the corruption of Israel's kings, priests, and citizens caused God to send them into exile, as the Babylonians sacked Jerusalem and destroyed the temple in 586 BC (2 Kings 25:1–30).[30] The prophets focus on priestly corruption and defilement as a major reason for the exile (Jer. 2:5–8; 5:31; Lam. 4:13; Ezek. 22:26; Hos. 4:6–9; Zeph. 3:4; Mal. 3:1–4). The priests were not holy and did not lead the people toward holiness. Josiah's reform sought to remove pagan priests from Judah (2 Kings 23:1–20). Jeremiah warned the people to repent from such unholy practices, lest they incur God's wrath (Jer. 5:1–6:30; 15:1–16:13). Ezekiel gives particular attention to how God abandons his dwelling place before its destruction by Nebuchadnezzar (Ezek. 9:3; 10:15–22; 11:23), highlighting how the sins of the people defiled the temple (8:1–18). This is devastating since the temple is much more than a magnificent building; this is where God's special presence dwelt amongst his people.[31] Many of the priests are deported and later executed during the Babylonian invasion (2 Kings 25:18–21; Jer. 52:24–27), although some Levites and subordinate priests remain and offer sacrifices in the remains of the temple.[32]

While the situation looks quite bleak, not all hope is lost. The temple is eventually rebuilt after the exiles return to the land, though that work was neglected for a time, much to the detriment of Israel (Hag. 1:3–9).[33] Ezekiel looks beyond the departure of God's glory from the temple to a time when God will reside in a new temple (Ezek. 40–48). God would do a permanent kind of work, such that he would forever dwell among us as our God, and we would be his people. God's people would receive new hearts (Jer. 31:31–34; Ezek. 36:25–27) and a temple would be built that would be a house of prayer for all the nations (Isa. 56:7; cf. 60:4–7; 66:18–21). This temple would have great glory (Hag. 2:9) and the nations would worship there (Zech. 14:10, 16–21). This was the expectation coming into the time of Jesus.

---

30. There were both faithful and unfaithful kings and priests throughout Israel's history. According to Averbeck, "Second Kings 23:4–20 lists five categories of priests that existed in ancient Israel before Josiah's reformation, and arranges them according to their proximity to the Jerusalem temple: (1) the high priest (v. 4), (2) the second-order priests (v. 4), (3) the idolatrous priests in the cities of Judah and in the area surrounding Jerusalem (v. 5); (4) the priests of the high places in the cities of Judah from Geba to Beersheba (vv. 8–9); and (5) the priests of the high places in Samaria (i.e., the remnants of the priests of the former northern kingdom, v. 20). According to this passage, a significant feature of Josiah's religious reformation was his eradication of all priests (and their cultic accouterments) except those who functioned legitimately within the Jerusalem temple. Therefore, only the first two categories of priests in 2 Kings 23 retained their office: the "high priest" (v. 4, here Hilkiah) and "the priests of the second order" (v. 4; i.e., other descendants of Aaron)." Averbeck, "Priest, Priesthood," 632.
31. McKelvey comments, "Jerusalem became the type of the final and universal salvation of the eschatological age (Isa. 2:2–4; Mic. 4:1–3; Zech. 14:16–19). One can understand therefore the sense of distress and loss felt as a result of the destruction of the temple in 587 BC. This meant nothing less than the loss of God's presence (Ezek. 9:3; 10:4–5; 11:23)." McKelvey, "Temple," 807.
32. Ellingworth, "Priests," 699.
33. See Petrotta, "Temple," 760.

Temple and Priesthood in the Writings

References to God's covenantal presence, which the temple symbolizes, fill the Psalms (e.g., Pss. 16:7–8; 21:5–6; 23:6; 26:8; 27:4–10; 31:20; 42:5; 44:1–3; 63:2; 65:4; 84:1–2; 91:14–16).[34] The Psalms demonstrate the reality that "the history of redemption, the covenant, and the prophetic word from God are not merely religious ideas or statements about the past but encounters with the living God."[35] In light of God's work with Israel in the past, the psalmists confidently and expectantly call upon the Lord to be present with them (68:7–12; 78:14–72; 97:1–5; 144:5–8). David greatly rejoices in seeking the Lord in his temple (27:4), but even after the decimation of the temple the psalmist still rejoices, declaring, "Yet God my King is from of old, working salvation in the midst of the earth" (74:12). As Lister avers, "Based on the Psalms, the God of David is the God who comes near in the exodus and in the exile as well."[36]

As one continues in the Writings there is an account of the return to the land in Ezra–Nehemiah. When Cyrus the Persian emperor allows the exiles to return to Israel (Ezra 1:1–2; cf. Isa. 44:24–45:25; Jer. 25:12; 29:10; 32:36–38), they begin the task of rebuilding Jerusalem and the temple. Through Nehemiah's leadership the temple is reconstructed. During this rebuilding phase priests and Levites return to the land, offer the Passover lamb (Ezra 6:19–21), teach the Law (Neh. 8:7–8), and assist in the covenant renewal (Neh. 9:38). The temple is again in Jerusalem and the people are in the land as it comes under God's covenant (at least temporarily). However, postexilic Jerusalem is a far cry from the days of Solomon. This new temple falls short of everything the prophets anticipated (cf. Ezek. 40–48), and the people of Jerusalem possess hearts that are still far from God (Neh. 13:1–31).[37] The restoration was partial; more must happen. Something greater was yet to occur, which would involve the restoration of the Davidic monarchy, a new temple, and a priesthood that was faithful to God.

Chronicles highlights David, Solomon, and the building of the temple as key points in its narrative (1 Chron. 11:1–2 Chron. 9:31). When David made Solomon king, he assigned the Levites to supervise the temple's construction (1 Chron. 23:1–4) and designated priests and Levites to serve as temple officials, judges, gatekeepers, or musicians (1 Chron. 23:1–26:28; cf. 1 Chron. 6:31–47). Averbeck elaborates:

> Initially, the duties of the Levites in assisting the priests focused on such tasks as the transportation of the tabernacle (see, e.g., Num. 3–4; 1 Chron. 15:2) and guarding the doorway to the tabernacle (see, e.g., 1 Chron. 9:19, 22–27). David assigned them

---

34. Lister, *Presence of God*, 232.
35. Graeme Goldsworthy, *According to Plan: The Unfolding Revelation of God in the Bible* (Downers Grove: InterVarsity, 2002), 177.
36. Lister, *Presence of God*, 234.
37. As Dempster states, "The reality depicted in Ezra-Nehemiah—compromise, assimilation to pagan culture, unfaithfulness, and devotion to their own pursuits instead of the kingdom of God—paints a very bleak picture of the restoration and return. See *Dominion and Dynasty*, 224.

other tasks in assisting the priests within the sanctuary (e.g., purification procedures, preparing the showbread and other grain offerings, leading in the praising of the Lord through song, special responsibilities for festival burnt offerings, etc., 1 Chron. 23:27–32; 25:1–8). The importance of the Levites in the priestly functions of the sanctuary are well illustrated by their involvement in the reforms of Hezekiah (2 Chron. 29–31) and Josiah (2 Chron. 34:9; 35:10–15).[38]

Unfortunately, while there were high points for the priesthood and temple worship in the era of the kings, subsequent rulers as well as the priests and the people chose to rebel against God and engage in sin and idolatry (2 Chron. 36:14–16). The temple is destroyed and the people are taken into exile (2 Chron. 36:17–21). Yet hope remains, as Cyrus proclaims the people can return to the land (2 Chron. 36:22–23). The end of the Old Testament points to a future work of God to bring about a better temple and priest.

Temple and Priesthood in the Gospels

In Jesus we see a new revelation regarding God's plans for humanity and all of creation. While the priesthood is present in Jesus's day, it is often referenced by the Gospel writers in a pejorative fashion (e.g., Mark 8:31; 10:33; 15:11, 31; John 11:49–52). Jesus comes as both the temple and great high priest. When John writes, "And the Word became flesh and dwelt among us" (John 1:14), he compares Jesus's body to the Old Testament tabernacle. The Greek verb "dwelt" (*skēnoō*) can be more literally rendered "tabernacled," and thus makes a concrete connection between the Old Testament dwelling place of God and the incarnation of Christ.[39] When Jesus remarks, "Destroy this temple, and in three days I will raise it up," John interprets this as referring to Jesus's body regarding his death and resurrection (John 2:19–21). The clearing of the temple represents a sign of God's judgment on Israel's religious system due to their hypocrisy and corruption and points to a new temple, the God-man Jesus Christ. Jesus also stands as the true high priest, who offers a better sacrifice and inaugurates a better covenant.[40] He declared the standard of true "cleanness" (Matt. 15:1–11; Mark 7:1–23; cf. Lev. 10:10–11; Acts 10:9–16, 28) and authoritatively interpreted the law (Matt. 5:17–48; Luke 24:27).

---

38. Averbeck, "Priest, Priesthood," 634.
39. This verb can be rendered "to pitch one's tent." This rare term, used elsewhere in the New Testament only in the book of Revelation (7:15; 12:12; 13:6; 21:3), suggests that in Jesus, God has come to take up residence among his people once again in a way more intimate than when he dwelt in the midst of wilderness in the tabernacle. See Carson, *John*, 127.
40. For further thoughts on the priesthood of Jesus in the gospel of John, see Helen Bond, "Discarding the Seamless Robe: The High Priesthood of Jesus in John's gospel," in *Israel's God and Rebecca's Children: Christology and Community in Early Judaism and Christianity: Essays in Honor of Larry W. Hurtado and Alan F. Segal*, ed. D. B. Capes et al., (Waco: Baylor University Press, 2007), 183–94. For a more general summary of Jesus's priestly work as connected to and surpassing that of Old Testament priests, see Stephen J. Wellum, *Christ Alone: The Uniqueness of Jesus as Savior; What the Reformers Taught . . . and Why It Still Matters*, Five Solas Series (Grand Rapids: Zondervan, 2017), 137–45. Most scholars agree the definitive place in the New Testament to see details regarding Jesus's priesthood is in the book of Hebrews.

The entry of Jesus into Jerusalem is also interpreted as "the eschatological hope of the coming Messiah (Matt. 21:9; Mark 11:9–10; Luke 19:38; John 12:14–15)."[41] Jesus comes as the Messiah, but rejects the present temple system for a better and more glorious temple, namely, himself.[42] In his death, the veil of the temple is torn in two (Mark 15:38). The death of Jesus "stands for the removal of the temple of Jerusalem and its replacement by a new means of forgiveness."[43] Thus, in Jesus, a new temple is acknowledged and God's purposes for the priesthood are fulfilled. Additionally, the sacrifice Jesus offers for sin is his own sinless life, the only true means of permanent atonement (Mark 10:45; Luke 22:19–20; cf. John 1:29).

Temple and Priesthood in Acts and the Letters

In Acts, the fledgling church anchored in Jerusalem is led by the apostles and eventually appoints seven men to serve the church (6:1–6). Stephen is one of those servants who preaches with wisdom and in the power of the Spirit (6:8–10). He is accused by the authorities of never ceasing to "speak words against the holy place" (i.e., the temple; 6:13–14). Stephen clearly affirms that God was in the midst of Old Testament Israel doing great works, but he will not bring his covenant presence to bear amongst a sinful people (7:44–53). Additionally, God is not confined to a building; his presence surpasses such confines (7:49–50; cf. Isa. 66:1–2). Thus, Stephen makes clear that the temple was certainly brought about by God's initiative as a means of fellowship with his people. However, as a structure the temple is useless if the people of God lack the hearts to worship him.[44] God has brought about his presence through Christ and his Spirit indwelling his people. Loyalty to the temple is thus replaced by pledging allegiance and placing faith in Jesus.

The uniqueness of the Old Testament temple as a structure was that God's presence dwelt there. The New Testament refers to Jesus as the temple, which fits quite well since "all the fullness of deity dwells in him bodily" (Col. 2:9; cf. 1:19). As Moo states, "God in his fullness has not taken up residence in and therefore revealed himself in a building but in a body."[45] The temple acted as a symbol, reminding people of the fact that God had chosen to

---

41. McKelvey, "Temple," 808.
42. See Bill Salier, "The Temple in the Gospel According to John," in *Heaven on Earth: The Temple in Biblical Theology*, ed. T. Desmond Alexander and Simon Gathercole (Waynesboro: Paternoster, 2004), 121–125, who claims that the New Testament writers "portray Jesus as not only revealing the divine presence in the midst of the Temple, but also replacing the Temple as the locus of divine presence" (125). See also Hoskins, *Fulfillment of the Temple*, 124.
43. McKelvey, "Temple," 808.
44. See Darrell L. Bock, *Acts*, Baker Exegetical Commentary on the New Testament (Grand Rapids: Baker, 2007), 302–7.
45. Douglas J. Moo, *The Letters to the Colossians and to Philemon*, Pillar New Testament Commentary (Grand Rapids: Eerdmans 2008), 193–94. Further, Moo maintains, "According to 1:19, 'God was pleased to have all his fullness dwell in him [Christ].' The dependence of 2:9 on 1:19 is clear from the tautologous repetition all the fullness and from the use of the same verb, *katoikeō*, 'dwell'. . . . In contrast to 1:19, however, Paul explicitly indicates that the "fullness" has to do with God by adding the qualification 'of the Deity.' The particular Greek word Paul uses here— *theotēs*—focuses on the divine nature, as opposed to the divine essence (which would be expressed with *theiotēs*).

make his special presence manifest in that place. Now in Christ one recognizes the presence of God in a man, more precisely the God-man who "tabernacled" among us (John 1:14). The incarnation denotes the fact that God is with us (Isa. 7:14).[46]

Furthermore, Jesus also acts as a perfect high priest, entering upon his ascension into the heavenly temple to make intercession for us (Heb. 4:14; 7:1–8:13; 9:24). The author of Hebrews focuses specifically on the idea of Jesus as priest. Jesus is the one who has come to our aid as our high priest by making "propitiation for the sins of the people" (2:17). He suffered the same sorts of temptations that we face, is a "merciful and faithful" high priest (2:17–18), and as such is "the apostle and high priest of our confession" (3:1). The author later exhorts us to "hold fast" to our sympathetic high priest (4:14–16) because in him we receive mercy and grace in our need.

The author then makes a comparison between the Levitical priests and Jesus. Averbeck maintains, "Old Testament high priests could sympathize with the people for whom they mediated because they had to offer sacrifices for their own sins before they could offer for the people (5:2–3; 7:27; and cf. Lev. 16:11–14 with Lev. 16:15–19). Jesus as our New Testament high priest is sympathetic because, even though he was the son of God, he suffered agony in the face of death (Heb. 5:7–8)."[47] Additionally, Jesus is a high priest after the order of Melchizedek, who is the first recorded priest in Scripture (5:5–6; cf. Gen. 14:18; Ps. 110:4). In Genesis 14, Abraham gives tithes to Melchizedek and receives a blessing from him. For the author of Hebrews, this demonstrates that "the inferior is blessed by the superior" (7:4–10). Jesus is not a Levitical priest, but a priest in the order of Melchizedek, signaling a change in law and covenant by means of a new priesthood (7:11–8:13). Jesus is superior in his priesthood in that he is a priest forever (6:20) and perfection in the priesthood and sacrifice comes through him (7:11).[48] He entered the most holy place and offered himself as a perfect and eternal sacrifice for our sins (9:1–10:18).

In summary of the argument in Hebrews, Ellingworth claims:

> Jesus is for the writer both a new and better kind of high priest, and also the sacrifice which he himself offers to God (Heb. 9:11–14, 23–28). The writer sees in the

As we noted in the comments on 1:19, this language of "dwelling" probably alludes to Old Testament teaching about the dwelling of God in the Temple (esp. Ps. 68:16). And this background may help explain why Paul qualifies the "dwelling" here with the adverb *sōmatikōs* (TNIV, 'in bodily form')" (193).

46. See Stephen J. Wellum, *God the Son Incarnate: The Doctrine of Christ*, Foundations of Evangelical Theology (Wheaton: Crossway, 2016), 237.

47. Averbeck, "Priest, Priesthood," 636–37.

48. Some puzzle over the connection between Melchizedek and Christ, but Ellingworth clarifies, "However, the main point in chap. 7 will be, not any personal characteristic of Melchizedek or indeed of Jesus, but the fact that this type of priesthood, unlike the Levitical institution, is 'permanently effective.'" Paul Ellingworth, *The Epistle to the Hebrews: A Commentary on the Greek Text*, New International Greek Testament Commentary (Grand Rapids: Eerdmans, 1993), 284.

mysterious figure of Melchizedek (Heb. 7:1–17) a foreshadowing of a priesthood higher than that of Aaron, and fulfilled in Jesus. His death supersedes the OT cultus, as reality supersedes a mere foreshadowing (10:1–4); it effects in the conscience of the believer the forgiveness and purification that the OT cultus [i.e., OT system of worship] could effect only in an external manner (10:5–18). In particular, Jesus carries out on a cosmic scale the functions repeatedly and ineffectually performed by the high priest of the earthly sanctuary on the Day of Atonement.[49]

Jesus perfectly embodies the concepts of temple and priest, and God's people are also called to operate under these same terms.

Anticipated by various iterations of the temple, especially the incarnation of Jesus Christ, the church becomes the new temple of God, extending God's presence throughout the earth.[50] As the temple of God (1 Cor. 3:16–17; 6:18–20; 2 Cor. 6:14–18; Eph. 2:19–22; 1 Peter 2:4–10), made up of both Jews and Gentiles, the church is indwelt with the Spirit and called to reflect and proclaim the glory of God in word and deed. The Holy Spirit, McKelvey remarks, is "the divine gift of the new age" (Ezek. 37:14; Joel 2:28–29; Acts 2:1–4).[51] The church is thus to be holy and unified. Jesus Christ is the cornerstone and we are the living stones under construction that comprise the "building" (Eph. 2:20–21; 1 Peter 2:4–5). As Christians both individual (1 Cor. 6:18–20) and corporate (1 Cor. 3:16–17; 2 Cor. 6:14–18), the church showcases the greatness of God. Christians do this knowing that, at Christ's second coming, the earth will be filled with the knowledge of the glory of the Lord as the waters cover the sea (Hab. 2:14).

In addition to identifying believers as the temple, Scripture also refers to us as priests. From Adam onwards, God's plan has always involved a restoration of the holy status originally intended for humanity as his image-bearers. Jesus is our great high priest and by his work all Christians are joined in a priesthood dedicated to God and his purposes.[52] As believers we are made holy by the shed blood of Jesus (1 Peter 1:18–19), to be a holy kingdom

---

49. Ellingworth, "Priests," 700. See also Bavinck, *Reformed Dogmatics*, 466–67.
50. This corresponds with portions of the Dead Sea Scrolls, as the Qumran community believed the people that comprised the community were in fact a temple (1QS 5.5–6; 8.4–10; 9.3–6).
51. McKelvey, "Temple," 809.
52. Calvin notes regarding the relationship between Christ's priesthood and our own, "Thus we see, that if the benefit and efficacy of Christ's priesthood is to reach us, the commencement must be with his death. Whence it follows, that he by whose aid we obtain favor, must be a perpetual intercessor . . . Christ now bears the office of priest, not only that by the eternal law of reconciliation he may render the Father favorable and propitious to us, but also admit us into this most honorable alliance. For we, though in ourselves polluted, in him being priests (Rev. 1:6) offer ourselves and our all to God, and freely enter the heavenly sanctuary, so that the sacrifice of prayer and praise which we present are grateful and of sweet odor before him." John Calvin, *Institutes of the Christian Religion*, ed. John T. McNeill, trans. Robert L. Battles, 2 vols., Library of Christian Classics 20–21 (Philadelphia: Westminster John Knox, 1960), 2:432.

of priests proclaiming the excellencies of God (1 Peter 2:9–10).[53] Jesus is the cornerstone upon which we are built, the source of the church's life and growth (1 Peter 2:4–8). As a priesthood in this era of the temple, believers offer spiritual sacrifices (1 Peter 2:4–5), which consist of their very lives (Rom. 12:1–2) as well as their worship (Heb. 9:14), praise (Heb. 13:15), and grace-wrought good works (Heb. 13:16).[54]

Temple and Priesthood in Revelation

This temple imagery flows from Eden to the tabernacle (Exod. 25–31), then to the temple (2 Chron. 2–7), but is also seen subsequently in Jesus as temple (John 2:19–22), the church (1 Cor. 3:16–17; 6:19–20; 2 Cor. 6:14–18; Eph. 2:19–22; 1 Peter 2:4–6), and finally culminates in the new heaven and new earth as the dwelling place of God (Rev. 21:1–4). John's vision reveals a city of enormous size shaped as a cube, which is indicative of the Most Holy Place within the Jerusalem temple, which was also shaped as a cube and plated with gold (1 Kings 6:19–32).[55] The new heaven and the new earth will exist as a holy place for God and his people where sin and destruction will never penetrate.

We are called now to function as priests, and we will one day serve in that capacity eternally (Rev. 1:5–6; 5:10; 20:6; 22:4–5). Hamilton reminds us that priests serve and worship God and mediate the knowledge of God to others.[56] We presently proclaim the person and work of Jesus and serve him in every aspect of our lives. And when the new creation fully flowers, we will serve and worship the living God in his presence forever as a "regal priesthood."[57]

John goes on to say, "And I saw no temple in the city, for its temple is the Lord God the almighty and the Lamb" (Rev. 21:22). Where one expects to find a temple they discover instead God the Father and the Son. This suggests that the whole city exists as the

---

53. Carson maintains, "The notion of a royal priesthood has less to do with establishing the authority of the covenant people of God (old covenant or new) than with themes of obedience, holiness, privilege, mission, self-identity under the good purposes of God." D. A. Carson, "1 Peter," in *Commentary on the New Testament Use of the Old Testament*, ed. G. K. Beale and D. A. Carson (Grand Rapids: Baker, 2007), 1031. Jobes concurs: "The kingdom of God is composed of believers who must think of themselves as holy with respect to the world, set apart for purity and a purpose demanded by God. This is the priesthood that serves the king of the universe." See Karen H. Jobes, *1 Peter*, Baker Exegetical Commentary on the New Testament (Grand Rapids: Baker, 2005), 161. See also Alex T. M. Cheung, "The Priest as the Redeemed Man: A Biblical-Theological Study of the Priesthood," *Journal of the Evangelical Theological Society* 29.3 (1986): 265–75.
54. As Averbeck observes, "Moreover, our ministry in the gospel can be described as an offering of our very life in priestly service to the church (Phil. 2:17), by which we can produce a harvest of sanctified people whom we present to God as an acceptable offering." See "Priest, Priesthood," 637.
55. See Akin, *Exalting Jesus in Revelation*, 338; Beale, *Revelation*, 1074; Hamilton, *Revelation*, 395
56. Hamilton, *Revelation*, 37.
57. For further detail on the relationship between kingship and priesthood in Revelation and elsewhere, see Malone, *God's Mediators*, 153–63.

holy of holies, where God's glory resides.[58] This is the culmination of the constant refrain throughout Scripture: I will be your God and you will be my people. In this holy city no barriers exist between God and humanity. Worship of the true and living God will prevail as they enjoy uninterrupted communion with the triune God. We will reign as a kingdom of priests in God's presence forever.

58. See Alexander, *City of God*, 152; Richard Bauckham, *Book of Revelation*, 140; Beale, *New Testament Biblical Theology*, 640–41; Lister, *Presence of God*, 68–69; McKelvey, "Temple," 810.

Discussion Questions

1. What is the relationship between the temple and the priesthood?

2. What is the job of the priest in the Old Testament? What does that teach us in relation to our own ministries as we consider that fact that Peter refers to us as a "kingdom of priests" (1 Peter 2:9)?

3. When looking across the testaments, what is the trajectory of God dwelling with his people? In other words, where and how did God dwell among us from creation to today? How will God dwell among us to the very end of time?

4. What Old Testament passage or set of passages most informed and/or impacted your thinking on this topic? Why?

5. What New Testament passage or set of passages most informed and/or impacted your thinking on this topic? Why?

Resources for Further Study

Alexander, T. Desmond. *The City of God and the Goal of Creation*. Short Studies in Biblical Theology. Wheaton: Crossway, 2018.

Beale, G. K. *The Temple and the Church's Mission: A Biblical Theology of the Dwelling Place of God*. New Studies in Biblical Theology 17. Downers Grove: InterVarsity, 2004.

Beale, G. K., and Mitchell Kim. *God Dwells among Us: Expanding Eden to the Ends of the Earth*. Downers Grove: InterVarsity, 2014.

Lister, J. Ryan. *The Presence of God: Its Place in the Storyline of Scripture and the Story of Our Lives*. Wheaton: Crossway, 2015.

Malone, Andrew S. *God's Mediators: A Biblical Theology of Priesthood*. New Studies in Biblical Theology 43. Downers Grove: InterVarsity, 2017.

CHAPTER 16

WORSHIP

WORSHIP STANDS OUT AS a central theme in Scripture because God, in his infinite greatness, is worthy of all glory, honor, and praise (Rom. 11:33–36; Rev. 4:11; 5:9–12). God has created all things for the praise of his glory (Ps. 19:1; Isa. 43:6–7; Eph. 1:3–14). Creation is intended to be the theater of God's glory, the dominion where his majestic holiness and love, his greatness and goodness, shine forth and are received and adored. He is the God who makes covenant with his people and acts redemptively within history. He is worthy and deserving of all praise.

The term "worship" most generally conveys the notion of "ascribing worth to something or someone." In a Christian understanding, worship is not just a set time of singing, but involves the whole life lived (Rom. 12:1). Block proposes a working definition of worship that "true worship involves reverential human acts of submission and homage before the divine Sovereign in response to his gracious revelation of himself and in accord with his will."[1] There is no room for ambivalence toward God, or rebellion in his presence. The very essence of who he is calls for unadulterated worship in all that we do (1 Cor. 10:31; Col. 3:17).[2] Humanity is

---

1. Daniel I. Block, *For the Glory of God: Recovering a Biblical Theology of Worship* (Grand Rapids: Baker, 2014), 23. Peterson similarly argues that worship is "an engagement with [God] on the terms that he proposes [in his Word] and in the way he alone makes possible" (*Engaging with God*, 20). Ross offers a definition with further detail: "True worship is the celebration of being in covenant fellowship with the sovereign and holy triune God, by means of the reverent adoration and spontaneous praise of God's nature and works, the expressed commitment of trust and obedience to the covenant responsibilities, and the memorial reenactment of entering into covenant through ritual acts, all with the confident anticipation of the fulfillment of the covenant promises in glory." Allen P. Ross, *Recalling the Hope of Glory: Biblical Worship from the Garden to the New Creation* (Grand Rapids: Kregel, 2006), 67–68.
2. For a helpful diagram displaying the various dimensions of worship in life, disposition, corporate gatherings, work, etc., see Block, *For the Glory of God*, 26.

called to engage with God in the way he deems appropriate as set out in Scripture. He has made worship possible by divine revelation regarding who he is, what proper worship consists of, and the grace to engage with him in such a fashion.

The most common term seen in Scripture for "worship" literally means to "bend over" or "bow down." It describes a gesture of respect or submission (Gen. 24:26–27; Exod. 34:8–9) performed by a lesser party to one who is greater. Other terms used for "worship" connote service, fear, and reverence.[3] Worship is an attitude of the heart, an expression of awe and grateful submission conveyed particularly in cultic rites, but expressed in every aspect of life. God has shown himself in revelation and redemption, and therefore calls for humanity to engage with him acceptably, on his terms.[4] Our God is incomparable and indescribable, holy and loving, transcendent and immanent. There is no one like him in heaven, on earth, or under the earth, and thus he is worthy of all glory and honor and praise.[5]

However, while God's glory is displayed and should be the center of our worship, we also see that it can be rejected with disastrous results. Worship is inevitable. We will all set our affection and allegiance on something or someone, and we will become like what we worship (Ps. 115:1–9; 2 Cor. 3:18).[6] However, with the presence of sin in the world there is no guarantee that worship will center on God. In fact, much of what is seen in creation is actually worship that is idolatrous in nature, bent toward worshipping the creation rather than the Creator (Rom. 1:24–25). Since certain expressions of worship are unacceptable to God (Gen. 4:3–5; Isa. 1:10–17; Heb. 12:28–29; Rev. 9:20–21; 13:1–18), and since our worship is indicative of our allegiances—which have eternal consequences—it is essential to know what pleases God and how he wants us to respond and relate to him. What God has revealed to us in Scripture must dictate and direct our worship.

Worship in the Law

In the beginning God created all things and called them "good" (Gen. 1:1–31). Adam and Eve were to be stewards of Eden, exercising dominion for the glory of God's name, worshipping him in all they did.[7] However, this worship did not last; instead Adam and

---

3. David G. Peterson, "Worship," in *New Dictionary of Biblical Theology*, ed. T. Desmond Alexander and Brian S. Rosner (Downers Grove: InterVarsity, 2000 [855–63]), 856–57.

4. Peterson, *Engaging with God*, 72–73.

5. For more detail on how God's character calls for fitting worship, see Ross, *Recalling the Hope of Glory*, 41–60.

6. Beale's fundamental thesis in relation to this point is "we resemble what we revere, either for ruin or for restoration." G. K. Beale, *We Become What We Worship: A Biblical Theology of Idolatry* (Downers Grove: InterVarsity, 2008), 49. Lints likewise maintains that "Human identity is rooted in what it reflects." Richard Lints, *Identity and Idolatry*, 30.

7. The goal of creation is worship of and communion with God. Adam and Eve fully enjoyed God's immediate presence with undiminished capacity. Communion with God is at the heart of worship, and even when sin enters the world God graciously makes a way for us to enjoy mediated access with him.

Eve turned to self-exaltation. Genesis 3:1–7 is the description of humanity's fall into sin. Though Adam was charged with working and keeping the Garden (2:15), an abdication of responsibility follows. Thus, humanity's demise occurs in a series of steps: the temptation and lie of the serpent (Satan; cf. Rev. 12:9), the twisted response of the woman and the man, the appeal of temptation, and the choice to rebel and disobey. In essence, humanity chooses to listen to a created being, rebel, and ascribe worship to themselves as opposed to their Creator God. Thus, "the witness of the Bible and the evidence from the pagan world clearly shows that Satan not only brought about the disobedience of Adam and Eve, but also set the pattern for the perversion of worship for all time."[8]

Man's disobedience of God's instruction to not eat of the fruit of the tree of knowledge of good and evil has far-reaching consequences, as shown in the remainder of Genesis 3. First, humanity experiences separation from God because of their sin. They will not know him with the same kind of intimacy, and actually manifest fear in his presence (3:8–10). Second, they become aware that they are naked, and so they cover themselves (3:7). They have shame rather than purity and thus are alienated from God and one another. The serpent is cursed and told that one day his head would be crushed by an offspring of the woman (3:14–15). The woman will have pain in childbearing (3:16), relational tension will exist between the man and the woman (3:16; cf. 4:7), the land will easily yield thorns and thistles (3:17–19), and death is now inevitable (3:19). Finally, they are driven from the garden and thus alienated from its security (3:20–24).[9]

While a measure of hope is offered in the promise of an offspring who will crush the head of the serpent as well as the provision of clothing, the catastrophic reality of this event is that sin and death have now been unleashed on God's good creation with insidious results. In Adam's sin, death and condemnation spread to all men because all now share in his sin (Rom. 5:12–21). We are sinful in our own nature (Eph. 2:3) from the time we are conceived (Ps. 51:5), and thus we naturally deviate from the moral law of God in a comprehensive way, including our attitude, motivation, word, and deed.

God created image-bearers to reflect his glory, but the fall inverts our reflective capacity. Humanity, beginning with the rebellion of Adam and Eve, gives itself over to idolatry, reflecting the image and likeness of idols instead of its Creator (cf. Rom. 1:18–25). Adam revered his own counsel and the counsel of the serpent, and prized that guidance more than the word of God. In doing so, Adam was not representing or reflecting God, but, in fact, looked more like the serpent. Because all of humanity has been affected by the fall, we see a pattern throughout redemptive history of humanity revering and

---

8. Ross, *Recalling the Hope of Glory*, 113.
9. Wenham points out that the pattern of the history of worship, beginning with Adam and Eve, is that when people sin they forfeit access to the sanctuary, the place God chose to make his presence known, until the sin is dealt with. See *Genesis 1-15*, 86.

reflecting creation rather than the Creator. Thus, humanity naturally glorifies idols instead of the living God.[10]

Worship began to take more definitive shape during the days of the patriarchs. God takes initiative with Noah and Abraham to call them to specific tasks and covenant relationship (Gen. 6:8–22; 8:21–9:17; 12:1–3), and they respond with worship through sacrifice (8:20; 13:18). Ross notes, "When God called Abraham (Gen. 11:27–12:9; 15:7; Acts 7:2–4), Abraham's family was living in a major religious center and had a history of worshipping other gods (Josh. 24:2)."[11] His worship had to be redirected towards the only one worthy of glory, and God was going to covenant with him so that his family, as well as the nations, would recognize and worship the one true God. As Hill maintains, "Often this expression of worship took the form of altar building (Gen. 33:20) and sometimes combined prayer (Gen. 26:25) or animal sacrifice (Gen. 31:54; 46:1). Other expressions of patriarchal worship included the erection of stone pillars and the pouring of drink offerings (Gen. 28:18, 22), taking of vows in response to divine revelation (Gen. 28:20; 31:13), ritual purification (Gen. 35:2), the rite of circumcision as a sign of covenant obedience (Gen. 17:9–14), and prayers of praise and thanksgiving (Gen. 12:8; 13:4), petition (Gen. 24:12; 25:21), and intercession (Gen. 18:22–33; 20:7)."[12] These beginnings of worship would come to fuller fruition as the descendants of the patriarchs came out of slavery in Egypt and were called to be God's covenant people.

The people of Israel were saved from slavery in Egypt so that they could "serve the Lord" (Exod. 3:12; 4:23; 8:1).[13] As they are delivered by God in the crossing of the Red Sea, they sing praises to the Lord, declaring his greatness (15:1–21).[14] In the exodus to their new land, they are brought into covenant with God, redeemed and set apart to obey his word (19:1–20:21).[15] God redeems and tasks Israel with a specific calling, demonstrating the close relationship that exists between worship and covenant. God gave them the law so that Israel might worship

10. Only by God's grace and faith in his person and work can a person be freed from slavery to sin and idolatry and be renewed in knowledge after the image of their Creator (cf. Col. 3:10) and be restored to a place of reflecting and glorifying him. This topic will be taken up in greater detail once we come to the New Testament.
11. Ross, *Recalling the Hope of Glory*, 135. See also Marten H. Woudstra, *The Book of Joshua*, New International Commentary on the Old Testament (Grand Rapids: Eerdmans, 1981), 344.
12. Andrew E. Hill, "Worship," in *Evangelical Dictionary of Biblical Theology*, ed. Walter A. Elwell (Grand Rapids: Baker, 1996 [837–44]), 839.
13. The parallel expressions "offer sacrifices to the Lord" (Exod. 3:18; 5:3, 8, 17; 8:8, 25–29) and "hold a festival" (5:1) indicate that some form of ritual service was immediately in view. See Peterson, "Worship," 856.
14. Stuart highlights, "The ingredients of Israelite hymns may almost always be summarized by the initials SRR: summons to praise, reasons to praise, recapitulation. All three elements are present in abundance in the Song of Moses." Stuart, *Exodus*, 348. In other words, worship is centered on revealed knowledge of God's character and works.
15. Peterson rightly claims, "Such terminology (e.g., 'treasured possession,' 'kingdom of priests,' 'holy nation') suggests that the engagement with God at Sinai was to inaugurate a total-life pattern of service or worship for the nation . . . A common factor in the three terms describing Israel's vocation here is the note of separation from the nations in order to be uniquely at God's disposal. The Israelites were drawn into a special or sanctified relationship with God from amongst the nations." Peterson, *Engaging with God*, 28. See also Dumbrell, *Covenant and Creation*, 84–90; Durham, *Exodus*, 263.

him in proper fashion. At the heart of the commands God gives, he directs his people to put no other gods before him, to make no idols, and to not take his name in vain (Exod. 20:3–7; cf. Deut. 5:7–11).[16] Above all else and embedded in each command of the Mosaic covenant, God calls for exclusive devotion from his people and for them to live as a distinct people dedicated to Yahweh alone (e.g., Exod. 23:13; Lev. 11:44; 18:3; 19:4; Deut. 7:25; 12:29–13:18; 27:15).

The legal code forming the stipulations of the Sinai covenant formally organized Hebrew worship. The Mosaic law standardized the form and the institutions of Israelite worship.[17] God provides the sacrificial system, for example, to enable Israel to receive cleansing from sin, consecration to God's service, and expressions of gratitude to God (Lev. 1–7; cf. Exod. 29:42–46).[18] The exodus and the covenant ratified at Mount Sinai also reshaped the Hebrew understanding of time and reordered the life of Israel according to a specific religious calendar. They were a people set apart unto God to worship him alone.

Central to Israel's worship was the establishment of the tabernacle/temple and the priesthood.[19] No common Israelite could come into God's presence, due to the fact that he is holy and the people are not. The temple, therefore, was set up as a place where God would dwell with his people, and the priesthood was established as a means of atoning for the sins of the people and reminding them to live in accordance with God's holy law. Peterson affirms, "The tabernacle was intended to provide a portable expression of God's presence with his people, to be located at the very center of Israel's life on the march from Sinai to the promised land (cf. Exod. 40:36–38; Num. 2)."[20] Yahweh reminded the people through these institutions, as well as the regular observances and annual feast days (Sabbath, Lev. 23:3; Passover, Lev. 23:4–8; Feast of Firstfruits, Lev. 23:9–14; Feast of Weeks, Lev. 23:15–22; Feast of Trumpets, Lev. 23:23–25; Day of Atonement; Lev. 16:1–34; 23:26–32; Feast of Booths, Lev. 23:33–43) commemorating his faithfulness to Israel as a people and his call for their covenant fidelity.[21]

---

16. Frame maintains that these commands forbid worship of tangible images and the belittling of God. Instead, there must be reverence for God, exclusive and loyal love, consecration to his purposes, and separation from all that would keep us from this exclusive worship. Frame, *Doctrine of the Christian Life*, 409–20.

17. Hill maintains regarding the various forms of worship in Israel, "Worship as recitation for the ancient Hebrews included liturgical responses like "Amen!" (1 Chron. 16:36) or "Hallelujah!", singing (Ps. 92:1), prayer (Ps. 5:3), vows and oath taking (Ps. 66:13–19), and the reading and teaching of God's Law (Deut. 31:9–13). Worship as ritual drama for the ancient Hebrews included sacrificial worship (Lev. 1–7), the Sabbath (Exod. 20:8–11), the seasonal festivals (Lev. 23), the pilgrimage festivals (Exod. 23:14–17), incense offerings and libations (Exod. 30:7–9), penitential rites (Lev. 16:29), purification rites (Lev .12:1–8), the tithe (Lev. 27:30–32), and artistic responses (e.g., music 2 Chron. 5:11–14; dance, Ps. 30:11; and sign and symbol, Exod 28:6–30). See Hill, "Worship," 839–40.

18. Peterson, "Worship," 856.

19. For more on the central theme of temple and priesthood, see chapter fifteen.

20. Peterson, *Engaging with God*, 31–32.

21. For more detail on the sacrificial system in general, see Alexander, *Promised Land*, 201–8, 237–58. For a more specific study on the Sabbath see D. A. Carson, ed., *From Sabbath to Lord's Day: A Biblical, Historical, and Theological Investigation* (Grand Rapids: Zondervan, 1982).

However, despite their verbal agreement, we see a nation who rejects the glory of God for idols in rather rapid fashion. While Moses receives the moral precepts of the law from God on Mount Sinai, Israel grows tired of waiting for his return. In an event that marks a major turning point in the narrative—a "fall" of Israel reminiscent of Adam and Eve in Genesis 3—the people request that Aaron make gods who will go before them.[22] Aaron complies and collects gold from the people and fashions a golden calf, saying this was the god who brought them out of Egypt, and even proclaims the next day as a feast to Yahweh (Exod. 32:1–6). The people worship this idol, commit sexual immorality, and profane the name of the Lord, breaking the first two of the Ten Commandments (Exod. 20:2–4; cf. 1 Cor. 10:7). God expresses his wrath (Exod. 32:7–10), Moses intercedes (32:11–14), and God displays his greatness and goodness in both judgment and mercy (32:15–35).[23] Appealing to the covenant God made with Abraham, Moses petitions God's glorious, holy, loving character. God hears Moses's intercession and his presence remains with Israel (Exod. 33:12–17). Moses then renders proper worship to God, as Israel should have (Exod. 34:1–8). In their act of idolatry, however, Israel rejects God's glory and exchanges it for an idol, receiving, revering, and reflecting its attributes instead of God's.[24]

This idolatrous moment in Israel's history is indicative of an attitude seen throughout the Pentateuch: hardness of the heart and a refusal to worship Yahweh in a fitting manner. Numbers 14 speaks of rebellion after the spies have been sent into Canaan before the taking of the promised land (cf. Exod. 17:1–7). Here the nation refuses to trust God's promise to give them the land, and threatens to kill the leaders who are faithful to God. God appears to bring judgment on the people. After Moses's intercession God proclaims, "I have pardoned, according to your word. But truly, as I live, and as all the earth shall be filled with the glory of the Lord, none of the men who have seen my glory and my signs that I did in Egypt and in the wilderness, and yet have put me to the test these ten times and have not obeyed my voice, shall see the land that I swore to give to their fathers. And none of those who despised me shall see it" (Num. 14:20–23). Due to their hardness of heart and lack of worship, God brings severe judgment upon Israel.

Numbers 20 describes a later moment in the wilderness wanderings, but Israel has still not learned. Much like in Exodus 17, the Israelites grumble (the very antithesis of worship) and shows no faith in God concerning their need for water. Even Moses displays a lack of faith in God and does not "uphold him as holy" in the way he approaches the rock to obtain

---

22. Regarding the parallels between this moment in Israel's history and the original rebellion of Adam and Eve, see Ross, *Recalling the Hope of Glory*, 181.

23. See J. Gary Millar, *Calling on the Name of the Lord: A Biblical Theology of Prayer*, New Studies in Biblical Theology 38 (Downers Grove: InterVarsity, 2016), 35–36.

24. Beale notes, "Oxen are commonly depicted as being out of control (Exod. 21:28–29, 32, 35–36; 23:4; Deut. 22:1) or running loose when they are wild and untrained (Num. 23:22; 24:8; Deut. 33:17; Job 39:9–10; Ps. 29:6; 92:10)." Beale, *New Testament Biblical Theology*, 368. The point is that Israel was reflecting what it was receiving and revering.

water (Num. 20:12). For this, Moses is also not allowed to enter the land God had promised Israel. God does not want to see rebellion, grumbling, and quarreling from his people; he wants to see faith, trust, submission, and praise, all signs of worship.

In a fitting end to the Pentateuch, Israel is called upon to fulfill all the words of the law in the land that God is giving them (Deut. 32:45–47) and not fall prey to the peoples of the land and their idolatry. Earlier in Deuteronomy Moses states, "And now, Israel, what does the Lord your God require of you, but to fear the Lord your God, to walk in all his ways, to love him, to serve the Lord your God with all your heart and with all your soul, and to keep the commandments and statutes of the Lord, which I am commanding you today for your good?" (10:12–13). Israel must reflect God's glory and walk in his ways, not in the ways of false gods.[25] But to do this, Israel must attain a circumcised heart that is no longer stubborn (10:16). Even more emphatically, Moses tells the people, "the Lord your God will circumcise your heart and the heart of your offspring, so that you will love the Lord your God with all your heart and with all your soul, that you may live" (30:6). God will continue to faithfully display his glory in creation, but until his people acquire new hearts they will not receive and reflect his glory as they ought. Instead they will reject his glory, revere idols, and reflect their nature (cf. Ps. 115:1–8). However, as promised in Deuteronomy 30, and as we will see in subsequent Scripture, God will bring about the means by which people will have the eyes to see his glory, embrace it with joy, and be progressively transformed into God's image so as to magnify his greatness.

Worship in the Prophets

As Israel comes into the land to take it as their own possession they are explicitly commanded to remove all of the people from the land (Josh. 23:4–13). This command is given because God knows the danger awaiting Israel. They will be tempted to put him aside and worship the gods of these other nations. Israel, however, does not completely obey this directive, leaving some of the inhabitants in the land (Judg. 1:1–36) with disastrous consequences concerning the exclusive worship of Yahweh.

Stuck in a cycle of idolatry (i.e., false worship), foreign oppression, pleas for help, and deliverance by means of a judge God provided, Israel descends a downward spiral throughout the narrative of the Old Testament. Miller notes, "In the scope of literary genre, Judges is a tragedy. . . . In just a single generation, the whole nation forgot their redeemer (2:12) and 'did what was evil in the sight of the Lord' (2:11; 3:7, 12; 4:1; 6:1; 10:6). Whereas at Sinai 'the Lord became king' of all Israel's tribes (Deut. 33:5), now it could be said, 'In those days there was no king in Israel. Everyone did what was right in his own

---

25. See J. Gary Millar, *Now Choose Life: Theology and Ethics in Deuteronomy*, New Studies in Biblical Theology 6 (Downers Grove: InterVarsity, 1999).

eyes (Judg .17:6; 21:25; cf. 18:1; 19:1)."[26] Even after Israel obtains a king, there are certainly seasons of obedience and proper worship, but many of the kings lead the people astray. Israel is ultimately driven into exile because they "walked in the customs of the nations" and they committed idolatry gave to idols what rightfully belonged to God rather than render true worship to the Lord (2 Kings 17:7–23).

Besides affirming and guiding the worship of God in Israel, the prophets often critique their illicit worship practices. Peterson claims, "Numerous passages in the prophetic writings condemn priests and people for their corruption of the sacrificial system (e.g., Amos 4:4–13; Hos. 8:11–13; Jer. 7:21–26; Ezek. 16:15–21; 20:25–31). Sometimes these deal with the introduction of pagan ideas and practices into Israelite worship, or the attempt to worship other gods whilst still claiming to serve the Lord. Often they attack the hypocrisy of engaging in the sacrificial ritual without genuine repentance or a desire to live in obedience to God's moral law."[27] The prophets speak of Israel's debauchery in strong terms and maintain that God will brook no rivals. Just as all idols are blind, deaf, dumb, and powerless (Isa. 42:10–25; 44:9–20; cf. Ps. 115:1–8), so too those who worship these idols will indeed become disempowered like them (Isa. 6:8–13; cf. Matt. 13:14–15).[28]

Clear and forthright in their denunciation of idolatry, the prophets recognize that it robs God of the glory only he deserves (Isa. 48:9–11). God despises false worship and often tells the people of his abhorrence (e.g., Isa. 1:10–15; Jer. 7:1–29; Ezek. 8:1–9:11; Hos. 1:1–2:13). The prophets describe God as both transcendent and utterly holy, as well as near and loving. God is the "Holy One in your midst" (Hos. 11:9), a God who at once dwells "in the high and holy place, and also with him who is of a contrite and lowly spirit" (Isa. 57:15). Therefore, he calls his covenant people to repentance and true worship (Isa. 1:16–20).[29] God is not pleased with mere sacrifices (Hos. 6:6; Mic. 6:6–8; cf. Ps. 51:16–17); he wants hearts that are fully committed to him (Hos. 6:1–3). God promised the restoration of Israel (Ezek. 20:40–44), but not as they once were. He would come to them with a new covenant, giving them new hearts and putting his Spirit within them, so that they would be enabled to worship God fittingly (Jer. 31:31–34; Ezek. 36:25–27). This coming worship was meant not only for Israel, but for the gathering of the nations as well (Isa. 2:1–5).

---

26. Chris A. Miller, "Judges," in *What the Old Testament Authors Really Cared About: A Survey of Jesus' Bible*, ed. Jason S. DeRouchie (Grand Rapids: Kregel, 2013), 198.
27. Peterson, "Worship," 858–59. For more on the prophets' response to Israel's idolatry, see Ross, *Recalling the Hope of Glory*, 308–39.
28. See Beale, *We Become What We Worship*, 36–70.
29. Ross, in summarizing the plea of the prophets for true worship, states that God is calling for submission, repentance, recognition of divine discipline, and a shunning of worldliness in all of its forms. When faith is operating effectively it will form proper manifestations of worship. See Ross, *Recalling the Hope of Glory*, 340–41.

Worship in the Writings

The Law laid out the proper means by which one should worship Yahweh, but it is the Psalter that shows us the beauty of praise. The Psalms are a collection of poems, songs, and prayers that were used by individual worshippers, as well as in corporate settings. Regarding the contents of the Psalms, Mays avers, "the Psalms themselves . . . contain more direct statements about God than any other book of the two testaments of the Christian canon. . . . The works of God and the attributes of God are the constant agenda of the Psalms."[30] All throughout this book, the people of God express their praise to God because of the worthiness of God.

Psalms is divided into five books (Book 1: Psalms 1–41; Book 2: Psalms 42–72; Book 3: Psalms 73–89; Book 4: Psalms 90–106; Book 5: Psalms 107–150), which seem to trace out an implicit storyline of David's rise to power, the fall of Jerusalem, and a call to trust in God regarding future salvation.[31] Whether a word of lament (e.g., 3; 44; 60; 74; 79; 80), thanksgiving (e.g., 30; 32; 34; 67; 100; 124), wisdom (e.g., 1; 37; 49), or praise (e.g., 8; 95; 98; 149; 150), the Psalms focus on the greatness of the glory of God. Even when the psalmist asks "How long O Lord?" (13:1), he nevertheless rejoices, sings, and trusts God because he recognizes that the Lord has dealt bountifully with him (13:5–6). Psalm 145 also serves as a helpful example, wherein the psalmist extols the Lord continually because of his great deeds (145:5), grace and mercy (145:8–9), and his provision (145:14–20). The Psalter thus serves as a faithful guide for the worship of Yahweh.

Like the Hebrew patriarchs, Job appears to function in the role of a priest as the head of his family and offers sacrifices on their behalf (Job 1:5). He reminds the reader that we should worship and fear God for who he is. Confession and repentance (42:6), and petition and intercessory prayer (6:8–9; 42:8–9) were routine practices for Job as he sought to worship God.[32] The Preacher of Ecclesiastes also reminds us of the ultimate end of our lives, namely, "Fear God and keep his commandments" (Eccl. 12:13). This parallels the call to fear the Lord in Proverbs (e.g., 1:7), and serves as a definitive way of worshipping God.[33]

---

30. James Luther Mays, "The God Who Reigns: The Book of Psalms," in *The Forgotten God: Perspectives in Biblical Theology: Essays in Honor of Paul J. Achtemeier on the Occasion of his Seventy-Fifth Birthday*, ed. A. Andrew Das and Frank J. Matera (Louisville: Westminster John Knox, 2002), 29–30.

31. For more detail on this view of Psalms as having an overarching and intentional structure, see Hamilton, *God's Glory in Salvation*, 276–78; House, *Old Testament Theology*, 405–6; Gordon Wenham, "Towards a Canonical Reading of the Psalms," in *Canon and Biblical Interpretation*, ed. Craig G. Bartholomew et al., Scripture and Hermeneutics Series 7 (Grand Rapids: Zondervan, 2006), 333–51.

32. Hill, "Worship," 840.

33. Reverence of God should lead to obedience to God. Peterson maintains, "To fear God is to keep his commandments (e.g., Deut. 5:29; 6:2, 24; Eccl. 12:13), to obey his voice (e.g., 1 Sam. 12:14; Hag. 1:12), to walk in his ways (e.g., Deut. 8:6; 10:12; 2 Chron. 6:31), to turn away from evil (e.g., Job 1:1, 8; 2:3; 28:28; Prov. 3:7), and to serve him (e.g., Deut. 6:13; 10:20; Josh. 24:14)." Peterson, *Engaging with God*, 71. For more on glorifying God by means of our Spirit-wrought obedience that stems from our reverence of him, see Wayne Grudem, "Pleasing God by Our

Elsewhere in the Writings, the Jews are shown repenting of sin, celebrating the festivals, and covenanting to obey God's commands, all as signs of worship (Esther 9:20–32; Ezra 6:19–22; 10:1–17; Neh. 8:1–10:39). However, the refrain "He did what was evil in the eyes of the Lord" (e.g., 2 Chron. 36:5, 9, 12) is a common reference to Israel's wicked kings, and though God sends prophets to warn them (2 Chron. 36:15–16), their typical response is hardness of heart, mockery, and ongoing idolatry. A new work would be done, wherein a new heart would be given not just to Israel, but people from every tribe, tongue, nation, and language (cf. Rev. 5:9–10).

When considering the teachings on worship in the Old Testament, although connections exist on a number of levels, one must acknowledge the discontinuity that exists regarding worship in the Old and New Testaments. Old Testament worship is tied specifically to the ark of the covenant, the temple, sacrifice, and the priesthood, and was designed to serve as a tangible means of living in God's presence as a nation in a specific locale. Its cultic rituals and rites are distinctive and tied to a national/political reality, as well as specific covenant stipulations. The Mosaic covenant is not a permanent way God relates to his people, as it gives way to new covenant realities (Heb. 8:1–13), and thus the Old Testament means of worship are not entirely applicable to believers in the New Testament era.

However, while particular in nature and tied to specific covenant regulations that would give way to new covenant realities, Old Testament worship paves the way toward the kind of worship one would see in the New Testament era. Hill summarizes the essence of Hebrew worship as the anticipation of Christian worship in theological principle, in that Hebrew worship required conscious preparation, encouraged private and family worship as a complement to corporate public worship, demanded the response of the "whole person" to God as Creator and Redeemer, promoted congregational worship that was active and participatory, focused on the redemptive acts of God in human history (e.g., the Passover/exodus event), employed symbolism to enhance worship aesthetically and improve worship didactically, observed a liturgical calendar that heightened the worshiper's anticipation of and participation in worship, and assumed that a lifestyle of obedience in service to God was necessary for integrity in worship.[34] These key facets pave the way for how worship would be understood in the New Testament era.

Worship in the Gospels

The Gospels use the terminology of "worship" to show that Jesus Christ is worthy of the reverence and devotion due to the Lord God of Israel (Matt. 14:33; 28:9, 17; Luke 24:52;

Obedience: A Neglected New Testament Teaching," in *For the Fame of God's Name: Essays in Honor of John Piper*, ed. Sam Storms and Justin Taylor (Wheaton: Crossway, 2010), 272–92.
34. Hill, "Worship," 842.

John 9:38; cf. Heb. 1:6; Rev. 5:8–14). Jesus is the son of David and the son of Abraham
(Matt. 1:1), the promised messianic ruler who will rescue the nations (Isa. 11:1–11; Jer.
23:5–6). He is the Son of Man (John 12:34) who will inherit nations and rule with a rod
of iron (Ps. 2:7–9; Dan. 7:13–14). He is worthy of praise and glory. Whereas the Old Testament held to a theocentric approach to worship (Deut. 6:4–5), the New Testament expands on who God is, revealing that proper worship must also be Christocentric (1 John
2:22–23).[35] Jesus Christ was with God and is God, the Word made flesh (John 1:1, 14),
such that when we see him, we have seen the Father (John 14:9). He is the greater temple
(Matt. 12:6; John 2:18–22), the definitive lawgiver (Matt. 5–7), the enactor of a new covenant (Luke 22:20), and the ultimate atoning sacrifice (John 1:29). In his death Jesus
opens up a way of worship that signifies greater access to God (Matt. 27:51). Jesus is God
incarnate and thus is rightly the recipient of our adoration and praise.

New covenant worship acknowledges Jesus as the one who finally and fully reveals the
truth about the Father and his purpose for Israel and the nations (John 8:45; 12:32; 14:6;
18:37). It also responds to the Spirit he gives to transform hearts and lives (John 3:5–8;
7:37–39; cf. 4:13–14).[36] Jesus is God incarnate. We dare not ascribe praise to Jesus while our
hearts are far from him (Matt. 15:8–9; cf. Isa. 29:13). The Spirit glorifies him (John 16:14),
and points us to him, so that worship may reach its proper terminus.

In John 4:20–24, a Samaritan woman dialogues with Jesus, eventually bringing the conversation around to the appropriate place of worship. Jesus bypasses this inquiry and speaks
more directly about how one should worship. The Father seeks "true worshipers" who will
worship the Father in "spirit and in truth" (John 4:23–24). Commenting on this passage,
Hill affirms, "True worship takes place on the inside, in the heart or spirit of the worshiper
(cf. Ps. 45:1; 103:1–2). Worship pleasing to God must be unfeigned and transparent, offered
with a humble and pure heart (Ps. 24:3–4; Isa. 66:2)." This is worship "in spirit." However,
worship in spirit is not enough. "Worship "in truth," Hill continues, "connects the heart or
spirit of worship with the truth about God and his work of redemption as revealed in the
person of Jesus Christ and the Scriptures. David understood the importance of worshiping
in truth and the necessary linkage between 'truth' and the Word of God when he wrote,
'Teach me your way, O Lord, and I will walk in your truth; give me an undivided heart,

---

35. Certainly there is a plurality to be observed within the Old Testament (e.g., Gen. 1:1–3, 27; 3:22; 11:7; Pss. 45:6–7;
110:1; Isa. 48:16–17), but what is alluded to in the Old Testament is made explicit in the New Testament, which
describes God as one being existing in three persons as Father, Son, and Holy Spirit (Matt. 3:13–17; 28:19–20; John
1:1–14, 33–34; 8:58; 14:16, 26; 16:15; 20:21–23; Rom. 8:15–17; 15:30; 1 Cor. 12:4–6; 2 Cor. 13:14; Gal. 4:4–6; Eph.
1:3–14; 3:14–19; 4:3–6; Titus 3:4–6; 1 Peter 1:2; Jude 20–21). Thus, as Ross claims, true worship must come from a
fresh awareness of the glory of God the Father, with explicit and direct reference to God the Son, and be empowered and enabled by God the Spirit. Ross, *Recalling the Hope of Glory*, 66–67. For more on this point see Letham,
Holy Trinity, 407–24.
36. Peterson, "Worship," 860.

that I may fear [i.e., worship] your name' (Ps. 86:11; cf. Ps. 145:18). Here both the Old and New Covenants agree! The true worship of God is essentially internal, a matter of the heart and spirit rooted in the knowledge of and obedience to the revealed Word of God."[37] Proper worship comes from a mind and heart that are enthralled with the living God.

Worship in Acts and the Letters

The Book of Acts indicates that the first church gathered daily for worship in the Jerusalem temple and the homes of believers, devoting themselves to instruction in the apostles' doctrine, fellowship, prayer, and the Lord's Supper (2:42–47). Bock notes that "devoting themselves" carries the idea of "persistence or persevering in something."[38] The apostles' teaching would likely have included all kinds of instruction—doctrinal, ethical, practical— all grounded in what God had accomplished in Christ.[39] Fellowship pointed to the unity of this community, a mutuality shared around their common confession of Christ. This fellowship was made manifest as they broke bread together (cf. Luke 24:35)[40] and prayed, seeking God's direction and demonstrating their dependence on him. At the heart of all of this communal worship was the resurrected and ascended Jesus Christ.

Worship in the New Testament era means "responding with repentance and faith to the person and work of the Lord Jesus Christ" (Acts 2:36–39; 10:36–43; cf. Rom. 10:9–13).[41] Such worship involves praying to Jesus (Acts 7:59–60; 1 Cor. 16:22; 1 Thess. 3:11), calling on his name (1 Cor. 1:2; Heb. 13:15), and obeying him.[42] We do this now in anticipation of the day when he will return and "every knee will bow in heaven and on earth and under the earth, and every tongue will confess that Jesus Christ is Lord, to the glory of God the Father" (Phil. 2:10–11; cf. 2 Thess. 1:5–10). The essential symbols of worship in the Christian church are baptism and the Lord's Supper. This pattern of celebrating these two ordinances is seen in the book of Acts (Acts

---

37. Hill, "Worship," 837–38. Carson elaborates, "To worship the Father 'in spirit and truth' clearly means much more than worship without necessary ties to particular holy places (though it cannot mean any less). The prophets spoke of a time when worship would no longer be focused on a single, central sanctuary, when the earth would be full of the knowledge of the Lord as the waters cover the sea. The Apocalypse concludes with a vision of the consummated kingdom, the new Jerusalem, in which there is no temple to be found, 'because the Lord God Almighty and the Lamb are its temple' (Rev. 21:22). The fulfillment of that vision has not yet arrived in its fullness. Even so, Jesus insists, through his own mission the hour was dawning when the principal ingredients of that vision would be set in operation, a foretaste of the consummation to come. 'God is spirit, and his worshippers must (Gk. *dei*, here the divine 'must') worship him in spirit and truth.'" D. A. Carson, *John*, 226.
38. Bock, *Acts*, 149.
39. Bock, *Acts*, 149.
40. A number of commentators agree that "the breaking of bread" is a technical term used in Luke–Acts for the Lord's Supper. See F. F. Bruce, *The Book of Acts*, rev. ed., New International Commentary on the New Testament (Grand Rapids: Eerdmans, 1988), 79; I. Howard Marshall, *Acts: An Introduction and Commentary*, Tyndale New Testament Commentaries 5 (Downers Grove: InterVarsity, 2008), 83; John B. Polhill, *Acts*, New American Commentary 26 (Nashville: Broadman, 1992), 119.
41. Peterson, "Worship," 860.
42. Peterson, "Worship," 860.

2:38–41; 8:12, 36–38; 9:18; 10:47–48; 16:31–33; 20:7), and referenced by Paul, who speaks of their significance. Baptism is an outward expression of an inward reality; namely, that one has died to sin and been raised to life with Christ (Rom. 6:1–4; Col. 2:12).[43] Baptism signifies that anyone who places faith in Jesus as Messiah is a child of God (Gal. 3:25–27). The church also celebrates the Lord's Supper in remembrance of Christ's death (1 Cor. 11:23–26) and in anticipation of the marriage supper of the Lamb that is to come (Rev. 19:9–10).[44] Much like Passover, the Lord's Supper reminds us of the redemptive work Christ accomplished for us (1 Cor. 5:7) and how we are now called to sojourn to a land not yet seen (Heb. 11:10; 1 Peter 1:17; 2:11–12).

Responding with faith and repentance to the person and work of Jesus Christ in all of life in a persevering manner also requires the edification and building up of the body of Christ by preaching and teaching Scripture. Paul tells Timothy to devote himself to "the public reading of Scripture, to exhortation, to teaching" (1 Tim. 4:13). He is to "Keep a close watch on himself and the teaching" because by doing so he will save himself and his hearers (1 Tim. 4:16). Paul also instructs Timothy to preach the God-breathed Word in and out of season (2 Tim. 3:16–4:2). Thus, preachers are to herald the truth of God's Word in corporate gatherings as an act of worship.[45]

There were, however, disputes over the proper forms of worship due to the clash that occurred between Jews and Gentiles on these matters (e.g., Acts 15:1–35). Many of Paul's letters aim to establish guidelines for resolving these problems surrounding Christian worship. Primarily, Paul advocates that the unity and edification of the congregation gathered for worship be of central importance (1 Cor. 12:7; Eph. 4:12–13). Peace should govern the overall practices of worship (1 Cor. 14:33, 40), and one should have a clear conscience and individual accountability before the Lord in certain matters related to personal freedoms and preferences in worship (Rom. 14:1–12).[46]

By the time of Paul's third missionary journey, the church met for corporate worship on the first day of the week (i.e., Sunday; Acts 20:7; 1 Cor. 16:2), likely in celebration of Christ's resurrection.[47] In addition to the weekly observance of the Lord's Supper (1 Cor. 11:17–34), the New Testament records indicate worship in the apostolic church also included the singing of

43. See John S. Hammett, *40 Questions About Baptism and the Lord's Supper* (Grand Rapids: Kregel, 2015), 115–21.
44. See Brian J. Vickers, "The Lord's Supper: Celebrating the Past and Future in the Present," in *The Lord's Supper: Remembering and Proclaiming Christ until He Comes*, eds. Thomas R. Schreiner and Matthew R. Crawford (Nashville: B&H, 2010), 313–40 (see 338–39).
45. Piper elaborates on this point: "Preaching as *expository exultation* is peculiarly suited for corporate worship. For corporate worship is the visible, unified knowing, treasuring, and showing of the supreme worth and beauty of God. Preaching fits that gathering, because that's what preaching is. Preaching shows God's supreme worth by opening Scripture to make the glories of God known, while treasuring them as supremely valuable." John Piper, *Expository Exultation: Christian Preaching as Worship* (Wheaton: Crossway, 2018), 70–71.
46. Hill, "Worship," 843.
47. For more detail concerning this point see Richard J. Bauckham, "The Lord's Day," in *From Sabbath to Lord's Day: A Biblical, Historical, and Theological Investigation*, ed. D. A. Carson (Grand Rapids: Zondervan, 1982), 221–50.

"psalms, hymns, and spiritual songs" (Eph. 5:19; Col. 3:16), prayer (1 Tim. 2:1–2), the giving of gifts to those in need (1 Cor. 16:1–4), the reading and teaching of the Old Testament and apostolic doctrine (1 Tim. 4:11–13), and the manifestation of a variety of spiritual gifts (1 Cor. 12:1–11).[48] Thus, teaching, exhortation, and prayer became significant ways to worship and glorify God as well as build up of the body of Christ.

In response to what God has done for us in Christ, we are to present our bodies to him as "a living sacrifice, holy and acceptable to God, which is your spiritual worship" (Rom. 12:1). Christ's obedience to God empowers a new obedience for the people of God (1 Peter 2:24). We daily and continually offer ourselves to God as a "living sacrifice," living for his purposes, accomplishing his will, bringing him glory, and worshipping him alone. As Peterson remarks, "Acceptable worship is the service rendered by those who truly understand the gospel and want to live out its implications in every sphere of life" (cf. Rom. 12:2–21).[49] And not only do we see ourselves as a sacrifice of praise to God, we minister to others as "priestly service of the gospel of God" seeing those we minister to as an acceptable offering (Rom. 15:16; cf. Col. 1:27–29).

Christ's unique sacrifice secures for believers all the blessings of the new covenant and enables them to serve him wholeheartedly with consciences cleansed from sin (Heb. 9:11–14; 10:11–22; 12:28–29).[50] Gratitude expressed in worship is evidence that people grasp and appreciate the grace of God. However, acceptable worship should also be characterized by "reverence and awe" (Heb. 12:28) because of the holiness and righteousness of God (cf. Heb. 13:1–16). We gather corporately as Christians to exhort one another, expose ourselves to the ministry of the Word, and stir one another up to love and good works (Heb. 3:12–13; 10:24–25).

We also gather to worship with eschatological expectation. In Hebrews a comparison is made between the earthly Sinai (Exod. 19:1–25) and the heavenly Zion (Heb. 12:18–24). This textual unit is marked by the double use of the perfect indicative verb *proseleluthate* ("you have come," 12:18, 22).[51] As Christians, we have not come to Sinai, the place of the Mosaic covenant, but to the presence of God administered by means of the new covenant. We are now in a permanent relationship with God through Christ.[52] Allison rightly remarks, "That living Christ-followers 'have

---

48. Hill, "Worship," 843. Further affirmation of such practices can be found in early Christian writings such as the Didache and The Epistle to Diognetus. For further detail and commentary on these texts, see Steven A. McKinion, ed., *Life and Practice in the Early Church: A Documentary Reader* (New York: New York University Press, 2001).
49. Peterson, "Worship," 861.
50. Peterson, "Worship," 862.
51. David L. Allen, *Hebrews* New American Commentary 35 (Nashville: B&H, 2010), 589. See also Ellingworth, *Epistle to the Hebrews*, 669.
52. Allen remarks, "If the perfect tense verb 'you have come' in v. 22 indicates the readers have come now to this place of permanent relationship with God in Zion, and if the perfect tense verb in v. 23 attests to the fact that their names have been permanently enrolled in heaven, then the possibility of apostasy would seem to be ruled out for the readers." Allen, *Hebrews,* 593. For more on this topic see Christopher W. Cowan, "The Warning Passages of Hebrews and the New Covenant Community," in *Progressive Covenantalism: Charting a Course Between Dispensational and Covenantal Theologies*, eds. Stephen J. Wellum and Brent E. Parker (Nashville: B&H, 2016), 189–214.

come' (Heb. 12:22) to this gathering that is 'both heavenly and eschatological' is significant. In one sense the heavenly city is still the goal of the Christian's pilgrimage. . . . In another sense, they have already reached Mt. Zion, the heavenly Jerusalem, the city of the Living God."[53] Thus, we worship the Lord with reverence and awe, recognizing our God is a consuming fire (Heb. 12:28–29), but we also await the fullness of his presence that is to come.

Worship in Revelation

The book of Revelation offers a window into the true realities of worship. Bringing glory to God is worthwhile and the path to life, but worship of the world, flesh, and devil is bankrupt. Hamilton reminds us regarding the beast and the prostitute as depicted in Revelation 17–18, "The idea is that the powers at work in the world are enticing people to commit spiritual adultery against the one to whom they owe their faithfulness and devotion. Have you noticed that the world wants to lead you away from God?"[54] There is a distinct call for perseverance, such that we are not deceived but endure in the worship of God with all of our lives (Rev. 13:10; 14:12).

John portrays God as infinitely glorious and the Lamb as worthy of all praise (4:8–11; 5:9–14). One of the key terms for "worship" (*proskynein*) is used twenty-four times in Revelation, indicating the centrality of the theme to the book as a whole.[55] The redeemed and heavenly beings render praise to God (7:11; 11:1, 16; 14:7; 15:4; 19:4, 10; 22:9), but the earthly scenes show various forms of idolatry (9:20; 13:4, 8, 12). There are thus those who worship the beast and those who worship the Lamb (14:1–11), and the respective results of such worship will be either eternal death or eternal life (19:11–20:15).

Someday the Lamb will return in all of his glory and he will usher in the new creation (19:11–21:8). Here God will dwell with his people (21:9–22:21) and all of his people, as a kingdom of priests, will render worship to him forever (22:3). This book is intended to prompt us to worship the true God as we anticipate the day of his return. Ross claims, "the ultimate picture of worship after the end of this age is one of eternal worship. It will be centered on the marvelous reality of the presence of the Lord with his people and his provisions for all their needs. . . . And in this glorious new creation, the people of God will serve the Lord and worship him forever. That is the hope of glory."[56] Revelation, therefore, is a stark reminder that worship of the living God is not a mere choice, but a divine imperative. God has been calling us to worship from the very beginning, and as we engage in a life that exalts the Creator God, we find satisfaction in him and he is glorified in our praise (Ps. 67:3–5; Phil. 1:18–26).

---

53. Allison, *Sojourners and Strangers*, 154.
54. Hamilton, *Revelation*, 285.
55. See Peterson, "Worship," 863.
56. Ross, *Recalling the Hope of Glory*, 500.

Discussion Questions

1. Define the term "worship." What is its meaning according to Scripture?

2. Do the forms of worship change from the Old Testament to the New Testament? How so? If yes, why?

3. Read John 4:20–24. What does it mean that we must worship the Father in spirit and in truth?

4. Read Hebrews 12:18–29. What does this passage say about worship? How does it contrast New Testament worship from Old Testament worship? How does this depiction practically impact the way we worship God during church services and in everyday life?

5. Read Revelation 4–5. List all of the reasons why God the Father and God the Son are so worthy of worship.

Resources for Further Study

Beale, G. K. *We Become What We Worship: A Biblical Theology of Idolatry*. Downers Grove: InterVarsity, 2008.

Block, Daniel I. *For the Glory of God: Recovering a Biblical Theology of Worship*. Grand Rapids: Baker, 2016.

Chappell, Bryan. *Christ-Centered Worship: Letting the Gospel Shape Our Practice*. Grand Rapids: Baker, 2017.

Peterson, David. *Engaging With God: A Biblical Theology of Worship*. Downers Grove: InterVarsity, 2002.

Ross, Allen P. *Recalling the Hope of Glory: Biblical Worship from the Garden to the New Creation*. Grand Rapids: Kregel, 2006.

CHAPTER 17

MESSIAH AND ATONEMENT

fROM THE BEGINNING, GOD had a plan to redeem his people by means of his Messiah. The term "Messiah" refers to persons who were "anointed" and had been "elected, designated, appointed, given authority, qualified, and equipped" for a specific office and the tasks that came along with that office.[1] Kings and priests were examples of those who were anointed for a specific purpose, but there is one anointed figure that takes precedence over all others. Humanity was ultimately in need of a person sent and set apart by God to accomplish his will on our behalf. This is due to the fact that, because of sin, we are incapable of coming to God and relating to him in a way that pleases him. We are separated, living under his wrath, and therefore in need of messianic rescue.

Biblical revelation anticipates and details the character and work of this figure. A genealogical line can be traced from Adam through to Jesus the Messiah (Luke 3:23–38), with progressively detailed descriptions of his identity and work. Thus, from start to finish it appears that the Old Testament is a "messianic document, written from a messianic perspective to maintain a messianic hope," and this hope is interpreted and elucidated with candid detail in the New Testament (Luke 24:27, 44–45; cf. Matt. 5:17; John 5:46).[2] Indeed,

---

1. Gerard Van Groningen, "Messiah," in *Evangelical Dictionary of Biblical Theology*, ed. Walter A. Elwell (Grand Rapids: Baker, 1996), 523. See also Walter Grundmann, "Χριστός," 493–580 in G. Kittel, G. W. Bromiley, G. Friedrich, eds., *TDNT (Grand Rapids: Eerdmans, 1977), 9:497*; I. Howard Marshall, "Jesus Christ," in *New Dictionary of Biblical Theology*, eds. T. Desmond Alexander and Brian S. Rosner (Downers Grove: InterVarsity, 2000), 593.
2. Hamilton, "Inner-Biblical Interpretation of Genesis 3:15," 30. See also J. J. M. Roberts, "The Old Testament's Contribution to Messianic Expectations," in *The Messiah: Developments in Earliest Judaism and Christianity*, ed. J. H. Charlesworth (Minneapolis: Fortress, 1992), 31–51 (esp. 41). This assessment is also in agreement with John Sailhamer, who writes, "I believe the messianic thrust of the OT was the *whole* reason the books of the Hebrew Bible were written. In other words, the Hebrew Bible was not written as the national literature of Israel. It probably also

345

the biblical picture will demonstrate that the promises and prophecies related to the Messiah are fulfilled in the person and work of Jesus Christ. Considering the progressive nature of revelation and taking the Bible on its own interpretive terms, one can observe the ways in which the biblical authors, by inspiration of God, made use of promises, prophecies, and types to point to God's anointed one.[3] There was messianic expectation from the very beginnings of the Old Testament, and it is important that as one seeks to understand who Jesus is to begin with a picture of his reality that is consonant with the descriptions seen in the Old Testament. Because of who Jesus is and what he has accomplished, in keeping with Old Testament revelation, God's wrath against us has been assuaged and through faith in Christ we can be brought into right relationship with the Father.

Messiah in the Law

In the beginning God created all things by his powerful word (Gen. 1:1–3), bringing about their existence and giving order to all things.[4] When humanity rebelled against God and chose to disobey his express command, they along with the rest of creation experienced terrible consequences. Yet, in the midst of judgment, God made a solemn promise, saying that an offspring of the woman would have his heel bruised by the serpent, but that he would ultimately crush the head of the serpent (Gen. 3:15).[5] This "seed" of the woman would overcome the serpent and bring about salvation for his people.[6] It is a vague promise at the beginning of the canon, but one that receives increasing attention as the storyline of Scripture progresses.

As the narrative of Genesis progresses, God calls Abraham, a descendant of Shem (9:25–27),[7] and makes his covenant with him, promising him land, offspring, and blessing

---

was not written to the nation of Israel as such. It was rather written, in my opinion, as the expression of the deep-seated messianic hope of a small group of faithful prophets and their followers." See Sailhamer, "Messiah and the Hebrew Bible," 23.

3. For more detail on how one's endeavors in epistemology, interpretation, and biblical and systematic theology affect one's approach to Christology, see Wellum, *God the Son Incarnate*, 79–104.

4. Carson rightly connects Genesis 1:1–3 to how John picks up on the concept of "word" in John 1:1: "God's 'Word' in the Old Testament is his powerful self-expression in creation, revelation and salvation, and the personification of that 'Word' makes it suitable for John to apply it as a title to God's ultimate self-disclosure, the person of his own Son." Carson, *John*, 116. See also Gerald L. Borchert, *John 1-11*, New American Commentary 25A (Nashville: B&H, 1996), 104.

5. Hamilton shows the conflict between the seed of the woman and the seed of the serpent pervades the entirety of Scripture, leading up to the time of Christ and beyond. See "Inner-Biblical Interpretation of Genesis 3:15," 33–43.

6. The term "seed" can be understood as referring to a collective group of people or to an individual. For an overview of the different usages of the term "seed" within the Old Testament, see Jason S. DeRouchie, "Counting Stars with Abraham and the Prophets: New Covenant Ecclesiology in OT Perspective," *Journal of the Evangelical Theological Society* 58.3 (2015): 447-50. *See also* Alexander, "'Seed' in Genesis"; Collins, "Woman's Seed"; Max Wilcox, "The Promise of the 'Seed' in the New Testament and the Targumim," *Journal for the Study of the New Testament* 5 (1979): 2–20. As will be seen, this concept of "seed" is applied to the offspring of Abraham as the nation of Israel, but will find its ultimate fulfillment in Jesus the Messiah as the true "seed."

7. For a clear outline and chart that traces the essential genealogy of Genesis, highlighting especially Adam, Noah, Shem, Terah, Abraham, Isaac, Jacob, Joseph, and Judah, see Alexander, *Promised Land*, 137.

(12:1–3). In other words, for the specific purposes of this chapter, "God covenanted in a special manner with Abraham, assuring him that via his seed God would carry out his redemptive/restorative work."[8] As such, Abraham was the next step in the messianic seed-bearing line through which God was bringing about his redemptive plan. Through Abraham and his offspring, all the nations of the earth would be blessed (12:3; cf. 15:1–21; 22:17–18; Gal. 3:7–16). Kings would come from Abraham's line (Gen. 17:6), and one seed in particular would "possess the gate of his enemies" (22:17).[9]

This offspring of the woman, coming to fruition through Abraham, and then Isaac and Jacob, takes on greater focus in Jacob's son, Judah. As Jacob blesses his sons before his death, he says "Judah is a lion's cub; from the prey, my son, you have gone up. He stooped down; he crouched as a lion and as a lioness; who dares rouse him? The scepter shall not depart from Judah, nor the ruler's staff from between his feet, until tribute comes to him; and to him shall be the obedience of the peoples" (49:9–10). The focus continues to narrow in on this messianic figure, the seed of the woman, who is to descend from Abraham and now specifically from Judah. This seed would be royal. Mathews maintains, "The 'scepter' symbolizes the monarchy that will be Judah's inheritance (e.g., Num. 24:17; Ps. 2:9; 45:6; Amos 1:8), which was historically realized in David's kingship (e.g., 2 Sam. 7:8–16; Ps. 89:3–4, 20). The kingdom is a permanent possession that 'will not depart [*sûr*] from Judah,' as it was promised to David's lineage in Nathan's oracle (sûr [2×] in 2 Sam. 7:15; cf. Ps. 89:33–37)."[10] Thus, an offspring from Judah will conquer his enemies and his reign will extend not just to his own nation, but over all of the peoples of the earth. More will be said of David later, but it is important to trace the genealogical trajectory of this messiah in Genesis, along with the specific role he will play in God's plan, in order to see how this picture progresses going forward.[11]

Later in the Pentateuch Israel is redeemed by God from the land of Egypt, brought into covenant relationship with him, and sent to the land God promised them. On the borders of Canaan, Balak the king of Moab sees how Israel has defeated their enemies in recent days, and along with the rest of Moab was in "great dread of the people" (Num. 22:3). Thus, Balak hires the diviner Balaam to curse Israel (Num. 22:4–21). However, each time Balaam attempts to curse Israel, he actually proclaims a blessing over them (Num. 23:1–24:25). Within these blessings more details are given concerning this coming seed of the woman. Balaam narrows his proclamation concerning the entire nation of Israel in Numbers 23 to refer specifically to a coming king who is "higher than Agag," (cf. Exod. 17:8–16; 1 Sam. 15:8) with great strength and through whom blessing comes (Num. 24:5–9).

---

8. Van Groningen, "Messiah," 524.

9. For further details on this point see Gentry and Wellum, *Kingdom through Covenant*, 285–89.

10. Kenneth A. Mathews, *Genesis 11:27–50:26*, New American Commentary 1B (Nashville: B&H, 2005), 892.

11. See Dempster, *Dominion and Dynasty*, 91.

Thus, the writer's purpose appears to be to view the reign of this future messianic king in light of God's acts of salvation in the past.[12] Drawing from Eden and exodus imagery, Balaam looks forward to the day when an Israelite seed would become an exalted king.[13] Later Balaam claims, "I see him, but not now; I behold him, but not near; a star shall come out of Jacob, and a scepter shall rise out of Israel; it shall crush the forehead of Moab and break down all the sons of Sheth" (Num. 24:17). Clear references are made to promises of the Messiah, showing the trajectory of his coming royal rule. Thus, the previous allusions in Genesis to a seed of the woman who would become a messianic ruler over Israel as well as the nations are reiterated here. Sailhamer deftly summarizes the pertinent allusions in this section:

> This entire section of Balaam's oracle is a quotation of Jacob's prophecy of the king who will come from the tribe of Judah [Gen. 49:9]. When Balaam says of this future king, "Those who bless you will be blessed and those who curse you will be cursed," he clearly applies to this future king the blessing to the seed of Isaac [Gen. 27:29] and that of Abraham [Gen. 12:3]. Finally, Balaam's description of the future victory of the coming king [Num. 24:17] draws heavily on God's words of promise and judgment spoken to the serpent in Genesis 3:15.[14]

The readers of these texts continue to be drawn forward in anticipation of this coming one.

At the end of the Pentateuch, Moses speaks of a future prophet that God will raise up from among his people. This prophet is differentiated from those who speak falsely on God's behalf (Deut. 13); rather he will speak all that God commands (18:15, 18). While prophets have been seen previously in the Pentateuch (Gen. 20:7; Num. 11:29; 12:6–8), and there is certainly a line of prophets in the Old Testament that speak God's words faithfully, Moses's prophetic office was unique in certain ways (Num. 12:8). Thus, while this passage can allude to a declaration of God's establishment of the prophetic office in Israel, it also seems to point beyond that, promising "the coming of the great prophet who is the Messiah."[15] This reading is supported by the New Testament (John 6:14; 7:40; Acts 3:19–23), and even within the Old Testament itself this passage was taken to refer to a specific individual who was to come (Deut. 34:10).[16] As such, the Pentateuch guides the reader toward

---

12. Sailhamer, *Pentateuch as Narrative*, 408.
13. Dempster, *Dominion and Dynasty*, 116.
14. Sailhamer, *Pentateuch as Narrative*, 408–9. See also Blaising and Bock, *Progressive Dispensationalism*, 217–18; Dempster, *Dominion and Dynasty*, 116–17; Schreiner, *King in His Beauty*, 77–78; and Trent Hunter and Stephen J. Wellum, *Christ from Beginning to End: How the Full Story of Scripture Reveals the Full Glory of Christ* (Grand Rapids: Zondervan, 2018), 152–53;
15. John Currid, *A Study Commentary on Deuteronomy* (Webster: Evangelical, 2006), 322.
16. Sailhamer writes in support of this point, "In Deuteronomy 34:10, for example, the final words of the book recall the promise of Moses in 18:18 and look far into the future to a single individual for its fulfillment. Thus by the

greater understanding of the identity of the seed of the woman, prompting great anticipation of his arrival.

Messiah in the Prophets

Israel comes into the land of Canaan and settles there. The priesthood is established, judges are put in place to lead God's people, and eventually the kings of Israel govern the nation under God's sovereign rule. The kingship of Saul passes and, in many ways, is unsuccessful as he fails to walk in the ways of Yahweh (1 Sam. 9:1–31:13). While David also demonstrates his propensity toward sin (e.g., 2 Sam. 11:1–27), he is still a king that pleases God and to whom virtually every other king in Israel would be compared. After several military victories and the triumph of the ark being brought back to Jerusalem (2 Sam. 2:1–6:23), God makes a covenant with David.

God promises David that he will make his name great (2 Sam. 7:9), "plant" Israel in the land (7:10), and give them victory over their enemies and rest (7:11). Moreover, God promises to make David a "house" (dynasty) by means of his seed (7:12). David's son would build God a temple, and God would "establish the throne of his kingdom forever" (7:13). God would relate to David's seed as a father relates to his son (7:14) and his steadfast love would not depart from him (7:15; cf. 1 Chron. 1–15). Dempster states, "David will not build a house for Yahweh (his son will), but Yahweh will build a house for David, a royal house, that is, a dynasty. This Davidic covenant establishes and confirms a relationship with David and God in which David is regarded as a son and God as a father, and in this relationship lies the key to Israel's national redemption and ultimately the world's as well."[17] God's mercy will not be removed from David's house, culminating in a particular seed, a son, who as a representative and mediator is faithful to God's purposes and accomplishes his will in totality. This covenant promise clearly builds upon the covenant with Abraham, in that

---

time the last verses of Deuteronomy were attached to the Pentateuch, these verses in Deuteronomy 18 were already being understood eschatologically and messianically." Sailhamer, *Pentateuch as Narrative*, 456.

17. Dempster, *Dominion and Dynasty*, 143. According to Wellum: "Within the covenant with Israel, God covenants with King David and his sons by making two main promises: to relate to the Davidic kings as a father to a son (2 Sam. 7:14; 1 Chron. 17:13; cf. Psalm 2; 89:26–27) and to establish David's house forever (2 Sam. 7:12–16; 1 Chron. 17:11–14). The sonship that was applied to the nation of Israel (Exod. 4:22–23; cf. Hos. 11:1) is now applied to David and his sons. As an individual, the Davidic king takes on the representative role of Israel as a nation. The king of Israel becomes the administrator and mediator of God's covenant with Israel, thus representing God's rule to the people and representing the people as a whole to God (2 Sam. 7:22–24). And this representative role of the Davidic king takes on significant implications for the coming of God's kingdom when God himself promises, "your house and your kingdom shall be made sure forever before me. Your throne shall be established forever" (v. 16). The eternal reign of the Davidic king, moreover, takes on a universal dimension. The Davidic covenant further narrows and defines the lineage of the promised offspring of Eve and Abraham: he will be not just any Israelite, but a king of Israel and a son of David. But the Davidic king also inherits the role of Adam as son of God and covenant head of all humanity." Wellum, *God the Son Incarnate*, 140.

David is promised a great name (2 Sam. 7:9; cf. Gen. 12:1–3) and there are also "echoes of universal blessing through his line in the rest of the Hebrew Bible."[18]

This royal, prophetic, messianic figure from the line of Abraham, Isaac, Jacob, Judah, and now David is spoken of in even greater detail throughout the Major Prophets. Summarizing Isaiah's foretelling of the Messiah, Van Groningen states, "Consider Isaiah's proclamation of the birth by a virgin (7:14), the wise, all-knowing ruling son of David (9:1–6), the fruitful branch who would bring redemption, restoration, and blessings in life (chap. 11). It was Isaiah who proclaimed that the Messiah was to be the light to the Gentiles (49:6), the suffering, exalted One (52:13–53:12). The Messiah was to be the great comforting preacher of freedom, the healer and bringer of joy (61:1–3)."[19] Isaiah 52:13–53:12 offers the reader a detailed prophetic look into the work the Messiah would accomplish on behalf of humanity. The death of the servant (Isa. 52:13) occurs in the place of others' sin, as he is offered up as a substitutionary sacrifice to propitiate God's wrath against us (53:3–5).[20] He is crushed on our behalf and offered up as a guilt offering (53:10). Thus, the servant takes the place of humanity, wounded and crushed by God the Father and thus suffers the fate that sinners deserved because of their rebellion against God.

This is essential to consider, as the notions of substitution and sacrifice link the Messiah to the Old Testament sacrificial system. Just as Israel sacrificed the Passover lamb—a substitute on behalf of their firstborn children—just prior to the exodus (Exod. 12:1–51), so too the Messiah would be offered on behalf of humanity (cf. 1 Cor. 5:7). When Isaiah states that the Servant was "pierced for our transgressions," "crushed for our iniquities," and bore chastisement and our wounds, these clearly reference the sacrifices made in Israel. Put forward as a guilt offering (Isa. 53:10; cf. Lev. 5:1–6:7), the Messiah would be a once and for all sacrifice so that we might be forgiven by God.[21] Atonement is made through his substitutionary sacrifice. This messianic prophecy in Isaiah also takes the reader back to the Day of

---

18. Dempster, *Dominion and Dynasty*, 143.
19. Van Groningen, "Messiah," 525.
20. Smith offers further detail: "The first half of the verse indicates that the reason for this suffering was 'because of our rebellion' and 'because of our iniquities.' This forthright confession of guilt plainly states that the Servant suffered the consequences for 'our' . . . sinful acts. This act was penal, for it involved a just punishment for rebellious acts. It was also substitutionary because the punishment that should have fallen on the Israelites who sinned were (*sic*) transferred instead to the Servant. The second half of the verse addresses the consequent benefits that this transfer of punishment brought to 'us.' This punishment is specifically described in the last line as 'his welts, wounds,' possibly the consequence of being beaten (53:4). The phrase, 'the punishment that brought our peace' (NIV), is an appropriate paraphrase of a construct relationship (lit 'the punishment of our peace') that expresses a genitive of purpose. This punishment was designed for the purpose of securing our peace, implying that peace was achieved with God because the just punishment he required was suffered by the Servant." Gary V. Smith, *Isaiah 40-66*, New American Commentary 15B (Nashville: B&H, 2009), 450. As such, this death signifies a substitutionary atoning sacrifice that satisfies God's wrath that stands against humanity.
21. See J. Alec Motyer, *Isaiah: An Introduction and Commentary*, Tyndale Old Testament Commentaries (Downers Grove: InterVarsity, 1999), 338.

Atonement (Lev. 16:1–34). During this holy festival in Israel two goats are taken, one to give up its life as a sin offering, the other to be a substitute who bears the sins of the nation and goes outside the camp so the people can be in right standing with God. These practices are intended to make atonement for the nation of Israel and are taken up by Isaiah in reference to the work of the servant.

As Van Groningen writes, elsewhere in the prophets:

> Micah prophesied that the Messiah was to come through the royal Davidic seedline to shepherd his people and bring them security (5:1–4). Amos likewise proclaimed that the Messiah of Davidic lineage would fulfill Yahweh's covenant promises to the nations (9:11–15). Jeremiah prophesied of the Messiah, the one of Davidic lineage who was to be the king of righteousness (23:5–6). Ezekiel called the exiles' attention to the Son of Man, the covenant mediator who would restore and shepherd his people (chapters 34 and 36). Postexilic prophets spoke of the Messiah as the royal, redeeming, restoring One to come (Hag. 2:20–22; Zech. 4:1–14; 6:9–15; 9:9–10). Malachi spoke of the Messiah as a cleansing agent who, as messenger of the covenant, would bring healing in his wings (3:1–4; 4:1–3).[22]

These are key metaphors, images, and examples that the New Testament authors would use to demonstrate how one particular individual was indeed the Messiah and fulfilled all of these prophecies and promises.

Messiah in the Writings

Additional images and details can be adduced regarding the Messiah in the Psalms. Psalm 2 refers to an anointed one, God's Son (Ps. 2:2, 7). This Son is given the nations as an inheritance and will rule with a rod of iron (2:8–9; cf. Rev. 12). All are told to bow before this anointed one, pay homage, and take refuge in him (2:10–12) since Yahweh has vested his authority in him.[23] In Psalm 16 David speaks of how God will not "abandon my soul to Sheol or let your holy one see corruption" (16:10). The feebleness of death to destroy this relationship with God is David's confidence.[24] This confidence of David would be seen not only in the death of the Messiah, but also in his being raised from the dead (cf. Acts 2:25–28; 13:35–37). Psalm 22, another psalm of David, prophesies of one who will come to suffer and die on our behalf. He speaks of being forsaken by God (22:1–2) and surrounded

---

22. Van Groningen, "Messiah," 525.

23. See C. Hassell Bullock, *Encountering the Book of Psalms: A Literary and Theological Introduction*, 2nd ed. (Grand Rapids: Baker, 2018), 22–23; Sidney Greidanus, *Preaching Christ from Psalms: Foundations for Expository Sermons in the Christian Year* (Grand Rapids: Eerdmans, 2016), 218–19.

24. See Eichrodt, *Theology of the Old Testament*, 2:524–25.

by enemies (22:12–15). These enemies pierce his hands and feet (22:16) and cast lots for his clothing (22:18), treating him with utmost contempt. This mistreatment corresponds to the Messiah's own suffering to come, though the consequences and results were far greater. In Psalm 110, David speaks as a prophet, "who declaims the enthronement oracle to the Messianic king, corresponding to the oracle given to other kings at their anointing or crowning (cf. 1 Sam. 10; 2 Kings 11:12)."[25] Yahweh speaks to David's Lord[26] and invites him to sit in enthronement, scepter in hand, over his enemies (Ps. 110:1–2). A divine oath is given that this messianic figure will not just reign as king, but also as priest, forever in the order of Melchizedek (110:4). In Melchizedek (Gen. 14:18–20) priesthood and kingship were united, as they will be in the Messiah (cf. Heb. 7:11–19).[27]

One other crucial passage found in the Writings regarding the Messiah is found in Daniel 7:13–14. Within Daniel's vision of four beasts (Dan. 7:1–8), Daniel sees the "Ancient of Days," a glorious depiction of God the Father sitting on his throne (7:9–10). Then Daniel beheld, "with the clouds of heaven there came one like a son of man, and he came to the Ancient of Days and was presented before him. And to him was given dominion and glory and a kingdom, that all peoples, nations, and languages should serve him; his dominion is an everlasting dominion, which shall not pass away, and his kingdom one that shall not be destroyed" (Dan. 7:13–14). This "son of man," whose description aligns with the other Old Testament accounts of the Messiah, will come from heaven to earth and will be given an everlasting kingdom. Since this "son of man" was "given" a kingdom and authority to rule, this scene evidently describes the coronation of the "son of man" by the Ancient of Days. As Miller writes, "According to the text, therefore, this individual will be crowned as the sovereign ruler of the world. His reign will never end."[28] Thus, as Wellum points out, "we have in this son of man who comes from heaven the promised Son-king who will bring covenantal reconciliation between God and man, restoring man's righteous vice-regent rule over God's

25. Derek Kidner, *Psalms 73-150*, Tyndale Old Testament Commentaries (Downers Grove: InterVarsity, 1973), 392.
26. The beginning of this psalm uses the terms *Yahweh* and *Adonai*, referring to two distinct people in addition to David (see the superscription and use of "my"). Ross states regarding the use of *Adonai* in 110:1, "The title emphasizes the authority and superiority of the king. A prophet addressing David as his master would not be difficult; but David was referring to his descendant as his master, which would be more unusual in dynastic pronouncements. David clearly sees this future coming king, who is the one to whom God is speaking, as his sovereign master." Allen Ross, *A Commentary on the Psalms: 90-150*, Kregel Exegetical Library (Grand Rapids: Kregel, 2016), 346. Jesus picks up on this point when addressing the religious leaders after his triumphal entry (Matt. 22:41–46).
27. Kidner, *Psalms 73-150*, 394. This is a crucial psalm in regards to understanding the role of the Messiah, and is one of the most often cited Old Testament passages in the New Testament (Matt. 22:43–45; 26:63–64; Mark 12:35–37; Luke 20:41–44; Acts 2:33–36; 5:30–31; 7:55–56; Rom. 8:34; 1 Cor. 15:24–25; Eph. 1:20–22; Heb. 1:3, 13; 8:1; 10:12–13; 12:2; 1 Peter 3:21–22). Ross confirms that these passages "refer to Jesus's exaltation between the ascension and the second advent. He now awaits the second coming to receive his kingdom (Matt. 26:64)." Ross, *Commentary on the Psalms*, 359.
28. Stephen R. Miller, *Daniel*, New American Commentary 18 (Nashville: B&H, 1994), 207.

creation."[29] The "son of man" is a favorite self-designation of the Messiah in the Gospels, and his understanding of his person and work interfaces specifically with this description (e.g., Mark 14:61–62; cf. Heb. 2:5–9).[30] The Messiah's reign would extend over all for all time.

Thus it can be seen from analyzing the Old Testament and examining how the New Testament reads the Old Testament that Jesus of Nazareth is the seed of Abraham that blesses all families of the earth (Gen. 12:2). He is the ruler from the tribe of Judah (Gen. 49:10) and the Son that establishes the house of David forever (2 Sam. 7:12–16). His virgin conception (Isa. 7:14), birth in Bethlehem (Mic. 5:2), even the date of his birth (Dan. 9:25) are foretold. His death is prophesied in exacting detail (Isa. 53; cf. Ps. 22), and David himself foresaw the resurrection of the Messiah (Ps. 16:10; cf. Acts 2:25–28). Christ is seen as the seed of the woman who crushes the seed of the serpent (Gen. 3:15; cf. Rom. 16:20). Thus, the predictive prophecies, types, and promises of the Old Testament form the indispensable background for understanding his life and ministry.

Messiah in the Gospels

"You are the Christ [i.e., Messiah, anointed one], the Son of the living God" (Matt. 16:16). These words, spoken by Peter, are "the most basic and universal Christological belief in the early church."[31] The Gospels take pains to demonstrate that Jesus is none other than the Messiah the Old Testament predicted. An exhaustive analysis of the Gospels on this matter is beyond the purview of this chapter, but certain key points will receive treatment.

Jesus is the Word who was "with God" and "was God," demonstrating his divine status, being "of one substance with the Father" (John 1:1; cf. 5:18; 8:58; 10:22–33).[32] He was born

---

29. Wellum, *God the Son Incarnate*, 164. Schreiner likewise affirms this point: "Indeed, the son of man in Daniel does not grasp rule through military conquest by which he brutally rules over other human beings. He is given the kingdom of God himself, and thereby he fulfills the role for which human beings were created (Psalm 8)." Schreiner, *New Testament Theology*, 216.

30. The phrase "son of man" is especially common in the eschatological passages of the New Testament (e.g., Matt. 16:27–28; 19:28; 24:30; 25:31). Other passages portray Christ with the same kind of glory and authority as set forth in Daniel 7 (e.g., Isa. 2:2–4; 9:6–7; 11:1–10; Ezek. 34:23–24; Matt. 28:18; Phil. 2:9–11; Rev. 19:1–10; 20:4–6). See Miller, *Daniel*, 208.

31. Michael F. Bird, *Jesus Is the Christ: The Messianic Testimony of the Gospels* (Downers Grove: InterVarsity, 2012), 1.

32. A great amount of historical detail could be supplied here, but is beyond the purview of the chapter. For work on the early church councils and their affirmation of Jesus as divine by means of his being *homoousios* (Latin: "of one substance") with the Father, see for example John Behr, *The Way to Nicaea*, Formation of Christian Theology 1 (Crestwood: St. Vladimir's Seminary Press, 2001); Behr, *The Nicene Faith*, Formation of Christian Theology 2 (Crestwood: St. Vladimir's Seminary Press, 2004); Donald Fairbairn, *Life in the Trinity: An Introduction to Theology with the Help of the Church Fathers* (Downers Grove: InterVarsity, 2009). Also, some may quibble about equating biblical language (e.g., Son of God, Son of Man, etc.) with later theological terminology (e.g., *homoousios*). Vanhoozer helpfully maintains that categories of systematic theology "preserve the same thought world of the biblical authors" in "new interpretive categories and with different conceptual terms." Vanhoozer continues and states, "Doctrine is faithful to biblical discourse not when it simply repeats the same terms and contexts but when it renders the same judgments by using different terms." See Vanhoozer, "Theology of the New Testament," 27. Vanhoozer's "concept/judgment distinction" is rooted in David S. Yeago, "The New Testament and the Nicene

of a virgin, as was prophesied (Matt. 1:18–25; Luke 1:26–38; cf. Isa. 7:14). He and his family had to flee a tyrannical ruler to avoid execution, and as God's Son he was called back to Israel (Matt. 2:13–23; cf. Hos. 11:1; Jer. 31:15).[33] At his baptism (Matt. 3:13–17; Mark 1:9–11; Luke 3:21–22; John 1:31–34) Jesus fulfilled all righteousness (Matt. 3:15), as the Spirit descended on him and God the Father, quoting Psalm 2:7 and Isaiah 42:1, identified his Son as the long awaited Messiah. Regarding this event, Wellum avers, "Jesus knew that to have the Spirit from the Father for the sake of righteousness signaled that he was the promised Messiah and that the messianic age had dawned—an age identified, as we saw in previous chapters, with God's sovereign, saving rule (Isa. 61:1–2; Luke 4:16–21; cf. Ezek. 34; Jonah 2:9). Therefore, to be the Spirit-anointed Messiah according to the storyline of Scripture is to be identified with God himself, who must act to fulfill the Old Testament expectation of redemption and restoration (Isa. 9:6–7)."[34] Thus, it is plainly seen that Christ comes as the promised Davidic Son to announce and fulfill God's covenantal promises, to save a people for himself and reign over all.[35]

In his temptation (Matt. 4:1–11; Mark. 1:12–13; Luke 4:1–13) Jesus overcomes all tests, trials, and enticement to sin, which is necessary for the Father's work to be accomplished in him.[36] As the Spirit-filled God-man, Jesus obeys God the Father where Adam, Eve, and Israel failed (Gen. 3:1–6; Deut. 6:13, 16; 8:3). The serpent did not deceive him or cause him to stumble; rather, Jesus as Messiah and our representative perfectly obeyed the Father's will and was making ready to crush his head (Gen. 3:15).

In his life, ministry, and miracles (Matt. 9:35–37), Jesus further demonstrates his messianic claims. He lived a life of perfect conformity to the will of God, fulfilling the law in every aspect (Matt. 5:17; John 17:1–5). Jesus preaches and inaugurates the kingdom of God, showing the kingdom to be both present and future. As the Davidic king (Matt. 21:1–11;

Dogma: A Contribution to the Recovery of Theological Exegesis," in *The Theological Interpretation of Scripture: Classic and Contemporary Readings*, ed. Stephen Fowl (Oxford: Blackwell, 1997), 87–100.

33. For more on this point, see Bird, *Jesus Is the Christ*, 65–67. Here he argues that Jesus is in effect beginning a new exodus for his people.

34. Wellum, *God the Son Incarnate*, 151. See also See R. T. France, *The Gospel of Matthew*, New International Commentary on the New Testament (Grand Rapids: Eerdmans, 2007), 121–22; Carson, "Matthew," 106–10; Schreiner, *New Testament Theology*, 172–73; Max Turner, *The Holy Spirit and Spiritual Gifts: In the New Testament Church and Today* (Peabody: Hendrickson, 1997), 19–30; Sinclair B. Ferguson, *The Holy Spirit*, Contours of Christian Theology (Downers Grove: InterVarsity, 1996), 45–52; Graham A. Cole, *He Who Gives Life: The Doctrine of the Holy Spirit*, Foundations of Evangelical Theology (Wheaton: Crossway, 2007), 149–77.

35. See David F. Wells, *The Person of Christ: A Biblical and Historical Analysis of the Incarnation* (Wheaton: Crossway, 1984), 39.

36. Treat maintains, "[Jesus] comes as a human to set right what Adam set wrong," obeying where Adam and Israel had not, and thus showing himself to be a faithful Son and worthy sacrifice. He continues, "Christ had to be fully human in order to save us because he had to fulfill the covenant as our representative, make an offering of atonement on our behalf, and bear the penalty in our place." See *Crucified King*, 213. See also Michael Scott Horton, *Lord and Servant: A Covenant Christology* (Louisville: Westminster John Knox, 2005), 171.

cf. Zech 9:9), Jesus makes present the kingdom of God (Matt. 12:28; Luke 17:21).[37] In other words, in Jesus the ruling and reigning power of God becomes present. Yet the theme of Jesus's parables was that his presence did not signal the immediate end of oppression, the overthrow of Rome, or the final victory of righteousness. Rather, the mustard seed must grow; the leaven must work all the way through the dough. We must wait until the harvest at the end of the age (Matt. 13:1–50). Thus, the kingdom has already been inaugurated, but not yet consummated. The point to be seen, however, is that Jesus did in fact come as the seed of Abraham, Judah, and David to rule and reign in God's kingdom.

Jesus also performed miracles. His miracles are important to note since they speak to his identity. Demons confront him and he casts them out; the sick seek him and he brings them healing (Matt. 4:23–25). Jesus performs these miracles as a sign of the presence of the kingdom of God (Matt. 12:28), as a response to human faith (Matt. 9:2, 22), because he was moved with compassion (Matt. 9:35; Luke 7:12–15) and to serve as witness to his status as the Son of God (John 2:11). His life, ministry, and miracles proclaim his status as God's anointed one sent to proclaim good news to the poor, liberty to the captive and oppressed, recovery of sight to the blind, and the year of the Lord's favor (Luke 4:18–19; cf. Isa. 61:1–2). As such, in Jesus "the saving rule and reign of God himself has finally come into the world."[38]

As the prophesied Messiah, Jesus's death and resurrection are of great significance (cf. Isa. 52:13–53:12; Ps. 16:9–11). Jesus knew his purpose and often spoke of his impending death to his disciples (Mark 8:31; 9:31; 10:33–34). Stott comments, "The Synoptic evangelists bear a common witness to the fact that Jesus both repeatedly foresaw and repeatedly foretold his coming death."[39] He came as the "lamb of God," not to be served, but to serve those in need of salvation (Matt. 20:28, Mark 10:49, John 1:29). At his last supper with his disciples, a Passover meal, Jesus institutes the Lord's Supper, which will commemorate his atoning work on behalf of humanity and his inauguration of the new covenant (Luke 22:14–20). In his death, Jesus died as a substitute on our behalf, for our sin (John 19:1–37). In his resurrection, Jesus is vindicated and death is defeated (John 20:1–10; cf. 1 Cor. 15:50–57).[40]

---

37. Goldsworthy argues, "We can grasp the idea of 'son of God' only when we see that it is inseparable from the whole structure of the kingdom of God." See Goldsworthy, *Son of God*, 71.
38. Wellum, *God the Son Incarnate*, 166. See also Carson, "Matthew," 222.
39. John R. W. Stott, *The Cross of Christ* (Downers Grove: InterVarsity, 2006), 28.
40. In summary, Wellum states, "Jesus understood, moreover, that by his death, 'everything that is written about the Son of Man by the prophets will be accomplished' (Luke 18:31). Thinking along the epochal and covenantal development of the Old Testament, Jesus knew that as the Son of God his death would bring divine judgment upon the world, depose Satan as "the ruler of this world," and install himself as king over all creation for the sake of all people (John 12:31–33). And as the Son of Man, Jesus understood that he could accomplish these divine works that would reconcile God and man because he had authority on earth to forgive sins (Mark 2:5–12; Luke 5:20–26)." Wellum, *God the Son Incarnate*, 155.

Messiah in Acts and the Letters

In the sermons contained in the book of Acts, there is ample evidence that the apostles understood Jesus of Nazareth to be the Messiah. For example, on the Day of Pentecost Peter declares to the crowd that Jesus's resurrection and heavenly enthronement are proof of his identity as Messiah (Acts 2:22–35; cf. Pss. 16:8–11; 110:1). God, Peter proclaims, "has made him both Lord and Christ, this Jesus whom you crucified" (Acts 2:36).[41] In other words, God the Father has demonstrated to all humanity through the life, death, resurrection, and ascension of Jesus that he is the Messiah whom the Old Testament prophets foretold, and that, as the expected hope of Israel, all should repent of their sin and believe in him (Acts 2:37–41). In a sermon in Acts 3, Peter refers to Jesus as God's "servant" (3:13, 26) a probable allusion to the servant figure of Isaiah 53.[42] Combining a reference to Jesus as "Christ" (3:20) alongside allusions to Jesus as the prophet (3:21–24; cf. Deut. 18:15, 18, 19) and the blessing of Abraham (3:25–26; cf. Gen. 22:18), one observes how deeply Peter roots his identification of Jesus as the Messiah in Old Testament promises.[43]

Later in Acts, Peter preaches to the Gentiles and identifies Jesus as "Jesus Christ" and "Lord of all" (10:36). He points out how God "anointed Jesus of Nazareth with the Holy Spirit and with power" (10:38) and how Jesus was whom the prophets bore witness (10:43). Another example of this can be found in Paul's preaching in Acts 13. After citing Old Testament history to his audience, Paul refers to Jesus as the offspring of David, a savior, and a promised one (13:22–23). Thus, as Marshall points out, "God has brought to Israel a savior from the seed of David in accordance with his promise. The promise probably refers to 2 Sam. 7:12 (cf. 22:51; Ps. 89:29, 36–37; 132:11), now understood to include not merely the immediate continuation of the royal line through Solomon and later kings, but also the renewal of the line in raising up the Messiah."[44] In Jesus's death and resurrection, Paul declares, the good news is that he has fulfilled "what God promised to the fathers" (Acts 13:32–33). He is the true Son of God (13:33; cf. Ps. 2:7) who has fulfilled the law (Acts 13:39) and brought about the opportunity for the forgiveness of sins through faith in him (13:38).

---

41. Bock comments concerning Jesus as "Lord" and "Christ," "The term 'Lord' in this context shows in particular Jesus's lordship over salvation and the distribution of salvation's benefits. Jesus as 'Lord' often appears in Acts (4:33; 8:16; 11:17, 20; 15:11, 26; 16:31; 19:5, 13, 17; 20:21, 24, 35; 21:13; 28:31). The sharing of the title with God led the church to apply to Jesus OT passages that were about Yahweh, as Acts 2:21 shows . . . 'Christ' is a key title for Luke (Luke 2:11, 26; 3:15; 4:41; 9:20; 20:41; 22:67; 23:2, 35, 29; 24:26, 46; Acts 2:31, 36, 38; 3:6, 18, 20; 4:10, 26; 5:42; 8:5, 12; 9:22, 34; 10:36, 48; 11:17; 15:26; 16:18; 17:3; 18:5, 28; 24:24; 26:23; 28:31). The Christ is the figure of deliverance." See Bock, *Acts*, 136.
42. Bock, *Acts*, 169. See also I. Howard Marshall, "Acts," in *Commentary on the New Testament Use of the Old Testament*, eds. G. K. Beale and D. A. Carson (Grand Rapids: Baker, 2007), 545; Ben Witherington, *The Acts of the Apostles: A Socio-Rhetorical Commentary* (Grand Rapids: Eerdmans, 1998), 179–80.
43. Bock helpfully summarizes how this depiction of Jesus in Acts 3 describes him as "the promised seed-servant-prophet-leader like Moses who is the Author of life." See *Acts*, 182.
44. Marshall, "Acts," 584.

The letters of the New Testament speak frequently to the identity of Jesus as Messiah. In Romans 1:3–4 Paul bears witness to the identity of Jesus, who was "descended from David according to the flesh and was declared to be the Son of God in power according to the Spirit of holiness by his resurrection from the dead, Jesus Christ our Lord." Wellum summarizes this passage, saying Jesus is "the eternal Son of God [who] became the incarnate Son of God to then become the Davidic Son of God through his life, death, and resurrection. The Redeemer we need—one who can undo the work of Adam, accomplish our forgiveness, and usher in God's kingdom and the new creation—must be God the Son incarnate."[45] He has offered himself as an atoning sacrifice, such that the Father is just and the justifier (Rom. 3:21–26). He is "the Christ, who is God over all" (Rom. 9:5), the source of our salvation and the object of our confession (Rom. 10:9–10).

The resurrection of the Messiah lies clearly at the heart of the Christian faith in the New Testament documents (1 Cor. 15:3–8). Without it, the cross loses its importance and, as Paul says, our faith is in vain (1 Cor. 15:17). The resurrection vindicates the work of the cross, openly proclaims Christ as God's Son (cf. Rom. 1:4; 1 Peter 1:3–4), guarantees our resurrection and victory over death (1 Cor. 15:12–57), and is the basis for Christ's ascension and exaltation.[46] Paul also reminds his readers that it is through the promised seed, Jesus Christ, that blessing comes to both Jews and Gentiles as well as our reception of the promised Holy Spirit (Gal. 3:10–16; cf. Gen. 12:1–3). Christ, as the seed of the woman (Gen. 3:15), became a curse for us and died as our satisfaction to assuage God's wrath toward our sin and bring us blessing. As such, in Jesus the Messiah, as relates to salvation, there is no differentiation between ethnicities, classes, or gender; rather, "if you are Christ's, then you are Abraham's offspring, heirs according to promise" (Gal. 3:29).[47] Jesus is the eternal divine Son who "emptied himself, by taking the form of a servant, being born in the likeness of men" (Phil. 2:7). That is, Jesus "emptied himself" by taking on a human nature, manifesting the form of God in the form of a servant (Phil. 2:6–8).[48] Because of this, the

---

45. Wellum, *God the Son Incarnate*, 174. In agreement, and speaking more specifically to the use of "son" language in this passage so as to avoid adoptionism, Schreiner concludes, "The one who existed eternally as the Son was appointed the Son of God in power as the Son of David . . . In other words, the Son reigned with the Father from all eternity, but as a result of his incarnation and atoning work he was appointed to be the Son of God as one who was now both God and man." Thomas R. Schreiner, *Romans*, Baker Exegetical Commentary on the New Testament (Grand Rapids: Baker, 1998), 38–9. See also Moo, *Romans*, 48–9.

46. See Gordon D. Fee, *The First Epistle to the Corinthians*, New International Commentary on the New Testament (Grand Rapids: Eerdmans, 1987), 746–51.

47. For more on Jesus as the seed of Abraham who brings about blessing, especially in conversation with N. T. Wright who puts emphasis on the believing community, see Jason S. DeRouchie and Jason C. Meyer, "Christ or Family as the 'Seed' of Promise: An Evaluation of N. T. Wright on Galatians 3:16," *Southern Baptist Journal of Theology* 14.3 (2010): 36–48. Therein they argue that the emphasis of the passages is "Paul's proper stress on the coming of Christ as Abraham's "seed" (v. 16) in order to enable Gentile individuals to be granted the same title (v. 29)" (36).

48. Wellum, *God the Son Incarnate*, 176–77. See also Simon J. Gathercole, *The Preexistent Son: Recovering the Christologies of Matthew, Mark, and Luke* (Grand Rapids: Eerdmans, 2006), 25; Schreiner, *New Testament Theology*, 325.

Father has exalted the Son above all (Phil. 2:9–11). Jesus is the "image of the invisible God," firstborn, sovereign ruler over all, creator, sustainer, and the one through whom all things are reconciled to God (Col. 1:15–20; 2:9).[49]

Similarly, as one comes to Hebrews and the Catholic Epistles, one finds similar exaltation of Jesus as Messiah. Jesus is the divine Son, appointed heir of all things, "the radiance of the glory of God and the exact imprint of his nature," who reigns over all and is superior to angels (Heb. 1:1–4). Thus, as Messiah, he is divine in his identity, and yet also relates to and represents his people in his humanity as their great high priest (Heb. 2:9–18; 4:14–16).[50] Jesus is the priest in the order of Melchizedek (Heb. 7:1–28; cf. Ps. 110:4) who inaugurates a new covenant (Heb. 8:1–13) by means of his perfect, once-for-all atoning sacrifice (Heb 9:1–18). In so doing, he makes a way for salvation and awaits the day when "his enemies will be made a footstool for his feet" (Heb. 10:13; cf. Ps. 110:1).[51] Jesus, as Messiah, is our atoning sacrifice and reigning king, bearing our sins as the righteous one, standing forth as the "Shepherd and Overseer" of our souls (1 Peter 2:22–25; cf. Isa. 53:4–6).

Messiah in Revelation

While people look to the final book of Scripture for many other reasons, the "Revelation of Jesus Christ" (Rev. 1:1) is intended to show God's people that who Jesus is in future days is completely aligned with the Old Testament and New Testament witness. John testifies of Jesus as "the faithful witness, the firstborn of the dead, and the ruler of kings on earth" (Rev. 1:5). Indeed, Jesus "persevered as a faithful witness to the Father in the face of persecution even to death, which he conquered, and then he became the cosmic ruler."[52] To him belongs "glory and dominion," and "he is coming with the clouds, and every eye will see him, even those who pierced him, and all the tribes of the earth will wail on account of him" (Rev. 1:6–7; cf. Dan. 7:13; Zech. 12:10).[53] He died and rose again, and he has the key of death

---

49. Tipton argues, based on these points, that the Son is the climax of the history of creation, and at the same time the starting point of the new creation, fulfilling the purposes of God in humanity and the cosmos. See Lane G. Tipton, "Christology in Colossians 1:15-20 and Hebrews 1:1-4: An Exercise in Biblico-Systematic Theology," in *Resurrection and Eschatology: Theology in Service of the Church: Essays in Honor of Richard B. Gaffin, Jr*, eds. Lane G. Tipton and Jeffrey C. Waddington (Phillipsburg: P&R, 2008), 193–94.

50. See Richard Bauckham, *Jesus and the God of Israel: God Crucified and Other Studies on the New Testament's Christology of Divine Identity* (Grand Rapids: Eerdmans, 2008), 236.

51. For more on the high volume of Old Testament quotations and allusions seen in Hebrews 7–10, see George H. Guthrie, "Hebrews," in *Commentary on the New Testament Use of the Old Testament*, edited by G. K. Beale and D. A. Carson (Grand Rapids: Baker, 2007), 968–79.

52. Beale, *Revelation*, 190.

53. Beale maintains regarding the usage of both the Daniel and Zechariah quotations and why they are found together here, "The Zechariah quotation perhaps connotes the climax of the historical process expressed in the Daniel 7 allusion. But John 19:37 quotes Zechariah 12:10 in reference to the Gentile soldier near the cross who "pierced" Jesus and then apparently repented (cf. John 19:34–37; Mark 15:39). A strikingly similar application of Zechariah 12:10 is found in Revelation 1:7. Consequently, the Zechariah 12 quotation could also include application to a

and Hades (Rev. 1:18). Thus, as Patterson points out, "Christ, through his atoning death and triumphant resurrection, has shown that he holds suzerainty even over the archenemy of the race and that he will unlock the prison doors for those who follow him."[54]

Later in the book, when looking for someone to open the scroll of God (Rev. 5:1–4), Jesus is referred to as "the Lion of the tribe of Judah" and "the Root of David" (5:5). These two descriptions of Christ are respectively taken from Genesis 49:9 and Isaiah 11:1, 10 (cf. Jer. 11:19; 23:5; 33:15; Zech. 3:8) and remind us that Jesus is the promised seed spoken of from the very beginning (Gen. 3:15). Jesus is the messianic figure who has and will conquer his enemies by means of his sacrificial death and royal reign (Rev. 5:6–14). Thus, as Beale points out, "Christ's overcoming of the enemy places him in a sovereign position to affect the divine plan of redemption and judgment, as symbolized by the opening of the book and its seals."[55] Jesus is the Lamb of God, slain for the sins of the world (Rev. 13:8), and he is the coming, conquering King (Rev. 19:11–21) who will stand in judgment over all (Rev. 20:11), "the root and the descendant of David, the bring morning star" (Rev. 22:16).

From beginning to end, the Messiah is a crucial theme within Scripture, and Jesus embodies every promise and prophecy of the Messiah in perfect measure. Within the message of Scripture, Jesus, as the promised Messiah, is the promised seed of the woman, overcomes the sin of Adam, receives and enacts the blessing of Abraham, comes forth as the true Davidic son and king, and suffers to pay the penalty for God's people and represent everyone who believes in him.[56]

---

period preceding the final parousia when Gentiles believe in the Messiah. If so, "see" would have to be taken more figuratively and perceived as future only from John's standpoint" See *Revelation*, 198.

54. Paige Patterson, *Revelation*, New American Commentary 39 (Nashville: B&H, 2012), 70.
55. Beale, *Revelation*, 350. See also Patterson, *Revelation*, 165–66.
56. See Chris Bruno, *The Whole Message of the Bible in Sixteen Words* (Wheaton: Crossway, 2017), 77.

Discussion Questions

1. The beginning of this chapter contained the following quote from James Hamilton: "The Old Testament is a messianic document, written from a messianic perspective to maintain a messianic hope." Do you agree with this assessment? Why or why not?

2. Name several Old Testament promises, prophecies, and types that point to the Messiah. Describe how they do so.

3. What is the significance of Daniel 7:13–14 (and the wider context of the entire chapter) for understanding the identity of the Messiah?

4. What were some frequent themes in the Peter's sermons in Acts 2–3 as it relates to the Messiah?

5. What role does the Messiah play in Revelation? How is he described and what does he do?

Resources for Further Study

Bird, Michael F. *Jesus Is the Christ: The Messianic Testimony of the Gospels.* Downers Grove: InterVarsity, 2013.

Cole, Graham A. *The God Who Became Human: A Biblical Theology of Incarnation.* New Studies in Biblical Theology 30. Downers Grove: InterVarsity, 2013.

Johnson, Dennis E. *Walking with Jesus through His Word: Discovering Christ in All the Scriptures.* Phillipsburg: P&R, 2015.

Wellum, Stephen J. *Christ Alone: The Uniqueness of Jesus as Savior; What the Reformers Taught . . . and Why It Still Matters.* Five Solas Series. Grand Rapids: Zondervan, 2017.

Wellum, Stephen J. *God the Son Incarnate: The Doctrine of Christ.* Wheaton: Crossway, 2016.

CHAPTER 18

SALVATION AND JUDGMENT

GOD IS A GREAT AND GLORIOUS GOD. His perfections shine forth in his creation (Ps. 19:1), his mighty deeds (Ps. 145:4–7), and his perfect word (Ps. 12:6). His glory is paramount in his own mind and will (Isa. 48:9–11) and that glory will cover the earth as the waters cover the sea (Isa. 11:9; Hab. 2:14). God's glory is displayed in his character and work in redemptive history, but is predominantly displayed in the lives of humanity by means of his judging of sin and saving of those who look to him in faith.

This can be clearly seen in a statement made by God after Israel committed idolatry with the golden calf. After making intercession for the nation, Moses asks to see God's glory (Exod. 33:8). God responds with his divine presence and by making a declaration to Moses: "The Lord, the Lord, a God merciful and gracious, slow to anger, and abounding in steadfast love and faithfulness, keeping steadfast love for thousands, forgiving iniquity and transgression and sin, but who will by no means clear the guilty, visiting the iniquity of the fathers on the children and the children's children, to the third and the fourth generation" (Exod. 34:6–7). Wagner rightly maintains, "These words are invoked repeatedly throughout Israel's sacred writings as a way of characterizing the intimate connection between God's very nature and his commitment to his people."[1] God is merciful, gracious, and loving, and he will by no means clear the guilty. He is a merciful God who upholds justice, and in this manifest love and holiness expressed toward humanity, he is glorified.

---

1. J. Ross Wagner, *Heralds of the Good News: Isaiah and Paul in Concert in the Letter to the Romans*, Supplements to Novum Testamentum 101 (Leiden: Brill, 2003), 53. For an argument that this passage serves as a paradigm, especially in the Old Testament, see Hamilton, *God's Glory in Salvation*, 133–37; Hermann Spieckermann, "God's Steadfast Love: Towards a New Conception of Old Testament Theology," *Biblica* 81 (2000): 311.

Thus, as Hamilton maintains, "Yahweh's steadfast love and refusal to clear the guilty, then, are intrinsic to his identity and inform everything he does."[2] Salvation refers to God taking the initiative to rescue a people from sin and its consequences.[3] Judgment carries the idea of "setting things to rights," especially as it relates to the standard God has set forth in Scripture.[4] God is both holy (Isa. 6:3) and loving (1 John 4:7–12), and therefore these qualities of salvation and judgment are intrinsic to his very nature. They serve as a crucial "dual theme" in the Bible, giving explanatory power to the way in which God is at work amongst humanity and creation from Genesis to Revelation.

Salvation and Judgment in the Law

The biblical narrative begins with God's creation of the universe, climaxing in the creation of humanity (Gen. 1).[5] Man and woman are created in God's image to reflect his glory and exercise dominion over the face of the earth (Gen. 1:26–28). God blesses Adam and Eve, who are to function as his vice-regents, and places them in a garden where they will experience blessing and God's presence, provided they obey God's command to not eat from one particular tree in the garden (Gen. 2:15–17). They, however, succumb to temptation, rebel, and eat from the tree of the knowledge of good and evil (Gen. 3:1–7). While the prospect of death—along with other negative results of the fall—is made clear as a consequence (Gen. 3:8–19), what the reader sees happen at that moment is the exile of Adam and Eve from Eden (Gen. 3:23–24).

God proclaims, due to Adam and Eve's choice to rebel against his command, that humans are now in a sinful state, and, seemingly, if they eat from the tree of life they will live forever in this state (Gen. 3:22). Therefore, he drives Adam and Eve from the garden of Eden and places an angel at the entrance of the garden to keep people from partaking of the tree of life (Gen. 3:23–24). Thus, God removes humanity from his blessing, immediate presence, and protection.[6] In other words, he renders judgment.

If the story ended there it would be a rather morbid conclusion; however, there is hope to be seen in this passage, as well as God's gracious character in his salvific work. He promises that the seed of the woman will come and crush the head of the serpent (Gen. 3:15). As such, "Adam and Eve's only hope of salvation is the judgment that God promises will fall on the

---

2. Hamilton, *God's Glory in Salvation*, 63.
3. Bruce Demarest, *The Cross and Salvation: The Doctrine of Salvation*, Foundations of Evangelical Theology (Wheaton: Crossway, 1997), 26.
4. See J. A. Motyer, "Judgment," in *New Dictionary of Biblical Theology*, eds. T. Desmond Alexander and Brian S. Rosner (Downers Grove: InterVarsity, 2000), 613.
5. Select portions of this chapter, especially pertaining to the theme of judgment, are derived from Kimble, *Church Discipline*, 16–62. Used by permission of Wipf and Stock Publishers.
6. See John H. Sailhamer, "Genesis," in *The Expositor's Bible Commentary* (Grand Rapids: Zondervan, 1990), 94.

snake through their seed."[7] God would bring about salvation by means of judgment. House also asserts, "With the consequences of sin clearly stated and with a long-term promise of the serpent's defeat in place, God acts in mercy to sustain the fallen couple. God clothes them (3:21). The Lord also removes them from the garden to protect them from eating of the tree of life, which had not been forbidden previously, so that they will not live forever in a sinful condition (3:22–24). Not even their sin can separate them from God's concern for and commitment to the well-being of the people he has created."[8] God, therefore, demonstrates his justice and grace, showing that sin is a grotesque affront to his holiness, while also providing for humanity in a temporal and eternal fashion.[9]

The themes of salvation and judgment are seen throughout the remainder of the Pentateuch. In Exodus God saves his people Israel by judging Egypt, a people who reject Yahweh, typified in Pharaoh (Exod. 4–12; see especially 5:2). Both Israel and Egypt would recognize by means of his salvation and judgment that he is Lord of all (Exod. 6:1–8; 7:5; 14:18). When Israel rebels against God in the wilderness and at Sinai, God brings about judgment because of sin (Exod. 32:1–35). However, for the glory of his name, God shows mercy to the people in not wiping them out completely (Exod. 32:7–14; 33:12–17). This pattern is seen throughout Israel's history.

The book of Leviticus begins by addressing the laws that relate to the various kinds of sacrifices that will be offered on a consistent basis by the nation of Israel (Lev. 1:1–6:7). The priests serve in accordance with God's holy law (Lev. 6:8–7:38), mediating between the nation of Israel and God.[10] Aaron and his sons, Nadab and Abihu, are consecrated as priests, and they offer sacrifices as God requires (Lev. 8:1–9:22). In response to this obedient act of worship, God displays his glory to all the people by consuming the sacrifices with fire, denoting his approval of the offerings, and all the people bow in worship (Lev. 9:23–24).[11] In the institution of the sacrificial system, God has brought about a way for people to atone

---

7. Hamilton, *God's Glory in Salvation*, 80. See also Calvin, who asserts that, for Adam, a "solemn excommunication" was administered not so the Lord would cut him off from all hope of salvation, but rather would cause individuals to seek new assistance elsewhere. He continues, "From the moment in which he became alienated from God, it was necessary that he should recover life by the death of Christ, by whose life he then lived." John Calvin, *Genesis*, Crossway Classic Commentaries (Wheaton: Crossway, 2001), 51.

8. House, *Old Testament Theology*, 66.

9. Ciampa argues that the arc of redemptive history can be seen in the pattern of "sin, exile, and restoration," both at a macro-level, as well as various micro-levels. Roy E. Ciampa, "The History of Redemption," in *Central Themes in Biblical Theology: Mapping Unity in Diversity*, ed. Scott J. Hafemann and Paul R. House (Grand Rapids: Baker, 2007), 254–308.

10. See Gordon J. Wenham, *The Book of Leviticus*, New International Commentary on the Old Testament (Grand Rapids: Eerdmans, 1979), 4.

11. One can note a key trajectory here. In Exodus 24 the glory of the Lord rests on the mountain at Sinai. In Exodus 40 the glory of the Lord fills the tabernacle, indicating that the tabernacle has become a portable Sinai. Now in Leviticus 9 the presence of God's glory indicates that God has established and approved the sacrificial system. See Mark F. Rooker, *Leviticus*, New American Commentary 3A (Nashville: B&H, 2000), 154.

for sin, saving them from its dire consequences by placing the judgment on an unblemished animal, if they come with contrition and faith.[12]

What we see here is an example of the display of God's glory in salvation and a proper response by God's people. However, this correct response is soon overshadowed by rejection, disobedience, and judgment. While the details are somewhat obscure, Nadab and Abihu, the sons of Aaron, offer unauthorized fire before the Lord (Lev. 10:1; cf. 16:1; Num. 3:4; 26:61; 1 Chron. 24:2). As the fire of God went out in approval in Leviticus 9:24 to celebrate the obedient priestly response to God's instructions for the inauguration of the priesthood, so here it is meted out in judgment as a response to disobedience (Lev. 10:2). God gives the reason for this, saying, "Among those who are near me, I will be sanctified, and before all the people I will be glorified" (Lev. 10:3). This narrative reminds the reader that God demands to be worshipped according to his prescribed means, and the leaders of Israel must take this seriously and pursue holiness (Lev. 11:44–45) lest he break out against them (cf. Exod. 19:22).[13] Again, one can observe God glorifying himself in kind reception of the obedient worship of Israel, and in proportionate judgment toward sin.

Following the history of the nation of Israel further into the Pentateuch, one can observe various moments of grumbling and rebellion. One particular episode comes on the heels of spies being sent into Canaan, the majority of who pessimistically report about the impossibility of conquering the people there (Num. 13:1–33). The people raise a loud cry, weep, and grumble against Moses and Aaron, calling for a return to Egypt where they had been in captivity (Num. 14:1–4). Moses and Aaron fall on their faces, and Joshua and Caleb call for renewed faith in the power of God to bring them into the land, but at this point the people are ready to stone the faithful outliers (Num. 14:5–10a). As the execution is about to commence, the glory of God appears at the tent of meeting to all of Israel and God speaks, ready to exact holy wrath on the people for their lack of faith in him (Num. 14:10b–12).

Moses intercedes for the people, reminding God of his covenant, power, and character (Num. 14:13–19; note the quotation of Exod. 34:6–7 in v. 18 and the appeal there to the glory of God displayed in mercy). However, the Lord is incensed because the people have seen the display of his glory numerous times—both in Egypt and in the wilderness—and yet they have rejected him (Num. 14:20–25). He pardons the people, in that he will not wipe them out and start over again with Moses (Num. 14:12), and in this way displays his glory through forgiveness and grace. However, God does not stop there. He states, "But truly, as

12. For more on the idea of sacrificial, substitutionary atonement, see David Peterson, ed., *Where Wrath and Mercy Meet: Proclaiming the Atonement Today* (Carlisle: Paternoster, 2001); S. Jeffery, Michael Ovey, and Andrew Sach, *Pierced for Our Transgressions: Rediscovering the Glory of Penal Substitution* (Wheaton: Crossway, 2007), 42–50, 214–15; 226–28; Frank S. Thielman, "Atonement," in *Central Themes in Biblical Theology: Mapping Unity in Diversity*, ed. Scott J. Hafemann and Paul R. House (Grand Rapids: Baker, 2007), 102–27.
13. See Wenham, *Leviticus*, 26.

I live, and as all the earth shall be filled with the glory of the Lord, none of the men who have seen my glory and my signs that I did in Egypt and in the wilderness, and yet have put me to the test these ten times and have not obeyed my voice, shall see the land that I swore to give to their fathers. And none of those who despised me shall see it" (Num. 14:21–23). The people have seen his glory manifested numerous times and disdained it. God showed grace, but with the surety of his existence and the end-time covering of the earth with his glory, he declares that this generation will not enter Canaan, the land promised to them.[14]

At this point, God's chosen people are not acting in accordance with what the display of his glory should produce. It is God's kindness that leads us to repentance (Rom. 2:4), and thus his mercy and grace should lead them to a life lived in obedience to him. In their rejection and lack of faith, they are not positioning themselves to reflect the glory of God as image-bearers, to see his glory and salvation extend to the ends of the earth. God thus rebukes and judges his people for their lack of conformity to his ways, and, eventually, God will call on a new generation to respond rightly and reflect his glory.

Eventually the first generation of Israel freed from Egypt dies off without inheriting the land, and a new generation comes of age. Having established the boundaries of the land, leadership structure, as well as the standard for the people's worship, moral virtue, and life together as the people of God, Israel is now called to prepare to depart into Canaan. Deuteronomy begins with a recounting of Israel's history (1:1–3:29),[15] followed by the stipulations of the law (4:1–26:19), the specific blessings and curses that will accompany obedience to this law or lack thereof (27:1–30:20), and the arrangement of succession in leadership from Moses to Joshua (31:1–34:12). Fundamentally, these stipulations found in Deuteronomy appear to flow from the command to Israel to love the Lord with their entire being (6:1–9).[16]

Moses reminds the people of Mount Sinai and the way God spoke and revealed his glory to them (Deut. 5:24). He then goes further and shows that while they have seen God's glory, especially in the tabernacle, now they will see how the Promised Land itself will be the abode of his glory. Specifically, in reference to Israel's worship (Deut. 12:5, 11, 21) and the giving of tithes (Deut. 14:22–24) and the celebration of various festivals (Deut. 16:2, 6, 11), there is the mention of the "name of the Lord" dwelling among his people (cf. Pss. 90:1; 91:9, which state that God actually is the dwelling place of his people). While not specified precisely in this context, this land will be set apart for God's people as distinctive from the nations who do not know God. The reader can also look ahead and see that God's name (i.e.,

---

14. Hamilton concurs: "Mercy will be shown [to Israel], but it will be a mercy that comes through judgment. Israel will not be wiped out—mercy—but the generation that came out of Egypt will die in the wilderness—judgment (14:22–23, 29)." Hamilton, *God's Glory in Salvation*, 116.
15. Millar points out that this section "is not simply a history lesson," but is intended to remind Israel of their past failures and motivate them toward obedience of God and his commands. Millar, *Now Choose Life*, 70.
16. Alexander, *Promised Land*, 167.

glory) will reside in Jerusalem in the temple (2 Chron. 7:1–3). In making his name dwell in a particular place amongst a particular people, God is again establishing a dwelling place—specifically, a kingdom—for his glory to be displayed, received, and reflected, wherein he will judge his enemies and save his people.

After highlighting the distinctiveness of God dwelling in the land, reiterating the precepts of the law, and pronouncing both the covenant blessings (i.e., salvation) and curses (i.e., judgment) for obedience and disobedience respectively, Moses declares a song to the Lord (Deut. 32:1–47). Here Moses directs attention to the name of the Lord and greatness of God (Deut. 32:3). He wants to take one last opportunity to proclaim to Israel that God is a glorious God, no one is like him, that God would be faithful both to save and to judge, and that the nation must learn from its history and respond accordingly.[17] The Lord God is a rock (Deut. 32:4; cf. 32:15, 18, 30; Hab. 1:12), perfect in character (Ps. 18:30), just (Dan. 4:37), upright (Ps. 111:7), faithful (Isa. 25:1), and without iniquity (Hab. 1:13). And yet, Israel has repaid his upright character and work in their lives with rebellion, though they are the heritage of the Lord (Deut. 32:5–9). While God cared for Israel (Deut. 32:10–14), they forsook and scoffed at God as they revered idols instead (Deut. 32:15–18). This rejection of God's glory for the sake of idols earned the Lord's righteous anger and judgment (Deut. 32:19–38).

God, however, would not be finished with his people, as Moses recounts. Similar to Moses' dialogue with God at Horeb (Exod. 32:11–14), God declares that he did not wipe out his people to demonstrate to the enemies of his people that they were not in control (Deut. 32:26–27). God orchestrated all things in the work he did in and through his people, showing both judgment and mercy, revealing the greatness of his glory. He would in fact bring judgment on his people for disobedience according to his covenant with them (Deut. 32:28–30), but he would also deliver them from the hand of their enemies (Deut. 32:31–42). He would work within his people new hearts (Deut. 30:6; cf. 10:16). God calls all nations to look to him and see that he is the only God, he is sovereign, he will deliver his people, and take vengeance on his enemies (Deut. 32:39, 43). Thus, as the God who brings about salvation and judgment he is worthy of all worship, and humanity must come to God on his terms to avoid his wrath and come under his saving grace.

Salvation and Judgment in the Prophets

In Joshua 1 God calls Joshua, the new leader of Israel, to focus on the truth of his Word and to "be strong and courageous" (Josh. 1:6, 7, 9) as he guarantees his presence with Israel (Josh. 1:5, 9). The people cross the Jordan on dry ground (Josh. 3:5–17), much like the

---

17. Vogt affirms this reading of Deuteronomy, stating, "At the core of Deuteronomy is a theology of the supremacy of Yahweh, expressed in the life of Israel through adherence to Torah." Peter T. Vogt, *Deuteronomic Theology and the Significance of Torah: A Reappraisal* (Winona Lake: Eisenbrauns, 2006), 5–6.

crossing of the Red Sea, as God continues to provide for his people. In this way, God demonstrates his presence among them and shows he will provide them blessing and salvation by means of the judgment of the Canaanites.[18] The peoples of the land must be removed because of their wickedness (Deut. 9:5) and so that their idolatrous ways do not spread and contaminate Israel (Deut. 20:16–18). Israel must also be faithful to God's ways, lest the judgment that will befall the Canaanites come upon them.[19]

As the conquest takes place and the land is divided between the various tribes of Israel (Josh. 13–22), Joshua reminds the people of God's greatness and his mighty acts done on their behalf and exhorts them to be strong and serve God alone, lest they face judgment (Josh. 23:1–13). Joshua recounts the faithfulness of God that has been shown to Israel from the days of Abraham and calls the people to covenant fidelity (Josh. 24:1–15). The people declare that they will indeed follow the Lord and serve him alone (Josh. 24:16–18), but Joshua tells the people they are not able to serve God since he is "a holy and jealous God" (Josh. 24:19). This moment serves as a replay of the people's covenant commitment at Sinai, where Moses tells the people to choose life (Deut. 30:11–14), though they do not have the heart to do so (Deut. 29:4; cf. 30:6).[20] Waltke rightly asserts, "Ironically, their confession of fidelity is at the same time a confession of their infidelity. They trust themselves, not I AM, to keep faith . . . The book of Joshua implicitly looks forward to the need for a new covenant even as the book of Deuteronomy explicitly prophesies a new covenant after exile."[21] These episodes preview the way God would bring about the judgment of his people, bring them through that judgment, and then accomplish salvation on their behalf.

The narrative picks up in Judges where Israel continues to take portions of the land of Canaan (Judg. 1:1–26), but also fail to "drive out" the people from these portions of the land (Judg. 1:27–36). As a result of their disobedience, an angel pronounces judgment on the Israelites and declares that God would not drive out the Canaanites, but that they would become thorns in the sides of Israel (Judg. 2:1–3). The author then unveils a cycle repeated throughout the book (2:11–3:6): sin, judgment, pleading with God, salvation, temporary obedience to God, and then back to sin.

Throughout Judges, whether its narrative speaks of Othniel (Judg. 3:7–11), Ehud (3:12–30), Shamgar (3:31), Deborah and Barak (4:1–5:31), Gideon (6:1–8:35), Tola (10:1–2), Jair (10:3–4), Jephthah (10:6–12:7), Ibzan (12:8–9), Elon (12:11–12), Abdon (12:13–15), or Samson (13:1–16:31), God keeps his word in saving and judging his people (Deut. 31:16–21). Israel

---

18. For more on this point, particularly in showing how this event serves as a polemic against the power of Baal, see J. Michael Thigpen, "Lord of All the Earth: Yahweh and Baal in Joshua 3," *Trinity Journal* 27 (2006): 245–54.
19. This is the case with the account of Achan in Joshua 7 where Israel is defeated in battle by the Canaanites because of Achan's violation of the covenant to not take any goods from Jericho.
20. Hamilton, *God's Glory in Salvation*, 153.
21. Waltke, *Old Testament Theology*, 533.

does evil in the sight of the Lord, and God responds—as he said he would—by strengthening an enemy to stand against Israel. After years of oppression the people cry out to God for deliverance,[22] and God has mercy (cf. Deut. 4:29; 30:2; 32:36) on his people by bringing about a judge to deliver them. Once the judge delivers Israel, the land has "rest" for a time, until Israel chooses to rebel once again.[23] By the end of the book it is clear that the people have no king, and everyone does what is right in their own eyes (Judg. 17:6; 18:1; 19:1; 21:25). God was faithful to save his people from oppression by means of judges, but he would surely judge them when they rebelled and worshipped other gods. As such, the book of Judges anticipates the days of a king over Israel, who would guide them toward obedience, know God's law, and uphold it within the land (Deut. 17:14–20).[24]

The book of Samuel is structured around three distinct, but topically overlapping poems (1 Sam. 2:1–10; 2 Sam. 1:19–27; 2 Sam. 22:1–23:7). These poems remind the reader that God judges the proud and saves the humble. More specifically, Hamilton observes, "Reversal is the rhyme and rhythm of these poems: the mighty, handsome, and seemingly impressive people of the world (such as Peninnah, Saul, Goliath, and Absalom) are exposed as bankrupt, while the small, weak, infertile, and unimpressive (such as Hannah, Samuel, Jonathan, and David) are exalted."[25] The book's narrative is designed to show the greatness of God and the way he humbles the proud, like Saul, and exalts the humble, like David. The king of Israel, functioning as God's representative, is responsible for leading the people toward obedience. When they go astray, the nation is quick to follow, and judgment is rendered. However, when the king obeys the instruction of God, the people flourish under God's saving grace. Even David, the prototype of coming righteous kings, fails and comes under divine judgment (see 2 Sam. 11–20). But through his confession of sin, David is forgiven by God and God's grace shines through David and Bathsheba's offspring, Solomon (2 Sam. 12:25).

The book of Kings describes the covenant blessings and curses (Deut. 28–30) that come to Israel and Judah based on their obedience or disregard for the law. After Solomon's reign—who displayed obedience to God's law early in his reign (1 Kings 1–10), but later

---

22. After Jephthah there is no indication that the people cry out to God when they are oppressed by an enemy. Waltke observes the deterioration of Israel's character throughout the book of Judges. See *Old Testament Theology*, 601. See also Gregory T. K. Wong, *Compositional Strategy of the Book of Judges: An Inductive, Rhetorical Study*, Supplements to Vetus Testamentum 111 (Leiden: Brill, 2006), 158–85.
23. Hamilton asserts, "This rest enjoyed by the land resonates with God's rest upon the completion of his work—shades of Eden." See *God's Glory in Salvation*, 156.
24. For more on this point see Alexander, *Servant King*, 47; Dempster, *Dominion and Dynasty*, 133; Eugene H. Merrill, *Everlasting Dominion: A Theology of the Old Testament* (Nashville: B&H, 2006), 423–24.
25. Hamilton, *God's Glory in Salvation*, 158. See also Robert D. Bergen, who states regarding the first of these poems, "Hannah's prayerful song eloquently affirms core concepts of Israelite faith: the Lord is the great judge and overseer of human destinies and a rewarder of those who earnestly seek him (cf. Heb. 11:6). He is the source of empowerment and victory for those who fear him, but for all others he is the overpowering authority who dispenses fearful judgment." See *1, 2 Samuel*, New American Commentary 7 (Nashville: B&H, 1996), 75.

had his heart turned toward idols by his many wives (1 Kings 11)—the land is split into the Northern (Israel) and Southern (Judah) Kingdoms. In the Northern Kingdom, Israel is ruled by nineteen kings, and not one of them lives an obedient life before God. Instead they commit idolatry, follow the ways of pagans, and lead the people astray, despite the best efforts of prophets such as Elijah (1 Kings 17–2 Kings 2) and Elisha (2 Kings 2–8). Israel is eventually conquered by Assyria (2 Kings 17:1–6) because they did not obey God's commands and would not listen to his prophets, but plunged into sin and idolatry instead (2 Kings 17:7–23). House summarizes, "Israel's most fundamental error all along has been covenant breaking, the most obvious manifestation of which is idolatry. The people forgot the exodus and all it stood for: God's power and grace, God's acts on their behalf, and their responsibility to reciprocate God's goodness with faith, undivided allegiance, and pure worship. Instead, they worshiped local deities, adopted corrupt ethical practices, and ignored the Lord's prophets who were sent to warn them. By the time God's patience was exhausted and judgment fell, the rebellion was two hundred years old, thus fully mature."[26] Again, the reader can perceive that those who rely in human power, their own ingenuity, and other gods will be judged, while those who rely on God will be saved.

In the south, of the twenty kings who reign in Judah, there are eight who did what was right in the eyes of the Lord. However, like the north, eventually Judah succumbed to idolatry and God rendered judgment in the form of exile to Babylon (2 Kings 25:1–26). This narrative upholds that "Israel is a sinful people and deserves the punishment it has received from the hands of God."[27] However, the story does not end there. Speaking of the release of Jehoiachin, Israel's king who had been imprisoned by Nebuchadnezzar (2 Kings 25:27–30), House avers, "What does the writer tell the reader? Trust the Lord and find hope in him. If God can give the land once, God can give it again. If the Lord can raise up one David, another can come to take his ancestor's place. If people could be faithful during Hezekiah's and Josiah's reigns, then they can be obedient again."[28] This passage, in addition to the decree for Israel to return to the land (2 Chron. 36:22–23), and the long-awaited Messiah of God, indicates a future for Israel. Judgment falls, but mercy will come to Israel again, all because God keeps his covenant with his people.

Commenting on the events recounted in the Former Prophets,[29] the Latter Prophets assert that the people have put themselves under the covenant curses of God, and therefore

26. Paul R. House, *1, 2 Kings*, New American Commentary 8 (Nashville: B&H, 1996), 341.
27. See John Barton, "Historiography and Theodicy in the Old Testament," in *Reflection and Refraction: Studies in Biblical Historiography in Honor of A. Graeme Auld*, eds. Robert Rezetko, Timothy H. Lim, and W. Brian Aucker, Supplements to Vetus Testamentum 113 (Leiden: Brill, 2007), 30.
28. House, *1, 2 Kings*, 402.
29. See Dempster, *Dominion and Dynasty*, 273.

need to repent.[30] Two key themes emerge in these books that relate to salvation and judgment: the Messiah and the day of the Lord. Having already spent ample space on the theme of the Messiah,[31] it is fitting here to point to the most overt prophecy in the Old Testament regarding the Messiah that deals explicitly with salvation and judgment: Isaiah 52:13–53:12. Here, the "servant" (cf. Isa. 42; 49–50; 52–53) is mistreated and disfigured in a shocking way.[32] The physical mutilation he endures is astonishing (Isa. 52:14). He is a root out of dry ground (Isa. 53:2; cf. 11:1), despised, grief-stricken, rejected, and shunned (Isa. 53:2–3). But in this suffering, the servant bears the transgressions and sins of the people in his death (Isa. 53:4–6). The people have strayed like sheep, but God puts all their iniquity upon the servant (Isa. 53:6–7). He is cut off and makes his soul a sin offering, and in this way satisfies God's wrath against his people. Through the divine judgment that falls on the servant the people are saved.

The day of the Lord is a frequent theme in the prophets (Isa. 2:6–22; 13:1–22; 22:1–25; 24:1–23; 34:1–17; Jer. 25:30–38; 46:1–12; Ezek. 7:1–27; 38:1–39:29; Joel 1:1–20; 2:1–11, 28–32; 3:1–21; Amos 5:16–27; Obad. 1–21; Nah. 1:1–15; Hab. 3:1–16; Zeph. 1:1–18; 2:1–15; 3:8–13; Zech. 12:1–9; 14:1–15; Mal. 3:1–5; 4:1–3) and denotes judgment for God's enemies, as well as salvation for his people (Zeph. 3:11–13). Specific imagery, such as darkness and gloom, earthquakes, fire, terror, labor pains, famine, desolation, as well as repentance and salvation, accompanies these various texts when speaking of this day to come. The prophets often point to present-day circumstances wherein God acts in their midst, yet also foretell a great day when God's eschatological judgment of his enemies and salvation of his people will take place.[33]

Salvation and Judgment in the Writings

The Writings take up the theme of salvation and judgment through worship, wisdom, and historical narratives. The Psalms focus on the Torah and the coming messiah frequently (for the former category see e.g., Psalms 1, 19, 119; for the latter category see e.g., Psalms 2, 22, 110, 118). Introducing the entire Psalter,[34] Psalms 1 and 2 offer delight-filled medita-

---

30. Noting the pattern of salvation and judgment, Hamilton summarizes the "story" of the Latter Prophets as follows: "Isaiah—After the judgment of the exile, Yahweh will return to Zion in glory, and a shoot from the stump of Jesse will reign in Edenic splendor. Jeremiah—After the judgment of the exile, Yahweh will make a new covenant with his people, and a righteous branch from David will be called 'Yahweh is our righteousness.' Ezekiel—After the judgment of the exile, Yahweh will inhabit his eschatological temple, and 'his servant David shall be king over them.' The Twelve—Hosea-Micah: Denunciation of covenant and cosmic sin; Nahum-Zephaniah: Announcement of covenant and cosmic punishment; Haggai-Malachi: Announcement of covenant and cosmic restoration." Hamilton, *God's Glory in Salvation*, 191.
31. For more on the theme of Messiah, see chapter seventeen.
32. For a helpful summary of this section of Isaiah and the irony of the suffering of the servant, see John N. Oswalt, "The Book of Isaiah: A Short Course in Biblical Theology," *Calvin Theological Journal* 39.1 (2004): 65–66.
33. For more textual detail on the day of the Lord, see Craig A. Blaising, "The Day of the Lord: Theme and Pattern in Biblical Theology," *Bibliotheca Sacra* 169.1 (2012): 3–19.
34. Many argue that these psalms function as a lens through which the rest of the book is to be read. See, for example, Jamie A. Grant, *The King as Exemplar: The Function of Deuteronomy's Kingship Law in the Shaping of the Book of*

tions on God's Word (1:2) and the call to serve the Lord and pay homage to his Son (2:7–12). The wicked will not be found innocent before God and will be judged (1:4–6). Those who refuse to submit to God and take counsel against him (2:1–3) will be held in derision by God and experience his fury (2:4–5). However, those who look to God's king will inherit the nations and the ends of the earth as their possession (2:6–9),[35] and those who serve and take refuge in him will receive salvation (2:10–12). Throughout the remainder of the Psalter, God's people are called to continually meditate on God's Word and happily submit to the coming messiah. In this way salvation will come, but the wicked who refuse to follow this course will be judged by God.

The prominent call in Proverbs is "Hear, my son" (Prov. 1:8, 10, 15; 2:1; 3:1, 11; 4:1, 20; 5:1; 6:1, 20; 7:1; 10:1; 13:1; 15:20; 19:13, 26, 27; 23:15, 19, 24, 26; 24:13, 21; 27:11; 28:7; 31:2). There is wisdom to be imparted and one must be ready to receive it. The fear of the Lord is "the beginning of wisdom" (1:7), and this fear of God leads one away from the path of fools, who will inherit destruction, to the path of life, obedience, and reward (e.g., 8:1–9:13).[36] Books like Job and Ecclesiastes remind us, however, that while reward and life come through wisdom and obedience, God does not always save and judge at the exact pace one would prefer. Instead, we must wait on the Lord and continue to fear God and walk in faithfulness (Job 1:22; 2:7; 40:3–5; Eccl. 1:2; 12:13–14). There are times when "the man of faith has to live with crushing questions,"[37] but the people of God must entrust themselves to the Lord and his promises of judgment and salvation.

Song of Songs shows "the Solomonic king, who is seed of the woman, seed of Abraham, seed of Judah, seed of David, overcoming the alienation of the fall [i.e., judgment] and renewing the intimacy of Eden [i.e., salvation]."[38] The book of Ruth depicts famine in the land in the days of the judges (Ruth 1:1), which leads to loss and bereavement for Naomi. Yet God works through these circumstances to bring about mercy and new life as Boaz, an unexpected kinsman-redeemer from the tribe of Judah, marries the Moabite Ruth who

---

Psalms, Society of Biblical Literature Academia Biblica 17 (Atlanta: Society of Biblical Literature, 2004), 10, 41–70, 230–31; Hamilton, *God's Glory in Salvation*, 280–82; John H. Walton, "Psalms: A Cantata about the Davidic Covenant," *Journal of the Evangelical Theological Society* 34.1 (1991): 23–24.

35. See Blaising and Bock, *Progressive Dispensationalism*, 217–18.

36. Proverbs 1–9 has an introductory structure that exhorts the hearer to choose the path of wisdom rather than folly, noting the reward that comes with wisdom. For detail on the chiastic structure of Proverbs 1–9, see Bruce K. Waltke, *The Book of Proverbs: Chapters 1-15*, New International Commentary on the Old Testament (Grand Rapids: Eerdmans, 2004), 12. The remainder of Proverbs offers more specific detail about the nature and content of wisdom.

37. Robert S. Fyall, *Now My Eyes Have Seen You: Images of Creation and Evil in the Book of Job*, New Studies in Biblical Theology 12 (Downers Grove: InterVarsity, 2002), 37.

38. Hamilton, *God's Glory in Salvation*, 307. For more on this interpretation see Iain D. Campbell, "The Song of David's Son: Interpreting the Song of Solomon in the Light of the Davidic Covenant," *Westminster Theological Journal* 62.1 (2000): 17–32; James M. Hamilton, "The Messianic Music of the Song of Songs: A Non-Allegorical Interpretation," *Westminster Theological Journal* 68.2 (2006): 331–45.

conceives and bears a son named Obed.[39] This Obed would be the grandfather of David, king of Israel (Ruth 4:13–21). Lamentations describes the judgment that has fallen on Jerusalem due to their ongoing disobedience (Lam. 1:1–3). The author of Lamentations acknowledges that Israel deserves God's judgment (Lam. 3:39–42) but rejoices that salvation will still come: "The steadfast love of the Lord never ceases; his mercies never come to an end; they are new every morning; great is your faithfulness. 'The Lord is my portion,' says my soul, 'therefore I will hope in him.' The Lord is good to those who wait for him, to the soul who seeks him" (Lam. 3:21–25).

Though never explicitly mentioned throughout the book, God works in Esther when his people are endangered and brings judgment upon Haman to save the Jews from utter destruction (Esther 7–9). Daniel, Ezra–Nehemiah, and Chronicles show how judgment has fallen on Israel (Dan. 1:1–7), describe the people's return to the land (Ezra 1:1–11), and prophesy of future salvation (Dan. 2:44; 12:1–4). Chronicles recounts the Old Testament story and ends with the exile and judgment of Judah, but also proclaims salvation and hope in the days to come through the edict of Cyrus (2 Chron. 36:22–23).

Salvation and Judgment in the Gospels

While depictions of salvation and judgment dominate the landscape of the Old Testament, there is an intensification and narrowing of scope when the New Testament conceives these concepts, as it looks predominantly to the realm of one's spiritual status before God. Since the fall, we operate under the wrath of God (John 3:36) and need something or someone to restore our relationship with God the Father. Jesus of Nazareth, the Son of God and Son of Man, is "the Jewish Messiah who brings salvation to its climax, saving his people from their sins."[40] God the Father will bring the judgment that we deserve upon his Son in order that we might receive salvation, if we will respond to him in faith (John 14:1).

When speaking of responses to his teaching, Jesus calls us to hear his words and do them, thus building our house upon the rock and not sand (Matt. 7:24–27). People are called to receive Jesus's teaching because he is the Son of God, the Son of Man, and the Messiah sent by God. He is the cornerstone of God's new temple, but he is a stumbling block and a stone that will crush those who reject him in judgment (Luke 20:9–18; cf. Ps. 118:22).[41] While the Jewish scribes and religious leaders expect that they are the ones who will receive

---

39. See House, *Old Testament Theology*, 462; Barry G. Webb, *Five Festal Garments: Christian Reflections on the Song of Solomon, Ruth, Lamentations, Ecclesiastes, and Esther*, New Studies in Biblical Theology 10 (Downers Grove: InterVarsity, 2000), 53, 57.
40. Strauss, *Four Portraits*, 214.
41. Stein asserts, "Strongly emphasized in the account is Israel's rejection of the prophets sent to them and especially their rejection of God's Son. Israel's rejection of its Messiah, taught throughout the Gospel, will soon climax in 22:66–23:25. The coming judgment about to fall upon Israel has also been taught throughout the Gospel and will climax in the events of A.D. 70 and in the coming mission to the Gentiles when the vineyard will be given

God's salvation, Jesus speaks out against them, saying the kingdom will be taken from them, the tenants, and given to those who produce its fruits (Matt. 21:43–44).

Most prominently in the Gospels, the reader observes Jesus taking judgment upon himself for our salvation in his atoning death. The extended passion accounts in each of the Gospels demonstrate that Jesus's death and resurrection serves as the climax of the story. Jesus fulfills the prophecy of Isaiah 53 as the suffering servant who gave his life as a ransom for many (Matt. 20:28; cf. Isa. 52:14–15; 53:11–12).[42] Jesus would be "lifted up" (John 3:14; 8:28; 12:32, 34), and in so doing would save the world.[43] Hamilton summarizes:

> Jesus upholds the truth and righteousness and holiness of God's justice, establishing his covenant and redeeming with perfect equity. Balancing this is the display of mercy, love, steadfast loyalty, and kindness in the Father's plan and the willingness of Jesus to die for his people. This salvation that is achieved as judgment falls on Jesus opens the way for sins to be forgiven. . . . Those who humble themselves and pray to the Lord will find that their faith has saved them, they will go in peace, and they will have been saved through judgment to live for the kingdom Jesus brings.[44]

Thus, Jesus announces the kingdom of God (Matt. 4:17), perfectly fulfills the law (Matt. 5:17), bears the Father's wrath and makes atonement for sin (Matt. 27:32–54), is raised from the dead (Matt 28:1–10), and calls people to be saved and follow him as disciples (Matt. 28:18–20).

Salvation and Judgment in Acts and the Letters

Jesus accomplished salvation for humanity by bearing our judgment as our substitute, and the remainder of the New Testament comments and elaborates on all that he accomplished. In the life of the early church, the apostles preached sermons that proclaimed Jesus as the crucified, resurrected, and ascended Messiah. Peter states, "This Jesus, delivered up according to the definite plan and foreknowledge of God, you crucified and killed by the hands of lawless men. God raised him up, loosing the pangs of death, because it was not possible for him to be held by it" (Acts 2:23–24). Paul likewise affirms, "And when they had carried out all that was written of him, they took him down from the tree and laid him in a tomb. But God raised him from the dead, and for many days he appeared to those who had come up with him from Galilee to Jerusalem, who are now his witnesses to the people. And we bring you the good news that what God promised to the fathers, this he has fulfilled to

---

to others." Stein, *Luke*, 494. This does not mean there is not a future for ethnic Israel (cf. Rom 11:25–32), but that judgment will decisively fall.

42. Schreiner, *New Testament Theology*, 265–67.
43. Schreiner, *New Testament Theology*, 282–83.
44. Hamilton, *God's Glory in Salvation*, 404–5.

us their children by raising Jesus" (Acts 13:29–33). Again and again, salvation is declared in Acts, noting that Jesus bore our judgment, and there is a call to repent and believe in him.[45]

As one surveys the New Testament Epistles, several passages explore these two central themes. In Romans 3:21–26, Paul addresses the fact that sin cannot be shrugged off by God; rather it must be dealt with by means of an atoning sacrifice. Jesus came as this ultimate Lamb of God to bear our punishment, and thus God is both "just and the justifier of the one who has faith in Jesus" (Rom. 3:26).[46] Paul exhorts the Corinthians to pursue purity as those saved and set apart by God (1 Cor. 1:2), since "Christ, our Passover lamb, has been sacrificed" (1 Cor. 5:7; cf. Exod. 12:43–13:16; Deut. 16:1–8). Jesus, for our sake, became poor (i.e., experienced God's judgment on our behalf), so that we might become rich (i.e., experience salvation; 2 Cor. 8:9). Paul also proclaims, "Christ redeemed us from the curse of the law by becoming a curse for us—for it is written, 'Cursed is everyone who is hanged on a tree'—so that in Christ Jesus the blessing of Abraham might come to the Gentiles, so that we might receive the promised Spirit through faith" (Gal. 3:13–14; cf. Deut. 21:23). Paul thus teaches that Christ took the curse of sin upon himself and absorbed humanity's punishment.[47] By repentance and faith in Jesus's accomplished work one can be saved, but to those who refuse to turn to him, "they will suffer the punishment of eternal destruction, away from the presence of the Lord, and from the glory of his might" (2 Thess. 1:9).

Elsewhere in the Epistles, there is celebration of Jesus's accomplished work (Heb. 12:1–2) and a call to render him proper worship (Heb. 12:28–29). Jesus suffered in order to save and sanctify a people (Heb. 13:12; cf. 8:1–13). Jesus bore our sins in his body on the cross for the purpose that we would die to sin and live to righteousness (1 Peter 2:24). Christians are called to recognize the saving work of Christ and live accordingly, refuting false teaching, fleeing the judgment to come, and living in holiness (2 Peter 3:1–14).[48]

Salvation and Judgment in Revelation

The final book of the biblical canon depicts salvation and judgment in profound ways. God makes himself known to all of creation by means of increasingly intensified judgments and the final salvation of his people. The judgment of God comes upon an unbelieving

45. For further thoughts on how the salvation accomplished by Jesus connects to the beginnings of a new exodus, journeying as sojourners to our promised inheritance of a new heavens and a new earth, see David W. Pao, *Acts and the Isaianic New Exodus* (Grand Rapids: Baker, 2002).
46. See Brian Vickers, *Jesus' Blood and Righteousness: Paul's Theology of Imputation* (Wheaton: Crossway, 2006), 100.
47. See Timothy George, *Galatians*, New American Commentary 30 (Nashville: B&H, 1994), 240–42; Thomas R. Schreiner, *Galatians*, Zondervan Exegetical Commentary on the New Testament (Grand Rapids: Zondervan, 2010), 216–17.
48. See John Dennis, "Cosmology in the Petrine Literature and Jude," in *Cosmology and New Testament Theology*, eds. Jonathan T. Pennington and Sean M. McDonough, Library of New Testament Studies 355 (London: T&T Clark, 2008), 177.

world in the breaking of the seven seals (Rev. 6:1–17), the blowing of the seven trumpets (Rev. 8:6–9:21), and the pouring out of the seven bowls (Rev. 16:1–21).[49]

Babylon falls (Rev. 18:1–24), the armies arrayed against the Lord are defeated (Rev. 19:17–21), and the beast and the false prophet are overthrown (Rev. 19:20). Satan is finally conquered (Rev. 20:1–10) and those who did not believe in Christ for salvation are judged and cast into the lake of fire (Rev. 20:11–15). This place for unbelievers is described as a fiery abyss where the fire never goes out (Mark 9:43) for the wicked and unbelieving. It is an eternal fire (Matt. 25:41, 46), dark and full of weeping (Matt. 8:12). It is the place of torment (Rev. 14:10–11), a second death (Rev. 21:8), and a lake of burning sulfur (Rev. 14:10; 19:20; 20:10; 21:8). It is better to lose body parts now than go into hell forever (Matt. 5:29–30), for it is a place of eternal conscious torment.

Though God's people suffer immensely during this time of tribulation, he promises them that they will not be hurt by the second death (Rev. 2:11). Jesus returns for his bride (Rev. 19:1–10) and God will dwell with his people in a new heaven and a new earth (Revelation 21–22). This salvation is final and eternal, with God dwelling among his people.

Beale summarizes the center of Revelation and states, "The main idea of the entire book may be roughly formulated as follows: The sovereignty of God and Christ in redeeming and judging brings them glory, which is intended to motivate saints to worship God and reflect his glorious attributes through obedience to his word."[50] Revelation showcases the beauty of God's glory displayed both in salvation and judgment. The Bible is indeed God's story, and all of history functions in such a way as to show forth his greatness. From creation to consummation, God displays his glory by bringing judgment on those who refuse to bow in worship, of which he is so worthy (Revelation 4–5), and by bringing about salvation for an undeserving people by his grace.

---

49. For a comparison of these judgments to what God did in Egypt (Exodus 7–12), see Hamilton, *God's Glory in Salvation*, 547.
50. Beale, *Revelation*, 151. See also Bauckham, *Revelation*, 6; Osborne, *Revelation*, 31–32.

Discussion Questions

1. Read Exodus 34:1–7. What does this text tell us about God's attributes? How do these attributes relate to salvation and judgment?

2. How does salvation and judgment relate to the covenants God makes with his people? Read, for example, Deuteronomy 28–29 to see details regarding one covenant.

3. What is the significance of Jesus atoning work as it relates to God's saving and judging humanity?

4. What Old Testament passage or set of passages most informed and/or impacted your thinking on this topic? Why?

5. What New Testament passage or set of passages most informed and/or impacted your thinking on this topic? Why?

Resources for Further Study

Demarest, Bruce. *The Cross and Salvation: The Doctrine of Salvation.* Foundations of Evangelical Theology. Wheaton: Crossway, 1997.

Hamilton, James M., Jr. *God's Glory in Salvation through Judgment: A Biblical Theology.* Wheaton: Crossway, 2010.

Hoekema, Anthony A. *Saved by Grace.* Grand Rapids: Eerdmans, 1986.

Horton, Michael. *Justification.* 2 vols., New Studies in Dogmatics. Grand Rapids: Zondervan, 2018.

Morgan, Christopher W. and Robert A. Peterson, eds., *Hell under Fire: Modern Scholarship Reinvents Eternal Punishment.* Grand Rapids: Zondervan, 2004.

CHAPTER 19

HOLY SPIRIT

IN CONCEIVING OF THE GLORIOUS truths of the gospel, one must understand who God is and how he has acted on our behalf. Our triune God has planned and executed the greatest rescue in all of history. God the Father "chose us in [Christ] before the foundation of the world, that we should be holy and blameless before him" (Eph. 1:4). He adopts us as sons (Eph. 1:5), and does so through the work of his Son, Jesus Christ. In Christ we have redemption, forgiveness, and riches of grace lavished upon us (Eph. 1:7–8). Jesus, as the ultimate fulfillment of all the promises of God, has set us free from sin and death and given us life.

Finally, we are sealed with God the Spirit,[1] who is "the guarantee of our inheritance" (Eph. 1:13–14). In other words, the Spirit is a "stamp" or "protecting sign" that signifies that our God has marked us at salvation for a final inheritance that we will receive at glorification. We are his people, and he will keep us in all things to the very end.[2] This is one facet of the role the Holy Spirit plays in the life of God's people. From creation to new creation, the ministry of the Spirit is significant and necessary for accomplishing God's overall plan of creation and redemption. This is a needful theme to take up—perhaps, more accurately, a divine person to describe. People understand that God is Father, given that they have earthly fathers, and that Jesus came in the flesh as a human being, which is also relatable,

---

1. Very little space in this chapter will be spent to demonstrate that the Holy Spirit is divine. In brief, one can note, in relation to the Spirit's divinity, that there are ascriptions of deity (Matt. 28:19; John 14:16; 2 Cor. 3:17; Acts 5:3–4), actions of deity where the Spirit is described as doing things only God can do (e.g., convicting: John 16:8–11; regenerating: John 3:5; Titus 3:5; and sanctifying: 1 Cor. 6:11), and finally attributes of deity used for the Spirit (such as eternal: Heb. 9:14). For further data concerning the deity of the Spirit, see Grudem, *Systematic Theology*, 226–56; Letham, *Holy Trinity*, 52–72.
2. See Peter T. O'Brien, *The Letter to the Ephesians*, Pillar New Testament Commentary (Grand Rapids: Eerdmans, 1999), 119.

but the idea of the Spirit can perplex and mystify. However, such understanding is essential, as the ministry of the Spirit is central to who and what we are as the people of God.

Holy Spirit in the Law

As the Father and the Son are involved in creation, so also is the Spirit. God created in the beginning, and the Spirit of God was "hovering over the face of the waters" (Gen. 1:2, cf. Deut. 32:11; Job 26:13; 33:4; Pss. 33:6; 104:29–30).[3] While a great amount of detail is not included in terms of the Spirit's exact function at the initial creation of the world,[4] one can observe that the Spirit is "extending God's presence into creation in such a way as to order and complete what has been planned in the mind of God."[5] It is also a reason to recognize his divinity and give him praise (Psalm 104).

Beyond the initial creation, the Spirit is seemingly involved with God in bringing Adam to life as he "breathed into his nostrils the breath of life" (Gen. 2:7; cf. Ps. 104:27–31; Job 33:4; note that "Spirit" and "breath" are linguistically connected). This reading is supported by Ezekiel 37:1–14, as Ezekiel prophesies to the bones and the breath, and God brings about life. God then says that he will put his Spirit within them as a new covenant promise, connecting the realities of "breath," "life," and "the Spirit."[6] The Spirit is God's source of all life for his creation, giving life to all that lives and breathes.[7]

Due to the sin originated in Genesis 3, all of humanity is estranged from God and under his wrath. In Genesis 6:3, just prior to the flood, it is said that God's Spirit will not abide with humanity forever. However, God the Father, in his grace, will accomplish a plan through God the Son, and the Holy Spirit is key in enacting this process starting in the Old Testament. Thus, one can observe that he was especially active in the life of God's people, Israel. The Spirit empowered Joseph with the ability to interpret dreams (Gen. 41:38), and gave abilities to craftsmen, such as Bezalel and Oholiab, to design the tabernacle (Exod 31:1–11, 35:30–36:1). He enabled Moses to lead Israel and also came upon seventy of the elders who prophesied to Israel (Num. 11:17–30; cf. Neh. 9:20). The Spirit also enabled Balaam to prophesy according to God's decree (Num. 24:2). He also came upon Joshua, who would

---

3. The history of interpretation on Genesis 1:2 is extensive and goes beyond the purview of this chapter. While the term *ruah* can refer to "wind" or "breath", it is also the term used to denote the Spirit. Contextually, it is accurate to see Genesis 1:2 as referring to the Holy Spirit and not generically to the wind (cf. Deut. 32:11). For further warrant regarding this position, see Sailhamer, "Genesis," 24–25; Sinclair B. Ferguson, *The Holy Spirit*, Contours of Christian Theology (Downers Grove: InterVarsity, 1996), 19–20.

4. Indeed, as Hawthorne states, "this is a feature of the Spirit's activity that is easily overemphasized." Gerald F. Hawthorne, *The Presence and the Power: The Significance of the Spirit in the Life and Ministry of Jesus* (Dallas: Word, 1991), 20.

5. Ferguson, *Holy Spirit*, 21. Ferguson supports this point by saying that this is precisely the role the Spirit plays elsewhere in Scripture (cf. Eph. 1:13–14; 1 Tim. 3:16; 1 Peter 1:1–2).

6. See Graham A. Cole, *He Who Gives Life*, 137.

7. The Nicene Creed refers to the Spirit as "The Lord and Life-giver."

lead Israel into Canaan to settle into the land God promised them (Num. 27:18–20; Deut. 34:9; cf. Isa. 11:2).[8] In these various ways we see the Spirit at work in creation as well as in the beginnings of the redemption and governance of God's people.

Holy Spirit in the Prophets

The Spirit also came upon certain judges, warriors, and prophets in a way that gave them extraordinary power and the ability to lead God's people. He enabled, for example, Othniel (Judg. 3:10), Gideon (Judg. 6:34), Jephthah (Judg. 11:29), and Samson (Judg. 14:6, 19) to serve as judges in Israel. The Holy Spirit also came upon the first kings of Israel, Saul (1 Sam. 10:6–10; 11:6) and David (1 Sam. 16:13–14; 2 Sam. 23:2). Saul, however, fails in his kingship as he directly disobeys God's commands (1 Sam. 13:8–15; 15:1–35). His disobedience costs him his throne and his life, as well as the presence of the Spirit (1 Sam. 16:14).[9] The Spirit came upon David, but, likely due to Saul's experience he recognized his need of the Spirit and the possibility that he may leave him due to his sin against Bathsheba and Uriah, and thus prayed for him to remain (Ps. 51:11).[10]

The Spirit, according to Isaiah, was in the midst of Israel in the wilderness wanderings. God showed pity on Israel in their affliction and redeemed them from Egypt (Isa. 63:7–9), "but they rebelled and grieved his Holy Spirit" (Isa. 63:10). This is so, even though God put his Holy Spirit in the midst of them as they passed through the Red Sea, went to Sinai, and settled in the land (Isa. 63:11–12). Even after the exile, Israel is assured the Spirit "remains in your midst" (Hag. 2:5), recognizing God's presence by means of his Spirit and anticipating a day when that presence would be full and lasting.

One of the key functions of the Holy Spirit as seen in the Prophets is to speak the word of the Lord by means of the prophets. The Spirit of God is "the motivating force in the inspiration of the prophets," the person who works in them in such a way that they proclaim

---

8. See Cole, *He Who Gives Life*, 119.
9. There are two important differences to note between the giving of gifts in the Old Testament and New Testament: first, in the Old Testament it appears that the gifts given were temporary and given for a specific purpose; in the New Testament, gifts appear to be given permanently and a general purpose is stated. Second, in the Old Testament only certain individuals (e.g., judges, kings) received gifts; in the New Testament, all believers are gifted. As such, it is important to recognize both the continuity and discontinuity that is present in this doctrine. For further thoughts on these points see Millard J. Erickson, *Christian Theology*, 3rd ed. (Grand Rapids: Baker, 2013), 881–92; Grudem, *Systematic Theology*, 1016–18.
10. There is scholarly debate regarding whether Old Testament believers were regenerated or indwelt by the Spirit, as were New Testament believers. For a survey of scholarship on this topic, see James M. Hamilton Jr., "Old Covenant Believers and the Indwelling Spirit: A Survey of the Spectrum of Opinion," *Trinity Journal* 24.1 (2003): 37–54. This connects to the temporary way in which the Spirit seemed to operate with Old Testament believers, coming upon them in strategic moments of ministry or leadership. It would seem, as one views the data, there is support for the position that Old Testament believers were regenerated, but not yet indwelt by the Spirit (John 14:17). See Cole, *He Who Gives Life,* 143–45; James M. Hamilton, *God's Indwelling Presence: The Holy Spirit in the Old and New Testaments*, NAC Studies in Bible and Theology (Nashville: B&H, 2006).

"thus says the Lord."[11] In other words, the Old Testament prophets are Spirit-inspired agents who receive the words of God and deliver them to the people. Many of the preexilic writing prophets did not claim to speak by the Spirit of the Lord explicitly. But during and after the exile, prophets more readily attributed their prophecies to the work of the Spirit (e.g., Ezek. 2:1–2; 3:24; 11:5; Mic. 3:8), and Zechariah looks back on all the former prophets and sees the Spirit speaking through them (Zech. 7:12; cf. 2 Sam. 23:2; Ezek. 2:2).

The prophets also anticipate a time when God, who is holy (Hos. 11:9), will pour out the Holy Spirit on a multitude of men and women (Isa. 11:1–2; Ezek. 37:14; Joel 2:28–32)—not only some of Israel's leaders (cf. Num. 11:24–29)—who will themselves become holy. This will come about by virtue of the new covenant, wherein God's law would be written on hearts (Jer. 31:31–34), the heart of stone removed and replaced by a heart of flesh, and the Spirit of God residing within his regenerated people (Ezek. 36:24–27).[12] Further, Ezekiel prophesies of a day when Israel will be enlivened by the Spirit, returned to the land, and cleansed of all idolatry (Ezek. 37:1–23).[13] The Spirit will do a new work amongst God's people, and this will take place by means of God's Messiah.[14]

The Old Testament prophets look to the coming Messiah as the one who will be specially anointed by the Spirit.[15] Isaiah proclaims that God will raise up an agent of his purpose from the line of David, upon whom the Holy Spirit would rest (Isa. 11:1–2). His rule will be just, full of integrity, and will bring about universal peace (Isa. 11:3–10; cf. 32:15–20; 44:1–5). He would be the anticipated ruler provided by God and empowered by the Spirit.[16] This servant of God would have the Spirit upon him as he brings forth justice, acts as a light to the nations, opens blind eyes, and sets the captive free (Isa. 42:1–9; cf. Matt. 3:17). The Spirit of the Lord will be upon this Messiah, to empower him to preach good news, bind up broken hearts, and proclaim the year of the Lord's favor and the day of God's vengeance

---

11. See T. S. Caulley, "Holy Spirit," in *Evangelical Dictionary of Theology*, 2nd ed., ed. Walter A. Elwell, (Grand Rapids: Baker, 2001), 568.
12. See Cole, *He Who Gives Life*, 136–37; William J. Dumbrell, *The Search for Order: Biblical Eschatology in Focus* (Eugene: Wipf and Stock, 2001), 104. This indicates that, under the new covenant, God's people would be a "saved" people, not a mixed community as Israel was. For an excellent essay detailing this point, see Stephen J. Wellum, "Baptism and the Relationship Between the Covenants," in *Believer's Baptism: Sign of the New Covenant in Christ*, eds. Thomas R. Schreiner and Shawn D. Wright, NAC Studies in Bible and Theology (Nashville: B&H, 2006), 97–161.
13. Daniel I. Block, "The Prophet of the Spirit: The Use of RWḤ in the Book of Ezekiel," *Journal of the Evangelical Theological Society* 32.1 (1989): 39; House, *Old Testament Theology*, 341–42.
14. Turner captures this point well, stating, "As the self-manifesting, transforming presence of God amongst his people, the Spirit is expected to accomplish deep existential renewal that recreates the very heart of humankind in obedience (Jer. 31:31–40; Ezek. 36:24–29; cf. Ps. 51:10–14; Isa. 44:3–5). In some expressions of this hope, it is to be fulfilled through a righteous prophetic liberator (Deut. 18:15; Isa. 42:61) and king endowed with the Spirit of wisdom and power (Isa 11:1–9)." Max Turner, "Holy Spirit," in *New Dictionary of Biblical Theology*, eds. T. Desmond Alexander and Brian S. Rosner (Downers Grove: InterVarsity, 2000), 552.
15. See Caulley, "Holy Spirit," 568.
16. See Cole, *He Who Gives Life*, 133; Charles H. Scobie, *Ways of Our God*, 316.

(Isa. 61:1–2; cf. Luke 4:17–19). Israel (and the nations) have a future because of the hope of this Spirit-empowered ruler. As Welker claims, "The power and authority of the person who bears God's Spirit lie in the fact that this person establishes justice, mercy, and the knowledge of God and gives them a universal extension."[17] And these prophecies clearly point to one figure: Jesus of Nazareth.

Holy Spirit in the Writings

In the Writings, the Spirit appears most frequently in the Psalms. In speaking of God's provision for the created order, the psalmist recognizes that if God "hides his face," they are dismayed, but when he "send[s] forth his Spirit, they are created" (Ps. 104:29–30). In other words, the Spirit is directly involved in sustaining the created order.[18] In Israel's history, when they rebelled against God, the psalmist describes the event as rebellion against God's Spirit who dwelt among them (Ps. 106:33; cf. Num. 20:1–13; 25:1–18). Moreover, the Spirit functions as "God's presence on earth," such that wherever we might go, he is there (Ps. 139:7–10).[19] The psalmist also understands the Spirit as a teacher and guide who leads him toward righteousness (Ps. 143:10). One can thus observe the personal and pervasive ministry of the Spirit in the lives of his people.

Elsewhere in the Writings, one observes that when Elihu speaks to Job and his three friends, it is "the breath of the almighty" that gives a person understanding (Job 32:8). He also declares that the Spirit of God has made him, and the breath of the Almighty gives him life (Job 33:4). In this allusion to the creation of Adam (Gen. 2:7), Elihu affirms how being made in God's image by means of the Spirit enables him to speak wise words to Job and his companions.[20] Daniel is spoken of as one in whom dwells the Spirit of God and he is able to interpret Nebuchadnezzar's dream (Dan. 4:8–9; cf. Gen. 41:1–39). In their prayer of confession during the time of Nehemiah, the Levites recall how God gave Israel the Spirit to instruct and warn the people through the prophets (Neh. 9:20, 30).[21] Chronicles also gives us one last look at the Spirit's role in prophetic utterance as it describes Zechariah as being "clothed" with the Spirit of God when he addresses the people (2 Chron. 24:20). The Spirit's ministry is essential, particularly in the lives of the leaders of Israel, but more is to come as we move into the era of the Messiah.

---

17. Michael Welker, *God the Spirit*, trans. John F. Hoffmeyer (Minneapolis: Fortress, 1994), 109.
18. See Leslie C. Allen, *Psalms 101-150*, Word Bible Commentary 21 (Dallas: Thomas Nelson, 2002), 135; Ferguson, *Holy Spirit*, 21.
19. Frame, *Systematic Theology*, 925.
20. Robert L. Alden, *Job*, New American Commentary 11 (Nashville: B&H, 1994), 322.
21. This first reference to the Spirit in Nehemiah 9 makes it sound as though the Spirit was given to all Israel to instruct each person, something that sounds more like what would occur under the auspices of the new covenant. Hamilton, however, rightly asserts "The reference to the Spirit probably recalls the way the Lord put the Spirit on the 70 elders who assisted Moses in leading the people (Num. 11)." Hamilton, *Ezra and Nehemiah*, 175.

Holy Spirit in the Gospels

Jesus is the Spirit-anointed God-man (cf. Acts 10:38). Wellum maintains, "Anyone steeped in the Old Testament would immediately recognize two important points: (1) the stress on the agency of the Holy Spirit tied to the expectation of the coming Messiah and messianic age (see Isa. 11; 42; 61; Joel 2:28–32); (2) the fact that this child will save his people from their sins according to the new covenant promise of Jeremiah 31:34."[22] As such, the Gospels—along with the rest of the New Testament—are key for recognizing the role of the Spirit in the lives of both the Messiah as well as God's people.

Both Matthew and Luke attribute the virginal conception of Jesus to the Holy Spirit (Matt. 1:20; Luke 1:35; cf. Isa. 7:14). Mary was "overshadowed" by the Holy Spirit, and in this way Jesus was conceived. This is a clear reminder that "the conception of Jesus by the Holy Spirit is the mode by which the Father's sending of the Son is effected," confirming that each person of the Trinity was engaged in the reality of the incarnation.[23]

Matthew, Mark and Luke all record the descent of the Spirit upon Jesus at his baptism (Matt. 3:13–17, Mark 1:10–11, Luke 3:21–22). John 1:32–33 also describes the descent of the Spirit, but does not explicitly identify the context as Jesus's baptism. Here Jesus is identified by the Father as the beloved Son with whom he is well pleased, a clear reference back to Isaiah 42:1 (cf. Ps. 2:7). The Synoptic Gospels also mention the Spirit leading Jesus into the desert (Matt 4:1, Mark 1:12, Luke 4:1). There he prepares for his earthly ministry and overcomes Satan's temptations, full of the Spirit (Luke 4:1).[24] After his time in the wilderness, Jesus "returned in the power of the Spirit to Galilee," (Luke 4:14), reads of his fulfillment of prophecy as the Spirit-anointed Messiah (Luke 4:18–19; cf. Isa. 61:1–2), and does ministry (e.g., healing, casting out demons) by the Spirit (Matt. 12:15–28). Jesus's public ministry is done as the divine Son of God, who is—in at least certain aspects of his ministry—empowered by the Spirit of God.[25]

---

22. Wellum, *God the Son Incarnate*, 237. Regarding Wellum's second point, the Spirit is also key in terms of the inauguration of the new covenant (Ezek 36:25–27).
23. Ferguson, *Holy Spirit*, 42–43.
24. Hawthorne avers, "Thus, at the outset of his ministry, Jesus is depicted as overcoming the evil one who stands in opposition to the work of the kingdom (Luke 11:19, 20) through the all-sufficient energizing power of the Spirit of God." Hawthorne, *Presence and the Power*, 139. See also Cole, *He Who Gives Life*, 159–60.
25. There is recent debate regarding the function of the Spirit in the life of Christ and to what degree Jesus acts in the power of the Spirit as opposed to his divinity when it comes to his miracles and life on earth. Crisp and Wellum each divide up these positions into "ontological kenotic Christology" (the divine Son gave up certain divine attributes or properties normally belonging to deity, thus limiting himself); "functional kenotic Christology" (the divine Son never or occasionally uses his divine attributes, but predominantly lives as we do, namely, in his humanity and dependence on the Spirit); and the classical view (Jesus is God the Son incarnate, all his attributes are essential to him, and he exercises these divine attributes while incarnate). See Oliver D. Crisp, *Divinity and Humanity: The Incarnation Reconsidered* (Cambridge: Cambridge University Press, 2007), 118–53; Stephen J. Wellum, "Evangelical Christology and Kenotic Influences: A 'New' and 'Better' Way?" in *Building on the Foundations of Evangelical Theology: Essays in Honor of John S. Feinberg*, eds. Gregg R. Allison and Stephen J. Wellum (Wheaton:

John's gospel offers some significant insight into the person and work of the Holy Spirit. He is the means of new life, the agent by whom we must be born again (John 3:1–8; cf. Titus 3:5). He is the river of living water flowing within the person who believes in Jesus (John 7:37–39; cf. Isa. 44:3; Ezek. 36:25–27; Joel 2:28). Of particular note in John's gospel regarding the Spirit are chapters 14–16. First, note the new name given to the Spirit here: *paraklētos*. This Greek title can take the meaning of advocate, helper, teacher, comforter, defender, or exhorter, but it is perhaps best to see the function of this name for the Spirit within the context of John 14–16.[26] Thus, one must observe the role of the Spirit, or *paraklētos*, in these chapters, which is essentially to continue and expand the ministry of Jesus. He is called "another Helper" (John 14:16) and the "Spirit of truth" (John 14:17). He is sent from the Father and will teach them (i.e., the apostles) all things, relating the work of the Spirit to the production of the Scriptures (John 14:26; 15:26; 16:13).[27] He will testify and make much of Jesus, participating in what Packer refers to as a "floodlight ministry," with Jesus as the one illumined by the beam (John 15:26; 16:14).[28]

Jesus even asserts, "Nevertheless, I tell you the truth: it is to your advantage that I go away, for if I do not go away, the Helper will not come to you. But if I go, I will send him to you" (John 16:7). When Jesus ascends, the ministry of the Spirit will commence with increased distinction, as was foretold by the prophets. He will convict the world of sin, righteousness, and judgment (John 16:8–11). John also connects the coming of the Spirit with the glorification of Jesus (John 7:37–39; 16:7; 20:22), recognizing that after Jesus died, rose again, and ascended he would send the Spirit to be in his people (John 14:17). The Spirit,

---

Crossway, 2015), 206–34. Both Crisp and Wellum cite advocates for each position and lay out the details and nuance in a beneficial manner. While a full-scale argument is beyond the purview of this chapter, it would seem the classical view of Trinitarian relations and agency is better able to make sense of the biblical data. As Wellum states, "We must explain the actions of the incarnate Son as his actions and the outworking of the triune relations in light of the incarnation and his redemptive work. The Son, then, acts in and through his two natures in *filial relation* (obedience and dependence) to his Father and *through* the Spirit. As *the Son* who continues to possess the divine nature, he is able to exercise his divine attributes and does so, for example, in his ongoing cosmic actions. Yet, the Son, even as the incarnate Son, never acts on his own; the Son always acts in filial relation to his Father *and* through the Spirit, which he has always done. Thus, in the incarnation, even though it is the Son who added to himself a human nature, the Son's relations and actions continue to be done according to his mode of subsistence, *as the Son*. The divine, *ad intra* personal relations never change, but we come to know these relations on the stage of history as the Son becomes incarnate, acts in obedience to his Father's will *through* the Spirit, and lives and dies as our new covenant representative and substitute." Wellum, *God the Son Incarnate*, 411.

26. So Dumbrell, *Search for Order*, 255, who states that while the term *paraklētos* has been translated in various ways, "it is perhaps best to leave it untranslated and focus on the function of the one that will come."

27. Ferguson maintains, "No doubt these words [are directly applicable to the apostles but] have a continuing significance for Christians today, but not in the direct way in which they are often understood (the Spirit will lead *me* into all truth in an unmediated way). Rather, they indicate that it is by means of the apostolic witness (now inscripturated in the New Testament), not by direct revelation of the Spirit to individual believers or by corporate revelation to teaching officers." Ferguson, *Holy Spirit*, 71.

28. J. I. Packer, *Keep in Step with the Spirit: Finding Fullness in Our Walk with God*, rev. ed. (Grand Rapids: Baker, 2005), 65–66.

therefore, was seen in the ministry of Messiah, and the promised bestowal of the Spirit on God's people was about to come to fruition.

Holy Spirit in Acts and the Letters

The book of Acts contains a great deal of information as it relates to the Holy Spirit. Jesus has ascended to the Father in heaven (Acts 1:6–11), and here one observes the beginnings of this distinctive ministry of the Spirit within all believers. The importance of the book of Acts to the understanding of the Holy Spirit can be seen in the fact that the word *pneuma* appears here seventy times (more than Matthew, Mark, and John combined). It is here, after the accomplished work of Christ, that the church receives the Spirit and embarks on its mission to make disciples of Jesus Christ (Acts 1:8; cf. Matt. 28:18–20).

Even before his ascension Jesus gives commands to the apostles "through the Holy Spirit" (Acts 1:2). The apostles were to remain in Jerusalem, since they were to be "baptized with the Holy Spirit" and would "receive power" when the Holy Spirit came upon them (Acts 1:4–5, 8). Shortly after Jesus's ascension on the day of Pentecost, the apostles gathered together in one place, as was their custom (Acts 2:1; cf. 1:12–14). While there the Spirit came upon them, manifested as a mighty rushing wind (cf. Ezek. 37:9), tongues of fire (cf. Exod. 3:2–5; 19:18), and the proclamation of the message of God in diverse languages (Acts 2:1–13). The crowd, comprised of Jews from various nations, heard the gospel message in their own language,[29] which Peter explains is not drunkenness, but the manifestation of the Spirit on God's people as was prophesied (Acts 2:13–21; cf. Joel 2:28–32). Thus, "The events here are preached as part of God's long-awaited promise in fulfillment of new covenant hope. . . . Luke sees the start of the decisive eras of fulfillment as happening in these recent events."[30]

With the arrival of the "last days" (Acts. 2:17; cf. Heb. 1:1–2; 9:26; 1 Peter 1:20; 2 Peter 3:3; 1 John 2:18; Jude 18) the Spirit is not given to a select few, but is poured out on believers, regardless of gender, class, age, and even ethnicity (cf. Acts 8:1–17; 10:1–11:18). Peter then preaches the glories of Jesus the Messiah, including the way in which he mediates the presence of the Holy Spirit to the people of God by means of their faith in the gospel (Acts 2:33).[31] Through repentance, signified by baptism (1 Peter 3:21), they would

---

29. Some scholars see this event as the beginnings of the reversal of Babel, when God confused the languages of humanity due to their arrogance in making a name for themselves (Gen. 11:1–9). See, for example, Cole, *He Who Gives Life*, 192; Ferguson, *The Holy Spirit*, 60. George T. Montague, *The Holy Spirit: The Growth of a Biblical Tradition* (Eugene: Wipf and Stock, 2006), 282. Bock, however, does encourage some caution when making connections between the two events. "The verb [*synechythē*] shows up in Genesis 11:7, 9 in the LXX. . . . [However,] one should not press the Babel analogy too much to argue for the reversal of that judgment, as the terms are common and the confusion is not ended by the act alone." See *Acts*, 101.
30. Bock, *Acts*, 112.
31. Bock, *Acts*, 133. See also Hamilton, *God's Indwelling Presence*, 190.

receive the principle gifts God had to offer, namely, forgiveness and the outpouring/baptism/gift of the Spirit (Acts 2:38).[32]

Soon after Pentecost a lame man is healed and Peter preaches to the masses that assemble (Acts 3:1–26). Peter and John are arrested by the Jewish officials and called on to give an account of their actions the next day (Acts 4:1–7). Peter again preaches Jesus as the Messiah, and Luke specifically says that he does this "filled with the Holy Spirit" (Acts 4:8; cf. 1 Cor. 2:4).[33] He proclaims the good news (Acts 4:8–20), is threatened to not speak again in the name of Jesus (Acts 4:21), and thus joins with fellow Christians to pray for boldness to continue speaking of Jesus and his gospel (Acts 4:22–31). In praying for boldness, God answers their prayers by filling them afresh with the Holy Spirit such that they continued to speak God's Word with boldness (Acts 4:31).[34]

Later in the book the apostles are again arrested and called to give an account of the rapid spread of the Christian faith. Peter declares Jesus's resurrection and lordship, saying they are witnesses to him, and the Holy Spirit is also witness (Acts 5:32; cf. John 15:26). As the narrative progresses, one observes that individuals can exhibit the filling of the Spirit in their lives (Acts 6:3–6; 7:55; 11:24; 13:9, 52). The Spirit gives guidance to God's people (Acts 8:29; 10:19; 13:2–4; 15:28; 16:6–7; 20:22–23), comforts (Acts 9:31), and gives words of prophecy to be spoken to God's people (Acts 11:28; 21:10–11). The book of Acts is thus significant in identifying a shift in the ministry of the Spirit brought about by the work of Christ, inaugurating his kingdom and a new covenant.

Moving on, the New Testament Epistles give more details regarding the person and work of the Spirit. One will see that the Spirit had a significant role in the resurrection of Jesus (Rom. 1:4; 8:11; 1 Tim. 3:16; 1 Peter 3:18).[35] Paul's trust in preaching the gospel was not in his cleverness, but the power of the Spirit to produce conviction of sin and faith in

---

32. See Bock, *Acts*, 141, 144. The language of baptism in the Holy Spirit is used seven times, four of which are parallel accounts (Matt. 3:11; Mark 1:8; Luke 3:16; John 1:33; Acts 1:5; 11:15–17; 1 Cor. 12:13). Since Acts 2 signifies the fulfillment of what Jesus discussed in the Gospels, and since terms such as "pour out" (Acts 2:17, 33) and "gift" (Acts 2:38) are used to describe the manifestation of the Spirit, it can be surmised that these terms refer to one event wherein one receives the Spirit at conversion. For more on this point, see Malcolm B. Yarnell III, "The Person and Work of the Holy Spirit," in *A Theology for the Church*, rev. ed., ed. Daniel. L. Akin (Nashville: B&H, 2014), 490–92.

33. The filling of the Spirit is mentioned 10 times in the book of Acts (2:4; 4:8, 31; 6:3, 5; 7:55, 9:17; 11:24; 13:9; 13:52), compared to baptism of the Spirit, mentioned only twice (1:5 and 11:16). The filling of the Spirit is seemingly not a one-time event (cf. Acts 4:8, 31), and is in connection with effective gospel ministry. Filling can be a habitual characteristic of individuals, and is visible to others (e.g., the deacons of Acts 6; Barnabas in Acts 11:24). The evidence of the Spirit's filling seems to be the Spirit's fruit (e.g., boldness, wisdom, goodness, full of faith, full of joy; cf Gal. 5:16–26; Eph 5:18). For more on the filling of the Spirit, see Gregg R. Allison, "Baptism with and Filling of the Holy Spirit," *Southern Baptist Journal of Theology* 16.4 (2012): 4–21.

34. See Cole, *He Who Gives Life*, 245.

35. For further detail regarding the role of the Spirit in the resurrection, see Gordon D. Fee, *God's Empowering Presence: The Holy Spirit in the Letters of Paul* (Grand Rapids: Baker, 2009), 483; Ferguson, *The Holy Spirit*, 53, 250-51; Moo, *Romans*, 49–51.

the human heart (1 Cor. 2:4; 12:3; 1 Thess. 1:5). He understands that apart from the Spirit, there is no conversion that takes place. The Spirit also illumines our understanding of the Scriptures, such that, to our heart and mind, they are wisdom and truth to be lived in obedience to God (1 Cor. 2:6–16).[36] The Spirit offers gifts to the church, so that they can serve one another for the common good (1 Cor. 12:7; cf. Rom. 12:3–8; 1 Peter 4:10–11). Again, in distinction to the Old Testament ministry of the Spirit, we see a pervasive gifting to all of God's people in the church; specifically, a variety of gifts that represent the various parts of the body of Christ (1 Cor. 12:12–26).[37]

Paul also declares, "For in one Spirit we were all baptized into one body—Jews or Greeks, slaves or free—and all were made to drink of one Spirit (1 Cor. 12:13). At conversion we are baptized in the Spirit, come into the body of Christ, and mark out our union with Christ.[38] We are sealed with the promised Holy Spirit, recognizing the assurance we have in his work in our lives, for God's glory (Eph. 1:13–14). The Spirit bears witness to our spirit that we are in fact children of God, fellow heirs with Christ (Rom. 8:14–17; cf. 1 John 3:24; 4:13). As believers, we are also "letters from Christ" written not with ink but with the Spirit of God on the tablets of the human heart (2 Cor. 3:3). This marks an "epochal development from the old to the new, precisely in terms of the ministry of the Spirit."[39] There is a diverse development from the Old Testament to the New Testament in regards to the Spirit as Jesus inaugurates the new covenant (Luke 22:20). The ministry of the Spirit has dawned for all believers with great glory, transforming God's people increasingly and progressively into the image of Christ (2 Cor. 3:4–18).

The indwelling Holy Spirit is also the source of our sanctification (2 Thess. 2:13, 1 Peter 1:2). We are called not to walk according to the flesh, but according to the Spirit, and to put to death the deeds of the body by means of the Spirit (Rom. 8:9–13; cf. Gal. 5:16–26). Moo deftly remarks, "While the Christian is made responsible for this 'mortification' of sins, he or she accomplishes this only 'through the Spirit.' Holiness of life, then, is achieved neither by our unaided effort—the error of 'moralism' or 'legalism'—nor by the Spirit apart from participation—as some who insist that they key to holy living is 'surrender' or 'let go and let God' would have it—but by our constant living out the 'life' placed within us by the Spirit

---

36. For a comprehensive study of the doctrine of illumination, see Kevin D. Zuber, "What Is Illumination? A Study in Evangelical Theology Seeking a Biblically Grounded Definition of the Illuminating Work of the Holy Spirit" (PhD Diss., Trinity Evangelical Divinity School, 1996). Kaiser avers that illumination does not merely mean cognitive understanding. Instead, he claims, "the Spirit's ministry is one of aiding the believer to apply, to see the value, the worth, and significance of a text for his own person, situation, and times." Walter C. Kaiser Jr., "A Neglected Text in Bibliology Discussions: 1 Corinthians 2:6-16," *Westminster Theological Journal* 43.2 (1981): 301-19.

37. The extent and continuation or cessation of certain spiritual gifts is beyond the purview of this chapter. For further discussion see Wayne A. Grudem, ed., *Are Miraculous Gifts for Today? Four Views* (Grand Rapids: Zondervan, 1996); Schreiner, *Spiritual Gifts*.

38. See Fee, *First Epistle to the Corinthians*, 603–6; Ferguson, *Holy Spirit*, 195.

39. Ferguson, *Holy Spirit*, 26.

who has taken up residence within."[40] The Spirit is "placed within" the believer in such a way that Paul refers to God's people as the temple of the Holy Spirit (1 Cor. 3:16–17; 6:18–20; cf. 2 Cor. 6:16). McKelvey rightly summarizes, "God no longer dwells in a house *with* his people; he dwells *in* them, they are his temple."[41] The goal of sanctification (i.e., being conformed to the image of Christ; Rom. 8:28–29) is a life characterized by the fruit of the Spirit (Gal. 5:22–23), and the means to sanctification is to increasingly walk in the fullness of the Spirit or be filled with him (Gal. 5:16–26; Eph. 5:18; cf. Col. 3:16).

Other New Testament epistles agree with Paul and Luke's testimony and speak of the Spirit as essential in the Christian life. The author of Hebrews refers to the gifts that are distributed by the Holy Spirit to believers "according to his will" (Heb. 2:4). In quoting Psalm 95 the author contends that the Holy Spirit speaks (Heb. 3:7; cf. 10:15–17). This correlates with Peter's testimony of the Spirit's work and his assertion that "no prophecy of Scripture comes from someone's own interpretation. For no prophecy was ever produced by the will of man, but men spoke from God as they were carried along by the Holy Spirit" (2 Peter 1:20–21; cf. Acts 1:16; 4:25). Thus, the Spirit is involved in the inspiration of Scripture, ensuring that its words are in fact God's words.[42] Regarding the old covenant, the Spirit reveals that the holy place (i.e., the holy of holies; the place of God's presence) was inaccessible (Heb. 9:8–10), but that through Christ, our great high priest, we have access to eternal redemption (Heb. 9:11–14). This is because the blood of Christ was shed, and Jesus "who through the eternal Spirit offered himself without blemish to God," purified our conscience to serve the living God (Heb. 9:14).[43] The Holy Spirit thus anointed Jesus as high priest for every aspect of his ministry, including his sacrificial death.[44]

Holy Spirit in Revelation

While often not the main focus of studies on the book of Revelation, as it is specifically "The revelation of Jesus Christ" (Rev. 1:1), the Spirit nevertheless plays a key role in John's

---

40. Moo, *Romans*, 495–96.
41. R. J. McKelvey, *The New Temple: The Church in the New Testament* (Oxford: Oxford University Press, 1969), 180. Theologians typically refer to this aspect of the Spirit's ministry as the "indwelling" of the believer.
42. Cole maintains, "This Petrine text should not be used to suggest that all Scripture is prophecy or that the Spirit is limited to prophetic texts. That is not the logic of the text. In fact in the last chapter of 2 Peter we find that Paul's letters are described as Scripture (2 Peter 3:15–16). Moreover there is some evidence that prophecy in Judaism was a wide enough category to cover the range of OT genres." Cole, *He Who Gives Life*, 263. See also Fee, *God's Empowering Presence*, 794.
43. There is grammatical difficulty in determining whether the reference to "Spirit" is a reference to Jesus's own spirit, the divinity of Christ, or the Holy Spirit. O'Brien claims this is a reference to the Holy Spirit: "Apart from 4:12, the preceding references in Hebrews to 'spirit' in the singular have been to 'the Holy Spirit'. The listeners, then, could be expected to identify *the eternal Spirit* with the Holy Spirit (3:7; 6:4; 9:8; see 10:15, 29)." P. T. O'Brien, *The Letter to the Hebrews*, Pillar New Testament Commentary (Grand Rapids: Eerdmans, 2010), 324. See also Ellingworth, *Hebrews*, 456.
44. O'Brien, *Hebrews*, 324. See also George H. Guthrie, *Hebrews*, NIV Application Commentary (Grand Rapids: Zondervan, 1998), 312.

apocalyptic letter to the churches. The Spirit is mentioned at the very beginning in the opening benediction as "the seven spirits who are before [the Father's] throne" (Rev. 1:4), bestowing grace and peace alongside of the Father and the Son.[45] The Spirit thus shares divine prerogatives with the Father and the Son as the third person of the Trinity (cf. 2 Cor. 13:14). The reader also sees a reference to Jesus as the one who "has the seven spirits of God and the seven stars" (Rev. 3:1). Earlier, the "seven stars" are interpreted as referring to the angels of the seven churches (Rev. 1:20). Thus, this verse seems to refer to Jesus as one "in relationship" with both the Spirit as well as the angels of these churches to communicate his authority.[46] In the vision of the throne room of heaven, John sees before the throne "seven torches of fire, which are the seven spirits of God" (Rev. 4:5; cf. Ezek. 1:13; Zech. 4:2, 6). The seven spirits before the throne may refer to God's judgment, holiness, and power (cf. Isa. 4:4).[47] The Spirit is also in this scene as John remarks about the Lamb that was slain who had "seven horns and seven eyes, who are the seven spirits of God sent out into all the earth" (Rev. 5:6). Again, Jesus is the Spirit-endowed Messiah, and the picture here is of the atoning work accomplished by Jesus as well as the "perfection, completeness, and fullness of the Spirit who goes out over the whole earth."[48] The Spirit is sent into all the earth to do his work as it relates to the witness of the gospel and the sanctification of God's people.

The Spirit enables John to receive his visions (Rev. 1:10; 4:2; 17:3; 21:10), such that the repeated phrase "in the Spirit" bears clear resemblance to Ezekiel's visionary experiences (Ezek. 2:2; 3:12, 14, 24; 11:1; 43:5). This would seem to indicate that John's revelation has "prophetic

---

45. Commentators have questioned whether the "seven spirits" refers to the Holy Spirit, or to the seven angels seen later in the book. The evidence for this phrase referring to the Holy Spirit is well-attested. Beale maintains, "Although some identify these spirits with the seven archangels, mentioned in Jewish writings (e.g., *1 En.* 20:1–8) or with the seven angels of the trumpets and bowls (Rev. 8:2; 15:1, 6–8), the expression is more likely a figurative designation of the effective working of the Holy Spirit, since this is the characteristic identification of πνεῦμα in the NT when found in conjunction with or as part of an apparent formula with God and Christ . . . The phrase is expanded in 4:5, where 'seven lamps of fire burning *before the throne*' are equated with 'the seven spirits of God.' It is not too speculative to understand these 'lamps' from John's metaphorical perspective as burning on 'the seven golden lampstands' (i.e., the churches, 1:12ff.). Therefore, the Spirit is what empowers the church to be effective as a burning lamp of witness in the world, which is why it is included in v 4 . . . The Spirit is the means by which God affects "grace and peace" and by which the church is encouraged to obedience and witness (cf. v 3). Indeed, the wording 'seven spirits' is part of a paraphrased allusion to Zechariah 4:2–7 (as is evident from Rev. 4:5 and 5:6), which identifies the 'seven lamps' as God's one Spirit, whose role is to bring about God's grace (cf. Zech 4:7) in Israel through the successful completion of the rebuilding of the temple (see further on 1:12; 4:5; 5:6)." Beale, *Revelation*, 189. Schreiner also mentions that the number "seven" is used to denote "fullness and perfection," typical in this kind of apocalyptic literature. Schreiner, *New Testament Theology*, 502.
46. Patterson, *Revelation*, 121. Schreiner also maintains that the rationale behind the reference to Jesus and the seven spirits is to point to Jesus as "the one endowed by the Spirit. Perhaps there is an allusion here to Isaiah 11:2, where seven different qualities are related to the Spirit, and the one upon whom the Spirit rests is none other than the descendant of Jesse—the messianic king." Schreiner, *New Testament Theology*, 502–3.
47. Osborne claims, "The perfect Spirit is the means by which God will oversee and judge his creation." Osborne, *Revelation*, 231.
48. Akin, *Exalting Jesus in Revelation*, 126. Akin goes on to say this is a reference to the omnipresence of the Spirit.

authority like that of the OT prophets."[49] The references to John being "in the Spirit" come at decisive moments in the book—the beginning of the book, John's vision of the heavenly throne room, and the contrast between Babylon and the New Jerusalem—clearly indicating that the Spirit ensured that what John saw and wrote was in fact the word of God.[50]

The Spirit is also the source for the messages to the seven churches (Rev. 2–3). John addresses these churches in Asia Minor, and ends each address with the phrase, "He who has an ear, let him hear what the Spirit says to the churches" (Rev. 2:7, 11, 17, 29; 3:6, 13, 22; cf. Isa. 6:9–10; Jer. 5:21; Ezek. 3:27; 12:2). The Old Testament prophets used this warning to decry participation in the idolatry of the nations. Given the context of the book of Revelation, it would seem this warning still applies and is intended to have the same effect (cf. Rev. 13:1–10; 18:1–5).[51] Each of these brief exhortations also begins with the phrase "the words of . . ." (Rev. 2:1, 8, 12, 18; 3:1, 7, 14), which refers to the words of Jesus Christ. Thus, the words of Jesus Christ, who died, was raised, and has all authority are also the words of the Holy Spirit. The message brought by the Spirit to the churches is the message of Jesus Christ (cf. John 16:13–15).[52]

The Spirit, finally, is one of the heavenly speakers John overhears.[53] The Spirit proclaims, in response to an angelic announcement, that those who have labored in the Lord will be blessed and find rest (Rev. 14:13). He also joins voices with the bride of Christ, the people of God, inviting the readers to come and satisfy their spiritual thirst in Christ (Rev. 22:17; cf. Isa. 55:1–2). The antichrist is coming, and even now many antichrists have come (1 John 2:18). We are not to be swayed by false teaching or engage in false forms of worship, but instead take part in the invitation of the Spirit to glorify Jesus and make much of him in all of life.

---

49. Beale, *Revelation, 203*. See also G. K. Beale and Sean M. McDonough, "Revelation," in *Commentary on the New Testament Use of the Old Testament*, eds. G. K. Beale and D. A. Carson (Grand Rapids: Baker, 2007), 1091. While detail is not given, Patterson notes "Most commentators believe the expression *en pneumati* suggests that John was in an ecstatic trance. While this is possible, even probable, the first use of the expression in 1:10 may mean no more than that John, when the events unfolded, was seeking God through worship. The same is possible here, though without question what follows has much in common with Paul's experience recorded by the apostle in 2 Corinthians 12:1–6. Paul confessed that he was unable to delineate his exact state, in or out of the body. John's situation seems similar." Patterson, *Revelation*, 150. Whatever the exact situation, readers can see John as operating in the line of prophets that have gone before him, with the Holy Spirit "carrying him along" (2 Peter 1:20–21).
50. See Schreiner, *New Testament Theology*, 501.
51. See Beale and McDonough, "Revelation," 1093.
52. See Schreiner, *New Testament Theology*, 501–2.
53. See Craig L. Blomberg, "Holy Spirit," in *Evangelical Dictionary of Biblical Theology*, ed. Walter A. Elwell (Grand Rapids: Baker, 1996) 347.

Discussion Questions

1. How does the Spirit specifically minister and empower people in the Old Testament?

2. How does the Spirit specifically minister and empower people in the New Testament? (In these first two questions, be sure to point out similarities and differences regarding the work of the Spirit in the Old Testament and the New Testament.)

3. In what specific ways did the Spirit minister in the life of Jesus? Was this necessary, seeing that Jesus is divine? Why or why not?

4. In what specific ways does the Spirit help us overcome sin and pursue righteousness?

5. What is the role of the Spirit in the book of Revelation?

Resources for Further Study

Cole, Graham. *He Who Gives Life: The Doctrine of the Holy Spirit*. Wheaton: Crossway, 2007.

Ferguson, Sinclair. *The Holy Spirit*. Contours of Christian Theology. Downers Grove: InterVarsity, 1996.

Hamilton, James M., Jr. *God's Indwelling Presence: The Holy Spirit in the Old and New Testaments*. NAC Studies in Bible and Theology. Nashville: B&H, 2006.

Horton, Michael. *Rediscovering the Holy Spirit: God's Perfecting Presence in Creation, Redemption, and Everyday Life*. Grand Rapids: Zondervan, 2017.

Schreiner, Thomas R. *Spiritual Gifts: What They Are and Why They Matter*. Nashville: B&H, 2018.

CHAPTER 20

MISSION

KÖSTENBERGER IS CERTAINLY RIGHT in saying "The subject of mission is often absent from treatments of systematic theology, and is frequently neglected even in theme studies of biblical books. But mission is an exceedingly important motif pervading virtually the entire course of biblical revelation."[1] Every organization has a mission, something they seek to accomplish for fiscal gain, humanitarian aid, or the promotion of a new initiative. In whatever way marketing strategies proclaim the prominence of such initiatives, however, the church has the most important mission of all. While seemingly weak and, in some cultures, utterly irrelevant to the details of life, the church declares the message of the risen Christ, a message that penetrates all aspects of reality on both a personal and cosmic level.

Supremely, the purpose of everything that exists in the universe is to glorify God (Ps. 19:1; Isa. 43:6–7; Phil. 2:10–11). God will be glorified in both the salvation and the judgment rendered to those who believe in Christ and his finished work (salvation), and those who do not (judgment). As such, since the fall, God has been on a distinctive mission to seek out and save that which is lost, and to restore his creation.[2] Throughout the storyline of the Bible one can observe how God has gone about the accomplishment of

---

1. A. J. Köstenberger, "Mission," in *New Dictionary of Biblical Theology*, eds. T. Desmond Alexander and Brian S. Rosner (Downers Grove: InterVarsity, 2000), 663.
2. As will be seen, God's mission provides the impetus, framework, and trajectory for the church's mission. However, the church's mission is not identical to God's mission, His is more comprehensive (e.g., total restoration of the cosmos). We must be careful not to confuse our mission with God's, nor with the ministries and ethical realities that are a result of that mission.

this mission, bringing about his kingdom through covenants and a dynasty, all of which culminate in Jesus Christ.[3]

As a result of the work of Christ, the church is now charged with two particular tasks aimed at glorifying God: making disciples of all nations (Matt. 28:18–20) and edifying believers (Eph. 4:11–16).[4] The latter task focuses on those already within the church and their continued growth in Christ-likeness by means of preaching, teaching, and fellowship. The former task is primarily focused on reaching people with the gospel of Jesus Christ and bringing them from darkness to light (Col. 1:13–14). This mission of reaching people with the gospel and making disciples of Jesus Christ is accomplished, by God's grace, through those who are fully committed to living their lives as disciples of Jesus Christ.

Mission in the Law

God created all things, and the pinnacle of that creation is humanity, which was made in his image (Genesis 1). All of creation, including humanity, was very good and made to proclaim the majesty of God. Genesis 1:27–28 highlights how the function of humanity as image-bearers was to expand the boundaries of the Garden until the entire earth became filled with the glory of God (cf. Hab. 2:14). Adam would "work" and "keep" the Garden (Gen. 2:15), thus serving as a priest-king in God's garden sanctuary (i.e., temple; cf. Num 3:7).

Adam however failed his commission, rebelling against God's command not to eat of the tree of the knowledge of good and evil. No longer did humans enjoy direct communion with God; they now needed to be liberated from sin and reconciled with their Creator. A promised offspring is named (Gen. 3:15) and the story now turns to God reclaiming a people for himself with whom he would dwell and be in covenant relationship. Following the fall, humanity continues to decline morally, going in the way of sin and rebellion against God. God calls Noah, who is, in many ways, like a new Adam (Gen. 9:1, 7) called to fill the earth and subdue it for God's glory. However, Noah also fails (Gen. 9:20–24). This is likewise true of the people at Babel as they sought to make a name for themselves rather than God (Gen. 11:1–9).

God then calls Abram (Gen. 12:1–3) and promises him a land, descendants, and blessing to him and through him for all nations.[5] God's covenant with Abram refers to

---

3. Thoughts concerning the nexus of the kingdom of God, the biblical covenants, and the dominion of God brought about through the specific bloodline of Adam, Abraham, Judah, and David have come about initially through interactions with Gentry and Wellum, *Kingdom through Covenant* and Dempster, *Dominion and Dynasty*.

4. Details will be noted throughout the chapter regarding the mission God has for his people in the Old Testament and its continuity and discontinuity with his mission for the New Testament church.

5. Bauckham rightly remarks, "In Genesis 12 Abraham is *singled out* by God. This is perhaps the most remarkable of all the instances of divinely chosen singularity in the Bible. For it follows immediately the thoroughly universal narrative of the first eleven chapters of Genesis, a narrative that concluded in chapter 10, with the great catalog of all the nations, seventy of them, descended from the three sons of Noah, and then, in chapter 11, with the story of Babel, from which the human race was scattered over all the earth to form the various nations, divided now by language and geography. Genesis 10–11 sets, as it were, the international scene for the whole of the rest of the

Israel as the seed of Abraham in the land of Canaan (though it also becomes clear, as will be seen, there is one particular "seed" coming through whom the nations are blessed; cf. Gal. 3:16). There are some who think of this text as a "Great Commission," revealing the heart of God's mission as well as the mission of Israel and the church to go out into the world and be a blessing.[6] However, this reading might import too much into the text grammatically and may also keep the reader from seeing the progressive nature of revelation and the distinctive nature of God's call to his people in the Old Testament era.[7] This does not mean it is wrong for Christians to bless others, but one should be cautious when seeking to equate this kind of text with the commission found at the end of the Gospel accounts. Those called by the Lord were to "display God's own character and rule" as a witness to the surrounding nations.[8] God unilaterally promises to bless Abraham and Israel, and in Abraham's offspring—the ultimate promised seed—all the nations of the earth would also be blessed (Gen. 22:17–18).[9]

In the book of Exodus, Israel is redeemed from Egypt and called by God to be a "kingdom of priests" and a "holy nation" (Exod. 19:1–6). In other words, as a nation that God formed and set apart to be distinct from the other nations, Israel was to display God's character to all the surrounding people, mediating God's presence and blessings to them and summoning them to participate in the renewal of all things by worshiping God alone.[10] As a

Bible's story. But from this emphatically universal scope the story suddenly narrows to just one man, Abraham, and his immediate family, called by God to leave his place in the international order (or disorder), to move to a new country and into a new future of which he knows only from God." Richard Bauckham, *Bible and Mission: Christian Witness in a Postmodern World* (Grand Rapids: Baker, 2003), 28. In addition, Abraham is to "leave his place in the international order" to be used of God to bless them.

6. See for example Walter C. Kaiser, "Israel's Missionary Call," in *Perspectives on the World Christian Movement: A Reader*, 4th ed., eds. Ralph D. Winter and Steven C. Hawthorne (Pasadena: William Carey Library, 2013), 25–34; Kaiser, *Mission in the Old Testament: Israel as a Light to the Nations*, 2nd ed. (Grand Rapids: Baker, 2012); Reggie McNeal, *Missional Renaissance: Changing the Scorecard for the Church* (San Francisco: Jossey-Bass, 2009), 27; Christopher J. H. Wright, *The Mission of God: Unlocking the Bible's Grand Narrative* (Downers Grove: InterVarsity, 2006), 194–221.

7. For details concerning the grammatical construction and its implication for mission, see Eckhard J. Schnabel, *Early Christian Mission*, 2 vols. (Downers Grove: InterVarsity, 2004), 1:61–66.

8. See Jonathan Leeman, "Soteriological Mission: Focusing in on the Mission of Redemption," in *Four Views on the Church's Mission*, ed. Jason S. Sexton (Grand Rapids: Zondervan, 2017), 24. Dumbrell further asserts concerning the nature of the term "blessed" and how it applies to Israel's mission, "This climactic rendering [of 12:3] would mean that the peoples of the world would find blessing by coming to the Abrahamic descendants, rather than by later Israel's outreach. And this interpretation is consistent with the way mission is presented in the Old Testament—nations coming in pilgrimage to Israel's God." See Dumbrell, *Search for Order*, 35. See also Andreas J. Köstenberger and Peter Thomas O'Brien, *Salvation to the Ends of the Earth: A Biblical Theology of Mission*, New Studies in Biblical Theology 11 (Downers Grove: InterVarsity, 2001), 30. This does not negate Israel serving as a light to the nations, as will be seen, but shows the Old Testament emphasizes a "come and see" mission, whereas the New Testament displays a "go and tell" mission.

9. Kevin DeYoung and Greg Gilbert, *What Is the Mission of the Church? Making Sense of Social Justice, Shalom, and the Great Commission* (Wheaton: Crossway, 2011), 33.

10. Köstenberger, "Mission," 663.

kingdom of priests they would be positioned at the crossroads of two major geographical regions (Egypt and Mesopotamia) such that the nations of the world would see displayed how to rightly relate to the true God, and thus Israel would serve as "a vehicle for bringing the nations to the divine presence and rule."[11] As a holy nation, Israel recognizes how God himself is set apart and that they too must be set apart from the nations around them (Lev. 11:44; 19:2). They are to live as a "model or paradigm before the world of what God intends for all."[12] Their placement allows them to challenge the idolatry of the surrounding nations as they live according to God's Torah.

It seems, therefore, that Israel's mission is mainly centripetal, drawing people to their land to worship God in the temple as they live as a light in following God's law. Köstenberger and O'Brien helpfully delineate this mission as happening "*historically* through incorporation" and "*eschatologically* through ingathering."[13] In other words, people in the Old Testament are "incorporated" into Israel's covenant relationship with God and choose to worship him (e.g., Rahab in Josh. 6:25; Ruth; foreigners in David's kingdom, see 2 Sam. 11:3; 15:19–23). Regarding "eschatological ingathering," the blessing of the nations through Abraham's seed becomes an increasingly frequent theme later in the Prophets and Writings and denotes the coming day when nations will stream to Jerusalem in worship (cf. Isa. 2:1–4; Mic. 4:1–2). The nation of Israel would live in this manner specifically in the land of Canaan, and would be blessed in their obedience, but cursed if they disobeyed (Deut. 28–30). If they became like the nations, succumbing to idolatry and immorality, and did not maintain their holy and priestly status as the people of God, they would be taken into exile by the nations, supplanting the mission God had for them.

Mission in the Prophets

Joshua eventually leads God's people into the Promised Land, and there they establish a nation in covenant with God. After the judges and Israel's first monarch, Saul, David reigns as king over Israel. God makes a covenant with him (2 Sam. 7:1–29; cf. 1 Chron. 17:1–15) and states that from David will come the promised seed (cf. Gen. 3:15; 12:1–3; 22:17; 49:10) who will reign as king forever. Thus, through this covenant, God will demonstrate his kingship

---

11. See Gentry and Wellum, *Kingdom through Covenant*, 321.
12. Michael W. Goheen, *A Light to the Nations: The Missional Church and the Biblical Story* (Grand Rapids: Baker, 2011), 39. Gentry sees these phrases as being recursive in nature: "A holy nation is a nation completely *devoted* to loving God and serving him. A kingdom of priests is a group of priests exhibiting the rule of God and in their ministry bringing others to experience God's rule in their lives—bringing others to devote themselves to *devote* themselves to the worship of God." Peter J. Gentry, *How to Read and Understand the Biblical Prophets* (Wheaton: Crossway, 2017), 43.
13. Köstenberger and O'Brien, *Ends of the Earth*, 35–36. See also Charles H. H. Scobie, "Israel and the Nations: An Essay in Biblical Theology," *Tyndale Bulletin* 43.2 (1992): 286–92.

over creation by means of this coming ruler who will serve as his son and representative, and under whose rule life and blessing will be found.[14]

During the rule of David's son Solomon, various promises to Abraham and David were fulfilled: the land ruled by Israel's king expanded to its fullest extent, Israel became a great nation, and the Jerusalem temple was built (1 Kings 3–8; cf. Deut. 12:5–11).[15] Even in his prayer of dedication for the temple, Solomon articulates a vision that demonstrates mission as a key part of Israel's existence, so that all people would know their God (1 Kings 8:41–43, 59–60; 2 Chron. 6:32–33). Witnessing Solomon and Israel's worship of God and observance of the Torah, the nations would recognize the greatness of God, as illustrated by the queen of Sheba (1 Kings 10:1–13). This is the ideal scenario: Israel would live as a kingdom of priests and a holy nation so that the surrounding nations would see and be drawn to the one true God. However, Israel fails to keep the covenant, and instead of drawing the nations to God through their worship of God, Israel is drawn away by the nations to other gods.

Israel is warned again and again in the Latter Prophets that they need to turn from their idolatry to serve the living God. Isaiah is one such prophet who testifies to these things. Isaiah makes clear that the Lord would bring about a new exodus by means of his servant (cf. Isa. 42:1–4; 49:1–6; 50:4–9; 52:13–53:12; cf. Luke 9:31).[16] This "servant" is Davidic and thus royal,[17] is distinct from Israel in that he will bring Israel back, and will be a light and salvation to the nations (Isa. 42:6–7; 49:6).[18] The servant's work for Israel will also affect the whole world. This servant, who delights God the Father (Isa. 42:1; cf. Matt. 3:17) and is anointed by the Spirit (Isa. 42:1; cf. 61:1; Luke 4:18–19), will also be a suffering servant (Isa. 52:13–53:12). Israel will reject this suffering servant, thinking him to be justly judged by

---

14. It is crucial to recognize the progression and interrelationship of the covenants. God told Abraham he would make his name great (Gen. 12:2), and does so with David (2 Sam. 7:9). The land promise of the Abrahamic covenant is taken up with the Davidic covenant as well (2 Sam. 7:10). In terms of the Mosaic covenant, sonship language used to refer to Israel (Exod. 4:22) is now applied to David and his seed (2 Sam. 7:14). It is in keeping the Torah that Israel and her king would be blessed, and this does not change in the covenant made with David, but comes into sharper focus.

15. See Köstenberger, "Mission," 664.

16. For examples of studies on the topic of the new exodus as prophesied of in Isaiah, see Pao, *Isaianic New Exodus*; Rikki E. Watts, *Isaiah's New Exodus in Mark*, Biblical Studies Library (Grand Rapids: Baker, 2000).

17. For more on this point see Daniel I. Block, "My Servant David: Ancient Israel's Vision of the Messiah," in *Israel's Messiah in the Bible and the Dead Sea Scrolls*, eds. Richard S. Hess and M. Daniel Carroll (Grand Rapids: Baker, 2003), 17–56.

18. See Motyer, *Isaiah*, 310–11. Gentry and Wellum concur: "The new covenant, then, will bring about the Abrahamic blessing in that it will benefit both Israel and the nations and thus have universal implications . . . Within the Old Testament, the new covenant is viewed as both national (Jer. 31:36–40; 33:6–16; Ezek. 36:24–38; 37:11–28) and international (Jer. 33:9; Ezek. 36:36; 37:28). In fact, its scope is viewed as universal, especially in Isaiah (42:6; 49:6; 55:3–5; 56:4–8; 66:18–24)." Gentry and Wellum, *Kingdom through Covenant*, 645. See also Bruce A. Ware, "The New Covenant and the People(s) of God," in *Dispensationalism, Israel and the Church: The Search for Definition*, eds. Darrell L Bock and Craig A Blaising (Grand Rapids: Zondervan, 1992), 72–73; Robert L. Saucy, *The Case for Progressive Dispensationalism: The Interface Between Dispensational and Non-Dispensational Theology* (Grand Rapids: Zondervan, 1993), 127–34.

God (Isa. 53:3–4). And yet, it is by this servant's death and the willingness of the Lord to crush him (Isa. 53:10) that we might receive healing (Isa. 53:4–5). Köstenberger and O'Brien note, "This Servant is both priest, who 'sprinkles' the unclean (52:15), and sacrifice ('guilt offering', 53:10) through whose priestly work God's people are cleansed and made fit for priestly service themselves.... The Servant is the vehicle of God's grace to sinners, and the key to the divine salvation reaching to the ends of the earth."[19] While Israel failed in their mission to be a light to the nations, this servant will come and fulfill a key role regarding the fulfillment of God's mission (cf. Isa. 54–55) to both Israel, as well as the nations.

This failure of Israel and the extension of God's grace to them and the nations are illustrated in the book of Jonah. Here God commands the prophet Jonah to proclaim a message to Nineveh, but the prophet's outright refuses to do this (Jonah 1:1–3). In response, God brings Jonah to a point of repentance inside the belly of a fish and urges him once again to go and preach to Nineveh (Jonah 1:4–3:2). The prophet obeys, preaches a brief message, and Nineveh repents (Jonah 3:3–10). God shows mercy to the people of Nineveh because of their repentance, which displeases Jonah though he also had been a recipient of God's grace (4:1–11).[20] Jonah's anger stems from his knowledge of God's character, knowing him to be "gracious and merciful, slow to anger and abounding in steadfast love" towards even the enemies of Israel (Jonah 4:2; cf. Exod. 34:6–7). God's heart for the nations is revealed at the end of the book, as he shows how his love for the people of Nineveh is much greater than Jonah's compassion and love for the plant that shaded him (Jonah 4:11).[21] God will work in and through his people Israel. He will raise up his servant and bring the nations to salvation such that "the earth will be filled with the knowledge of the glory of the Lord as the waters cover the sea" (Hab. 2:14; cf. Isa. 11:9).

Mission in the Writings

The Psalms remind us that Israel was to be a beacon and a centerpiece among the nations that displayed the greatness of God. And the center of life in Israel was found in Jerusalem, the place of the temple wherein God's presence dwelt among his people (Pss. 5:7; 11:4; 48:1–14; 65:4; 76:1–12; 78:67–69). The name Zion, which came to be "applied variously to the sanctuary or temple, the holy mountain, Jerusalem, as well as the nation or remnant within it,"[22] refers to Israel's place of worship in the Old Testament. God's presence dwells there and invites both Israel and the nations to honor and glorify God

---

19. Köstenberger and O'Brien, *Ends of the Earth*, 48–49.
20. For more on the theme of grace and judgment within the book of Jonah, see Bryan D. Estelle, *Salvation through Judgment and Mercy: The Gospel according to Jonah* (Phillipsburg: P&R, 2005).
21. See Gregory Coswell, "Jonah among the Twelve Prophets," *Journal of Biblical Literature* 135.2 (2016): 283–99; Michael B. Shepherd, *A Commentary on the Book of the Twelve: The Minor Prophets*, Kregel Exegetical Library (Grand Rapids: Kregel, 2018), 236.
22. Köstenberger and O'Brien, *Ends of the Earth*, 51.

at that place. Thus, Zion is an Old Testament geographical center where God not only resides, but also calls for repentant, contrite, and faith-filled hearts eager to worship him (Pss. 72:8–11; 102:12–22).

However, there is no guarantee that God's presence remains in Jerusalem. If Israel turns away from God and walks in the ways of the nations, thus breaking covenant with him, then God's presence will depart from his people (cf. Ezek. 10:1–11:25). This would extinguish the light intended to shine for the nations, which is why the work of the servant prophesied in Isaiah is so necessary. A horn will "sprout for David" whom God will honor for the great work of salvation he accomplished, and whose enemies God will shame (Ps. 132:13–18). This salvific work is aimed initially at Israel, but ultimately shifts to an eschatological time when the nations would be glad in God and praise him (Ps. 67:1–7). Israel is to serve as a channel of blessing to the nations (Ps. 67:1–2)[23] thus fulfilling what God promised through Abraham so that the gladness of the peoples would be rooted in the greatness of God.[24]

One other mention of this concept occurs toward the end of the Hebrew Bible. In 1 Chronicles 16 the ark of the covenant is returned to Jerusalem and the Levites praise God and make offerings to the Lord (16:1–7). A song of thanks is then offered to God (1 Chron. 16:8–36; cf. Ps. 105:1–15). This song appeals for the deeds of God to be declared "among the peoples" (1 Chron. 16:8), signaling a clear call to display the greatness of God beyond the confines of the Jewish people. A reminder is given to Israel of their humble beginnings with the patriarchs and how God has been faithful to his people and displayed his wondrous works (1 Chron. 16:9–22). Israel should rejoice in God, but this call also goes out to "all the earth" (1 Chron. 16:23). Because God is great and greatly to be praised, and because any other god is false and worthless, the glory of God and his marvelous work should be declared by the nations (1 Chron. 16:24–27).[25] Next, a prayer is made for Israel to be saved and delivered from among the nations (1 Chron. 16:35), but the call is clearly made for all the "families of the peoples" to worship the Lord (1 Chron. 16:28–34). While Israel worships the Lord as his people, the nations are still clearly in view as God aims to receive worship from all people.[26]

---

23. There is a definite tension in place here. Israel fails to be the light they are called to be, but the servant will fulfill this role, thus operating in the way that Israel should have all along. See Goheen, *Light to the Nations*, 58.

24. See John Piper, *Let the Nations Be Glad! The Supremacy of God in Missions*, 3rd ed. (Grand Rapids: Baker, 2010), 231.

25. See John A. Thompson, *1, 2 Chronicles*, New American Commentary 9 (Nashville: B&H, 1994), 140.

26. Bauckham points to the movement of the Old Testament from particular to the universal. God works with Abraham, Israel, and in Zion, but ultimately with a broader framework in mind: "God's purpose in each of these of these singular choices was universal: that the blessing of Abraham might overflow to all the families of the earth, that God's self-revelation to Israel might make God known to all the nations, that from Zion his rule might extend to the ends of the earth." Bauckham, *Bible and Mission*, 46. These Old Testament trajectories pave the way for a theology of mission that is much more explicit in the New Testament.

Mission in the Gospels

God's mission to fill the earth with his glory comes into full display in the life, death, resurrection, and ascension of Jesus. In his first coming, Jesus came with an express purpose and mission. He follows the Old Testament pattern of going to the people of Israel, but Gentiles are also impacted by his ministry (Mark 5:1–20; 7:24–30).[27] He preaches the kingdom of God and proclaims liberty as the Spirit-anointed Messiah (Luke 4:16–21; cf. Isa. 61:1–2). The extent of his ministry and work in his life, death, and resurrection would enable disciples of Jesus to be made in all nations (Matt. 28:19–20; cf. Mark 13:10).

Jesus proclaims and inaugurates the gospel of the kingdom (Matt. 4:17; 12:28) and exercises kingly authority as he heals and casts out demons (Matt. 4:23–25). He takes upon himself the curse due to Adam, Israel, and all humanity (Matt. 20:28; Mark 10:45). He makes atonement (Luke 22:19–20; 23:44–49; cf. Rom. 3:21–27) and, in his resurrection, stands as the Son of Man (Dan. 7:13–14) and the seed from the line of Abraham (Gen. 12:1–3), Judah (Gen. 49:9–10), and David (1 Chron. 17:11–14). Jesus lives a perfect life in full obedience to the will of the Father (John 4:34; 6:38), dies an atoning death, and rises from the dead, demonstrating his fulfillment of the call to be a "light to the nations" as he accomplishes salvation for all who will believe (Matt .12:15–21; Luke 2:29–32; cf. Isa. 42:1–3; 49:6).[28]

The salvation Jesus accomplished as his mission and the kingdom he inaugurated would be announced by his disciples.[29] As the Father sent Jesus, now Jesus would send his people in the power of the Spirit (John 20:21–22).[30] As their distinct mission, God's new covenant people, the church, will proclaim the good news of Jesus's person and his accomplished work. This good news "will be proclaimed throughout the whole world, as a testimony to all nations" (Matt. 24:14). God's covenant presence would be not just with the Jews, but with all people who call on the name of Jesus in faith (Mark 11:17; cf. Isa. 56:7).[31] Therefore, this gospel must be proclaimed to all nations.

---

27. Köstenberger, "Mission," 665.
28. Bauckham, *Bible and Mission*, 48. Pao and Schnabel, in reference to Luke's quotation of Isaiah 49:6 in Luke 2:32, comment that while this salvation will be for the glory of the people of Israel, "with the arrival of Israel's deliverer, Gentiles will be able to participate in the people of God." David W. Pao and Eckhard J. Schnabel, "Luke," in *Commentary on the New Testament Use of the Old Testament*, eds. G. K. Beale and D. A. Carson (Grand Rapids: Baker, 2007), 272–73.
29. See Schnabel, *Early Christian Mission*, 1:378, who states, "Jesus was sent by God in order to do the 'work' that the Father had entrusted to him, and Jesus faithfully carried out this work, with unreserved engagement and unselfish willingness to suffer, until it was 'finished' in his death. And it is this work that the disciples are commissioned to continue." Here Schnabel does not mean atoning death as the continued work, but the disciples serving as envoys and representatives of Jesus, who may in that pursuit suffer and die as Jesus did.
30. See Leon Morris, *The Gospel according to John*, New International Commentary on the New Testament (Grand Rapids: Eerdmans, 1995), 746–47.
31. Watts states regarding this quotation of Isaiah 56:7, "the inclusion of proselytes from the ends of the earth (e.g., 45:22; 49:6; 52:10) in a restored Zion will be a central feature of a new thing that Yahweh was doing (56:4–7; 60–62; cf. 42:1–6; 49:1, 6; 52:15; also 14:1; 19:19–25). . . . For the sake of his glory, Yahweh will bring such ones [i.e. Gentiles]

Gilbert and DeYoung further delineate this definition of mission, focusing specifically on the "Great Commission" texts coming at the end of the Gospels, stating, "The mission of the church is to go into the world and make disciples by declaring the gospel of Jesus Christ in the power of the Spirit and gathering these disciples into churches, that they might worship the Lord and obey His commands now and in eternity to the glory of God the Father (Matt. 28:18–20; Luke 24:45–49; John 20:21; Acts 1:8)."[32] Certainly, in a broad sense this means that disciples of Jesus are commissioned to live, love, and serve in ways commensurate to the example of Jesus through the power and grace he supplies. But in a narrower sense, our mission is to make disciples of Jesus Christ, baptizing them and teaching them to observe all that Jesus commanded.[33]

Jesus sends his followers into the world as the Father sent him into the world (John 17:18), in order that they would bear much fruit (John 15:16) in accomplishing the mission of making disciples of Jesus. Christ gives this directive and ascends to the Father in heaven, but will one day return. In the meantime, "mission is the church's primary task between Christ's first coming and his return. The striking open-endedness of the commissioning scene, similar to the open-endedness of the book of Acts, is pregnant with anticipation and potential. The eleven, as representatives of later generations of believers, embark on their mission, at the command and on the basis of the authority of the exalted Christ, the eschatological ruler, the Son of God."[34]

Mission in Acts and the Letters

With the commission of Jesus ringing in their ears and hearts and his call to be his Spirit-empowered witnesses in Jerusalem, Judea, Samaria, and even the ends of the earth (Acts 1:8),[35] the fledgling church devoted themselves to prayer (Acts 1:14). Köstenberger maintains, "In a major paradigm shift from a centripetal movement to a centrifugal one, the Twelve are to function as 'witnesses' to Israel (in place of the restoration of the kingdom of Israel, 1:6),

---

to his holy mountain, for it is his intention that his house be a house of prayer for all peoples, universal and without restriction (cf. Isa. 2:1–4; note also the language of Solomon's prayer in 1 Kings 8:41–43, which seems to be used here)." Rikk E. Watts, "Mark," in *Commentary on the New Testament Use of the Old Testament*, eds. G. K. Beale and D. A. Carson (Grand Rapids: Baker, 2007), 209. As Watts later states, the temple was corrupt in Jesus's day (Mark 11:15–19), but that temple would be destroyed and a new temple raised up, which was embodied in Jesus Christ and his people, and made up of believing Jews and Gentiles (212).

32. DeYoung and Gilbert, *Mission of the Church*, 62. Elsewhere DeYoung and Gilbert argue for the strategic importance of these Great Commission texts, stating that these are direct commands about the mission of the church, their placement as Jesus's last words suggests their significance, and the work of Jesus dictates what we are now to do regarding mission (40–45).

33. This distinction between a broad (i.e., *being* disciples) and narrow (i.e., *making* disciples) mission is marked out in Leeman, "Soteriological Mission," 19–20. Leeman further argues for the "foregrounding" of Jesus's priestly work, which would then emphasize the narrow mission for his disciples (29–35).

34. Köstenberger and O'Brien, *Ends of the Earth*, 108–9. See also Carson, "Matthew," 670.

35. These places serve essentially as geographic concentric circles.

and subsequently Paul acts as 'witness' to the Gentiles."[36] This ever-expanding mission would begin at Pentecost when the Spirit would come upon God's people in a new way.

While the disciples are gathered on the day of Pentecost, they are filled with the Holy Spirit and begin to speak the gospel in different languages (Acts 2:1–12). Peter addresses the crowd and explains how this phenomenon is attributable to the ministry of the Spirit, as prophesied in Joel 2:28–32 (Acts 2:14–21). The crowd of Jews, who come from a variety of nations,[37] hear the truth regarding the crucified and resurrected Jesus, who is indeed Lord and Messiah and calls all to repent and believe in him (Acts 2:22–41). Three thousand believed in the truth of the gospel that day, and the good news continues to spread in Jerusalem through the bold proclamation of Peter, John, and the other disciples (Acts 3:1–7:60). Those who received Jesus would experience times of refreshment (Acts 3:20), but those who refused him would suffer judgment and eternal condemnation (Acts 3:23).

The persecution of the church drove its mission beyond Jerusalem into Judea and Samaria (Acts 8:1–4). Philip serves as the initial evangelist to the Samaritans (Acts 8:5–25). This was surprising since Jews did not typically interact with Samaritans (John 4:9), but also completely expected given Jesus's commission to his disciples (Acts 1:8). As Samaritans began believing in Christ, the apostles sent Peter and John to pray that the Samaritans would also receive the Holy Spirit (Acts 8:14–17).[38] Travelling southwest toward Gaza, Philip speaks to an Ethiopian eunuch concerning the gospel of Jesus Christ (Acts 8:26–40). Finally, Luke informs his readers that Philip goes to Azotus, near the Mediterranean coast, and then north to Caesarea (Acts 8:40).

In similar fashion, Peter expands the scope of the gospel mission by visiting the Roman centurion Cornelius after being told in a dream to not consider unclean what God considers clean and then instructed by the Spirit to accompany Cornelius's men (Acts 10:1–23). When Peter preaches to this group of Gentiles, he begins by acknowledging that the gospel was the word "sent to Israel" (Acts 10:36; cf. Isa. 52:7) but then declares to them the truth about Jesus's death and resurrection and the call to receive "forgiveness of sins through his name (Acts 10:36–43). Those in attendance believe the word Peter preaches and they receive the Holy Spirit (Acts 10:44–48). When Peter is later questioned by the apostles about why he

---

36. Köstenberger, "Mission," 666.
37. These nations approximately parallel the table of nations in Genesis 10 (cf. Isa. 66:18–19), seemingly signifying a beginning work that would extend to the Gentiles within those nations and beyond. See J. M. Scott, "Luke's Geographical Horizon," in *The Book of Acts in its First Century Setting: Volume 2. Graeco-Roman Setting*, eds. D. W. J. Gill and C. Gempf (Grand Rapids: Eerdmans, 1994), 527–30; John Michael Penney, *The Missionary Emphasis of Lukan Pneumatology* (Sheffield: Sheffield Academic, 1997), 82.
38. Bock avers, "Baptism with a later coming of the Spirit is exceptional and not normative." See *Acts*, 331. It would seem there are unique moments where the Spirit fills those who believe in Jerusalem (Acts 2), Samaria (Acts 8), as well as the Gentile region of Caesarea (Acts 10), signifying the mission of the church and the reach of the gospel would include the nations, as prophesied. See Köstenberger and O'Brien, *Ends of the Earth*, 139–40.

went to the Gentiles, he recounts to them everything that occurred (Acts 11:1–18). Luke's narrative emphasizes that Cornelius and his company are not the only Gentiles who receive salvation, stating that the Holy Spirit was poured out on the Gentiles (Acts 10:45) and God has granted repentance to them (Acts 11:18). Wright notes, "The outpouring of the Spirit and granting repentance and forgiveness were among the key signs of the eschatological reign of God. If God were now granting these things to the nations, then that era must have dawned, with all its universal implications for all the nations."[39] The Gentiles would not need to worship at a temple in Jerusalem; Jesus is the cornerstone of a new temple made of Jews and Gentiles who believe in him and are Spirit-indwelt.[40] Thus, the Word of God continues to increase and spread (Acts 6:7; 12:24; 19:20).

The conversion of Saul of Tarsus is also a key moment in the book of Acts as it relates to mission. Formerly a persecutor of the disciples of Jesus, Saul comes into contact with the risen Christ on the road to Damascus and converts (Acts 9:1–19). God tells Ananias that Saul—soon to be referred to as Paul—is "a chosen instrument of mine to carry my name before the Gentiles and kings and the children of Israel" (Acts 9:15). Speaking in this way, claims Bock, it seems clear that Paul's ministry "will reflect the ultimate intent of Jesus's work: ministry to all people, both Jews and Gentiles."[41] As an apostle, Paul would be a primary means by which the gospel would continue to reach the nations in these early days of the church.

Paul and Barnabas are set apart by the church in Antioch for the work to which God called them: proclaiming the gospel to various regions of the empire (Acts 13:1–3). Luke records the various journeys of Paul (Acts 13:1–20:38) and also recounts several of Paul's key sermons in these different locations. One such sermon is found in Acts 13 as Paul preaches in a synagogue in Pisidian Antioch. He makes known that Jesus is in fact the Messiah prophesied in the Old Testament, but eventually the Jews revile and contradict him (Acts 13:44–45). As a result, Paul declares that from then on, Barnabus and him would go and proclaim Jesus to the Gentiles (Acts 13:46).

Paul states that proclaiming Jesus to the Gentile follows what the Lord commanded, quoting Isaiah 49:6: "I have made you a light for the Gentiles, that you may bring salvation to the ends of the earth" (Acts 13:47). This citation, according to Marshall, "serves to motivate and legitimize the mission to the Gentiles as part of God's plan foretold in Scripture."[42] When we consider the context of Isaiah 49:6, it is intriguing here that Paul and Barnabas adopt the role of Isaiah's servant (cf. Isa. 42:1–9; 49:1–13; 50:4–11; 52:13–53:12), a title which is normally tied to Jesus in the New Testament (Matt. 12:17–21; Luke 22:37).

---

39. Wright, *Mission of God*, 515–16. See also Bock, *Acts*, 410.
40. For more on the themes of temple, Spirit, and mission in the book of Acts, see Beale, *Temple*, 201–44.
41. Bock, *Acts*, 361.
42. Marshall, "Acts," 588.

Paul and Barnabas can thus be seen as an extension of Jesus's work, servants of the Servant spreading the message of the gospel to the nations.[43]

The Jerusalem council is also an important moment in Acts as it relates to mission (15:1–35). The advancement of the gospel to the Gentiles causes consternation among some Jews. The Jerusalem council addresses the issue of whether Gentiles needed to be circumcised according to Mosaic law to join the church (Acts 15:1–5). Three speeches are given. First, Peter reminds the council of his experience with Cornelius and how he and other Gentiles received the Holy Spirit through faith in Jesus (Acts 15:6–11). Second, Barnabas and Paul recount their own gospel work among the Gentiles (Acts 15:12). Third, James then calls the church to not burden the Gentiles with old covenant regulations, although they should abide by some specific principles (Acts 15:13–21). In James's speech he appeals to Amos 9:11–12 (cf. Isa. 45:21; Zech. 8:22) and asserts that reaching the Gentiles with the gospel fulfills the prophecy of the rebuilding of the "tent of David" (Acts 15:16–17). Jesus, the new temple (John 2:18–22), is the Messiah from David's line, the prophesied restoration from the seed of Abraham who blesses all the nations and builds them up as a temple (1 Cor. 3:16–17; 6:18–20; 2 Cor. 6:14–7:1; Eph. 2:20; 1 Peter 2:4–10).[44] Thus, as Bauckham asserts, "The Gentiles do not have to become Jews in order to join the eschatological people of God and to have access to God in the Temple of the Messianic age."[45] The message of Jesus Christ would continue to spread and reach various regions. Acts concludes with Paul in Rome, a clear example of the gospel going to the ends of the earth (Acts 1:8), which serves as a kind of invitation to continue to take the gospel as a light to all the nations (Isa. 49:6).[46]

The New Testament Epistles are situational and speak to issues experienced by particular churches in specific places. Many of these issues relate in some way to the gospel mission. Paul's plan was to establish Christian congregations with qualified leadership in strategic cities from which the gospel could reach surrounding regions.[47] In Romans, Paul clearly states that he is not "ashamed of the gospel, for it is the power of God for salvation to everyone who believes, to the Jew first and also to the Greek" (Rom. 1:16). Paul still seeks to minister the gospel to fellow Jews (Rom. 9:1–5; 10:1–3), but also recognizes that Gentiles who believe in Jesus have been grafted into God's people (Rom. 11:17–24; cf. Eph. 2:11–22).

---

43. See Bock, *Acts*, 464.
44. See Kenneth L. Barker, "The Scope and Center of Old Testament Theology and Hope," in *Dispensationalism Israel, and the Church: The Search for Definition*, eds. Craig A. Blaising and Darrell L. Bock (Grand Rapids: Zondervan, 1992), 327; Köstenberger and O'Brien, *Ends of the Earth*, 150–51; Marshall, "Acts," 592–93.
45. Richard Bauckham, "James and the Gentiles: Acts 15:13-21," in *History, Literature, and Society in the Book of Acts*, ed. Ben Witherington III (Cambridge: Cambridge University Press, 1996), 178.
46. See T. S. Moore, "'To the End of the Earth': The Geographical and Ethnic Universalism of Acts 1:8 in Light of Isaianic Influence on Luke," *Journal of the Evangelical Theological Society* 40.3 (1997): 389–99; Brian Rosner, "The Progress of the Word," in *Witness to the Gospel: The Theology of Acts*, eds. I. Howard Marshall and David Peterson (Grand Rapids: Eerdmans, 1998), 217–19.
47. See Köstenberger, "Mission," 667.

He states that he is in the priestly service of the gospel so that the offering of the Gentiles might be acceptable (Rom. 15:16).[48] Paul ministers as a servant to both Jews and Gentiles (Rom. 15:8–13; cf. 2 Sam. 22:50; Ps. 18:49; Deut. 32:43; Ps. 117:1; Isa. 11:10) and looks to preach in places where the gospel has not yet been proclaimed so that, "Those who have never been told of him will see, and those who have never heard will understand" (Rom. 15:20–21; cf. Isa 52:15).[49]

In Galatians Paul deals directly with the propagation of false gospels, saying that if different "gospels" are being proclaimed, those who do so are accursed (Gal. 1:6–9). He deals with various other gospel distortions in Colossians, 1–2 Thessalonians, 1–2 Timothy, and Titus, and does so because he sees himself as a steward of the gospel (Eph. 3:1–6; Col. 1:25).[50] Paul is concerned that these churches not err regarding the content of the gospel, whether it be in the direction of legalism or laxity. Being entrusted with a stewardship to preach the gospel (1 Cor. 9:16–17), whether verbally or in writing, Paul strives to keep the churches in line with proper gospel doctrine.

The book of Hebrews exhorts believers to persevere in their faith. At key junctures Hebrews urges its readers to "pay much closer attention" to the message of Jesus (Heb. 2:1), "consider Jesus" (Heb. 3:1), and look to Jesus (Heb. 12:1–2), and not "shrink back" but hold onto their faith, even in the midst of trials (Heb. 10:32–39). They must look to Jesus as they run the race and follow him outside the camp (Heb. 12:1–3; 13:12–14). By returning to Judaism, the readers of Hebrews would neglect this great salvation only to their peril (Heb. 2:1–3).

Peter reminds the church, using the language already seen in Exodus 19:6, that we are "a chosen race, a royal priesthood, a holy nation, a people for [God's] own possession, that

---

48. This is the only place in the New Testament where someone—besides Christ—speaks of their own ministry in priestly terms. Wright asserts that the allusion to the priestly office here by Paul could likely refer to Isaiah 66:18–21. "For there God promises that the emissaries to the nations will bring in both Jews and Gentiles as an offering to the Lord, and the language used is that of priesthood and sacrifice. This would fit with Paul's probable echo of Isaiah 66 later in Romans 15 when he describes his own missionary intentions as going in a great arc from Jerusalem, through Asia Minor, via Macedonia and Illyricum, and onward to the farthest west." Wright, *Mission of God*, 525–26. See also Daniel Jong-Sang Chae, "Paul's Apostolic Self-Awareness and the Occasion and Purpose of Romans," in *Mission and Meaning: Essays Presented to Peter Cotterell*, ed. Anthony Billington, Tony Lane, and Max Turner (Carlisle: Paternoster, 1995), 116–37.

49. Moo maintains that Paul likely cited that particular Old Testament text for three reasons: "First, it justifies Paul's decision not 'to build on another's foundation' (v. 20); for the text speaks of bringing a message to those who have not yet heard. Second, it accords with Paul's sense of calling to Gentiles, since the ones who have not had it announced to them and have not yet heard are 'kings' and 'nations' (v. 15a). Third, it alludes to the content of Paul's gospel. For Isaiah 52:15 is part of the famous fourth 'servant' passage, and the 'him' concerning whom these Gentiles have not been told is the Servant of the Lord. Paul's pioneering church-planting ministry among the Gentiles is fulfilling the OT prediction about Gentiles coming to see and understand the message about the Servant of the Lord." Moo, *Romans*, 897–98.

50. For more on stewardship language in the New Testament and how it relates to the proclamation of the gospel, see Jeremy M. Kimble, "The Steward of God: Exploring the Function and Role of Elders," *Southeastern Theological Review* 6.1 (2015): 83–112.

you may proclaim the excellencies of him who called you out of darkness and into his marvelous light" (1 Peter 2:9). The church now functions as mediators of God's blessings to the nations, by means of gospel proclamation.[51] As Gladd and Harmon state, "Through us Jesus is being fruitful and multiplying his people so that the earth will be filled with his glory."[52] These Gentile believers were not God's people and had not received his mercy, but now they receive both through their belief in the gospel, and are to make it known to others as their distinct mission (1 Peter 2:10; cf. Hos. 1:10; 2:23).[53]

Later epistles, such as 2 Peter, 1–3 John, and Jude speak of mission as it relates to dealing with false teaching within the church. As Köstenberger maintains, these letters "display an essential prerequisite for mission: zeal for the 'faith once for all entrusted to the saints' (Jude 3)."[54] False prophets and teachers must be identified and denounced (2 Peter 2:1–22; Jude 3–16). Christians should not receive false teachers into their homes or give them any greeting (2 John 1:10), but should support "workers for the truth" who have gone out to proclaim the gospel (3 John 1:5–8). Finally, Christians should persevere in their faith, building themselves up in the most holy faith, praying in the Spirit, and keeping themselves in the love of God (Jude 20–21). Christians must also do what they can to rescue those who have erred or are attracted by the doctrines of false teachers, showing mercy while keeping themselves unstained by the world (Jude 22–23; cf. James 1:27).[55]

Mission in Revelation

In the final book of the biblical canon, mission continues to be a key emphasis. Early in the book we see examples of churches beset by two distinct challenges: persecution and deceptive teaching (Rev. 2:2–3, 10, 13–16, 20–23; 3:4, 8–10). This should not be surprising to the reader, given that Daniel depicted the time of tribulation as being filled with the persecution of the saints as well as the propagation of false doctrine (Dan. 7:1–28; 11:29–37; cf. Matt. 24:3–28). The gospel will reach the nations,[56] and Christ's return culminates this mission. Meanwhile, the people of God are called to persevere and continue to share the good news.

The great enemy of God, Satan, who is depicted as a dragon (Rev. 12:1–17), appears alongside two other "beasts" ("the man of lawlessness" and the false prophet; Rev. 13:1–18;

---

51. See Thomas R. Schreiner, *1, 2 Peter, Jude*, 114.
52. Benjamin L. Gladd and Matthew S. Harmon, *Making All Things New: Inaugurated Eschatology for the Life of the Church* (Grand Rapids: Baker, 2016), 167.
53. See Jobes, *1 Peter*, 163–64.
54. Köstenberger, "Mission," 667.
55. Peter H. Davids, *The Letters of 2 Peter and Jude*, Pillar New Testament Commentary (Grand Rapids: Eerdmans, 2006), 100.
56. See Richard Bauckham, *The Climax of Prophecy: Studies on the Book of Revelation* (London: T&T Clark, 1999), 238–337, who contends that the conversion of the nations is a central theme of Revelation.

cf. 2 Thess. 2:1–12) who speak deceptively and lead many astray from God's ways. Those who do not follow them are persecuted and even killed (Rev. 13:11–18). This is depicted by the two witnesses who prophesy and give testimony on behalf of God, and are then killed by the beast and his followers (Rev. 11:1–10). However, God will raise them up and bring judgment on those who persecuted them. Likewise, the 144,000 who live faithfully in the midst of a world dominated by evil are redeemed as a "firstfruits for God and the Lamb" (Rev. 7:1–8; 14:1–5).

The mission of proclaiming the gospel, as depicted in Revelation, is opposed by many, but nevertheless advances. This is why John records these details: to give a call "for the endurance of the saints, those who keep the commandments of God and their faith in Jesus" (Rev. 14:12). The dragon, the beasts, and the prostitute (the great city of Babylon that has dominion) oppose God and his people and do all they can to deceive and persecute (Rev. 17:1–18). As such, believers in Jesus are called to depart Babylon, lest they share in her sins and cease to persevere in their faith (Rev. 18:4–5).[57] Representing the world system opposed to God, Babylon will fall, but Jesus will return and render judgment, and God's people will be finally and eternally saved (Rev. 18:1–20:15). Believers in Jesus will be ushered into a new creation where they will reign with God forever (Rev. 21:1–22:1).

In the end, the book of Revelation finally shows people from every nation gathered in heaven to worship God and Jesus, "the Lamb" (cf. Rev. 4:10–11; 5:6–9; 7:9–10). John describes the new heaven and new earth as "a city-temple where God's glorious presence dwells in its fullness with humanity. . . . Nations and kings reflect to God his own glory as they worship the Lamb who sits on the throne. God's redeemed people serve as priest-kings who rule over a renewed creation as they were originally intended to do."[58] This

---

57. While describing the final return and judgment of Jesus Christ here in Revelation, even now we are instructed to go out from the midst of the world and be separate (2 Cor. 6:17; cf. Isa. 52:11). Alexander maintains, "For those who are united to Jesus Christ, eternal life begins here and now, as does citizenship of the city that will one day be created by God on a renewed earth. Jesus challenges his followers to look forward in faith, to pray and work for the spread of God's rule here and now. They are to exercise true humility, remembering that they have been redeemed from evil only by the grace of God and not by their own achievements or piety. They are to witness to an alternative worldview that promotes belief in a Creator God, highlighting the inadequacy of a purely materialistic view of human existence. They are to be peacemakers, reconciling those who are alienated, especially from God. They are to make disciples of Jesus Christ, extending God's kingdom throughout the world through self-sacrificial love. They are to hunger and thirst after righteousness, caring for the oppressed and promoting social justice for the benefit of the marginalized. They are to resist the powers of evil, arming themselves for the spiritual battle that continues to rage until Christ returns. They are to consider themselves exiles and pilgrims in 'Babylon,' holding lightly to this life but living in this absurd and evil world in confident anticipation of all that God will yet do. They are to live holy lives, aiming for personal moral perfection and purity. They are to love others wholeheartedly, including their enemies, as an expression and outworking of their sincere love for God. They are to fulfill their creative capacity as home and city builders but ever recognizing the temporary nature of this present world." Alexander, *City of God*, 163. Again, while Alexander emphasizes the present focus, one must not forget the climactic judgment of Babylon and the call for endurance at the end as well.
58. Gladd and Harmon, *Making All Things New*, 167–68.

fulfills God's covenants with Abraham and David and completes the journey from the original creation to the new creation, where redeemed humanity will live forever in the presence of God and where, in keeping with the prophetic vision, he will be their God and they will be his people (Rev. 21:3).[59] Thus, God's mission will be finally and completely accomplished and realized.

---

59. See Köstenberger, "Mission," 667. In noting the culmination of the covenants in the book of Revelation, Wright aptly summarizes: "Noah is there in the vision of a new creation, and new heavens and a new earth after judgment (Rev. 21:1). Abraham is there in the ingathering and blessing of all nations from every tongue and language (Rev. 7:9). Moses is there in the covenantal assertions that 'they will be his people, and God himself will be with them and be their God,' and 'the dwelling of God is with men, and he will live them' (Rev. 21:3). David is there in the holy city, the new Jerusalem, and the expansion of the temple to include the whole creation (Rev. 21), and in the identity of Jesus as the Lion of Judah and the Root of David (Rev. 5:5). And the new covenant is there in the fact that all of this will be accomplished by the blood of the Lamb who was slain (Rev. 5:12)." Wright, *Mission of God*, 530.

Discussion Questions

1. What is the mission of God? How is this mission put on display in the Old Testament? The New Testament?

2. What is the mission of the church?

3. What are some specific Old Testament and New Testament passages that highlight the fact that God wants to see people in his kingdom from every tribe, people, and nation?

4. In the Catholic Epistles (e.g., 2 Peter, Jude), what is the relationship between the mission of the church and the refutation of false teaching?

5. Often the mission of the church is related to evangelism and rightly so. How does perseverance in the faith factor into discussions about mission?

Resources for Further Study

DeYoung, Kevin and Greg Gilbert. *What Is the Mission of the Church? Making Sense of Social Justice, Shalom, and the Great Commission.* Wheaton: Crossway, 2011.

Piper, John. *Let the Nations Be Glad! The Supremacy of God in Missions.* Grand Rapids: Baker, 2010.

Sexton, Jason S., ed. *Four Views on the Church's Mission.* Grand Rapids: Zondervan, 2017.

Tennent, Timothy. *Invitation to World Missions: A Trinitarian Missiology for the Twenty-First Century.* Grand Rapids: Kregel, 2010.

Wright, Christopher J. H. *The Mission of God: Unlocking the Bible's Grand Narrative.* Downers Grove: InterVarsity. 2006.

BIBLICAL THEOLOGY IN THE CHURCH AND THE ACADEMY

CHAPTER 21

BIBLICAL THEOLOGY IN THE LIFE OF THE CHURCH

THE CHURCH IS CHRIST'S BRIDE (Eph. 5:22–27), the institution Jesus proclaimed that the gates of hell would not prevail against (Matt. 16:18). Yet, one can observe within the pages of the New Testament, as well as throughout church history, that the church can veer from the course set out for her by Jesus. The tenets of Scripture can be forgotten, resulting in doctrinal infidelity and moral laxity. Thus, the discipline of biblical theology is essential to the health and vitality of the church.

So far, this book has explored the canonical shape, storyline, and key themes of Scripture. These points are crucial to understand cognitively, but we as Christians are also called to relate and apply these truths to real life. Knowing God by means of his Word will profoundly affect the way in which we live as individual Christians and operate corporately as a church. This chapter will address several ways biblical theology impacts our Christian living, beginning with our own individual habits of grace[1] and culminating with the impact of biblical theology on the life of the church.

Bible Reading

The blessed man is the one who forsakes the way of wickedness and instead delights in meditating on God's law day and night (Ps. 1:1–2). This key emphasis marks out the people of God. In fact, the need to study Scripture in an ongoing fashion is visible within

---

1. For an excellent book on this topic see David Mathis, *Habits of Grace: Enjoying Jesus through the Spiritual Disciplines* (Wheaton: Crossway, 2016).

the structure of the Old Testament itself. The beginning of each grouping of the Old Testament (Law, Prophets, and Writings) stresses the power of the Word of God (cf. Gen. 1:3, 6, 9, 11, 14, 20, 24, 26, 28, 29; Josh. 1:8; Ps. 1:2).[2] One can also observe how the seams between the Old Testament books commend the reader to obtain knowledge and wisdom through careful study of Scripture (cf. Deut. 34:5–Josh. 1:9; Mal. 4:4; Ps. 1).[3] Thus, on both the micro and macro levels, Scripture calls the reader to take up its contents, meditate on them constantly, and be a doer of the Word (James 1:22).

This call to read and study Scripture is not merely to obtain knowledge of its content, but to know the author himself. God is there, and he is not silent. He has made himself known by means of his creation (Ps. 19:1; Rom. 1:18–20) and most especially by means of his divinely inspired Word (2 Tim. 3:16–17; 2 Peter 1:20–21). Here one encounters God as omniscient, omnipotent, and omnipresent, the creator and sustainer, holy and loving, transcendent and immanent. He is revealed in all of his glory, greatness, and goodness as Scripture unveils the truth of who he is. This is all true, but one must also have eyes to see it.

Conversion is when God shines light in a person's heart to see the "light of the knowledge of the glory of God in the face of Christ" (2 Cor. 4:6) so that they can behold the beauty of Christ in the gospel (2 Cor. 4:4). However, beholding Christ in the gospel at conversion is not the end of the matter. With unveiled faces (i.e., as converted people) we are to continually behold the glory of the Lord, and in so doing we will be transformed from "one degree of glory to another" (2 Cor. 3:18). We do not presently see Jesus face-to-face; rather we behold Christ in the gospel (2 Cor .4:4, 6), which is acknowledged and highlighted throughout the Scriptures (cf. Luke 24:27, 44; John 5:39). Thus, joyfully and expectantly beholding Christ in the Scriptures is the means to becoming like him.[4]

When one understands how to skillfully read Scripture—not randomly or haphazardly, but in continuity with the principles learned in the discipline of biblical theology—and beholds the glory of God in Christ in their study of his Word, and delightfully meditates on this Word day and night, they will be firmly established like a tree (Ps. 1:3; cf. Jer. 17:5–8; Dan. 11:32). Biblical theology helps our reading of the Bible to more readily see the glory

---

2. See Dempster, *Dominion and Dynasty*, 33; Hamilton, *God's Glory in Salvation*, 139.
3. Shepherd elaborates, "The similarity and uniqueness of the language at these strategic junctures can hardly be coincidental. Furthermore, this seam work sends an eschatological message that had and has a global impact on the reading of the lower levels of the canon. The text commends itself as the object of study for the wise person (Deut. 34:9; Josh. 1:8; Ps. 1:2) who waits in expectation for the messianic prophet like Moses (Deut 34:10) whose forerunner, the prophet like Elijah (Mal. 3:23 [Eng. 4:5]), will prepare the way before the Day of YHWH (cf. Luke 1:17; Acts 3:22)." Michael B. Shepherd, *Textuality and the Bible* (Eugene: Wipf and Stock, 2016), 27–28. See also Sailhamer, *Old Testament Theology*, 239–51.
4. For more commentary concerning 2 Corinthians 3:18–4:6 see David Peterson, *Transformed by God: New Covenant Life and Ministry* (Downers Grove: InterVarsity, 2012), 117–22. Beale also expounds on this point, pointing more toward idolatry, but also referring to worship of God, arguing that "What you revere you resemble, either for ruin or for restoration." See Beale, *We Become What We Worship*, 11.

of God in Christ and thus be conformed to the image of Christ (Rom. 8:29). As Hamilton states, "Understanding the story's plot and purpose enriches our reading and our living."[5] Knowing the storyline, structure, and key themes of the Bible opens up the overall content of the Bible to our understanding and affections, which summons our hearts to worship God and our hands to serve him.

Prayer

As we come to know God and are conformed to the image of Christ by hearing from him in his Word, we are also further compelled to reply to his words by means of prayer. As we increase in our knowledge of God, our desire to cry out to him in adoration and worship should only increase. We call out to him because he is a merciful and gracious God, slow to anger, abounding in steadfast love, rendering justice on those who are guilty, but also forgiving iniquity, transgression, and sin (Exod. 34:6–7). The character of God shows us his heart and thus how we ought to live and pray. Thus, there is a direct correlation between our understanding of Scripture and the precision and depth available to us as we pray, which is why biblical theology is of such value for our prayers.

Biblical theology helps us understand the structure and themes of Scripture so that we can pray in accordance with the microstructures and macrostructures seen therein. In other words, one learns to pray from specific passages that contain focused prayers, as well as from the overarching storyline of Scripture as a whole. Concerning specific passages, many throughout the history of the church have been helped by praying through the Psalter.[6] Jesus's prayers in the Gospels, particularly the Lord's Prayer (Matt. 6:9–13), show his followers what and how to pray. The apostle Paul also includes specific prayers within his letters that provide insight regarding how we address God (Rom. 15:14–33; Eph. 1:15–23; 3:14–21; Phil. 1:9–11; Col. 1:9–14; 1 Thess. 3:9–13; 2 Thess. 1:3–12).[7] Specific passages containing actual prayers, or those that teach about prayer, can serve as wonderful guides for growth in this area.

Biblical theology also shows us the overarching structure of Scripture so as to teach us to pray in accordance with God's will. Thinking with a biblical-theological lens enlightens our understanding of the identity and character of the creating, sustaining, redeeming, Trinitarian God who is over all. He created all things for his glory (Ps. 19:1; Isa. 43:6–7), but humanity quickly rebelled against his will and ushered in sin and death as dominant realities within the world. God chose Abraham and his offspring, comprising the nation of

---

5. Hamilton, *God's Glory in Salvation*, 569.
6. See Christopher J. H. Holmes, *The Lord is Good: Seeking the God of the Psalter* (Downers Grove: InterVarsity, 2018); Timothy Keller, *The Songs of Jesus: A Year of Daily Devotions in the Psalms* (New York: Viking, 2015).
7. For an excellent study regarding the prayers of Paul and how they serve as a model for Christians today see D. A. Carson, *Praying with Paul: A Call to Spiritual Reformation*, 2nd ed. (Grand Rapids: Baker, 2014).

Israel, to be a people for his own possession as well as a light and blessing to the nations. However, like Adam, Israel failed in this enterprise and suffered exile from the land. Redemption could come neither through the nation of Israel nor through the personal practice of the Mosaic law. Rather, redemption would come through the Messiah, Jesus of Nazareth, who lived a perfect life in conformity to God's law, died as an atoning sacrifice, and rose from the dead three days later. The New Testament church, a people of the new covenant and the temple of God indwelt by the Spirit, are to make disciples of all nations until the day Christ returns to usher in his kingdom fully in the new creation.

Knowing that macrostructure of Scripture shapes the way in which we pray. We address God as our creator, sustainer, and redeemer, and recognize our dependence on him. We affirm and confess the reality of sin in the world and in our own lives, and we pray for God to keep us far from temptation and continue to form us into the image of Christ by means of the power of the Spirit (Rom. 8:28–29; 2 Cor. 3:18). We acknowledge that Jesus is our great priest who intercedes for us and we go to the throne with confidence (Heb. 4:14–16). We beseech God to assist us in our efforts to make disciples, knowing that we can plant and water, but only God can cause the growth (1 Cor. 3:5–9). We seek the Lord in prayer, praying at all times in the Spirit, knowing that every day we are in a spiritual war (Eph. 6:10–18). And we pray for God's kingdom to come and his will to be done on earth as it is in heaven (Matt. 6:9–13), awaiting a day where there is no more pain, sorrow, tears, or death (Rev. 21:1–4). Our prayers are, thus, profoundly shaped by our interaction with biblical theology.

Evangelism

We are conceived and born spiritually dead in our transgressions and sins (Eph. 2:1). The wages for that sin is death, and not just physical death, but eternal spiritual death in a place of torment called hell (Rom. 6:23; cf. John 3:36; Rev. 20:11–15). While one could conceive of themselves as doing good deeds or being "better" than some fellow human being, the reality is that all fall short of the glory of God (Rom. 3:23). We are in desperate need of grace and mercy from the God of the universe, because we can do nothing in and of ourselves to bring about our own redemption (cf. Rom. 3:27–31).

Biblical theology as a discipline reminds us of the plight of humanity and the plan of God to save by means of Jesus Christ. We are reminded as we engage in the systematic study of the Scriptures that the bad news of our sin cannot be glossed over, as it portends our eternal separation from God. Without this knowledge of the bad news of God's judgment for sin, the good news of salvation has no real meaning or substance. Thinking along the grain of the Bible instructs us that God is both holy and loving, and thus we are under condemnation for sin, but a way has been made in Christ (John 14:6). God's wrath is real and intense in his judgment of sin, but this makes the mercy, grace, and love seen in the gospel shine out all the more brightly.

Our world is filled with deceptive teachings and false teachers (1 John 2:18) and thus we must be ready to "test the spirits" to see whether or not they are from God (1 John 4:1). Biblical theology prepares us to spot counterfeit teaching and counteract false worldviews with the truth of the gospel.[8] Satan works to blind the minds of unbelievers to prevent them from seeing "the light of the gospel of the glory of Christ, who is the image of God" (2 Cor. 4:4). It is our job to know the details and contours of the gospel message outlined in Scripture so as to portray the whole truth of the identity and work of Jesus. Biblical theology is a valuable tool in that endeavor.

Discipleship

The standard definition of a "disciple" is a follower or learner who adheres to the teachings of another person.[9] It refers to someone who takes up the ways of someone else. Applied to Jesus, a disciple is someone who learns from him to live like him. It is someone who, because of God's awakening grace, conforms his or her words and ways to the words and ways of Jesus.[10] As others have said in early days of the church, disciples of Jesus are themselves "little Christs" (Acts 11:26; 26:28). Parnell wisely observes, "We follow Jesus [in conversion] into a new world, not as mere pedagogy, but as fellowship. We come not as objective pupils, but as rebellious creatures made alive for the first time—rebellious creatures now reconciled to God by the death of his Son. Discipleship—following Jesus—is to live before God's face, to dwell in his presence, to be satisfied in all that he is."[11] Most fundamentally, to follow Jesus means to worship and obey him exclusively.

The task before us is to make more disciples of Jesus from all nations (Matt. 28:18–20), and discipleship is about training for growth in godliness (1 Tim. 4:7). The church works such that disciples increasingly look like Jesus. When we disciple others, our aim is to express love for God and for others that flows from "a pure heart and a good conscience and a sincere faith" (1 Tim. 1:5). To say it another way, the aim of discipleship is maturity: "Him we proclaim, warning everyone and teaching everyone with all wisdom, that we may present everyone mature in Christ" (Col. 1:28). Or, we might talk about being conformed to the image of God's Son (Rom. 8:29). This involves denying one's self (i.e., worldly pleasure

---

8. Helpful treatments on evangelizing and defending the faith in the midst of a world riddled with deceptions and counterfeits include Mark Dever, *The Gospel and Personal Evangelism* (Wheaton: Crossway, 2007); John S. Feinberg, *Can You Believe It's True? Christian Apologetics in a Modern and Postmodern Era* (Wheaton: Crossway, 2013).

9. Much of this section is derived from Kimble, *40 Questions About Church and Discipline*, 72–73. Used by permission of Kregel Publications.

10. Lunde offers a more detailed definition: "Covenantal discipleship is learning to receive and respond to God's grace and demand, which are mediated through Jesus, the Servant King, so as to reflect God's character in relation to him, to others, and to the world, in order that others may come to experience this same grace and respond to this same demand. Lunde, *Following Jesus*, 276.

11. Jonathan Parnell, "The Heart of Discipleship," *Desiring God* (blog), May 25, 2012, http://www. desiringgod.org/articles/the-heart-of-discipleship/.

to get the greatest treasure, namely, Jesus Christ), taking up the cross, and following Jesus in every aspect of life (Matt. 16:24).

There are a number of means to growth as a disciple: worship, preaching, the church's missional enterprise, baptism, the Lord's Supper, counseling, community groups, and personal mentoring.[12] While all of these aspects merit attention, the focus here will be more general in nature. When looking at the list above, one can observe that there are two distinct aspects of discipleship. First, discipleship involves instruction on the part of the teacher and hearing and thinking on the part of the follower (2 Tim. 2:2, 7). The instruction involved in discipleship is the gospel along with the exhortations, commands, warnings, and promises that flow from it. Therefore, discipleship encompasses biblical instruction, correction, rebuke, and admonishment (2 Tim. 3:16–17).

Secondly, discipleship involves modeling on the part of the teacher and seeing and practicing on the part of the disciple (1 Cor. 11:1; Phil. 4:9; 2 Tim. 3:10–11). Paul was not shy about calling people to imitate his faith, as long as they imitated the ways in which he was imitating Christ. In fact, part of Christian leadership is living in such a way that people can look at your life and seek to imitate the facets that are consistently conforming to the character and ways of Christ (Heb. 13:7). So again, for the teacher, discipleship involves modeling; and for the disciple, it involves seeing, practicing, and forming habits of virtue that spring from new life in Christ (2 Cor. 3:18) and the indwelling Holy Spirit (1 Cor. 6:18–20).[13]

Biblical theology is a key factor for effective discipleship. By means of instruction and imitation a disciple may grow in their conformity to Christ. In a sense, embracing the teaching of Scripture sets us on a lifelong pilgrimage. Biblical theology supplies the disciple with the content—the storyline, structure, and themes of the Bible—that will guide them in their doctrine and practice. To be a disciple is to become immersed in what and how the Bible speaks as we increasingly understand and embrace the interpretive perspective set out by the biblical authors.[14] To make disciples, according to Jesus's commission, is to engross people in what and how the Bible speaks and show them how it affects your own life so they can learn to better live, love, and lead like Jesus. Biblical theology

---

12. See Allison, *Sojourners and Strangers*, 441.
13. For more detail on this approach to discipleship, see Michael Horton, *The Gospel Commission: Recovering God's Strategy for Making Disciples* (Grand Rapids: Baker, 2012); James G. Samra, *Being Conformed to Christ in Community: A Study of Maturity, Maturation and the Local Church in the Undisputed Pauline Epistles*, Library of New Testament Studies 320 (London: T&T Clark, 2006).
14. This way of speaking of biblical theology can be found in James M. Hamilton, *What Is Biblical Theology? A Guide to the Bible's Story, Symbolism, and Patterns* (Wheaton: Crossway, 2014), 15. This is similar to Vos, who defines biblical theology as "that branch of Exegetical Theology which deals with the process of self-revelation of God deposited in the Bible." See *Biblical Theology*, 5. Graeme Goldsworthy also speaks of biblical theology as "theology as the Bible reveals it." Biblical theology traces the progression seen within the canon, relates every passage of the Bible to the whole, shows the relationship of all parts of the Old Testament to the person and work of Jesus, and enables us to map out unity and diversity seen within the Bible. See Goldsworthy, *According to Plan*, 20–24.

is thus a useful tool for raising up disciples who know and love God and seek to conform their lives to Christ by means of his Word.

Preaching and Teaching

The proclamation of God's Word to people is one of the greatest privileges and responsibilities we have as pastors and ministry leaders. In the process of preparing to preach and teach, one must always remember that we are constantly asking what the passage is about, analyzing its book-level meaning, and discerning how the text fits within the context of the entire canon of Scripture.[15] As such, preaching a passage of Scripture demands that we understand the rest of the Bible so that we can properly see how it fits within the grand scope of God's providential actions and purposes. To rightly interpret a particular passage, it is necessary to have a clear understanding of the Bible as a whole and its individual books.

Like Paul, we are responsible to proclaim the "whole counsel of God" (Acts 20:26–27) to people so that they are aware of God's authoritative Word and how it impacts the way they think, feel, and live. Hamilton notes, "Biblical theology helps us get our arms around the big picture that ties together everything from Leviticus to Esther, and we see how Amos, John, Romans, and Revelation fit, too. Knowing what the forest looks like enables understanding of the individual trees. If we are to preach the whole counsel of God, we need biblical theology."[16] This is true for those who interpret and preach, but also for the people who are called to faithfully study the Word of God. The Bible is not some anthology, but a cohesive collection where the parts must be seen and understood in light of the whole.

A robust understanding of biblical theology would also demand that all the books of the Bible are worthy of being included in our preaching and teaching ministry. Many pastors tend to default to the Pauline Epistles as their primary (if not virtually exclusive) preaching content. While Paul's writings are essential and excellent, if we are to proclaim the whole counsel of God, there also needs to be sermon series derived from books such as Leviticus, Isaiah, Ezekiel, Ecclesiastes, Chronicles, Jude, and Revelation.[17] This will demonstrate that all Scripture is breathed out by God, profitable (2 Tim. 3:16), and equips us, as well as gives people a clear guide for their own study of the Scriptures.

---

15. See Michael Lawrence, *Biblical Theology in the Life of the Church: A Guide for Ministry* (Wheaton: Crossway, 2010), 182–83. There is a host of literature dealing with the meaning of individual passages, and more books continue to come out regarding out understanding of the Bible as a whole. Often what can be neglected in prep work is the recognition of how a text fits within the context of a given book. For numerous examples of this point dealing with the Prophets, see Gentry, *Biblical Prophets*.
16. James M. Hamilton Jr., "Biblical Theology and Preaching," in *Text-Driven Preaching: God's Word at the Heart of Every Sermon*, eds. Daniel L. Akin, David Lewis Allen, and Ned Lee Mathews (Nashville: B&H, 2010), 197.
17. See the excellent series done by 9Marks ministries that encourages pastors to preach from books of the Bible that do not always receive the greatest amount of attention. *Preaching through the Bible* (blog), *9Marks* https://www.9marks.org/tag/preaching-through-the-bible/. Accessed October 30, 2018.

As preachers and teachers of God's Word we must take biblical theology into account in both our study as well as our actual delivery. This means that in our study we must take into account what the passage is about, how it fits in the overall message of the book, and how the passage fits in the whole of the canon. The study of Scripture is a daunting and blessed task to which we must dedicate ourselves, and involves the fine details of textual analysis and the broad strokes of the macrostructures seen within books of the Bible and the themes that run across the canon. In study, therefore, one will want to consider structural features, key cross references, the Old Testament's use of other Old Testament texts, the New Testament's use of the Old Testament, intertextual connections, repeated words and phrases, key themes, and what the text tells us about God.[18] These features will be essential for understanding a passage within its textual, epochal, and canonical context.[19]

In our delivery we want to shape people by reading the Bible holistically with a biblical-theological lens. Hamilton helpfully describes how one would go about preaching while modeling how biblical theology affects our reading and application of the Bible: introduce the message; raise the audience's awareness of their real need for what the passage being preached provides; state the main point of the passage/message; preview and then work through the structure of the passage/message; give the wider context of the passage within the book; and address the passage's canonical context (i.e., how it fits in the overall storyline of the Bible).[20] As you do this, you will model how to read Scripture, taking into account near textual context as well as the progression of the story and the climaxing of all things in Christ. This will be essential as we continue to formulate our thinking and our living in light of the teaching of Scripture.[21]

---

18. Preaching textbooks often go through these features in greater detail. For some examples see Daniel L. Akin, David Lewis Allen, and Ned Lee Mathews, eds., *Text-Driven Preaching: God's Word at the Heart of Every Sermon.* *(Nashville: B&H, 2010)*; Bryan Chapell, *Christ-Centered Preaching: Redeeming the Expository Sermon*, 2nd ed. (Grand Rapids: Baker, 2005); Mark Dever and Greg Gilbert, *Preach: Theology Meets Practice* (Nashville: B&H Books, 2012); Graeme Goldsworthy, *Preaching the Whole Bible as Christian Scripture: The Application of Biblical Theology to Expository Preaching* (Grand Rapids: Eerdmans, 2000); Sidney Greidanus, *The Modern Preacher and the Ancient Text: Interpreting and Preaching Biblical Literature* (Grand Rapids: Eerdmans, 1988); Dennis E. Johnson, *Him We Proclaim: Preaching Christ from All the Scriptures* (Phillipsburg: P&R, 2007); Jason C. Meyer, *Preaching: A Biblical Theology* (Wheaton: Crossway, 2013).

19. For further detail on these three levels of biblical meaning see Richard Lints, *The Fabric of Theology: A Prolegomenon to Evangelical Theology* (Grand Rapids: Eerdmans, 1993), 290–311.

20. Hamilton, "Preaching and Biblical Theology," 214.

21. One of the challenges often noticed in preaching is applying the Old Testament to the life of a Christian. One must recognize that there is both continuity and discontinuity when it comes to the relationship between the Old Testament and the New Testament. For examples of detailed studies on various themes in Scripture that deal with what differs and what remains when working through the canon of Scripture in its progression from the Old Testament to the New Testament, see John S. Feinberg, ed., *Continuity and Discontinuity: Perspectives on the Relationship Between the Old and New Testaments: Essays in Honor of S. Lewis Johnson, Jr* (Wheaton: Crossway, 1988). As one understands the progression of these themes across the canon they are in a better position to understand how to apply the text to the life of a Christian, individually and corporately. Analysis on how application works in preaching while taking biblical theology into account can be found in Lawrence, *Life of the Church*, 181–98.

Elder Leadership

Some within our churches are called by God to serve as shepherds of the flock to guide God's people faithfully. The office of pastor/elder serves as a crucial means for the church to receive sound doctrine (2 Tim. 4:1–5), oversee God's people (Acts 20:28), and equip the church for the work of ministry (Eph. 4:11–12).[22] Elders in the local church serve as stewards of God's grace and overseers of God's Word and people (1 Cor. 4:1–2; 9:17; Eph. 3:2; Col. 1:25; Titus 1:7; cf. 1 Tim. 3:15).[23] In other words, they are called to shepherd God's flock toward maturity in Christ (Col. 1:28–29) and proclaim to them the whole counsel of God (Acts 20:27–32). In many ways, as Beale states, the office of elder is essential to the church in dealing with the ongoing realities of false teaching and deception so prevalent among us (1 John 2:18).[24] As such, this office must operate in light of the truth seen through the discipline of biblical theology.

In local church life there are a number of business items that must be attended to, including nomination for various offices, annual budgets, building upkeep, Sunday schedules, and church-wide events. If they are not careful, elders can spend the vast majority of their time on such matters. However, their primary task is to preach and teach the Word of God, pray for their congregations, exhibit godly character, and oversee and lead the flock that God has entrusted to them (1 Tim. 3:1–7; 1 Peter 5:1–5). Elders will have to think through specific strategies to orient themselves biblically when they meet together, preach and teach, and engage in their shepherding ministry.

First, in relation to pastor-elders meeting together, while business must be dealt with, the mutual sharpening of each others minds and hearts with the content of biblical theology must be a priority. There must always be continued growth in our knowledge and application of biblical truths, and communities of pastors would benefit from challenging one another in this way. One way to pursue such an initiative would be to agree upon a

---

22. I am using the terms of "pastor," "elder," and "overseer" interchangeably (cf. Acts 20:17–35; Titus 1:5–9; 1 Peter 5:1–5). For a thorough argument in favor of the elder and overseer being one office in Scripture, see Benjamin L. Merkle, *The Elder and Overseer: One Office in the Early Church*, Studies in Biblical Literature 57 (New York: Peter Lang, 2003). See also Mark E. Dever, "The Church," in *A Theology for the Church*, ed. Daniel L. Akin, David P. Nelson, and Peter R. Schemm Jr. (Nashville: B&H, 2007), 800–805; John S. Hammett, *Biblical Foundations for Baptist Churches: A Contemporary Ecclesiology* (Grand Rapids: Kregel, 2005), 159–89; Phil A. Newton, *Elders in Congregational Life: Rediscovering the Biblical Model for Church Leadership* (Grand Rapids: Kregel, 2005); Alexander Strauch, *Biblical Eldership: An Urgent Call to Restore Biblical Church Leadership*, rev. ed. (Littleton: Lewis and Roth, 1995); Samuel E. Waldron, "Plural-Elder Congregationalism," in *Who Runs the Church? Four Views on Church Government*, ed. Steven B. Cowan (Grand Rapids: Zondervan, 2004), 212–21. This list is certainly not comprehensive, but gives the reader an ample starting point. While not all will agree with this particular form of church polity, the focus here is how biblical theology shapes the role of the pastor.
23. For more detail on this point see Kimble, "Steward of God."
24. See Beale, *New Testament Biblical Theology*, 822. While I do not agree with every facet of Beale's argument about the extent of the inauguration of end-time tribulation, his point is helpful in recognizing the reality of false teaching and the need for pastor-elders to teach and preach Scripture faithfully to God's people.

particular book dealing with biblical theology, read it individually, and then take some time in the elder meeting to discuss the content read for that session.[25] This can produce lively conversation amongst church leaders and serve as a means of dialoguing over matters that matter to our interpretation and living out of the text of Scripture. These discussions can also settle into our minds and hearts and strengthen our teaching and shepherding to the benefit of our congregations. Elder meetings are also an opportunity to think about all the realities of church life through a biblical-theological lens, reminding us that all areas of our lives fall under the authority of Christ by means of his Word.

The ministry of preaching and teaching has already been mentioned, but perhaps one facet to consider is how biblical theology prepares us to refute error as we teach what is biblically true (Acts 20:28–32; 1 Tim. 1:3–7). False teaching abounds and people are susceptible. We must be diligent in renewing our own minds (Rom. 12:2; Phil. 4:8) and thinking God's thoughts after him, but this will only happen when we immerse ourselves in the text, memorize Scripture, and meditate joyfully on its contents day and night (Ps. 1:1–2). We must be cognizant of God's teaching by means of a robust biblical theology, and also aware of the ideologies that pervade our culture. Our teaching and preaching ministry must aim to refute arguments and opinions raised against God and teach our communities to "take every thought captive to obey Christ" (2 Cor. 10:5).

Finally, in shepherding ministry, pastor-elders must recognize the importance of biblical theology in their personal ministry. There will be opportunities to visit the sick, comfort the grieving, counsel the hurting, and encourage the fainthearted. In these dire moments, people do not need mere opinion or sentiment; rather they need the deep and abiding truth of God's Word applied to their specific situation. Therefore, biblical theology serves as a helpful guide to remind people of the grand storyline, of which they are a part. We will have the resources to gently tell them of the key themes of Scripture, their specific trajectories across the canon, and how these matters come into play in that respective moment of their lives. The Word of God serves as our guide as we speak into the various situations our communities will face, and this is crucial as we ponder how we must think, feel, and live in moments that are profoundly difficult or confusing. Biblical theology serves as an antidote to the world's supposed wisdom and offers truth and life.

---

25. In some ways this exercise would depend on the biblical-theological level of the group in terms of which book would be selected, particularly if there are lay-elders who may not have the same level of education as vocational elders. While there are numerous biblical theologies one could choose from, here are several representing different levels of difficulty. Basic: Vaughan Roberts, *God's Big Picture: Tracing the Storyline of the Bible* (Downers Grove: InterVarsity, 2002). Intermediate: Schreiner, *King in His Beauty*; Advanced: Childs, *Biblical Theology* or Hamilton, *God's Glory in Salvation*. For a more comprehensive bibliography of biblical theologies a group could go through see https://www.zondervan.com/p/biblical-theology/bibliography/.

Seeing Life through the Lens of Scripture

Scripture reveals the one and only true God and shows us the reality of creation, the fall into sin, redemption through Christ, and the coming new creation. This is why it is of such importance that we give ourselves to delightfully meditating on Scripture day and night (Ps. 1:1–2). The world constantly tells us various kinds of narratives, draws us away from the living God, and competes for our allegiance and affection. We are called to not love the world or the things of the world (1 John 2:15) and to keep ourselves from idols (1 John 5:21). God, in his grace, gave us Scripture so that we would know how to rightly interpret all of reality through the lens of his revealed Word.

In the overall life of the church, this demands that the understanding and application of God's Word are our utmost priorities that we allow to shape us as we gather and scatter. When we gather corporately, our services must draw us back again and again to the truth contained in God's Word. As such, in our corporate gatherings we must be committed to read the Word of God publicly (1 Tim. 4:13), preach the entire counsel of God (Acts 20:26–28), pray in accordance with Scripture, sing songs that convey the truths taught in the Bible (Eph. 5:18–19; Col. 3:16), and see the truths of the gospel displayed in the ordinances (Rom. 6:1–4; 1 Cor. 11:23–26).[26] Reading the Bible each week, even without explanation or comment, demonstrates the authoritative value of Scripture for our lives. It also reminds us that we do not live by bread alone, but "by every word that comes from the mouth of the Lord" (Deut. 8:3). Preaching the Bible must be constantly done, "in season and out of season" (2 Tim. 4:2). To shape people who know and obey God's will, we must continually lay before them the truth of God's Word.[27]

Our churches should also pray and sing the Bible. The shape of public prayers can help our congregations understand how to pray effectively and in accordance with Scripture, leading us to worship God, confess sin, give thanks, and make requests aligned with God's will.[28] We are also called to build one another up by singing psalms, hymns, and spiritual

---

26. See D. A. Carson, *Worship by the Book* (Grand Rapids: Zondervan, 2002), 25, 54–55; Mark Dever and Jamie Dunlop, *The Compelling Community: Where God's Power Makes a Church Attractive* (Wheaton: Crossway, 2015), 77–88; and J. Ligon Duncan III, "Does God Care How We Worship?" and "Foundations for Biblically Directed Worship," in *Give Praise to God: A Vision for Reforming Worship*, eds. Philip Ryken, Derek Thomas, and J. Ligon Duncan III (Phillipsburg: P&R, 2003), 17–73.

27. One important point, therefore, concerning preaching, would be whether it is done in a topical or expository fashion. Certainly there is room for topics to be addressed at various points in our congregations, but given the nature of biblical theology our sermons should be leading our people to know how to better study, comprehend, and apply Scripture in every area of life. As such, expository preaching should be the norm within our churches. For more on this point, see Abraham Kuruvilla, *A Vision for Preaching: Understanding the Heart of Pastoral Ministry* (Grand Rapids: Baker, 2015), 13–30; Meyer, *Preaching*, 292–97.

28. The evangelist George Mueller gives helpful commentary on how meditation over the Word gives way to biblically-based prayers: "The point is this: I saw more clearly than ever that the first great and primary business to which I ought to attend every day was to have my soul happy in the Lord. The first thing to be concerned about was not how much I might serve the Lord, how I might glorify the Lord; but how I might get my soul into a happy state, and

songs together (Eph. 5:19). As biblical theology takes up residence in the life of the church, it demands that we think theologically about the songs that we sing and focus on lyrics that accurately convey the truth about God and his Word. Finally, we see the gospel displayed in the ordinances, which are palpable reminders of Christ's redeeming work. The ordinances, in essence, make the church visible through the initiation of its members through baptism (Matt. 28:19–20) and the renewal of their commitment to Christ and one another via the Lord's Supper (1 Cor. 11:17–26).

As we scatter as God's people, the Word of God must continue to be central. We gather, stir up, encourage, and exhort one another (Heb. 3:12–13; 10:24–25) and then go out proclaiming and showcasing the truth of Scripture, always ready to give an answer regarding the hope within us (1 Peter 3:15–16).[29] Church members should see their leaders asking spiritual questions and discussing biblical matters and recognize this as normal Christian behavior. The Word of God will be part of us as we labor in our workplaces, attend small group meetings, and have discussions over the fence with our neighbors. It will be what we read, study, memorize, and meditate on throughout the days, weeks, months, years, and decades of our lives.[30]

If Scripture has the words of eternal life (John 6:68) and is the only true interpretation of all of life, it is then worthy of our attention corporately as well as in our everyday lives as individuals. Our lives must be ever increasingly shaped by the truths of the Word of God; no substitute should overtake it as the dominant influence on our minds, affections, and actions. We want to think God's thoughts after him and embrace the interpretive perspective

---

how my inner man might be nourished. . . . Before this time my practice had been at least for ten years previously as a habitual thing to give myself to prayer after having dressed in the morning. Now I saw that the most important thing I had to do was to give myself to the reading of the word of God and to meditation on it, that thus my heart might be comforted, encouraged, warned, reproved, instructed; and that thus, while meditating, my heart might be brought into experimental communion with the Lord. I began, therefore, to meditate on the New Testament from the beginning early in the morning. The first thing I did, after having asked in a few words the Lord's blessing upon his precious word, was to begin to meditate on the word of God, searching as it were into every verse to get blessing out of it; not for the sake of the public ministry of the word; not for the sake of preaching on what I had meditated upon; but for the sake of obtaining food for my soul. The result I have found to be almost invariably this, that after a very few minutes my soul has been led to confession, or to thanksgiving, or to intercession, or to supplication; so that though I did not, as it were, give myself to prayer but to meditation, yet it turned almost immediately more or less into prayer. When thus I have been for a while making confession or intercession or supplication or have given thanks, I go on to the next words or verse, turning all, as I go on, into prayer for myself or others, as the word may lead to it; but still continually keeping before me that food for my soul as the object of my meditation." George Mueller, *A Narrative of Some of the Lord's Dealing with George Müller, Written by Himself, Jehovah Magnified. Addresses by George Müller Complete and Unabridged,* 2 vols. (Muskegon: Dust and Ashes, 2003), 1:272–73.

29. A helpful work that traces the centrality of the Word of God in both gathering and scattering is Jonathan Leeman, *Word-Centered Church: How Scripture Brings Life and Growth to God's People* (Chicago: Moody, 2017).

30. One of the surest ways to meditate on Scripture, as Psalm 1 exhibits, is to memorize Scripture. Andy Naselli gives practical advice on this topic and why and how we should memorize the Bible. See Andrew David Naselli, *How to Understand and Apply the New Testament: Twelve Steps from Exegesis to Theology* (Phillipsburg: P&R, 2017), 338–42.

of the biblical authors. Biblical theology offers us the storyline, structure, symbols, and themes that lead to the articulation of clear doctrine, resulting in a particular culture that is embodied by God's people in the church. Therefore, we should give ourselves to frequent, delight-filled meditation on God's Word (Ps. 1:1–2). As Peter writes, "All flesh is like grass, and all its glory like the flower of grass. The grass withers and the flower falls, but the word of the Lord remains forever" (1 Peter 1:24–25; cf. Isa. 40:6, 8).

Discussion Questions

1. What are some practical ways we can ensure that our reading of Scripture and use of prayer contribute to and build upon the discipline of biblical theology?

2. How does biblical theology assist us in our efforts of evangelism and discipleship?

3. As local church members, how should biblical theology permeate the culture of our churches? What kind of effect would that have on the way we worship and fellowship?

4. In what ways should biblical theology manifest itself in our preaching and teaching in the local church? What will this require of us?

5. What functions do elders perform in the local church? How does biblical theology help them in their endeavors?

Resources for Further Study

Billings, J. Todd. *The Word of God for the People of God: An Entryway to the Theological Interpretation of Scripture.* Grand Rapids: Eerdmans, 2010.

Lawrence, Michael. *Biblical Theology in the Life of the Church: A Guide for Ministry.* Wheaton: Crossway, 2010.

Roark, Nick and Robert Cline. *Biblical Theology: How the Church Faithfully Teaches the Gospel.* Wheaton: Crossway, 2018.

Roberts, Vaughan. *God's Big Picture: Tracing the Storyline of the Bible.* Downers Grove: IVP, 2003.

Vanhoozer, Kevin. *Hearers and Doers: A Pastor's Guide to Making Disciples through Scripture and Doctrine.* Bellingham: Lexham, 2019.

CHAPTER 22

BIBLICAL THEOLOGY IN THE
LIFE OF THE ACADEMY

IN 2 TIMOTHY 3, Paul speaks highly about the nature of the Scriptures. He also outlines several ways that the Scriptures are vital and useful for the life of the Christian and for the health of the churches (3:14–17). In 2 Timothy 4, Paul writes, "I solemnly charge you in the presence of God and of Christ Jesus, who is to judge the living and the dead, and by His appearing and His kingdom: preach the word!" (4:1–2, NASB). Consider how much theology is already packed into this basic description of who God is and who Jesus is. God is a being who is present. Jesus is the Christ. And, this Christ is one who has the power to judge both the living and the dead. Not only this, but this Christ has made himself known; he has appeared and will appear again, bringing his kingdom with him.

In just a few short words, Paul marshals a freight load of theology and Christology in order to make the simple but profound exhortation: Preach the Word! From this starting point he continues, "Be ready in season and out of season; reprove, rebuke, exhort, with great patience and instruction. For the time will come when they will not endure sound doctrine; but wanting to have their ears tickled, they will accumulate for themselves teachers in accordance with their own desires, and will turn away their ears from the truth and will turn aside to myths. But you, be sober in all things, endure hardship, do the work of an evangelist, fulfill your ministry" (4:2–5, NASB). Here, Paul connects the grand storyline of the Bible (Jesus is the Christ!) to the preaching of the gospel message, the ministry of the word in the life of believers, and the defense of the faith.

This necessary and smooth connection that Paul envisions between theological and practical realities sets the stage for our final discussion concerning the relationship between the academy and the churches in the study of biblical theology.

The Relationship between the Academy and the Churches

As a Topic in the Field of Biblical Theology

Throughout the history of the discipline of biblical theology, the relationship between the academy and the church has often been debated. In particular, when biblical theology is conceived as a historical-critical endeavor aimed at examining not only the biblical literature but also the historical settings of the biblical events, the discipline becomes relegated to a purely academic endeavor.[1] Moreover, when no distinction is made between biblical theology and systematic theology, the task of interpretation becomes a wholly theological endeavor pursued only in a church context or without any formal academic parameters.

Klink and Lockett summarize this dynamic in their discussion of contemporary biblical theology. As they note, "Much of this question depends on who may claim the rights to a religious 'text.' By asking whether biblical theology is a task for the church or the academy, one must consider whether biblical theology is prescriptive or descriptive. If it is prescriptive—that is, the theology of the Bible must be understood as both speaking to our modern world and authoritative for Christian life and practice—then one would assume that the church must necessarily be committed to biblical theology."[2] Conversely, "if biblical theology is descriptive—namely, only the historical task of outlining what ancient peoples believed about their God—it would only be of antiquarian interest and thus fail to be central to the modern church's task."[3]

We do not need to rehearse here our previous discussion of the history of the discipline of biblical theology. Rather, I simply highlight that the conversation about the relationship between the academy and the churches regarding the study of the Bible is one that is well-established in the field of biblical theology and touches on an enduring commitment for evangelicals.

---

1. For example, consider Wrede, "Task and Methods," 73: "The questions and needs of the church can be a legitimate influence only in a limited sense—and probably least of all in the biblical field. On the whole it is not within the historical researcher's power to serve the church through his work. The theologian who obeys the historical object as his master is not in a position to serve the church through his properly scientific-historical work, even if he were personally interested in doing so." Barr also states directly that "biblical theology is something that is done by biblical scholars" (*Concept of Biblical Theology*, 2–3).
2. Klink and Lockett, *Understanding Biblical Theology*, 20.
3. Klink and Lockett, *Understanding Biblical Theology*, 20. Cf. also Sailhamer's treatment of the "Descriptive or Confessional" choice in *Introduction to Old Testament Theology, 115–83*.

As an Enduring Commitment for Evangelicals

For an evangelical approach to biblical theology, the relationship between the academy and the churches is in some ways a settled question.[4] Biblical theology is never a purely academic endeavor as the study of the Scriptures involves a series of theological presuppositions and faith claims. This close relationship between the academy and the churches is one of the key features of a "confessional" approach to the discipline.

Because of this confessional approach, biblical theology is an interdisciplinary program that integrates exegesis on the one hand and systematic theology on the other. Biblical theologians will necessarily pursue the biblical-theological task from different starting points. If they take a confessional approach to the task as a whole, however, they will also have an eye toward the interdisciplinary implications of their work. As Childs envisions, "There is little hope of the biblical and theological disciplines interacting in a beneficial way unless biblical scholars are working constructively in theology, and conversely challenging the theologians to come to grips with the material described by the biblical disciplines."[5] Childs also urges "biblical scholars to be more systematic, and systematic theologians to be more biblical, *and to get on with the task.*"[6] Miroslav Volf echoes this sentiment, observing that "the return of biblical scholars to the theological reading of the Scriptures, and the return of systematic theologians to sustained engagement with the scriptural texts—in a phrase, the return of both to theological readings of the Bible—is the most significant development in the last two decades."[7]

This blend of confessional commitment and higher education runs directly counter to the prevailing conventional wisdom in some sectors of contemporary American educational

---

4. For example, note the articulation of the evangelical position on this question in Nick Roark and Robert Cline, *Biblical Theology: How the Church Faithfully Teaches the Gospel* (Wheaton: Crossway, 2018), 26: "Biblical theology is for the church, begins with the Bible, and ends with King Jesus and his church." Further, they argue that "if the story of Scripture is all about Christ the King, this reality ought to impact the preaching and teaching ministry of the local church directly" (75). Biblical theology, then, functions as "a guard" and as "a guide" for the churches. See also Michael Lawrence's sustained argument to this effect in *Life of the Church*, including his broad statement that "everything in the life and ministry of the local church is affected by a proper use of biblical theology" (199).

5. Childs, *Biblical Theology in Crisis*, 93. For a recent set of essays seeking to envision this sort of interdisciplinary work under the banner of theological interpretation, see Craig G. Bartholomew and Heath A. Thomas, *A Manifesto for Theological Interpretation* (Grand Rapids: Baker, 2016).

6. Childs, *Biblical Theology*, 89; emphasis added. Childs's larger comment (which comes at the end of his proposal for a canonical approach) is worth quoting in full: "In sum, at this juncture probably little more precision in theory is required other than to urge biblical scholars to be more systematic, and systematic theologians to be more biblical, and to get on with the task. The ultimate test of the success of co-operation between the two fields lies in the degree to which the biblical text and its subject matter are illumined. Neither Biblical Theology nor dogmatic theology is an end in itself, but rather they remain useful tools by which to enable a fresh access to the living voice of God in sacred Scripture" (89).

7. Miroslav Volf, *Captive to the Word of God: Engaging the Scriptures for Contemporary Theological Reflection* (Grand Rapids: Eerdmans, 2010), 14. Volf also clarifies, "True, because the Bible can be misused and because it has been badly misused over the centuries, the value of rediscovering the theological reading of the Bible will ultimately depend on how well it is read. But still, being read well depends on its being read in the first place" (14–15).

culture. For example, in a recent article in *The Chronicle of Higher Education* about the role of accreditation, Peter Conn asserts that an "important objection to accreditation as codified and practiced now" is that "by awarding accreditation to religious colleges, the process confers legitimacy on institutions that systematically undermine the most fundamental purposes of higher education. Skeptical and unfettered inquiry is the hallmark of American teaching and research. However, such inquiry cannot flourish—in many cases, cannot even survive—inside institutions that erect religious tests for truth." For Conn, "the contradiction is obvious."[8] Conn's editorial articulates the contemporary general consensus regarding the validity and value of Christian higher education within a confessional context.

Accordingly, Christian educators must carefully consider the nature of their professional and academic goals. Positively, a strong confessional framework frees evangelical academics to pursue *responsible* academic work rather than striving for *respectability* in the eyes of secular intellectual gatekeepers. In the words of Carson and Woodbridge's fictional senior evangelical scholar, "I doubt very much that evangelicals are wise to pursue academic respectability. What we need is academic responsibility. There is a world of difference."[9] In this vein, Köstenberger pleads with evangelical academics "not to sacrifice their scholarly integrity for the sake of attaining academic respectability."[10] Recognizing the strategic role of theological commitments in Christian higher education, Köstenberger asserts that "believing scholarship is not only possible but in fact is more virtuous than critical, unbelieving, or supposedly objective academic work."[11]

8. See Peter Conn, "The Great Accreditation Farce," *The Chronicle of Higher Education*, June 30, 2014. For a wide-ranging historical study of the steady secularization of higher education, see George M. Marsden, *The Soul of the American University: From Protestant Establishment to Established Nonbelief* (Oxford: Oxford University Press, 1994).

9. D. A. Carson and John D. Woodbridge, *Letters along the Way: A Novel of the Christian Life* (Wheaton: Crossway, 1993), 174. Their character explains, "Elevating academic respectability to the level of controlling desideratum is an invitation to theological and spiritual compromise. I do not find Jesus angling to become a member of the Sanhedrin in order to gain a more public voice; I do not find Paul pursuing academic respectability in the categories of his day, for then he could not have written the kinds of things he did about rhetoric (e.g., 1 Corinthians 2:1ff.). Academic responsibility is something else. This means that we pursue integrity in debate, that we eschew harangues, that we seek to give an answer to everyone for the hope that is in us, that we persuade people with the truth. Academic respectability, in my vocabulary, has too much self-interest in it for me to trust it; academic responsibility, on the other hand, calls me to discipline and work" (174). For a recent reflection on this particular issue (employing these categories), see Andy Naselli, "Three Reflections on Evangelical Academic Publishing," *Themelios* 39.3 (2014): 428–54.

10. Andreas J. Köstenberger, *Excellence: The Character of God and the Pursuit of Scholarly Virtue* (Wheaton: Crossway, 2011), 24. Cf. Craig Bartholomew, *Introducing Biblical Hermeneutics: A Comprehensive Framework for Hearing God in Scripture* (Grand Rapids: Baker, 2015), 484: "Let us not despise the day of small things but be faithful in the opportunities available to us, continually aspiring to excellence in genuinely Christian scholarship that seeks to contribute to the flourishing of all. Such excellence will not be possible without a recovery of Scripture as foundational to Christian scholarship." Exploring the relationship between Scripture and the University, Bartholomew discusses "the ecology of Christian scholarship" (463–84).

11. Köstenberger, *Excellence*, 24. On the relationship between Christian beliefs and higher education, see also George Marsden, *The Outrageous Idea of Christian Scholarship* (Oxford: Oxford University Press, 1997) and

Scholarship, the Churches, and Trickle-Down Academics

Academic Ministry Works for the Churches

The goal of theology is to produce a product that glorifies God and edifies the churches. The former goal can be effectively accomplished by means of the latter goal. The best theology is to be done *for the churches*.[12]

As long as churches bear the mark of the right preaching of the Word, biblical theology will always have a foundational place in this context. Pastors must grapple with the issues addressed by biblical theology whether they realize it or not. Theologians should aim to foster a theological dialogue within the church. If biblical theologians can enable their students and members of the local church to think biblically and theologically about their lives and the world around them, then they have succeeded in this task. As Vanhoozer argues, "to correspond to revelation and to the substance of the gospel, the theologian must not only speak but act."[13] Further, the theologian who provides a big picture framework that enables students and church members to read their Bibles better and apply the message of Scripture more faithfully has accomplished the ultimate objective of the biblical theology quest.

When interpreting Scripture, theologians are caught up in a process that extends beyond themselves. Obviously, as a reader of small and large portions of the Scriptures, you must find a way to transfer the insights you glean to your students in the classroom and your fellow church members. Otherwise, the interpretive process will remain woefully incomplete.[14]

Academic Ministry Works within the Church

If theology is for the church, then it only makes sense that theology would also be done *from within the context of the church community*. Indeed, the interpreter who has a vested

---

Jeffry C. Davis, "The Countercultural Quest of Christian Liberal Arts," in *Liberal Arts for the Christian Life*, eds. Jeffry C. Davis and Philip G. Ryken (Wheaton: Crossway, 2012), 31–43. For a distinctly theological approach to this issue, see also Daniel J. Treier, *Virtue and the Voice of God: Toward Theology as Wisdom* (Grand Rapids: Eerdmans, 2006); and Kevin J. Vanhoozer and Daniel J. Treier, *Theology and the Mirror of Scripture: A Mere Evangelical Account* (Downers Grove: IVP, 2015), especially the final two chapters ("In Fellowship with the Saints," 192–220; and "In Pursuit of Scholarly Excellence," 221–61).

12. For a sampling of recent theologians who consider the role of the "pastor-theologian" in light of the relationship between the academy and the church, see Kevin J. Vanhoozer and Owen Strachan, *The Pastor as Public Theologian* (Grand Rapids: Baker, 2015); Gerald Hiestand and Todd Wilson, The Pastor Theologian: Resurrecting an Ancient Vision (Grand Rapids: Zondervan, 2015); and Todd Wilson and Gerald L. Hiestand, eds., *Becoming a Pastor Theologian: New Possibilities for Church Leadership* (Downers Grove: InterVarsity, 2015).

13. Vanhoozer, *The Drama of Doctrine: A Canonical-Linguistic Approach to Christian Theology* (Louisville: Westminster John Knox, 2005), 59. Vanhoozer characterizes the "primary role of the theologian" as bearing "witness, in word and deed, to the meaning and significance of God's communicative action in Jesus Christ, in order to enable others to understand and participate in it too" (58).

14. D. A. Carson, "The Role of Exegesis in Systematic Theology," in *Doing Theology in Today's World*, 71, states strongly that if the message of the interpreter is not transferred to the people of God, then "the entire exercise is such a distortion of the *purposes* of revelation as to approach profanity."

interest in the outcome of the theological process is well-positioned to do faithful and informed theology. Ideally, the theology produced by the theological educator will transform him or her into the image of Christ. As theologians shape their theology, this very theology must shape them. As Childs notes, "The true expositor of the Christian Scriptures is the one who awaits in anticipation toward becoming the interpreted rather than the interpreter. The very divine reality which the interpreter strives to grasp is the very One who grasps the interpreter."[15]

When theological educators communicate the truth they find in Scripture, they personify "the transformation that is created through encounter with revelation."[16] Thus, their lives must bear witness to the truth they have found through the interpretive process. In this way, theologians remain tethered to the community of faith and fulfill the ultimate goal of their vocation.

In the discipline of biblical theology in particular, there should never be a gaping chasm between the academy and the churches. There is simply no way to compensate for the loss that occurs when the biblical or theological scholar is cut off from the local church. Vocational theologians exist to build up and edify their churches. There should be a natural and organic connection between academic and ecclesial classrooms. This crucial task cannot be accomplished if there is an ugly ditch or relational rift between the churches and the academy. Theologians should be doing the best theology *for the churches* and *from within the churches*. Pastors and church members, professors and students, and all other participants in Christian ministry or theological education should benefit from the meaningful fellowship and discussion that arises within the context of a God-centered, Word-saturated, gospel-oriented local church.

---

15. Brevard S. Childs, *Biblical Theology: A Proposal* (Minneapolis: Fortress, 2002), 69. Cf. Childs's similar comment to this regard: "It might also be refreshing for the pastor to be told that the interaction between the university and the parish is not a one-way street. It may well be that some of the direction for the new biblical theology of the future will come from the experience of pastors on the front lines of the church's confrontation with the world. It was not by accident that a working pastor in the forgotten Swiss village of Safenwil [i.e., Karl Barth] first discovered what Romans could mean to a congregation before dropping his theological bomb on the scholarly community. Fortunately God still has a way of making use of the Bible which is not synchronized to the publication schedule of the religious press" (*Biblical Theology in Crisis*, 96).

16. Gerhard Maier, *Biblical Hermeneutics*, trans. Robert Yarbrough (Wheaton: Crossway, 1994), 408. Maier observes further that "in passing along the interpretation that has transformed him and made him into a witness, his interpretation itself becomes testimony" (408). In developing a "special hermeneutic," Maier emphasizes the necessary connection between the academy and the local church community. For him, any interpretive approach "must orient itself in an ongoing way with a careful eye to its object and to the necessities of its service in the Christian community" (377). The interpreter must be fully "embedded in faith and in the Christian community" (279). Maier states strongly that no scholar should think he or she lives "in an open zone beyond the concerns of the community" nor pursue theology "as if the holy congregation did not exist" (380). An academic theologian should be embedded and also engaged in "discussion with the Christian church." Moreover, "no amount of myriads of secondary literature is able to offset the lack that arises from sundering the interpreter from the church."

Trickle-Down Academics:
Why Scholarship for the Churches Is Often, but Not Always, to the Churches

An important distinction to consider in this particular discussion relates to the audience of any given scholarly study. In short, scholarship *for* the churches is often but not always *to* the churches. In other words, the intended audience of a given study might not immediately be a particular local church or a group of local churches. This particular study or scholarly project, though, can still be *for the church.*

This observation recognizes the "trickle-down" effect that scholarship has within both higher education and ecclesial academic communities. The "general consensus" in a particular area of study often has a wide-ranging but largely unacknowledged influence upon teaching and preaching. What is considered "common sense" is either taken for granted or must be consciously argued against in a particular message or scholarly argument. Either way, the general consensus exerts influence and makes its presence felt on teaching or preaching.

A study of biblical theology that contributes to the field or a subdiscipline of biblical or theological studies may have far-reaching implications for the churches, but it may simply take a few steps to make its presence felt. When a consensus forms at the highest academic level, this consensus typically is reflected in major peer-reviewed journal articles and scholarly monographs. These academic publications are then read by authors who write books for those who train theological students and pastors. Those individuals, in turn, are often the ones who write the commentaries and popular-level works read by those doing church ministry. Thus, a broad approach to reading the Scriptures, a particular hermeneutical principle, a distinct theological position, or a unique interpretation of a biblical passage that becomes pervasive among the churches often does not have a single point of origin.

This scenario highlights the fact that it is often inadequate to pit technical academic work over against popular-level writing solely on the basis of audience. For, many times the consensus that an academic work contributes to or operates within will, at some point, impact or influence the popular-level publications or preaching ministry of the churches. This discussion helps explain how a work that is not intended for a popular audience can nevertheless greatly impact that audience (i.e., the churches).

This phenomenon also helps explain why there is sometimes a "gap" when a particular interpretation or theological position is roundly rejected among evangelical scholars, but nevertheless remains relatively widespread among evangelical churches. What is sometimes missing are individuals who have the dual skill set to both access, process, and evaluate high-level scholarly discussions and then effectively communicate such information to a broader audience. When done well, this process avoids a loss of meaning or nuance while shifting the rhetorical situation and communicative context of a particular publication or teaching scenario. There is an enduring need for this type of work in evangelical scholarship that bridges the academy and the churches in the exegetical, biblical-theological, and systematic theology fields.

This recognition is both a *challenge* but also an *encouragement*. We need preachers, teachers, and scholars at every level working in the field of biblical theology who consciously strive to produce careful and faithful work for the churches.

The Universal Academy and the Local Academy

Another helpful angle from which to approach this relationship between the academic study of the Bible and the life of the churches borrows from a key distinction in discussions of ecclesiology. When studying the nature of the "church," an important distinction is the one between the universal church and the local church. The universal church refers to the people of God in the broadest possible terms, both temporally and physically (Eph. 1:22–23; 1 Cor. 12:28; Col. 1:18). The past, present, and future believers in the gospel make up the universal church. The local church, then, would be a specific group of believers who serve the Lord in a particular place and hold to a particular confession (1 Thess. 1:1; 1 Cor. 4:17). In the New Testament, the notion of a universal church undergirds its vision of the global reach of the gospel and connects to the cosmic scope of God's revelation in Christ. At the same time, the New Testament overwhelmingly stresses the nature and function of the gathered local church of believers.[17]

This textual pattern within the New Testament Epistles can provide theological guardrails for how we conceptualize the tasks of teaching, preaching, and "cultural" engagement. Especially in the context of social media, there is an ever-present draw to engage and speak to the "church in America" or "the church" in general (the universal church or "generic" church) rather than address the nitty-gritty reality of ministering to the actual individuals present within a local church congregation.

A parallel movement sometimes happens in the evangelical scholarly world where a scholar's focus might drift toward speaking only to the *universal academy* (e.g., conference presentations, the "guild at large," or a networking event) rather than the work of the *local academy* (e.g., students in a current course, email responses to questions, course preparation, or follow-up student meetings). These contexts, of course, are not at odds with one another. Making this distinction, however, can perhaps help the pastor-theologian or the pastoral theologian maintain a set of priorities. The relationship between the academy and

---

17. A particularly instructive example of the relationship between these two senses occurs in 1 Corinthians 1:1–3. Here Paul writes "to the church of God that is in Corinth, to those sanctified in Christ Jesus, called to be saints" (i.e., the local church) and connects this address to the broader context of believers: "together with all those who in every place call upon the name of our Lord Jesus Christ, both their Lord and ours" (i.e., the universal church). On the pattern of the New Testament's affirmation of the universal church and emphasis on the local church see Thomas White, "The Universal and Local Church," in *Upon This Rock: A Baptist Understanding of the Church*, eds. Jason G. Duesing, Thomas White, and Malcolm B. Yarnell III (Nashville: B&H, 2010), 208–39; and D. A. Carson, "Why the Local Church is More Important than TGC, White Horse Inn, 9Marks, and Maybe Even ETS," *Themelios* 40.1 (2015): 1–9.

the churches might be easier to delineate in practice if there is a clear role for both the local church and the local academy present in the minister or scholar's vision of their vocation.

Addressing the disposition required to maintain focus within the local academy, Jason Duesing uses two helpful metaphors: shepherds who lead with gentleness and Sherpas (climbing guides) who patiently instruct, serve, and pursue the success and intellectual development of their students.[18] Theological educators care best for their students, Duesing notes, when they adopt "the lowly posture of a Sherpa."[19] With this mindset, "the educator can serve without conceding any ounce of experience or rank." Inside and outside of the classroom setting, then, an educator can serve students "by taking time with them and by making time for them."[20] Adopting this perspective allows the formative endgame of the local academy to remain a fixture on the horizon of a Christian professor's career ambitions. As Duesing urges, "The theological educator, in this sense, should at some point in the student's life and career, be forgotten, even while what was taught and given to the student remains. The theological educator's legacy is not that he is remembered, but that the students have adopted what was taught and are changed by it for the service of others."[21]

Pedagogical Goals for the Local Academy: Inform, Persuade, Inspire

Within the context of the local academy or a teaching setting within the local church, biblical and theological reasoning can directly enhance the task of teaching. Three goals worth pursuing by a Christian educator are to inform, to persuade, and to inspire. Drawing on the ancient rhetorical tradition, Augustine cites these aims as the goal of the Christian teacher. He explains, "Now of these three, the one first mentioned, the teaching, which is a matter of necessity, depends on *what* we say; the other two on the *way* we say it."[22] For Augustine, to *inform* is central, but to *persuade* and *inspire* are organically connected to the central task of teaching.

The student must be moved to act as well as possess the competency to gain knowledge: "When . . . the truth taught is one that must be carried into practice, and that is taught for

---

18. See Jason G. Duesing, "Gentlemen Shepherds and Invisible Sherpas: The Task of Theological Educators," *Permanent Things 1.1 (2019): 58–65.*

19. Duesing, "Gentlemen Shepherds and Invisible Sherpas," 62.

20. Duesing, "Gentlemen Shepherds and Invisible Sherpas," 62. This particular practice can relate to major situations but also to the mundane rhythms of the academic life. In this vein, Duesing notes that "often this is as simple as modeling patience and understanding with any question asked in class or in public. When students see that even the most mundane of questions are taken with seriousness and without smirk in public, they are more willing to ask their vital questions in private." Further, even the willingness to modify teaching styles can participate in this act of service: "The theological educator as Sherpa assists students best when he strives to communicate in multiple ways, many venues, and with repetition to ensure that even that one student, who seems to care the least, comes to appreciate the course and subject matter" (62).

21. Duesing, "Gentlemen Shepherds and Invisible Sherpas," 63.

22. See Augustine, *On Christian Doctrine*, in *NPNF*, First Series, Volume 2, 4.13.27. Emphasis mine.

the very purpose of being practiced, it is useless to be persuaded of the truth of what is said, it is useless to be pleased with the manner in which it is said, if it be not so learnt as to be practiced."[23] Accordingly, as teachers, we must not "only teach so as to give instruction, and please so as to keep up the attention," but we must also "sway the mind so as to subdue the will."[24] These ancient teaching principles stand the test of time and serve as a helpful template for the contemporary educator. In our biblical-theological classrooms, we must seek to deliver the most strategic content in the most strategic manner.

Pedagogical Virtues for the Local Academy: Boldness and Humility

In pursuing these goals, we also seek to develop the pedagogical virtues of boldness and humility. We need boldness to teach with confidence and lead students as they access and grapple with new concepts and material. We also need humility to keep us reliant on God's grace and also mindful of the learning levels of our students. Both of these traits are necessary and are necessarily connected for the believing academic. This emphasis on the character of the educator is recognized in both secular and confessional contexts.[25] In a classroom or mentorship setting, we must be bold to explain or deliver the material in a way that demonstrates the truth of its content and our competency to do such a task. We must also be humble and acknowledge both where we lack knowledge and where we must accommodate our teaching level to the needs of our students.

To study, teach, or preach the brand of biblical theology put forward in this volume requires us to maintain this dialectic between boldness and humility. We need boldness in order to speak with confidence about the meaning of individual texts, biblical books, and the biblical canon as a whole. We also need humility because of the size and challenge of this kind of task. As we recognize that our own presuppositions guide and govern our analysis, we must reckon with the possibility that we have an incomplete grasp of this textual and theological material and our own sinful nature may be subtly informing what we see when we read. A disposition that includes both boldness and humility can help keep us rooted within the biblical-theological circle, where we read and reread both the parts and the whole of Scripture in prayerful submission to its authority and the guidance of the Holy Spirit.

---

23. Augustine, *On Christian Doctrine*, 4.13.29.
24. Augustine, *On Christian Doctrine*, 4.13.29.
25. For a recent evangelical treatment of the importance of character and the "scholarly virtues," see Köstenberger's discussion in *Excellence*. Köstenberger treats these traits under the categories of vocational excellence (diligence, courage, passion, restraint, creativity, eloquence), moral excellence (integrity, fidelity, wisdom), and relational excellence (grace, humility, interdependence, love). From a secular perspective, see James M. Banner and Harold Cannon, *The Elements of Teaching* (New Haven: Yale University Press, 1977). Banner and Cannon focus on "the qualities, both natural and cultivated, of those who teach rather than on the techniques they use because far too much attention has been given to explaining the process of teaching and not nearly enough to describing the people responsible for that process" (vii).

While much more could be said along these lines and many practical examples could be produced, these broad categories can serve as a helpful way to begin thinking through this urgent area of concern.

The Function of a Course on Biblical Theology

One way to illustrate the relationship between the academy and the churches is to reflect briefly upon a few examples of the way they can directly intersect. The following are three case studies, which include sample assignment prompts and areas for further research. Each of these case studies begin with an example of a teaching moment from a real-life ministry scenario and then is followed by a series of possible exercises that might equip someone to handle these types of discussions.

Case Study One: Acts and the Shape of the New Testament

When I was in seminary, for several months I met with an older man who was part of a halfway house ministry that helped people transition into the workforce after being homeless or in prison. He had been a believer for a few years, but he had never read much of the Bible. When I started meeting with him, we read several chapters from John's gospel each week. As we made our way through the story he became interested in Peter, so for our next book study he picked Peter's letters. That sounded good to me, so the next week we met to discuss 1 Peter. When we began talking about the letter, though, an odd thing began to happen. He kept giving a very negative reading of Peter's message and tone in his letter. He would say things like, "Well, Peter is sad in this letter. He's unsure of himself. He doesn't really feel like he has a right to speak to these people." This line of conversation went on for a few minutes. Confused as to why he was reading this very specific psychological profile into what is a strongly worded and confident letter, I simply asked him why he thought Peter would be thinking these things. He then said, "Well, Peter betrayed Jesus and abandoned him. How could you ever recover from something like that?"

Now I saw the issue more clearly. What had happened is that he was reading Peter's letter in light of only half of Peter's story. He was familiar with the Gospel narrative of Peter's denial of Jesus, and his last memory of Peter before reading 1 Peter 1:1 was Peter cursing Jesus and the shame and horrifying betrayal exposed by the sound of the rooster's crow. After realizing that this is where he was coming from, I told him, "Well, that's not the end of Peter's story!" We then returned to the closing chapters of John's gospel to revisit Peter's restoration with Jesus along the shore, and then briefly surveyed Peter's prominent role in the book of Acts as a confident preacher of the gospel. We saw Peter explain the new covenant, preach to thousands, follow the guidance of the Holy Spirit, shape the direction of the early church, and boldly serve the resurrected Christ. "Well," he said, "that changes everything. Knowing this about Peter changes how I read his letter for sure!"

I have thought of this conversation often when considering the role of Acts in relation to the rest of the New Testament. The narrative and theology of the book of Acts shapes our understanding of much of the New Testament. Several possible research projects or classroom activities can be built around this biblical-theological topic:

Exercise 1

How does the book of Acts function in the shape of the New Testament canon? In particular, when considering the structure and message of the book of Acts as a whole, how does this book compare and contrast first with the Gospel corpus and then with the two major letter collections of the New Testament?

Exercise 2

First, describe the scholarly discussion about the unity of Luke–Acts. Second, investigate the manuscript evidence for the independent circulation of Luke and Acts. Third, consider the hermeneutical impact of Luke's location in the Gospel grouping and Acts's association with the New Testament letters.

Exercise 3

Luke's gospel and the book of Acts are two important places in the New Testament where we see the role of the Holy Spirit developed. In the shape of the New Testament, John's gospel appears between Luke and Acts. For this reflection, consider the contribution that John's gospel makes to Luke and Acts's development of the person and work of the Holy Spirit.

Use these passages as a starting point for your analysis: Luke 1–4: John 14–17; Acts 1–5. After reading these passages, use the following questions as a basis for your analysis:

- According to Luke (in his Gospel and Acts), what are some of the distinctive aspects of the person and work of the Holy Spirit?
- According to John, what are some of the distinctive aspects of the person and work of the Holy Spirit?
- Reflect upon the relationship between John and Luke's portrayal of the Spirit. What would be lost if you isolated one strand of the New Testament's portrayal of the Spirit? How are you able to articulate both the unity and the diversity exhibited in these passages?

Case Study Two: The Gospel and the Grand Storyline

The study of salvation is an attempt to trace out the contours and shape of the gospel. Reflecting upon the question, "What is the Gospel?" is one of theology's primary tasks. The gospel should be the starting point, the guardrails, and the blazing center of all our theological reflection. Considering the nature of the gospel reminds us how much is connected to this "good news."

This discussion reminds me of an evangelism encounter I had a number of years ago. We were in a small Asian fishing village located near two small mountains in the area. One day, our group decided to climb one of them. Once we reached the top, we asked someone to take our picture. This young man and I then struck up a conversation. When we finished our climb, he invited me to climb the other mountain the next day. I agreed, and after we managed to accomplish this feat (he much more ably than I!), I needed to take a break, so on the way down we stopped at a small Buddhist temple that was built into the side of the mountain. Our conversation turned to spiritual things, and I asked if I could share the gospel with him. He said I could, and as I began, I started by saying that Jesus had died for our sins. His immediate question to me was, "What is sin?"

At this point, I quickly realized that I was going to have to find a different starting point than the one I had planned. I had assumed too much common ground and too much of the biblical storyline in our conversation. So, after pausing for a few seconds, I basically just started over, and began "in the beginning" with a basic presentation of who I believe God is as the creator of all things and rightful ruler over all that he has created. I then gave a simple account of the initial entrance of human rebellion against God's purposes into the world (essentially a paraphrase of Genesis 1–3).

After beginning where the biblical story begins, we were then able to continue our conversation. We now had common ground to discuss the sinfulness of humanity in general and also the sinfulness of every person. We needed to establish the *bad news* of the deceptive and pervasive reality of sin so that we could consider the claim that the gospel of Jesus Christ is *good news*. We needed to hear about the curse before we could consider news about the cure. We had to hear about paradise lost before we could hear the promise that paradise has been restored.

This encounter reminds me of the importance of studying the gospel within view of the grand storyline of the Bible. It also encourages me to continue thinking about the way the gospel is one of those theological areas that demonstrate the interconnection between exegesis, biblical theology, systematic theology, and the heartbeat of Christian ministry.

Exercise 1

In the study of salvation, we encounter many different images for salvation and a variety of ways to articulate what it means to be saved. Because each of us are different people with different experiences, we tend to gravitate toward certain ways of articulating the gospel and salvation. One of the ways to make sure our understanding of the gospel and salvation is anchored in the big picture of God's work in the world is to think about these realities in light of biblical theology. Trying not to abstract the gospel message from its home within the grand storyline of the entire Bible, a biblical theology of salvation seeks to account for God's work on behalf of his people from beginning to end. A common way of sharing the gospel with others is called the "Romans Road," which is a series of verses taken from Paul's Letter to the Romans that outline a basic gospel presentation. For this assignment, you will briefly articulate the features of salvation and the gospel from these verses. Then, you will set this gospel message within the framework of the entire biblical storyline.

First, read Genesis 1–3; Then, read the following verses from Romans: Romans 3:10–12, 23; 6:23; 5:8; 10:9–10, 13; 5:1; 8:1; 8:38–39. Finally, read Revelation 21–22.

Second, in one or two well-written paragraphs, write out a gospel presentation that follows the sequence of these passages. Make sure to include details from these texts in your presentation.

Finally, in one or two well-written paragraphs, reflect on the following questions:

- What difference does it make when you intentionally integrate Genesis 1–3 and Revelation 21–22 into your understanding and presentation of the gospel?
- Would you be able to understand the "Romans Road" without Genesis 1–3 and Revelation 21–22? Which specific elements would be missing or susceptible to being misunderstood? In other words, how does Paul draw upon these textual and theological elements in his letter to the Romans?
- What would be lost if you did not include these elements?

Exercise 2

Using the tools outlined in chapters two and eleven, compare and contrast the opening chapters of Genesis with the concluding chapters of Revelation. In particular, identify and analyze the intertextual connections that are present in Revelation 21–22. Then, address the following questions:

- What central themes of biblical theology are mentioned in these chapters?
- What aspects of the biblical storyline are mentioned here?
- How are these aspects connected and what textual links are present?

Exercise 3

In several places Paul describes the gospel message that he preaches. In these strategic passages, he connects his articulation of the gospel to the grand storyline of the Bible and the textual witness of the Old Testament. Pick two of the following passages: Romans 1:1–7; 1 Corinthians 15:1–11; 2 Corinthians 4:1–6; 2 Timothy 2:1–10. Next, discuss the way that Paul connects the proclamation of the gospel message to themes of biblical theology and address how the discipline of biblical theology helps us understand Paul's emphasis in these passages.

Case Study Three: Biblical Theology and the History of Interpretation

Several years ago, a student asked to meet with me to discuss something that was troubling her. Over the previous few weeks, she had been introduced through a friend to a particular teacher that had posted several brief but engaging video lectures online. She told me, "I know something is wrong about these videos, but I'm not sure what that is, or why it is so hard to figure that out!" "But," she continued, "if what he is saying is correct, then it means much of what I believe to be true is actually false. Can you help?" After watching several of these online lectures (which turned out to be not so brief!), I could see what my student was talking about. These videos described a new way of understanding biblical language that utilized different definitions of God, love, and humanity. The teacher said he was going to reinterpret everything you thought you knew about the gospel and how it works. His basic point was that salvation involves not God's redeeming work on behalf of humanity, but rather each human's realization of the saving light that is already within them.

In follow-up conversations with my student, we discussed several issues. One reason responding to these videos was so difficult was the way they employed biblical terms and then filled them with new meaning. In this situation, a biblical or theological formulation (like humanity's need for God's redemption in order to experience salvation) became a tool that taught a very different version of the gospel. One of the most helpful dialogue partners in this discussion (and what led to a breakthrough for this student) was Irenaeus and his "rule of faith." As we noted in chapter one, in his discussion of the "rule or faith" Irenaeus harnesses the metaphor of a mosaic of previous jewels arranged in the image of a beautiful king, but later are repositioned into a poorly executed dog or fox. Like those who rearrange the image of the king into an ugly dog, false teachers use biblical language but disregard the "order and connection" of the Scriptures. This, it turns out, was an excellent way to respond to this contemporary teaching.

Now, this online lecturer did not mention Gnosticism or draw directly upon the writings of the patristic period. However, working through the *way* Irenaeus responded to the reinterpretation of biblical language by the gnostic teachers of his day provided a conceptual tool that immediately illustrated what this modern teacher was asserting and why it was so problematic.

This anecdote is particularly instructive for me as I teach my students about the value and strategic significance of the great tradition. The biblical-theological issues at stake in this scenario involved the characterization of the nature of the gospel, the big picture of what God is doing in the world, and the interpretation of individual phrases from the New Testament. There is thus a long history and an enduring relevance for this type of analysis.

Exercise 1

One of the ways the theologians of the early church brought the totality of the biblical witness to God's work in the world to bear on their defense of the faith and the preaching of the gospel was a "rule of faith." For this reflection, read the following three places where two early Christian theologians—Irenaeus and Tertullian—articulate this rule of faith:

- Irenaeus, *Against Heresies*, 1.10.1–2
- Irenaeus, *Demonstration of the Apostolic Preaching*, 6–7
- Tertullian, *Prescription against Heretics*, 13

How is the "rule of faith" being used in each instance, and what are its essential contents and characteristics? How does the rule relate to the message, story, and/or canon of Scripture? Finally, how does this use of the rule of faith in the early church relate to contemporary approaches to the discipline of biblical theology?

Exercise 2

A perennial concern of biblical readers and the discipline of biblical theology is the relationship between the Testaments and the nature of the Mosaic covenant. For this reflection, compare and contrast the way that Thomas Aquinas, Martin Luther, and John Calvin discuss the relationship between the old covenant and the new covenant in the following brief selections:

- Thomas Aquinas, *Summa Theologica*, First Part of the Second Part, Question 107 ("The new law as compared with the old")
- Martin Luther, "How Christians Should Regard Moses" (*Luther's Works,* Vol. 35: *Word and Sacrament I*, 155–74)
- John Calvin, *Institutes of the Christian Religion*, Book 2, Chapters 10–11 ("Similarity and Difference between the Two Testaments")

Next, address the following questions: How would you characterize the overall argument being advanced in each of these selections? How are they using biblical texts and features of the canonical context in their discussion? Moreover, how does the way they go about addressing this question compare or contrast with contemporary approaches to the discipline of biblical theology?

For a broader framework (either in a class discussion or a larger research-based assignment), pursue this question: How do Aquinas, Luther, and Calvin each address these biblical-theological connections within the context of their larger works? For this line of reflection, you might consult these further selections: Aquinas's *Hic est Liber* (discussion point: relevance of canonical shape); Luther's "Prefaces" to his biblical translations (discussion point: hermeneutical strategies for reading); Calvin's prefaces/introductions to the various editions of his *Institutes* (discussion point: relationship between theological and biblical studies).

Exercise 3

An important turning point to consider in the study of biblical theology as a discipline is the effect of the modern period on biblical and theological studies. For this reflection, you will analyze several influential articulations of the discipline:

- Read J. P. Gabler's influential address, "An Oration on the Proper Distinction between Biblical and Dogmatic Theology and the Specific Objectives of Each."
- Describe and discuss the strategic significance of Gabler's address for the history of biblical interpretation and the emergence of the modern discipline of biblical theology. Even though Gabler's address does not *establish* this distinction for the first time, what about his discussion and formulations make his address a common starting point for telling the story of the modern period's effect on biblical and theological studies?
- Compare and contrast Gabler's address with either William Wrede's address, "The Task and Methods of 'New Testament Theology,'" or James Barr's chapter on "Definitions: The Many Faces of Biblical Theology." These three readings represent a span of over two centuries. What remains the same across these three works, and what do you notice that develops from one work to the next?
- For an introduction and bibliographic information for Gabler, Wrede, and Barr, see chapter one.

Discussion Questions

1. Why is the relationship between the academy and the churches a relevant issue for the discipline of biblical theology in general and evangelical scholarship in particular?

2. What is "trickle-down academics?" What are some recent examples of this type of phenomenon in scholarly discussions or ministry contexts?

3. Describe the difference between the "universal academy" and the "local academy." What does this distinction mean, and why might it be an important way to think about academic ministry?

4. What are the central reasons to maintain *both* boldness and humility in the discipline of biblical theology? What are some additional theological reasons for this basic disposition when studying the Scriptures?

5. Consider the initial anecdote in the three case studies at the end of this chapter. What are some of the real-life ministry situations you have encountered that the study of biblical theology might inform or assist?

Resources for Further Study

House, Paul R. *Bonhoeffer's Seminary Vision: A Case for Costly Discipleship and Life Together.* Wheaton: Crossway, 2015.

Köstenberger, Andreas J. *Excellence: The Character of God and the Pursuit of Scholarly Virtue.* Wheaton: Crossway, 2011.

Treier, Daniel J. *Virtue and the Voice of God: Toward Theology as Wisdom.* Grand Rapids: Eerdmans, 2006.

Vanhoozer, Kevin J. *Pictures at a Theological Exhibition: Sources for the Church's Worship, Witness and Wisdom.* Downers Grove: InterVarsity, 2016.

Webster, John. *The Culture of Theology.* Edited by Ivor J. Davidson and Alden C. McCray. Grand Rapids: Baker, 2019.

CONCLUSION

IN ACTS 17, PAUL AND SILAS arrive in Berea under the cover of night after a serious conflict in Thessalonica. When they arrive they enter the Jewish synagogue and proclaim the gospel message (Acts 17:10–11). Luke recounts that "these Jews were more noble than those in Thessalonica" because they "received the word with all eagerness, examining the Scriptures daily to see if these things were so" (17:11). The message the Bereans examine here is likely the same one that Paul preached in Thessalonica. Luke notes that over the course of three Sabbaths in Thessalonica, Paul "reasoned with them from the Scriptures, explaining and proving that it was necessary for the Christ to suffer and to rise from the dead" (17:2–3). Paul explains in his preaching, "This Jesus whom I proclaim to you, is the Christ" (17:3).

These ancient Bereans can be a model for contemporary believers and biblical theologians. A Berean brand of biblical theology argues that the study of the whole Bible on its own terms is organically connected to the preaching of the gospel and the ministry of the churches. The Berean practice of reading the Scriptures in light of the risen Christ can shape both our understanding of the big picture of the Bible and also our exegetical practice. This scene also illustrates several of the principles developed throughout this volume: The gospel is a story that takes two testaments to tell. The biblical authors were also biblical readers. The task of biblical theology requires reading and rereading.

As mentioned at the beginning of this volume, we took seriously the goal of providing an invitation to the discipline and practice of biblical theology. Accordingly, this book is neither a full-scale or exhaustive account of these areas of inquiry, nor only a surface-level introduction to basic elements. Rather, we have sought to introduce some of the central aspects of biblical theology as a discipline, explain some of the strategic tools that are used in the practice of biblical theology, and provide a series of studies that highlight the payoff to this approach for understanding the Scriptures. In these discussions, we have taken certain positions and made several specific proposals, but the overall aim of the endeavor has been to orient you to this type of study and way of thinking about the Bible's message as a whole.

The approach taken in this volume focuses on and directly relates the canon, the covenants, and the Christ. The Scriptures were composed, gathered, and circulated in such a way that they are able to communicate God's revelation of his saving message for future generations. This canonical context, then, is where we encounter the biblical writings. Moreover, a grand storyline arises from the many narratives comprising this canonical collection. The heartbeat of this storyline can be heard in the biblical covenants. Both the canonical collection and the biblical covenants point to Jesus as the Christ. These three interconnected categories—the canon, the covenants, and the Christ—have structured our attempt to capture the crucial components of biblical theology.

The heart of the biblical theologian's task is to explore these three categories and their interrelationship. As we have developed, these important areas of emphasis are interwoven throughout the Scriptures and encompass many of the main features of the Bible. This approach resonates with several recent trends in evangelical scholarship on biblical theology, especially those that stress the importance of textual features, the storyline of the Bible as a whole, and the strategic function of the biblical canon.

In chapter one, we considered the nature and definition of biblical theology as a discipline. We also considered several approaches to the task of biblical theology. In chapter two, we outlined a specific approach to biblical theology that took as its orienting framework the canonical context of the Bible, the narrative flow of the biblical storyline, and the strategic place of the biblical covenants in that storyline. We also discussed several of the tools that are necessary for the practice of biblical theology. These tools help you read individual passages well and present biblical-theological themes cogently. In chapter three, we moved to consider the final part of our framework for biblical theology. The culminating feature of this biblical-theological framework is its conviction that one of the main purposes of Scripture is to display Jesus Christ. In chapter four, we examined some of the theological commitments we make about Scripture that enable us to approach biblical theology in this manner.

In chapters five through ten, we considered the story of Scripture from beginning to end. Each major grouping in the biblical canon moves along the grand storyline of the Bible and develops the central themes that bind the Scriptures together. In chapters eleven through twenty, we surveyed several of these central themes that appear throughout the Bible. In these studies, we sought to make use of the biblical-theological tools discussed in the first part of the volume. In the final two chapters, we considered the way that the study of biblical theology can function within the churches and within the academy.

The work done in this volume is not designed to be exhaustive but rather to serve as a warm invitation to doing biblical theology along these lines. We hope you accept this invitation as you serve the churches, study the Scriptures, and seek to understand what you are reading.

1. SELECT INFLUENTIAL ORDERINGS OF THE HEBREW BIBLE

Talmudic Tradition	Masoretic Tradition	Medieval and Modern Jewish Tradition
The Law	***The Law***	***The Law***
Genesis	Genesis	Genesis
Exodus	Exodus	Exodus
Leviticus	Leviticus	Leviticus
Numbers	Numbers	Numbers
Deuteronomy	Deuteronomy	Deuteronomy
The Prophets	***The Prophets***	***The Prophets***
Joshua	Joshua	Joshua
Judges	Judges	Judges
Samuel	Samuel	Samuel
Kings	Kings	Kings
Jeremiah	Isaiah	Isaiah
Ezekiel	Jeremiah	Jeremiah
Isaiah	Ezekiel	Ezekiel
The Twelve	The Twelve	The Twelve
The Writings	***The Writings***	***The Writings***
Ruth	Chronicles	Psalms
Psalms	Psalms	Proverbs
Job	Job	Job
Proverbs	Proverbs	Song of Songs
Ecclesiastes	Ruth	Ruth
Song of Songs	Song of Songs	Lamentations
Lamentations	Ecclesiastes	Ecclesiastes
Daniel	Lamentations	Esther
Esther	Esther	Daniel
Ezra (includes Nehemiah)	Daniel	Ezra–Nehemiah
Chronicles	Ezra–Nehemiah	Chronicles
Attesting Evidence:	***Attesting Evidence:***	***Attesting Evidence:***
• Babylonian Talmud Baba Bathra 14b • 12–15 manuscripts dated from the twelfth through the fifteenth century.	• Aleppo Codex • Leningrad Codex	• Liturgical manuscripts dated to the twelfth or thirteenth century. • Jewish Publication Society Tanakh (1917 & 1985)

2. SELECT INFLUENTIAL ORDERINGS OF THE NEW TESTAMENT

Codex Sinaiticus (01)	Codex Alexandrinus (A 02)	Codex Vaticanus (B 03)	Athanasius, *39th Festal Letter* (AD 367)
Matthew	Matthew	Matthew	Matthew
Mark	Mark	Mark	Mark
Luke	Luke	Luke	Luke
John	John	John	John
Romans	Acts	Acts	Acts
1 Corinthians	James	James	James
2 Corinthians	1 Peter	1 Peter	1 Peter
Galatians	2 Peter	2 Peter	2 Peter
Ephesians	1 John	1 John	1 John
Philippians	2 John	2 John	2 John
Colossians	3 John	3 John	3 John
1 Thessalonians	Jude	Jude	Jude
2 Thessalonians	Romans	Romans	Romans
Hebrews	1 Corinthians	1 Corinthians	1 Corinthians
1 Timothy	2 Corinthians	2 Corinthians	2 Corinthians
2 Timothy	Galatians	Galatians	Galatians
Titus	Ephesians	Ephesians	Ephesians
Philemon	Philippians	Philippians	Philippians
Acts	Colossians	Colossians	Colossians
James	1 Thessalonians	1 Thessalonians	1 Thessalonians
1 Peter	2 Thessalonians	2 Thessalonians	2 Thessalonians
2 Peter	Hebrews	Hebrews	Hebrews
1 John	1 Timothy	(manuscript breaks off)	1 Timothy
2 John	2 Timothy		2 Timothy
3 John	Titus		Titus
Jude	Philemon		Philemon
Revelation	Revelation		Revelation
Barnabas	1 Clement		
Hermas	2 Clement		

3. SELECT BIBLIOGRAPHY OF RESOURCES TO HELP BEGIN

THE STUDY OF BOOK ORDERINGS

The following works include information on relevant manuscripts, ordering traditions, and/or ancient lists of biblical books. These resources can provide a starting point for further research and reflection on the extant orderings of the biblical material and also the patterns of continuity and discontinuity between the various orderings of the collections found in the biblical canon.

Beckwith, Roger T. *The Old Testament Canon of the New Testament Church: And Its Background in Early Judaism*. London: SPCK, 1985.

Comfort, Philip Wesley. *A Commentary on the Manuscripts and Text of the New Testament*. Grand Rapids: Kregel, 2015. (See esp. 43–126)

Gallagher, Edmon L., and John D. Meade. *The Biblical Canon Lists from Early Christianity and Analysis*. Oxford: Oxford University Press, 2017.

Hurtado, Larry. *The Earliest Christian Artifacts: Manuscripts and Christian Origins*. Grand Rapids: Eerdmans, 2006. (See esp. "Appendix 1: Christian Literary Texts in Manuscripts of the Second and Third Centuries," 209–29)

McDonald, Lee Martin. "Lists and Catalogues of Old Testament Collections" and "Lists and Catalogues of Old Testament Collections." In *The Canon Debate*, edited by Lee M. McDonald and James A. Sanders, 585–98. Peabody: Hendrickson, 2002.

Metzger, Bruce. *The Canon of the New Testament: Its Origin, Development, and Significance*. Oxford: Oxford University Press, 1987. (See esp. "Variations in the Sequence of the Books of the New Testament," 295–300)

Trobisch, David. *The First Edition of the New Testament*. Oxford: Oxford University Press, 2000. (See esp. 8–44)

BIBLIOGRAPHY

Aalen, Sverre. "*Doxa.*" In *New International Dictionary of New Testament Theology,* edited by Colin Brown, 4 vols., 2:44–48. Grand Rapids, Zondervan, 1971.

Akin, Daniel L. *Exalting Jesus in Revelation.* Christ-Centered Exposition Commentary. Nashville: B&H, 2016.

Akin, Daniel L., David Lewis Allen, and Ned Lee Mathews, eds. *Text-Driven Preaching: God's Word at the Heart of Every Sermon.* Nashville: B&H, 2010.

Akin, Daniel L., David P. Nelson, and Peter R. Schemm, eds. *A Theology for the Church.* Nashville: B&H, 2007.

Alden, Robert L. *Job.* New American Commentary 11. Nashville: B&H, 1994.

Alexander, T. Desmond. *The City of God and the Goal of Creation.* Short Studies in Biblical Theology. Wheaton: Crossway, 2018.

———. *From Eden to the New Jerusalem: An Introduction to Biblical Theology.* Grand Rapids: Kregel, 2009.

———. *From Paradise to the Promised Land: An Introduction to the Pentateuch.* 3rd ed. Grand Rapids: Baker, 2012.

———. "Further Observations on the Term 'Seed' in Genesis." *Tyndale Bulletin* 48.1 (1997): 363–67.

———. *The Servant King: The Bible's Portrait of the Messiah.* Vancouver: Regent, 1998.

Alexander, T. Desmond, and Brian S. Rosner, eds. *New Dictionary of Biblical Theology.* Downers Grove: InterVarsity, 2000.

Allen, Leslie C. *Psalms 101-150.* Word Bible Commentary 21. Dallas: Thomas Nelson, 2002.

Allison, Gregg R. *The Baker Compact Dictionary of Theological Terms.* Grand Rapids: Baker, 2016.

———. "Baptism with and Filling of the Holy Spirit." *Southern Baptist Journal of Theology* 16.4 (2012): 4–21.

———. *Historical Theology: An Introduction to Christian Doctrine.* Grand Rapids: Zondervan, 2011.

———. "The Kingdom and the Church." In *The Kingdom of God*, edited by Christopher W. Morgan and Robert A. Peterson, Theology in Community 4, 179–205. Wheaton: Crossway, 2012.

———. *Roman Catholic Theology and Practice: An Evangelical Assessment.* Wheaton: Crossway, 2014.

———. *Sojourners and Strangers: The Doctrine of the Church.* Wheaton: Crossway, 2012.

Allison, Gregg R., and Chris Castaldo. *The Unfinished Reformation: What Unites and Divides Catholics and Protestants after 500 Years.* Grand Rapids: Zondervan, 2016.

Allison, Gregg R., and Stephen J. Wellum, eds. *Building on the Foundations of Evangelical Theology: Essays in Honor of John S. Feinberg.* Wheaton: Crossway, 2015.

Auerbach, Erich. *Mimesis: The Representation of Reality in Western Literature.* Translated by Willard R. Trask. Princeton: Princeton University Press, 1953.

Austin, J. L. *How to Do Things with Words.* Cambridge: Harvard University Press, 1962.

Averbeck, R. E. "Priest, Priesthood." In *Evangelical Dictionary of Biblical Theology*, edited by Walter A. Elwell, 632–38. Grand Rapids: Baker, 1996.

Baglow, Christopher T. "Rediscovering St. Thomas Aquinas as a Biblical Theologian." *Letter and Spirit* 1 (2005): 137–46.

Banner James M., and Harold Cannon. *The Elements of Teaching*. New Haven: Yale University Press, 1977.

Barker, Kenneth L. "The Scope and Center of Old Testament Theology and Hope." In *Dispensationalism, Israel, and the Church: The Search for Definition*, edited by Craig A. Blaising and Darrell L. Bock, 293–328. Grand Rapids: Zondervan, 1992.

Barr, James. *Bible and Interpretation: The Collected Essays of James Barr, Volume I: Interpretation and Theology*. Edited by John Barton. Oxford: Oxford University Press, 2013.

———. *The Concept of Biblical Theology: An Old Testament Perspective*. London: SCM Press, 1999.

Barrett, Matthew. *God's Word Alone: The Authority of Scripture*. Grand Rapids: Zondervan, 2016.

Barth, Karl. *Church Dogmatics, Volume I: The Doctrine of the Word of God, Part One*. Translated by G. W. Bromiley. Edinburgh: T&T Clark, 1975.

Bartholomew, Craig G., and Heath A. Thomas. *A Manifesto for Theological Interpretation*. Grand Rapids: Baker, 2016.

Bartholomew, Craig G., Scott Hahn, Robin Parry, Christopher Seitz, and Al Wolters, eds. *Canon and Biblical Interpretation*. Scripture and Hermeneutics Series 7. Grand Rapids: Zondervan, 2006.

Barton, John. "Historiography and Theodicy in the Old Testament." In *Reflection and Refraction: Studies in Biblical Historiography in Honor of A. Graeme Auld*, edited by Robert Rezetko, Timothy H. Lim, and W. Brian Aucker, Supplements to Vetus Testamentum 113, 27–33. Leiden: Brill, 2007.

———. *Holy Writings, Sacred Text: The Canon in Early Christianity*. Louisville: Westminster John Knox Press, 1997.

———. *The Nature of Biblical Criticism*. Louisville: Westminster John Knox, 2007.

Bauckham, Richard. *Bible and Mission: Christian Witness in a Postmodern World*. Grand Rapids: Baker, 2003.

———. *The Climax of Prophecy: Studies on the Book of Revelation*. London: T&T Clark, 1999.

———, ed. *The Gospels for All Christians: Rethinking the Gospel Audiences*. Grand Rapids: Eerdmans, 1997.

———. "James and the Gentiles: Acts 15:13-21." In *History, Literature, and Society in the Book of Acts*, edited by Ben Witherington III, 154–84. Cambridge: Cambridge University Press, 1996.

———. *Jesus and the God of Israel: God Crucified and Other Studies on the New Testament's Christology of Divine Identity*. Grand Rapids: Eerdmans, 2008.

———. "The Lord's Day." In *From Sabbath to Lord's Day: A Biblical, Historical, and Theological Investigation*, edited by D. A. Carson, 221–50. Grand Rapids: Zondervan, 1982.

———. "Reading Scripture as a Coherent Story." In *The Art of Reading Scripture*, edited by Ellen Davis and Richard Hays, 38–53. Grand Rapids: Eerdmans, 2003.

———. *The Theology of the Book of Revelation*. Cambridge: Cambridge University Press, 1993.

Bavinck, Herman. *Reformed Dogmatics: Abridged in One Volume*. Edited by John Bolt. Grand Rapids: Baker, 2011.

Beale, G. K. *The Book of Revelation: A Commentary on the Greek Text*. New International Greek Testament Commentary. Grand Rapids: Eerdmans, 1999.

———. "Eden, the Temple, and the Church's Mission in the New Creation." *Journal of the Evangelical Theological Society* 48.1 (2005): 5–31.

———. *The Erosion of Inerrancy in Evangelicalism: Responding to New Challenges to Biblical Authority*. Wheaton: Crossway, 2008.

———. *Handbook on the New Testament Use of the Old Testament: Exegesis and Interpretation.* Grand Rapids: Baker, 2012.

———. *John's Use of the Old Testament in Revelation.* Library of New Testament Studies 166. London: T&T Clark, 2015.

———. *A New Testament Biblical Theology: The Unfolding of the Old Testament in the New.* Grand Rapids: Baker, 2011.

———, ed. *The Right Doctrine from the Wrong Texts? Essays on the Use of the Old Testament in the New.* Grand Rapids: Baker, 1994.

———. *The Temple and the Church's Mission: A Biblical Theology of the Dwelling Place of God.* New Studies in Biblical Theology 17. Downers Grove: InterVarsity, 2004.

———. *We Become What We Worship: A Biblical Theology of Idolatry.* Downers Grove: InterVarsity, 2008.

Beale, G. K., and D. A. Carson, eds. *Commentary on the New Testament Use of the Old Testament.* Grand Rapids: Baker, 2007.

Beale, G. K., and Mitchell Kim. *God Dwells among Us: Expanding Eden to the Ends of the Earth.* Downers Grove: InterVarsity, 2014

Beale, G. K., and Sean M. McDonough. "Revelation." In *Commentary on the New Testament Use of the Old Testament,* edited by G. K. Beale and D. A. Carson, 1081–1161. Grand Rapids: Baker, 2007.

Behr, John. *Irenaeus of Lyons: Identifying Christianity.* Oxford: Oxford University Press, 2013.

———, trans. *On the Apostolic Preaching.* Crestwood: St Vladimir's Seminary Press, 1997.

———. *The Nicene Faith.* Formation of Christian Theology 2. Crestwood: St Vladimir's Seminary Press, 2004.

———. *The Way to Nicaea.* Formation of Christian Theology 1. Crestwood: St Vladimir's Seminary Press, 2001.

Bergen, Robert D. *1, 2 Samuel*. New American Commentary 7. Nashville: B&H, 1996.

Bird, Michael F. *Jesus Is the Christ: The Messianic Testimony of the Gospels*. Downers Grove: InterVarsity, 2012.

Bird, Michael F., and Michael W. Pahl, eds. *The Sacred Text: Excavating the Texts, Exploring the Interpretations, and Engaging the Theologies of the Christian Scriptures*. Piscataway: Gorgias, 2010.

Blackburn, W. Ross. *The God Who Makes Himself Known: The Missionary Heart of the Book of Exodus*. Downers Grove: InterVarsity, 2012.

Blaising, Craig A. "A Case for the Pretribulation Rapture." In *The Rapture: Pretribulation, Prewrath, or Posttribulation*, edited by Stanley N. Gundry, 25–73. Grand Rapids: Zondervan, 2010.

———. "The Day of the Lord: Theme and Pattern in Biblical Theology." *Bibliotheca Sacra* 169.1 (2012): 3–19.

Blaising, Craig A., and Darrell L. Bock. *Progressive Dispensationalism*. Grand Rapids: Baker, 1993.

Blenkinsopp, Joseph. *Prophecy and Canon: A Contribution to the Study of Jewish Origins*. Notre Dame: Notre Dame University Press, 1977.

Block, Daniel I. *The Book of Ezekiel: Chapters 25–48*. New International Commentary on the Old Testament. Grand Rapids: Eerdmans, 1998.

———. *For the Glory of God: Recovering a Biblical Theology of Worship*. Grand Rapids: Baker Academic, 2014.

———. "The Prophet of the Spirit: The Use of RWḤ in the Book of Ezekiel." *Journal of the Evangelical Theological Society* 32.1 (1989): 27–49.

———. "My Servant David: Ancient Israel's Vision of the Messiah." In *Israel's Messiah in the Bible and the Dead Sea Scrolls*, edited by Richard S. Hess and M. Daniel Carroll, 17–56. Grand Rapids: Baker, 2003.

Blomberg, Craig L. "Holy Spirit." In *Evangelical Dictionary of Biblical Theology*, edited by Walter A. Elwell, 344–47 Grand Rapids: Baker, 1996.

Blowers, Paul M. "The *Regula Fidei* and the Narrative Character of Early Christian Faith." *Pro Ecclesia* 6 (1997): 199–228.

Bock, Darrell L. *Acts*. Baker Exegetical Commentary on the New Testament. Grand Rapids: Baker, 2007.

Bock, Darrell L., and Craig A Blaising, eds. *Dispensationalism, Israel and the Church: The Search for Definition*. Grand Rapids: Zondervan, 1992.

Bond, Helen K. "Discarding the Seamless Robe: The High Priesthood of Jesus in John's Gospel." In *Israel's God and Rebecca's Children: Christology and Community in Early Judaism and Christianity: Essays in Honor of Larry W. Hurtado and Alan F. Segal*, edited by David B. Capes, April D. DeConick, Helen K. Bond, and Troy A. Miller, 183–94. Waco: Baylor University Press, 2007.

Borchert, Gerald L. *John 1-11*. New American Commentary 25A. Nashville: B&H, 1996.

Bray, Gerald L. *The Doctrine of God*. Contours of Christian Theology. Downers Grove: InterVarsity, 1993.

———. "God." In *New Dictionary of Biblical Theology*, edited by T. Desmond Alexander and Brian S. Rosner, 511–21. Downers Grove: InterVarsity, 2000.

Bright, John. *The Kingdom of God: The Biblical Concept and its Meaning for the Church*. Nashville: Abingdon, 1953.

Brown, Jeannine K. *Scripture as Communication: Introducing Biblical Hermeneutics*. Grand Rapids: Baker, 2007.

Bruce, F. F. *The Book of Acts*. Rev. ed. New International Commentary on the New Testament. Grand Rapids: Eerdmans, 1988.

———. *The Canon of Scripture*. Downers Grove: InterVarsity, 1988.

Bruno, Chris. *The Whole Message of the Bible in Sixteen Words*. Wheaton: Crossway, 2017.

Bullock, C. Hassell. *Encountering the Book of Psalms: A Literary and Theological Introduction.* 2nd ed. Grand Rapids: Baker, 2018.

Calvin, John. *Commentaries on the First Book of Moses, Called Genesis.* Translated by John King. 2 vols. Grand Rapids: Eerdmans, 1948.

———. *Institutes of the Christian Religion.* Edited by John T. McNeill. Translated by Ford L. Battles. 2 vols. Library of Christian Classics 20–21. Philadelphia: Westminster John Knox, 1960.

Campbell, Iain D. "The Song of David's Son: Interpreting the Song of Solomon in the Light of the Davidic Covenant." *Westminster Theological Journal* 62.1 (2000): 17–32.

Carson, D. A. "1 Peter." In *Commentary on the New Testament Use of the Old Testament,* edited by G. K. Beale and D. A. Carson, 1015–45. Grand Rapids: Baker, 2007.

———. "A Biblical-Theological Overview of the Bible." In *NIV Biblical Theology Study Bible,* edited by D. A. Carson, 2325–27. Grand Rapids: Zondervan, 2018.

———. "Biblical Theology." In *Dictionary of Biblical Criticism and Interpretation,* edited by Stanley E. Porter, 35–41. London: Routledge, 2007.

———, ed. *The Church in the Bible and the World: An International Study.* Grand Rapids: Baker, 1987.

———. "Current Issues in Biblical Theology: A New Testament Perspective." *Bulletin for Biblical Research* 5 (1995): 17–41.

———. *Exegetical Fallacies.* Grand Rapids: Baker, 1996.

———, ed. *From Sabbath to Lord's Day: A Biblical, Historical, and Theological Investigation.* Grand Rapids: Zondervan, 1982.

———. *The Gagging of God: Christianity Confronts Pluralism.* Grand Rapids: Zondervan, 2002.

———. *The Gospel according to John.* Pillar New Testament Commentary. Grand Rapids: Eerdmans, 1991.

———. "John and the Johannine Epistles." In *It Is Written: Scripture Citing Scripture: Essays in Honour of Barnabas Lindars, SFF*, edited by D. A. Carson and H. G. M. Williamson, 245–64. Cambridge: Cambridge University Press, 1988.

———. "Matthew." In *The Expositor's Bible Commentary*. Vol. 9. Grand Rapids: Zondervan, 2010.

———. "New Testament Theology." In *Dictionary of the Later New Testament and Its Developments*, edited by Ralph Martin and Peter Davids, 796–811. Downers Grove: InterVarsity, 1997.

———. *Praying with Paul: A Call to Spiritual Reformation*. 2nd ed. Grand Rapids: Baker, 2014.

———. "Systematic Theology and Biblical Theology." In *New Dictionary of Biblical Theology*, edited by T. D. Alexander and Brian S. Rosner, 89–104. Downers Grove: InterVarsity, 2000.

———. "Why the Local Church Is More Important Than TGC, White Horse Inn, 9Marks, and Maybe Even ETS." *Themelios* 40.1 (2015): 1–9.

———. *Worship by the Book*. Grand Rapids: Zondervan, 2002.

Carson, D. A., and John D. Woodbridge, eds. *Scripture and Truth*. Grand Rapids: Baker, 1992.

Carter, Craig A. *Interpreting Scripture with the Great Tradition: Recovering the Genius of Premodern Exegesis*. Grand Rapids: Baker, 2018.

Caulley, T. S. "Holy Spirit." In *Evangelical Dictionary of Theology*, edited by Walter A. Elwell, 568–73. Grand Rapids: Baker, 2001.

Chae, Daniel Jong-Sang. "Paul's Apostolic Self-Awareness and the Occasion and Purpose of Romans." In *Mission and Meaning: Essays Presented to Peter Cotterell*, edited by Anthony Billington, Tony Lane, and Max Turner, 116–37. Carlisle: Paternoster, 1995.

Chapell, Bryan. *Christ-Centered Preaching: Redeeming the Expository Sermon*. 2nd ed. Grand Rapids: Baker, 2005.

Chapman, Stephen B. *The Law and the Prophets: A Study in Old Testament Canon Formation.* Grand Rapids: Baker, 2019.

Charnock, Stephen. *Discourses Upon the Existence and Attributes of God.* Grand Rapids: Baker, 1979.

Cheung, Alex T. M. "The Priest as the Redeemed Man: A Biblical-Theological Study of the Priesthood." *Journal of the Evangelical Theological Society* 29.3 (1986): 265–75.

Childs, Brevard S. *Biblical Theology in Crisis.* Philadelphia: Westminster Press, 1970.

———. *Biblical Theology of the Old and New Testaments: Theological Reflection on the Christian Bible.* Minneapolis: Fortress, 1992.

———. *The Church's Guide for Reading Paul: The Canonical Shaping of the Pauline Corpus.* Grand Rapids: Eerdmans, 2008.

———. *Introduction to the Old Testament as Christian Scripture.* Philadelphia: Fortress, 1979.

———. *The New Testament as Canon: An Introduction.* Philadelphia: Fortress, 1984.

———. *Old Testament Theology in a Canonical Context.* Philadelphia: Fortress, 1985.

———. "The One Gospel in Four Witnesses." In *The Rule of Faith: Scripture, Canon, and Creed in a Critical Age*, edited by Ephrain Radner and George Sumner, 51–62. Harrisburg: Morehouse, 1998.

Chou, Abner. *The Hermeneutics of the Biblical Writers: Learning to Interpret Scripture from the Prophets and Apostles.* Grand Rapids: Kregel, 2018.

Chrupcala, Leslaw. *The Kingdom of God: A Bibliography of 20th Century Research.* Jerusalem: Franciscan, 2007.

Ciampa, Roy E. "The History of Redemption." In *Central Themes in Biblical Theology: Mapping Unity in Diversity*, edited by Scott J. Hafemann and Paul R. House, 254–308. Grand Rapids: Baker, 2007.

Clowney, Edmund P. "The Biblical Theology of the Church." In *The Church in the Bible and the World: An International Study*, edited by D. A. Carson, 13–87. Grand Rapids: Baker, 1987.

Cole, Graham A. *The God Who Became Human: A Biblical Theology of Incarnation.* New Studies in Biblical Theology 30. Downers Grove: InterVarsity, 2013.

———. *He Who Gives Life: The Doctrine of the Holy Spirit.* Foundations of Evangelical Theology. Wheaton: Crossway, 2007.

———. "Why a Book? Why This Book? Why the Particular Order within This Book? Some Theological Reflections on the Canon." In *The Enduring Authority of the Christian Scriptures*, edited by D. A. Carson, 456–76. Grand Rapids: Eerdmans, 2016.

Collins, C. John. "*Kabod.*" In *New International Dictionary of Old Testament Theology and Exegesis*, edited by Willem VanGemeren, 5 vols., 2:577–87. Grand Rapids: Zondervan, 2012.

———. "A Syntactical Note (Genesis 3:15): Is the Woman's Seed Singular or Plural?" *Tyndale Bulletin* 48.1 (1997): 139–48.

Conn, Peter. "The Great Accreditation Farce." *The Chronicle of Higher Education*, June 30, 2014.

Cook, W. Robert. "The 'Glory' Motif in the Johannine Corpus." *Journal of the Evangelical Theological Society* 27.3 (1984): 291–97.

Coswell, Gregory. "Jonah among the Twelve Prophets." *Journal of Biblical Literature* 135.2 (2016): 283–99.

Cowan, Christopher W. "The Warning Passages of Hebrews and the New Covenant Community." In *Progressive Covenantalism: Charting a Course between Dispensational and Covenantal Theologies*, edited by Stephen J. Wellum and Brent E. Parker, 189–214. Nashville: B&H, 2016.

Cowan, Steven B., ed. *Who Runs the Church? Four Views on Church Government.* Grand Rapids: Zondervan, 2004.

Crisp, Oliver D. *Divinity and Humanity: The Incarnation Reconsidered*. Cambridge: Cambridge University Press, 2007.

Currid, John. *A Study Commentary on Deuteronomy*. Webster: Evangelical Press, 2006.

Davids, Peter H. *The Letters of 2 Peter and Jude*. Pillar New Testament Commentary. Grand Rapids: Eerdmans, 2006.

Davies, John A. *A Royal Priesthood: Literary and Intertextual Perspectives on an Image of Israel in Exodus 19.6*. Journal for the Study of the Old Testament 395. London: T&T Clark, 2004.

Davis, Jeffry C. "The Countercultural Quest of Christian Liberal Arts." In *Liberal Arts for the Christian Life*, edited by Jeffry C. Davis and Philip G. Ryken, 31–43. Wheaton: Crossway, 2012.

Demarest, Bruce. *The Cross and Salvation: The Doctrine of Salvation*. Foundatons of Evangelical Theology. Wheaton: Crossway, 1997.

Dempster, Stephen G. "Canon and Old Testament Interpretation." In *Hearing The Old Testament: Listening for God's Address*, edited by Craig G. Bartholomew and David J. H. Beldman, 154–79. Grand Rapids: Eerdmans, 2012.

———. *Dominion and Dynasty: A Biblical Theology of the Hebrew Bible*. New Studies in Biblical Theology 15. Downers Grove: InterVarsity, 2003.

———. "The Prophets, the Canon and a Canonical Approach: No Empty Word." In *Canon and Biblical Interpretation*, edited by Craig G. Bartholomew, Scott Hahn, Robin Parry, Christopher Seitz, and Al Wolters, Scripture and Hermeneutics Series 7, 293–329. Grand Rapids: Zondervan, 2006.

———. "The Servant of the Lord." In *Central Themes in Biblical Theology: Mapping Unity in Diversity*, edited by Scott J. Hafemann and Paul R. House, 128–78. Grand Rapids: Baker, 2007.

Dennis, John. A. "Cosmology in the Petrine Literature and Jude." In *Cosmology and New Testament Theology*, edited by Jonathan T. Pennington and Sean M. McDonough, Library of New Testament Studies 355, 157–78. London: T&T Clark, 2008.

———. "Glory." In *Dictionary of Jesus and the Gospels*, 2nd ed., edited by Joel B. Green, Jeannine K. Brown, and Nicholas Perrin, 314. Downers Grove: InterVarsity, 2013.

DeRouchie, Jason S. "Counting Stars with Abraham and the Prophets: New Covenant Ecclesiology in OT Perspective." *Journal of the Evangelical Theological Society* 58.3 (2015): 445–85.

———. *How to Understand and Apply the Old Testament: Twelve Steps from Exegesis to Theology.* Phillipsburg: P&R, 2017.

DeRouchie, Jason S., and Jason C. Meyer. "Christ or Family as the 'Seed' of Promise: An Evaluation of N. T. Wright on Galatians 3:16." *Southern Baptist Journal of Theology* 14.3 (2010): 36–48.

Dever, Mark. "The Church." In *A Theology for the Church*, edited by Daniel L. Akin, David P. Nelson, and Peter R. Schemm Jr., 766–856. Nashville: B&H, 2007.

———. *The Gospel and Personal Evangelism.* Wheaton: Crossway, 2007.

Dever, Mark, and Jamie Dunlop. *The Compelling Community: Where God's Power Makes a Church Attractive.* Wheaton: Crossway, 2015.

Dever, Mark, and Greg Gilbert. *Preach: Theology Meets Practice.* Nashville: B&H, 2012.

DeYoung, Kevin, and Greg Gilbert. *What Is the Mission of the Church? Making Sense of Social Justice, Shalom, and the Great Commission.* Wheaton: Crossway, 2011.

Dockery, David S. *Christian Scripture: An Evangelical Perspective on Inspiration, Authority, and Interpretation.* Eugene: Wipf and Stock, 2004.

Doriani, Daniel M. *Putting the Truth to Work: The Theory and Practice of Biblical Application.* Phillipsburg: P&R, 2001.

———. "A Redemptive-Historical Model." In *Four Views on Moving beyond the Bible to Theology*, edited by Gary T. Meadors, 75–149. Grand Rapids: Zondervan, 2009.

Driver, Daniel R. *Brevard Childs, Biblical Theologian: For the Church's One Bible.* Forschungen zum Alten Testament 2.46. Tübingen: Mohr Siebeck, 2010.

Duesing, Jason G. "Gentlemen Shepherds and Invisible Sherpas: The Task of Theological Educators." *Permanent Things* 1.1 (2019): 58–65.

Dumbrell, William J. *Covenant and Creation: An Old Testament Covenantal Theology.* Carlisle: Paternoster, 1984.

———. *The End of the Beginning: Revelation 21-22 and the Old Testament.* Homebush West: Lancer, 1985.

———. "Genesis 2:1-17: A Foreshadowing of the New Creation." In *Biblical Theology: Retrospect and Prospect*, edited by Scott J. Hafemann, 53–65. Downers Grove: InterVarsity, 2002.

———. *The Search for Order: Biblical Eschatology in Focus.* Eugene: Wipf and Stock, 2001.

Duncan III, J. Ligon. "Does God Care How We Worship?" In *Give Praise to God: A Vision for Reforming Worship*, edited by Philip Ryken, Derek Thomas, and J. Ligon Duncan III, 17–50. Phillipsburg: P&R, 2003.

———. "Foundations for Biblically Directed Worship." In *Give Praise to God: A Vision for Reforming Worship*, edited by Philip Ryken, Derek Thomas, and J. Ligon Duncan III, 51–73. Phillipsburg: P&R, 2003.

Durham, John I. *Exodus.* Word Biblical Commentary 3. Waco: Word, 1987.

Ebeling, Gerhard. "The Meaning of 'Biblical Theology'." *Journal of Theological Studies* 6.2 (1955): 210–25.

Ebert, Daniel J. "The Chiastic Structure of the Prologue to Hebrews." *Trinity Journal* 13 (1992): 163–79.

Edwards, Jonathan. "A Dissertation Concerning the End for Which God Created the World." In *The Works of Jonathan Edwards: Volume 8*, edited by Paul Ramsey, 405–536. New Haven: Yale University Press, 1989.

Eichrodt, Walter. *Theology of the Old Testament.* 2 vols. Philadelphia: Westminster, 1961.

Ellingworth, Paul. *The Epistle to the Hebrews: A Commentary on the Greek Text*. New International Greek Testament Commentary. Grand Rapids: Eerdmans, 1993.

———. "Priests." in *New Dictionary of Biblical Theology*, edited by T. Desmond Alexander and Brian S. Rosner, 696–701. Downers Grove: InterVarsity, 2000.

Elliott, Mark W. "Pietism," in *New Dictionary of Theology: Historical and Systematic*, edited by Martin Davie, Tim Grass, Stephen R. Holmes, John McDowell, and T. A. Noble, 676–77. Downers Grove: InterVarsity, 2016.

———. "The Pure and the True Gabler: Questioning a Received Image in the History of Biblical Theology." In *Biblical Theology: Past, Present, and Future*, edited by Mark W. Elliot and Carey Walsh, 3–17. Eugene: Cascade, 2016.

Emerson, Matthew Y. *Christ and the New Creation: A Canonical Approach to the Theology of the New Testament*. Eugene: Wipf and Stock, 2013.

Emerson, Matthew Y., and Christopher W. Morgan. "The Glory of God in 2 Corinthians." *Southern Baptist Journal of Theology* 19.3 (2015): 21–39.

Erickson, Millard J. *Christian Theology*. 3rd ed. Grand Rapids: Baker, 2013.

Estelle, Bryan D. *Salvation through Judgment and Mercy: The Gospel according to Jonah*. Phillipsburg: P&R, 2005.

Evans, Craig A. "Inaugurating the Kingdom of God and Defeating the Kingdom of Satan." *Bulletin for Biblical Research* 15 (2005): 49–75.

Fairbairn, Donald. *Life in the Trinity: An Introduction to Theology with the Help of the Church Fathers*. Downers Grove: InterVarsity, 2009.

Fee, Gordon D. *God's Empowering Presence: The Holy Spirit in the Letters of Paul*. Grand Rapids: Baker, 2009.

Feinberg, John S. *Can You Believe It's True? Christian Apologetics in a Modern and Postmodern Era*. Wheaton: Crossway, 2013.

———, ed. *Continuity and Discontinuity: Perspectives on the Relationship between the Old and New Testaments: Essays in Honor of S. Lewis Johnson, Jr.* Wheaton: Crossway, 1988.

———. *No One Like Him: The Doctrine of God.* Foundations of Evangelical Theology. Wheaton: Crossway, 2001.

Feinberg, John S., and Paul D. Feinberg. *Ethics for a Brave New World.* 2nd ed. Wheaton: Crossway, 2010.

Feinberg, Paul. "The Meaning of Inerrancy." In *Inerrancy,* edited by Norman L. Geisler, 267–304. Grand Rapids: Zondervan, 1980.

Ferguson, Sinclair B. *The Holy Spirit.* Contours of Christian Theology. Downers Grove: InterVarsity, 1996.

Fesko, J. V. *Last Things First: Unlocking Genesis 1-3 with the Christ of Eschatology.* Fearn, Ross-shire: Mentor, 2007.

Frame, John M. *The Doctrine of God.* A Theology of Lordship 2. Phillipsburg: P&R, 2002.

———. *The Doctrine of the Word of God.* A Theology of Lordship 4. Philipsburg: P&R, 2010.

———. *An Introduction to Christian Belief.* Phillipsburg: P&R, 2013.

———. "Presuppositional Apologetics." *Frame-Poythress.org.* May 23, 2012. https://frame-poythress.org/presuppositional-apologetics/.

———. *Systematic Theology: The Doctrine of the Christian Life.* A Theology of Lordship 3. Phillipsburg: P&R, 2008.

France, R. T. *The Gospel of Matthew.* New International Commentary on the New Testament. Grand Rapids: Eerdmans, 2007.

Frei, Hans W. *The Eclipse of Biblical Narrative: A Study in Eighteenth and Nineteenth Century Hermeneutics.* New Haven: Yale University Press, 1974.

Gaffin, Richard B., Jr. "Glory." In *New Dictionary of Biblical Theology,* edited by T. Desmond Alexander and Brian S. Rosner, 507–8. Downers Grove: InterVarsity, 2000.

———. "The Glory of God in Paul's Epistles." In *The Glory of God*, edited by Christopher W. Morgan and Robert A. Peterson, Theology in Community 2, 127–52. Wheaton: Crossway, 2010.

Gage, Warren Austin. *The Gospel of Genesis: Studies in Protology and Eschatology*. Winona Lake: Carpenter, 1984.

Gallagher, Edmon L. and John D. Meade, *The Biblical Canon Lists from Early Christianity and Analysis*. Oxford: Oxford University Press, 2017.

Gathercole, Simon J. *The Preexistent Son: Recovering the Christologies of Matthew, Mark, and Luke*. Grand Rapids: Eerdmans, 2006.

Gentry, Peter J. *How to Read and Understand the Biblical Prophets*. Wheaton: Crossway, 2017.

———. "Kingdom through Covenant: Humanity as the Divine Image." *Southern Baptist Journal of Theology* 12.1 (2008): 16–42.

Gentry, Peter J. and Stephen J. Wellum. *Kingdom through Covenant: A Biblical-Theological Understanding of the Covenants*. Wheaton: Crossway, 2012.

George, Timothy. *Galatians*. New American Commentary 30. Nashville: B&H, 1994.

German, Brian T. *Psalms of the Faithful: Luther's Early Reading of the Psalter in Canonical Context*. Bellingham: Lexham, 2017.

Gerstenberger, Erhard. *Theologies in the Old Testament*. London: T&T Clark, 2001.

Gladd, Benjamin L., and Matthew S. Harmon. *Making All Things New: Inaugurated Eschatology for the Life of the Church*. Grand Rapids: Baker, 2016.

Goheen, Michael W. *A Light to the Nations: The Missional Church and the Biblical Story*. Grand Rapids: Baker, 2011.

Goldsworthy, Graeme. *According to Plan: The Unfolding Revelation of God in the Bible*. Downers Grove: InterVarsity Press, 2002.

———. *The Goldsworthy Trilogy.* Carlisle: Paternoster, 2000.

———. "Ontology and Biblical Theology. A Response to Carl Trueman's Editorial: *A Revolutionary Balancing Act.*" *Themelios* 28.1 (2002): 37–45.

———. *Preaching the Whole Bible as Christian Scripture: The Application of Biblical Theology to Expository Preaching.* Grand Rapids: Eerdmans, 2000.

———. *The Son of God and the New Creation.* Short Studies in Biblical Theology. Wheaton: Crossway, 2015.

Goppelt, Leonhard. *Typos: The Typological Interpretation of the Old Testament in the New.* Translated by Donald H. Madwig. Grand Rapids: Eerdmans, 1982.

Gorman, Frank J. *Leviticus: Divine Presence and Community*, International Theological Commentary. Grand Rapids: Eerdmans, 1997.

Goswell, Greg. "The Johannine Corpus and the Unity of the New Testament Canon." *Journal of the Evangelical Theological Society* 61.4 (2018): 717–33.

———. "The Order of the Books in the Hebrew Bible." *Journal of the Evangelical Theological Society* 51.4 (2008): 673–88.

———. "The Order of the Books of the New Testament." *Journal of the Evangelical Theological Society* 53.2 (2010): 225–41.

———. "The Place of the Book of Acts in Reading the NT," *Journal of the Evangelical Theological Society* 59.1 (2016): 67–82.

Grant, Jamie A. *The King as Exemplar: The Function of Deuteronomy's Kingship Law in the Shaping of the Book of Psalms.* Society of Biblical Literature Academia Biblica 17. Atlanta: Society of Biblical Literature, 2004.

Green, Joel B., Jeannine K. Brown, and Nicholas Perrin, eds. *Dictionary of Jesus and the Gospels.* 2nd ed. Downers Grove: InterVarsity, 2013.

Greidanus, Sidney. *The Modern Preacher and the Ancient Text: Interpreting and Preaching Biblical Literature.* Grand Rapids: Eerdmans, 1988.

———. *Preaching Christ from Psalms: Foundations for Expository Sermons in the Christian Year*. Grand Rapids: Eerdmans, 2016.

Grudem, Wayne A. *The Gift of Prophecy in the New Testament and Today*. Rev. ed. Wheaton: Crossway, 2000.

———. "The Perspicuity of Scripture." *Themelios* 34.3 (2009): 288–308.

———. "Pleasing God by Our Obedience: A Neglected New Testament Teaching." In *For the Fame of God's Name: Essays in Honor of John Piper*, edited by Sam Storms and Justin Taylor, 272–92. Wheaton: Crossway, 2010.

———. *Systematic Theology: An Introduction to Biblical Doctrine*. Downers Grove: InterVarsity, 1994.

Grundmann, Walter. "Χριστὸς," In *Theological Dictionary of the New Testament*, edited by G. Kittel, G. W. Bromiley, and G. Friedrich, 493–580. Grand Rapids: Eerdmans, 1977.

Guthrie, George H. *Hebrews*. NIV Application Commentary. Grand Rapids: Zondervan, 1998.

———. "Hebrews." In *Commentary on the New Testament Use of the Old Testament*, edited by G. K. Beale and D. A. Carson, 919–97. Grand Rapids: Baker, 2007.

Hafemann, Scott J., ed. *Biblical Theology: Retrospect and Prospect*. Downers Grove: InterVarsity, 2002.

———. "The Covenant Relationship." In *Central Themes in Biblical Theology: Mapping Unity in Diversity*, edited by Scott Hafemann and Paul House, 20–65. Grand Rapids: Baker, 2007.

Hafemann, Scott J., and Paul R. House, eds. *Central Themes in Biblical Theology: Mapping Unity in Diversity*. Grand Rapids: Baker, 2007.

Hamilton, James M., Jr. "Biblical Theology and Preaching." In *Text-Driven Preaching: God's Word at the Heart of Every Sermon*, edited by Daniel L. Akin, David Lewis Allen, and Ned Lee Mathews, 193–218. Nashville: B&H, 2010.

———. "The Center of Biblical Theology in Acts: Deliverance and Damnation Display the Divine," *Themelios* 33.3 (2008): 34–47.

———. *Exalting Jesus in Ezra and Nehemiah*, Christ-Centered Exposition Commentary. Nashville: B&H, 2014.

———. *God's Glory in Salvation through Judgment: A Biblical Theology*. Wheaton: Crossway, 2010.

———. *God's Indwelling Presence: The Holy Spirit in the Old and New Testaments*. NAC Studies in Bible and Theology. Nashville: B&H, 2006.

———. "The Messianic Music of the Song of Songs: A Non-Allegorical Interpretation." *Westminster Theological Journal* 68.2 (2006): 331–45.

———. "Old Covenant Believers and the Indwelling Spirit: A Survey of the Spectrum of Opinion." *Trinity Journal* 24.1 (2003): 37–54.

———. *Revelation: The Spirit Speaks to the Churches*. Preaching the Word. Wheaton: Crossway, 2012.

———. "The Seed of the Woman and the Blessing of Abraham." *Tyndale Bulletin* 58.2 (2007): 253–73.

———. "The Skull Crushing Seed of the Woman: Inner-Biblical Interpretation of Genesis 3:15." *Scottish Journal of Theology* 10.2 (2016): 30–54.

———. "Still *Sola Scriptura*: An Evangelical Perspective on Scripture." In *The Sacred Text: Excavating the Texts, Exploring the Interpretations, and Engaging the Theologies of the Christian Scriptures*, edited by Michael F. Bird and Michael W. Pahl, Gorgias Precis Portfolios 7, 215–40. Piscataway: Gorgias, 2010.

———. *What Is Biblical Theology? A Guide to the Bible's Story, Symbolism, and Patterns*. Wheaton: Crossway, 2014.

———. *With the Clouds of Heaven: The Book of Daniel in Biblical Theology*. New Studies in Biblical Theology 32. Downers Grove: InterVarsity, 2014.

Hammett, John S. *40 Questions About Baptism and the Lord's Supper*. Grand Rapids: Kregel, 2015.

———. *Biblical Foundations for Baptist Churches: A Contemporary Ecclesiology*. Grand Rapids: Kregel, 2005.

Hasel, Gerhard. *New Testament Theology: Basic Issues in the Current Debate*. Grand Rapids: Eerdmans, 1978.

Hawthorne, Gerald F. *The Presence and the Power: The Significance of the Spirit in the Life and Ministry of Jesus*. Dallas: Word, 1991.

Hays, Richard B. *Echoes of Scripture in the Gospels*. Waco: Baylor, 2016.

Helmer, Christine. "Introduction: Multivalence in Biblical Theology." In *The Multivalence of Biblical Texts and Theological Meanings*. edited by Christine Helmer, Society of Biblical Literature Symposium Series 37, 1–10. Atlanta: Society of Biblical Literature, 2006.

Hiestand, Gerald L. and Todd Wilson, eds. *Becoming a Pastor Theologian: New Possibilities for Church Leadership*. Downers Grove: InterVarsity, 2015.

———. *The Pastor Theologian: Resurrecting an Ancient Vision*. Grand Rapids: Zondervan, 2015.

Hill, Andrew E. "Worship." In *Evangelical Dictionary of Biblical Theology*, edited by Walter A. Elwell, 837–45. Grand Rapids: Baker, 1996.

Hill, C. E. *Who Chose the Gospels? Probing the Great Gospel Conspiracy*. Oxford: Oxford University Press, 2010.

Hoekema, Anthony A. *Created in God's Image*. Grand Rapids: Eerdmans, 1986.

Holmes, Christopher J. H. *The Lord Is Good: Seeking the God of the Psalter*. Downers Grove: InterVarsity, 2018.

Horton, Michael. *The Christian Faith: A Systematic Theology for Pilgrims on the Way*. Grand Rapids: Zondervan, 2011.

———. *God of Promise: Introducing Covenant Theology*. Grand Rapids: Baker, 2006.

———. *The Gospel Commission: Recovering God's Strategy for Making Disciples*. Grand Rapids: Baker, 2012.

———. *Justification*. 2 vols. New Studies in Dogmatics. Grand Rapids: Zondervan, 2018.

———. *Lord and Servant: A Covenant Christology*. Louisville: Westminster John Knox, 2005.

———. *Rediscovering the Holy Spirit: God's Perfecting Presence in Creation, Redemption, and Everyday Life*. Grand Rapids: Zondervan, 2017.

Hoskins, Paul M. *Jesus as the Fulfillment of the Temple in the Gospel of John*. Milton Keynes: Paternoster, 2006.

———. *That Scripture Might Be Fulfilled: Typology and the Death of Christ*. Longwood: Xulon Press, 2009.

House, Paul R. *1, 2 Kings*. New American Commentary 8. Nashville: B&H, 1996.

———. "Biblical Theology and the Wholeness of Scripture: Steps toward a Program for the Future." In *Biblical Theology: Retrospect and Prospect*, edited by Scott J. Hafemann, 267–79. Downers Grove: InterVarsity, 2002.

———. *Bonhoeffer's Seminary Vision: A Case for Costly Discipleship and Life Together*. Wheaton: Crossway, 2015.

———. "The Day of the Lord." In *Central Themes in Biblical Theology*, edited by Scott J. Hafemann and Paul R. House, 179–224. Grand Rapids: Baker, 2007.

———. *Old Testament Theology*. Downers Grove: InterVarsity Press, 1998.

Howard, David M., Jr. *Joshua*. New American Commentary 5. Nashville: B&H, 1998.

Hunter, Trent, and Stephen J. Wellum. *Christ from Beginning to End: How the Full Story of Scripture Reveals the Full Glory of Christ*. Grand Rapids: Zondervan, 2018.

Jeffery, Steve, Michael Ovey, and Andrew Sach. *Pierced for Our Transgressions: Rediscovering the Glory of Penal Substitution*. Wheaton: Crossway, 2007.

Jensen, Peter F. "God and the Bible." In *The Enduring Authority of the Christian Scriptures*, edited by D. A. Carson, 477–96. Grand Rapids: Eerdmans, 2016.

Jobes, Karen H. *1 Peter*. Baker Exegetical Commentary on the New Testament. Grand Rapids: Baker, 2005.

Johnson, Dennis E. *Him We Proclaim: Preaching Christ from All the Scriptures*. Phillipsburg, NJ, 2007.

Jones, David W. *An Introduction to Biblical Ethics*. B&H Studies in Biblical Ethics. Nashville: B&H, 2013.

Jones, Mark. *God Is: A Devotional Guide to the Attributes of God*. Wheaton: Crossway, 2017.

Kaiser, Walter C., Jr. "The Blessing of David: The Charter for Humanity." In *The Law and the Prophets: Oswald T. Allis Festschrift*, edited by John H. Skilton, 298–318. Philadelphia: P&R, 1974.

———. "Israel's Missionary Call." In *Perspectives on the World Christian Movement: A Reader*, 4th ed., edited by Ralph D. Winter and Steven C. Hawthorne, 25–34. Pasadena: William Carey Library, 2013.

———. *Mission in the Old Testament: Israel as a Light to the Nations*. 2nd ed. Grand Rapids: Baker, 2012.

———. "A Neglected Text in Bibliology Discussions: 1 Corinthians 2:6-16." *Westminster Theological Journal* 43.2 (1981): 301–19.

Kant, Immanuel. "What Is Enlightenment?" In *The Enlightenment: A Sourcebook and Reader*, edited by Paul Hyland, 54. London: Routledge, 2003.

Keathley, Kenneth D. and Mark F. Rooker. *40 Questions About Creation and Evolution*. Grand Rapids: Kregel, 2014.

Keller, Timothy. *The Songs of Jesus: A Year of Daily Devotions in the Psalms.* New York: Viking, 2015.

Kidner, Derek. *Psalms 73-150*, Tyndale Old Testament Commentaries. Downers Grove: InterVarsity, 1973.

Kilner, John F. *Dignity and Destiny: Humanity in the Image of God.* Grand Rapids: Eerdmans, 2015.

Kimble, Jeremy M. *40 Questions About Church Membership and Discipline.* Grand Rapids: Kregel, 2017.

———. "The Steward of God: Exploring the Function and Role of Elders." *Southeastern Theological Review* 6.1 (2015): 83–112.

———. *That His Spirit May Be Saved: Church Discipline as a Means to Repentance and Perseverance.* Eugene: Wipf and Stock, 2013.

Kline, Meredith G. *Kingdom Prologue: Genesis Foundations for a Covenantal Worldview.* Overland Park: Two Age, 2000.

Klink, Edward W. and Darian R. Lockett. *Understanding Biblical Theology: A Comparison of Theory and Practice.* Grand Rapids: Zondervan, 2012.

Knuteson, Roy E. *Calling the Church to Discipline: A Scriptural Guide for the Church That Dares to Discipline.* Nashville: Action, 1977.

Kolb, Robert. *Luther and the Stories of God: Biblical Narratives as a Foundation for Christian Living.* Grand Rapids: Baker, 2012.

Koorevaar, Hendrik J. "The Torah Model as Original Macrostructure of the Hebrew Canon: A Critical Evaluation." *Zeitschrift für die Alttestamentliche Wissenschaft* 122.1 (2010): 65–80.

Köstenberger, Andreas J. *Excellence: The Character of God and the Pursuit of Scholarly Virtue.* Wheaton: Crossway, 2011.

———. "The Glory of God in John's Gospel and Revelation." In *The Glory of God*, edited by Christopher W. Morgan and Robert A. Peterson, Theology in Community 2, 107–26. Wheaton: Crossway, 2010.

———. "Mission." In *New Dictionary of Biblical Theology*, edited by T. Desmond Alexander and Brian S. Rosner, 663–68.Downers Grove: InterVarsity, 2000.

———. *A Theology of John's Gospel and Letters*. Biblical Theology of the New Testament. Grand Rapids: Zondervan, 2009.

Köstenberger, Andreas J., and Peter Thomas O'Brien. *Salvation to the Ends of the Earth: A Biblical Theology of Mission*. New Studies in Biblical Theology 11. Downers Grove: InterVarsity, 2001.

Köstenberger, Andreas J., and Richard D. Patterson. *Invitation to Biblical Interpretation: Exploring the Hermeneutical Triad of History, Literature, and Theology*. Grand Rapids: Kregel, 2011.

Kruger, Michael J. *Canon Revisited: Establishing the Origins and Authority of the New Testament Books*. Wheaton: Crossway, 2012.

Kuruvilla, Abraham. *A Vision for Preaching: Understanding the Heart of Pastoral Ministry*. Grand Rapids: Baker, 2015.

Ladd, George Eldon. *The Presence of the Future: The Eschatology of Biblical Realism*. Grand Rapids: Eerdmans, 1974.

———. *A Theology of the New Testament*. Grand Rapids: Eerdmans, 1993.

Lane, Daniel C. "The Meaning and Use of the Old Testament Term for 'Covenant': With Some Implications for Dispensational and Covenant Theology." PhD Diss., Trinity International University, 2000.

Lane, William L. *Hebrews 1-8*. Word Biblical Commentary 47A. Grand Rapids: Zondervan, 2015.

Lau, Peter H. W. and Greg Goswell, *Unceasing Kindness: A Biblical Theology of Ruth*. New Studies in Biblical Theology 41. Downers Grove: InterVarsity, 2016.

Lawrence, Michael. *Biblical Theology in the Life of the Church: A Guide for Ministry*. Wheaton: Crossway, 2010.

Leeman, Jonathan. *Don't Fire Your Church Members: The Case for Congregationalism*. Nashville: B&H, 2016.

———. "Soteriological Mission: Focusing in on the Mission of Redemption." In *Four Views on the Church's Mission*, edited by Jason S. Sexton, 17–45. Grand Rapids: Zondervan, 2017.

———. *Word-Centered Church: How Scripture Brings Life and Growth to God's People*. Chicago: Moody, 2017.

Legaspi, Michael C. *The Death of Scripture and the Rise of Biblical Studies*. Oxford Studies in Historical Theology. Oxford: Oxford University Press, 2010.

Letham, Robert. *The Holy Trinity: In Scripture, History, Theology, and Worship*. Phillipsburg: P&R, 2004.

Link, Peter J., Jr., and Matthew Y. Emerson. "Searching for the Second Adam: Typological Connections between Adam, Joseph, Mordecai, and Daniel." *Southern Baptist Journal of Theology* 21.1 (2017): 123–44.

Lints, Richard. *The Fabric of Theology: A Prolegomenon to Evangelical Theology*. Grand Rapids: Eerdmans, 1993.

———. *Identity and Idolatry: The Image of God and Its Inversion*. New Studies in Biblical Theology 36. Downers Grove: InterVarsity, 2015.

Lister, J. Ryan. *The Presence of God: Its Place in the Storyline of Scripture and the Story of Our Lives*. Wheaton: Crossway, 2015.

Lockett, Darian R. *Letters from the Pillar Apostles: The Formation of the Catholic Epistles as a Canonical Collection*. Eugene: Pickwick, 2017.

———. "Limitations of a Purely Salvation-historical Approach to Biblical Theology." *Horizons in Biblical Theology* 39.2 (2017): 211–31.

———."Some Ways of 'Doing' Biblical Theology: Assessments and a Proposal." In *Biblical Theology: Past, Present, and Future*, edited by Mark W. Elliot and Carey Walsh, 91–107. Eugene: Cascade, 2016.

Longenecker, Richard N. *Biblical Exegesis in the Apostolic Period*. Rev. ed. Grand Rapids: Eerdmans, 1999.

Longman III, Tremper. "The Glory of God in the Old Testament." In *The Glory of God*, edited by Christopher W. Morgan and Robert A. Peterson, Theology in Community 2, 47–78. Wheaton: Crossway, 2010.

Lunde, Jonathan. *Following Jesus, the Servant King: A Biblical Theology of Covenantal Discipleship*. Biblical Theology for Life. Grand Rapids: Zondervan, 2010.

Luther, Martin. "How Christians Should Regard Moses." In *Luther's Works*, Vol. 35, edited by E. Theodore Bachmann, 155–74. Philadelphia: Fortress, 1960.

———. "Treatise on the Last Words of David: 2 Samuel 23:1-7." In *Luther's Works*, Vol. 15, translated by Martin H. Bertram, 265–352. St Louis: Concordia, 1972.

Lyotard, Jean-Francois. *The Postmodern Condition: A Report on Knowledge*. Minneapolis: University of Minnesota Press, 1984.

MacArthur, John. *The Battle for the Beginning: Creation, Evolution, and the Bible*. Nashville: Thomas Nelson, 2012.

MacArthur, John, and Richard Mayhue, eds. *Biblical Doctrine: A Systematic Summary of Bible Truth*. Wheaton: Crossway, 2017.

MacDonald, Nathan. "Israel and the Old Testament Story in Irenaeus's Presentation of the Rule of Faith." *Journal of Theological Interpretation* 3.2 (2009): 281–98.

Maier, Gerhard. *Biblical Hermeneutics*. Translated by Robert Yarbrough. Wheaton: Crossway, 1994.

Malone, Andrew S. *God's Mediators: A Biblical Theology of Priesthood*. New Studies in Biblical Theology 43. Downers Grove: InterVarsity, 2017.

Marsden, George M. *The Outrageous Idea of Christian Scholarship*. Oxford: Oxford University Press, 1997.

———. *The Soul of the American University: From Protestant Establishment to Established Nonbelief*. Oxford: Oxford University Press, 1994.

Marsh, William M. *Martin Luther on Reading the Bible as Christian Scripture: The Messiah in Luther's Biblical Hermeneutic and Theology*. Princeton Theological Monograph Series. Eugene: Pickwick, 2017.

Marshall, I. Howard. *Acts: An Introduction and Commentary*. Tyndale New Testament Commentary 5. Downers Grove: InterVarsity, 2008.

———. "Acts." In *Commentary on the New Testament Use of the Old Testament*, edited by G. K. Beale and D. A. Carson, 513–606. Grand Rapids: Baker, 2007.

———. "Jesus Christ." In *New Dictionary of Biblical Theology*, edited by T. Desmond Alexander and Brian S. Rosner, 592–602. Downers Grove: InterVarsity, 2000.

Martens, Elmer A. "Tackling Old Testament Theology." *Journal of the Evangelical Theological Society* 20.2 (1997):123–32.

Mathews, Kenneth A. *Genesis 11:27-50:26*. New American Commentary 1B. Nashville: B&H, 2005.

Mathis, David. *Habits of Grace: Enjoying Jesus through the Spiritual Disciplines*. Wheaton: Crossway, 2016.

Mays, James Luther. "The God Who Reigns: The Book of Psalms." In *The Forgotten God: Perspectives in Biblical Theology: Essays in Honor of Paul J. Achtemeier on the Occasion of his Seventy-Fifth Birthday*, edited by A. Andrew Das and Frank J. Matera, 29–38. Louisville: Westminster John Knox, 2002.

McCartney, Dan G. "'Ecce Homo': The Coming of the Kingdom as the Restoration of Human Viceregency." *Westminster Theological Journal* 56.1 (1994): 1–21.

McComiskey, Douglas S. "Exile and the Purpose of Jesus' Parables (Mark 4:10-12; Matt 13:10-17; Luke 8:9-10)." *Journal of the Evangelical Theological Society* 51.1 (2008): 59–85.

McConville, J. G. "Ezra-Nehemiah and the Fulfillment of Prophecy." *Vetus Testamentum* 36 (1986): 205–24.

McGuckin, Terence. "Saint Thomas Aquinas and Theological Exegesis of Sacred Scripture." *New Blackfriars* 74.870 (1993): 197–213.

McInerny, Ralph, ed. and trans. *Thomas Aquinas: Selected Writings*. London: Penguin Books, 1998.

McKelvey, R. J. *The New Temple: The Church in the New Testament*. Oxford: Oxford University Press, 1969.

———. "Temple." in *New Dictionary of Biblical Theology*, edited by T. D. Alexander and Brian S. Rosner, 806–11. Downers Grove: InterVarsity, 2000.

McKinion, Steven A., ed. *Life and Practice in the Early Church: A Documentary Reader*. New York: New York University Press, 2001.

McNeal, Reggie. *Missional Renaissance: Changing the Scorecard for the Church*. San Francisco: Jossey-Bass, 2009.

Mead, James K. *Biblical Theology: Issues, Methods, and Themes*. Louisville: Westminster John Knox, 2007.

Meadors, Gary T, ed. *Four Views on Moving Beyond the Bible to Theology*. Grand Rapids: Zondervan, 2009.

Merkle, Benjamin L. *The Elder and Overseer: One Office in the Early Church*. Studies in Biblical Literature 57. New York: Peter Lang, 2003.

———. "The Meaning of Ekklēsia in Matthew 16:18 and 18:17." *Bibliotheca Sacra* 167.667 (2010): 281–91.

Merrill, Eugene H. *Everlasting Dominion: A Theology of the Old Testament*. Nashville: B&H, 2006.

Meyer, Jason C. *Preaching: A Biblical Theology*. Wheaton: Crossway, 2013.

Metzger, Bruce. *The Canon of the New Testament: Its Origin, Development, and Significance.* Oxford: Clarendon, 1987.

Millar, J. Gary. *Calling on the Name of the Lord: A Biblical Theology of Prayer.* New Studies in Biblical Theology 38. Downers Grove: InterVarsity, 2016.

———. *Now Choose Life: Theology and Ethics in Deuteronomy.* New Studies in Biblical Theology 6. Downers Grove: InterVarsity, 1999.

Miller, Chris A. "Judges." In *What the Old Testament Authors Really Cared About: A Survey of Jesus' Bible,* edited by Jason S. DeRouchie, 186–99. Grand Rapids: Kregel, 2013.

Miller, Stephen R. *Daniel.* New American Commentary 18. Nashville: B&H, 1994.

Mohler, R. Albert. "When the Bible Speaks, God Speaks: The Classical Doctrine of Biblical Inerrancy." In *Five Views on Biblical Inerrancy,* edited by J. Merrick and Stephen M. Garrett, 29–58. Grand Rapids: Zondervan, 2013.

Moo, Douglas J. *The Epistle to the Romans.* New International Commentary on the New Testament. Grand Rapids: Eerdmans, 1996.

———. "The Law of Christ as the Fulfillment of the Law of Moses." In *The Law, the Gospel, and the Modern Christian: Five Views,* edited by Wayne G. Strickland, 319–76. Grand Rapids: Zondervan, 1993.

———. *The Letters to the Colossians and to Philemon.* Pillar New Testament Commentary. Grand Rapids: Eerdmans 2008.

Moore, Russell. *The Kingdom of Christ: The New Evangelical Perspective.* Wheaton: Crossway, 2004.

Moore, T. S. "'To the End of the Earth': The Geographical and Ethnic Universalism of Acts 1:8 in Light of Isaianic Influence on Luke." *Journal of the Evangelical Theological Society* 40.3 (1997): 389–99.

Montague, George T. *The Holy Spirit: The Growth of a Biblical Tradition.* Eugene: Wipf and Stock, 2006.

Morales, L. Michael. *Who Shall Ascend the Mountain of the Lord? A Biblical Theology of the Book of Leviticus*. Downers Grove: InerVarsity, 2015.

Moreland, J. P., Stephen C. Meyer, Christopher Shaw, Ann Gauger, and Wayne Grudem, eds. *Theistic Evolution: A Scientific, Philosophical, and Theological Critique*. Grand Rapids: Zondervan, 2017.

Morgan, Christopher W. "Toward a Theology of the Glory of God." In *The Glory of God*, edited by Christopher W. Morgan and Robert A. Peterson, Theology in Community 2, 153–88. Wheaton: Crossway, 2010.

Morgan, Christopher W., and Robert A. Peterson, eds. *The Glory of God*. Theology in Community 2. Wheaton: Crossway, 2010.

———, eds. *Hell under Fire: Modern Scholarship Reinvents Eternal Punishment*. Grand Rapids: Zondervan, 2004.

———, eds. *The Kingdom of God*. Theology in Community 4. Wheaton: Crossway, 2012.

Morris, Leon. *The Gospel according to John*. New International Commentary on the New Testament. Grand Rapids: Eerdmans, 1995.

Motyer, J. Alec. *Isaiah: An Introduction and Commentary*. Tyndale Old Testament Commentaries. Downers Grove: InterVarsity, 1999.

———. "Judgment." in *New Dictionary of Biblical Theology*, edited by T. Desmond Alexander and Brian S. Rosner, 612–15. Downers Grove: InterVarsity, 2000.

Mueller, George. *A Narrative of Some of the Lord's Dealing with George Müller, Written by Himself, Jehovah Magnified. Addresses by George Müller Complete and Unabridged*. 2 vols. Muskegon: Dust and Ashes, 2003.

Muller, Richard A. *Dictionary of Latin and Greek Theological Terms: Drawn Principally from Protestant Scholastic Theology*. Grand Rapids: Baker, 1986.

Naselli, Andrew David. *How to Understand and Apply the New Testament: Twelve Steps from Exegesis to Theology*. Phillipsburg: P&R, 2017.

———. "Three Reflections on Evangelical Academic Publishing." *Themelios* 39.3 (2014): 428–54.

Naudé, J. A. "*Qadosh*." In *New International Dictionary of Old Testament Theology and Exegesis*, edited by Willem VanGemeren, 5 vols., 3:877–87. Grand Rapids: Zondervan, 2012.

Newton, Phil A. *Elders in Congregational Life: Rediscovering the Biblical Model for Church Leadership*. Grand Rapids: Kregel, 2005.

Nichols, Stephen. "The Kingdom of God: The Kingdom in Historical and Contemporary Perspectives." In *The Kingdom of God*, edited by Christopher W. Morgan and Robert A. Peterson, Theology in Community 4, 25–48. Wheaton: Crossway, 2012.

Nienhuis, David R. and Robert W. Wall. *Reading the Epistles of James, Peter, John, and Jude as Scripture: The Shaping and Shape of a Canonical Collection*. Grand Rapids: Eerdmans, 2013.

O'Brien, Peter T. *The Letter to the Ephesians*. Pillar New Testament Commentary. Grand Rapids: Eerdmans, 1999.

———. *The Letter to the Hebrews*. Pillar New Testament Commentary. Grand Rapids: Eerdmans, 2010.

Osborne, Grant R. *Revelation*. Baker Exegetical Commentary on the New Testament. Grand Rapids: Baker, 2002.

Oswalt, John. "The Book of Isaiah: A Short Course in Biblical Theology." *Calvin Theological Journal* 39.1 (2004): 54–77.

———. *The Book of Isaiah. Chapters 40-66*. New International Commentary on the Old Testament. Grand Rapids: Eerdmans, 1998.

Packer, J. I. "Infallible Scripture and the Role of Hermeneutics." In *Scripture and Truth*, edited by D. A. Carson and John D. Woodbridge, 321–56. Grand Rapids: Baker, 1992.

———. *Keep in Step with the Spirit: Finding Fullness in Our Walk with God*. Rev. ed. Grand Rapids: Baker, 2005.

Pao, David W. *Acts and the Isaianic New Exodus*. Grand Rapids: Baker, 2002.

Pao, David W. and Eckhard J. Schnabel. "Luke." In *Commentary on the New Testament Use of the Old Testament*, edited by G. K. Beale and D. A. Carson, 251–414. Grand Rapids: Baker, 2007.

Parnell, Jonathan. "The Heart of Discipleship." *Desiring God* (blog). May 25, 2012, http://www.desiringgod.org/articles/the-heart-of-discipleship/.

Penney, John Michael. *The Missionary Emphasis of Lukan Pneumatology*. Sheffield: Sheffield Academic, 1997.

Pennington, Jonathan T. *Heaven and Earth in the Gospel of Matthew*. Supplements to Novum Testamentum 126. Leiden: Brill, 2007.

———. "The Kingdom of Heaven in the Gospel of Matthew." *Southern Baptist Journal of Theology* 12.1 (2008): 44–51.

———. *Reading the Gospels Wisely: A Narrative and Theological Introduction*. Grand Rapids: Baker, 2012.

Peterson, David G. *Engaging with God: A Biblical Theology of Worship*. Downers Grove: InterVarsity, 2002.

———. *Transformed by God: New Covenant Life and Ministry*. Downers Grove: InterVarsity, 2012.

———, ed. *Where Wrath and Mercy Meet: Proclaiming the Atonement Today*. Carlisle: Paternoster, 2001.

———. "Worship." In *New Dictionary of Biblical Theology*, edited by T. Desmond Alexander and Brian S. Rosner, 856–57. Downers Grove: InterVarsity, 2000.

Petrotta, A. J. "Temple." In *Evangelical Dictionary of Biblical Theology*, edited by Walter A. Elwell, 759–61. Grand Rapids: Baker, 1996.

Philpot, Joshua. "See the True and Better Adam: Typology and Human Origins." *Bulletin of Ecclesial Theology* 5.2 (2018): 79–103.

Piper, John. *Expository Exultation: Christian Preaching as Worship*. Wheaton: Crossway, 2018.

———. *Let the Nations Be Glad! The Supremacy of God in Missions*. 3rd ed. Grand Rapids: Baker, 2010.

———. *The Pleasures of God: Meditations on God's Delight in Being God*. Rev. ed. Sisters: Multnomah, 2000.

Plummer, Robert L. *40 Questions About Interpreting the Bible*. Grand Rapids: Kregel, 2010.

Polhill, John B. *Acts*. New American Commentary 26. Nashville: Broadman, 1992.

Porter, Stanley E. and Andrew W. Pitts. *Fundamentals of New Testament Textual Criticism*. Grand Rapids: Eerdmans, 2015.

Postell, Seth D. "The Old Testament in the Old Testament." In *The Moody Handbook of Messianic Prophecy: Studies and Expositions of the Messiah in the Old Testament*, edited by Michael Rydelnik and Edwin Blum, 103–117. Chicago: Moody Publishers, 2019.

———. "Typology in the Old Testament." In *The Moody Handbook of Messianic Prophecy: Studies and Expositions of the Messiah in the Old Testament*, edited by Michael Rydelnik and Edwin Blum, 161–75. Chicago: Moody Publishers, 2019.

Reeves, Michael. *Delighting in the Trinity: An Introduction to the Christian Faith*. Downers Grove: InterVarsity, 2012.

Reynolds, Benjamin E., Brian Lugioyo, and Kevin J. Vanhoozer, eds. *Reconsidering the Relationship between Biblical and Systematic Theology in the New Testament: Essays by Theologians and New Testament Scholars*. Wissenschaftliche Untersuchungen zum Neuen Testament 2.369. Tübingen: Mohr Siebeck, 2014.

Roark, Nick and Robert Cline. *Biblical Theology: How the Church Faithfully Teaches the Gospel*. Wheaton: Crossway, 2018.

Roberts, J. J. M. "The Old Testament's Contribution to Messianic Expectations." In *The Messiah: Developments in Earliest Judaism and Christianity*, edited by James H. Charlesworth, 31–51. Minneapolis: Fortress, 1992.

Roberts, Vaughan. *God's Big Picture: Tracing the Storyline of the Bible*. Downers Grove: InterVarsity, 2002.

Rogers, Jack B. and Donald K. McKim. *The Authority and Interpretation of the Bible: An Historical Approach*. San Francisco: Harper & Row, 1979.

Robertson, O. Palmer. *The Christ of the Covenants*. Phillipsburg: P&R, 1987.

Rooker, Mark F. *40 Questions About Creation and Evolution*. Grand Rapids: Kregel, 2014.

———. *Leviticus*. New American Commentary 3A. Nashville: B&H, 2000.

Rosner, Brian S. "Biblical Theology." In *New Dictionary of Biblical Theology*, edited by T. Desmond Alexander and Brian S. Rosner, 3–11. Downers Grove: InterVarsity, 2000.

———. *Paul and the Law: Keeping the Commandments of God*. Downers Grove: InterVarsity, 2013.

———. "The Progress of the Word." In *Witness to the Gospel: The Theology of Acts*, edited by I. Howard Marshall and David Peterson, 215–33. Grand Rapids: Eerdmans, 1998.

Ross, Allen P. *A Commentary on the Psalms: 90-150*. Kregel Exegetical Library. Grand Rapids: Kregel, 2016.

———. *Recalling the Hope of Glory: Biblical Worship from the Garden to the New Creation*. Grand Rapids: Kregel, 2006.

Rowe, C. Kavin. "For Future Generations: Worshipping Jesus and the Integration of the Theological Disciplines." *Pro Ecclesia* 17.2 (2008): 186–209.

Routledge, Robin. "Is There a Narrative Substructure Underlying the Book of Isaiah?" *Tyndale Bulletin* 55.2 (2004): 183–204

Rydelnik, Michael. *The Messianic Hope: Is the Hebrew Bible Really Messianic?* Nashville: B&H, 2010.

Sailhamer, John. "Cosmic Maps, Prophecy Charts, and the Hollywood Movie: A Biblical Realist Looks at the Eclipse of Old Testament Narrative." *Criswell Theological Review* 7.2 (1994): 65–81.

———. "The Canonical Approach to the OT: Its Effect on Understanding Prophecy." *Journal of the Evangelical Theological Society* 30.3 (1987): 307–15.

———. *First and Second Chronicles*. Chicago: Moody, 1983.

———. "Genesis." In *The Expositor's Bible Commentary*, Vol. 2. Grand Rapids: Zondervan, 1990.

———. *Introduction to Old Testament Theology: A Canonical Approach*. Grand Rapids: Zondervan, 1995.

———. "Johann August Ernesti: The Role of History in Biblical Interpretation." *Journal of the Evangelical Theological Society* 44.2 (2001): 193–206.

———. *The Meaning of the Pentateuch: Revelation, Composition and Interpretation*. Downers Grove: InterVarsity, 2009.

———. "The Messiah and the Hebrew Bible." *Journal of the Evangelical Theological Society* 44.1 (2001): 5–23.

———. *The Pentateuch as Narrative: A Biblical-Theological Commentary*. Library of Biblical Interpretation. Grand Rapids: Zondervan, 1992.

Salier, Bill. "The Temple in the Gospel According to John." In *Heaven on Earth: The Temple in Biblical Theology*, edited by T. Desmond Alexander and Simon Gathercole, 121–34. Waynesboro: Paternoster, 2004.

Samra, James G. *Being Conformed to Christ in Community: A Study of Maturity, Maturation and the Local Church in the Undisputed Pauline Epistles*. Library of New Testament Studies 320. London: T&T Clark, 2006.

Sanders, Fred. *The Deep Things of God: How the Trinity Changes Everything*. Wheaton: Crossway, 2010.

———. *The Triune God*. New Studies in Dogmatics. Grand Rapids: Zondervan, 2016.

Sandys-Wunsch, John and Laurence Eldredge. "J. P. Gabler and the Distinction between Biblical and Dogmatic Theology: Translation, Commentary, and Discussion of His Originality." *Scottish Journal of Theology* 33 (1980): 133–58.

Saucy, Robert L. *The Case for Progressive Dispensationalism: The Interface between Dispensational and Non-Dispensational Theology*. Grand Rapids: Zondervan, 1993.

Schnabel, Eckhard J. *Early Christian Mission*. 2 vols. Downers Grove: InterVarsity, 2004.

Schreiner, Patrick. *The Kingdom of God and the Glory of the Cross*. Short Studies in Biblical Theology. Wheaton: Crossway, 2018.

Schreiner, Thomas R. *1, 2 Peter, Jude*. New American Commentary 37. Nashville: B&H, 2003.

———. *Covenant and God's Purpose for the World*. Short Studies in Biblical Theology. Wheaton: Crossway, 2017.

———. *Galatians*. Zondervan Exegetical Commentary on the New Testament. Grand Rapids: Zondervan, 2010.

———. *The King in His Beauty: A Biblical Theology of the Old and New Testaments*. Grand Rapids: Baker, 2013.

———. *New Testament Theology: Magnifying God in Christ*. Grand Rapids: Baker, 2008.

———. *Paul, Apostle of God's Glory in Christ: A Pauline Theology*. 2nd ed. Downers Grove: InterVarsity, 2020.

———. *Romans*. Baker Exegetical Commentary on the New Testament. Grand Rapids: Baker, 1998.

———. *Spiritual Gifts: What They Are and Why They Matter*. Nashville: B&H, 2018.

Schreiner, Thomas R., and Matthew R. Crawford, eds. *The Lord's Supper: Remembering and Proclaiming Christ Until He Comes*. Nashville: B&H, 2010.

Schreiner, Thomas R., and Shawn D. Wright, eds. *Believer's Baptism: Sign of the New Covenant in Christ*. Nashville: B&H, 2006.

Scobie, Charles H. H. "Israel and the Nations: An Essay in Biblical Theology." *Tyndale Bulletin* 43.2 (1992): 283–305.

———. *The Ways of Our God: An Approach to Biblical Theology*. Grand Rapids: Eerdmans, 2003.

Scott, J. M. "Luke's Geographical Horizon." In *The Book of Acts in Its First-Century Setting: Volume 2. Graeco-Roman Setting*, edited by D. W. J. Gill and C. Gempf, 483–544. Grand Rapids: Eerdmans, 1994.

Searle, John R. *Speech Acts: An Essay in the Philosophy of Language*. Cambridge: Cambridge University Press, 1969.

Seitz, Christopher R. "The Canonical Approach and Theological Interpretation." In *Canon and Biblical Interpretation*, edited by Craig G. Bartholomew, Scott Hahn, Robin Parry, Christopher Seitz, and Al Wolters, Scripture and Hermeneutics Series 7, 58–110. Grand Rapids: Zondervan, 2006.

———. *The Character of Christian Scripture: The Significance of a Two-Testament Bible*. Grand Rapids: Baker, 2011.

———. *The Elder Testament: Canon, Theology, Trinity*. Waco: Baylor University Press, 2018.

———. *Figured Out: Typology and Providence in Christian Scripture*. Louisville: Westminster John Knox, 2001.

———. *The Goodly Fellowship of the Prophets: The Achievement of Association in Canon Formation*. Grand Rapids: Baker, 2009.

———. *Prophecy and Hermeneutics*. Grand Rapids: Baker, 2007.

Sexton, Jason S., ed. *Four Views on the Church's Mission*. Grand Rapids: Zondervan, 2017.

Shepherd, Michael B. *A Commentary on the Book of the Twelve: The Minor Prophets*. Kregel Exegetical Library. Grand Rapids: Kregel, 2018.

———. *Daniel in the Context of the Hebrew Bible*. Studies in Biblical Literature 123. New York: Peter Lang, 2009.

———. *Text in the Middle*. Studies in Biblical Literature 162. New York: Peter Lang, 2014.

———. *Textuality and the Bible*. Eugene: Wipf and Stock, 2016.

———. *The Textual World of the Bible*. Studies in Biblical Literature 156. New York: Peter Lang, 2013.

Sheppard, Gerald T. "Canon Criticism: The Proposal of Brevard Childs and an Assessment for Evangelical Hermeneutics." *Studia Biblica et Theologica* 4 (1974): 3–17.

Silva, Moisés. *Biblical Words and Their Meaning: An Introduction to Lexical Semantics*. Grand Rapids: Zondervan, 1994.

Smith, Gary V. *Isaiah 40-66*. New American Commentary 15B. Nashville: B&H, 2009.

Spellman, Ched. "The Canon after Google: Implications of a Digitized and Destabilized Codex." In *Princeton Theological Review* 16.2 (Fall 2010): 39-42.

———. "The Drama of Discipline: Toward an Intertextual Profile of *Paideia* in Hebrews 12." *Journal of the Evangelical Theological Society* 59.3 (2016): 487–506.

———. "The Scribe Who Has Become a Disciple: Identifying and Becoming the Ideal Reader of the Biblical Canon." *Themelios* 41.1 (2016): 37–51.

———. "Nehemiah's New Shadow: Reading and Rereading the Ezra-Nehemiah Narrative." *Southeastern Theological Review* 9.1 (2018): 3–22.

———. *Toward a Canon-Conscious Reading of the Bible: Exploring the History and Hermeneutics of the Biblical Canon*. Sheffield: Sheffield Phoenix, 2014.

Spieckermann, Hermann. "God's Steadfast Love: Towards a New Conception of Old Testament Theology." *Biblica* 81 (2000): 305–27.

Spurgeon, Charles. "Christ Precious to Believers." The Spurgeon Archive, Midwestern Baptist Theological Seminary, http://archive.spurgeon.org/sermons/0242.php.

Stein, Robert H. *Luke*. New American Commentary 24. Nashville: Broadman, 1992.

Steinberg, Julius, and Timothy J. Stone with Rachel Stone, eds. *The Shape of the Writings*. Siphrut 16. Winona Lake: Eisenbrauns, 2015.

Sternberg, Meir. *The Poetics of Biblical Narrative: Ideological Literature and the Drama of Reading*. Bloomington: Indiana University Press, 1985.

Stone, Timothy J. *The Compilational History of the Megilloth: Canon, Contoured Intertextuality and Meaning in the Writings*. Forschungen zum Alten Testament 2.59. Tübingen: Mohr Siebeck, 2013.

Storms, Sam. *Practicing the Power: Welcoming the Gifts of the Holy Spirit in Your Life*. Grand Rapids: Zondervan, 2017.

Storms, Sam, and Justin Taylor, eds. *For the Fame of God's Name: Essays in Honor of John Piper*. Wheaton: Crossway, 2010.

Stott, John R. W. *The Cross of Christ*. 20th anniversary ed. Downers Grove: InterVarsity, 2006.

Strauch, Alexander. *Biblical Eldership: An Urgent Call to Restore Biblical Church Leadership*. Rev. ed. Littleton: Lewis and Roth, 1995.

Strauss, Mark L. *Four Portraits, One Jesus: An Introduction to Jesus and the Gospels*. Grand Rapids: Zondervan, 2007.

Stuart, Douglas. *Exodus*. New American Commentary 2. Nashville, B&H, 2006.

Stump, J. B. ed. *Four Views on Creation, Evolution, and Intelligent Design*. Grand Rapids: Zondervan, 2017.

Swain, Scott R. *Trinity, Revelation, and Reading: A Theological Introduction to the Bible and Its Interpretation*. London: T&T Clark, 2011.

Tabb, Brian J. *All Things New: Revelation as Canonical Capstone*. Downers Grove: InterVarsity, 2019.

Temple, William. *Nature, Man and God. London: Macmillan, 1934.*

Tennent, Timothy. *Invitation to World Missions: A Trinitarian Missiology for the Twenty-First Century.* Grand Rapids: Kregel, 2010.

Thielman, Frank S. "Atonement." In *Central Themes in Biblical Theology: Mapping Unity in Diversity*, edited by Scott J. Hafemann and Paul R. House, 102–27. Grand Rapids: Baker, 2007.

Thigpen, J. Michael. "Lord of All the Earth: Yahweh and Baal in Joshua 3." *Trinity Journal* 27 (2006): 245–54.

Thompson, Alan J. *The Acts of the Risen Lord Jesus: Luke's Account of God's Unfolding Plan.* Downers Grove: InterVarsity, 2011.

Thompson, Mark D. *A Clear and Present Word: The Clarity of Scripture.* New Studies in Biblical Theology 21. Downers Grove: InterVarsity, 2006.

———. "The Generous Gift of a Gracious Father: Toward a Theological Account of the Clarity of Scripture." In *The Enduring Authority of the Christian Scriptures*, edited by D. A. Carson, 615–43. Grand Rapids: Eerdmans, 2016.

———. *A Sure Ground on Which to Stand: The Relation of Authority and Interpretive Method in Luther's Approach to Scripture.* Carlisle: Paternoster, 2004.

Thompson, John A. *1, 2 Chronicles.* New American Commentary 9. Nashville: B&H, 1994.

Tipton, Lane G. "Christology in Colossians 1:15-20 and Hebrews 1:1-4: An Exercise in Biblico-Systematic Theology." In *Resurrection and Eschatology: Theology in Service of the Church: Essays in Honor of Richard B. Gaffin, Jr.*, edited by Lane G. Tipton and Jeffrey C. Waddington, 177–202. Phillipsburg: P&R, 2008.

Tipton, Lane G., and Jeffrey C. Waddington, eds. *Resurrection and Eschatology: Theology in Service of the Church: Essays in Honor of Richard B. Gaffin, Jr.* Phillipsburg: P&R, 2008.

Todd III, James M. *Sinai and the Saints: Reading Old Covenant Laws for the New Covenant Community.* Downers Grove: InterVarsity, 2017.

Tõniste, Külli. *The Ending of the Canon: A Canonical and Intertextual Reading of Revelation 21-22*. Library of New Testament Studies 526. London: Bloomsbury, 2016.

Tov, Emanuel. *Textual Criticism of the Hebrew Bible*. 3rd ed. Minneapolis: Fortress, 2011.

Treat, Jeremy R. *The Crucified King: Atonement and Kingdom in Biblical and Systematic Theology*. Grand Rapids: Zondervan, 2014.

Treier, Daniel J. *Virtue and the Voice of God: Toward Theology as Wisdom*. Grand Rapids: Eerdmans, 2006.

Trobisch, David. *The First Edition of the New Testament*. Oxford: Oxford University Press, 2000.

———. *Paul's Letter Collection: Tracing the Origins*. Minneapolis: Fortress, 1994.

Trueman, Carl. "Editorial: A Revolutionary Balancing Act." *Themelios* 27.3 (2002): 1–4.

Turner, Max. "Holy Spirit." In *New Dictionary of Biblical Theology*, edited by T. Desmond Alexander and Brian S. Rosner, 551–58. Downers Grove: InterVarsity, 2000.

———. *The Holy Spirit and Spiritual Gifts: In the New Testament Church and Today*. Peabody: Hendrickson, 1997.

VanDrunen, David. *God's Glory Alone: The Majestic Heart of Christian Faith and Life*. Five Solas Series. Grand Rapids: Zondervan, 2015.

VanGemeren, Willem. *The Progress of Redemption: The Story of Salvation from Creation to the New Jerusalem*. Grand Rapids: Baker, 1988.

Van Groningen, Gerard. "Messiah." In *Evangelical Dictionary of Biblical Theology*, edited by Walter A. Elwell, 523–28. Grand Rapids: Baker, 1996.

Vanhoozer, Kevin J. *Biblical Authority after Babel: Retrieving the Solas in the Spirit of Mere Protestant Christianity*. Grand Rapids: Brazos, 2016.

———. *The Drama of Doctrine: A Canonical-Linguistic Approach to Christian Theology*. Louisville: Westminster John Knox Press, 2005.

———. *Faith Speaking Understanding: Performing the Drama of Doctrine.* Louisville: Westminster John Knox, 2014.

———. "Is the Theology of the New Testament One or Many? Between (the Rock of) Systematic Theology and (the Hard Place of) Historical Occasionalism." In *Reconsidering the Relationship between Biblical and Systematic Theology in the New Testament*, edited by Benjamin E. Reynolds, Brian Lugioyo, and Kevin J. Vanhoozer, Wissenschaftliche Untersuchungen zum Neuen Testament 2.369, 17–38. Tübingen: Mohr Siebeck, 2014.

———. *Is There a Meaning in This Text? The Bible, the Reader, and the Morality of Literary Knowledge.* Grand Rapids: Zondervan, 2009.

———. "May We Go Beyond What Is Written After All? The Pattern of Theological Authority and the Problem of Doctrinal Development." In *The Enduring Authority of the Christian Scriptures*, edited by D. A. Carson, 745–92. Grand Rapids: Eerdmans, 2016.

———. *Pictures at a Theological Exhibition: Sources for the Church's Worship, Witness and Wisdom.* Downers Grove: InterVarsity, 2016.

———. "Systematic Theology." In *New Dictionary of Theology: Historical and Systematic*, edited by Martin Davie, Tim Grass, Stephen R. Holmes, John McDowell, and T. A. Noble, 885–86. Downers Grove: InterVarsity, 2016.

Vanhoozer, Kevin J. and Daniel J. Treier. *Theology and the Mirror of Scripture: A Mere Evangelical Account.* Studies in Christian Doctrine and Scripture. Downers Grove: InterVarsity, 2015.

Vanhoozer, Kevin J. and Owen Strachan. *The Pastor as Public Theologian.* Grand Rapids: Baker, 2015.

Vickers, Brian J. *Jesus' Blood and Righteousness: Paul's Theology of Imputation.* Wheaton: Crossway, 2006.

———. "The Lord's Supper: Celebrating the Past and Future in the Present." In *The Lord's Supper: Remembering and Proclaiming Christ Until He Comes*, edited by Thomas R. Schreiner and Matthew R. Crawford, 313–40. Nashville: B&H, 2010.

Vogt, Peter T. *Deuteronomic Theology and the Significance of Torah: A Reappraisal.* Winona Lake: Eisenbrauns, 2006.

Volf, Miroslav. *Captive to the Word of God: Engaging the Scriptures for Contemporary Theological Reflection.* Grand Rapids: Eerdmans, 2010.

Vos, Geerhardus. *Biblical Theology: Old and New Testaments.* Grand Rapids: Eerdmans, 1948.

———. "The Idea of Biblical Theology as a Science and as a Theological Discipline." In *Redemptive History and Biblical Interpretation: The Shorter Writings of Geerhardus Vos,* edited by Richard B. Gaffin Jr., 3–24. Phillipsburg: P&R, 2001.

Wagner, J. Ross. *Heralds of the Good News: Isaiah and Paul in Concert in the Letter to the Romans,* Supplements to Novum Testamentum 101. Leiden: Brill, 2003.

Waldron, Samuel E. "Plural-Elder Congregationalism." In *Who Runs the Church? Four Views on Church Government,* edited by Steven B. Cowan, 185–252. Grand Rapids: Zondervan, 2004.

Waltke, Bruce K. *The Book of Proverbs: Chapters 1-15.* New International Commentary on the Old Testament. Grand Rapids: Eerdmans, 2004.

———. "The Kingdom of God in the Old Testament: Definitions and Story." In *The Kingdom of God,* edited by Christopher W. Morgan and Robert A. Peterson, Theology in Community 4, 49–71. Wheaton: Crossway, 2012.

———. *An Old Testament Theology: An Exegetical, Canonical, and Thematic Approach.* Grand Rapids: Zondervan, 2007.

Walton, John H. "Psalms: A Cantata about the Davidic Covenant." *Journal of the Evangelical Theological Society* 34.1 (1991): 21–31.

Ward, Timothy. *Words of Life: Scripture as the Living and Active Word of God.* Downers Grove: InterVarsity, 2009.

Ware, Bruce A. *God's Greater Glory: The Exalted God of Scripture and the Christian Faith.* Wheaton: Crossway, 2004.

———. "The New Covenant and the People(s) of God." In *Dispensationalism, Israel and the Church: The Search for Definition*, edited by Darrell L. Bock and Craig A. Blaising, 351–72. Grand Rapids: Zondervan, 1992.

Warfield, Benjamin B. "The Divine and Human in the Bible." In *Selected Shorter Writings of Benjamin B. Warfield*, edited by John E. Meeter, 2 vols., 2:542–48. Philipsburg: P&R, 2001.

———. *Revelation and Inspiration*. Grand Rapids: Baker, 2003.

Watson, Francis. *The Fourfold Gospel: A Theological Reading of the New Testament Portraits of Jesus*. Grand Rapids: Eerdmans, 2016.

Watts, Rikki E. *Isaiah's New Exodus in Mark*. Biblical Studies Library. Grand Rapids: Baker, 2000.

———. "Mark." In *Commentary on the New Testament Use of the Old Testament*, edited by G. K. Beale and D. A. Carson, 111–250. Grand Rapids: Baker, 2007.

Webb, Barry G. *Five Festal Garments: Christian Reflections on the Song of Solomon, Ruth, Lamentations, Ecclesiastes, and Esther*. New Studies in Biblical Theology 10. Downers Grove: InterVarsity, 2000.

Webster, John. *The Culture of Theology*. Edited by Ivor J. Davidson and Alden C. McCray. Grand Rapids: Baker, 2019.

———. *The Domain of the Word: Scripture and Theological Reasoning*. London: Bloomsbury, 2012.

———. "What Makes Theology Theological?" *Journal of Analytic Theology* 3 (2015): 17–28.

Weinandy, Thomas G., Daniel A. Keating, and John P. Yocum, eds. *Aquinas on Scripture: An Introduction to His Biblical Commentaries*. London: T&T Clark, 2005.

Welker, Michael. *God the Spirit*. Translated by John F. Hoffmeyer. Minneapolis: Fortress, 1994.

Wells, David F. *The Person of Christ: A Biblical and Historical Analysis of the Incarnation*. Wheaton: Crossway, 1984.

Wellum, Stephen J. "Baptism and the Relationship between the Covenants." In *Believer's Baptism: Sign of the New Covenant in Christ*, edited by Thomas R. Schreiner and Shawn D. Wright, NAC Studies in Bible and Theology, 97–161. Nashville: B&H, 2006.

———. "Beyond Mere Ecclesiology: The Church as God's New Covenant Community." In *The Community of Jesus: A Theology of the Church*, edited by Kendall H. Easley and Christopher W. Morgan, 183–212. Nashville: B&H, 2013.

———. *Christ Alone: The Uniqueness of Jesus as Savior; What the Reformers Taught . . . and Why It Still Matters*. Five Solas Series. Grand Rapids: Zondervan, 2017.

———. "Evangelical Christology and Kenotic Influences: A 'New' and 'Better' Way?" In *Building on the Foundations of Evangelical Theology: Essays in Honor of John S. Feinberg*, edited by Gregg R. Allison and Stephen J. Wellum, 206–34. Wheaton: Crossway, 2015.

———. *God the Son Incarnate: The Doctrine of Christ*. Foundations of Evangelical Theology. Wheaton: Crossway, 2016.

———. "The Importance of the Nature of Divine Sovereignty for Our View of Scripture." *Southern Baptist Journal of Theology* 4.2 (2000): 76–91.

Wenham, Gordon J. *The Book of Leviticus*. New International Commentary on the Old Testament. Grand Rapids: Eerdmans, 1979.

———. *Genesis 1-15*. Word Biblical Commentary 1A. Nashville: Thomas Nelson, 1987.

———. "Sanctuary Symbolism in the Garden of Eden Story." In *"I Studied Inscriptions from before the Flood": Ancient Near Eastern, Literary, and Linguistic Approaches to Genesis 1-11*, edited by Richard S. Hess and David Toshio Tsumara, Sources for Biblical and Theological Study 4, 399–404. Winona Lake: Eisenbrauns, 1994.

———. "Towards a Canonical Reading of the Psalms." In *Canon and Biblical Interpretation*, edited by Craig G. Bartholomew, Scott Hahn, Robin Parry, Christopher Seitz, and Al Wolters, Scripture and Hermeneutics Series 7, 333–51. Grand Rapids: Zondervan, 2006.

Westphal, Merold. *Overcoming Onto-Theology: Toward a Postmodern Christian Faith*. New York: Fordham University Press, 2001.

White, Thomas. "The Universal and Local Church." In *Upon This Rock: A Baptist Understanding of the Church*, edited by Jason G. Duesing, Thomas White, and Malcolm B. Yarnell III, 208–39. Nashville: B&H, 2010.

Wilcox, Max. "The Promise of the 'Seed' in the New Testament and the Targumim." *Journal for the Study of the New Testament* 5 (1979): 2–20.

Williams, Joshua E. "The Message of the Pentateuch." *Southwestern Journal of Theology* 52.1 (2009): 2–16.

Williamson, Paul R. "Covenant." in *New Dictionary of Biblical Theology*, edited by T. Desmond Alexander and Brian S. Rosner, 419–29. Downers Grove: InterVarsity, 2000.

———. *Sealed with an Oath: Covenant in God's Unfolding Purpose*. Downers Grove: InterVarsity, 2007.

Witherington, Ben. *The Acts of the Apostles: A Socio-Rhetorical Commentary*. Grand Rapids: Eerdmans, 1998.

Wolters, Albert. "Metanarrative." In *Dictionary for Theological Interpretation of the Bible*, edited by Kevin J. Vanhoozer, 506–7. Grand Rapids: Baker, 2005.

Wong, Gregory T. K. *Compositional Strategy of the Book of Judges: An Inductive, Rhetorical Study*. Supplements to Vetus Testamentum 111. Leiden: Brill, 2006.

Woodbridge, John D. *Biblical Authority: A Critique of the Rogers/McKim Proposal*. Grand Rapids: Zondervan, 1982.

Woodbridge, John D. and Frank A. James III, *Christ History, Volume Two: From Pre-Reformation to the Present Day*. Grand Rapids: Zondervan, 2013.

Woudstra, Marten H. *The Book of Joshua*. New International Commentary on the Old Testament. Grand Rapids: Eerdmans, 1981.

Wrede, William. "The Task and Methods of New Testament Theology." In *The Nature of New Testament Theology: The Contribution of William Wrede and Adolf Schlatter*, edited and translated by Robert Morgan, 68–116. Eugene: Wipf and Stock, 1973.

Wright, Christopher J. H. *The Mission of God: Unlocking the Bible's Grand Narrative*. Downers Grove: InterVarsity, 2006.

Wright, N. T. *The New Testament and the People of God*. Minneapolis: Fortress, 1992.

Yarbrough, Robert W. "The Kingdom of God in the New Testament: Matthew and Revelation," In *The Kingdom of God*, edited by Christopher W. Morgan and Robert A. Peterson, Theology in Community 4, 95–124. Wheaton: Crossway, 2012.

Yarnell III, Malcolm B. "The Person and Work of the Holy Spirit." In *A Theology for the Church*. Rev. ed., edited by Daniel. L. Akin, 483–540. Nashville: B&H, 2014.

Yeago, David S. "The New Testament and the Nicene Dogma: A Contribution to the Recovery of Theological Exegesis." In *The Theological Interpretation of Scripture: Classic and Contemporary Readings*, edited by Stephen Fowl, 87–100. Oxford: Blackwell, 1997.

Zuber, Kevin D. "What Is Illumination? A Study in Evangelical Theology Seeking a Biblically Grounded Definition of the Illuminating Work of the Holy Spirit." PhD Diss., Trinity Evangelical Divinity School, 1996.

Scripture Index

Acts

Romans

Name Index